DESIGNING SALESFORCE AGENTS: THE PATTERN-BASED GUIDE TO AGENTFORCE

ENTERPRISE READY PATTERNS FOR BUILDING EFFECTIVE SALESFORCE AGENTS

CYNTHIA QIAO

ANDY FORBES

Roadmap Press
Hillsboro, Virginia, United States

ISBN: 978-1-969489-16-7 (paperback)
ISBN: 978-1-969489-03-7 (ebook)

Cover design by: Roadmap Press

This was an exciting and educational endeavor for me, and I thank Andy for his encouragement and support. A great gratitude to my husband for his never ending support, guidance, advice and love.
Cynthia Qiao

To my wife, Claudia - thank you for your unwavering support and for understanding the long hours I spent on this book. Your patience and encouragement made it possible.
Andy Forbes

To Lara Wasowski and Cameron Stewart, thank you for reviewing this book and helping make it the best book it could be.
Cynthia Qiao and Andy Forbes

"I have not invented anything. I have only discovered what was already there."

— Nikola Tesla

CONTENTS

FOREWORD

"I'm a member of the last generation of CEOs to manage an all-human workforce"

So said Marc Benioff, co-founder and CEO of Salesforce, in his Foreword to my book Agentforce (Wiley 2025) – and he's swarming the company around this insight.

I wrote Agentforce when AI Agents were relatively new, and customers were asking basic questions, building their first working agents. In fact, it's not difficult to build a single, relatively simple agent – a few minutes at a Dreamforce demo booth was enough.

But very quickly customers (and Salesforce product teams) noticed there was a meaningful learning curve between initial adoption and the ultimate goal: a working multi-agent, cross-channel platform.

The question is: How to get there from here? How can the hard-working enterprise go from agent-curious to agent-adept? Agentic implementation is not always easy; no technology is, particularly in its early phase. Success requires trial and error, testing, laborious improvement.

And success in the long-run requires managing expectations. When I worked as a Research VP at Gartner, we produced the "Hype Cycle," describing the lifecycle of expectations around new technology categories, like Customer Data Platforms. Agents and AI itself are going through their own Hype Cycles, which glide predictably from the Peak of Inflated Expectations to the Trough of Disillusionment (using Gartner's terms) ... followed by the mature Plateau of Productivity. Agents are not yet in this final stage.

So what is Agentforce? Not a simple application or a marketing concept, it is a comprehensive, rapidly-developing platform – itself built on top of Salesforce's global, metadata-driven CRM platform – that enables enterprises to design, test, implement, monitor and govern a network of agents to do almost anything.

Singular AI uses prompts and responses, and one-off results can be impressive. But Agentforce is much more ambitious. It understands intent, takes actions, learns and pivots, pulling real-time first-party data from internal systems, all in a context of trust, audit-logs and confidence.

Ultimately, Agentforce helps companies to build and run a robust "Agent Factory," one that scales as agents are more embedded in their daily workflows. Since launching Agentforce in 2024, Salesforce has stressed the mantra, "Don't DIY Your AI." This simply means that AI success -- particularly agentic AI success -- is not as easy as it looks. We are all surrounded by startups and established players offering impressive tools. These can assemble striking agents but fall short of providing a trusted, grounded, audited, governed, multi-LLM platform that provides tools to help build and test agents and a Command Center to monitor human and robot workers. And Agentforce is the only platform now that can enable and empower the emerging human-agent hybrid workforce.

The co-authors of this book, Cynthia Qiao and Andy Forbes, do an impressive job moving the Agentforce conversation to the next level. They detail the primary patterns we've seen for AI Agents, how they differ and how they thrive. In the process, they demystify the agentic agenda and provide practical tools and tips to set the stage for your success.

Crucially, these patterns apply to Agentic AI in general as well as to Agentforce. As the authors say, the patterns are "abstract enough to apply anywhere," while Agentforce users enjoy additional concrete guidance. Meanwhile, the authors catalog so-called "Patterns in the Wild," considering the roles of various well-known tools such as LangChain, Microsoft AutoGen, OpenAgents / CrewAI, and Model Context Protocol.

Among the eight major patterns are:

- Sentinel (monitor-react) – as an example, this pattern could monitor internal channels for policy violations and alert HR
- Conductor (orchestration) – e.g., coordinate the creation of a marketing campaign from brief writing through audience definition, media planning and optimization
- Presenter (UX optimization) – perhaps, pull data from multiple disparate systems and present a rolled-up real-time view
- Action (task doer) – automatically handle routine returns for an online retailer, say
- Coach (insights/advisory) – e.g., analyze a salesperson's upcoming pitch and suggest improvements

For each pattern, the authors provide detail around use cases spanning the entire enterprise – from Finance and HR to Marketing and Customer Care, – along with event sources, evaluation logic, agentic actions, tools and tech. The latter spans platform events, Apex/Flow, Agent Builder, MuleSoft, APIs and more, at times including code.

In fact, this is the book Agentforce users have been waiting for. Subsequent sections dive into topics such as managing agents with trust; handling memory and context; designing and governing multi-agent systems. The authors provide convincing advice on how to deploy AI agents, starting from your first-ever try, and how to develop a portfolio of agentic solutions. Not to mention swarming orchestration – my favorite term, describing a phalanx of agents, each with a specific task, invested in accomplishing a shared goal. It's like science fiction, but it's real: Salesforce already uses agent swarms within its Atlas Reasoning Engine, the so-called "brain" of the platform, handling deliberation and learning in context.

Following the more disciplined approach presented in this book, the AI agent practitioner can improve modularity and composability – the ability to draw clear lines of responsibility around particular agents so they can function in teams. This modularity is particularly important in the rapidly-emerging scenarios of agent-to-agent cooperation among very different entities, like different companies and customers.

What's both exciting and disturbing is how much managing an agentic workforce resembles managing a human one. In Chapter 18, the authors describe the steps to grow "companion agents into daily work partners," and the steps are understandably anthropomorphic: agents move from suggesting ideas to handling more delegated tasks on their own, gradually enjoying autonomy as trust is earned and learning advances. So AI agents are a lot like human interns, at first; and in time – like some interns, – some of them become star performers. But it is definitely a process. No person and no agent starts their career as a seasoned practitioner.

There is no doubt that Marc Benioff is right and the Agentic Enterprise describes the future of business. Succeeding as an agent-centric organization is not guaranteed to anyone and requires thought and considered action. The stakes are high. Certainly, companies that aren't actively working on their agentic, hybrid human-agent future are already behind.

There's plenty in here for readers from the merely agent-curious to the agent-adept, from business line users to Salesforce Architects and Admins. After all, we're all on the same agentic AI journey together, whether we know it or not.

Martin Kihn (mkihn@salesforce.com)
Senior Vice President Strategy, Salesforce
New York, NY – October 2025

The views expressed in this foreword are my own and reflect my personal perspective as a practitioner, not an official position or endorsement of Salesforce, Inc. or its affiliates.

We are in the middle of one of the biggest shifts in enterprise technology since the cloud. We've also never experienced such rapid change and technological progression - welcome to the AI -evolution! In just a few short years, we've progressed from Predictive AI, powered by scripts and deterministic rules, to Generative AI, fueled by data patterns and creative algorithms that generate dynamic content, and now to Agentic AI, where systems still follow rules but can reason, decide, and converse in natural language. With that, we've entered the age of assistive and collaborative software, where agents augment the human workforce, changing how we work, how decisions get made, and how value is delivered. At Salesforce, we've seen this evolution unfold through Agentforce, our agentic platform that brings together trusted data, AI, and automation. What started as copilots and assistants is rapidly becoming something much more powerful, a network of intelligent teammates that operate alongside people across every function, in the flow of work. This isn't a future vision, it's happening now. But as the number of agents grows, so does the complexity.

Enterprises are realizing that building one great agent is not the same as scaling to a multi-agent ecosystem while maintaining safety, consistency, and alignment to the "jobs to be done." And that this is a real challenge that must be addressed to succeed in the Agentic Enterprise era. Enterprises may have tens or even hundreds of thousands of employees, yet those roles map to a much smaller number of role types, such as seller, service rep, recruiter, analyst, manager, and leader for example. The same will be true for AI agents. As companies orchestrate vast numbers of agents, those agents will naturally align into a smaller set of recurring patterns, which is the digital equivalent of those human roles. Some will monitor, some will execute, others will guide or coach.

This book captures that structure beautifully. This book is one of the first serious attempts to define those standard agent patterns that are becoming the shared language we will use as we design, deploy, and scale agentic systems. The patterns: Sentinel, Supervisor, Conductor, Companion, Presenter, Curator, Action, and Coach are the building blocks of the agentic enterprise. They provide consistency where it matters most: trust, safety, and interoperability.

Cynthia Qiao and Andy Forbes have created something that's both thoughtful and actionable. It's not a theoretical exploration of AI; it's a framework for building responsibly at scale. Cynthia's perspective as one of Salesforce's most respected technical architects shines through on every page, grounded in real-world architecture, governance, and customer-facing deployment experience. Andy's clarity and systems thinking make complex ideas accessible. Together, they've written what every architect, developer, and business leader needs right now, which is a field guide to building intelligent, safe, and repeatable agent systems on Salesforce.

As organizations shift from experimentation to AI adoption at scale, the greatest risk isn't failure, it's fragmentation. Companies might face situations where multiple well- intentioned teams build agents in isolation, with no shared design principles or guardrails. This is common during periods of fast-paced innovation and experimentation. Patterns solve that. They help teams move fast and at the same time stay consistent. They define what an agent does, how it behaves, and how it interacts with humans and other agents. They create a common foundation for scaling responsibly, similar to object models, data schemas, and design systems in earlier eras of enterprise architecture.

If a company is serious about becoming an agentic enterprise, which more and more companies are, it needs to be intentional about how it brings multiple agents into its ecosystem. This means that agents become part of the digital workforce and core to how work happens. Given this, building right and building the right agents becomes foundational to the success of the business, and this framework can help balance innovation with structure, autonomy with accountability, and intelligence with trust.

That's exactly what this book provides, a practical, deeply informed guide written by two practitioners who've been in the trenches helping customers bring AI to life.

Irina Gutman
Vice President Forward Deployed Engineering, Salesforce
New York, NY – November 2025

The views expressed in this foreword are my own and reflect my personal perspective as a practitioner, not an official position or endorsement of Salesforce, Inc. or its affiliates.

Two decades at Salesforce have afforded me a front-row seat to some of the most profound transformations in enterprise technology. From the early days of moving CRM to the cloud, through the rise of mobile and analytics, to today's era of generative AI, one truth has remained constant - innovation only matters when it drives meaningful business outcomes. The launch of Agentforce marks the next great inflection point in that journey - a shift from systems of record to systems of intelligence, from static automation to dynamic, reasoning agents that act as trusted members of the enterprise.

Across every industry I've worked with — from financial services and manufacturing to healthcare, public sector, and retail — the same question surfaces - How can we scale intelligence responsibly? Agentforce provides the answer. It translates the power of AI into comprehensible, repeatable, and governable business capability. Just as the Salesforce Platform democratized development through clicks, not code, Agentforce democratizes autonomy — enabling teams to design, deploy, and refine AI agents safely within business and compliance guardrails. This book is a landmark contribution to that mission. Cynthia Qiao and Andy Forbes have distilled the complexity of AI agent design into practical, human-centered frameworks anyone can apply. The eight core agent patterns presented here — from Sentinel and Supervisor to Conductor, Companion, and Coach — are more than technical constructs. They're archetypes of how intelligence can work alongside people. Each pattern reflects a different relationship between humans and machines, tailored to the rhythm of real-world processes: observing, advising, executing, learning.

What resonates most for me, after years of guiding customers through digital transformation, is the pattern mindset this playbook instills. Enterprises succeed when they move from experimentation to intentional design — when AI becomes an operating discipline rather than a collection of prototypes. Patterns give organizations that structure. They accelerate innovation while ensuring trust, security, and reuse. Whether you are a Salesforce admin, architect, developer, or business leader, this book equips you to scale AI not through chance, but through craft.

Agentforce also redefines the very fabric of work. We are entering an age where digital teammates will manage workflows, interpret context, and anticipate needs in ways that mirror human collaboration. But this future will only be realized when design meets governance — when creativity meets accountability. The frameworks in these pages show how to balance both. They make AI approachable, auditable, and adaptable — the qualities that have always set Salesforce innovation apart.

As you explore the chapters ahead, I invite you to see beyond technology. What you'll discover here is a blueprint for the Agentic Enterprise — one where every employee, partner, and customer is augmented by intelligence that listens, learns, and acts with purpose. Agentforce is not just a new capability; it's a new way of thinking about business itself.

Welcome to the era of the Agentic Enterprise — and to your playbook for leading it.

Pat Fischer
Vice President Global Industry Center of Excellence, Salesforce
Basking Ridge, NJ – November 2025

The views expressed in this foreword are my own and reflect my personal perspective as a practitioner, not an official position or endorsement of Salesforce, Inc. or its affiliates.

The Agentforce platform provides a framework for digital labor as autonomous, reasoning agents that augment and collaborate with human teams across systems of record, engagement, and insight. Many organizations are now moving beyond early proofs of concept on this platform toward programs that deliver measurable value at scale. Success in this phase requires moving fast but not recklessly—balancing urgency with architectural and organizational discipline to ensure digital and human teammates can reliably and coherently operate together.

For organizations on this journey, achieving value depends less on any single innovation and more on how well efforts are coordinated across people, processes, and the interconnected systems of applications, data, and integrations they depend on. Alignment is essential. It requires a shared language—a consistent way for architects, developers, and business leaders to design, govern, and evolve agentic capabilities. Without it, even the most promising initiatives risk fragmentation and duplication.

That is where this book delivers its greatest value. Beyond implementation guidance, it provides structure for how to think and communicate about agents. The patterns here can serve as components of an enterprise-wide language, a starting point for one, or a litmus test for evaluating existing plans. The resulting alignment, streamlined governance, and cohesion of agentic capabilities across the enterprise are critical to success.

The authors, Cynthia Qiao and Andy Forbes, balance practical experience with conceptual depth. I've had the privilege of working closely with Cynthia for years driving a practice guiding complex, AI-centric Salesforce programs, and as mutual members of the elite Salesforce Certified Technical Architect (CTA) community which collaborates across the ecosystem to solve cutting-edge enterprise challenges. Cynthia exemplifies this community's best qualities, and her influence is evident throughout this work. Andy complements her Salesforce expertise with broad knowledge of the AI ecosystem and a clear, accessible style that makes complex ideas actionable. Their combined perspective is rigorous, readable, and valuable.

For enterprises pursuing Agentic AI–centric transformation programs, this book is a great companion. It helps teams validate strategies, refine thinking, and identify ways to accelerate responsibly. Above all, it promotes a shared understanding—enabling organizations to move from experimentation to coherent, large-scale adoption with confidence and clarity.

Wayne Blair

Vice President Head of Technical Consulting for Manufacturing, Automotive, Energy & Utilities, Salesforce
Hamden, Connecticut – October 2025

The views expressed in this foreword are my own and reflect my personal perspective as a practitioner, not an official position or endorsement of Salesforce, Inc. or its affiliates.

PROLOGUE

By the time you open this book, the ground will already have shifted beneath our feet. That's the nature of artificial intelligence. It moves fast, then faster, then all at once. Ray Kurzweil calls it the law of accelerating returns; we call it the reason every business leader and technologist feels like they're sprinting on a treadmill that keeps nudging the speed up a half-step at a time.

Agentforce sits squarely in the middle of that acceleration. When we started writing this, the feature set looked one way. By the time we finished editing, it had shifted again. And at the moment you're reading this, it has almost certainly changed once more. That isn't a flaw in the platform—it's the point. We are all living through the transition from software that updates quarterly to intelligence that updates continuously.

So take what's here as patterns, as a way of thinking, as a framework you can use no matter what label Salesforce attaches to a feature next month. The specifics will evolve. The core ideas—how agents interpret intent, how they coordinate work, how designers shape behavior, how teams control risk—will hold.

Now, if you run into something in these pages that you think needs an update, or sparks an idea, or simply makes you want to argue, good. That's a sign you're leaning forward, not backwards. We're active in the Salesforce community, and we can always be found on LinkedIn. If you want to talk about Agentforce, or AI design, or the very strange future we're moving into together, reach out. This space moves too quickly for any single book to have the last word.

What we do know is this: artificial intelligence is about to reshape business and society in ways that will feel abrupt only to those who weren't paying attention. Work, decision-making, customer experience, operations—every part of the modern enterprise is on the verge of being rewritten.

We're heading into interesting times.

This book is one way to get ready.

1

INTRODUCING AGENT PATTERNS

AI agents are rapidly becoming digital teammates in the modern Salesforce enterprise. With the rise of Salesforce Agentforce – a platform for building autonomous AI agents – teams are moving beyond simple chatbots and static automations to agents that can reason, act, and continually learn. In this new era, developers face a challenge familiar from classic software engineering: how do we avoid reinventing the wheel every time we build an AI agent? The answer is agent patterns – reusable blueprints for designing and deploying AI agents effectively.

Just as software design patterns provide proven solutions for recurring coding challenges, agent patterns provide proven strategies for recurring AI agent scenarios. They give Salesforce professionals a common language and set of templates for building agents that are scalable, trustworthy, and aligned with business needs. This is crucial because the biggest risk in the AI era isn't simply building a "bad" agent – it's letting teams build disconnected, inconsistent agents that don't follow best practices. Imagine every team in your org crafting their own AI sidekick with no guidelines: one service bot might handle escalations cautiously while another sales bot sends customers off the rails with overzealous automation. Without patterns, agent development can devolve into an inconsistency nightmare.

Salesforce's Agentforce platform has already seen explosive adoption. But early on, many lacked the tooling and governance to scale these agents safely. Agent patterns address this by embedding governance and consistency into design. They ensure that whether you're building a customer-facing assistant or an internal automation, you follow a blueprint that's proven to work and to play nicely with others. Patterns offer a common language across your enterprise to avoid "agent sprawl" – that proliferation of siloed bots – and instead promote reuse, safety, and maintainability.

Moreover, agent patterns help bridge the gap between high-level AI capabilities and real-world business requirements. A Salesforce AI agent is far more sophisticated than a simple chatbot. Chatbots follow predefined scripts and can't truly take action; an Agentforce agent, by contrast, understands user intent and can take actions, pivot mid-conversation, and draw on real-time data. It's the difference between a FAQ bot that parrots knowledge articles and an autonomous agent that can troubleshoot an issue, query your ERP system for data, and even initiate a follow-up task. With such power comes complexity – and the need for structured patterns to harness it. You'll notice even smart code assistants sometimes suggest sloppy solutions – e.g. autopredicting Apex DML inside a loop – because without a guiding pattern, AI can easily go off-track. Patterns keep both humans and AI on the rails.

In this chapter, we introduce the concept of agent patterns and lay the foundation for using them in Salesforce development. First, we'll define what an agent pattern is in the context of autonomous AI systems, comparing them to traditional software patterns and showing how they shape an agent's design. Next, we'll explore why these patterns matter, from preventing chaotic agent deployments to building trust and reuse across teams. We'll then discuss how patterns accelerate team productivity – making onboarding, testing, and maintenance easier for developers and architects. From there, we'll look at how agent patterns apply across business functions, extending beyond CRM into areas like HR, Finance, and Legal, with examples of each core pattern in action. We'll zoom out to see agent patterns in the broader AI ecosystem, drawing parallels to frameworks like LangChain and CrewAI and standards like the Model Context Protocol (MCP). After that, we'll map the patterns to Salesforce's own tools – such as Agent Builder, Flow, Invocable Apex, and more – to show how you implement these blueprints in practice. Finally, we'll present a quick-reference matrix of the eight core agent patterns we'll be exploring: Sentinel, Supervisor, Conductor, Companion, Presenter, Curator, Action, and Coach. Think of these as the fundamental "roles" that AI agents can play. Teams can combine and extend these patterns as needed, but these eight give you a starting toolbox for almost any situation.

By the end of this chapter, you'll understand what agent patterns are and why they're indispensable for anyone building AI agents on Salesforce. More importantly, you'll be ready to identify which pattern (or mix of patterns) fits a given use case, ensuring your AI agents are built on solid, repeatable foundations rather than whim or improvisation.

Next, let's define exactly what we mean by an agent pattern and how this concept applies to autonomous AI agents...

WHAT IS AN AGENT PATTERN?

To put it simply, an agent pattern is a reusable design blueprint for a type of AI agent. It encapsulates the structure, behavior, and best practices that an agent should follow to solve a certain class of problems. If you come from a software background, think of how the Model-View-Controller (MVC) pattern defines roles for UI applications, or how a trigger framework in Salesforce enforces consistent handling of database events. In the same way, an agent pattern defines the "shape" of an AI agent's reasoning and actions. It's a template for how the agent perceives inputs, how it processes decisions (perhaps using an LLM-based reasoning engine), and how it produces outcomes or actions.

Just as classic design patterns describe object interactions or data flow, agent patterns describe cognitive and interactive structure. They guide both the internal structure of the agent (its planning, tool use, memory, etc.) and its external interaction (the way it responds to user input or other events). For example, one pattern might define an agent that primarily observes and reacts (listening for certain triggers and responding – akin to an event handler), whereas another pattern might define an agent that plans a multi-step workflow to achieve a goal. These are very different behaviors, and patterns help us categorize and design for them explicitly.

It helps to compare this to familiar territory. In Salesforce development, we often use patterns even if we don't call them that. Consider the "trigger handler" pattern: you don't write raw trigger logic in one monolithic block; you use a framework to route events to handler classes. Or consider the Invocable Apex pattern: writing an Apex class with a standardized @InvocableMethod signature so it can be called from a Flow. These are patterns – they solve recurring problems (like ensuring triggers are bulk-safe or allowing code reuse in Flows) with consistent structure. An agent pattern is similar but at a higher level: it's about the architecture of decision-making and action in an AI agent.

Concretely, defining an agent pattern involves specifying things like: What inputs does the agent focus on? (e.g. customer utterances, or streaming events, or database changes), What reasoning does it apply? (e.g. does it use a single prompt to an LLM, or an iterative reflection loop, or a set of business rules plus AI?), and What outputs/actions does it produce? (e.g. a final answer to a user, an automated change in Salesforce, an alert to a human, etc.). By answering these questions, a pattern provides a template for the agent's construction.

For instance, one of the patterns we'll explore is the Supervisor pattern. This pattern's idea is that the agent generates a draft output or recommendation, but a human has the final say. If we analogize to real life, it's like an AI peer reviewer or assistant: it prepares something (a draft email reply, a risk assessment, etc.), then a human supervisor reviews and approves or tweaks it. Knowing this pattern, we immediately know the structure of such an agent: it needs a step for generating the draft (AI reasoning), and a mechanism for human review/approval (perhaps integrating with a Salesforce approval process or sending a task to a queue). That's very different from, say, the Action pattern (another we'll cover) where the agent is trusted to execute a specific task directly with no human in the loop. By naming these patterns, Supervisor vs. Action in this case, everyone on the team knows the expected behavior and constraints of the agent being built.

Importantly, agent patterns are technology-agnostic blueprints. Whether you implement an agent with Salesforce's low-code Agent Builder, with Apex code, or even on another platform entirely, the pattern concept still applies. For example, the "Supervisor" pattern could be implemented in Salesforce using a Flow for the human approval step and an Agentforce topic for the draft generation – or it could be implemented in a Python-based framework like LangChain with a chain that pauses for human feedback. The pattern remains recognizable in either implementation. In fact, many modern AI frameworks have independently arrived at similar patterns. LangChain's agents, for instance, often use a ReAct pattern (Reason + Act) behind the scenes – which is basically an agent pattern where the AI reasons about which tool to use, uses it, then reasons again. Microsoft's Autogen or the open-source OpenAgents framework might use patterns for multi-agent collaboration that map to what we'll discuss here. The key point: agent patterns aren't proprietary to Salesforce; they are grounded in how autonomous AI systems are built, generally.

Salesforce Agentforce, however, has made patterns first-class citizens by providing built-in tools to realize them. The Agent Builder in Agentforce

Studio, for example, lets you declaratively set up an agent's topics (the subject areas it can handle), instructions (constraints or guidelines for the AI), and actions (the operations it can execute). These roughly correspond to pattern components – for a given pattern, you'll configure topics/instructions differently. An agent pattern can essentially be "wired up" using these building blocks. If you prefer code, Agentforce also offers an Agentforce SDK and support for Apex/Flows, so you can implement the pattern logic programmatically if needed. The idea is that the pattern guides your implementation approach.

Pro Tip: Treat agent patterns as part of your development language. When teammates share an agent design, identify the pattern (or combination of patterns) it follows. This shared vocabulary reduces thrash. For example, if everyone knows a new "Onboarding Helper" agent is following the Companion pattern, they'll anticipate it lives in the UI and augments a user's workflow, rather than, say, autonomously doing back-end batch jobs. Using consistent patterns (and even naming conventions in your configs and code) makes debugging and onboarding new team members much easier.

At its core, an agent pattern answers: "What kind of problem is this agent solving, and what's the proven way to solve that kind of problem?" By defining patterns up front, you avoid ad-hoc designs. Instead of every developer crafting agents in completely different ways, your organization can say: "This agent will be a Sentinel type," immediately communicating a whole set of expectations about its behavior (monitoring something and reacting) and implementation (likely using event triggers, etc.). Now that we've defined what agent patterns are, let's explore why using patterns makes such a difference in practice – especially as you scale up the number of agents in your Salesforce org.

WHY AGENT PATTERNS MATTER

As we venture into building AI agents, a fair question is: do we really need formal patterns? Can't an experienced developer just whip up an agent with some prompts and call it a day? The reality is that without patterns, organizations risk and inconsistency. Early AI projects at many companies produced a wild west of agents: marketing built a lead-qualifying bot one way, sales ops built a forecasting assistant another way, each with different levels of oversight and safety checks. This unstructured approach leads to overlapping functionality, contradictory behaviors, and maintenance headaches. One agent might happily overwrite a Salesforce record in the name of automation while another similar agent, built by a cautious team, only ever suggests changes for humans to approve. Multiply that by dozens of agents, and you have an unpredictable system – not exactly what you want in an enterprise setting.

Agent patterns matter because they impose order and consistency on this process. By picking a pattern, you're also picking up a set of best practices. For instance, if you choose the Supervisor pattern for an agent handling expense report approvals in Finance, that implies certain safety guards: the agent shouldn't auto-approve anything without human review; its role is to assist, not fully automate. On the other hand, if you identify an opportunity for a fully automated task resolution, you might choose the Action pattern – and everyone will understand that agent is allowed to complete tasks end-to-end on its own. In other words, patterns define clear boundaries of autonomy. This prevents the scenario where an agent inadvertently does more (or less) than stakeholders expect. It's much easier to get buy-in from business owners when you can say "Don't worry, this agent follows a Coach pattern – it will advise your team, not replace their decisions," versus trying to explain a one-off custom design.

Another reason patterns are crucial: risk management and trust. Enterprise AI adoption faces rightful scrutiny around safety, ethics, and reliability. Patterns help bake in repeatable trust mechanisms. If every agent is built ad-hoc, you might forget a guardrail here or a logging step there. But if you know, for example, that the Sentinel pattern (which we'll detail later) always involves a "evaluate significance before acting" step, you will consistently include checks to avoid false alarms or overly aggressive actions. Patterns essentially come with a checklist of considerations. The Supervisor pattern's checklist includes "how does a human provide feedback or approval?" The Curator pattern's checklist includes "ensure data filtering criteria are well-defined to avoid junk in outputs." By following patterns, teams embed these considerations from the start, rather than rediscovering them through painful trial and error.

Patterns also enhance modularity and composability. This becomes vital as you scale to multiple agents or multi-step processes. If agents are built on known patterns, it's easier to have them work together or hand off tasks. For example, you might have a Sentinel agent monitoring for an event (say, a spike in support cases), which then triggers a Conductor agent to run a multi-step workflow in response. If both agents were built with patterns, the integration is smoother: you know what to expect from the Sentinel's output and the Conductor's input because each adheres to a template of behavior. In contrast, if each agent were a bespoke creation, you'd worry about mismatched assumptions (e.g., does this monitoring agent just alert, or does it also try to fix things? Does this other agent expect to be triggered with raw data, or a summarized insight?). Patterns make these contracts clear.

From a maintainability perspective, agent patterns align with good development practice. It's analogous to coding standards or frameworks. An agent built following a known pattern is easier to debug and extend because you understand its structure. Imagine joining a new team and seeing 10 agents in production. If their designs are all over the map, you'll spend weeks unraveling each one's logic. But if each agent's documentation (you do have docs, right?) simply states its pattern and any customizations, you can quickly grok what each does. For example: "Agent A – Pattern: Companion. This agent lives in the sales dashboard and offers on-screen tips to reps, pulling data via curated prompts." Immediately you know Agent A isn't making database changes or running unattended at midnight – by pattern definition, it's user-facing and assistive. This context speeds up troubleshooting (you wouldn't chase a data corruption bug in a Companion agent, because it shouldn't be writing data in the first place).

Patterns also help cross-functional teams collaborate on AI projects. Not everyone is an AI expert or a Salesforce developer; business stakeholders, compliance officers, etc., need to understand what an agent will do. Pattern names become a shared shorthand. A legal department might be wary of AI, but if you explain, "We're deploying a Coach pattern agent in Legal – it will suggest contract improvements but final decisions stay with the attorney," that clarity can win trust. It's a lot easier than diving into prompt engineering details or LLM jargon. The pattern communicates the agent's role in plain terms.

One more subtle but important aspect: patterns mitigate the risk of blind spots. When you have a library of known patterns, and you're designing a new agent, you naturally check against those patterns – it's almost a review process. If none of the standard patterns fit, that's a flag to be very deliberate: are you sure your agent isn't just a combination of existing patterns? If truly novel, fine, but at least you did the diligence. Many times, teams start designing something from scratch ("We need an agent that does X") and a pattern mindset helps them realize X is essentially a Conductor plus a Presenter working together, for example. You then know to incorporate everything those patterns entail (or use two agents in tandem). Patterns hence serve as a design checklist to ensure you're not missing pieces like error handling, human escalation, etc., that an ad-hoc approach might overlook.

Pro Tip: Use patterns as a review tool. Whenever you're about to deploy a new agent, ask: Which pattern (or mix of patterns) does this agent follow? If the answer is fuzzy, that's a red flag. Forcing this question can reveal design gaps. If you claim it's a Supervisor agent but realize there's no mechanism for human review in your design – oops, you better add one or rethink the pattern. This practice not only catches oversights, it also helps others in code or design review quickly understand your agent's intended behavior.

In summary, agent patterns matter because they bring coherence, safety, and efficiency to AI agent development. They tame the Wild West of AI experimentation into a structured practice more akin to traditional software engineering (with all the benefits of reliability that come with it). As agent development accelerates – and Salesforce reports it truly is, with companies deploying more and more AI workers – patterns will be what keep your AI workforce from turning into an unruly mob. They ensure your agents are singing from the same songbook, so to speak. Next, let's look at how this translates into concrete benefits for development teams and operations – in other words, how patterns can supercharge your team's productivity and effectiveness.

HOW PATTERNS ACCELERATE TEAMS

Agent patterns don't just impose discipline; they actively make life easier for development teams, QA, and operations. By adopting a pattern-based approach, teams find that many aspects of the AI agent lifecycle – from onboarding new developers to testing and deployment – become faster and more predictable. Let's break down a few ways patterns act as a force multiplier for your Salesforce teams.

1. Faster Onboarding and Knowledge Transfer: When a new developer or tester joins the project, there's a lot of tribal knowledge to absorb. Patterns give newcomers a shortcut to understanding the system. Instead of reading 50 pages of documentation per agent, a new team member can start with the pattern glossary: "Agent X is a Conductor, Agent Y is a Sentinel, Agent Z is a Companion," and so on. Immediately, they have a mental model for each. It's like joining a well-architected software project that uses MVC – once you know which classes are Controllers vs. Models, you already get the division of responsibilities. We've seen this in practice: a junior developer who knows the patterns can look at an Agentforce configuration or a Flow and say, "Oh,

this is following the Curator pattern, I expect it's gathering and filtering data for something." That understanding might take days to derive if each agent were a unique snowflake. In a Salesforce context, this means less time spelunking through Flow diagrams or Apex classes to figure out what the heck the agent is supposed to do – the pattern orientates you instantly.

2. Reuse of Components (Low-Code and Pro-Code): Patterns inherently encourage reuse because similar agents share skeletons. If you've built one Supervisor pattern agent, the next one can likely reuse a lot of the same Flow structures, Apex invocables, or even prompt templates. For example, many Action pattern agents (fully autonomous task doers) will need to call APIs or perform Salesforce updates. You might create an invocable action (Apex or Flow) that does a specific operation (say, create an Order record from a quote) and then reuse that across multiple agents of Action type. Agentforce's design facilitates this – the Agent Builder lets you build a library of actions that agents can share. Patterns accelerate this by making those actions broadly applicable. Without patterns, teams sometimes build very siloed actions (because each agent was conceived in isolation). With patterns, you identify common needs. A Presenter pattern agent, for instance, often needs to format output nicely for end-users; you might develop a reusable "response formatter" utility that any Presenter-type agent can use. Essentially, patterns help you build a catalog of building blocks (Flows, Apex, prompts) that can be mixed and matched, rather than one-off logic buried in each agent.

Salesforce developers will appreciate that this is akin to avoiding the old "copy-paste integration" anti-pattern. Instead of duplicating logic in multiple places, you centralize it. If your Coach pattern agents (which provide guidance) all use a common set of business rules, you can implement those rules once in an Apex class or Decision table and invoke it from all Coach agents. When policy changes, update that one spot – and all agents adhere to the new rule. This modular reuse is a huge time-saver and quality booster, and patterns effectively highlight where the seams between modules should be.

3. Streamlined Testing and Debugging: Knowing an agent's pattern gives strong clues about what to test. Each pattern comes with its typical failure modes and edge cases. For example, a Sentinel pattern agent (monitoring and reacting) needs to be tested for false positives and false negatives (does it trigger when it should, and stay quiet when it should?). A Conductor pattern (orchestrating a multi-step process) needs thorough testing of each branch and step, including what happens if one step fails. A Companion pattern (user-facing helper) should be tested for UX: does it give useful help without

being intrusive? Because you recognize the pattern, you have a ready-made testing checklist. This means QA engineers can develop standardized test suites for each pattern. In Salesforce terms, you might have a set of flow test cases or Apex tests that target generic pattern behavior. Indeed, Salesforce's own Agentforce Testing Center encourages simulating agent behaviors with test cases before going live. If your agent follows a known pattern, creating those simulations is easier – you know what scenarios to throw at it.

Debugging likewise benefits. When an agent misbehaves in production, you can narrow down the cause faster by thinking in pattern terms. "Our companion agent is suggesting oddly irrelevant tips – where could that be going wrong?" If it's a Companion pattern, you know it likely relies on context data and maybe a bit of profile info about the user. So the issue might be that it's not getting the right context (maybe a field mapping issue), rather than, say, a logic bug in a transaction (since a Companion shouldn't be doing transactions). In contrast, if the same symptom (irrelevant output) came from a Curator pattern agent, you'd suspect the data filtering or retrieval logic first. This intuition guided by pattern can save hours of guesswork.

4. Consistent Documentation and Training: Patterns allow you to templatize your documentation. Each agent can have a one-pager that says "Pattern: [Name]. Purpose: ... Inputs: ... Outputs: ... Key considerations: ...". In fact, by the end of this book you'll likely have a reference matrix that serves as an outline for documenting any new agent. When training users or operators (like your support team overseeing AI agents), you can explain behaviors by pattern. "All Supervisor-type agents will require your approval if they're unsure" or "All Sentinel agents will create a Service Cloud alert when they flag something." Consistency builds trust with the broader organization – they learn what to expect from AI. It's much like how end-users learned that "scheduled Apex" means something runs daily or hourly – once familiar, it's not a mystery. Patterns give that predictability for AI behavior, which in turn makes adoption smoother.

5. Alignment with Salesforce DevOps Tools: Modern Salesforce development uses source control, CI/CD, and monitoring. Patterns align nicely with these practices because they encourage modular, testable units. For example, if each agent pattern corresponds to a set of metadata (flows, Apex classes, etc.), you can organize your source repository by pattern. Maybe all Supervisor agents' components live in a certain folder structure or share a naming prefix. Your continuous integration can run pattern-specific test suites. Even Salesforce's metadata deployment tools can benefit: companies

like Gearset have started to support Agentforce deployments, and having a structured approach (where, say, you treat each agent pattern as a package or unlockable module) could simplify promotion through environments. Additionally, Salesforce's Event Monitoring and the new Agentforce Command Center give you telemetry on agent performance. If you tag or label agents by pattern, those dashboards could be filtered (imagine being able to see, "How are my Sentinel agents doing overall on response times vs. my Conductor agents?"). Patterns essentially introduce an attribute you can track and manage at scale.

Let's not forget developer happiness: there's a morale benefit when things are structured. It's no fun diving into a confusing bot built by someone who left the company, with no rhyme or reason to its logic. Patterns provide a sense of order and professionalism – you feel like you're working with a well-designed system, not a hacky collection of scripts. And when developers feel in control, they work faster and with fewer errors.

To illustrate acceleration in action, consider a scenario: your team is tasked with building ten new AI agents after a successful pilot. If you had no patterns, that could be an overwhelming prospect – ten completely separate designs. But with patterns, you might realize those ten break down into, say, three Sentinels, two Conductors, a Supervisor, and four Action-type agents. Immediately, you've scoped the project: you know you can build one base Sentinel then clone/tweak it for the other two similar use cases. You can plan common test approaches for the four Action agents together. You might assign developers by familiarity ("Alice is great with Flows and Invocable Apex – let her handle the Conductors; Bob has a knack for UX, he'll do the Companion if we need one."). Essentially, patterns help project manage the proliferation of agents.

Finally, Salesforce has provided tools like Agentforce for Developers which has features for debugging and simulating agent logic. These tools can take advantage of patterns too. For example, a developer console might allow you to simulate a Supervisor agent by providing a test input and then letting you step through where a human would intervene. When you use patterns consistently, such tooling becomes more effective because it can make assumptions (perhaps the console has built-in templates for common patterns).

In sum, patterns save time and headaches by turning what could be a messy art into a repeatable craft. Teams move faster because they're not solving the same design problems over and over – they solved it once (in the pattern), and now they just implement. As a result, you get to focus on higher-level improvements (like refining the quality of your AI's recommendations) rather than constantly reinventing the plumbing. Next, we'll broaden our view and see how these agent patterns apply beyond the usual CRM scenarios – demonstrating that this playbook isn't just for Sales or Service use cases, but for any domain in the enterprise.

PATTERNS ACROSS FUNCTIONS – NOT JUST CRM

One of the most exciting aspects of AI agents is their versatility. While the Salesforce world often talks about Sales, Service, and Marketing use cases (since those are core CRM domains), the truth is the same agent patterns can be applied in virtually every department and function. In fact, some of the highest ROI opportunities for AI agents lie in internal or non-customer-facing processes – areas like HR, Finance, Legal, IT, and Operations. Let's explore how our eight core patterns can manifest in a variety of business contexts.

To make this concrete, here's a quick tour of patterns in action beyond CRM:

Sentinel in HR: Think of a Sentinel agent as a watchful guard. In HR, a Sentinel-pattern agent could monitor company chat channels or HR case logs for policy violations or urgent employee issues. For example, it could scan for keywords that indicate harassment or safety concerns (within agreed privacy boundaries) and immediately flag a human HR representative when something needs attention. It's similar to how a Sentinel might watch customer support queues for SLA breaches; here it's watching internal signals for compliance breaches or employee well-being issues. The agent's core behavior (monitor events, evaluate significance, react) is the same, just pointed at a different domain.

Supervisor in Finance: In Finance, you might deploy a Supervisor-pattern agent to streamline expense approvals or budget requests. The agent could review incoming expense reports, cross-check them against policy (maybe using an LLM to spot out-of-policy purchases), and then make a recommendation: approve, reject, or flag for review. A human finance manager then quickly approves or adjusts those recommendations. The agent is effectively acting like a junior auditor. It doesn't have final say – that's why it's Supervisor pattern – but it dramatically reduces the time humans spend on grunt work. The human-in-the-loop ensures that any questionable calls (like an ambiguous case that the AI isn't sure about) are handled correctly. This pattern could also apply in compliance (recommend if a transaction looks fraudulent, but let an analyst confirm) or in procurement (suggest contract tweaks for savings, then legal reviews).

Conductor in Supply Chain: A Conductor-pattern agent is an orchestrator of processes, which is perfect for complex, cross-system workflows common in Supply Chain management. Picture an agent that manages an order fulfillment process: when a big order comes in, it needs to check inventory, schedule manufacturing if stock is low, arrange shipping, and notify the sales team. A Conductor agent could autonomously perform these steps across SAP, Salesforce, and a shipping API by invoking multiple actions in sequence, handling the logic of what to do if, say, inventory is insufficient (maybe escalate to a human or switch to an alternate supplier). Here the agent is like a supply chain coordinator that never sleeps. It follows a script, but can also adapt – if manufacturing is delayed, it could reschedule shipping and inform the customer proactively. This is a pattern not just for supply chain: any multi-step business process (onboarding a new employee across IT and HR systems, for example) could leverage a Conductor agent to ensure all the right tasks happen in order.

Companion in IT (or Anywhere): A Companion-pattern agent is one that works side-by-side with a human, often embedded in an application or interface to provide live assistance. Imagine an internal IT help portal with an embedded AI assistant that guides employees through troubleshooting before filing a ticket. This Companion agent might ask questions ("What issue are you facing? Let me see if I can resolve it."), perform some checks (look up the user's device info or recent login errors), and either fix simple things (reset a password automatically if policy allows, using an Action subcomponent) or gather info to hand off to a human technician. It's very similar to a customer-facing chatbot experience, but pointed internally. The key is the Companion pattern's defining trait: it's interactive and user-centric, always waiting in the wings to help the user perform tasks more effectively. Outside of IT, you could have a Companion agent in a procurement system guiding managers on how to create purchase orders, or in a training system guiding new employees through orientation ("Next, fill out this form. Need help? Here's an example."). Because it's pattern-based, these diverse applications all share common design elements (context-awareness, helpful prompts, ability to step back if the user chooses to do things manually, etc.).

Presenter in Analytics/Reporting: The Presenter pattern agent's job is to take raw information and deliver it in a clear, digestible format to a user, often adding explanation or emphasis. Consider a Finance scenario: end of quarter, dozens of reports and metrics are flying around. A Presenter-pattern agent could be tasked with generating an "executive summary" of key financial metrics each morning. It might pull numbers from Salesforce (opportunities, revenue), from an ERP (expenses, receivables), maybe from Data Cloud for some product usage metrics, and then compile a narrative report: "Good morning CFO, here's today's brief – Revenue is 5% above target, driven by X; one anomaly: expenses in marketing spiked 10% – likely due to event spend." It's essentially acting as a robo-analyst that presents information. The pattern ensures the agent doesn't introduce new transactions or decisions; it focuses on communication. Another example: a Presenter agent in Legal could read through a long contract and produce a one-page summary with key points and risks (a huge time-saver for busy attorneys). Different departments, same pattern of digesting and presenting information in a human-friendly way.

Curator in R&D or Knowledge Management: A Curator-pattern agent excels at sifting through large volumes of data to find relevant nuggets. In a Research & Development context, suppose a pharmaceutical company has thousands of research papers and experimental results. A Curator agent could take a query like "Find any research related to compound ABC's stability in high temperature" and go through internal knowledge bases, documents, maybe even external databases, to collate the top relevant pieces of information. It might summarize each finding and perhaps exclude data that isn't credible or is out-of-date. Essentially it curates a knowledge feed for the researcher. In an internal knowledge management scenario, a Curator agent could auto-tag and organize content. For instance, at the end of each project, it could take all documents and communications and produce a "knowledge pack," filtering out trivial items and highlighting lessons learned. This pattern ensures the agent's role is well-bounded: it collects and filters information; it's not acting on the world, just organizing knowledge. Nearly any department drowning in data (legal with case files, HR with resumes, etc.) could use such an agent.

Action in Procurement: The Action pattern agent is the autonomous doer. In Procurement, a simple but high-impact agent might watch inventory levels and automatically place restock orders with approved vendors when thresholds are crossed. This agent doesn't chat, doesn't explain – it just performs a specific transactional job very efficiently. For example, if widget stock falls below 500, it creates a purchase order in Salesforce (or an external system) to buy more, maybe even signs it digitally if that's within its authority, and notifies the procurement officer. Because it's an Action agent, it was designed with the trust that it can carry out that operation without human approval each time (likely after careful testing and with guardrails like spending limits). Other examples could be IT automation agents (automatically scaling server capacity when load is high) or Facilities agents (automatically scheduling maintenance if sensor data indicates a machine's running hot). In each case, the pattern is about single-focus autonomous action. It's straightforward, but extremely powerful in aggregate – these are your digital workers handling grunt work continuously.

Coach in Legal (or Sales, or HR): A Coach-pattern agent provides guidance and expertise, often personalized to the user, to help them improve or make better decisions. In Legal, a Coach agent could assist junior lawyers by reviewing their draft contracts or briefs and giving feedback: "This clause might be legally weak because of X precedent" or "Usually, we include a confidentiality clause here; consider adding it." It's like a mentor that has read all the firm's past contracts and knows the playbook. Importantly, a Coach agent doesn't generally execute changes itself; it advises. Similarly, in Sales, you might have a Coach agent analyzing a salesperson's pipeline and nudging them: "Deals in healthcare are stagnating 20% longer – maybe prioritize those" or giving tips like a real sales coach would. In HR, a Coach could guide managers on leadership ("Your last 1:1 was 60 days ago, it's good to check in more often – here are some conversation starters."). The Coach pattern ensures the agent's tone and role is advisory. It often uses a lot of context about the person it's coaching (their past performance, profile, etc.) to tailor the advice – much like a human coach would adjust feedback per person. This pattern can directly uplift skills and compliance (imagine a Coach agent reminding a manager of labor law considerations during employee termination processes, for instance).

As you can see, each pattern is like a mold that can be applied to many use cases across different fields. The specifics differ, but the underlying blueprint is recognizable. The list below gives a quick snapshot of each core pattern paired with an example outside the traditional CRM realm:

Sentinel

- **Non-CRM use case:** HR policy watchdog.
- **Description of use:** Continuously monitors internal communications for potential policy violations and alerts HR teams early, allowing intervention before issues escalate.

Supervisor

- **Non-CRM use case:** Expense report assistant (Finance).
- **Description of use:** Reviews employee expense submissions, flags exceptions, and recommends approval or denial based on policy, while leaving final decisions to managers.

Conductor

- **Non-CRM use case:** Order fulfillment orchestrator (Operations).
- **Description of use:** Coordinates multi-step order processing across inventory, manufacturing, and shipping systems to ensure smooth execution and timely delivery.

Companion

- **Non-CRM use case:** Employee IT helpdesk assistant (IT).
- **Description of use:** Guides employees through troubleshooting steps in real time, embedded directly in the IT support experience to reduce tickets and resolution time.

Presenter

- **Non-CRM use case:** Executive briefing agent (Analytics).
- **Description of use:** Aggregates key performance indicators from multiple systems and delivers a concise, daily summary tailored for leadership consumption.

Curator

- **Non-CRM use case:** Research literature digester (R&D).
- **Description of use:** Scans, filters, and summarizes large volumes of research material to surface relevant findings on demand for scientists and researchers.

Action

- **Non-CRM use case:** Auto-reorder bot (Procurement).
- **Description of use:** Automatically places supply orders when inventory falls below predefined thresholds, following established rules and approval constraints.

Coach

- **Non-CRM use case:** Contract review advisor (Legal).
- **Description of use:** Analyzes draft contracts and provides suggestions to legal professionals to improve clarity, mitigate risk, and strengthen terms.

Each of these illustrates a unique value proposition of AI agents beyond the usual suspects of sales and customer service. In many cases, these internal or cross-functional applications can be less risky testing grounds for AI. As one pro tip: the fastest path to proving ROI with AI agents is often in internal operations. Deploying a well-contained agent for, say, internal IT support can show clear productivity gains without the pressure of customer-facing perfection. A successful internal Sentinel or Conductor agent can then build confidence for more ambitious projects.

Cross-departmental adoption of agent patterns also has a side benefit: it starts to standardize AI thinking across the organization. If HR and Finance and Legal are all using, say, a Supervisor pattern for various approval workflows, they can share experiences and even components. Your company might develop an internal "ApprovalBot" template (Supervisor pattern) and then every department adapts it for their needs – HR for leave requests, Finance for expenses, etc., all consistent. This reduces duplication of effort and accelerates AI familiarity organization-wide. It's akin to when companies rolled out Salesforce years ago beyond Sales – suddenly having a common platform and approach (like every department having similar page layouts and automations) made it easier to onboard users and admins alike.

Looking ahead, each of the agent patterns we've introduced will get its own deep dive in upcoming chapters, with more examples and technical how-tos. But even here, you can start envisioning which patterns might address pain points in your area of work. The main takeaway: agent patterns are broad and flexible. Don't pigeonhole AI agents as just chatbots for customers. Whether it's a factory floor or a corporate legal office, if there's information to analyze, decisions to make, or tasks to do, there's likely a pattern-based agent that can help.

With a sense of how these patterns play out across the enterprise, let's now step back and see how they connect to the wider AI ecosystem. In the next section, we'll examine how Salesforce's agent patterns align with what's happening outside of Salesforce – in open-source frameworks, industry standards, and multi-agent systems at large.

AGENT PATTERNS IN THE BROADER AI ECOSYSTEM

Salesforce may have formalized these agent patterns for its platform, but the ideas behind them resonate throughout the AI world. It's reassuring (and not coincidental) that the patterns we use in Agentforce echo patterns observed in other AI frameworks and research. This means when you learn to design a Sentinel or Conductor agent in Salesforce, you're also gaining insight into how to structure AI agents generally, whether it's with Python libraries, cloud AI services, or other enterprise AI tools.

Let's draw some parallels. One prominent framework in the AI community is LangChain, which many developers use to build complex LLM-driven applications. LangChain doesn't explicitly list "Sentinel" or "Coach" as patterns, but it provides primitives that let you implement similar concepts. For instance, LangChain supports the ReAct (Reason+Act) loop, which underpins agents that can use tools based on intermediate reasoning. This is very much in line with our Action or Conductor patterns, where an agent plans and executes steps to fulfill a task. Another example: the Reflection pattern (sometimes called "reflexion") is gaining popularity – where an AI agent stops to reflect on its output and improve it iteratively. That idea maps into our patterns too; a Supervisor agent could be seen as adding a reflection step via a human, or an advanced Coach agent might internally reflect on the advice it gives.

Then there's CrewAI, an open-source framework specifically for multi-agent orchestration. CrewAI introduces the concept of a "crew" of agents with different roles collaborating on tasks. If you look at those roles, they mirror patterns: one agent might play a Planner role (similar to a Conductor), another might play a Critic or Reviewer (sounds a lot like a Supervisor or Coach), and so on. The framework's focus on orchestrating multiple agents aligns with how we imagine patterns can be combined. For example, in CrewAI you might have a Researcher agent and a Writer agent working together. In our terms, a Researcher agent might be a Curator pattern (gather info) and the Writer a Presenter pattern (format info), and the multi-agent orchestration itself is akin to a Conductor that manages the interplay. This shows that patterns aren't isolated; in complex scenarios you'll have multiple patterns interacting – something CrewAI is designed to handle. Salesforce's Agentforce also anticipates this; it's why having clear patterns helps (so two agents handing off tasks know what to expect from each other, as mentioned earlier).

Consider Microsoft's Autogen (from Microsoft Research). It's designed for creating "auto-GPT" style agents, often involving multiple specialized sub-agents (like a scenario with a Solver agent and a Critic agent in a loop). Those correspond to planning and feedback patterns – essentially the Reflection or Supervisor ideas – one agent generating solutions, another reviewing and guiding. The nomenclature differs, but conceptually they are implementing pattern-based roles for agents.

Another emerging piece of the ecosystem is the Model Context Protocol (MCP). MCP is often described as an open standard for connecting AI agents to external tools and each other – a kind of "USB-C for AI" where any agent can plug into any tool or service if both speak MCP. The relevance of MCP to patterns is interoperability. If your Salesforce agent follows a clear pattern, it's easier to expose its capabilities via MCP to the outside world in a predictable way. For example, a Sentinel agent might expose an MCP endpoint that essentially says "send me events, I'll send back alerts." Meanwhile, an external system (maybe a monitoring tool or another platform's agent) can connect to that because it understands the pattern of interaction (continuous input, occasional output on trigger). Salesforce Agentforce 3 natively supports MCP for connecting agents to third-party systems, so a well-designed pattern-based agent can become part of a larger multi-platform agent ecosystem with minimal friction. In practice, you might have a Salesforce agent handling CRM data, and an AWS-hosted agent doing heavy data analysis, coordinating via MCP. Patterns help here: if both sides adhere to known paradigms (like "I'm a Presenter agent expecting curated data" vs "I'm a Curator agent providing data"), they can work together without stepping on each other's toes.

Open-source initiatives like OpenAgents (not to be confused with the generic term, there is an actual OpenAgents project) aim to enable millions of AI agents to collaborate by standardizing their communication and roles. They define specialized agent types such as "Data Agent," "Web Agent," etc., which excel at certain tasks. These are essentially patterns by another name – a Data Agent might correspond to our Curator or Presenter depending on how it's used; a Web Agent might be akin to a Sentinel scanning the web for certain info. The fact that such projects exist underscores that the community recognizes recurring agent roles and is working to formalize them.

From an architectural standpoint, Andrew Ng and others have described key "design patterns" for AI workflows: Reflection, Tool use, Planning, and Multi-agent collaboration. These can be thought of as ingredients that combine into our higher-level patterns. Reflection is embedded in patterns like Supervisor (human reflection) or any pattern where the AI double-checks itself. Tool use is a given in Action/Conductor patterns (they call external tools to act). Planning is core to Conductor (planning steps) and to any complex agent that has to figure out a sequence. Multi-agent collaboration we see in scenarios where multiple patterns are deployed together for a solution. So while Salesforce gives friendly names like Coach or Sentinel, under the hood we are leveraging those fundamental design ideas that experts identify as crucial for advanced AI systems. It's a nice validation that, for example, our Conductor pattern isn't just a Salesforce concept – it embodies the "Planning + Tool Use" patterns that are widely deemed best practice for complex tasks.

Interoperability is another big theme. Salesforce knows Agentforce won't exist in a vacuum. Real enterprises might have an Agentforce agent working alongside an IBM Watson Orchestrate bot, a custom Python agent someone whipped up, and so on. Patterns provide a lingua franca. If you tell your integration team that the Watson bot is essentially playing a Coach role and the Salesforce agent is a Conductor, they can devise the integration points more clearly (e.g., the Conductor might call out to the Coach at a certain step for advice). And with standards like MCP, this could even be a dynamic discovery: one agent could query a registry for "any Coach agents available?" and find one to leverage. We're painting a picture of a mixed-stack, multi-agent system where clear patterns on each side smooth out the collaboration.

One might ask, will patterns become standardized across industry? It's possible. We already see common patterns emerging in literature and tools (everyone independently inventing a "let LLM self-reflect" approach, etc., which indicates a pattern). Salesforce's eight patterns might not match 1-to-1 with another platform's list of patterns, but they'll rhyme. By learning the concept in Salesforce, you'll readily understand analogous agent types elsewhere.

Finally, consider governance. Outside Salesforce, AI governance tools are being built that track what agents do, log their decisions, and audit outcomes. If those tools can tag actions by pattern, it provides immediate context for risk analysis. For example, a log entry like "Agent34 executed Action XYZ" could be interpreted differently if Agent34 is known as an Action pattern agent (we expect it to execute things autonomously) versus if it were a Companion (which normally shouldn't execute without user input). In the broader ecosystem, this kind of pattern-aware monitoring can catch anomalies (like "hey, this Presenter agent just tried to call an external

API – that's out of pattern for a Presenter, maybe something's off or it's compromised").

To summarize, the patterns we apply in Agentforce resonate with patterns and best practices seen in frameworks like LangChain (tool-using planners), CrewAI (multi-agent orchestration of specialized roles), Autogen (reflective, multi-step agents), and standards like MCP (which facilitates patterns working together). This broader alignment means you're not just learning something proprietary to Salesforce; you're learning general principles of agent design.

In practical terms, as you design Salesforce agents, keep an eye on these external developments. If a new technique in the community emerges (say a better way to do reflection or a new planning algorithm), you'll often be able to incorporate it into the corresponding pattern in Salesforce. For example, if a new "self-check" prompt technique becomes popular, you might incorporate that into your Supervisor or Coach agents' instruction set. Salesforce's openness to standards like MCP suggests they want Agentforce to play nicely in the sandbox with others, so pattern-aligned agents will be ready to plug into those future ecosystems.

Having situated agent patterns in the wider world, let's turn our focus back home. In the next section, we'll map these patterns to the Salesforce tools and features that help implement them. We've been hinting at Flows, Apex, and Agent Builder throughout – now we'll get specific about which tools are best suited for each pattern and how Salesforce's platform accelerators tie in.

AGENT PATTERNS AND SALESFORCE TOOLS

Designing an agent pattern is one side of the coin; implementing it with the right Salesforce tools is the other. Fortunately, the Salesforce ecosystem offers a rich toolbox – from low-code builders to pro-code options – and each agent pattern tends to align naturally with certain tools. Here we'll break down how each of our core patterns maps to Salesforce development tools and features, ensuring you know the go-to implementation approach once you've chosen a pattern.

First, let's list the major tools at our disposal in Agentforce and the Salesforce Platform:

Agent Builder (in Agentforce Studio): A low-code interface to create and customize agents using topics, instructions, and actions. It's great for declaratively defining what an agent should do without writing a lot of code.

Flow Builder: Salesforce's beloved click-and-drag process automation tool. In Agentforce context, flows (particularly Invocable Flows) can be used as actions that agents invoke to do things in Salesforce (update records, send emails, etc.).

Apex (especially Invocable Apex): Custom code for logic that's too complex for Flows or needs fine control. By making Apex invocable, you expose that logic as an action or decision point an agent can call.

Lightning Web Components (LWC) and other UI components: Useful for embedding agents in UIs (for Companion pattern) or creating custom interaction forms.

Flow Orchestration: A tool to orchestrate multi-step, long-running processes. This might not be explicitly branded under Agentforce, but it's relevant for patterns like Conductor that need to manage stateful workflows or wait conditions.

Agentforce Testing Center & Dev Console: Tools for testing and debugging agents. Not an implementation tool per se, but worth leveraging for quality.

Telemetry and Command Center: Monitoring tools (like the Agentforce Command Center dashboards) to observe agent performance and events – important for any pattern in production.

Now, how do these pair with patterns? We can map each pattern to a primary implementation approach:

Sentinel Pattern → Invocable Apex + Event Triggers (plus some Flow): Sentinel agents monitor signals (platform events, data changes, etc.). Often, writing Apex triggers or using Platform Events with Apex subscribers is the most efficient way to catch those signals. An Invocable Apex class can serve as the agent's "brain" to evaluate if an event is noteworthy (e.g., check if a case is breaching SLA). Once a decision is made, a Flow can be invoked to take the action (like create an alert or escalate the case). Agent Builder can help tie these pieces together, but Sentinel logic usually lives in code or formulas because it's condition-heavy. For instance, you might use a CDC (Change Data Capture) event on an object, handled by an Apex trigger that calls an Agentforce action. In Agentforce Studio, you'd configure the agent's topic to listen on that event and an action that maps to your Apex/Flow logic. Salesforce Event Monitoring or real-time events feed seamlessly into this pattern – an example is hooking a Sentinel agent up to the event bus to watch for certain sequences of events (security events, etc.). In short:

Sentinel = lots of Apex logic to detect and decide, with Flows or Agent actions to execute responses.

Supervisor Pattern → Agent Builder + Flow for human loop: The Supervisor pattern involves generating AI output and then having a human review. Salesforce Agentforce shines here because you can define an Agent Topic for the scenario (e.g., "Expense Approval Draft") and an Agent Action that uses a prompt to have the AI generate a recommendation. That prompt might be implemented via an LLM call (which under the hood Agentforce handles with the Atlas engine). Once the draft decision is made, you'd likely use a standard Salesforce Approval Process or just a screen Flow to present it to a human. The tools: Agent Builder to orchestrate the prompt generation (maybe using Prompt Builder for the template), then a Flow that the agent triggers to create a Task or Notification for a human. The human's input (approve/reject) can feed back – possibly via updating a record that the agent monitors or calling an invocable method to finalize the process. Invocable Apex might come in if the evaluation logic is complex (like "how to weigh different factors in the recommendation") but often this can be done with a combination of prompt instructions and some Flow logic. Notably, Agentforce for Developers in VS Code can help if you want to write custom code to refine how the agent forms its recommendation, but many Supervisor agents can be done mostly declaratively. In testing, you'd use the Testing Center to simulate various input cases and ensure the AI's draft plus the human override produce the right outcomes.

Conductor Pattern → Flow Orchestration + Apex for integration: Conductor agents handle multi-step flows, possibly over time or involving external systems. Salesforce Flow Orchestration is a natural fit to visually layout the steps, especially if some steps wait on events or have complex branching. You might design a flow orchestrator that, say, checks inventory, then calls an external API (using an Apex action), then creates an order, etc. Each of these steps can be an invocable action, making it modular. The Agent Builder can encapsulate this orchestrated flow as a single agent action (or a series of actions under one topic). If the orchestration is entirely within Salesforce, an autolaunched Flow might suffice; for cross-system, you'll lean on MuleSoft or Apex callouts (MuleSoft can even make those APIs available as MCP endpoints now). Invocable Apex is often needed to perform things not easily done in Flow (complex data transformation, error handling with retries, etc.). In fact, for Conductor agents, a best practice is to implement robust retry and compensation logic (e.g., if step 3 fails, roll back step 2) – Apex gives you that flexibility. These agents also benefit from Custom Metadata to store configuration (like what systems to call, thresholds, etc.), so you're not hardcoding. Agentforce's ability to use Heroku or external endpoints via MCP means a Conductor agent could orchestrate non-Salesforce tasks as well. For instance, a Conductor agent might trigger a Heroku-hosted microservice to perform a complex computation, then wait for the result. Tools like Platform Events or Async Apex might be used to allow the agent to pause and resume when external info comes back. So, in mapping: Conductor = heavy use of Flow Orchestration + Apex invocables + possibly MuleSoft for external steps. Agent Builder ties it together at a high level (the topic could be something like "Fulfill Order" and the actions sequence is defined).

Companion Pattern → LWC and Embedded Service + Agent APIs: Companion agents live in the UI. The primary tool here is often building a Lightning Web Component (or utilizing the Einstein Copilot UI) to embed the agent's interface in a Salesforce app (e.g., on a dashboard or record page). The LWC can call the Agentforce API (there's an Agent API for invoking agents programmatically) or reference an Agent through an Aura component if provided. Essentially, you need a front-end that can pass the user's context and input to the agent and display its responses. Embedded Chat or Slack integration can also be channels for Companion agents – think of Slack bots powered by Agentforce (Salesforce has Agentforce for Employees that integrates with Slack). Under the hood, the Companion agent likely uses a combination of prompt (for what to say to the user) and data queries (maybe via the agent's actions pulling data). Agent Variables in Agentforce can feed the agent context like the current record or user info, which is crucial for personalization. So, the tools stack: LWC for the UI, Agentforce API to talk to the agent, possibly some Apex controller to facilitate that. The agent itself is defined in Agent Builder with topics tuned to common user questions or tasks. If it needs to perform actions on behalf of the user, you could integrate flows or Apex actions triggered by the agent (but typically a Companion suggests and the user clicks "yes do it" which then might call an invocable flow). For example, a Companion agent on a case record could suggest: "Shall I draft an email to the customer with the latest update?" If user says yes, the agent might invoke a Presenter action to draft the email and show it. The heavy lifting is in the UI and experience design; the pattern ensures the agent doesn't run off and do stuff without user direction. Salesforce provides design guidelines for embedding AI assistants (like making sure it doesn't cover critical UI or can be easily dismissed – that's UX, beyond our scope, but worth noting for Companion implementations).

Presenter Pattern → Invocable Flows (for formatting) + Agent Builder: Presenter agents produce outputs for humans, often summarizing or explaining data. A lot of this can be done with Prompt templates (using Prompt Builder) combined with data retrieval actions. For instance, you might have an agent action that runs a SOSL or uses the Data Cloud to grab relevant data, then the prompt templatizes how to present it ("Summarize the following account status and recent activity..."). Agent Builder allows you to set this up declaratively: you define an action that uses a prompt with certain inputs, maybe chained with a small flow that prepares those inputs (like querying the data and passing it into the prompt). Invocable Flows are great here – one flow to gather data, then an Agentforce action that calls an LLM to generate the summary from that data. The output then is sent to the user (maybe via a screen or a record update). If the presentation is interactive (say the user can ask follow-up questions on the presented report), this bleeds into Companion territory; but pure Presenter is often one-shot. Tools like Einstein GPT (for auto-summarization) were basically Presenter pattern under the hood (taking CRM data and producing text), so hooking those capabilities via Agentforce is natural. Also, if building this purely with core platform, you might use Apex to do some formatting (though LLMs can handle natural language generation quite well, Apex could add charts or HTML formatting if needed). One could also leverage Lightning Components to display the result nicely (like embedding a chart), but the "agent" part is the generation of content. So, Presenter agents = heavy use of prompt engineering via Agentforce actions, fed by Flows/Apex that collect info. They likely rely on the Einstein Trust Layer for data access and compliance in generation, but that's mostly behind the scenes. If you want the agent to read attachments or non-SF data, you might utilize Data Cloud or MCP connectors to feed that in.

Curator Pattern → Data Cloud + Apex/Flow for filtering: Curator agents shine when dealing with large datasets or knowledge bases. Salesforce's Data Cloud is a boon here because it can index and retrieve data for AI (they mention it powers RAG – retrieval augmented generation – in Agentforce). A Curator agent likely uses a combination of Vector database queries (to find relevant unstructured info) and rule-based filtering. Tools: you might use the Data Cloud's APIs to fetch segments of data, or if the data is in Salesforce objects, an Apex query or SOSL search. Then the agent (via a prompt or Apex logic) filters and synthesizes the results. The output could be passed to a Presenter agent or directly to the user. Agent Builder can orchestrate this: e.g., define an action that calls an Apex class to do a search (or an external MCP service like a Box connector for documents) and returns snippets, then another action that summarizes or compiles these snippets. Essentially, Curator might split into two sub-actions: retrieve then summarize. In terms of mapping to Salesforce features: if curating across different data sources, MuleSoft with new MCP connectors can unify those sources for the agent. Also, Einstein Search capabilities might be leveraged behind the scenes. It's plausible to use Invocable Actions for external search (Salesforce may provide or one can build an invocable action to query SharePoint, for example). The key tool is anything that can gather data; the "curation" logic can be partly prompt (e.g., prompt: "Given these 10 pieces of info, pick the 3 most relevant.") and partly code (e.g., filter out duplicates or known irrelevant pieces via Apex). Once again, custom metadata could define what sources to search or how to rank relevance – making the agent configurable without code changes. Curator pattern, due to dealing with a lot of content, might also use Lightning Quill or similar to handle large text fields, but that's more in the weeds.

Action Pattern → Invocable Apex & Flows as atomic actions: Action agents are straightforward – they do one thing autonomously. Often this means invoking a single Apex method or Flow that performs the transaction. For example, an Action agent for auto-order might directly call a Flow that creates the order record and then maybe sends a confirmation. In Agentforce, you could configure an agent with a single topic "AutoReorder" and one action that is basically "Create Order via Flow". Because trust is key (it runs without asking permission each time), you might incorporate checks in the Apex/Flow (like ensure the order amount is below a threshold). But generally, the Salesforce tools used are the standard automation tools we've had for years – just triggered by the agent rather than a button click. Agentforce here provides the AI reasoning if needed (though in many Action cases, the logic could be simple rules). For example, an Action agent might still use an LLM to interpret a request: say you have a Slack bot where an employee can type "order more laptops", the agent uses AI to parse that (maybe figure out how many, what type from context) then executes the action. That front part would use Agentforce NLU capabilities, the back part uses an Apex action to interface with your ordering system. Another scenario: a scheduled Action agent (maybe runs nightly) – you could schedule an Agentforce agent or just schedule an Apex that invokes the agent. The tools are flexible here. But one important Salesforce feature for Action agents is Permission Sets and Security – since these agents act autonomously, you want to restrict them to what they should do. For instance, give an Action agent its own integration user or a permission set that only allows the object it needs to touch. Salesforce's Einstein Trust

Layer ensures the LLM doesn't do unauthorized things, but you also want your configuration to be tight (e.g., if it's creating orders, it shouldn't also be able to delete accounts). In terms of mapping, Action pattern often equals one Invocable Action in Agentforce – which could be implemented by an Apex method or Flow. If it involves external systems, then an Apex callout or MuleSoft call is part of that action. Essentially, think of these agents as glorified "if condition met, then perform X" automations – not too different from a workflow rule of old, except with more brains possibly deciding if condition met (the AI could decide an action is needed based on unstructured input).

Coach Pattern → Agent Builder + Apex (for analysis) + LWC (for delivery): Coach agents deliver guidance, which often means analyzing a user or scenario and then pushing advice. Tools wise, a Coach might run periodically or be triggered by an event (like a new opportunity created triggers a Sales Coach agent to analyze it). You'd use Apex or an AI prompt to generate the guidance content. For example, an Apex class might compare an opportunity's fields to a set of best-practice criteria and produce suggestions (like "Close Date is a Monday, those usually slip – consider moving to last business day of quarter."). Or an LLM action might evaluate the text of a customer email and suggest a response approach for the support rep. The output then needs to be delivered in context. Often, that's via a Toast notification, Chatter post, Slack message, or even inserting a note on a record. A Coach could use something like Next Best Action framework (though NBA is more rule-based; an AI Coach could be seen as an advanced NBA). Lightning Web Components can be used to show the coaching tips on a record page in a nice format (like a "Tips" component that queries the agent's output). Agent Builder would orchestrate triggers and actions, but likely you also incorporate scheduling (maybe via a scheduled Apex that invokes the agent for each relevant record/user). For instance, to coach managers, a batch job could run weekly, call the Coach agent for each manager (passing their team's data) and post a private message to them with insights. Tools like Einstein Analytics (Tableau CRM) might even be used by the agent indirectly – e.g., use a dataset to derive some metric then present advice. If you want real-time proactive advice, you might integrate with the UI similar to Companion: e.g. when a sales rep is viewing an opportunity, a behind-the-scenes call could fetch Coach agent tips for that opp. In terms of mapping: Coach pattern uses multi-faceted tools – it might combine data analysis (via Apex/Analytics), natural language generation (via LLM prompts to phrase the advice nicely), and a delivery mechanism (via UI or notifications). It also benefits from contextual awareness: Salesforce's context variables (like

$User, $Profile) can be fed into the agent's logic to tailor advice. The Atlas Reasoning Engine in Agentforce can take instructions like "adapt tone to user's role" which is perfect for a Coach that should speak differently to a new employee vs. a veteran. Implementation could also use Custom Metadata to store coaching rules or thresholds (so business folks can tweak when the agent should comment on something).

Given these mappings, it's clear that Agentforce doesn't operate in isolation – it builds on core Salesforce capabilities. Patterns essentially dictate which combination of tools you'll lean on. As you design, always ask: what's the appropriate tool for each part of this agent? For instance, if it's "decide if threshold breached -> alert user", threshold check might be Apex, alert might be Flow creating a Task. If it's "summarize data -> provide to user", maybe Data Cloud + Prompt, then output via LWC.

One strategy teams use is to annotate or tag components with the pattern. For example, you might include a prefix or keyword in Flow names like "Sentinel – Case SLA Monitor Flow" or in Apex classes like "CoachOpportunityHelper". This makes it easy to identify in the org which components belong to which pattern/agent. It can also feed into observability: the Agentforce Command Center could allow tagging agents by type, then you could filter dashboards by "show me all Supervisor agents and their average human escalation rate," etc. If not yet a feature, you can DIY by using a naming convention or custom metadata on each agent record.

Pro Tip: Annotate your implementations with pattern info. Drop a brief note in your Flow descriptions or Apex class comments: e.g., "Pattern: Curator – gathers knowledge base articles for agents to answer FAQs". This will help code reviewers and future maintainers instantly know the context. It also opens up possibilities like pattern-specific static code analysis rules (e.g., a lint rule that flags if a Presenter pattern Apex class is trying to do DML – that might indicate a wrong approach, since Presenters typically shouldn't change data). By tagging components, your observability and governance gets a boost; you can quickly run an audit "show all Apex classes used by Sentinel agents" if an incident arises.

To illustrate an end-to-end example, consider building a Sentinel agent for high-value account changes. You'd use a Platform Event or trigger on Account updates (Tool: Apex trigger), funnel that into an Agent action (Agent Builder config with an Invocable Apex that checks "if account value > $1M and important fields changed"), and if conditions meet, the Apex calls a Flow (Tool: Flow) to create an Alert record and maybe send an email to the account owner. You'd tag the Apex as "SentinelAccountWatcher". In testing, you simulate account changes (maybe using the Agentforce Testing Center to inject events). In production, you monitor via logs or the Command Center to see how often this Sentinel fires and ensure it's not spamming (tweaking thresholds via Custom Metadata without changing code if needed). We just used at least four tools (Triggers, Apex, Flows, Email Alerts) in one agent – typical for an enterprise scenario.

As you design each pattern, you'll get a feel: e.g., anything with heavy AI text generation, lean on Prompt Builder and LLM actions; anything with complex decision logic, likely Apex; anything user-interactive, think LWC/Slack; anything multi-step, think Flow Orchestration or even Salesforce Scheduler. By aligning the right tool to the right pattern, you also make sure you're using Salesforce tech as intended (which usually yields better scalability and less hackiness).

In conclusion, Salesforce provides the ingredients, and agent patterns are the recipe guiding how to mix them. A robust agent will often involve a dash of Flow, a pinch of Apex, maybe a sprinkle of Data Cloud, all glued by Agentforce's orchestration. The patterns tell you which ingredients dominate the dish. Now that we've covered design and implementation, let's consolidate our understanding of the eight core patterns themselves. In the next section, we'll present them side-by-side in a quick-reference format, summarizing each pattern's essence, ideal use cases, typical inputs/outputs, and the Salesforce tools we just discussed that map to each.

THE EIGHT CORE PATTERNS AT A GLANCE

To wrap up this introductory chapter, let's summarize the eight core agent patterns we'll be working with throughout the playbook. Below is a handy at-a-glance list that captures each pattern's key characteristics. You can use this as a quick reference as you plan projects or communicate designs with your team. The list outlines each pattern's core function, the kind of problems it's ideal for, typical inputs and outputs, and which Salesforce tools are commonly used to implement it.

Sentinel

- **Core function:** Monitors signals and events, then reacts
- **Ideal use cases:** Event monitoring, anomaly detection, SLA enforcement (for example, HR policy violations, system errors)
- **Typical inputs:** Streaming events, data changes, system logs

- **Typical outputs:** Alerts, incident creation, automated escalation
- **Key Salesforce tools:** Platform Events, Change Data Capture triggers, Invocable Apex for evaluation logic, Flow for alerts and escalation, Command Center for monitoring

Supervisor

- **Core function:** Produces AI recommendations while deferring final decisions to humans
- **Ideal use cases:** Human-in-the-loop tasks such as expense approvals, content moderation, compliance checks
- **Typical inputs:** User submissions or queries, business rules, contextual data
- **Typical outputs:** Draft decisions or recommendations with approval requests
- **Key Salesforce tools:** Agent Builder topics and actions with LLM prompts, Flows for approval routing, Apex for complex policy checks, Salesforce Approval Processes

Conductor

- **Core function:** Orchestrates multi-step workflows and tool calls
- **Ideal use cases:** Complex, multi-system or long-running processes such as order fulfillment or employee onboarding
- **Typical inputs:** Triggers such as record changes or schedules, plus state from previous steps
- **Typical outputs:** Coordinated execution of multiple actions and a consolidated outcome
- **Key Salesforce tools:** Flow Orchestration, MuleSoft connectors for external steps, Invocable Apex for integration and error handling, Custom Metadata for configuration

Companion

- **Core function:** Assists users in real time and in context
- **Ideal use cases:** Interactive guidance such as internal copilots, live form assistance, guided in-app help
- **Typical inputs:** User input combined with current screen or contextual data

- **Typical outputs:** Contextual suggestions, step-by-step guidance, automated entries with user consent
- **Key Salesforce tools:** Lightning Web Components or Visualforce for UI, Agentforce APIs for dialogue handling, Prompt Builder for contextual responses, Embedded Chat or Slack integration

Presenter

- **Core function:** Summarizes and explains information for easy consumption
- **Ideal use cases:** Reporting, executive briefings, status updates such as daily KPI summaries or case wrap-ups
- **Typical inputs:** Structured data from CRM or Data Cloud, query results, knowledge articles
- **Typical outputs:** Human-readable summaries, explanations, visual report content
- **Key Salesforce tools:** Agent actions with LLMs for summarization, Flow or Apex to retrieve data, Einstein query capabilities, Lightning components for display

Curator

- **Core function:** Gathers, filters, and organizes data or knowledge
- **Ideal use cases:** Knowledge management, research assistance, assembling FAQs or document collections
- **Typical inputs:** Large datasets, document repositories, search queries
- **Typical outputs:** Filtered information sets, curated collections, consolidated knowledge artifacts
- **Key Salesforce tools:** Data Cloud indexing and queries, SOSL and search, Agent Builder actions to fetch multiple sources, Apex or Flow for filtering logic, optional external integrations

Action

- **Core function:** Executes a task autonomously
- **Ideal use cases:** Straight-through processing and simple automation such as auto-creating orders or resetting passwords
- **Typical inputs:** Triggering conditions or direct requests, thresholds, or commands

- **Typical outputs:** Completed transactions or updates with minimal user interaction
- **Key Salesforce tools:** Invocable Apex or Flow for execution, Agent Builder for topic-to-action mapping, Apex triggers or schedulers, Permission Sets and Trust Layer controls

Coach

- **Core function:** Provides personalized advice and feedback
- **Ideal use cases:** Skill coaching and decision support such as sales deal coaching, manager feedback, compliance reminders
- **Typical inputs:** User profile data, behavioral signals, situational context such as pipeline metrics or document content
- **Typical outputs:** Tailored guidance, next-best-action suggestions, warnings delivered as notifications or inline prompts
- **Key Salesforce tools:** Agentforce topics with rich instructions, Analytics or Apex for performance evaluation, Lightning components or Slack/Chatter for delivery, Custom Metadata for advice rules, Einstein Conversation Insights

Each pattern is a starting template. In real projects, you might combine patterns or evolve them. For instance, a single agent could embody both Presenter and Coach behaviors (presenting data then giving advice on it), or a Sentinel might hand off to a Conductor (detect an issue, then launch an orchestration to resolve it). That's fine – patterns are modular by design. But it's valuable to articulate which patterns are in play so you ensure you cover all the responsibilities implied by each.

It's also useful to share this matrix with your stakeholders. When everyone from developers to product owners to execs understands these eight agent archetypes, discussions become clearer. A product owner might say, "We need an agent to help in onboarding – likely a Companion pattern," which immediately sets expectations. Or an architect might caution, "We're trying to make this single agent do too much – it's part Sentinel, part Coach; maybe we should split those roles." Posting this list on your internal wiki or including it in design docs can foster that shared understanding (feel free to do so as a quick-reference cheat sheet for your team).

Finally, remember that each of these patterns will be explored in depth in upcoming chapters. There we'll dive into detailed examples, implementation steps, and advanced tips for each one. The quick summary above is your map; the next chapters are the turn-by-turn directions.

Having laid out the agent pattern landscape – the why, what, how, and where – you should now have a solid conceptual foundation. We've identified the recurring agent "types" and how to build them on Salesforce. The stage is set. Next, we will zoom in on the first (and perhaps most vigilant) of our patterns: the Sentinel. In Chapter 2, we'll learn how Sentinel agents monitor, detect, and act in various business contexts, and how to design and deploy a Sentinel step by step. But before we dive into that, let's recap the key takeaways from this chapter.

SUMMARY

In this opening chapter, we introduced the concept of AI agent patterns and established why they are a game-changer for designing and deploying AI agents on the Salesforce platform. Much like software design patterns, agent patterns serve as reusable blueprints – they help teams avoid one-off, inconsistent bot builds by providing proven templates for common scenarios. We emphasized that the real risk in the era of Agentforce isn't just building technically "bad" agents, but building a hodgepodge of agents with no common standards. Patterns offer a remedy by giving everyone a common language and structure for AI agents, thereby reducing chaos and improving alignment across developers, admins, architects, and business stakeholders.

We defined what agent patterns are in practical terms: they outline an agent's role, decision-making approach, and interaction style. By comparing them to familiar Salesforce patterns (like trigger frameworks or invocable Apex usage), we saw that patterns guide both how an agent is built internally and how it behaves externally. A quick real-world analogy (e.g., a Supervisor agent acting like an AI peer reviewer) helped cement these ideas. We also touched on the tools – such as Agent Builder, Flow, Apex, and more – showing that Salesforce provides the building blocks to implement any pattern once you know which one you're following.

Next, we dove into why patterns matter. Patterns help prevent agent sprawl by ensuring new agents fit known molds instead of doing redundant or contradictory things. They embed trust and safety by carrying forward best practices (for example, every Supervisor pattern agent naturally includes a human check step, reducing risk). We noted how patterns enhance composability (agents can work together more easily) and maintainability (teams can understand and update agents faster when they recognize the pattern).

A pro tip highlighted using patterns as a checklist in design reviews, to catch any missing pieces before agents go live.

We then explored how patterns accelerate team performance. From onboarding new talent faster (because patterns convey design intent quickly), to reusing components (flows, Apex classes, prompt templates) across agents, to streamlining testing (each pattern suggests what to test and monitor), the benefits were clear. We saw that aligning Agentforce development with standard Salesforce DevOps (CI/CD, source control, etc.) is easier when agents are pattern-based, since they tend to be more modular and predictable. Essentially, patterns help teams move faster with confidence, turning AI development from art into more of a science.

Crucially, we demonstrated that these patterns apply beyond the usual CRM departments. Through examples in HR, Finance, Legal, Procurement, IT, and more, we showed an agent pattern can add value anywhere there's data and decisions. HR could use Sentinel agents for policy compliance, Finance could use Supervisor agents for approvals, Legal could use Coach agents for contract guidance, and so on. A quick list illustrated a non-CRM use case for each of the eight patterns, underlining that AI agents are enterprise-wide helpers, not just chatbots for sales or service. We also gave the advice that internal use cases are often a safe and high-ROI proving ground for agent technology.

Zooming out, we connected agent patterns to the broader AI ecosystem. We saw that frameworks like LangChain, CrewAI, and Microsoft's Autogen are leveraging similar ideas (planning, tool use, reflection, multi-agent orchestration) – meaning the patterns we adopt in Salesforce are in harmony with industry trends. We discussed interoperability standards like Model Context Protocol (MCP), which Salesforce Agentforce 3 supports, enabling Agentforce agents to plug into multi-platform workflows. The takeaway is that learning these patterns in Salesforce gives you insight applicable to AI systems in general – patterns are the common denominator that will let different AI platforms collaborate.

We then mapped each pattern to the Salesforce tools and features best suited for implementation. For instance, Sentinel agents lean on event triggers and Apex, Supervisor agents pair well with Flow and approval processes, Conductor agents may use Flow Orchestration and MuleSoft for cross-system steps, and Companion agents involve LWCs or Slack integrations for a great UI experience. We broke down how Agent Builder and other tools configure to support each pattern, and provided tips like tagging your components with pattern names to improve governance and clarity.

Finally, we presented a quick-reference list of all eight core patterns, summarizing their core function, use cases, inputs/outputs, and relevant Salesforce tools side by side. This matrix is both a cheat sheet for you and something to share with your team to establish a shared vocabulary around these patterns. It's essentially the "catalog" of the Agentforce Agent Pattern Playbook: Sentinel, Supervisor, Conductor, Companion, Presenter, Curator, Action, and Coach – each with its niche in the AI agent universe and each to be detailed in its own chapter.

With this foundational knowledge, you're now prepared to dive deeper. We've set the stage by explaining the why, what, and how of agent patterns. From here, we'll transition into the part of the book where each chapter will focus on one pattern in detail – starting with one of the most fundamental patterns: the Sentinel. In the next chapter, we'll explore the Sentinel pattern's intricacies, learning how to design agents that act as vigilant watchdogs over your business processes, detecting important signals and reacting autonomously (but appropriately) to keep things on track. Get ready to meet the digital watchtower of your AI agent arsenal! Chapter 2 will equip you with everything you need to implement Sentinel agents effectively and responsibly, kicking off our deep dive into the Agentforce patterns.

2

THE SENTINEL PATTERN (MONITOR AND REACT)

Imagine an AI that never sleeps – tirelessly watching logs, events, and signals across your business for the faintest sign of trouble or opportunity. This is the essence of the Sentinel pattern. A Sentinel agent is distinct within the Agentforce ecosystem as the vigilant monitor: it listens to a continuous stream of signals, detects notable events, evaluates their significance, and then reacts according to policy. In simpler terms, a Sentinel is the digital equivalent of a perimeter watchtower. But unlike a passive alert system, a Sentinel doesn't just ring an alarm – it can also take action (or trigger downstream actions) to address what it has detected. This combination of signal listening, evaluation logic, and execution is what makes the Sentinel pattern so powerful and broadly useful.

Sentinel agents have cross-functional relevance. In IT operations, a Sentinel might watch deployment logs for failures and automatically roll back a release or notify on-call staff. In finance, a Sentinel can flag suspicious spending patterns or duplicate invoice payments as soon as they occur. In HR, a Sentinel monitors for policy violations or critical employee events (for example, alerting HR if a high performer submits a resignation). In customer support, a Sentinel keeps an eye on open cases and catches looming SLA breaches before they escalate into incidents. The pattern appears in nearly every domain: wherever there are streams of data or events, a Sentinel can stand guard.

What truly sets Sentinel agents apart is their ability to thrive in event-rich environments. Modern enterprise systems generate continuous signals – database changes, application logs, API calls, IoT sensor readings, you name it. A Sentinel agent is designed to reduce response time and increase reliability by reacting to these signals in real time without flooding the system with noise. In practice, that means implementing the right filtering and logic so that humans or downstream processes only get alerted when it really matters. The Sentinel should catch the needle in the haystack (or the smoke before the fire), not spam everyone whenever any minor log entry appears.

To achieve this, Sentinel agents typically rely on tight integrations between event sources, decision logic, and action handlers. On the Salesforce platform, this might look like: a platform event listener (such as a Change Data Capture event or custom Platform Event) picks up the signal, some evaluation logic runs (maybe via an Apex class or even an embedded ML model/LLM call), and then an execution pathway kicks off (perhaps a Flow or an Invocable Apex action to perform a task or call an external service). Salesforce's Agentforce tooling makes these designs approachable – for example, you might use Agent Builder to define the event subscription and outline the agent's policy, an Invocable Apex method to code complex evaluations, and the Command Center observability dashboard to monitor all these agent-triggered actions in one place. (We'll discuss Command Center more – it's essentially a "mission control" for agents, giving a unified view of their health and actions.)

By combining declarative platform features with custom logic and AI capabilities, Sentinel agents can be both nimble and smart. They can execute straightforward rules (e.g. "if server CPU > 90% for 5 minutes, launch a new server instance") and also handle nuanced judgments (e.g. using a language model to read an error message and classify its severity). This blend of always-on vigilance and decision-making intelligence is what makes the Sentinel pattern a foundation for autonomous operations.

In the pages ahead, we'll dive into the Sentinel pattern in depth. First, we need to clearly define the Sentinel's role and how it differs from other agent patterns in our playbook. Understanding the structure and purpose of a Sentinel is crucial before attempting to build one. The next section will define the Sentinel pattern and outline its core lifecycle and variants, setting the stage for applying it effectively.

DEFINING THE SENTINEL PATTERN

What exactly is a Sentinel agent? At its core, a Sentinel is an autonomous agent that monitors a source of events or signals and reacts when certain conditions are met. In many ways it's analogous to a watchdog or an automated sentinel guard: continuously observing, evaluating significance, and then responding according to predefined rules or learned policies. The Sentinel pattern is characterized by a simple loop of: Signal → Evaluation → Decision → Action. Let's break that down:

Signal (Monitor): A Sentinel continuously listens for input events. These could be platform events (like a Salesforce Platform Event message or Change Data Capture on an object), system logs, external webhooks (e.g. an incoming HTTP callback from another system), or even streaming data from APIs. The key is that the Sentinel is passive until an event arrives – it doesn't initiate work on its own, but it's always waiting and ready.

Evaluation (Analyze): When a signal comes in, the Sentinel evaluates it. This could be a simple check (e.g. compare a field value to a threshold), a complex rule set, or even an AI-based analysis (like running the text of an event through an ML model to detect sentiment or anomalies). The evaluation step might also involve context enrichment – for example, fetching additional data to make a more informed decision. A Sentinel watching a "new case created" event might query the account's history to see if this is a high-value customer or if similar cases happened recently. Evaluation can produce a result like "notable event" vs "ignore," or categorize the event's severity.

Decision (Policy): Based on the evaluation, the Sentinel decides what to do. In many cases, this is entwined with evaluation (e.g. the logic might directly decide "if X then trigger alert Y"). But conceptually, it's useful to think of a policy layer: given the analysis (and perhaps a confidence score), does this event warrant action? The policy could implement thresholds ("if error severity >= HIGH, then act") or patterns ("if three failed logins from the same user in 1 minute, then act"). This step ensures the Sentinel doesn't overreact to low-significance signals – a good Sentinel is keen-eyed but level-headed.

Action (React): Finally, if the decision is to react, the Sentinel carries out one or more actions. This could be as simple as creating an alert record or sending a notification. Or it could kick off a chain of responses – for instance, launching a remediation flow, calling an external service, or even invoking another agent. In Salesforce Agentforce terms, the action might be executed via a Flow (e.g. an auto-launched Flow that creates tasks, posts to Slack, etc.), an Apex method (to perform complex updates or callouts), or by publishing another event that downstream systems subscribe to.

This lifecycle repeats continuously for each new signal. It's a pipeline that transforms raw events into decisions and actions. It's worth noting that some Sentinels implement a stateful memory of events – for example, to decide that "three events in X time" constitute a pattern. Others are stateless, treating each event in isolation. We'll discuss state considerations shortly.

One helpful way to understand Sentinel agents is to differentiate them from a couple of other patterns in this playbook: Conductor and Supervisor. If you recall from Chapter 1, a Conductor agent is an orchestrator – it coordinates multi-step processes or multiple agents (think of it as a project manager or workflow engine). A Supervisor agent, on the other hand, introduces a human-in-the-loop for validation – it generates recommendations or drafts but expects a person to review/approve (like a knowledgeable assistant that always seeks sign-off). The Sentinel is different from both:

The Sentinel is reactive and focused on detection. It doesn't necessarily perform a multi-step plan (that's the Conductor's job), nor does it inherently involve human approval (that's the Supervisor's realm). Instead, the Sentinel's responsibility is to keep watch and respond immediately to events according to predefined policy.

Think of it this way: if these agents were people in an organization, the Sentinel is the security guard or system monitor, the Conductor is the team lead coordinating a project, and the Supervisor is the quality control officer checking work. The Sentinel spots something and either handles it or raises the alarm; the Conductor marshals resources to execute a game plan; the Supervisor double-checks and fine-tunes the output of others. They have distinct roles, though in practice they might work in tandem (e.g. a Sentinel might hand off to a Conductor for complex responses, or a Sentinel might notify a Supervisor agent/human to review an event).

For example, in an incident response scenario: a Sentinel could detect an anomaly (like a server spike or security alert) and trigger a Conductor agent to handle the incident resolution steps. Meanwhile, a Supervisor pattern might come into play to have a human verify the final resolution or communications. But the Sentinel's part in that story was the detection and initial trigger.

It's also useful to compare the Sentinel pattern to classic software concepts. It resembles the Observer pattern from software design: something happens (subject changes state) and an observer is notified to react. In Salesforce terms, a close cousin is the trigger on a database object (or a platform event subscriber) – those are essentially built-in Sentinel mechanisms at a low level. In fact, implementing a Sentinel often involves writing a trigger or a Platform Event subscriber under the hood. The big difference is that a design pattern like Sentinel implies a higher-level architecture: it's not just one trigger on one object, but a coordinated agent that might handle multiple event sources, apply more sophisticated logic (possibly involving AI), and execute richer actions than a single trigger can. A well-designed Sentinel agent is also bulk-safe and scalable – just like a good trigger framework processes records in batches to handle high volumes, a Sentinel should be able to handle bursts of events gracefully without missing signals or causing performance issues. If 1000 events come in at once, a robust Sentinel will process them in bulk (perhaps via batch Apex or a Bulk API event handler) and produce the necessary outcomes, similar to how Salesforce triggers operate on batches of records for efficiency.

Speaking of scale, Sentinel agents can be layered watchers. This means you might have a hierarchy or sequence of checks. For instance, a simple layer might filter obvious noise (like ignore events below a certain severity), then a second layer adds context (attach related info to the event), then a third layer makes a decision (score it and act if score > threshold). You could implement this layering within one agent or via multiple agents working together (for example, a Curator agent – another pattern introduced in Chapter 1 – might act as a pre-filter for a Sentinel). An advanced Sentinel might incorporate a confidence scoring mechanism: for example, an LLM could evaluate an event description and give a probability that it's critical. The Sentinel can then decide, say, only to act if confidence is above 80% to reduce false alarms. We'll see more about combining Sentinel with Curator or AI filters later.

Pro tip: Before you start building any Sentinel agent, it's wise to define the "known unknowns" – the events or conditions the business cares about but currently isn't catching reliably. In other words, identify the blind spots or latency in your current monitoring. These will be prime candidates for a Sentinel pattern. For example, perhaps you know that customer support sometimes fails to notice when a VIP client's case is stuck (so a Sentinel for SLA breaches could fill that gap), or you suspect there are fraudulent expense reports slipping through in finance (so a

Sentinel for abnormal spend can help). By listing these out, you ensure your Sentinel agent's requirements are driven by real needs and you design it to catch those elusive but important scenarios. This also helps you set the right thresholds and actions – essentially encoding the tribal knowledge of "what do we wish we had known sooner?" into an automated watcher.

Having defined what the Sentinel pattern is and how it operates, we can now move from theory to practice. Next, we'll explore concrete use cases across various business functions to illustrate how Sentinel agents can be applied in different domains. This will give us a clearer picture of the pattern's versatility and value before we dive into designing and building one.

SENTINEL PATTERN USE CASES ACROSS FUNCTIONS

The Sentinel pattern isn't just a lofty concept – it delivers tangible benefits across a wide range of business scenarios. Let's tour through several realistic examples in different functions to see how Monitor and React agents can improve operations. In each of these cases, note the common thread: an event occurs (often something time-sensitive or anomaly-related), the Sentinel agent detects it quickly, and a responsive action is taken (often preventing a bigger issue or seizing an opportunity). We'll then summarize these examples in a handy list mapping each use case to its event source, logic, and tooling.

Customer Service – Preempting SLA Breaches: Imagine a global support center where certain customer cases have service-level agreements (SLAs) – for example, "Priority 1 cases must be resolved within 24 hours." A Sentinel agent can monitor all open support cases in real time. If a case is approaching its SLA deadline without resolution, the Sentinel detects this "ticking clock" event. The evaluation logic might check how much time is left and whether the case has seen recent activity. If it's, say, under 2 hours to go and no owner response in the last 4 hours, the Sentinel's policy deems it high risk. The action? Perhaps auto-escalate the case: update its status, notify a support manager via Slack or Salesforce notification, and maybe even invoke a Conductor agent to spin up a rapid response task force. The Sentinel essentially gives the support team a heads-up: "This case is about to breach its SLA – do something now." Without such an agent, teams often rely on periodic reports or someone manually checking the queue, which isn't real-time and can let things slip through. By having a Sentinel, customer service can dramatically reduce missed SLAs and the firefighting that follows.

Finance – Flagging Duplicate Payments or Anomalies: In accounts payable, duplicate vendor payments are costly mistakes that sometimes happen in large organizations (two departments accidentally pay the same invoice, for example). A finance Sentinel agent listens to payment transactions being recorded. When a new payment event comes in, the Sentinel quickly cross-references it against recent payments: same vendor, same amount, similar date? If it finds a likely duplicate, the agent flags it. The policy could be "two payments to the same vendor within X days for the same amount triggers an alert." The action here might be to create a finance case or notification for the accounts payable team to review and potentially cancel one of the payments. Similarly, the finance Sentinel could watch for abnormal spending – for example, an expense report that is 5x higher than usual, or a sudden spike in spend in a certain category. The event source could be an integration from an ERP system or expense system (via MuleSoft publishing an event to Salesforce when a payment is submitted). The Sentinel's evaluation might leverage an anomaly detection model or simple thresholds configured by finance (e.g. "flag any single expense over $10,000 or any daily total over $50,000"). The benefit here is catching errors or fraud within minutes of occurrence rather than during month-end reconciliation.

HR – Catching Critical Employee Events: Human Resources can use Sentinels to ensure important employee events get immediate attention. One example: if a high-performing employee (say one who's rated as "Key Talent" or in a critical role) submits a resignation via the HR system, that's a trigger the organization would want to know right now. A Sentinel can monitor the HR system (perhaps via a platform event or webhook when a resignation record is created). The Sentinel evaluates: "Is this employee a high performer or critical role?" – it could query the employee's profile or performance records. If yes, the decision is to react. The Sentinel's action might be multi-faceted: notify the HR business partner and the employee's manager immediately, perhaps create a "retain this employee" task force (invoking another agent or process to attempt an intervention or knowledge transfer plan). Another HR example: monitoring policy violations – say employees posting certain keywords on the company intranet that might indicate harassment or data leakage. A Sentinel could integrate with a collaboration platform's API to scan messages in real-time for triggers (like someone sharing a confidential client list publicly). That crosses into compliance territory as well.

Supply Chain – Detecting Delays and Disruptions: In a supply chain or operations context, a Sentinel agent can dramatically improve responsiveness to logistical issues. Consider a manufacturing company that relies on IoT sensors and shipping APIs. A Sentinel might subscribe to a stream of IoT events from factory machines (maybe via a Salesforce IoT Cloud event or an MQTT feed). If a critical machine sends a "temperature too high" or "unexpected shutdown" signal, the Sentinel immediately flags that the production line might stop. It could then trigger maintenance workflows (perhaps calling a Conductor agent to schedule a repair and re-route production to other machines). Or take shipping: the Sentinel listens to a third-party shipping status API (via MuleSoft pushing events into Salesforce whenever a status update comes). If a key delivery is marked as delayed beyond a threshold, the Sentinel reacts by alerting the supply chain manager and possibly reordering stock or sending notifications to customers about potential delays. In essence, the Sentinel acts as the bridge between external real-time data and internal action – ensuring the business isn't the last to know about a supply disruption.

Legal/Compliance – Real-Time Contract Clause Alerts: Legal teams often need to ensure that contracts or documents adhere to certain standards. Suppose your company has certain "non-negotiable" clauses that must appear (or forbidden clauses that must not appear) in all vendor contracts. A Sentinel can help by scanning each new contract as it's uploaded or generated. The event could be "new contract record created" in Salesforce (assuming contracts are stored or tracked in CRM), or even a document being added to a repository. The Sentinel could leverage an AI component – for example, use an LLM or NLP model to read the contract text and detect if any risky language is present (like an indemnification clause that's not standard). The evaluation might produce a score or list of issues. The policy might be: if any high-risk clause is found, flag legal. The action could be creating a Legal Task or Case in Salesforce, or even automatically sending the document to a legal queue for review, with a summary of what was flagged. Alternatively, for compliance, think of something like data privacy: a Sentinel could monitor data exports from Salesforce (using Event Monitoring logs as the signal source) and detect if someone exported a large number of contacts or ran a report with sensitive data. That could then trigger a security review action.

Security/IT – Correlating Low-Level Events into Alerts: IT Security is a classic domain for Sentinel-like logic. Often a single event (like one failed login) is benign, but a combination (several failed logins, followed by a new device login, followed by a data download) is a red flag. A Sentinel agent can be set up to correlate streams of security events. Salesforce itself generates event logs (e.g., LoginEvent records, Platform Event for security alerts, etc.). A Sentinel could subscribe to these or an external SIEM system feed. It might maintain a short-term memory (stateful evaluation) to aggregate events per user or per session. For example, if User X fails login 3 times in 5 minutes, then successfully logs in from a new IP – that pattern triggers the Sentinel. The response might be to automatically lock the account or create a high-priority security incident. Another case: monitoring configuration changes in Salesforce (via Setup Audit Trail events). A Sentinel could watch for a combination like "admin changed profile permissions" and "admin exporting data right after" which could be suspicious (maybe an insider threat scenario). The Sentinel can then notify the security team or even rollback the permission change via an automated flow if that's appropriate and safe. These multi-signal Sentinels are essentially doing what expensive security tools do – but you can implement them with Agentforce using event streams and Apex/Flow logic.

As we see, the Sentinel pattern finds utility from customer-facing processes to deep in the back office. The key benefits in all these examples are speed and proactive response. By catching events as they happen (or shortly after), Sentinels help organizations respond in minutes instead of hours or days. That can save revenue, improve customer satisfaction, prevent compliance breaches, and reduce manual monitoring workload.

To cement these examples, the list below maps each use case to (a) the typical event source, (b) the evaluation/logic applied, (c) the next action the Sentinel takes, and (d) which Salesforce/Agentforce tools could be used in the implementation. This can serve as a blueprint when you're brainstorming Sentinel opportunities in your own context.

Customer Service SLA Breach

- **Event source:** Case created or updated events; time-based checks via platform events or scheduled triggers
- **Evaluation logic:** Evaluate case priority, time open versus SLA threshold, and whether there has been recent activity
- **Sentinel action (next step):** Escalate the case by changing status, notify the support manager (for example via Slack), and invoke an escalation Flow or Conductor agent for incident management

- **Tools and tech:** Platform Events with Apex or Flow; Agent Builder configuration for SLA rules; Salesforce Flow for notifications

Finance Duplicate Payment

- **Event source:** Payment transaction event from ERP via MuleSoft or Change Data Capture on the Payment object
- **Evaluation logic:** Compare new payment to recent records with the same vendor and amount within a defined time window
- **Sentinel action (next step):** Create an alert record or task for the accounts payable team and optionally place the duplicate payment on hold via API
- **Tools and tech:** MuleSoft event to Salesforce with invocable Apex logic; Flow to create tasks; Agentforce developer tools for integration

Finance Spend Anomaly

- **Event source:** Expense report submission from a Salesforce object or external webhook
- **Evaluation logic:** Check whether the amount exceeds a defined threshold or deviates significantly from the user's typical spending pattern
- **Sentinel action (next step):** Notify a finance approver or create a compliance case and optionally trigger a Supervisor agent for manual review
- **Tools and tech:** Change Data Capture or Platform Event on Expense__c with Apex or Einstein Analytics for anomaly detection; Flow for alerts

HR High-Performer Resignation

- **Event source:** HR system event such as a Resignation record insert or webhook from Workday into Salesforce
- **Evaluation logic:** Evaluate employee performance rating and role criticality against defined criteria
- **Sentinel action (next step):** Immediately notify the HR business partner and manager, and trigger a retention Conductor to attempt counter-offer or knowledge transfer

- **Tools and tech:** Platform Event or Change Data Capture with Apex for employee lookup; Agent Builder invoking a Flow to start the retention process

Supply Chain Shipment Delay

- **Event source:** Shipping update from an external API via MuleSoft or Salesforce Connect
- **Evaluation logic:** Compare actual status or delivery date against expected timelines and assess whether the delay exceeds a threshold or impacts a critical order
- **Sentinel action (next step):** Alert the supply chain team and trigger a Conductor to evaluate alternatives such as sourcing from a backup supplier
- **Tools and tech:** MuleSoft streaming API into Platform Events; Apex for evaluation logic; Flow or Orchestration for follow-up actions

Manufacturing IoT Alert

- **Event source:** IoT sensor events via Salesforce IoT or a streaming API
- **Evaluation logic:** Evaluate sensor readings against safe operating ranges and optionally aggregate readings over a time window
- **Sentinel action (next step):** Trigger a maintenance workflow by creating a Field Service work order, notify technicians, and optionally issue a shutdown command via API
- **Tools and tech:** Salesforce IoT Explorer events with Apex threshold logic defined in Custom Metadata; Invocable Apex to create work orders; Flow for notifications; external callouts for device control

Legal Contract Clause Flag

- **Event source:** Contract document upload via Salesforce Files or creation of a Contract record
- **Evaluation logic:** Use NLP or an LLM to scan text for forbidden or required clauses or evaluate metadata for non-standard terms
- **Sentinel action (next step):** Create a legal review case, notify the legal team, and tag the contract record with a "Needs Review" status

- **Tools and tech:** Apex callouts to Einstein NLP or third-party AI; Invocable Apex or Flow to create cases; Agentforce Command Center for tracking flag frequency

IT Security Multi-Event Alert

- **Event source:** Security events such as LoginEvent or Transaction Security alerts streamed via Event Monitoring
- **Evaluation logic:** Correlate multiple events by user or session, such as repeated failures combined with data exports, using pattern logic stored in metadata
- **Sentinel action (next step):** Create a security incident record or ITSM ticket, auto-lock the account or disable the session if severe, and immediately notify the InfoSec team
- **Tools and tech:** Event Monitoring with Apex for stateful correlation logic using custom objects; Flow for incident creation; integrations with SIEM or ITSM tools; Command Center for real-time dashboards

As the list illustrates, implementing a Sentinel usually involves hooking into the right event source, applying the appropriate evaluation logic (which can range from simple if-then rules to AI-driven analysis), then taking an action which often is an integration point back into business processes. Salesforce provides many of the pieces out-of-the-box: Platform Events and Change Data Capture for event sources, Apex and Einstein APIs for logic, Flow and external service calls for actions. Agentforce's tooling (like Agent Builder and the upcoming Agentforce Dev Tools) can help glue these pieces together in a more guided way, so you don't have to custom-build every part.

Each department can have its own Sentinels, but an organization also gains a lot by standardizing how they build them – that's where the pattern concept shines. A Salesforce developer in IT and another in HR might not typically compare notes, but if both are building Sentinel agents, they can share a common approach (for example, using a similar template for how to write the Apex evaluation logic or how to structure alert messages). It also means a central platform team could provide some reusable components, like a base "Sentinel Alert" custom object or logging framework that all Sentinels use.

Now that we've seen the why and what through examples, you might be itching to build one of these Sentinels yourself. The next step is to dive into how to design the architecture of a Sentinel agent in Salesforce Agentforce. What components do you need? How do you ensure its scalable, configurable, and reliable? We'll tackle these questions in the next section, translating the use case ideas into a general architecture and design considerations for Sentinel agents.

DESIGNING SENTINEL AGENT ARCHITECTURE

Designing a Sentinel agent requires balancing responsiveness with maintainability. Based on our understanding of the Sentinel's role, we can outline a standard architecture for a Sentinel agent within Salesforce's ecosystem. The architecture generally comprises three core components (with potential sub-components): Signal Ingestion, Evaluation/Decision Logic, and Action Mechanism. Let's walk through each, then discuss cross-cutting concerns like temporal patterns, state, and configurability.

Signal Ingestion

This is the front door of the Sentinel. In Salesforce, there are a few common ways to ingest events:

Platform Events & CDC (Change Data Capture): Salesforce allows you to define custom Platform Events (pub/sub model) and to enable CDC on objects, which publishes events on data changes. A Sentinel can subscribe to these. For example, a "CaseStatusChange" platform event could be emitted whenever a case is nearing SLA, or CDC on the Case object could alert our agent to any new case or status update. Platform Events have the advantage of decoupling – different systems (or different parts of the org) can publish events that Sentinels subscribe to, which is great for modularity.

Streaming API / CometD: Under the hood, platform events and CDC use the Streaming API. But if needed, you could also directly use generic events or PushTopic events. However, these are older approaches; with Agentforce we'd likely stick to Platform Events or newer event types.

Triggers on Objects: This is a more tightly coupled approach, but effective for certain scenarios. For instance, an Apex trigger on the Expense__c object could directly call a Sentinel's logic when a new expense is inserted. This is immediate and doesn't require an event bus, though it runs synchronously in the transaction (which can be a consideration – we might prefer async for complex evaluation).

External Webhooks and API calls: Many external systems can call a Salesforce API when something happens (for example, an IoT platform could do an HTTP POST to a Salesforce endpoint on an event). Agentforce might also allow easier integration via MuleSoft or function services. In such cases, the Sentinel's ingestion point might be an Apex REST endpoint or a MuleSoft-initiated flow that receives the event data.

Scheduled Polling (as a fallback): If real-time events aren't available, a Sentinel might periodically run (using a scheduled Apex or cron job) to check for certain conditions. However, this is more "monitor and react" in a batch sense rather than true event-driven. It's an option but tends to be less responsive. Ideally, we use real event feeds.

For design, it's often best to decouple ingestion from processing. For example, a Platform Event could trigger a Flow or Queueable Apex to do the evaluation asynchronously. This way, your event capture is robust (the event can be replayed if the processing fails, etc.), and you're not doing heavy logic in a trigger context that could slow down a user's transaction.

Evaluation & Decision Logic

This is the brain of the Sentinel. We consider:

Rules vs. AI: Some sentinel conditions are straightforward (rules/thresholds), while others might benefit from AI/ML. For instance, to detect a spending anomaly, you could hardcode a threshold or use an Einstein Discovery model to flag statistically unusual entries. Salesforce's Einstein services or even an external ML model could be invoked here. With Agentforce, we can integrate such calls as agent "actions" or via Apex callouts.

Invocable Apex: A common pattern is to implement the evaluation logic as an Apex class method annotated with @InvocableMethod. This allows you to call it from a Flow or even from Agent Builder declaratively. It also makes it easy to reuse across different places. For example, you might have an invocable method AlertEvaluator.evaluateCaseSLA(List<Case> cases) that returns a list of cases that are at risk. The Flow subscribes to case CDC events, collects new/updated cases, passes them to this Apex, and then the Apex returns which ones need action. Invocable Apex methods can also be bulkified (taking a list input), aligning with Salesforce best practices. Below is a simplified snippet of what such an Apex might look like:

```
public class CaseSLAEvaluator {
```

```
    // Invocable method to evaluate SLA status for cases
    @InvocableMethod
    public static List<Id> checkCases(List<Id> caseIds) {
        List<Case> cases = [SELECT Id, Priority, Status, SLA_Due_Date__c, Last-
ModifiedDate
                            FROM Case WHERE Id IN :caseIds];
        List<Id> atRiskCases = new List<Id>();
        for (Case c : cases) {
            if (c.Priority == 'High' && c.SLA_Due_Date__c != null) {
                // If SLA due within next 2 hours and case not closed
                if (c.Status != 'Closed' &&
                    DateTime.now().addHours(2) > c.SLA_Due_Date__c) {
                    atRiskCases.add(c.Id);
                }
            }
        }
        return atRiskCases;
    }
}
```

Example: Invocable Apex logic for a Sentinel that monitors high-priority cases close to breaching SLA. It returns the list of case Ids that need attention (e.g., to be escalated).

In this snippet, we see bulk-safe logic iterating through multiple cases. This method could be invoked by a Flow that runs on a schedule or triggered by an event, and the Flow could then loop through the returned IDs to take action (like posting alerts). The logic here is simple threshold checking; more complex evaluation might involve additional queries or calls to AI services.

Custom Metadata for Config: Hardcoding values like "2 hours" or which priority to check isn't ideal. Instead, we design our Sentinel logic to use custom metadata or custom settings for easy adjustability. For example, we could have a Custom Metadata Type named SentinelPolicy__mdt with fields like Name (e.g., "Case_SLA"), ThresholdMinutes__c (e.g., 120 for 2 hours), ApplicablePriority__c ("High"). Then the Apex would retrieve that config record inside the method:

```
Integer threshold = SentinelPolicy__mdt.getInstance('Case_SLA').Threshold-Minutes__c;

...

if (c.SLA_Due_Date__c != null &&

  DateTime.now().addMinutes(threshold) > c.SLA_Due_Date__c) {... }
```

By using metadata, admins or architects can tune the Sentinel's sensitivity without modifying code. This makes the agent more flexible and fosters trust – you might start with a conservative threshold and later adjust it as you see how many alerts are generated.

Temporal patterns & state: As noted, some evaluations need to consider events over time (e.g., "3 failures in 5 minutes"). There are a few ways to handle this:

Keep an aggregator state in a custom object or static resource. For example, a custom object Login_Failure_Tally__c could log user failure counts, and the Sentinel's logic updates and reads from this object. If using Platform Events, sometimes you might accumulate events in a batch (the platform can deliver events in a batch to a subscriber).

Use an Apex static map or cache if the window is very short and within a single execution context. But in a distributed event system, that often won't cover all cases (multiple events might trigger separate transactions).

Employ an external tool: Salesforce Event Monitoring or Shield has transaction security policies that can detect patterns, or use something like an Einstein Analytics dataset to flag anomalies. However, those might not be real-time enough. Another approach is using Platform Cache or Redis (Heroku) to store counters for a short duration.

Design simplification: You could actually treat the detection of a pattern as its own "higher-level event". E.g., write an Apex that subscribes to the raw events and whenever the pattern condition is met, it fires a new Platform Event like "MultiFailAlertEvent" which a Sentinel then just treats like a normal single event. This splits the complexity (one part does pattern detection, the Sentinel proper does response).

The key is that stateful logic introduces complexity – you need to consider how to reset state, how to avoid infinite growth of records, etc. Sometimes it's perfectly fine to have a slightly delayed reaction: e.g., schedule a small Apex job to run every 5 minutes to check if "3 failures in last 5 min" happened. It's near-real-time and simpler than juggling state in memory.

Layering and filtering: As mentioned earlier, a Sentinel might incorporate multiple checks. A best practice is to design the evaluation logic in modular steps. For instance:

1. Filter out trivial signals quickly (cheap operations first).

2. Enrich with context (only for those that passed filter).

3. Apply heavier logic or AI (only on the enriched subset).

4. Decide and tag what needs action.

This way, you're efficient. If you have 100 events and only 5 matter, maybe you only call the AI on those 5 rather than all 100. This is analogous to how a security system might have a broad motion detector but then a finer camera analysis if motion is detected – you don't run face recognition on an empty room continuously.

Confidence and scoring: If using an ML model or if the outcome isn't a binary rule, you often get a score. Deciding the threshold for that score is important and again should be configurable. You might start with a low threshold to see what the Sentinel catches (and risk false positives) and then gradually raise it. Logging all scored events (even if below threshold) for a while is helpful, so you can review "events that were ignored" to see if you're missing things.

Action Mechanism

Once the Sentinel decides an event needs reaction, how does it actually do something? There are multiple mechanisms, and often a Sentinel might use more than one for different outcomes:

Invoke a Flow: Salesforce Flow (particularly auto-launched or record-triggered flows) can handle many actions declaratively – updating records, creating tasks, sending emails/alerts, posting to chatter or external systems (through

HTTP callouts or MuleSoft). If your Sentinel's response is a series of record updates or notifications within Salesforce, a Flow is a great choice. You can call an invocable Flow from Apex or subscribe a Flow directly to a Platform Event. Using Flow Builder also makes it easier for admins to visualize or adjust the process later. You might have a library of sub-flows like "NotifySupportManager" or "CreateSecurityIncidentRecord" that the Sentinel can trigger.

Apex actions: If the action involves complex logic or external API callouts that require transformations, Apex might be necessary. For example, automatically reversing a duplicate payment might mean calling an external payment API – an Apex @InvocableMethod or a trigger could handle that. Apex can also work in conjunction with Flow (Flow can call Apex and vice versa).

External Integration: Sometimes the "action" is actually handing off to an external system. For example, raising an incident in ServiceNow or sending a message to Slack/MS Teams. Salesforce offers tools like Outbound Message (older) or named credentials + Apex HTTP callouts (code approach) or External Services (low-code approach) or MuleSoft for complex integration. With Agentforce, one can envision an easier integration via Agentforce's model (maybe calling an MCP endpoint or using the Atlas integration to talk to other AI services).

Trigger another Agent (Agent Handoff): This is a powerful concept – a Sentinel might determine that a sequence of steps is needed and therefore invoke a Conductor agent (or any other appropriate pattern agent). For instance, the HR resignation Sentinel could invoke a Conductor agent to carry out the offboarding process (multiple steps including revoking system access, scheduling exit interview, etc.). In implementation terms, that might just mean the Sentinel creates a record or event that the Conductor agent is listening for. Because all Agentforce agents are ultimately working on the Salesforce platform, they can communicate through records or events easily.

Escalation vs. direct resolution: One design decision is whether the Sentinel should attempt to resolve the issue on its own or just alert/escalate. In many cases, a Sentinel in production does minimal direct changes beyond logging an alert and kicking off another process. This is to avoid a bad automated decision causing harm. For instance, an automatic payment reversal could be risky if the detection was a false positive – you wouldn't want the agent to yank money without human double-check. So a safer pattern is often: Sentinel detects -> creates an "Incident" or "Alert" record -> another process or person reviews -> maybe an Action agent (another pattern) actually does the fix if confirmed. However, in low risk scenarios (like a non-customer-facing internal cleanup), you might let the Sentinel act fully automatically. The level of autonomy vs. human oversight depends on the use case's tolerance for false positives and the maturity of the logic.

Temporal Logic Considerations

Sentinels can be point-in-time (each event treated independently) or time-series aware. We touched on stateful design above. If the requirement is to detect trends (like increasing error rate) or absence of something (like "no heartbeat received in 10 minutes"), you might incorporate a scheduler or a background job:

No event scenario: Sometimes the event to react to is actually the lack of an event (e.g., "a scheduled job failed to run" or "no data received from a device for X minutes"). This is harder because by definition you didn't get a signal. One approach: have a scheduled Apex job that periodically checks for gaps. This Apex could itself be considered a type of Sentinel (just not event-triggered but time-triggered). For example, every hour check if each IoT device sent at least one signal in the last hour – if not, raise an alert. This is a valid design, just not purely event-driven.

Chaining events: Another scenario: the first event doesn't require action by itself, but a combination does. You might design smaller Sentinels that each fire on one specific thing and log it, and a "master" Sentinel that reads the log. For example, one sentinel logs every failed login in a custom object, including timestamp. Another sentinel (or a scheduled job) queries that log for patterns (like 5 failures for same user in 5 minutes) and then reacts. This separation of duties can simplify logic (each piece is simple) at expense of a slight delay and more moving parts.

Bulk processing: When multiple events come in simultaneously, say via a Platform Event Bus, Salesforce might batch them up to 200 per transaction for a subscriber. Your evaluation logic should handle lists (as shown in the Apex snippet). If using Flow, the platform can pass a collection of records into the Flow. In designing the architecture, always ask "can this handle 200 events at once?" to ensure you don't break bulk rules (for example, don't do a SOQL query inside a loop for each event – do one query for all, etc.). If an event surge happens (like 1000 events), Salesforce will chunk them into multiple transactions, but your logic should ideally be idempotent and stateless between chunks unless you specifically incorporate state memory.

Configurability and Metadata

We already touched on using Custom Metadata Types to store thresholds or lists (like list of forbidden contract clauses, list of VIP customers for special handling, etc.). In the architecture, it's wise to design a Sentinel agent to be metadata-driven:

1. Have a metadata type for each Sentinel that defines key parameters (thresholds, who to notify, toggle on/off).

2. Possibly even store the actions to take in metadata (for example, a metadata record could say: "if this condition, then Action = 'EscalateCaseFlow'"). The agent could then dynamically choose which Flow to call. This is advanced but gives a very flexible framework – almost like building a mini rule engine.

3. The benefit is that changes can be made through deployments of metadata (or even in Setup UI if you expose it) without modifying code. Also, you can have different metadata in different environments (like less sensitive in a sandbox, more sensitive in prod).

Pro tip: For advanced use cases with high volume signals, consider pairing a Sentinel with a Curator pattern agent. The Curator (which we'll cover in a later chapter) is essentially a filter or prioritizer. It could sit between the raw firehose of events and the Sentinel's core logic. For example, a Curator agent might group related events or discard dupes, then feed a cleaner stream to the Sentinel. This can significantly reduce noise. Think of a Curator as a smart gatekeeper – if you find your Sentinel is getting overwhelmed or too chatty, a Curator can help dial it in. In practice, this might be implemented by having one agent subscribe to the raw events (perform grouping/filtering) and publish a new refined event that the actual Sentinel listens to. By splitting responsibilities, each agent stays simpler and you gain modularity (you can improve the filtering logic independently of the reaction logic).

Now that we've sketched out the architecture and key design principles for Sentinel agents, we're ready to get hands-on. In the next section, we'll walk through building a Sentinel agent in Agentforce, step by step. We'll use the Salesforce tooling where possible (Agent Builder, Flow, etc.) and illustrate with a specific scenario (monitoring customer churn signals) to show how the pieces come together in a real implementation.

BUILDING A SENTINEL AGENT IN AGENTFORCE

Time to roll up our sleeves and construct a Sentinel agent step-by-step. We'll use a running example as our guide: a Sentinel that watches for churn signals in customer accounts. Imagine we want an agent that monitors various data points (like account health score, support ticket sentiment, usage metrics) and alerts the account team if a customer is at risk of churning. This example will touch multiple tools: Agent Builder for the high-level setup, Apex for some logic, Flow for actions, and the Agentforce Dev Tools for testing. Even if your use case is different, the process will be similar.

Step 1: Define the Agent in Agent Builder

Salesforce's Agent Builder (part of the Agentforce suite) is a declarative interface to configure AI agents. While it's often used for conversational or user-facing agents, it also supports background agents like our Sentinel. In Agent Builder, you'd start by creating a new Agent with the pattern type "Sentinel" (we'll assume Agentforce has pattern templates or at least fields to indicate its role). Key things to configure:

Agent Name and Description: e.g. "Account Churn Sentinel – Monitors key signals from accounts to predict churn risk and trigger retention actions."

Event Sources (Triggers): In Agent Builder, we might specify one or multiple triggers. For instance:

Platform Event Trigger: Perhaps we use a custom Platform Event Account-Signal__e that is published whenever certain things happen related to an account (a nightly job might publish an event summarizing an account's usage drop, or a support case closure publishes an event with sentiment score).

Change Data Capture: We could also directly subscribe to Account field changes, like if Health_Score__c field on Account drops significantly.

We may combine triggers: Agent Builder could allow a trigger definition like "on Platform Event X or on change of Account field Y." If not, we might create a single composite event source via Apex.

Input Data Definition: We tell Agent Builder what data the agent will receive. For a Platform Event, it knows the fields from the event definition. For a CDC change, it would be the record Id (and possibly changed fields).

We ensure our agent knows to expect an Account Id and maybe some context (if the event includes a "changeType" or a score).

Parameters/Thresholds: If Agent Builder allows custom parameters (perhaps via associated custom metadata), we'd surface something like "Churn Risk Threshold = 0.4" (meaning 40% risk score) as a configurable field. We might also define who gets alerted (maybe link a Queue or a role for notifications).

Linked Actions (if any): Some agent platforms let you declaratively link to actions. We might declare that this Sentinel agent has an action "Trigger Retention Flow" and map it to a specific Flow (which we'll build in a moment). Or we might keep it general and handle in logic.

Essentially, Agent Builder is helping us scaffold the agent: establishing the event subscription and providing a place to plug in our logic. Under the hood, this might create a Platform Event subscriber (a Flows or Apex trigger) that routes events to the agent runtime.

Step 2: Implementing the Evaluation Logic

With the agent defined, we implement how it assesses churn risk. Let's say our strategy is:

If Account Health Score drops below a threshold and the account is a high-value tier, flag it as high risk. Or if a recently closed support case for the account had very negative feedback, that could also flag risk (maybe the agent got a sentiment score in the event). Possibly incorporate product usage metrics drop (if available).

We'll use Apex for this evaluation because it likely involves querying multiple objects and maybe calling an AI model for sentiment interpretation. We create an Apex class, e.g. AccountChurnSentinel, and perhaps an inner class to represent a result or action. Here's a snippet focusing on one rule (health score threshold) as an example:

```
public class AccountChurnSentinel {

    // Invocable method so it can be called from Flow or Agent Builder directly

  @InvocableMethod

  public static List<AlertAction> evaluateAccounts(List<Id> accountIds) {
```

```
    // Load configuration from custom metadata
    SentinelPolicy__mdt config = SentinelPolicy__mdt.getInstance('Account_Churn');
    Decimal threshold = config != null ? config.ThresholdValue__c : 0.5;
    String alertRecipient = config != null ? config.Alert_Target__c : 'AccountTeam';

    List<Account> accounts = [SELECT Id, Name, Health_Score__c, Tier__c
                FROM Account WHERE Id IN :accountIds];
    List<AlertAction> alerts = new List<AlertAction>();
    for (Account acc : accounts) {
      Boolean highRisk = false;
      String reason = '';
      if (acc.Health_Score__c != null && acc.Health_Score__c < threshold) {
        highRisk = true;
        reason = 'Health Score dropped below ' + threshold;
      }
      // (Additional checks could go here, e.g. recent case sentiment)
      if (highRisk) {
        alerts.add(new AlertAction(acc.Id, 'High churn risk: ' + reason, alertRecipient));
      }
    }
    return alerts;
  }

  // Inner class to represent an alert action with details
  public class AlertAction {
```

```
        @InvocableVariable public Id accountId;

        @InvocableVariable public String message;

         @InvocableVariable public String target; // could be a queue or user ID
or group identifier

        public AlertAction(Id acctId, String msg, String tgt) {

            accountId = acctId;

            message = msg;

            target = tgt;

        }

    }

}
```

EXAMPLE: Invocable Apex class for a Sentinel that evaluates accounts for churn risk. It retrieves a threshold from metadata, checks each account's health score against that threshold (and potentially other criteria), and returns a list of alert actions (each containing the account, a message, and a target recipient).

A few things to note here:

We used SentinelPolicy__mdt.getInstance('Account_Churn') to fetch config. Suppose our custom metadata has ThresholdValue__c = 0.4 (40%) and Alert_Target__c = 'AccountTeam' (maybe a keyword our Flow knows how to route, or an actual Queue name).

We made the return type a custom inner class AlertAction and annotated its fields with @InvocableVariable. This way, if a Flow calls this Apex, it can access the returned list of AlertAction and use those fields. For example, the Flow could iterate over each AlertAction, post the message to the appropriate target (mapping 'AccountTeam' to maybe the account owner or a chatter group).

We only implemented one simple rule for brevity. We could extend it with more signals: e.g., query recent Cases related to the account and see if any case has a CSAT_Score__c below some value or if any case was a high severity issue in last 30 days – each could contribute to setting highRisk = true or maybe increment a risk score that we compare to a threshold.

By returning a structured result (AlertAction), we decouple the evaluation from the action. The Apex isn't directly sending notifications or updating records; it's just telling us "here's what I think needs attention and why." This is a pattern we often use to keep logic and action separate. It makes testing easier too (we can write a unit test that feeds in some Account records and asserts that we get the expected AlertActions back, without having to inspect the database or chatter posts).

Step 3: Implement the Action Layer via Flows (or other mechanisms)

Now, how do we use that result? We create a Flow (using Flow Builder) that is launched by our Sentinel agent when needed. If using Platform Event trigger: We might have a Platform Event triggered flow that gets the event (with Account Id and maybe some raw data like new health score).

That flow will call our Apex invocable method AccountChurnSentinel.evaluateAccounts, passing in the Account Id (or a collection of them if multiple events batched). The Apex returns a collection of AlertAction records (as defined above). We add a Flow loop element to go through each AlertAction. Use a decision element if needed (maybe not, since presumably each returned is an alert to process).

Post a Slack or Chatter message: We can use the Flow's Slack integration or a core action to post to Chatter. The target could be interpreted: in our design, maybe Alert_Target__c in metadata could be a public group or queue name. The flow might do a lookup (e.g., if target equals 'AccountTeam', find the Account Owner or Team and post there).

Alternatively, create a Task or Case: The flow could create a Task assigned to the Account Owner saying "Attention needed: {{message}}". Or call another subflow, like "Begin Retention Playbook", which could be a more complex Flow or even an Orchestration (Conductor).

End the flow.

Agent Builder may allow linking this flow directly to the agent's action. In Agentforce, they might even have a concept of an Agent Action library. Agent Builder allows creating a library of actions for the agent. Perhaps we define an action like "AlertAccountTeam" that under the hood is our flow, and in Agent Builder we say: if evaluation result is alert needed, execute "AlertAccountTeam" with parameters (message, accountId).

If our agent needed to do something like call an external service (say, automatically send a "We miss you, here's a discount" email via Marketing Cloud to a churn-risk customer), that could be another action. Maybe an invocable action that creates a Marketing Cloud API call.

For our first iteration, let's assume we just notify internally.

Testing the Sentinel Agent

Salesforce provides the Agentforce Development Tools – which will likely include things like a Developer Console extension or a CLI plugin to simulate agent events. In absence of the actual product specifics, we do what a developer would do. We write unit tests for the Apex class (as mentioned, feed in sample accounts, verify output).

Use a Scratch Org or sandbox to deploy this agent and test in an isolated environment. Treat the agent like any code: use source control, deploy via CI (continuous integration). (Recall the old Salesforce mantra of no changes in prod without testing – this applies to agents too. Even though Agentforce encourages low-code, those configurations and flows are still metadata that should ideally flow through a sandbox -> UAT -> prod pipeline. CI-only deployments help maintain quality.) Manually trigger some events to see if it works. For example, in a test org, lower an Account's health score and see if the Platform Event fires and the agent responds. Agentforce Dev Console might have a feature where you can simulate an event or step through an agent's logic, similar to how you can debug a flow.

One tool likely to be in Agentforce Dev Tools is a visual debugger or tracer. Salesforce has something called the "Flow Orchestrator Debugger" and for agents they might extend that. You could see a trace of "Event received -> Apex executed -> returned X -> Flow posted Y". This is invaluable because multi-step asynchronous processes can be hard to follow otherwise.

Step 5: Versioning and Deployment

After testing, you'd promote this to higher environments. Because Sentinel agents can touch critical processes, it's important to version-control all parts: the Platform Event definition, the Apex class, the Flow, the Agent configuration. Agentforce may provide a way to export the agent definition (perhaps as metadata or a JSON) that can be checked into source control. If not, document the config thoroughly.

When deploying to production, monitor it closely initially. You might want to deploy the Sentinel in a "silent" mode first – e.g., have it log alerts to a custom object but not actually notify anyone for a week, just to gauge its behavior, then turn on notifications once you're confident. This can prevent embarrassing false alarms. It's analogous to deploying a new monitoring tool in shadow mode to tune it.

Our Account Churn Sentinel, once live, would start catching things like: "Health Score for Acme Corp dropped from 0.7 to 0.3 in a week" -> agent posts an alert "High churn risk: Health Score dropped below 0.4" to the Account Team's Slack channel. The account manager sees it and can proactively reach out to the customer. Perhaps concurrently, the Sentinel (or a linked process) could also create a playbook of tasks (schedule a check-in call, offer a discount, etc.). Those could be orchestrated by a Conductor agent, showing how patterns combine.

Example Outcome

To illustrate, let's follow a specific scenario with our built agent:

Day 1: Customer's health score is 0.8 (fine). They then encounter a major issue – multiple support cases are opened.

Day 2: The support cases get resolved but with low CSAT feedback. The health score algorithm (maybe updated by a batch job or an AI) drops the score to 0.3 due to recent dissatisfaction and reduced usage.

- A Platform Event AccountSignal__e is published with AccountId = AcmeCorpId, NewHealthScore = 0.3.
- Our Sentinel agent receives this event (via the subscription we set up in Agent Builder).
- It invokes the Apex evaluator with AcmeCorpId.
- The Apex queries Account, finds Health_Score__c = 0.3, threshold 0.4 -> marks highRisk, returns an AlertAction("AcmeCorpId", "High churn risk: Health Score dropped below 0.4", "AccountTeam").
- The Flow iterates that result, and posts a message to the AccountTeam (let's say it finds the Account Owner is Alice; it posts in a Chatter group that includes Alice and her manager: "Account Acme Corp flagged for high churn risk (Health Score 0.3 < 0.4). Consider proactive engagement.").
- It also creates a Task for Alice: "Follow up with Acme Corp - flagged for churn risk."

Because we were forward-thinking, we also integrated Salesforce Command Center to log this event. The Sentinel agent might, for instance, create a record in a custom "Agent Alert Log" object or emit a log event. Command Center picks it up, so on a dashboard, the AI Ops team sees a blip: 1 churn alert triggered today. (We'll cover more on Command Center in the next section.)

From this example, you can see multiple Agentforce components in play: Agent Builder configures it, Invocable Apex processes, Flow carries out actions, and underlying Salesforce platform (Events, Chatter, etc.) does the heavy lifting of delivery.

One more note: building a Sentinel often requires cross-team collaboration. The Salesforce developer might need input from the data science team (for what constitutes churn risk), from business stakeholders (what threshold is acceptable), and from IT (how to integrate any external signals). This is where having a clear pattern helps – people understand you're designing a "Sentinel" and that vocabulary speeds up discussions ("Okay team, we're going to implement a Sentinel for churn – data science will provide the model for health score, ops will set the alert threshold initially, sales management will define who gets notified..." etc.).

Now that our Sentinel is built and running, we need to ensure it operates reliably in the long haul. That's where observability, monitoring, and trust come into play. In the next section, we will discuss how to keep an eye on Sentinel agents (to make sure they are healthy and effective), how to handle errors or false positives gracefully, and how to maintain human trust in these automated watchers.

OBSERVABILITY AND TRUST IN SENTINEL AGENTS

Building a Sentinel agent is only half the story – running it in production is where the real learning begins. Just as we monitor our systems, we also need to monitor our monitors! In this section, we'll cover how to make Sentinel agents observable (so you can see what they're doing), how to handle their errors or "false alarms", and how to maintain trust with users who rely on them. We'll also look at how Salesforce's Command Center and other tools can provide a centralized view of your agent's activities.

Instrumenting Sentinel Agents (Logs, Audits, Dashboards)

A Sentinel agent acts autonomously, which means if it misfires at 3 AM, you want to know about it (and diagnose why) without relying on a user report. Key practices:

Logging: Within your Sentinel's logic (Apex or Flow), incorporate logging for critical decisions. For example, if the Sentinel decides to fire an alert, log a record of it. You might create a custom object like Sentinel_Alert__c with fields: AgentName, EventId, ActionTaken, Timestamp, Details. Each time the agent triggers, insert a record. This provides an audit trail. If someone asks "why did we alert on Acme Corp yesterday?", you can check the log record: it might say "Agent=AccountChurnSentinel, EventId=PE-12345, Action=AlertAccountTeam, Reason=Health Score dropped below 0.4, Timestamp=...".

Salesforce Event Logs: Another approach is using the built-in platform event monitoring. Salesforce can capture debug logs or platform event deliveries. However, parsing those can be complex. It's often easier to implement a simple custom log as above for domain-specific info.

Notifications of failure: Ensure that if the Sentinel encounters an error during execution (exception in Apex, flow fault), it doesn't fail silently. Use Flow fault paths or Apex try-catch to handle exceptions. For instance, in Flow Builder, every external action element (like an Apex call) can have a Fault connector. Connect that to an action that, say, writes to an "Agent Error Log" or sends an alert to the dev team. Here's a pseudo-view:

Apex Action: Evaluate Accounts (if this fails) -> Fault -> Create "Sentinel Error" record and Email admin.

Telemetry and metrics: Over time, you want to gather metrics: how often is the Sentinel triggering? How many events is it processing? What's the average throughput? Are errors increasing? This is where the Agentforce Command Center becomes extremely useful. The Command Center is essentially an observability dashboard for AI agents, providing a "unified pane of glass" to monitor agent health and performance. It can show real-time analytics like:

- Number of events processed by each agent (and any backlog if events are queuing).
- Alert frequency (how many alerts sent per day by the Sentinel).

- System metrics like average processing time per event, error rates, etc.
- Possibly even AI-specific metrics if our agent calls ML models (like how often it gets high vs low confidence).

Salesforce has built Command Center on top of OpenTelemetry standards, meaning you can even pipe these metrics to external monitoring tools (Splunk, Datadog, etc.) if your ops team prefers. In practice, enabling Command Center integration for our Sentinel might be as simple as flipping a setting or adding a few lines in Apex to instrument spans. But much of it could be automatic since Agentforce likely tracks each agent invocation. The key is that by using Command Center, you can correlate agent behavior with other system events – e.g., see if an agent spike coincided with a deployment, etc., which is crucial for debugging.

Dashboarding: You might create a custom dashboard or use Command Center's default. For example, a dashboard showing "Churn Sentinel Alerts by Week" to see trends (are we flagging more customers over time? Maybe something changed in input data or threshold). Another chart: "False Positive Rate" (if we have data on which alerts were dismissed vs acted on, more on that below).

Integration with Salesforce Command Center

Let's talk a bit more about this since it's a new concept in Salesforce's AI world. The Command Center for Agentforce is like an operations center for all your agents:

- It likely lists all agent instances running, their status, last run time, etc.
- For Sentinel agents, it could have a live feed of events being processed and whether actions were taken.

It might allow setting up alerts on the alerts (meta-alerting): e.g., if an agent fails 5 times in an hour, Command Center can notify the platform team.

Because Command Center is built with enterprise needs in mind, it emphasizes reliability and trust: For any given agent action, you should be able to trace back "what happened?" and "why?". This addresses the common question: if an AI agent did something wrong, how do we investigate? The

Sentinel's logs combined with Command Center's telemetry help answer that.

For our Account Churn Sentinel, if we open Command Center, we might see:

Agent Name: AccountChurnSentinel – Healthy (green) – 20 events processed today, 3 alerts triggered, 0 errors. Click in: see timeline of events and actions.

One event might be expanded: Event ID 12345 at 10:05: processed in 300ms, Alert triggered (AccountId X, message "...").

Another event: ID 12346 at 10:07: processed in 250ms, No action (health score above threshold).

This level of detail is incredibly helpful for trust and auditing. It's akin to how a security operations center monitors security alerts – here we monitor AI agent alerts.

Notifying Humans Without Overwhelming Them

A common pitfall with any monitoring system is alert fatigue. If your Sentinel spams people with too many notifications (especially false or low-value ones), users will start ignoring them – defeating the purpose. So how to manage this:

Severity levels: Incorporate severity or priority into alerts. For example, "High churn risk" vs "Moderate churn risk" could be distinguished, and maybe moderate ones are batched into a daily digest instead of immediate ping.

Aggregation of notifications: If 10 events happen in an hour for the same issue, perhaps send one summary alert. Our Sentinel design could handle this by either grouping in logic or via the notification mechanism. Salesforce Flow could be configured to append to an existing Chatter post or use a single Slack thread for related alerts.

User Preferences: If possible, integrate with user preferences – maybe an account manager can opt-out of immediate alerts and choose a daily summary. This might be beyond a single agent's scope, but a central mechanism (maybe Command Center or a "Notification Settings" custom metadata) could coordinate it.

Preventing loops: Ensure that notifying a human doesn't itself trigger another agent in a loop. For instance, if you send an email from the agent, that email shouldn't trigger another Salesforce case that the Sentinel listens to! This is an edge case but worth thinking through events filtering.

A practical tip is to start with notifications to a small group first (maybe just a system admin or pilot team) and gradually roll out to wider audience once tuned. For example, initially send all churn risk alerts just to the Customer Success Ops team, who can verify if they're legit. After a few weeks, once you trust the agent, have it notify the actual account owners. This phased approach saves embarrassment and builds credibility.

Building Confidence Over Time & Adjusting Thresholds

When you first deploy a Sentinel, it's based on assumptions (threshold = 0.4, etc.). Reality might show that threshold is too low or too high. For instance, we might find the churn Sentinel is alerting on 30% of accounts, which is far too noisy – maybe we need to lower sensitivity. Or maybe it missed a known churn case, so we need to be more aggressive or add another signal (like "if customer hasn't logged in in 30 days, alert").

Thus, treat the first 1-2 months as a learning period:

Collect feedback: If alerts go to humans, provide a way for them to give feedback. Perhaps the notification has two links: "Confirm risk" or "False alarm". If they click false alarm, we log that and maybe the Supervisor pattern (next chapter) can aggregate this feedback. Over time, this can even train an AI model: we could feed back into Einstein which alerts were actually true churn vs false. That might improve the model if one is used.

Adjust metadata: Using our metadata-driven design, adjusting thresholds is easy – just update the custom metadata in production (which can be done via deployment or possibly via the UI if you expose it safely). Just ensure you document changes (maybe note in the metadata description why it changed).

Versioning logic: Sometimes you need to change the logic itself (e.g., add a new check). That requires a deployment of Apex/Flow. It's important to follow normal dev practice: test in sandbox, etc., because ironically a bug in an agent can cause bigger impact than a bug in a normal app (if the agent is widespread, a logic error could spam 1000 people at midnight – not good!). So treat agent updates like critical code updates.

The goal is to reach a steady state where the Sentinel is trusted. Teams should feel, "If I got an alert from the Sentinel, I need to act, it's likely real" – much like how a well-calibrated smoke detector rarely false-alarms, so you take it seriously when it rings. Achieving this means ruthlessly eliminating sources of noise.

Incident Review Loops – Incorporating the Supervisor Pattern

Despite best efforts, false positives (or negatives) will happen. It's essential to have a process to review them:

False Positives: These are cases where the Sentinel cried wolf. Each false positive can erode trust. Set up a Supervisor agent or process to handle them. For example, create a simple form or Slack command where a user can flag "This alert was not useful." Those could create records that a human (maybe an AI Ops engineer or business analyst) reviews weekly. If patterns emerge (e.g., Sentinel always flags accounts that had a one-off low score but bounced back), you refine the logic to avoid that scenario.

False Negatives: Harder to catch, because it means the agent missed something. You usually find out because the bad thing happened without an alert (e.g., a customer churned and account team says "we had no warning!"). To capture these, you might have to do some retroactive analysis. For example, once a quarter, look at customers who did churn and see if our Sentinel should have flagged them (what was their health score? Did we set threshold too low?). This could be aided by analytics: if you have the data on actual churns, feed that into a model or simply analyze it in reports.

Continuous Improvement: Combine the above feedback loops with possibly machine learning. Salesforce has Einstein Discovery which could analyze a dataset of "alert triggered or not" vs "churn happened or not" and suggest a better predictive model. In future, you might upgrade your Sentinel to use an AI model rather than static rules, once you have enough data points.

Pro tip: Leverage Flow fault paths and custom logging in development to quickly isolate issues with your Sentinel. For instance, if the Sentinel's Apex throws an exception for a certain event (maybe a null pointer because some data was unexpected), a well-placed try-catch can log a clear error message to a log object: "ChurnSentinel failed for Account X: null health score". This is much easier than combing through debug logs. By proactively coding these fault handlers, you can resolve issues faster in production. Here's a mini-pattern for Apex:

```
try {
  //... agent logic...
} catch (Exception e) {
   System.debug('Sentinel Error: ' + e.getMessage());
   // Log to custom object
   Agent_Error__c err = new Agent_Error__c(
      Agent_Name__c = 'AccountChurnSentinel',
      Error_Detail__c = e.getMessage(),
      Event_Context__c = JSON.serializePretty(eventData)
   );
   insert err;
   // (Optional) send platform event or email to devOps
}
```

AND IN FLOW, always connect those fault connectors! For example, if a notification action fails (maybe Slack API was down), catch it and log it. This way, nothing disappears silently. In Command Center, these errors would also surface – a spike in errors would show in the health metrics.

By implementing strong observability and feedback, you create a virtuous cycle: the Sentinel gets better over time, and the business's trust in it grows. You move from skeptics ("Will this robot overwhelm us with junk?") to advocates ("This agent saved us twice last month by catching issues early!").

Our Sentinel is now well-monitored and (hopefully) well-behaved within its domain. But no agent is an island. Often, a Sentinel will be part of a larger multi-agent ecosystem, handing off to or receiving input from other agents. In the next section, we'll explore how Sentinels interact with other agent patterns (like Conductor, Coach, etc.) to form end-to-end intelligent workflows. We'll even outline a real-world example of multi-agent handoff (with a diagram of Sentinel → Conductor → Coach) to show how these patterns can work in concert.

SENTINELS IN MULTI-AGENT SYSTEMS

Sentinel agents shine on their own for catching specific events, but they often play an even more important role as part of a team of agents. In a multi-agent system, different pattern agents collaborate, each handling their specialty. Think of an orchestra: the Sentinel is like the percussionist giving the cue (bang the drum when it's time), the Conductor (pattern) is literally the conductor coordinating the symphony, and perhaps a Coach agent is like a mentor ensuring the orchestra learns and improves for the next performance. In practical terms, Sentinels frequently serve as the trigger that sets other processes in motion. Let's go through a few common interactions and then detail a concrete example with a diagram.

When a Sentinel Calls a Conductor

Conductor agents manage multi-step workflows or coordinate multiple agents/tasks (as we'll explore in a later chapter). It's very common for a Sentinel to hand off to a Conductor when the response to an event is complex. For instance, in a deployment pipeline scenario: A Sentinel in DevOps watches for a failed deployment event. The moment it detects a failure, it invokes a Conductor agent that orchestrates rollback steps, notifications to stakeholders, and creates a problem ticket. The Sentinel's job was just to notice the failure quickly; the Conductor takes over to handle the fallout through a scripted set of actions (maybe involving multiple teams or systems).

In our earlier support SLA example: The Sentinel detected an impending breach and could call a Conductor agent called "Urgent Case Resolution Orchestrator." That Conductor might do things like: reassign the case to a special team, escalate its priority, notify the account manager, and spin up a swarming channel for the support team. Each of those steps could involve different systems (Salesforce case reassignment, Slack for channel, PagerDuty for on-call alert). The Conductor coordinates all that. The Sentinel essentially says, "This case needs white-glove treatment now" and the Conductor knows what "white-glove treatment" entails step-by-step.

In Marketing: A Sentinel detects a trending topic on social media about your brand (maybe through Social Studio or an API feed). It triggers a Conductor agent that orchestrates a marketing response: drafts a quick blog post with a Presenter agent (pattern for content generation), gets legal approval via a

Supervisor agent (pattern for human approval), then posts it across channels. The Sentinel's detection kicked off a whole multi-agent dance.

The technical implementation of Sentinel→Conductor handoff might be:

- The Sentinel creates a record that the Conductor is watching (e.g., insert a new row in a custom "Incident" object marked as "deployment failure", which a Conductor agent is subscribed to).
- Or the Sentinel calls an Apex method of the Conductor (if allowed directly).
- Often easiest: use Platform Event or Salesforce record as the bridge.

This decoupling is healthy: it keeps the Sentinel lean and focused (detect & notify), and the Conductor can be more elaborate without burdening the detection logic.

When a Sentinel Flags a Coach

Coach agents (another pattern in our playbook) are those that provide guidance to humans, typically for improvement or training. They're less about doing tasks and more about advising or teaching. How might a Sentinel work with a Coach?

One scenario: The Sentinel observes some repeated pattern that suggests a human might need additional training. For example, a Sentinel in a call center monitors call transcripts (via events from Einstein Conversation Mining perhaps). It notices that a particular agent (human agent, not AI) frequently forgets to mention a required disclaimer on calls (this is detected by a text pattern in transcripts). The Sentinel flags this and invokes a Coach agent that interacts with that human agent – maybe via a chat message or email – providing guidance or resources ("Hey, I noticed on several calls the compliance disclaimer was missing. Here's a quick refresher on when and how to say it."). The Coach agent pattern is likely an AI that engages with an employee in a supportive way. The Sentinel essentially supplies the trigger ("this employee might benefit from coaching on X").

Another example: HR onboarding again – a Coach agent could be assigned to a new employee to guide them through their first week ("virtual buddy"). A Sentinel might feed the Coach with timely triggers ("new hire has not completed security training by day 3" – Sentinel picks that up and nudges the Coach agent to remind them or offer help).

Or consider sales: a Sentinel monitors that a salesperson hasn't updated any opportunities in 30 days. It could nudge a Coach agent to reach out to that salesperson with tips on pipeline management, or even schedule a 1:1 with their manager. The Coach agent could even be the manager's digital assistant which says "Your rep Jane hasn't updated her deals; maybe check in".

In all these, the Sentinel provides insight ("something might be off here"), and the Coach provides actionable guidance to a human. This is a powerful combination because it blends automated detection with human-centric remediation. It addresses the "last mile" problem: an AI can detect an issue, but often a human has to do something about it – a Coach helps that human do it better.

Sentinel Feeds Companion Agents

Companion agents are like personal assistants (think of an agent that sits with a user to help with tasks, context, etc., e.g., a sidebar in Salesforce that suggests next best actions). A Sentinel can act behind the scenes to keep companions up-to-date.

For example, a sales rep might have a Companion AI in their CRM that gives them insights about their accounts each morning. A Sentinel in the background monitors news feeds or internal data changes about those accounts overnight. When it finds something (a news article about a client, or a drop in usage), it doesn't directly notify the human, but instead feeds the info to the Companion agent. Next morning, the rep's Companion says, "Good morning! Noticed a news article about your customer Acme Corp announcing layoffs – might impact your deal. Also, their usage dropped 20% last week (Sentinel flagged this). Consider reaching out." Here the Sentinel is the researcher, the Companion is the presenter of info in context to the user.

IT example: An IT admin has a Companion agent in their dashboard that summarizes system health. Various Sentinels (security, performance) feed into that summary. So the Companion can say "Today's Overview: All systems nominal except the EU server had 3 high CPU alerts (flagged by SentinelX). These were auto-remediated."

Implementation: The Companion agent likely has some data store or context it refreshes. The Sentinel can update that context (maybe write to a custom object or Knowledge article that the Companion references, or call a service that the Companion queries). There might even be a direct API if the Companion is built on Agentforce: e.g., a Companion could subscribe to certain events or be invoked via Agentforce API.

Escalation Chains and Sentinel-of-Sentinels

It's worth noting you can have layered Sentinels too: one Sentinel could watch the output of another. This sounds strange but consider:

You have multiple local Sentinels monitoring different systems (Salesforce, an ERP, a website). You could have a higher-level Sentinel that correlates alerts from all of them into a single "global incident". This higher Sentinel might look for patterns like "Sentinel A and Sentinel B both triggered within 10 minutes – that means a broader issue". It then could call a Conductor for enterprise incident response.

Alternatively, one Sentinel could be designated as a load balancer or router for events: if it's an event of type X, route to Sentinel A, if type Y, route to Sentinel B. But that's more like a filtering mechanism (more of a Curator function as previously mentioned).

Real-World Example: HR Onboarding (Sentinel → Conductor → Coach)

Let's bring it all together with a narrative and a simple diagram of an HR onboarding scenario:

Event: A new employee has been added to the HR system (they accepted an offer and their start date is set, or they just completed day 1 orientation). This is a critical moment where many tasks should happen quickly.

Sentinel (Onboarding Sentinel): Monitors the HR system for new hire events. As soon as a "New Hire" record appears or status changes to Active, the Sentinel triggers. Its evaluation: "New hire in Sales department, role = Sales Rep".

Action by Sentinel: The Sentinel creates an "Onboarding Orchestration Request" (could be a custom object or directly calls a Conductor agent) with details of the new hire (name, role, department).

Conductor (Onboarding Orchestrator Agent): This agent kicks off a multi-step onboarding process:

1. Create IT tickets for account setup (email, laptop provisioning).

2. Assign mandatory training modules to the new hire in the LMS.

3. Schedule an orientation session event on their calendar (perhaps using an Action agent to interface with the calendar system).

4. Notify relevant people: email the manager with a 100-day onboarding plan template, notify the team that a new member joined.

5. Coordinate with a "Buddy" system: maybe assign a peer mentor.

This Conductor can utilize other agents too. For example, a Presenter agent could draft a welcome email to the new hire that HR will send, and a Companion agent could be set up for the manager to track onboarding tasks.

Coach (New Hire Coach Agent): Now enters a Coach agent. Let's say the company provides a chatbot for new employees (accessible via Slack or an internal portal) that can answer questions and also proactively check on them. Once the Conductor finishes certain steps, it "introduces" the Coach agent to the new hire. In practice, the Conductor might send a welcome message from the Coach ("Hi! I'm your onboarding buddy AI. I'm here to help you with any questions about the company for the next 30 days.").

Over the next days, the Coach agent will periodically reach out: "Day 1, have you setup your dev org access? Need help?", "Day 3, here's a tip about using Salesforce expense system", etc. It's guided by time triggers and also by signals (maybe the Sentinel monitors if the new hire completed their training – if not by day 5, it nudges via the Coach). Meanwhile, the Sentinel could continue to watch during the new hire's first weeks for any issues (like if no one completed their IT setup tasks for 3 days, the Sentinel might escalate to HR that something's stuck – essentially sentinel supervising the process).

Let's summarize that flow in a simplified list/diagram form:

New Hire Event – (HR system signals New Employee record created)

Sentinel Agent: Onboarding Watcher – detects the new hire event and classifies it (e.g., department, role).

Sentinel triggers Conductor – passes new hire info to next agent.

Conductor Agent: Onboarding Orchestrator – executes multi-step process:

- Creates IT setup tasks.
- Schedules orientation sessions.

- Assigns training.
- Notifies manager and team.
- Potentially uses other agents for specific tasks, e.g., a Presenter agent to draft welcome kit.

Conductor triggers Coach – after initial tasks, it initiates a Coach for the new hire.

Coach Agent: New Hire Buddy – engages with the new hire via chat:

Day 0: Introduces itself, offers help.

Day 1-30: Answers questions (like a chatbot FAQ), and nudges the hire on key tasks ("I see you haven't completed security training, here's why it's important...").

Feedback Loop – The Coach might feedback completion info (e.g., new hire finished all tasks) to the Conductor or Sentinel to mark the process complete. Sentinel could also monitor if tasks remain incomplete and prompt escalation to HR if necessary (e.g., "new hire has 3 overdue tasks – maybe their manager needs to step in").

To visualize a portion of this, particularly the handoff chain:

Sentinel (Onboarding Watcher) – :bell: detects new hire event → invokes Conductor (Onboarding Orchestrator).

Conductor – :gear: executes steps (IT setup, orientation scheduling, etc.) → upon completion, invokes Coach (New Hire Buddy).

Coach – :speech_balloon: engages new hire (provides guidance, answers Qs for first month).

We can describe it as a sequence:

NewHire Event --> [Sentinel: Onboarding Watcher] --> [Conductor: Onboarding Orchestrator] --> [Coach: New Hire Buddy]

Where each arrow "–>" represents a handoff or trigger. The Sentinel's arrow means it detected the event and kicked off the Conductor. The Conductor's arrow means after orchestrating tasks, it started the Coach's involvement.

This example shows how multiple agent patterns interconnect. The Sentinel ensures no new hire slips through without the proper process starting. The

Conductor ensures the process is thorough and standardized. The Coach ensures the human involved (the new hire) feels supported and that soft issues (questions, morale) are addressed – something a rigid workflow might miss.

In any multi-agent setup, careful design is needed to avoid confusion:

- You don't want redundant or conflicting actions (e.g., Sentinel and Conductor both sending notifications).
- You want clear ownership: Sentinel triggers, Conductor coordinates, Coach mentors – each has its lane.
- Use metadata or an "Agent Registry" to keep track of agents and their roles. Possibly the platform can enforce some of this (Agentforce might have an internal registry with agent names, types, and maybe even dependencies or tags like "this agent is a Sentinel for HR events").

One more benefit: multi-agent systems can evolve gradually. Maybe you start with just a Sentinel and humans did the rest. Then you automate steps with a Conductor. Then you add a Coach for extra support. Each pattern adds capability without having to redesign the whole system from scratch – that's the beauty of modular patterns.

Now, we've focused on Salesforce-centric scenarios. It's important to realize that Sentinel-like behavior appears in many AI ecosystems outside Salesforce too. In the next section, we will compare how other frameworks (LangChain, Microsoft's AutoGen, open-source Agent frameworks) implement similar "monitor and react" capabilities. We'll also discuss interoperability standards like the Model Context Protocol (MCP) which can allow a Salesforce Sentinel to coordinate with non-Salesforce agents, ensuring your Sentinel can signal across system boundaries when needed.

PATTERNS IN THE WILD – SENTINEL LOOKALIKES IN THE ECOSYSTEM

The concept of a "monitor and react" agent isn't unique to Salesforce Agentforce. As AI agent frameworks have emerged, many have components or patterns that mirror the Sentinel's behavior. Understanding these not only validates the pattern's importance but also helps when integrating Salesforce agents with external systems. Let's survey a few notable ones:

LangChain (Open-Source LLM Framework): LangChain primarily helps build chains and agents for LLMs (Large Language Models). While it doesn't personify agents in named patterns, it provides a callback system that effectively serves a sentinel role during chain execution. Callbacks in LangChain allow you to hook into events like a model starting/finishing, a tool being used, an error occurring, etc. This is explicitly for logging or reactive behavior. For example, you could set up a callback that monitors for when an agent in LangChain makes a certain decision and then execute custom code (like abort if it's going wrong or log a trace). In multi-agent setups, one agent can even oversee another by analyzing these callback events. Think of a LangChain callback handler as a mini-Sentinel embedded in the workflow – it watches the process and can react (usually by logging or stopping the process on certain conditions). Additionally, LangChain's newer observability tooling (LangSmith) provides debugging and monitoring dashboards, analogous to our Command Center but specific to LangChain apps. This shows that even in LLM-centric frameworks, monitoring and reactive hooks are crucial to manage agent behaviors.

Microsoft AutoGen (Multi-Agent Orchestration): AutoGen by Microsoft is designed for creating multi-agent systems where agents (LLMs) can converse or work together. Within AutoGen, the emphasis is on orchestration and having agents that can act as managers or workers. While they might not use the term Sentinel, AutoGen includes an AgentOps/Observability component (AgentOps) which provides metrics and monitoring for agent interactions. For example, AgentOps can track if an agent is stuck in a loop or if it's failing frequently. This is similar to having a watchdog thread observing the autonomous agents – again, a sentinel-like function. Also, one agent in AutoGen could be designated to watch certain triggers: e.g., a "monitor agent" that listens to the conversation and interrupts if necessary (maybe if the dialogue goes off track or a safe word is used). The framework supports event hooks and even human-in-the-loop breaks (like a user pressing a key to stop execution), which indicates the designers considered that agents might need oversight. In summary, AutoGen's approach reinforces the idea that monitoring, debugging, and triggers are first-class needs in agent frameworks.

OpenAgents / CrewAI (Open Multi-Agent Platforms): OpenAgents (and similarly CrewAI) are open-source platforms aiming to scale to many agents working together. They introduce concepts like distinct roles for agents and often have built-in logging and event systems. For instance, OpenAgents emphasizes detailed logs for understanding agent decisions. A pattern akin to Sentinel might be an agent role that monitors the environment or other agents. In some multi-agent simulations (like MetaGPT or similar "AI company" simulations), there is often a project manager agent role – one could argue that part of its job is sentinel-like: monitor the progress of others and intervene if things go off course. Also, these frameworks allow external triggers: for example, an external event can be fed in which agents then react to (e.g., new data arrives, agent must adjust plan). They don't always call it out as a separate pattern, but the functionality is there.

Model Context Protocol (MCP): This deserves special mention for cross-platform interoperability. The Model Context Protocol is an emerging open standard (spearheaded by Anthropic and supported by Salesforce, as of late 2024) for connecting AI models/agents to external data and tools. Think of it as a universal API for AI agents – analogous to how USB or HTTP are standards. Why is this relevant to Sentinels? Because MCP can allow a Sentinel agent in Salesforce to directly connect and send information to an agent outside Salesforce (or vice versa) in a standardized way. For example, suppose you have a sophisticated AI security system outside Salesforce that detects network intrusions (its own Sentinel). Via MCP, that system could send a standardized alert to your Salesforce Agentforce environment, and a Conductor agent there could log a case or orchestrate an internal response. Or your Salesforce Sentinel that catches say "customer upset sentiment" could use MCP to call an external agent that specializes in generating appeasement offers using a different AI model. MCP essentially makes agents more interoperable by standardizing context exchange. Salesforce's adoption of MCP (Agentforce has a native MCP client) means your Sentinel could theoretically plug into a larger multi-vendor agent ecosystem without heavy custom integration. It's like giving your Sentinel a common language to speak to external AI services or agents.

External Orchestration Tools (MuleSoft, etc.): Sometimes you might not build all agents in Salesforce. You might have a central orchestration engine (maybe a MuleSoft flow or an AWS Step Functions or Azure Logic App) that handles cross-system events. In these setups, you might let that external orchestrator act as the primary Sentinel for cross-system events (since it can see everything), and then have it invoke specific Salesforce agents as needed. For instance, MuleSoft could detect a pattern across Salesforce and SAP (two different systems) – something no single agent in one platform would see. It could then call a Salesforce agent via REST or Platform Event. Alternatively, MuleSoft could host an MCP server making it an interface to trigger Agentforce agents. The point here: architecture matters – if your enterprise uses multiple AI/automation platforms, you want to place Sentinels strategically. Some might be local (watching within Salesforce), while some global Sentinels might watch at a higher level and trigger actions across systems.

Reactive Engines in LLM Stacks: There are also libraries for complex event processing and reactive rules (e.g., Drools for business rules, or Esper for event streams). These aren't AI per se, but if integrated, they can act as Sentinels by doing the heavy event correlation and then handing off to AI agents. One could use something like Apache Kafka with stream processing to gather events and only notify the Salesforce Sentinel when a certain condition is met, rather than sending every raw event. This again parallels the Curator/Sentinel partnership we mentioned – some external systems might play the Curator role.

When dealing with multiple ecosystems, a few tips:

Clearly define boundaries: Decide which system owns detection vs response. Avoid duplicate detection in multiple places (leading to either double actions or each thinking the other will act).

Use standard protocols (MCP, webhooks): This reduces friction in connecting agents. For example, a Slack bot (external agent) could send an MCP message to Salesforce Agentforce indicating an event occurred in Slack (like a keyword mention), and a Salesforce Sentinel picks it up as if it were a platform event.

Keep security in mind: More agents and cross-system triggers mean more security considerations. Make sure events are authenticated and that one compromised system can't trick your agents into doing something harmful. (E.g., an external sentinel shouldn't be able to trigger a Salesforce agent to delete data unless properly vetted.)

Pro tip: If your enterprise operates multiple AI agent frameworks, Sentinel agents are prime candidates for cross-stack coordination. Why? Because by design they are the initiators rather than the heavy doers. A Sentinel can emit a simple signal that other systems listen for, without needing to deeply integrate business logic across platforms. For instance, your Salesforce Sentinel could publish a single JSON message "HighValueCustomerAtRisk" to a message bus. Other AI systems (maybe a Python-based agent on AWS) can subscribe and act accordingly, and vice versa. This loosely coupled approach means you can add or remove subsystems without rewriting the whole logic – each Sentinel just focuses on detection and broadcasting, trusting that any necessary responders (in any platform) will handle the broadcast. In technical terms, it's like making your Sentinels the publishers of events and designing your multi-agent architecture as a set of subscribers that may belong to different platforms. This mirrors event-driven microservice architecture, now applied to AI agents.

We've now surveyed the landscape and seen that the Sentinel pattern – in spirit if not name – is pervasive and vital across AI platforms. Whether it's a callback hook in LangChain or a metrics monitor in AutoGen, the idea of monitoring events and reacting intelligently underpins many robust AI solutions. The Salesforce Agentforce implementation benefits from the platform's strengths (declarative events, Apex, flows, Command Center telemetry, etc.), but it's encouraging to know that the pattern aligns with broader industry practice, meaning skills and designs here are transferable.

With this, we conclude our deep dive into the Sentinel pattern. You should now have a solid grasp of why Sentinels matter, how to build and tune them, and how they interact both within Salesforce and with the outside AI world. In the next chapter, we'll shift focus from the lone watcher to a partner pattern: the Supervisor, which brings humans into the loop to validate and approve AI-driven work. It's a natural next step – if Sentinel is the autonomous guard, Supervisor is the wise editor – and together they cover detection and validation for safe AI operations.

SUMMARY

In this chapter, we explored the Sentinel pattern in depth – the "monitor and react" agents that serve as vigilant watchdogs across the enterprise. We began with an introduction to what makes a Sentinel agent distinct: its ability to continuously listen for signals, intelligently evaluate events, and trigger immediate actions or escalations. We saw how this pattern applies cross-functionally, from IT and security to HR, finance, and customer service, by walking through realistic use cases where Sentinels catch issues like SLA breaches, spending anomalies, policy violations, and more before they escalate.

We then dove into designing and building Sentinel agents on Salesforce's Agentforce platform. Key design components include robust event ingestion (using Platform Events, CDC, webhooks), flexible evaluation logic (leveraging Invocable Apex, flows, and even AI models for analysis), and clear action pathways (like invoking flows, Apex routines, or other agents). We emphasized making Sentinels configurable and scalable – using custom metadata for thresholds and ensuring bulk-safe, state-aware logic – so that these agents remain maintainable as business needs evolve. Through a detailed example (an account churn Sentinel), we demonstrated how to implement the pattern using Agentforce tools (Agent Builder, Flow Builder, Invocable Apex) and how to test and deploy such agents with proper development lifecycle controls.

Crucially, we addressed observability and trust for Sentinels in production. We discussed instrumenting agents with logging and using Salesforce Command Center dashboards to monitor agent health and performance. Techniques like flow fault paths and custom error logs were highlighted to catch and debug issues quickly. We also covered strategies to fine-tune alerts and avoid notification fatigue – ensuring that human teams trust the Sentinel's outputs by minimizing false positives and involving them in feedback loops. In fact, we foreshadowed how a Supervisor pattern can be paired for reviewing Sentinel alerts, creating a human-in-the-loop safety net for autonomous monitoring.

The chapter also explored how Sentinels fit into larger multi-agent systems. We illustrated how a Sentinel might trigger a Conductor agent for orchestrating multi-step responses or hand off to a Coach agent to guide humans, using an HR onboarding scenario (Sentinel → Conductor → Coach) as a concrete example of agents working in concert. This demonstrated that Sentinels often act as the first domino in a chain of intelligent actions, proving their value as initiators in automated workflows.

Finally, we looked beyond Salesforce, comparing analogous mechanisms in other AI frameworks and reaffirming that the Sentinel pattern (in function, if not in name) is ubiquitous. From LangChain's callback hooks to Microsoft's AutoGen monitors and open standards like MCP for cross-platform signals, it's clear that the ability to monitor events and react is a cornerstone of effective AI agent systems. We provided insight into integrating Agentforce Sentinels with external tools, noting that Sentinels make excellent bridges between disparate systems due to their event-publishing nature.

The Sentinel pattern equips us with a reusable blueprint for building AI agents that serve as always-on guardians of our business processes. They reduce reaction time, catch the unseen, and trigger the right responses – all in a controlled, observable, and tunable manner. With Sentinels deployed, an organization moves closer to the vision of an autonomous enterprise nervous system, where important signals never go unnoticed and intelligent actions are initiated the moment they're needed.

Now that we've explored the watcher (Sentinel), our next step is to explore the reviewer – the Supervisor pattern. In Chapter 3, we'll learn how Supervisor agents provide a critical human-in-the-loop function, acting as AI assistants that draft or recommend while deferring final judgment to humans. This pattern ensures that AI-driven processes can maintain quality, compliance, and human oversight, complementing the autonomy of patterns like Sentinel with the wisdom of human judgment. It's time to see how AI and humans can form a checks-and-balances partnership in the Supervisor chapter to come.

3

THE SUPERVISOR PATTERN (HUMAN-IN-THE-LOOP VALIDATOR)

Imagine an AI agent that works like a diligent assistant – it drafts emails, flags suspicious transactions, or suggests hiring decisions – but always asks a human supervisor for the final "OK." This is the essence of the Supervisor pattern: an agent that generates a recommendation or draft action, then defers ultimate authority to a person. In enterprise environments, where automation must coexist with corporate policies, nuance, and accountability, the Supervisor pattern acts as a safety harness. It's the critical bridge between AI-generated output and trusted human oversight, ensuring that autonomous work doesn't outrun an organization's comfort with risk and quality control.

The Supervisor pattern shines in scenarios where full automation would be too risky or culturally unacceptable. Consider a few examples: a contract analysis agent might draft a new clause for a sales agreement, but a legal counsel must review and approve it. A claims-processing agent could classify an insurance claim as likely fraud, yet defer to a human adjuster to make the rejection call. In compliance and finance, AI can scour records for anomalies or policy violations, but sensitive decisions (denying a loan, flagging a transaction to regulators) require human judgment. Across domains like contract drafting, claims evaluation, compliance checks, financial approvals, and even hiring recommendations, Supervisor agents allow AI to do the heavy lifting while humans handle the final mile. This pattern is particularly valued in regulated or high-stakes areas where letting an AI act unchecked could expose the business to legal or ethical fallout. In fact, Salesforce's own

AI Acceptable Use Policy explicitly requires a human in the loop for any high-risk AI use case – a clear affirmation that some decisions should never be fully delegated to machines.

How does a Supervisor-type agent actually work? At a high level, it follows a loop with four stages: Suggest → Submit → Review → Decide. First, the agent produces an output based on input data – for example, an LLM (Large Language Model) generates a draft email response, or an Apex routine computes a risk score for a transaction. Next, instead of acting immediately, the agent submits this draft or recommendation to a human reviewer through a structured hand-off. This could be as simple as creating a task in a work queue or sending a Slack message, or as integrated as popping up a Screen Flow in Salesforce with the AI's output pre-filled. Then a human (the supervisor) reviews the suggestion. They might edit the drafted content, provide approval or rejection, or select a next-step path (approve the expense, escalate the case, etc.). Finally comes the decide stage: based on the human's input, the outcome is finalized – the email is sent if approved, the case is routed, or perhaps the AI's recommendation is overridden. Crucially, many Supervisor agents also include a feedback loop: the human's decision and any corrections can be captured to continually train models or adjust business rules. Over time, this means the AI gets better – for instance, refining its prompts or adjusting confidence thresholds – by learning from what the humans accepted or rejected.

Salesforce's Agentforce platform provides a rich toolbox to implement the Supervisor pattern in practice. Agent Builder can be used to declaratively define an agent's role and capabilities, giving you a head start in scaffolding the logic for suggestions and hand-offs. For the AI generation step, teams often use Invocable Apex (to execute custom server-side logic or call out to an LLM like Einstein GPT) as well as declarative tools like Prompt Templates. The hand-off to humans can leverage Flow Builder – for example, an orchestrated screen flow that surfaces the AI's draft in a friendly UI for review, with "Approve" and "Reject" paths. In Salesforce, you might also tap into native mechanisms: a Screen Flow or Slack integration can prompt users in real time, or a standard Approval Process can route records (e.g. a contract or case update) to the right approver. What's more, capturing the human feedback is made easier with platform features – you might log the review outcome in a custom "Feedback" object or use metadata tags on records to mark that an AI suggestion was human-validated. All of this is supported by Agentforce's emphasis on integration: for example, a Supervisor agent can send its draft decision to a manager via Salesforce Inbox or email, and wait for a response. Meanwhile, the Agentforce Command Center provides observability, tracking metrics like how often the agent's suggestions get accepted vs. overridden. The upshot is a comprehensive, human-in-the-loop workflow built with both low-code and pro-code tools – one that spans predictive AI generation and traditional workflow automation in harmony.

Because Supervisor agents sit at the intersection of AI and human decision-making, designing them often becomes a team sport. Architects and developers must set up the technical pieces (flows, Apex, data integrations) and ensure the system is robust (e.g. bulk-safe logic and alignment with trigger frameworks so it won't break under volume). Data scientists or prompt engineers might craft how the AI generates its suggestions (ensuring it's steerable and respects policies). Business stakeholders are key in defining the review criteria and threshold – for instance, which cases require human approval, what constitutes a "risky" recommendation, and who should be the reviewer. It pays to plan this upfront: a Supervisor agent is only as effective as the workflow around it.

Pro Tip: When building a Supervisor agent, design the feedback loop first. Knowing exactly how and by whom the AI's output will be evaluated helps shape the agent's prompts, model choices, and rule logic from the start.

In the rest of this chapter, we'll deep-dive into the Supervisor pattern. The next section begins by mapping out the structure and components of a Supervisor agent in detail – its anatomy. From there, we'll explore when to deploy this pattern (and when not to), walk through cross-functional use cases, and provide a how-to on building one using Salesforce tools (with examples of code and configuration). We'll discuss strategies for building trust and explainability into Supervisor agents so that human reviewers actually rely on them, and we'll survey how similar human-in-the-loop designs appear in other AI ecosystems (from Microsoft's Copilot to open-source frameworks like LangChain and CrewAI). Finally, we'll see how the Supervisor plays with other agent patterns in orchestrated workflows. By the end of this chapter, you'll have a clear blueprint for leveraging human-in-the-loop validators to deploy AI responsibly. Next, let's start with the fundamentals: what makes up a Supervisor agent's core structure?

THE STRUCTURE OF A SUPERVISOR AGENT

At its core, a Supervisor agent's lifecycle can be described as Suggest → Submit → Review → Decide. This section breaks down each part of that lifecycle and the key ingredients that make it work, from the inputs an agent consumes to the outputs it produces and the tools that glue everything together.

Lifecycle Stages. A Supervisor agent typically starts by suggesting an outcome or draft based on some input. For example, it might generate a suggested reply to a customer email, or produce a risk rating for a loan application. This suggestion stage is powered by the agent's internal logic and data: it could involve an LLM prompt (for a text draft) or an algorithmic rule (for a numeric score). Next, the agent submits this suggestion for human review instead of acting on it immediately. In practical terms, submission might mean creating a task or record that appears in a manager's approval queue, sending a notification via Slack/Teams, or opening a Salesforce Screen Flow that displays the AI's work. The human then reviews the suggestion. During review, the person can compare the AI's output against real-world context and policies – maybe editing text for tone, or checking that a recommended action is justified. Finally, based on the human input, a decision is made: the draft is approved and executed (e.g. the email is sent or the transaction is approved), or it's rejected/modified. If rejected, the workflow might loop back (maybe the agent is asked for a revised suggestion, or the process ends with a human-crafted response instead). The decision stage closes the loop for that task, and ideally logs the outcome.

Inputs and Outputs. What does a Supervisor agent take in, and what does it produce? The inputs can be any relevant context that the AI needs to make its initial suggestion. In Salesforce terms, this often includes record data (fields on a Case, Opportunity, Claim, etc.), relevant business rules or policy metadata, and possibly external data. For instance, an agent drafting a contract clause might ingest the deal's parameters and a library of standard clause templates. Or an agent evaluating an expense report might reference policy thresholds (stored in a custom metadata type) for allowable amounts. These inputs ensure the AI isn't hallucinating in a vacuum – it's grounded in the facts and rules of the business scenario. The output from the agent is usually a recommendation or draft content, often accompanied by some confidence or classification. For example, the agent might output: "Recommended approval of $5,000 budget increase – Confidence 82%" or "Draft email to customer (see text below)". In some cases, the output could be a simple flag or label (e.g. "High risk" versus "Low risk" classification of a case) which then dictates whether human review is needed at all. A well-designed Supervisor agent also hints at a proposed next step: for instance, a draft email output might include instructions like "(Send upon approval)", or a risk assessment might come with "(Escalate to Tier-2 review if rejected)". This way, the human reviewer knows what actions are available or recommended following their decision.

Common Forms of AI Suggestions. It's helpful to concretely imagine what a Supervisor agent might actually produce for review. In customer service, a prevalent form is a draft communication – such as an email or chat response composed by the agent (a bit like Gmail's smart compose on steroids) that an agent can tweak and send. In HR or hiring, a Supervisor agent might produce a score or recommendation (e.g. a rating for a job candidate, or a suggested compensation change) that a human manager must confirm. In finance, the agent could propose a field update (like adjusting a credit limit) or a transaction classification ("This expense looks out-of-policy, recommend rejection"). In compliance or security, the agent might output a risk flag with an explanation ("This contract clause deviates from standard terms; high-risk – please review"). The variety is wide, but what ties all these forms together is that the AI is not directly committing changes. Instead, it's producing something for a human to look at. Even in automated case routing (a task AI could do outright), a Supervisor-pattern twist might be to let the AI suggest a case priority or assignment, but route it to a dispatcher for confirmation if certain conditions are met (like VIP customers or edge cases). By structuring outputs as suggestions, the Supervisor agent ensures no irreversible action happens without a human's nod.

Enabling Tools in Salesforce. Under the hood, several Salesforce technologies typically cooperate to bring a Supervisor agent to life:

AI Generation (Suggest Stage): This can be handled by Invocable Apex or by calling an AI service. For instance, one might write an Apex invocable method generateDraftEmail(caseId) that collects case details and invokes an LLM (via the Salesforce Einstein AI APIs or an external service) to draft an email. Alternatively, Salesforce's Einstein GPT and Prompt Builder could be used declaratively – you define a prompt template for, say, "Draft a friendly resolution email for Case {Case.Id} using details X, Y, Z," and let the platform produce the text. The result of this generation is passed into the flow as a variable (e.g. the drafted email body or a recommended field value).

Routing to a Human (Submit Stage): Once the draft or recommendation is ready, the agent needs to find the right human and channel for review. Here, Salesforce offers many options. A simple approach is using a Screen Flow that pops up for an assigned user; for example, a support agent working a case hits a point where an "AI suggestion" screen appears with the draft response and an "Approve and Send" button. For asynchronous or background processes, one might create a Task record or Approval request assigned to a queue or specific user – leveraging Salesforce's standard Approval Process framework for things like expense approvals or contract changes (which automatically handles notifications and tracking). Modern enterprises might prefer real-time collaboration tools: using the Salesforce-Slack integration or email alerts to send the AI output to a human. For example, an agent could post to Slack: "AI Drafted a contract clause for Opportunity 123 – click here to review," and the human can respond in Slack to approve or request changes. There's also Omni-Channel routing in Service Cloud, which could treat "AI review needed" as a work item that online agents with the right skills pick up. The goal is to insert the AI's work into the normal workflow of the human reviewer as seamlessly as possible, so that using the Supervisor agent feels like a helpful assist rather than a hindrance.

Feedback Capture (Review/Decide Stage): When the human makes their decision, the outcome should be captured both to carry out the decision and to improve the agent. If the human approves the draft, the system might automatically take the approved content and execute it (send the email, save the changes, etc.). If the human edits the draft before approving, those edits are valuable data – the delta between AI output and final output can be logged (perhaps stored in a "Feedback" custom object or even fed back into model fine-tuning). If the human rejects the AI suggestion outright, that's also important information: was it a false positive flag? An incorrect draft? Many teams set up a brief feedback form as part of the rejection path, asking the reviewer to categorize why (e.g. "Tone not appropriate," "Wrong data used," "Policy issue"). Such structured feedback can later be analyzed to refine the agent's logic. In Salesforce flows, capturing feedback can be as simple as having different decision outcomes (path for accepted vs. rejected) and updating fields accordingly – e.g., mark an AI_Outcome__c field as "Accepted" or "Rejected" on the record the agent was handling, along with a text field for comments. Additionally, Salesforce's metadata can help here: you might use a Custom Metadata Type to define acceptable thresholds or approver roles and check which applied, making it easy to adjust those rules without changing code.

Pro Tip: Use custom metadata to drive who can approve and what conditions trigger review – for example, maintain a table of transaction types and amount limits above which VP approval is needed. This avoids hard-coding those thresholds in Apex or Flow, so the Supervisor pattern can scale and adapt across departments.

Learning Loop: Some of the feedback capture naturally feeds into a learning loop. A simple version of learning is manual: the team reviews all AI rejections in a sprint retro and updates the prompt or model. A more automated approach might use Salesforce's AI Analytics – for instance, Agentforce's Command Center logs every agent interaction. Supervisors can check the dashboard to see, say, that "this week, 40 AI suggestions were presented, 30 were accepted, 10 were overridden". If many suggestions are overridden for the same reason, that trend will surface. Indeed, Agentforce Command Center provides metrics like escalation frequency (how often the AI needed human help) and feedback tagging to pinpoint where the AI might be going off track. In future iterations, one could imagine these systems doing automated retraining – for now, it's typically a human data scientist in the loop for improving the AI. But even without full automation, the key is that the Supervisor agent is not a fire-and-forget solution; it's an evolving system that gets better with every cycle of human guidance.

Now that we have outlined the structure of a Supervisor agent – its lifecycle from suggestion to decision, the inputs and outputs involved, and the Salesforce tools that enable each step – you should have a mental model of how these agents function. Essentially, think of a Supervisor agent as an AI augmented junior employee: it can generate useful work product and follow predefined rules, but it always checks in with the "boss" (human) before finalizing anything. This structure ensures AI contributions are harnessed for efficiency, while human expertise guards the final quality and compliance.

Before diving into how to build such an agent, it's important to decide when the Supervisor pattern is the right approach. After all, not every task warrants human oversight – sometimes full automation is appropriate (the Action pattern), and sometimes an agent only needs to monitor and alert (the Sentinel pattern). In the next section, we'll discuss the scenarios where a Supervisor agent makes sense and provide guidance on choosing this pattern versus others. (In other words, how do you know when your AI agent needs a human chaperone?) Let's explore that decision next.

WHEN TO USE THE SUPERVISOR PATTERN

The Supervisor pattern is powerful, but it's not meant for every single AI-driven task. Injecting a human review step will slow things down and consume people's time – which is perfectly acceptable (even necessary) for some decisions, but overkill for others. This section will help you determine when to deploy a human-in-the-loop agent versus letting the AI roam free. In a nutshell: use a Supervisor agent when the cost of a wrong or unchecked AI action is high. If an error could cause meaningful harm – to a customer, to the business, to compliance – it's a good candidate for human oversight. If not, you might be better served by a fully autonomous agent pattern (or no AI at all).

Here are some guidelines and scenarios where the Supervisor pattern is typically the right choice:

Decisions with meaningful downside risk: Whenever an automated decision could have serious negative consequences if wrong, put a human in the loop. Classic examples include denying an insurance claim, canceling a customer's account, approving a large financial transaction, or any " irreversible" action. An AI might be very helpful in recommending such actions (it can process far more data than a human), but you'd want a person to double-check before pulling the trigger. The Supervisor agent handles the recommendation, and a human owner provides the final sign-off. Many financial services teams, for instance, use AI to scan loan applications or credit card transactions for fraud signals – but a human analyst reviews the high-risk flags before the account is actually frozen. The rule of thumb is: the higher the stakes, the stronger the case for a Supervisor agent. As one industry commentary put it, AI today "lacks real-world context, ethical reasoning, and the ability to understand regulatory nuances" – so if a mistake in context or nuance would be a big deal, don't let the AI system operate alone.

Communications requiring tone or legal accuracy: Generative AI is famously good at drafting text, but it can still stumble on tone or exact phrasing – especially in business communications that carry branding or legal implications. If an agent is tasked with writing content that must be right (polite in tone, legally vetted, on-brand), it's wise to use the Supervisor pattern. For example, an AI could draft an apology email to a customer after a service failure. That email better strike the right tone of empathy and not admit to anything that creates liability. A human-in-the-loop can ensure the tone and wording are spot-on before it's sent. Similarly, marketing teams might use AI to generate social media posts or ad copy, but they'll have a human review for brand compliance and factual accuracy before anything goes live. The Supervisor pattern here prevents the nightmare scenario of an AI-generated PR gaffe. It acts as a tone and quality filter, catching those subtle issues that AI often misses (like culturally inappropriate references or unintended connotations). It's no coincidence that Microsoft's Copilot for content generation always leaves the final insertion to the user – the pattern acknowledges that AI is a first drafter, not the final editor when nuance matters.

High-variance or edge-case scenarios: If your task involves a long tail of weird cases or exceptions that are hard to fully codify, a Supervisor agent can provide a safety net. For instance, consider an HR recruiting agent that screens resumes and suggests who to interview. Most resumes might be straightforward, but some candidates have non-traditional backgrounds that confuse the AI's training. Rather than risk missing a great but atypical candidate, the organization might mandate a human review for any recommendation to reject a candidate that the AI isn't highly confident about. These "edge" decisions – where the AI's confidence or the situation's novelty passes a threshold – are prime for human oversight. One could implement this as: if AI confidence < 90% or certain unusual attributes are present, route to human via Supervisor pattern; else if it's a routine scenario with high confidence, perhaps allow an automated decision (or a different pattern). Essentially, whenever automated thresholds are exceeded or uncertainty is high, bring in the humans. This is akin to how autopilot in airplanes hands back control to pilots in unusual weather – for the mundane, AI can handle it, but for the strange and unexpected, a person should step in.

Regulated processes with mandatory human review: In some industries, using the Supervisor pattern isn't just best practice – it's the law or policy. There are regulations (in healthcare, finance, aviation, etc.) that outright require a human to be accountable for certain decisions. For example, certain financial trades or medical diagnoses might legally need a human sign-off even if AI did 99% of the work. Salesforce's perspective aligns with this: even with advanced AI, humans remain "in the loop" for legal or significant decisions. If you're building an AI agent for a process that has an existing approval chain or compliance checkpoint, you will almost certainly incorporate the Supervisor pattern at those points. Think of an AI agent assisting with FDA approval document preparation – no matter how good it is, final submission to regulators would always involve a human expert reviewing every word. The pattern ensures you meet all governance requirements. Additionally, auditors and regulators tend to be much more comfortable knowing that AI outputs are vetted by humans before affecting customers or financial statements. A Supervisor agent provides a clear audit trail of who approved what, which can be critical for compliance reports.

Training wheels for full automation (scaffolding): Sometimes organizations use the Supervisor pattern as a transitional strategy. When rolling out a new AI capability, you might not trust it enough to let it run autonomously on Day 1. So you start with a human-in-the-loop for every decision, essentially shadowing the AI and catching mistakes. Over time, if the AI proves accurate and the team gains confidence, you can gradually loosen the reins – perhaps only spot-checking decisions or eventually moving to an Action pattern (fully automated) for that task. In this use, the Supervisor pattern acts like scaffolding around a building under construction: providing support and stability until the structure (the AI model and rules) are robust enough on their own. A real example could be an expense report auditor agent: in initial deployment, it flags 50 reports and humans review all 50; after a few months of tuning, if 45 out of 50 were consistently correct, the team might allow the agent to auto-approve low-value expenses and only send edge cases for review. By using human oversight as a learning phase, you mitigate risk upfront and gather data to eventually justify automation. It's a pragmatic approach in enterprises where trust in AI is earned, not assumed. (GPT may be a fast learner, but corporate trust-building moves at a human pace, often with good reason.)

To decide between a Supervisor agent and other patterns, it helps to have a decision framework or even a simple flowchart. One approach is to ask two questions of any potential AI-driven process: "What's the worst-case if the AI gets it wrong?" and "How frequently do we expect the AI to be wrong or uncertain?" If the worst-case is truly damaging (e.g. legal violation, loss of major account, safety issue), lean toward Supervisor. If the AI is likely to be wrong only in minor ways or very rarely, you might handle those with testing and an Action agent plus occasional human audit. Another question: "Is a human available and reasonably capable of adding value in this loop?" If humans would catch errors that AI would miss (like subtle context or common sense), that's a point for Supervisor. If humans wouldn't do much better (or the volume is so massive that human review is impractical), you may need to invest more in the AI's accuracy and go full automation. Many teams explicitly define criteria for human escalation as part of their agent design. For example, Decision Tree:

- If task is low-risk and AI confidence is high (above X%), then use autonomous Action agent (no human in loop).
- If task is high-risk or AI is unsure, then use Supervisor pattern (AI proposes, human approves).

- If task is purely about monitoring events with predefined rules (no decision needed, just alerts), then use Sentinel pattern.

Such a tree can be codified as configuration. Some orgs maintain an "oversight matrix" in a custom metadata: listing processes vs. required oversight level (none, spot-check, full approval). This helps governance and consistency in deciding patterns.

It's worth comparing the Supervisor pattern with its close cousin, the Action pattern. The Action pattern (covered later in the book) is for agents that execute autonomously – they take an input and directly perform an action in the system (create a record, send a notification, update a field) without asking permission each time. The Supervisor, by contrast, proposes rather than disposes; it's a recommender, not an executor. Both patterns can achieve similar business outcomes – e.g. closing a case or adjusting a record – but one does it with a human checkpoint and the other does it fully hands-off. When you have high confidence in the logic and low risk in the outcome, the Action pattern offers speed and simplicity. When in doubt, or when accountability is paramount, the Supervisor pattern provides reassurance. A practical combination in many systems is to start a process in Action mode and fall back to Supervisor mode for exceptions: for instance, an agent might auto-complete 90% of routine tasks, but when it encounters something outside the norm (like a very large transaction amount or a novel query), it switches to Supervisor behavior (draft a response, then ask a human). Salesforce Agentforce makes it feasible to blend these – you could have a flow that normally goes straight through but invokes a human approval subflow on certain conditions.

To summarize, use the Supervisor pattern to mitigate risks and uncertainties in AI-driven work. As a Salesforce executive noted, trusted AI often "needs a human at the helm" for significant use cases, and the Supervisor architecture is exactly about keeping a human pilot in the cockpit while the AI copilot flies the plane. If you err, err on the side of oversight: teams generally prefer discovering they didn't need a human in hindsight (which can be fixed by more automation later) over wishing they had a human involved after a costly AI mistake. In practice, many organizations start new AI agent deployments with a Supervisor pattern unless it's blatantly low-risk – it's a confidence-building phase. You can always graduate an agent to more autonomy once it earns trust. On the flip side, avoid sticking a human review step in every single AI action "just because" – that leads to review fatigue and defeats the purpose of automation. The art is to right-size the oversight to the risk and maturity of the solution.

Now that we've identified when a Supervisor agent is appropriate, let's look at concrete examples across different business functions. In the next section, we will tour several cross-functional use cases to see how Supervisor agents operate in the wild – from HR to legal to marketing – and we'll summarize these scenarios in a handy list mapping outputs, reviewers, and success metrics. This will solidify your understanding of the pattern's versatility before we dive into building one.

CROSS-FUNCTIONAL USE CASES FOR SUPERVISOR AGENTS

One of the strengths of the Supervisor pattern is that it applies to many domains wherever AI and human decision-making intersect. Let's explore how different departments and industries are leveraging Supervisor agents as "AI co-pilots" with human oversight. We'll cover use cases in HR, legal, finance, compliance, and marketing, then summarize them in a list to highlight the key elements: the domain context, what output the agent generates, who the human reviewer is, and how success is measured. Along the way, we'll sprinkle in a few real-world metaphors and best practices (including Salesforce-specific angles) to illustrate each scenario.

HR (Recruiting and Talent Management): Hiring new employees is as much art as science, and getting it wrong can be costly – both financially and culturally. HR teams have started employing AI agents to assist with recruiting, but always with a human in the loop to maintain fairness and personal judgment. For example, an AI Interview Analysis Agent might review video interviews or written candidate answers and provide a preliminary assessment: "Candidate shows strong problem-solving, average communication; recommends proceeding to next round." This agent might even draft a short summary of the candidate's strengths and weaknesses. However, rather than auto-rejecting or advancing candidates, the agent routes its recommendations to a human hiring manager or recruiter (the reviewer). The human then validates the recommendation – checking, for instance, that the AI didn't overlook something important in the candidate's resume or display an unintended bias. In this Supervisor setup, the success metric could be time saved per candidate (maybe recruiters screen 50% more resumes per week thanks to AI suggestions) combined with quality of hire (ensure the AI isn't causing good candidates to be wrongly filtered out). A good outcome is that humans agree with, say, 80% of the AI's recommendations, indicating the AI is learning the organization's preferences, while the remaining 20% where humans override it provide valuable data to refine the model or adjust criteria. This approach aligns with Salesforce best practices around AI ethics – by keeping a person accountable, the company can better guard against things like algorithmic bias in hiring. (And let's face it, GPT-4 doesn't know your company's culture or team dynamics; a human does.)

Legal (Contract Review and Drafting): Legal departments deal with documents full of nuance and implications. A Contract Review Agent is a perfect example of the Supervisor pattern in action. Such an agent can scan a new contract draft and flag any anomalies or risky clauses compared to the company's standard playbook. It might highlight, "Clause 7 deviates from template – adds unlimited liability; suggest replacing with standard liability cap clause." The AI could even draft the suggested replacement clause text. This is immensely helpful given the volume of contracts, but no sane General Counsel will let an AI approval stand on its own. Instead, the agent's findings and drafted edits are forwarded to a legal counsel or contract manager for review. That human sees all the highlights (perhaps through a nice Salesforce screen showing redlined clauses the AI flagged) and the AI's recommended text changes. The lawyer then makes the call: accept the suggestions, modify them, or override them (maybe there's context the AI couldn't know, such as a negotiated concession). The metrics of success here revolve around review efficiency and risk reduction: for instance, contract throughput time (did deals close faster because lawyers spent less time on first-pass reviews?) and error avoidance (did the AI+human combo catch risky clauses that a rushed human might have missed alone?). We might also track AI precision – how often it flagged clauses that the human agreed were problematic. An interesting Salesforce best practice to apply: use Custom Metadata to store a library of "legally acceptable clauses" and have the AI agent reference that. This way, the AI's suggestions are based on official company policy, and updating the policy (metadata) automatically tunes the agent's behavior without re-coding. In sum, the AI is like a junior legal associate scanning the contract and marking it up, but the senior attorney always reviews those markups.

Pro Tip: For legal use cases, always provide the source or reasoning behind AI flags – e.g. a link to the policy it violated or a past case. This builds the lawyer's trust that the AI isn't just making things up.

Finance (Budgeting and Approvals): Finance teams often face decisions where strict rules meet business judgment. Picture a Budget Reallocation

Agent in a large company. Managers might request to move funds between departments or increase their budget mid-quarter. An AI agent can evaluate these requests against historical data and policy: "This request of $50K for marketing is 10% above the usual quarterly spend; similar past requests were approved when justified by pipeline data." The agent could then recommend approval if certain conditions are met (like the department under-spent in another area, or revenue projections justify it) – or recommend denial if it sees red flags. Instead of automatically moving money around (which could be dangerous), the agent compiles its recommendation and reasoning and forwards it to a Finance Director or CFO's delegate for sign-off. The human reviewer gets a concise summary: "AI suggests approving $50K transfer from Travel to Digital Marketing, confidence 75%, because travel budget under-run and campaign ROI is projected to be high." The human then considers intangibles the AI might not know (maybe there's a hiring freeze that changes the context) and clicks Approve or Reject in a custom Salesforce approval screen. Key metrics here include process speed (how much faster are budget changes processed?), compliance (no policy limits breached – the AI should catch those), and forecast accuracy (did these AI-suggested reallocations lead to better financial outcomes?). A well-tuned Supervisor agent in finance can dramatically reduce the back-and-forth for routine approvals while still leaving final control with humans who understand the strategic context. Salesforce Flow's role in this might be orchestrating a multi-step approval: the AI's recommendation could even auto-fill fields in an Approval Process record and dynamically choose the right approver based on amount (leveraging, say, a custom metadata of approval limits per role). The human approver sees "AI recommended – Yes" as a field, which might make them more comfortable trusting it (or conversely, prompt them to double-check AI logic – both reactions are understandable early on!). Over time, if they see the AI's right most of the time, trust grows and maybe threshold for auto-approval can be increased.

Compliance (Transaction Monitoring and PII review): Compliance officers are on the hook to ensure the company plays by the rules – be it financial regulations, data privacy laws, or internal policies. Here we find Supervisor agents acting as diligent watchdogs with human gatekeepers. Consider a Sensitive Data Detection Agent in a company that processes customer data. The agent scans data entries or documents for personally identifiable information (PII) or other sensitive content that shouldn't be there (e.g. someone accidentally uploaded a list of passwords or social security numbers into a case file). The agent might detect something and raise an alert: "Possible PII (credit card number) found in Case Attachment ID 5678 – recommended action: mask or delete the attachment." Rather than immediately deleting (which could be a mistake if the detection is a false positive or if that data is legitimately needed), the Supervisor pattern kicks in. The alert plus recommendation is sent to a Compliance Officer or Security Analyst to review. They open a dashboard (maybe a Lightning page summarizing the incident) to see what the AI flagged. The agent could even blur out the sensitive bits and show just enough context. The human then decides: yes, this is a violation – scrub it (and they click "Remove Data" which triggers a Flow to mask the info), or no, it's a false alarm / allowed exception – dismiss the alert. The success metrics in compliance scenarios are typically false positive/negative rates and incident response time. We want the AI to catch a high percentage of true issues (increase coverage), while not overwhelming humans with noise (precision matters so compliance officers don't get alert fatigue). With the Supervisor approach, one can measure how many AI flags were confirmed vs. overridden. If too many false alarms, you tune the model. If any false negatives slipped past both AI and human, that's serious and triggers retraining and perhaps process changes. Another use case: Anti-money-laundering (AML) Agent in banking – it scores transactions or customer behaviors for risk and forwards the risky ones to human compliance analysts with an explanation ("Customer X's transfer pattern matches known smurfing behavior"). Here the Supervisor pattern is essentially mirroring what many banks already do with rule-based systems, but with AI pattern recognition enhancements. It's important to note a pragmatic caveat: GPT still doesn't understand regulatory nuance or legalese like an experienced compliance officer does, so don't expect your AI to replace your compliance team – think of it as giving them a smart sieve that catches more potential issues and frees them to focus on analysis. The Supervisor agent ensures that no compliance action (or accusation) is taken by AI alone – preserving the principle that accountability rests with human staff, as regulators expect.

Marketing (Content and Campaign Approvals): Marketing organizations love creativity – but also carry the brand's reputation, so they tend to vet content carefully. Enter the Campaign Content Drafting Agent. Imagine an AI agent that can generate variants of marketing copy, social media posts, or even entire campaign briefs based on some initial parameters. It might produce a set of suggestions like, "Here are three tagline options for the new product launch, and a draft email to customers." This is a boon for marketers staring at a blank page. However, brand managers or editors will want to review anything outward-facing. Using the Supervisor pattern, the AI's content drafts are routed to a Marketing Manager or Brand Director for approval. In Salesforce, this could be managed through a custom content management object: the AI creates a "Proposed Content" record with fields for each channel's copy, and an approval process notifies the manager. The manager reviews each suggestion: maybe option A has the right tone, option B is off-brand, etc. They might approve one of the taglines as-is, edit the email draft (tweaking phrasing that the AI made too generic), and reject a social post altogether if it's not appropriate. The success metrics here include content production speed (did having AI drafts accelerate the campaign creation timeline?), engagement or quality scores (maybe measured by A/B tests or internal review ratings, to ensure AI-suggested content performs well), and consistency with brand voice (a subjective measure, but over time the AI should learn from the edits what the brand guidelines are). Marketing is an area where occasional dry wit from the AI might actually be welcome – but it can also produce tone-deaf mistakes, so human oversight is crucial. A fun metaphor: the Supervisor agent in marketing is like a junior copywriter that can spitball 100 ideas in an hour – a creative powerhouse – but the creative director (human) picks the one gem out of the rough and polishes it for the world to see. This partnership can yield more creative output without sacrificing brand integrity. From a Salesforce perspective, teams might integrate this with Content Management and CRM data; e.g., the AI drafts social posts that include personalized tidbits (pulled from Data Cloud about customer interests), then a human ensures none of those personalizations cross the line into "creepy" before approving the post. That balance of personalization and privacy is exactly why the human touch remains vital.

We've walked through five domains, but there are countless other examples: Healthcare might use Supervisor agents for AI-assisted diagnosis (AI suggests, doctor confirms), Customer Support might have an agent that drafts knowledge base articles from case resolutions (agent writes, support content manager reviews before publishing), and so on. In all cases, the pattern is consistent – AI generates something useful, human gatekeeper validates it.

To cement these examples, the list below summarizes each use case with key elements:

HR

- **Agent output (suggestion):** Recommended interview outcome or candidate ranking for a role (for example, "Candidate recommended for hire, score 8/10").

- **Human reviewer:** HR recruiter or hiring manager.
- **Success metrics:** Faster screening time per candidate; improved quality of hire and retention, with fewer strong candidates overlooked.

Legal

- **Agent output (suggestion):** Flagged contract clauses with suggested edits (for example, "Clause 5 is non-standard; replace with approved wording X").
- **Human reviewer:** Legal counsel or contract manager.
- **Success metrics:** Reduced contract review turnaround time; zero critical legal misses while maintaining compliance.

Finance

- **Agent output (suggestion):** Draft decision on approval of a transaction or budget change (for example, "Approve expense #1234: compliant with policy, low risk").
- **Human reviewer:** Finance director or designated approver such as a VP or CFO delegate.
- **Success metrics:** High rate of correct approvals with few false positives or negatives; measurable time savings in the approval process.

Compliance

- **Agent output (suggestion):** Risk classification or alert with recommended action (for example, "Transaction flagged as potential fraud; recommend hold and investigation").
- **Human reviewer:** Compliance officer or security analyst.
- **Success metrics:** Higher detection of true incidents; low false alarm rate; rapid response to flagged issues.

Marketing

- **Agent output (suggestion):** AI-generated content draft such as copy, taglines, or ads (for example, "Draft social post: 'Introducing our new feature...'").
- **Human reviewer:** Marketing manager or brand reviewer.

- **Success metrics:** Faster content creation cycles; content performance meets engagement standards; consistent brand voice as measured by review scores.

As the list illustrates, the reviewer persona varies by domain (it could be a manager, an analyst, a lawyer, etc.), but in all cases the reviewer is someone accountable for the decision's outcome. And success metrics blend efficiency gains from AI with maintenance of quality or compliance due to human oversight. Many teams find that introducing a Supervisor agent lets them handle a greater volume of work (because AI does the first pass) while actually improving quality (because the human focuses on final adjustments rather than drudge work). It's a sweet spot of human-AI collaboration.

In practice, rolling out these use cases requires change management. Teams must be trained on how to interact with the AI's suggestions (e.g. how to provide feedback in Salesforce after reviewing an AI draft). Also, a bit of dry but wise advice: don't let the presence of the AI make humans complacent. There's a risk that human reviewers become rubber-stampers if the AI is usually right – which undermines the safety net. To combat this, some companies randomly inject a few known "bad suggestions" or require periodic audits of approved items to ensure reviewers stay vigilant (sort of like quality control on the quality control). Over time, as trust grows, the process can be tuned to maximize throughput (maybe one human can oversee multiple agents' outputs in a command center style).

We've now seen the Supervisor pattern in action across a spectrum of business scenarios. These examples should spark ideas about where you can apply human-in-the-loop validators in your own organization. The beauty is that the pattern is consistent enough to be templated (reusable logic and components), yet flexible enough to adapt to everything from creative work to compliance drudgery.

Having covered the "why" with real examples, it's time to get hands-on. In the next section, we will walk through building a Supervisor agent with Salesforce Agentforce tools. We'll use an example (an agent that drafts a customer service email and seeks approval) to illustrate the technical implementation step by step – including how to generate the AI output, present it for review in a Flow, and capture the feedback. By the end, you should have a practical blueprint for creating your own human-in-the-loop AI agent on the platform.

BUILDING A SUPERVISOR AGENT WITH AGENTFORCE TOOLS

Now we get into the nuts and bolts of constructing a Supervisor pattern agent using Salesforce's Agentforce framework and related tools. Up to this point, we've discussed concepts – now it's implementation time. We'll follow a concrete example to make it tangible: suppose we want to build an agent that drafts an outbound case resolution email for a support case and then submits it for human approval before sending to the customer. This is a common scenario in customer support organizations, where AI can save agents time by writing the first draft of a response, but the company still wants a human to verify the message (to ensure accuracy of the solution and appropriate tone) before it goes out. We'll see how to create this Supervisor agent from scratch, referencing Salesforce tools like Agent Builder, Flow Builder, Invocable Apex, and more. Along the way, we'll highlight best practices (like making the solution bulk-safe and testable) and how to leverage metadata for flexibility. Let's break the build process into key steps: define the agent, implement the generation logic, design the review flow, handle versioning and logging, and finally test and deploy.

Step 1: Define the Agent with Agentforce Agent Builder. Agentforce's Agent Builder is a great starting point because it provides a declarative way to set up the scaffold of an agent without writing code. In Agent Builder, you create a new agent (let's call it "EmailDraftAgent") and give it a role/persona and basic instructions. For our example, the role might be "Support Email Drafter – an AI agent that prepares draft email responses for support cases." Using natural language, you could describe what the agent should do, e.g.: "When a support case is ready to close, draft a polite, concise resolution email to the customer summarizing the issue and solution, including any next steps or apology as needed. Do not send the email; mark it for agent review." Agent Builder may even suggest some topics or actions automatically by scanning metadata (for instance, it might detect you have email templates or knowledge articles and suggest those as resources). We confirm the agent's settings, such as what Salesforce object it will work with (Case) and ensure it has access to relevant fields (like Case Description, Case Resolution, Customer Name, etc.). At this stage, we're essentially configuring the scope of the agent – what it can see and what job we expect it to do. Agent Builder might allow us to choose an out-of-the-box "Human Handoff" topic as well, which ensures the agent knows it should not fully complete the task without escalation to a human. Think of this step as writing the job description for your AI co-worker. Once saved, we have an agent record which can be further extended with flows and Apex.

Step 2: Implement the Draft Generation Logic (Invocable Apex & LLM). While Agent Builder sets up the shell, the brains of our agent – drafting a high-quality email – will likely require either a large language model or some advanced templating. Salesforce provides Einstein GPT and Prompt Builder, but for illustration, let's assume we want full control and use an Invocable Apex action to generate the draft. We create an Apex class, e.g. CaseEmailDraftGenerator, with an @InvocableMethod that takes in a list of Case Ids and returns a list of draft email strings. Inside this method, we'd gather the necessary info from each Case (like the issue description, what the resolution code or text is, maybe related knowledge articles). Then we'd form a prompt for an LLM. For example:

```
public with sharing class CaseEmailDraftGenerator {
  @InvocableMethod
  public static List<String> generateDraftEmails(List<Id> caseIds) {
    List<String> emailDrafts = new List<String>();
    List<Case> cases = [SELECT Id, Contact.Name, Description, Solution__c
                FROM Case WHERE Id IN :caseIds];
    for (Case c : cases) {
      String prompt = 'You are a support agent drafting an email. '
        + 'Customer Name: ' + c.Contact.Name + '. '
        + 'Issue: ' + c.Description + '. '
          + 'Solution: ' + (c.Solution__c != null ? c.Solution__c : 'Solution not recorded') + '. '
          + 'Write a brief, polite closure email thanking the customer, summarizing the fix, and confirming resolution.';
        String draft = AiIntegration.promptLLM(prompt); // Pseudo-call to an AI service
      emailDrafts.add(draft);
    }
    return emailDrafts;
```

```
    }
}
```

IN THIS PSEUDO-CODE, AIIntegration.promptLLM stands in for whatever mechanism we use to call an LLM (it could be a callout to OpenAI/Anthropic, or using Salesforce's Einstein via AI.invoke if available on platform). We'd need to handle governor limits (e.g., callouts in Apex) and possibly do this asynchronously if using an external service. In a real implementation, you might use Einstein GPT's Apex SDK or an asynchronous queue. Importantly, note the method is bulk-aware: it handles a list of case IDs (Salesforce best practice: make invocables bulk-safe so if the flow passes multiple cases, we do one query and handle each).

Once this Apex is deployed, we register it as an Invocable Action in the Agent's design (Agent Builder likely can pick it up, or we simply call it from a Flow). We now have the ability for our agent to generate an email draft on command.

Step 3: Design the Human Review Flow (Screen Flow). With generation in hand, we turn to the Submit→Review→Decide part. Salesforce Flow is ideal for orchestrating this. We'll create a Screen Flow (or possibly an Auto-launched Flow triggered by some event, which then pops a screen via a quick action – multiple patterns are possible). For concreteness, let's say the trigger is a support agent clicking a "Draft AI Email" quick action on the Case. That action launches our flow. The flow does the following:

Call Apex: It invokes CaseEmailDraftGenerator.generateDraftEmails, passing in the case Id, and gets back the draft email text.

Display Draft on Screen: The flow then shows a Screen element to the support agent (the human reviewer). On this screen, we include a read-only text area (or perhaps a rich text component) showing the AI's drafted email. We might label it "AI-Suggested Email Draft". We also include editable fields or text areas if the human wants to tweak the content right there. Let's say we give an editable text area pre-populated with the draft so the support agent can edit wording. We also include two buttons: "Send (Approve)" and "Decline" (with maybe a third "Edit and Send" path if we want to distinguish that from straight send – but if we allow editing in place, the "Send" can cover that).

Decision Branch: After the screen, the flow checks which button was pressed. If "Send" (approve), the flow proceeds to actually send the email. This could be done via an Email Alert or a Core Action to send an email using the content. Or we could simply update the Case status to closed and post the email content to the Case Feed as a sent email. If "Decline", the flow could branch to a different path. On that decline path, we might ask for feedback: another screen "Please briefly explain why the draft was not used (optional)". This can help us collect data. The flow would then end, maybe leaving the case open for the support agent to manually write their own email – effectively the human decides to do it themselves.

Record Feedback: Regardless of approve or decline, the flow can record the event. For example, set Case.AI_Email_Used__c = true/false and log a record in a custom object "AI Email Review" with fields: Case Id, AI Draft text, Approved? (checkbox), Approved Timestamp, Reviewer Id, Comments. This is gold for later analysis. We'd also want to store if the agent edited the text significantly (maybe compute an edit distance or at least flag "edited" if they changed the draft text box). For now, capturing the final text and outcome is enough.

Execution: In the approve path, after sending the email (via whatever means – possibly invoking a send email action or integration with the Omni-Channel if it's a messaging platform), the flow might mark the case closed or trigger the next step in the process (maybe notify the customer, update a field that it was handled by AI assist). In a decline path, perhaps it notifies a supervisor or simply logs it. It's important that the flow gracefully handles either outcome without causing extra burden – e.g., if declined, perhaps prompt the human to proceed with their own solution.

This Screen Flow essentially implements the Supervisor UI. Salesforce's design considerations here: we likely embed this flow in a Lightning Component or as a utility bar item for support agents. There's also the approach of using Salesforce Inbox or Slack: for example, the AI draft could be sent via Slack to an expert team for approval. But for simplicity, an in-platform screen that the case owner themself sees (and they become the reviewer of the AI's draft) works well. This is like the Copilot model – the support agent is both the user and the supervisor, guiding the AI output. Alternatively, if policy says a manager must approve customer communications, the flow could assign the Screen to a manager user (perhaps using a redirect or a custom Approvals object). That adds complexity, so many teams let the frontline employee be the human-in-the-loop for their AI assistant.

Step 4: Version Control and Metadata-Driven Settings. As we build the agent, we should plan for maintainability. That means applying Salesforce dev practices: use source control (maybe the agent definition and flows are part of your SFDX project), and design the solution to be configurable via Metadata. For example, define a Custom Metadata Type "AI_Agent_Threshold__mdt" with fields like Agent_Name, Min_Confidence_To_AutoSend, etc. In our case email scenario, we might not auto-send anything, but imagine if confidence > 95% we wanted to skip human review (just hypothetical). We could store that threshold and check it in the flow: if the LLM or Apex returned a confidence metric and it exceeds a value from metadata, the flow could actually auto-send the email and just notify the agent after the fact. This hybrid allows high-confidence automations while still using Supervisor pattern for most cases. Even if we don't implement that now, baking in the ability to adjust behavior without changing code is prudent. Similarly, if we have roles involved (like maybe only cases for VIP customers require manager approval while others the support agent's own approval suffices), those rules can live in a Custom Metadata or Custom Setting (or even in the Role hierarchy with some apex logic). The main point: avoid hard-coding specifics into your flow or Apex that might change. Instead, externalize them. This makes the Supervisor pattern scalable across teams. Today it's used in Support, tomorrow Sales might use a similar flow for AI-drafted proposals – you can often reuse the components by just tweaking metadata (like the email template or approval condition).

Speaking of versioning – as you improve the AI model or prompts, track versions. A simple way: include a hidden field or comment in the AI output like "[Draft generated by EmailDraftAgent v1.2]" so when reviewing logs you know which iteration produced it. Or maintain a Custom Metadata "Agent Version" that you update with notes on changes (like prompt tweaks, model upgrades). This will help if suddenly the performance changes – you can correlate it with a version change.

Step 5: Telemetry and Command Center Integration. Once deployed, you'll want to monitor how the Supervisor agent is doing. We touched on logging each decision; those records can feed reports or dashboards. Salesforce's Agentforce Command Center in particular could be leveraged – it automatically captures agent interactions and outcomes if you instrument it. Ensure that the flow or Apex emits logs or events for key points (like an Apex System.debug or, better, use the Agent Telemetry API if provided). In our example, we might log an event "EmailDraftProposed" with metadata like caseId, lengthOfDraft, generationTime, etc., and another event "EmailDraft-

Outcome" with outcome=approved/rejected and maybe time-to-approve. The Command Center can aggregate such data. For instance, you might get a dashboard of acceptance rate – how often did agents use the AI draft vs. discard it? If the acceptance rate is low (say 20%), that signals the drafts aren't good enough or agents don't trust them; you'd then gather feedback to improve the model. If it's high (80-90%), that's great – maybe you can streamline further or eventually auto-send low-risk ones. Also, telemetry might show escalation frequency, which in this context could mean how often the AI needed significant human edits. It's analogous to how often a Supervisor agent's judgment is altered by the human. Monitoring this over time helps prove the ROI of the agent (e.g. "over 3 months, our AI drafting agent saved ~500 hours of writing time, with an acceptance rate climbing from 70% to 85% after prompt tuning"). These are wonderful stats to surface to stakeholders. Agentforce's Command Center can likely be configured to raise alerts if something unusual happens – like if the AI starts producing a lot of rejections (maybe a sign an upstream model changed or a bug introduced), you get alerted to investigate.

Step 6: Testing and Bulk Considerations. Before rolling out to users, test the Supervisor agent thoroughly. This means unit tests for your Apex (e.g. simulate the LLM response by mocking AiIntegration.promptLLM to return a deterministic string in a test context). You'll write Apex tests that cover both paths – simulate an approval and a rejection – asserting that after flow execution, the proper records were updated and no unintended side effects occurred. Also test bulk scenarios: what if someone selects 10 cases and runs the draft (if your flow or Apex can do batch)? Does it handle multiple properly? In our design, the invocable is bulk-ready, but our Screen Flow is single-record oriented. Still, ensure the Apex won't break if invoked with 200 cases (maybe from a future enhancement like a nightly batch that drafts emails for all near-breached cases and queues them for the morning team).

Another angle is UI/UX testing – put it in the hands of a few pilot users and see if the flow interface makes sense. Perhaps add guidance text on the screen: "This draft was generated by AI. Please review and edit as needed before sending. If you decline to use it, you'll need to compose a response manually." Setting the right expectations helps user adoption.

Finally, test failure modes: what if the AI service is down and no draft is generated? The flow should handle null draft gracefully (maybe show a friendly "Sorry, no draft available right now" and exit). Or if the AI output contains something it shouldn't (like it accidentally included a placeholder or offensive word), does the human know how to handle it? Likely yes (they'd just edit it out), but it's wise to instruct users during training that the AI isn't infallible or officially sanctioned content until they approve it.

With these steps, we have built a working Supervisor agent example. To recap in brief for our case: an agent monitors for a case closure scenario, uses Apex and LLM to draft an email, surfaces it via Screen Flow for the support agent to approve or edit, then acts based on the agent's input, and logs the results. All using standard Salesforce components that orchestrate AI and human interaction. The pattern can be replicated: if you wanted a Supervisor agent for expense approvals, you'd similarly create an Apex class to score/recommend, a flow to present to the manager, and capture the response. Or a Supervisor agent for code review (pair programming with AI) could generate code suggestions and have a developer approve them – possibly using a different interface like VS Code with a Salesforce plugin. The underlying steps remain analogous.

Before wrapping up this section, let's address bulk-safe logic and trigger alignment, since those were noted as best practices. Bulk-safe we did in Apex (taking list inputs). If our agent were invoked from triggers (say on Case update, trigger calls AI to draft something), we must ensure not to hit governor limits and to handle batches of records. In many cases, it might be better to decouple (e.g., trigger creates a "Pending AI Draft" record and a platform event picks that up to call AI asynchronously). This avoids slowing down the user save. For trigger frameworks: you could incorporate an AI evaluation in an after-save flow that only executes for certain criteria, again calling invocable in bulk. Always test with many records. One more consideration: Transaction control. If the human declines, and maybe closes the case manually after, ensure no open loops remain (e.g. an approval request record should be canceled). If they approve and an email is sent, ensure the email send is within the same transaction or clearly logged.

Alright, we've built our Supervisor agent! By following a structured approach – scaffold with Agent Builder, implement AI logic with Apex/LLM, design the human interface with Flow, use metadata for config, and instrument with logging – we've created a maintainable, enterprise-ready human-in-the-loop solution. You likely noticed we effectively combined declarative tools (Flow, Approval processes) with code (Apex, possibly LWC). This combo is typical for Agentforce implementations: use low-code for speed and visibility, and augment with code where needed for custom AI or complex logic.

With the agent built, the next crucial topic is trust: How do we ensure the humans actually trust and effectively work with the AI's suggestions? After all, a Supervisor agent is only useful if the human validators find the AI's output helpful and feel comfortable with the process. In the next section, we will discuss techniques for boosting human trust and understanding in Supervisor agents – from explainability and transparency features to setting up feedback loops that continually improve the agent. This will include some "pro tips" on things like showing reasoning, confidence scores, and using metadata to configure who approves what. Building the tech is one thing; getting humans to trust the AI assistant is another, and it's just as important for success.

SUPERVISOR AGENTS AND HUMAN TRUST

Deploying a Supervisor pattern agent is as much about people as it is about technology. Because these agents intentionally put a human in the loop, the overall system only works if the human reviewers trust the AI enough to use its suggestions, yet remain vigilant enough to catch its mistakes. It's a delicate balance: we want to speed things up with AI, but not at the expense of accuracy or accountability. In this section, we focus on how to build confidence in agent-generated recommendations and drafts. We'll cover techniques for making the AI's output more explainable, so humans understand why a suggestion was made and feel comfortable acting on it. We'll also discuss how to empower reviewers with options (overrides, escalations) so they never feel trapped by the AI's proposal. And we'll examine how capturing and leveraging feedback closes the loop to improve both AI performance and human trust over time. Think of this section as the "soft skills" and UI/UX side of the Supervisor pattern – features and practices that make a human reviewer say, "You know, I actually like having this AI assistant, it makes my job easier and I still have control."

Building Initial Confidence: When a human first encounters an AI recommendation, skepticism is natural. Is the AI correct? How did it come up with this? To build trust, transparency is key. One effective technique is providing a brief explanation or rationale alongside the suggestion – even if it's generated by the AI. This is sometimes called chain-of-thought prompting or explainable AI output. For example, if our Supervisor agent flags a transaction as fraud-risk, it should present not just a label but why it thinks so: "Flagged because amount is 3x average and from a new IP address." If it drafts an email, perhaps it highlights which knowledge article or case info it used to form the answer. Salesforce flows or UI can incorporate this by simply having an "AI's Reasoning" section. You might instruct the LLM to output a rationale (some architectures have the AI generate a hidden explanation for the human). Even a simple list of factors considered can help the human reviewer quickly gauge the suggestion's validity. Studies have shown that people trust AI more when they can see the logic – even a rudimentary explanation gives a sense of accountability ("the AI isn't a black box, it followed these steps"). In Agentforce, you could use the Plan Tracer or logs to surface how the agent reasoned, but ideally the user-facing interface has a clear snippet of why this output.

Confidence Scores and Highlights: Another way to calibrate trust is through confidence scoring. If the AI or algorithm can provide a confidence level or score with its recommendation, show that to the human. For instance: "Recommended Approval (Confidence: High)" or maybe a percentage or 3-star scale. Humans intuitively factor confidence into their decision – if the AI says it's only 60% sure, the human will likely scrutinize more carefully (as they should). If it's 99% and they know the model is usually good, they might be more lenient. However, you have to be careful: overconfidence from AI on wrong answers is a known issue. So ensure your confidence metrics are well-calibrated or even conservative. It might be better to use categories like High/Medium/Low rather than precise percentages, to avoid a false sense of precision. Additionally, in contexts like document or image analysis, highlighting relevant portions of input data that led to the output is extremely helpful. Salesforce AI, for example, might highlight the clause in a contract that it deemed risky, so the lawyer's eyes go straight to it. Or highlight the sentence in a customer email that triggered the tone-check. These visual cues make the reviewer's job easier and also validate the AI's focus ("Ah, the agent flagged this sentence – I agree that does look problematic."). If the agent is using any reference data (like knowledge articles), citing those sources (much as this text cites sources) can boost credibility. An agent that says "According to Knowledge Article 123, we should do X" immediately signals to the human that the suggestion is grounded in known information, not just hallucinated. (In fact, Salesforce is working on features to include citations for AI answers because it's such a trust enhancer.)

User Interface for Oversight: The design of the review interface itself can inspire trust or erode it. A few best practices gleaned from various deployments:

Clearly distinguish AI-generated content from user-entered content. For example, use a different font style or a subtle highlight background for AI draft text, so the reviewer knows what was AI-written vs. what they have modified. Slack's AI recap does this by letting you click through to original messages – in our case, showing sources or using quotation marks for AI text can help.

Provide an easy way to edit the AI's suggestion. If the human sees something minor to fix, it should be simpler to tweak it than to reject and start from scratch. This keeps them engaged and not frustrated. For instance, in a Screen Flow, the AI text could be in a rich text field the user can edit directly. If they have to copy-paste to another window to edit, that friction might lead them to just do it all themselves next time (losing trust in the AI's convenience).

Offer quick actions for common adjustments. Maybe the AI draft is good but a bit too formal – a button "Make it more casual" could trigger a re-prompt that adjusts tone. This is advanced, but some Supervisor agents include multiple options or a refine button ("Regenerate draft" if user isn't happy). However, multiple regenerations can also confuse or overwhelm the user, so use judiciously. Sometimes just having a second suggestion for comparison can increase confidence ("both AI options look okay, so I feel safer that it's not completely off-base").

Acknowledge limitations in the UI. A small note like "AI-generated suggestion – please review for accuracy" ironically increases trust, because it sets the expectation that the human is still in charge. It shows the tool is meant to assist, not replace judgment. This can reduce the psychological barrier where the reviewer might think "Am I supposed to just trust this blindly?" – the UI itself says no, you are the validator.

Overrides, Rejections, Escalations: A Supervisor agent must respect human authority at all times – that's the pattern's philosophy. So, ensure the system always allows the human to override or change the AI's output easily, and document that decision. If the human reviewer doesn't agree with the AI, their "reject" action should be final (with no nagging from the AI). In some sensitive workflows, you might even allow the human to escalate to another human if unsure – for example, if an agent doesn't trust the AI's draft and isn't confident in editing it, maybe they can forward it to a subject matter expert. That's an example of Supervisor pattern blending with normal human workflows (you don't have to implement that in every case, but in high-stakes ones it's a good option). Also consider partial overrides: maybe the AI suggests a $10,000 refund and the manager thinks that's too high, so they change it to $5,000 and approve that. The system should capture that adjustment. This ties into feedback – the agent should learn, hey, when scenario X comes up, my recommendation was scaled down by half, perhaps I should calibrate future suggestions. On the flip side, if the AI was too conservative and the human ups it (like AI said deny claim, human paid it out), that feedback is vital.

Capturing Structured Feedback: We've talked about logging outcomes, but let's emphasize how important structured feedback loops are. Every time a human interacts with a Supervisor agent's output, that's a learning opportunity. Encourage (or require) reviewers to provide a reason code when they override the AI. One approach: present a short picklist when they reject or heavily edit: e.g. "Reason for override: A) AI was factually incorrect, B) Tone/style issue, C) Business policy nuance missed, D) Other." It could be as simple as that. Over time, you gather statistics – perhaps 60% of rejections are due to tone. That means the AI drafts are technically right but not matching company voice, so you'd focus on improving that (maybe by giving the LLM more style guidelines). Or if many are due to factual errors, maybe integrate a better knowledge source or fix data. Without structured feedback, you're flying blind on why humans aren't accepting AI suggestions. With it, you have a goldmine for continuous improvement. This is essentially applying the concept of Reinforcement Learning from Human Feedback (RLHF) in a practical enterprise way. You might not retrain the model on the fly, but you're doing a form of supervised fine-tuning by analyzing these patterns and adjusting prompts or model parameters accordingly. Additionally, show the human reviewers that their feedback is valued and used. For example, after a few months, send a summary to the team: "We collected 50 pieces of feedback and updated the AI's knowledge base/prompting, resulting in a 30% drop in needed edits." This closes the loop with the users and encourages them to keep giving quality feedback rather than just silently fixing issues each time.

Pro Tip: Leverage Custom Metadata for Trust Settings. One clever way to maintain and scale trust configurations is to use custom metadata to define who can review and what thresholds trigger review. We mentioned this earlier in build, but here's a trust-related spin: Suppose you have a Supervisor agent that handles multiple types of outputs (or multiple departments). You could have a metadata table like: Pattern_Name, Confidence_Threshold, Approver_Level

For instance, "MarketingEmailDraft, 90, Marketing Director" means if confidence < 90, a Director must review; if >= 90, maybe a Coordinator can review or even auto-send with just a coordinator's click. Or "LegalContractReview, 100, GeneralCounsel" meaning no matter what, GC sign-off needed (some companies might say only GC final). The idea is to avoid scattering these rules in code. If next quarter policy changes that team leads can approve instead of VPs, you update metadata, not flows. This also helps maintain consistent governance across many Supervisor agents. You could even create an "Oversight Matrix" custom object where each row is a scenario and required oversight. The Supervisor agent flow then consults it to determine routing (like which user or group to send to for approval). By doing this, trust and compliance rules become part of your org's metadata, which is auditable and easily adjustable. This supports scaling the Supervisor pattern because as new processes adopt AI, you can quickly configure the appropriate human checkpoints.

Bulk Safe & Testing Strategy (Team-level insight): From a team perspective, emphasize a testing strategy around trust: simulate scenarios where the AI is wrong and ensure the system and people catch it. Do fire drills: deliberately feed a bad case through and see if the reviewer flags it. This can be part of training – e.g., show new users an obviously wrong AI suggestion and walk through how to handle it. Not only does this build user confidence in their authority, it also might reveal any UI shortcomings ("Oh, we realize we didn't give an easy way to correct this kind of mistake, let's improve that."). Always remember, trust is built over time. So start with the agent making small suggestions and gradually increase its role as users get comfortable. For example, an agent might initially only draft internal notes, not customer-facing ones, until it proves itself. Or it flags issues but doesn't suggest the fix for the first phase, letting humans get used to AI flagging correctly, then later you add auto-suggested fixes when trust is higher. This phased approach can be formalized in your deployment plan.

In summary, Supervisor agents should be designed with transparency, control, and continuous learning in mind. Give human validators the information (why and how) to trust an AI suggestion, the tools to easily correct or override it, and a voice in improving the AI via feedback. When done right, users come to see the AI not as a threat to their authority, but as a helpful colleague that does 90% of the grunt work and humbly asks, "Is this okay?" Consider a metaphor: a new hire on your team might be extremely fast and eager (the AI), but they need training and oversight from a seasoned employee (the human supervisor). Over time, as the new hire learns and the supervisor sees consistent good work, the supervisor will delegate more and micromanage less. The Supervisor pattern facilitates exactly this dynamic between AI and human – if we implement it thoughtfully, the result is a high-performing human-AI team where each trusts the other's strengths.

Having addressed the human trust factor within Salesforce and your organization, let's zoom out in the next section to the bigger picture: how does the Supervisor pattern appear in the broader AI ecosystem beyond Salesforce? We'll compare notes with other AI agent frameworks and industry examples – showing that whether you call it human-in-the-loop or something else, this pattern is emerging everywhere to keep AI on track. Understanding these external parallels will give you insight into best practices and perhaps reassure you that Salesforce's approach is aligned with global trends in responsible AI. Onward to the AI ecosystem perspective!

SUPERVISOR PATTERN IN THE AI ECOSYSTEM

The concept of an AI agent that proposes an action and waits for human approval is not unique to Salesforce or Agentforce. Across the AI industry, we see many implementations of human-in-the-loop validators under different names. By examining these, you can glean ideas and reassure stakeholders that the Supervisor pattern is a well-recognized best practice, not just something your team invented. In this section, we'll briefly tour a few notable ecosystems and how they incorporate this pattern: we'll look at LangChain, a popular framework for building agentic applications; CrewAI, an emerging open-source multi-agent orchestration platform; and Microsoft's Copilot experiences, which inherently rely on user approval for AI suggestions. We'll also touch on the Model Context Protocol (MCP) and other standards that allow agents on different platforms to signal the need for human validation. A theme will emerge: as AI agents become more autonomous and "smarter," wise designers are building safety boundaries – often in the form of Supervisor-like agents or explicit approval steps – especially when multiple agents are collaborating or operating with a lot of autonomy. In multi-agent "swarms," having one agent act as a gatekeeper or reviewer can prevent collective mistakes. Let's dive into each example:

LangChain's Reviewer Agents and Approval Workflow: LangChain is a framework many developers use to create complex AI agent behaviors in Python/JavaScript. One of its capabilities is designing agents that don't just blindly act, but can be configured to wait for human input or require confirmation at certain steps. In fact, LangChain's documentation highlights building "copilots that write first drafts for review, act on your behalf, or wait for approval before execution". This is essentially describing the Supervisor pattern. Using LangChain's LangGraph or callback system, developers can insert a checkpoint: for example, an agent plans a multi-step action, and before actually executing, it outputs the plan and yields control back for a human to say "yes, proceed" or modify the plan. Another approach in LangChain is the Critique and Revise pattern (sometimes called Reflexion or Self-critique) – where one agent generates an output and another agent (or human) critiques it, then it's revised. Often the "critiquing agent" could be replaced with a human for higher assurance. Additionally, LangChain introduced features like a tool to explicitly pause for human approval mid-run. This shows that even in code-centric AI development, designers consider human oversight a first-class feature. If you have teams experimenting with LangChain outside Salesforce (maybe building a quick prototype), you can align their approach with your Salesforce Supervisor agents by acknowledging it's the same pattern: one could even have a LangChain agent do some off-platform task (like generate a script or query) and then route the result into Salesforce for a Supervisor agent (human) to validate and maybe push into production. The key takeaway: The Supervisor pattern concept translates into code with constructs to pause and seek confirmation, which frameworks like LangChain support out-of-the-box, reflecting a broad recognition of its importance.

CrewAI's Human Gatekeeping and HITL Workflows: CrewAI is another framework focused on orchestrating multiple specialized agents (a "crew" of agents). They place significant emphasis on Human-in-the-Loop (HITL) workflows as a way to keep AI agents on track. In CrewAI, you can literally include a "human" as part of the agent flow. They provide features like a human_input flag on tasks which, when set, will pause an agent's execution and wait for a person to provide input or approval. For example, you might have an AI agent that, when it has a draft answer, automatically pings a human via a webhook, asking "Is this good to go?". The system then continues or retries based on the human feedback (the human might say "No, fix X and Y" and resume the agent with that feedback). This explicit HITL integration highlights how frameworks like CrewAI see human gatekeepers as a powerful tool for complex decision-making and sensitive operations. CrewAI even documents best practices like being specific and timely with feedback, and has mechanisms to loop the agent retry if negative feedback is given – essentially formalizing a training loop at runtime. Another concept in multi-agent setups is having a "moderator" or "manager" agent that oversees others. CrewAI allows customizing a manager agent – one could design that manager agent to be a sort of AI supervisor, but often you might just put a real human in the manager role via HITL. The notion of collaborative control is baked in. For our purposes, if someone in your enterprise is using CrewAI for something (maybe in a skunkworks project or R&D), you can share lessons: CrewAI's guidance that HITL is valuable for quality assurance, high-stakes ops, compliance, etc., mirrors why we have Supervisor pattern in Salesforce. It's encouraging to see that even cutting-edge multi-agent research frames human oversight not as a burden but as an enhancement for certain contexts.

Microsoft Copilot and Inline Approvals: Microsoft has been integrating "Copilot" AI assistants across many products (GitHub Copilot for code, 365 Copilot for Office documents, etc.), and their philosophy inherently uses a human-in-the-loop model. Copilot will suggest code or text, but it's up to the human developer or writer to accept, modify, or ignore those suggestions. This is a prime example of the Supervisor pattern in a UX context. The AI is essentially acting as a Supervisor agent's "Suggest" stage constantly, and the user is the reviewer/decider on the fly. For instance, in GitHub Copilot, the AI might complete a line of code; the developer reviews it and either tabs to accept or edits it if it's not quite right. Over time, developers learn when to trust it (e.g., for boilerplate code) and when to be cautious (e.g., complex logic or anything with security impact). One interesting development is Copilot for Pull Requests (in preview) where it can suggest descriptions or even review code changes and flag issues, but it's up to a human maintainer to accept those review comments or not. We can also look at Power Platform's AI features: when Copilot suggests a formula in Power Automate or a Flow, a human builder must explicitly insert it and can tweak it. The common thread is AI suggests, human validates – exactly Supervisor pattern. Microsoft even has settings where you can tune how assertive the AI is – effectively a confidence threshold for suggestions or when to auto-apply vs. wait. The reason Microsoft sticks to user-in-the-loop is clear: it prevents catastrophic errors (like an AI writing a wrong formula that goes live without oversight) and it engenders user trust by keeping them in control. When explaining your Salesforce AI agents to business stakeholders, you might draw this parallel: "Think of our Supervisor agents like Microsoft Copilot: it's there to help produce a draft or decision, but you (or your team) get the final say, just like hitting accept on a Copilot suggestion." This often clicks with people because many will have heard of or tried Copilot by now.

Model Context Protocol (MCP) and Cross-Platform Approvals: The Model Context Protocol (MCP) is an emerging standard aimed at allowing different AI agents and tools to interoperate in a standardized way. One aspect of MCP relevant to us is that it can carry context about roles and approval checkpoints across systems. For example, if a Salesforce Agentforce agent calls an external agent via MCP, it could indicate that a certain step requires human approval, so that the external system knows to pause and await a signal. Conversely, an external agent using MCP to call into Salesforce could trigger a Flow that involves a Supervisor pattern step. Essentially, MCP provides a common language, and it's up to implementers to decide to include human checkpoints as part of that language. Salesforce Agentforce 3's native support for MCP means we might see out-of-the-box ways to do things like "if external Agent X sends a completion with status 'needs_human', automatically create a Salesforce task for review." Already, we see hints of that in Agentforce's integration with systems like Slack (surfacing agent activity to human supervisors in real time). The point is the broader AI ecosystem isn't siloed – your Supervisor agent in Salesforce could be one part of a bigger chain. For instance, an AutoGPT-like agent might be crunching data and come up with a recommendation, but before finalizing, it calls a Salesforce Supervisor agent to have a manager give thumbs up. Or vice versa: a Sentinel in Salesforce detects something and calls an external orchestration which then calls back to a human gatekeeper. Interoperability will rely on clear signals for when human input is needed. MCP and similar standards are evolving to include such patterns.

A notable trend in AI circles is also the idea of "constitutional AI" or multi-agent debate – where AI agents critique each other to ensure rules are followed (e.g., one agent generates, another checks policy compliance). This is somewhat parallel to our pattern, except replacing the human with another AI. That can scale but has obvious limits (AI might miss nuance still). However, combining approaches can be powerful: e.g., have an AI do a first check, and only escalate to human if the AI itself is unsure or finds a policy hit. Some frameworks call this a "Moderator" agent or a "Referee". CrewAI, for instance, could allow a designated agent to have veto power, or use an evaluation tool like Patronus AI to rate outputs. These are exciting but I'll caution: relying on an AI to approve another AI is like hiring one newbie to review another newbie's work – it helps, but you still might want a manager oversight for the toughest decisions. So, in multi-agent systems ("swarms"), I often recommend having at least one human-in-loop agent or a final human checkpoint especially if the agents are doing something high impact (like coordinating a complex workflow that could fail in weird ways). In Salesforce context, if we ever orchestrate multiple patterns, likely the final step for critical outcomes will be a Supervisor style approval, just to be safe.

Summary of Ecosystem Learnings: The Supervisor pattern is everywhere, under various guises: Human-in-the-loop, HITL, approval gates, reviewer roles, trust boundaries. It's reassuring to know our pattern is not only a Salesforce thing but a widespread design for responsible AI. This means there's a community of practice out there – best practices from one domain can be adapted to another. For example, the UI ideas from Copilot (inline diff view for changes) might inspire features in Salesforce (imagine a future where a Flow can show "here's how the AI's suggested field values differ from current, accept changes?"). Or lessons from LangChain's critique agents might lead us to incorporate an automated check agent before handing to human (like a mini peer review by AI prior to human).

It also means when integrating Salesforce agents with others, you should keep the Supervisor concept in the architecture: ensure an external agent knows if it should wait for Salesforce human approval, etc. The open standards help – and Salesforce is actively building toward a world of "trusted agent interoperability" where these patterns can function across platforms securely.

To close this section, let's sprinkle a little pragmatic wit: In the grand future of AI, perhaps swarms of intelligent agents will self-organize and do our work while we sip coffee. But until GPT-n+1 truly understands nuance, it's comforting (and frankly entertaining at times) to have a human safety net. Think of the Supervisor pattern in a multi-agent world like the designated driver in a carpool of self-driving cars – you still want one human awake to take the wheel if all the Teslas start misreading the road. Many AI thought leaders assert that human oversight remains essential "especially where language model autonomy is high", to prevent, well, Skynet-esque misadventures. So, we see broad consensus: whether in Salesforce or elsewhere, keeping humans in the loop is not a bug – it's a feature, one that makes AI deployments viable and trustworthy.

Having examined how the Supervisor pattern fits into the wider AI landscape, let's turn in the next section to how the Supervisor works in concert with other agent patterns within the Salesforce Agentforce Playbook. Specifically, we'll look at scenarios combining Supervisor agents with Sentinels, Conductors, Companions, and more – painting a picture of a full end-to-end business process where multiple AI roles play their part. This orchestration view will help you envision larger solutions and tee up the next chapter on the Conductor pattern, which is all about coordination.

SUPERVISOR-TO-SWARM – ORCHESTRATING WITH OTHER PATTERNS

No agent is an island. In a robust enterprise AI architecture, different agent patterns often work together, each handling a piece of the puzzle. The

Supervisor pattern, with its human-in-the-loop focus, frequently acts as the trust anchor or gating mechanism in these orchestrations. In this section, we'll illustrate how Supervisor agents interact with other core patterns from this playbook – such as Sentinel (the monitor), Conductor (the orchestrator), Curator (the data aggregator), Action (the automator), and Companion (the user-facing assistant). We'll use a storyline of a claim handling process in an insurance context as a running example, since it naturally involves multiple stages and decision points that map well to different patterns. Consider it a swimlane diagram in prose: multiple agents passing the baton, with the Supervisor pattern ensuring that at critical junctures, a human review provides the final say. Through this, we aim to reinforce how the patterns can be composed and how the Supervisor pattern specifically complements others by adding a layer of oversight. By the end, you'll see how Chapter 3 (Supervisor) sets the stage for Chapter 4 (Conductor) – because coordinating agents often means deciding which tasks are autonomous and which require validation.

Sentinel → Supervisor: From Detection to Decision. Our scenario begins with a Sentinel agent (covered in Chapter 2) scanning for unusual events. In an insurance company, a Sentinel agent might watch incoming claims for potential fraud indicators or major incidents. Let's say this Claims Sentinel spots a new claim that looks suspiciously similar to a known fraud pattern (perhaps same repair shop, high amount, just after a new policy was opened – classic red flags). The Sentinel's job is to detect and alert, not to judge guilt – so what it does is raise an alert and trigger a follow-up action. In a traditional process, it might just notify a human fraud investigator. But with our AI toolkit, we can escalate it to a Supervisor agent specialized in fraud review. This Supervisor agent takes the alert and composes a recommended next step: for example, it might gather relevant info (claim details, claimant history, pattern matched) and suggest "Recommendation: Flag this claim for investigation and do not pay until review. Rationale: multiple fraud signals detected (listed). Please approve to initiate formal investigation." The human supervisor (fraud analyst) then reviews this recommendation. In effect, the Sentinel identified the case and handed it to the Supervisor agent to prepare the decision package, which the human must authorize. If the human agrees and approves, this might then trigger further automated actions (like notifying the special investigations unit, or sending a letter to the claimant about additional documentation – which could be handled by an Action agent once approved). If the human says "No, I see why the AI flagged it, but I recognize this case – it's actually legitimate due to X," they decline, and perhaps provide feedback which gets logged for both the Supervisor and Sentinel agents' learning. The combination here vastly speeds up detection-to-decision time: the Sentinel ensures no suspicious claim is missed, and the Supervisor ensures the response is appropriate and reviewed. This can be visualized as Sentinel (watcher) -> Supervisor (reviewer) -> Human -> outcome. It's similar to how in security, an intrusion detection system might flag something and a human then decides to block traffic – here AI is assisting on both flagging and proposing the block, with human final say. This duo reduces both false negatives (thanks to constant monitoring) and false positives (thanks to human validation).

Curator → Supervisor: From Data Synthesis to Approval of Summary. Now imagine another part of the insurance operation: after a major weather event, many claims come in rapidly. A Curator agent might collect and cluster these claims – for instance, grouping claims by geographic area and summarizing the overall impact ("100 claims of type X in Florida region, likely related to recent hurricane"). This Curator provides a summary report for management. However, before such a summary is used in a board meeting or sent to PR, a human might need to ensure its accurate and sensitive (especially if it goes public). Enter a Supervisor agent for quality control of AI-generated reports. The Curator agent passes its compiled summary to a Supervisor agent which then routes it to, say, a regional manager for validation. The Supervisor agent might also add a recommendation: "Based on these claims, we suggest allocating an extra $5M to the reserve for Florida this quarter. Please review the summary and approve the allocation." Here the Supervisor pattern ensures that aggregate AI outputs, which might come from complex data crunching, still get a human's eye before any big decisions or communications. The human reviewer checks that the summary isn't missing context (maybe they know half those claims are minor and shouldn't be framed as a huge catastrophe) and that the recommended action aligns with business strategy. They approve, modify, or reject. If approved, this could feed into a Conductor agent or process that then carries out the plan (e.g., the Conductor triggers finance workflows to reallocate funds, send notifications, etc., which are automated tasks beyond just a proposal). So in flow: Curator (gather & summarize) -> Supervisor (validate summary & decision) -> Conductor/Action (execute plan). The Supervisor stage is crucial because Curator agents, dealing with big data, may occasionally gloss over individual nuances. A human can catch if maybe one outlier claim skews the data or if the recommended $5M is overshooting. This pattern of "AI analysis then human-approved conclusions" is seen in many analytics scenarios. For example, some companies use AI to draft quarterly business reviews which managers then edit and approve. It speeds up prep but keeps accountability with the manager.

Supervisor → Action: Turning Approved Recommendations into Automated Actions. Let's assume our fraud case from earlier was approved for investigation. Previously, a human might then manually log a task for investigators, call the claimant, etc. But we can chain an Action agent to take over once the Supervisor's output is greenlit. The sequence: Supervisor agent (with human input) decides "Yes, investigate Claim #123." That decision can trigger an Action pattern agent that is configured to carry out predefined steps for an investigation: e.g., create a Case record in the Investigation system, send an email to the claimant requesting more info, notify the internal fraud team via Slack, and set a flag on the policy. Those are routine tasks that don't need further human creativity, just execution. Because a human already reviewed the decision, we're comfortable letting the Action agent do its thing in bulk-safe, automated fashion. Essentially, the Supervisor agent's output feeds the Action agent's input. In Salesforce terms, perhaps the Supervisor agent's Flow ends with an Apex action (or calling a sub-flow) that performs these updates. This highlights a key benefit: the Supervisor pattern doesn't mean everything is manual – it can still leverage full automation immediately after the checkpoint. We just insert a pause for human say-so, then unleash automation. Many approval processes in Salesforce work exactly this way (human approves, then an Apex trigger or Flow does a bunch of updates). We're just extending that with AI making the initial recommendation and then possibly orchestrating multi-step actions post-approval. One caveat: make sure the handshake is clean – i.e., the Action agent only triggers once the human explicitly confirms. We don't want an eager Action agent jumping the gun. Using record states or status fields (like an Approval Status) that the Action agent listens for can be effective: e.g., until Case.Investigation_Approved__c = true, Action agent is dormant.

Companion + Supervisor: AI Assistant with User Confirmation Loop. The Companion pattern (to be detailed in a later chapter) covers agents that work interactively with end-users, often in a conversational or real-time assistive manner (think: a chatbot helping a service agent or a Clippy-like aide). When you combine Companion and Supervisor, you get an agent that actively assists a user but still defers certain decisions back to the user for confirmation – effectively treating the user themselves as the human-in-the-loop validator. This is actually very common. For instance, Salesforce might have an Einstein Assistant (Companion) for sales reps that can draft an update to an opportunity or schedule a follow-up task via chat. The pattern can be that the Companion suggests: "Shall I update the opportunity stage to 'Negotiation' since the meeting went well?" and the user can just click "Yes, do it" or "No." In doing so, that Companion agent is following a Supervisor approach – it doesn't unilaterally change data; it asks the human. The difference from a pure Supervisor agent is primarily UX and timing: the suggestion is made in the flow of work dynamically. But conceptually, the user is playing the supervisor role. Many "copilot" style agents are exactly this: they appear alongside you (Companion), offer to do things (like draft an email or code snippet), and you approve/modify (Supervisor behavior). So designing good Companion experiences often involves embedding a mini Supervisor workflow in the UI. For example, you might implement an on-screen accept/reject for each suggestion the assistant gives. In terms of architecture, the Companion agent and Supervisor agent could be one and the same code, just interacting differently – or the Companion agent might internally call a Supervisor agent to log the feedback and decision. Imagine a Slack bot (Companion) that says: "I've drafted a response to the customer complaint; do you want to send it?" When the user replies, under the hood a Supervisor logic records that approval and an Action agent sends the email. The patterns blur at the edges, but the lesson is: Supervisor pattern principles enhance Companion agents by ensuring the user remains in control. From a metaphor standpoint, the Companion agent is the enthusiastic intern whispering in your ear, and the Supervisor pattern ensures you, the user, still make the final call on what to say or do. Users appreciate that because it makes them comfortable using the AI's suggestions without fear of it running off.

Let's tie these together in the context of a claim handling journey to visualize the multi-agent dance:

Intake & Monitoring: A Sentinel agent monitors new claims coming in. It detects Claim #123 has anomalies (maybe amount high for that customer profile).

Alert & Draft Response: The Sentinel triggers a Supervisor-Fraud agent which compiles a recommendation to investigate Claim #123. It attaches evidence (maybe courtesy of a Curator function that pulled similar past fraud cases).

Human Review: A fraud analyst (human) uses the Supervisor agent's interface to review and approves the recommendation to investigate.

Orchestration: Upon approval, a Conductor agent kicks off an investigation process. This Conductor might coordinate multiple steps: assign an investigator (could be via an Action to create a task), notify customer service to hold any payout (another Action), and perhaps inform a Companion chatbot that if the customer calls, route them to a special handler.

Companion Involvement: The customer actually calls in asking about their claim status. A Companion agent assisting the customer service rep pops up info: "This claim is under investigation for potential fraud. Suggest apologizing for delay and gathering additional info." The rep follows the suggestion (here the rep is implicitly approving the agent's guidance).

Investigation Outcome: The investigation completes (let's say it found it was actually a legitimate claim after verifying documents). Now a Supervisor agent could be used in deciding to release payment. The investigator might have an AI-generated summary of findings, which a Supervisor agent presents to a manager for final payment approval. The manager approves the payout.

Automated Resolution: An Action agent (or Conductor) then automates the payout transaction, sends the customer a notification email (maybe even drafted by an AI and approved by someone — Supervisor again for customer communication), and closes the case.

In that story, we saw Sentinel -> Supervisor, Supervisor -> Action/Conductor, and Companion weaving in, with Supervisor oversight at multiple decision points (investigate or not, pay or not, communicate this way or not). The Supervisor pattern is like the glue that ensures at each critical juncture, the right balance of AI help and human judgment is applied.

Such orchestration might sound complex, but Salesforce tools are well-suited for it: Flow Orchestration could manage multi-step approvals, Invocable actions connect agents' outputs to the next agent's inputs, and platform events could signal when an AI-driven process needs human attention (which a Supervisor agent could subscribe to). A visual diagram of this would show swimlanes for each agent type and arrows where they hand off. If one were drawn, the Supervisor agent's swimlane would often intersect with others, catching outputs from some and gating inputs to others.

As you design multi-agent systems, a practical tip is to explicitly mark which steps are autonomous and which are "HITL" (Human-in-the-loop). That's effectively mapping out Supervisor pattern applications. By doing so, you create a clear blueprint for where to place approvals in a Flow or Orchestration. Salesforce even allows screen flows to be assigned to queues or external users (communities) if needed, so you could involve customers as the human validators in some patterns (like verifying their own info – a sort of self-supervisor scenario!). The flexibility is there.

The interplay of patterns ensures that AI agents amplify each other's strengths while compensating for weaknesses. The Sentinel is fast but not nuanced – pair with Supervisor to add nuance. The Conductor can juggle many tasks but shouldn't decide high-level policy – let a Supervisor ensure the plan is sound. The Action is efficient but blind to context – let Supervisor confirm context. The Companion is friendly but could be overly eager – Supervisor (the user) keeps it in check.

By mastering these combinations, you're well on your way to architecting sophisticated AI-agent ecosystems that are both high-performing and high-trust. This also naturally leads us to the next chapter: The Conductor Pattern. In many ways, the Conductor (Chapter 4's focus) is the brains of a multi-agent operation, delegating tasks to specialists (like Sentinels, Actions, etc.). But even the best Conductor agent might sometimes ask: "Should I proceed with this complex operation?" – at which point it might consult a Supervisor pattern (or a human directly). Designing that interplay will be the art of chapters to come.

We'll wrap up now, reinforcing the main points about the Supervisor pattern and providing a segue into the world of orchestration with the Conductor pattern. The Supervisor pattern, as we've seen, is our AI safety net, the bridge between machine output and human judgment, ensuring that as we scale up the autonomy of agents, we do so responsibly and in alignment with enterprise trust requirements.

SUMMARY

In this chapter, we unpacked the Supervisor pattern – the bridge between machine suggestion and human judgment in AI agent workflows. We began by establishing why this pattern is essential: in high-stakes or sensitive processes, it's the safeguard that lets AI drive efficiency without compromising accuracy, ethics, or compliance. A Supervisor agent generates recommendations or drafts and then pauses, hand on the wheel, until a human gives the green light. This simple concept has profound implications for enterprise AI adoption.

You explored when to apply the Supervisor pattern, learning that it shines in scenarios with meaningful risk: critical decisions, customer communications needing finesse, edge cases, and regulated steps all benefit from a human-in-the-loop. We contrasted it with fully autonomous agents (Action pattern) and saw that often a hybrid approach yields the best of both worlds – speed with safety. We followed that with concrete use cases across HR, Legal, Finance, Compliance, and Marketing, showing how a Supervisor agent can augment roles from hiring managers to legal counsel to brand directors. Each use case highlighted how AI can do the heavy lifting (scanning, drafting, preliminary scoring) while humans make the final calls, and how success is measured (faster cycles, maintained quality, etc.).

On the practical side, we walked through building a Supervisor agent using Salesforce's tools. From Agent Builder to design the agent's role, to Invocable Apex for custom generation logic, to Flow Builder for orchestrating the approval UI, we demonstrated that creating a human-in-loop workflow is very achievable on the platform. We emphasized the importance of making these solutions maintainable – using metadata-driven thresholds, versioning, and embedding telemetry. By including code snippets and configuration tips, we illustrated that a Supervisor agent isn't a black box magic – it's an elegant combination of well-known Salesforce capabilities (screen flows, Apex actions, record-based approvals) with a dash of AI. Crucially, we stressed testing and governance: treat these agents like any other mission-critical system – bulk-safe logic, clear trigger points, and robust test coverage.

We then dove into the human dimension: trust and explainability. A Supervisor agent will only be embraced by teams if the human reviewers feel confident in the AI's outputs and comfortable in their control over the outcomes. Techniques like showing why an AI recommended something, providing confidence indicators, allowing easy edits/overrides, and capturing structured feedback all reinforce a virtuous cycle of trust. We included pragmatic caveats (yes, GPT still doesn't truly understand your business's nuances, so the human oversight isn't going away!) and "Pro Tips" like using custom metadata for approver roles, which help scale oversight consistently. The upshot is that a well-implemented Supervisor pattern not only prevents mistakes – it can actually build trust in AI over time, as users see that the AI assists rather than dictates.

Zooming out, we saw that Salesforce's approach aligns with broader industry practices. Whether it's LangChain agents waiting for human approval, CrewAI orchestrating human feedback loops, or Microsoft's Copilots requiring user confirmation, the world of AI is converging on the idea that human-in-the-loop is a feature, not a bug, for responsible AI. We discussed how standards like MCP might let these patterns play out across platforms, and how Supervisor agents might serve as safety valves in multi-agent "swarms" where autonomy runs high. The key takeaway: the Supervisor pattern isn't a Salesforce-specific notion – it's a fundamental design for aligning AI with human oversight, recognized across the ecosystem.

Finally, we illustrated how the Supervisor pattern interplays with other agent patterns in end-to-end workflows. In multi-agent orchestration, Supervisor agents act as the trust gateways at critical junctures – for example, a Sentinel can alert and a Supervisor decides what to do about it; a Conductor can draft a complex plan and a Supervisor (human) approves it; a Companion can advise a user and the user (as supervisor) confirms any actions. Through the lens of a claim handling example, we saw multiple patterns dance together, with the Supervisor pattern ensuring the performance of the whole ensemble stays in tune with business policy and human intent.

In short, the Supervisor pattern equips us to deploy AI responsibly, especially in the highest-stakes scenarios where we would never fully hand over the keys to an algorithm. Rather than slowing down innovation, it enables it – by building confidence among stakeholders that AI is being used with proper checks and balances. A well-implemented Supervisor agent can dramatically reduce workload (by handling the grunt work of analysis/drafting) while actually improving quality and consistency (because every AI output gets a final polish by a person). It's the pattern that turns AI into a true collaborator rather than a loose cannon.

With the Supervisor pattern covered, our next step is to shift from validation to coordination. Chapter 4 will introduce the Conductor pattern, where we move beyond single decisions to orchestrating complex multi-step processes across many agents and systems. The Conductor is like the project manager of agents – and as we hinted, it will often work hand-in-hand with patterns like Supervisor to decide which parts to automate and which to have reviewed. As we venture into the Conductor pattern, keep the lessons of the Supervisor in mind: even the grandest orchestration benefits from a few well-placed human checkpoints. Now, let's explore how to conduct our growing AI workforce to achieve outcomes in parallel and at scale, without missing a beat. The journey continues in Chapter 4: The Conductor Pattern (Orchestration Agent).

4

THE CONDUCTOR PATTERN (ORCHESTRATION AGENT)

The Conductor Pattern is the strategic orchestrator of multi-agent workflows. Just as a musical conductor coordinates many performers, a Conductor agent coordinates multiple AI agents (and systems) to complete a complex task that no single agent could handle alone. Unlike a simple automation script that performs one predefined sequence, a Conductor breaks down a complex job into smaller subtasks, delegates each subtask to specialized agents or services, and then reassembles the results into a coherent outcome. It's the difference between pressing "play" on a single instrument versus conducting an entire symphony.

This orchestration goes far beyond basic automation. Automation focuses on individual tasks, like automatically creating an email account for a new hire, whereas orchestration manages whole end-to-end processes. For example, onboarding a new employee isn't just one step – it involves setting up single sign-on credentials, assigning permissions, collecting tax forms, signing NDAs, provisioning a laptop and ID badge, and so on. A Conductor agent can oversee all these steps with built-in logic and decision points: ensuring one step's output becomes the next step's input, handling conditional branches (e.g. not every new hire needs every form), and invoking human intervention when needed. In essence, the Conductor pattern ensures that multi-step processes happen in the right order, under the right conditions, with robust error handling, something a single automation script would struggle to achieve alone.

Conductor agents are essential for enterprise-grade use cases where multiple agents or systems must collaborate to achieve a goal. Think of scenarios like processing a complex quote request that requires pricing approval, legal review, and inventory checks across different departments. Or imagine onboarding a new business partner: the Conductor would coordinate a background check, compliance verification, account setup in various systems, and notifications to relevant stakeholders. Other examples include regulatory compliance workflows (gathering data from legal, finance, and IT systems to ensure rules are met), orchestrating a multi-stage product launch (where marketing, sales, support, and supply chain tasks all need to sync up), or handling an internal process like an employee onboarding we described. In all these cases, the Conductor pattern provides a single point of coordination. It sequences and synchronizes work across disparate functions, ensuring nothing falls through the cracks and that each dependency is addressed in turn (with fallback paths if something fails).

Salesforce's Agentforce platform supports the Conductor pattern with a rich toolset for building these orchestration agents. Using Flow Orchestration, architects can lay out visual multi-step flows (including parallel branches and conditional stages) that represent the Conductor's game plan. With Invocable Apex (Apex methods annotated with @InvocableMethod) and External Services, a Conductor can delegate execution to code or call out to external APIs as needed. Agentforce encourages using a metadata-driven registry of available agents, so a Conductor can dynamically discover and call the right agent for each subtask. For example, a Conductor agent could invoke another agent's capabilities via an invocable Flow action or a REST API call exposed by that agent, then wait for the result. During execution, it might log progress to a custom Orchestration Tracker object or fire platform events to monitor each step. Once all subtasks complete, the Conductor aggregates the outputs into a final result or summary. That result might be passed on to a Supervisor pattern agent (for human review/approval) or presented via a Companion pattern agent to a user. In short, Agentforce provides the glue – flows, Apex hooks, events, and metadata – that Conductor agents use to integrate multiple AI components into one cohesive process.

In the rest of this chapter, we'll explore the Conductor pattern in depth. First, we'll break down the anatomy and lifecycle of a Conductor agent, to see how it initiates, delegates, and completes its work. From there, we'll discuss when to apply the Conductor pattern (versus a simpler single-agent approach), walk through use cases across different business functions, and then get hands-on with implementing a Conductor agent on Salesforce. We'll also cover how to make these orchestrations observable, auditable, and resilient, and how Conductor agents fit into the broader ecosystem of AI orchestration (comparing with frameworks like LangChain, CrewAI, and Microsoft's Copilot). By the end, you'll see how Conductor agents serve as the unifying force that makes an ensemble of narrow AI agents perform like a well-coordinated team.

ANATOMY OF A CONDUCTOR AGENT

At the heart of every Conductor agent is a well-defined workflow that it orchestrates from start to finish. In simple terms, a Conductor follows a core lifecycle with distinct stages: Initiate → Decompose → Dispatch → Monitor → Aggregate → Output. This lifecycle encapsulates how the Conductor takes in a request, breaks it into parts, delegates work, and composes the final result.

Figure: An example orchestration flow for a Conductor agent. After initiation, the Conductor decomposes a complex request into multiple subtasks (Task A, Task B, Task C) which can run in parallel or in sequence as needed. It dispatches each task to the appropriate specialized agent or external service, then monitors their progress (waiting for each to complete or report back). Once all subtasks finish (successfully or with handled exceptions), the Conductor aggregates the outcomes and produces a final output or next action.

To understand this better, let's walk through each phase of the Conductor's lifecycle:

Initiate: The Conductor agent is triggered by an event or request. This could be a user's action (e.g. a customer asking for a complex service via a chatbot) or a system event (e.g. a nightly batch job or platform event). At initiation, the Conductor gathers the initial input – such as the user's intent or a record identifier – and any relevant metadata about the process. It essentially asks: "What am I orchestrating, and what context do I have?"

Decompose: Next, the Conductor breaks down the overall goal into discrete subtasks or steps. It acts as a planner, determining which tasks need to happen, in what order or concurrency. For example, if the request is to "onboard a new vendor", the Conductor might decompose that into: (a) verify compliance documents, (b) set up the vendor in the finance system, and (c) notify the procurement team. Some of these can happen in parallel while others depend on prior results. The Conductor leverages any available process metadata (like an orchestration template for "vendor onboarding") to decide the task list.

Dispatch: The Conductor then delegates each subtask to the appropriate agent or service. It might call a specialized Agentforce agent for a task (e.g. invoke a Curator agent to analyze compliance documents, or an Action agent to create records via API). It could also call external APIs or trigger integrations – whatever is needed to get the task done. In this phase, the Conductor is effectively the central coordinator, invoking the right capabilities for each piece of work. In microservices terms, this pattern behaves like a real orchestra, where a single component (service 1) coordinates others by making requests to them. The Conductor ensures every subtask knows what to do by passing along the necessary data and instructions.

Monitor: After dispatching tasks, the Conductor doesn't go idle – it actively monitors progress. It may do this synchronously (waiting for each call to return) or asynchronously (setting up callbacks or subscribing to events). In a Salesforce context, a Conductor might spawn parallel Flow interviews or Apex queue jobs and then poll for their completion, or it might listen for Platform Events that signal a task's outcome. Monitoring includes error handling: if a subtask fails or times out, the Conductor catches that and can apply a retry or fallback logic. This stage is where the "orchestration" aspect shines – the Conductor is constantly conducting, making sure each part finishes in tune with the overall process.

Aggregate: Once all subtasks have either completed successfully (or been handled in case of failure), the Conductor collects the results. This could mean gathering data outputs from each agent, consolidating multiple responses into one, or determining an overall status (e.g. "3 of 5 checks passed"). For example, the Conductor would compile the outcomes from compliance, finance, and procurement checks into a single holistic view of "Vendor onboarding completed (with these details...)". Aggregation may involve transforming or formatting data so that it makes sense in context, such as summarizing findings or merging records.

Output: Finally, the Conductor produces an output or takes a final action to conclude the process. The nature of the output depends on the use case: it might update Salesforce records or create a new summary record, send a notification or email with the consolidated results, or call another agent to handle post-processing. Often the output includes a human-readable summary of what was accomplished, which can be passed to a Presenter agent or directly to a user interface. In many cases, the Conductor's output also triggers follow-on behavior. For example, after orchestrating an employee onboarding, the Conductor might signal a Supervisor pattern agent to review the setup or a Companion pattern agent to notify the hiring manager that everything is done. The output stage ensures the end result of the orchestration is delivered to the right place – whether that's a database, another system, or a person needing to take action.

This lifecycle is typically implemented with a combination of Salesforce tools and custom logic. Flow Orchestration provides a declarative way to define these steps, decision points, and parallel paths. Admins or architects can design an Orchestration Flow where each step corresponds to a subtask (calling a sub-flow or Apex action), and use stages and Decision elements to control sequencing. For example, one stage could contain two parallel steps (to perform Task A and Task B concurrently), followed by a decision that waits for both to finish, then a final step for aggregation. Salesforce's orchestration engine takes care of running steps sequentially or in parallel as configured.

For more complex delegations, Invocable Apex methods are a key tool. By writing an Apex method and marking it with @InvocableMethod, you can expose a unit of work that the Conductor can call as an action. This is useful when a subtask requires complex logic or external integration that a Flow alone can't handle. The Conductor's flow can invoke such an Apex action (for example, to call an external web service or perform a bulk calculation) and receive the result back. Additionally, Salesforce External Services and HTTP callouts can be used within flows to reach outside systems – the Conductor pattern often involves bridging Salesforce with other platforms, so these callouts become the "hands" by which the Conductor directs outside actors.

A Conductor agent generally has certain key traits that distinguish its design:

Stateless Initiation, Stateful Coordination: The Conductor is typically launched fresh for each new process instance – it doesn't carry over memory from one orchestration to the next (making it stateless at start). However, as it runs, it maintains state about the process. This state could be kept in variables within a Flow Orchestration or in a dedicated tracker object in the database. For example, the Conductor might write an "Orchestration Run" record with a unique ID, status of each step, timestamps, etc. This allows the orchestration to pause, resume, or recover if needed. The key point is that the Conductor doesn't rely on long-lived in-memory state (which could be lost on a crash); instead, it externalizes state to reliably coordinate multi-step work.

Parallelism and Sequencing Logic: A Conductor encodes the logic of what can run in parallel and what must happen in sequence. If tasks are independent, the Conductor will often launch them concurrently to save time. If one task depends on another's output, the Conductor enforces the order. This is not simply a linear checklist – it's a directed graph of activities with the Conductor as the manager. Flow Orchestration supports this with parallel paths and decision gates, and similarly in Apex you might spawn asynchronous processes and then join their results. The ability to intermix parallel execution with conditional branching is a hallmark of the Conductor pattern. It ensures efficiency (through concurrency) without sacrificing control over dependencies.

Delegation to Agents and APIs: Unlike some agents that do heavy AI computations internally, the Conductor is more of a traffic controller than a laborer. Its primary job is to invoke others. This means a well-designed Conductor has minimal business logic hardcoded; instead, it calls the appropriate agent or service for each function. One subtask might involve an LLM-based analysis (delegated to a Curator agent or an external AI service), another might involve a database update (delegated to an Action agent or an Apex routine). The Conductor pattern is inherently modular – if tomorrow a better tool or agent is available for a subtask, you can rewire the Conductor to use that, rather than changing its core logic. This also means the Conductor can orchestrate across boundaries: calling out to AWS or SAP via APIs in one step, and invoking a Salesforce agent in the next. It's not limited to a single platform.

In terms of inputs and outputs: a Conductor agent typically takes in a triggering context and produces a unified result. Inputs can include a user's request (structured as parameters), the record or object that kicked off the process (like an Order Id or Case Id), and any relevant configuration metadata. For example, a Conductor might read from a custom Metadata type which subtasks to run for a given "Process Type" – making it flexible to orchestrate slightly different flows for different scenarios without changing code. The outputs, as discussed, could be anything from updated records to a summary message. Often, the final output is designed to be human-friendly (e.g. a single Slack message summarizing "Vendor onboarding completed for XYZ"). Additionally, the Conductor might raise follow-on events or triggers; for instance, emitting a Platform Event like "Vendor_Onboarding_Completed__e" which other systems or agents listen to for further automation.

Because a Conductor coordinates many moving parts, robust error handling is vital. If one step fails (say an API is down or an approval is rejected), the Conductor should have logic to either retry that step, compensate (undo or adjust other steps), or gracefully exit and notify a human. This brings us to a crucial design tip:

Pro Tip: Design your Conductor agents with retry and failover logic from the start. In production scenarios, assume that one or more subtasks will fail or behave unexpectedly. Incorporate mechanisms like retry with backoff for transient errors, alternate execution paths if a service is unavailable, and human escalation points if automation cannot complete a step. For example, if an external compliance check API doesn't respond, the Conductor might retry twice, then fall back to flagging the task for manual review (and still continue with other steps if possible). By anticipating failures and building in resiliency, your Conductor agent ensures the overall process can still reach a safe outcome even when individual parts hit a snag.

With the anatomy of a Conductor agent defined, we have a blueprint of how it operates internally. Next, we'll consider when to apply this pattern. Not every problem needs a full orchestration agent – in the following section, we'll explore criteria to decide if the Conductor pattern is the right fit for a given job, or if a simpler single-agent (or different pattern) approach would suffice.

WHEN TO USE THE CONDUCTOR PATTERN

Not every scenario calls for an orchestration agent. Many simple tasks can be handled by a single well-designed agent without the overhead of multi-agent coordination. The Conductor pattern shines (and is worth the effort) when you're dealing with processes that are complex, multi-step, and cross-functional. To decide whether a Conductor agent is appropriate, teams should evaluate the nature of the job along several dimensions. Key considerations include the number of steps involved, the dependencies between those steps, the number of different systems or teams in the loop, how variable or conditional the process is, and what kind of failure handling is required. If the process is straightforward – say, just generating a report from one data source – a single Action agent or Curator agent might suffice. But if the process looks more like a project plan with multiple contributors and decision points, that's a strong sign that a Conductor is needed to orchestrate it.

The following decision framework can help determine if you should use a Conductor pattern or stick to a simpler single-agent pattern:

Process complexity

- **Single-agent fit:** Simple, atomic task or linear flow with few steps.
- **Conductor fit:** Complex workflow with multiple distinct steps or phases.

Dependencies

- **Single-agent fit:** Little or no interdependency between actions; one agent has all necessary context.
- **Conductor fit:** Many interdependent tasks where the output of one step becomes the input to another and coordination is required.

Systems and teams involved

- **Single-agent fit:** Self-contained within a single system or domain, such as all work occurring inside Salesforce.
- **Conductor fit:** Spans multiple systems, clouds, or teams, including CRM, ERP, and external APIs.

Variability of flow

- **Single-agent fit:** Fixed and predictable process that rarely changes or branches.
- **Conductor fit:** Dynamic process with conditional branching or parallel paths driven by data or decisions.

Failure handling

- **Single-agent fit:** Low risk if a step fails; errors can be handled with simple retries or are non-critical.
- **Conductor fit:** High-stakes or complex failure modes requiring rollback, human escalation, or alternate execution paths.

Process duration

- **Single-agent fit:** Short-lived process that completes in a single session or transaction, typically seconds or minutes.
- **Conductor fit:** Long-running process that may last minutes to days and involves waiting for approvals or external responses.

If most of the "Conductor Fit" characteristics apply, then implementing a Conductor agent is likely the right approach. You want an orchestrator when the job is multi-faceted and needs tight coordination across various parts. On the other hand, if the task is narrowly scoped and self-contained, using a single agent (or even just a simple automation) is often more efficient. As a rule of thumb, the more complex and interdependent the process, the more likely you are to benefit from orchestration. The Conductor pattern introduces overhead and complexity of its own, so you reserve it for when that overhead is justified by the complexity of the problem space.

For example, consider an employee onboarding process versus a simple data lookup. Onboarding has many steps (IT setup, HR paperwork, provisioning equipment, training scheduling) involving different departments – a clear candidate for a Conductor agent. In contrast, a data lookup (like fetching a customer record and summarizing it) might only involve one agent with access to the database, no orchestration needed. Teams should evaluate each use case with the above criteria to avoid over-engineering simple tasks or, conversely, underestimating the needs of complex ones. The goal is to apply the Conductor pattern only where it adds value by unifying what would otherwise be disjointed efforts.

USE CASES ACROSS FUNCTIONS

To see the Conductor pattern in action, let's explore several hypothetical scenarios in different business functions. In each case, a Conductor agent coordinates multiple agents or steps to accomplish a complex workflow that spans various teams and systems. These examples are clearly hypothetical (not descriptions of actual companies) but illustrate how one could apply the pattern:

HR – Onboarding a New Employee

Scenario: A new employee joins the company. The onboarding process involves IT provisioning (hardware and system access), HR tasks (benefits enrollment, policy acknowledgments), and managerial tasks (orientation scheduling, team notifications).

How a Conductor Helps: Rather than relying on checklists and people to pass the baton, an HR Onboarding Conductor agent can orchestrate all these steps. When HR submits a new hire form (the trigger event), the Conductor decomposes the onboarding into subtasks:

Hardware Setup: It calls an IT Action agent or integration to request the new hire's laptop, phone, and badge. This might be done via an API call to a procurement system or by creating tickets in an IT service queue.

Access Provisioning: In parallel, the Conductor invokes an identity management script (through an Apex call or External Service) to create accounts for email, Slack, Salesforce, and other applications. Specialized mini-agents handle each account creation (using provided details), while the Conductor tracks when all accounts are done. For example, once an Active Directory account is created (signaled via a platform event), the Conductor moves on to provision the next access.

Benefits Enrollment: The Conductor triggers a Curator-type agent that sends the new hire a benefits enrollment package (or interacts with an external HR portal via API) and waits for confirmation that forms were completed.

Manager & Team Notifications: Finally, the Conductor notifies the hiring manager and the team about the new hire's start date and any onboarding tasks they need to do (like assigning a mentor). This could be done by a Presenter/Companion agent that posts a welcome message or sends an email summary once all other steps are finished.

Throughout this process, the Conductor agent monitors each step. If the hardware order fails or an account cannot be created, it can escalate to a human HR coordinator (perhaps via a Supervisor pattern, flagging the issue in a dashboard). Once everything succeeds, the Conductor aggregates the outcomes (e.g. "Hardware ordered, accounts created, benefits email sent") and produces a summary. The hiring manager might get a final notification: "Onboarding Complete for Jane Doe – laptop is ordered, all accounts are active, and orientation is scheduled." The Conductor ensures no part of the onboarding is forgotten and that IT, HR, and managerial tasks are executed in harmony. This gives each new hire a consistent onboarding experience and saves the HR team from juggling multiple threads manually.

Finance – Approving a Large Purchase

Scenario: A department submits a capital expenditure request for a large purchase. Approving this purchase requires checking budget availability, assessing vendor risk, and obtaining legal approval for compliance. These steps involve Finance, Risk Management, and Legal – often working in different systems.

How a Conductor Helps: A Purchase Approval Conductor agent can orchestrate the end-to-end approval process across these functions:

Budget Check: When a purchase request is created, the Conductor first dispatches a budget verification task – for example, calling a Finance system via API (or an Agentforce Action that wraps a SOQL query) to ensure the expense is within the department's budget. Perhaps an invocable Apex method queries an ERP system or Salesforce budgets to get current spend vs. budget.

Risk Analysis: In parallel, the Conductor triggers a Risk Analysis agent to evaluate the vendor or the purchase itself. This might involve a Curator agent gathering data on the vendor's credit rating or past performance, and applying risk rules. If the purchase amount is above a certain threshold, the Conductor could also call an external risk assessment API or an AI service to score the risk.

Legal Review: Simultaneously, the Conductor invokes a Legal Review step. It could send the contract or purchase order details to a Legal AI agent that checks for compliance with company policies (e.g., does the contract have required clauses?). Alternatively, it might create a task for a human lawyer to approve if the AI finds any anomalies or if policy dictates human review for large contracts – effectively the Conductor acting as a smart routing mechanism.

The Conductor monitors all three streams (budget, risk, legal) and waits for their outcomes. If any comes back negative (budget exceeded, high risk score, or legal flagged an issue), the Conductor can either reject the request automatically or escalate to a higher authority (maybe using a Supervisor agent to get a CFO's approval despite the issues).

If all checks pass, the Conductor aggregates the approvals and marks the purchase as approved. It might then trigger an Action agent to perform the next step, such as generating a Purchase Order record in Salesforce or sending an approval notification to the requestor.

Without a Conductor, this process would involve multiple email threads and sequential approvals taking place slowly. The Conductor agent automates the coordination: budget, risk, and legal checks happen in parallel and consistently for every request, and the results are combined. The overall approval time is reduced, and nothing gets purchased without all proper checks completed. This demonstrates the Conductor pattern's value in multi-department workflows – it enforces that dependencies (here, approvals) are handled and recorded systematically, with much less chance of human error or oversight.

Legal – Orchestrating Contract Review

Scenario: The legal department needs to review a new contract with a partner. The review involves comparing the contract's clauses to standard approved clauses, verifying compliance with regulations, and summarizing any deviations for the legal team's decision. This entails multiple analyses, potentially using AI and human expertise together.

How a Conductor Helps: A Contract Review Conductor agent can streamline this multi-step analysis:

Clause Extraction: The Conductor takes the contract (maybe a PDF) as input. It first calls a Clause Extraction agent (using NLP) to identify key clauses in the contract – payment terms, liability limits, termination conditions, etc. This Curator-like sub-agent might label each clause with a category.

Clause Comparison: The Conductor then invokes a Clause Comparison agent. For each important clause, this agent checks it against the company's playbook of approved clause language. For example, it might determine if the "Limitation of Liability" clause in the contract matches the standard template or has changes. The Conductor can run these checks in parallel for different clauses since they're independent.

Compliance Checks: In addition, the Conductor triggers a Compliance Check step. It might send contract details (like jurisdiction, data privacy terms) to an external compliance service or use a rule-based AI (a Coach pattern agent for regulations) to ensure nothing violates laws or company policies. This could involve checking for banned provisions (e.g., violating GDPR if European data is involved) and getting a green/red signal.

As these analyses complete, the Conductor aggregates the findings. It could call a Summary Presenter agent (perhaps GPT-powered) to generate a concise report for the lawyers: highlighting any non-standard clauses, potential legal risks, and suggesting language changes.

Finally, the Conductor produces the output package for the human legal reviewer. This might be an email or a task in Salesforce that includes the original contract annotated with comments, the summary of issues, and a recommendation (e.g., "Clause 5 deviates from standard indemnity clause – needs approval or revision"). The human lawyer can then focus on the flagged areas rather than reading the whole contract line by line.

In this use case, the Conductor coordinates multiple AI assistants (clause finder, compliance checker, summarizer) and possibly human input. It ensures that the contract review is thorough and consistent – every clause was checked and no important aspect is overlooked – but also efficient, because the AI did the heavy lifting. The legal team receives a well-organized analysis rather than raw text. If the Conductor encounters something unexpected (say the clause extraction failed or a compliance API is down), it would log an error and could notify the legal ops team (e.g., spawn a task for a paralegal to manually gather that info), ensuring the process still moves forward. This hybrid of AI and human review under a Conductor's guidance significantly speeds up contract negotiations while managing risk.

Customer Operations – Managing a Product Recall

Scenario: A manufacturing company initiates a recall for a defective product. The operations team must identify all customers who bought the product, notify them with instructions, arrange return shipping or repairs, and ensure customer support is ready for inquiries. This is a coordination-heavy process involving customer data, logistics, and support teams.

How a Conductor Helps: A Product Recall Conductor agent can orchestrate the entire recall process:

Identify Affected Customers: The Conductor queries the order database (via an Action agent or direct SOQL query) to retrieve all customers and shipments of the recalled product. It might use a Curator agent to filter and format this list (e.g., prepare a CSV of names, contacts, purchase dates).

Customer Notifications: For each affected customer, the Conductor triggers a Notification agent (Presenter pattern) to send out an email (or SMS) with the recall notice and instructions. This could integrate with a marketing cloud or an external email service. The Conductor may batch customers into groups and send notifications in waves, monitoring delivery success and recording who has acknowledged the message (perhaps via link clicks or replies).

Logistics Coordination: In parallel, the Conductor interfaces with the logistics system. It could create return merchandise authorization (RMA) records or schedule pickup shipments for returning the product. For example, it might call a MuleSoft API that generates a UPS return label for each customer. Each label or tracking number returned from MuleSoft is captured by the Conductor and associated with the customer's case.

Customer Support Prep: The Conductor also alerts the support team. It might create a "Recall Case" in Salesforce for each customer or a single master case, and use a Presenter agent to post an internal announcement: "Recall XYZ initiated – support please be prepared to handle questions." If support agents need a script, the Conductor can provide one (maybe via a Curator that summarizes the issue and solution steps).

Follow-up and Tracking: The Conductor monitors responses. Using a time trigger, it could generate a follow-up task or email for customers who haven't returned their product after a few weeks. It also compiles statistics – e.g., how many units have been returned vs. still in the field – updating a dashboard (perhaps by creating a summary record or sending data to an analytics system).

During this recall, the Conductor agent touches multiple systems: CRM data, email/SMS, shipping, and support. It handles errors at each step: if generating a shipping label fails for a customer, the Conductor logs it and assigns a human to handle that one manually (ensuring one failed label doesn't halt the entire recall). By automating what can be automated and providing clear hand-offs for what can't, the Conductor speeds up the recall and ensures consistency – every customer gets notified and offered help, every returned product is tracked, and management can see the overall status in real time. It's a great example of orchestrating people, data, and things (physical shipments) through one unified process.

IT – Provisioning a New Environment

Scenario: An IT team needs to set up a new application environment for a development project. This involves provisioning servers or cloud services, configuring network and security settings, deploying the application, and registering the environment in monitoring and documentation systems. Multiple teams (DevOps, SecOps, QA) and tools are typically involved.

How a Conductor Helps: An Environment Provisioning Conductor agent can take a high-level request ("Set up a QA environment for Project X") and orchestrate all required steps:

Infrastructure Provisioning: The Conductor calls an automation script or cloud API (via Apex callout or using an existing integration) to create the necessary infrastructure – e.g., spin up virtual machines, databases, and load balancers on AWS or Azure. It waits for a success confirmation (perhaps polling the cloud's status or receiving an event when provisioning is done).

Network & Security Configuration: Next, the Conductor triggers a Security Config agent. For example, it might run a script to set up firewall rules or VPN access for the new environment. If using an external system (like a network automation tool), the Conductor calls that via API. These tasks could be done in parallel with server provisioning if the systems allow, or sequentially if network settings depend on server IPs.

Application Deployment: Once the environment is up, the Conductor calls a Deployment agent to deploy the application code. This might hook into a CI/CD pipeline (e.g., Jenkins, GitHub Actions) or use Salesforce DX if it's a Salesforce org. The Conductor provides necessary parameters (environment name, config values) and triggers the deployment job, then monitors its completion.

Monitoring & Documentation: As a final stage, the Conductor updates monitoring tools – for instance, using an API to register the new servers in the monitoring system (so alerts will cover them). It also creates or updates documentation: perhaps it logs the environment details in a Confluence page or a CMDB (Configuration Management Database) via an integration. These might be done via Presenter or Action agents (formatting and sending the data to the appropriate system).

Notification: The Conductor then notifies the requester (and relevant team members) that the environment is ready. This could be an automated email summarizing "Project X QA environment set up at URL ..., credentials here, monitoring enabled." A Companion agent could even present this info to the requester in a chat interface for convenience.

The IT Conductor ensures the environment setup follows a standardized process every time. If any step fails – say the deployment encountered an error – the Conductor can halt further steps, mark the overall provisioning as failed, and alert the DevOps team with the error details. Without a Conductor, setting up an environment might require an engineer to follow a lengthy checklist and coordinate with multiple people. With a Conductor agent, a single request triggers a reliable sequence of actions across systems, and the team gets a consistent, auditable outcome.

These examples demonstrate the breadth of contexts where Conductor agents add value. From HR to IT, whenever a process spans multiple people, systems, or sequential decisions, a Conductor can serve as the digital project manager that never forgets a step. Each use case involved breaking a big workflow into pieces, calling the right tool or person for each piece, and bringing it all together – exactly what the Conductor pattern is designed to do.

IMPLEMENTING A CONDUCTOR AGENT IN AGENTFORCE

Designing a Conductor agent on Salesforce's Agentforce platform involves combining declarative tools with Apex code to achieve a flexible orchestration. The process typically goes like this: you define the agent's interface (inputs and outputs) in Agent Builder, implement the orchestration logic either with a Flow Orchestration or an Invocable Apex class (or a mix of both), and configure the agent so it can be invoked (by users or other agents) as a single cohesive service. Let's break down some key steps and best practices:

Agent Definition with Agent Builder: Agent Builder is where you create a new agent and describe its purpose, inputs, and outputs. For a Conductor agent, you would specify what triggers it (e.g. an Apex action or an API call) and what data it needs to start. In Agent Builder, you might create a "Supplier Onboarding Conductor" agent, giving it input fields like Supplier Name, Supplier ID, etc., and output fields for the results (e.g. success flag, error message, IDs of records created). This metadata is important because Agentforce uses it to match user requests to the right agent and to document what the agent does. For example, marking a method with @InvocableMethod and providing a label/description makes it available in the Agentforce Studio for configuration.

Using Flow Orchestration for Logic: One way to implement the Conductor's workflow is via Salesforce Flow Orchestration (a declarative process tool). You can create an Orchestration that mirrors the lifecycle: with steps for each subtask (perhaps calling sub-flows or Apex actions), decision elements for conditional logic, and stages to organize sequential vs. parallel work. For instance, our supplier onboarding Conductor could be built as a Flow

Orchestration that first invokes a "Risk Check" flow, then a "Terms Approval" human step, then an "Account Setup" flow. You might use Decision elements that consult custom metadata to determine branching (say, if a supplier's risk score is above a certain threshold, add an extra approval step). Storing such rules in Custom Metadata means you can tweak conditions without altering the flow – a form of metadata-driven orchestration. Each step in the orchestration can be an invocable action (like a sub-flow or Apex method) representing one of the delegate agents.

Delegation via Invocable Apex and Named Agents: In many cases, you will implement specific subtask logic in Apex – either because it involves complex code or integration calls. By writing Apex with @InvocableMethod, you create reusable actions that flows (and other agents) can call. These Apex actions can themselves call out to external services or perform database operations. A Conductor agent may call other Agentforce agents too: for example, if you have a Curator agent for risk profiling, the Conductor could invoke it via an Apex method or even a platform event. Agentforce supports a registry where agents can expose endpoints (sometimes called "named agents"), so the Conductor might conceptually do something like Agent.invoke('RiskCuratorAgent', params) – but in practice, this is achieved by calling an invocable method or flow that triggers the desired agent's logic. The key is that the Conductor doesn't hard-code the details of each task; it delegates to modular components.

Monitoring and Aggregating in Apex: If you implement the orchestration with Apex, you'll likely create a single Apex class that coordinates the calls and handles results. In this SupplierOnboardingConductor class:

We define inner classes OnboardRequest and OnboardResult to structure the input and output data for our Conductor agent. The @InvocableVariable annotations expose those fields in Agentforce and Flow.

The @InvocableMethod onboardSuppliers is the entry point that Agentforce or a Flow will call to execute the orchestration. We provided a label and description so it's identifiable in Agent Builder. This method is bulkified to handle a list of requests, as required by invocable standards.

The code loops through each request and performs the orchestration steps inside a try-catch. In this case:

Risk Profile – calls a (hypothetical) RiskCuratorAgent.generateProfile method to get a risk assessment for the supplier (using a Curator pattern agent or external service).

Terms Approval – calls ContractSupervisorAgent.reviewTerms, which might implement a Supervisor pattern (potentially involving a human decision or a policy check) to approve or reject the supplier's terms based on the risk profile.

Account Setup – if terms are approved, calls SupplierActionAgent.createAccount to actually create the supplier's account in the system (an Action pattern agent performing the database insert or external API call).

We use a try-catch around the steps to catch any unexpected exceptions. If an error occurs, we mark the result as success=false and capture the error message. This way the Conductor provides a graceful output even if something fails, which is crucial for debugging and user feedback.

We also handle the scenario where the terms were not approved: in that case we set an appropriate error message ("Supplier terms not approved") and do not proceed to create the account. Each OnboardResult carries a success flag and either an accountId (on success) or an errorMessage if something went wrong.

This code-centric approach to building the Conductor could be used on its own or alongside Flow Orchestration. For example, you might have a Flow Orchestration that mostly coordinates user interactions or simple checks, and it calls an Apex Conductor like the above for heavy lifting or integrations. The benefit of using Apex is that you can leverage the full power of Salesforce's platform (SOQL, callouts, complex logic) within your orchestration. The benefit of Flow is that it's easier to visualize and update by declarative means (which is great for admins or rapid changes). In practice, many Conductor solutions use a mix: some steps as invocable Apex, stitched together by a declarative orchestration.

Version Control and Maintainability: It's important to manage changes to a Conductor agent carefully since it touches many parts. Use source control for your Flow and Apex (so you can track changes, roll back if needed) and adopt naming conventions for clarity. For instance, you might maintain a flow named "Supplier_Onboarding_Orchestration_v1" and create a new version (v2) when making major changes, rather than editing in place – ensuring old behavior can be restored if necessary. Using metadata-driven logic (as mentioned, custom metadata to drive which sub-agents to call or thresholds for decisions) makes the system more adaptable without code deployment. For example, you could have a Custom Metadata type mapping each "Process Step" to an agent name. The Conductor's Apex could read this to determine which agent to invoke for "RiskProfile" vs "CreditCheck" vs

"CreateAccount" – allowing you to swap out implementations via config instead of rewriting code.

Schema Layout for Orchestration Tracking: In many cases, Conductor agents benefit from having a custom object to track their progress or results. For example, you might create a Supplier_Onboarding__c record when a new supplier process starts, and update it as each subtask completes (store the Risk Score, whether Terms were approved, the new Account ID, etc.). This provides an audit trail and a quick dashboard of all ongoing or completed orchestrations. You can even build reports on this object to analyze how long each step typically takes or where failures occur most. Additionally, platform events can be used for tracking and notifications: the Conductor might publish events like Supplier_Onboarding_Step_Completed__e after each major step, which could be used to update UI in real time or trigger other agents (for example, a Presenter agent that updates a progress bar for a user). The main idea is to not treat the Conductor as a black box – design some data model around it (status fields, log records, events) so that you can observe and manage its work.

Implementing a Conductor agent requires careful thought, but Salesforce provides the building blocks to do it systematically. You clearly define the agent's role and interface, orchestrate with flows and/or Apex, delegate to specialized actions, and keep everything as configurable as possible. With our example in mind, we can now consider how to monitor and manage these orchestrations in production – ensuring we have visibility into each Conductor's operations and a plan for error handling and recovery.

OBSERVABILITY, AUDITING, AND RECOVERY

Building a Conductor agent is only half the battle – you also need to keep an eye on it in operation and be prepared for things to go wrong. Enterprise orchestrations require robust observability (knowing what's happening inside the agent), auditing (recording what happened for compliance or analysis), and recovery mechanisms (handling failures gracefully). Here are key practices in these areas:

Centralized Logging and Tracking: It's wise to log the Conductor's progress in a central place that admins and other systems can reference. As mentioned earlier, a common approach is to use a tracker object. For example, each time the Conductor runs, it could create or update a record (e.g., Supplier_Onboarding__c or Orchestration_Run__c) with fields for each step's status, timestamps, and key outputs. This provides a single at-a-glance view of where an orchestration is ("Waiting on Legal Approval" or "Completed Successfully"). Having a Salesforce record for each run makes it easy to query and report on agent performance (how many completed, how many failed, average durations, etc.). These logs also serve as an audit trail – months later you can answer "Which agents handled that supplier onboarding?" or "Who approved that purchase?" by looking at the stored data.

Human-Readable Summaries: While logs are important for system monitoring, it's also useful to provide summaries for human stakeholders. Often a Conductor agent will use the Presenter pattern to generate a digest of what it did, especially if a process ends with a human decision or notification. For example, after a Conductor finishes orchestrating a product recall, it might post a summary to a Slack channel or send an email report: "Recall Process Complete – 95 customers notified, 80 responses received, 15 pending." This closes the loop with team members and creates a clear narrative of what the automation accomplished. In Salesforce, you might implement this via an Email Alert or by integrating with Slack using a webhook. The key is that the outcome of the orchestration is communicated in plain language to the people who care about it – not just stored as fields in a database. These summaries also play a role in auditing by providing a human-friendly record of actions taken.

Partial Failure Handling and Recovery: A Conductor must be designed with the expectation that not every run will go perfectly. There are several strategies to handle partial failures:

Retries: If a subtask fails due to a transient issue (e.g., a network timeout or a temporarily down service), the Conductor should automatically retry it (perhaps after a short delay or using exponential backoff). For example, if a payment gateway call times out, try again in a few minutes. Flow Orchestration can implement retries with loop paths or scheduled triggers, and Apex can implement it with recursive Queueable jobs or tried-catch logic with setTimeout. The number of retries and interval might be configurable via metadata. Ensure you log the failure and final success or failure after retries, to maintain transparency.

Compensation and Rollback: If a later step fails after earlier steps succeeded, consider whether you need to roll back or compensate for those earlier actions. For instance, if a Conductor created a new account and then a subsequent verification step failed causing the process to abort, you might either deactivate that account or mark it for review to avoid having a partially onboarded account in the system. Designing compensation is process-specific (some processes can't easily be undone), but it's important to analyze your orchestration and decide: if it stops at step 4 of 5, do we leave steps 1-3 as-is or reverse them? Sometimes leaving partial results is fine; other times it can cause data integrity issues.

Escalation to Humans: If automation cannot complete the process after retries, the Conductor should hand off to a person. This could mean creating a Salesforce Task or Case assigned to a responsible team, with details about what failed and what remains to be done. For example, if an automated expense approval Conductor can't reach a definitive outcome (maybe due to conflicting rules or system unavailability), it could create a "Manual Approval Needed" case for Finance and notify them. By surfacing these exceptions, you ensure that the process still gets completed manually and that the right people are aware of it.

Graceful Degradation: In some workflows, it's better to complete most of the tasks and only fail the portion that's broken. A Conductor can be smart about this. For example, if during onboarding the equipment ordering system is offline, the Conductor might proceed to set up accounts and benefits, but log that hardware ordering failed and notify IT separately, rather than abort the entire onboarding. The new hire still gets most of their setup done on time, and a human can later handle the one missing piece. This approach ensures that one failed component doesn't nullify all the good work done by the other components.

End-to-End Telemetry (Command Center): In a production environment with many orchestrations running, you'll want a "single pane of glass" to monitor their health. Salesforce is introducing tools like an Agentforce Command Center for end-to-end telemetry of agents and orchestrations. These dashboards aggregate data on agent invocations, success/failure rates, execution times, and so on. They help identify bottlenecks (e.g., a particular step that frequently slows down) and highlight systemic failures (if an external API used by many agents is down, you'd see multiple Conductors failing around the same time). Flow Orchestration already provides an Orchestration Monitor for admins to track in-flight and completed flows, and similarly, Agentforce's Command Center would give an overview of multi-agent workflows. Even before such a native tool is available, you can achieve telemetry by using Platform Events or logging to an external system (like pushing log records to Splunk or CloudWatch). The goal is to never have a silent failure – every orchestration should either complete successfully or visibly alert someone (or something) that it didn't, with information about where and why.

Audit Trails of Agent Actions: When multiple agents and systems are involved in a process, keeping an audit trail of who did what when is crucial for compliance and trust. Your Conductor should record which sub-agent (or user, if a human step) performed each action. This could be done by writing to a child record like "Orchestration Step" records linked to the tracker object, each storing: Step Name, Executing Agent (or User), Start Time, End Time, Outcome. For example: "Step: Risk Check – Agent: RiskCuratorAgent – Completed 2025-07-04 10:00 – Result: High Risk". Such an audit log allows you to answer questions later like "Did we run the compliance check on that order? Which agent handled it? How long did it take?" Salesforce's Field Audit Trail or even just LastModified fields provide some of this implicitly, but a custom log gives you fine-grained detail. If a regulator or internal auditor comes knocking, you can generate a report from these logs to show every action taken in an automated process and whether a human reviewed any part. This builds confidence that your orchestration is doing things with accountability.

Pro Tip: Consider building a "debug mode" into your Conductor agents. This could be a configuration setting (e.g., a Custom Metadata flag) that, when turned on, makes the Conductor agent log verbosely or store additional debug details. In normal operation, you'd keep this off to avoid clutter and performance overhead. But if you're troubleshooting a tricky issue, enabling debug mode could cause the Conductor to record step-by-step inputs/outputs, API responses, or execution times in a debug log object or even just System.debug (viewable in Salesforce's logs). Just be careful not to expose sensitive data in these debug logs – maybe mask personal info or secrets. With a debug mode, you can get deep insights during development or a critical incident without permanently increasing the noise in your logs. It's like having a diagnostic switch that you can flip when needed to see inside the machine.

In summary, a Conductor agent should be treated as mission-critical infrastructure: you want real-time visibility into its workings and outcomes. By logging diligently, summarizing key results for humans, designing smart failure recovery, and monitoring continuously, you turn the Conductor from a "black box" into a transparent, trustworthy part of your enterprise. When something goes wrong, you'll not only be alerted – you'll have the information needed to respond and improve the process. This level of operational maturity is what transforms an experimental automation into a reliable enterprise asset.

CONDUCTOR AGENTS IN EXTERNAL ECOSYSTEMS

Salesforce's Conductor pattern doesn't exist in a vacuum. The idea of orchestrating multi-step, multi-agent workflows appears across the AI landscape. It's valuable to understand how Agentforce's approach compares to other ecosystems and how Conductor agents can integrate with external tools and platforms.

LangChain and Agent Chains: LangChain, a popular open-source framework, provides a form of orchestration for large language model applications. In LangChain, developers create chains of actions (e.g., "retrieve data -> call LLM -> process output") and can even define agents that use an LLM to decide which tool to use next. Essentially, a LangChain agent is like a reasoning engine that dynamically orchestrates sub-tasks and tool calls based on AI prompts. For example, a LangChain agent might determine: "The user asked for a financial forecast; I should query the database, then use an LLM to explain the results, then email them." This is similar in spirit to the Conductor pattern, though implemented very differently. LangChain's orchestration is code-centric and often relies on the LLM itself to make decisions about sequence, whereas Agentforce's Conductor is more explicit – you the architect define the flow (with perhaps some conditional logic). Each approach has its advantages. LangChain allows very fluid, on-the-fly tool use, which is powerful for unstructured problems. Agentforce's Conductor provides predictability and governance, which is essential in enterprise settings. These approaches aren't mutually exclusive: you might have a Salesforce Conductor invoke a LangChain agent as a sub-task when some flexible reasoning is needed, or conversely, a LangChain pipeline could call a Salesforce Conductor via API to perform a transactional step (like updating CRM records) within a larger AI-driven workflow. The interoperability potential means your orchestration can span across platforms when necessary.

CrewAI and Multi-Agent Coordination: CrewAI is another open-source framework aimed at orchestrating multiple AI agents working together. In CrewAI, you define individual agents with specific roles and goals (e.g., one agent is a "researcher", another is a "writer"), and CrewAI orchestrates their interactions to achieve a common goal. This directly parallels the Conductor concept: CrewAI effectively provides a coordinator agent that mediates a team of AI agents (each possibly an LLM with a persona). For example, using CrewAI you could have a "planner" agent break a task into subtasks and assign them to a "translator" agent, a "summary" agent, etc., then have the planner compile results. If that sounds like a Conductor, it is! The main difference is context: CrewAI runs in a Python environment and was born from the autonomous AI agent community (where agents converse in natural language and collaborate), whereas Agentforce runs within Salesforce's ecosystem with structured data and process rules. A Salesforce Conductor could incorporate CrewAI by calling out to a CrewAI process (imagine an Apex callout to a CrewAI API that kicks off a team of LLM-based agents for some creative brainstorming task, then returns results to Salesforce). On the flip side, the principles behind CrewAI's orchestrator – like balancing different AI agents' outputs – might inspire future features in Agentforce. The key takeaway is that the industry recognizes the need for an orchestrator (be it Conductor or CrewAI's coordinator) when multiple agents are involved. Agentforce provides that in a platform-governed way, while frameworks like CrewAI explore more free-form multi-agent collaboration. Both have their place, and an enterprise could even use them in tandem for different purposes.

Microsoft Copilot and Generative Orchestration: Microsoft's Copilot (in platforms like Microsoft 365 and Power Platform) has introduced the idea of generative orchestration, where an AI agent uses a large language model to orchestrate other functions. In Copilot Studio, an agent can choose the best tools, topics, or other agents to respond to a query or event. By default, Copilot uses this generative approach – meaning the orchestration logic itself is produced by AI on the fly, rather than a fixed workflow. For example, if a user asks a Microsoft 365 Copilot "Organize a team meeting and summarize our last project," the Copilot agent might dynamically decide to invoke the calendar, a summary of project documents, and an email draft function in sequence without that exact sequence being pre-programmed. This is like having a Conductor where the plan is created by an AI "planner" in real-time. The advantage is high flexibility (Copilot can handle multi-intent requests gracefully) at the cost of less predictable internals. Agentforce's Conductor pattern, in contrast, typically involves a classic orchestration approach – predetermined flows triggered by specific conditions (though it can have dynamic branches, we usually know the possible branches in advance). Both approaches can coexist. For instance, Microsoft's generative orchestration is great for user-facing assistants that need to handle whatever the user throws at them (similar to a Companion agent we'll discuss in Chapter 5). Salesforce's Conductor is great for back-office processes that need reliability and clarity. It's easy to envision a Copilot-style agent handing off a task to a Salesforce Conductor for execution of enterprise processes ("Copilot, onboard a new vendor for me" – Copilot calls Salesforce via API, where a Conductor does the actual orchestrating of vendor onboarding). Conversely, a Salesforce Conductor could call a Copilot or other generative service if some flexible decision-making is needed. The industry trend is toward these hybrid orchestrations: some parts generative, some parts deterministic. Salesforce's focus is ensuring the deterministic parts (the Conductor flows) integrate well with generative AI components, so that enterprises get the best of both worlds.

Integration via MuleSoft and APIs: A big part of orchestration is connecting beyond the Salesforce platform. MuleSoft, Salesforce's integration arm, often acts as a bridge between Conductor agents and other enterprise systems. If a Conductor needs to interact with an ERP like SAP or an HR system like Workday, it can call MuleSoft workflows or REST APIs that encapsulate those integrations. For example, our Finance Conductor might invoke a MuleSoft REST endpoint that queries SAP for budget data. From the Conductor's perspective, it's just one step (an HTTP call) in the flow, but MuleSoft handles the complexity of authenticating and querying SAP, then returns a simple response. MuleSoft itself has orchestration capabilities (it can do multi-step integrations), so an architect should decide which orchestration to do in Salesforce vs. in MuleSoft. A common strategy is to use Salesforce Conductor for orchestrating actions that involve Salesforce records or AI agents, and use MuleSoft to orchestrate multi-step interactions between external systems. The Conductor can call one MuleSoft flow that itself might call 3 different external APIs in sequence – effectively the Conductor outsources a chunk of work to MuleSoft when appropriate. Additionally, Conductor agents can directly call third-party APIs using Apex callouts or External Services without MuleSoft if it's a simple integration. For instance, using External Services, you can import an OpenAPI spec and then invoke an external operation in Flow with ease (no code). Whether via MuleSoft or direct callouts, a Conductor agent should be designed to treat external services as just another kind of sub-agent – it calls them, handles success/failure, and continues the orchestration. MuleSoft can also serve as an event broker: a Conductor might publish a Platform Event that MuleSoft's Anypoint Platform subscribes to, triggering a whole integration workflow. In short, Salesforce Conductors are integration-friendly by design, ensuring that orchestrations aren't limited to within Salesforce's walls.

Model Context Protocol (MCP) and Cross-Platform Agents: Industry players (like Anthropic, OpenAI, IBM) are working on standards such as the Model Context Protocol (MCP) to enable interoperability between different AI agent platforms. MCP is essentially an open protocol for connecting AI systems with external tools and data in a standardized way. Think of it as a lingua franca that lets a Salesforce agent, a Python agent, and a cloud service all communicate tasks and results. If Agentforce supports MCP in the future, a Conductor agent could, for example, query an MCP server to find available "skills" or tools provided by other systems, and invoke them as needed. For instance, a Salesforce Conductor might send an MCP request to a data science agent running on AWS to run a complex simulation, then get back the result and proceed. Conversely, an external AI agent following MCP could call into Salesforce – discovering that Salesforce has a "Conductor Agent for Order Processing" and telling it to execute (with necessary parameters) via the MCP interface. MCP essentially abstracts the API layer between AI services, allowing a network of heterogeneous agents to work together without tightly coupling their implementations. While still emerging, this concept aligns well with the Conductor pattern: the Conductor becomes not only the orchestrator of Salesforce processes, but potentially an orchestrator in a federation of agents across platforms.

To illustrate an MCP-style interaction, here's a hypothetical JSON request a Conductor might send to invoke an external agent via MCP:


```
{
"agent": "DocumentSummaryAgent",
"action": "summarize",
"parameters": {
  "document_url": "https://example.com/manual.pdf",
  "summary_length": "short"
}
}
```


In this example, our Conductor is asking an external agent (identified as "DocumentSummaryAgent") to perform a "summarize" action on a document, with a specified length. The Conductor wouldn't need to know how that agent works (it could be using GPT-4 or some proprietary model); it just trusts the MCP infrastructure to route the request and return the summary. Once returned, the Conductor could then, say, send that summary to a human or use it in the next step of an orchestration. MCP and similar efforts aim to make orchestrating across different AI ecosystems as straightforward as calling a local subroutine, which could greatly enhance the power of patterns like Conductor by extending their reach beyond a single platform.

Agentforce vs. External Orchestrators: To put it all in perspective, Agentforce's Conductor pattern emphasizes explicit, configurable workflows with strong integration into enterprise data and governance. External orchestration frameworks like LangChain and CrewAI provide more emergent or code-driven orchestration, often used in experimental or highly dynamic AI applications. Microsoft's Copilot introduces AI-driven orchestration that's user-facing and very flexible. Each has strengths: Agentforce Conductors shine for business-critical processes that need auditability, security, and clear control; LangChain/CrewAI shine for exploratory AI use cases that require extreme flexibility; generative orchestration shines for helping users in unpredictable scenarios. An enterprise might well use all of these: Salesforce Conductors for core business operations, and other frameworks for edge cases or user productivity tools. The good news is that Salesforce is not building a walled garden – through APIs, MuleSoft, and likely standards like MCP, Agentforce is ready to participate in a heterogeneous agent ecosystem. Your Conductor agents can call and be called by external services, making them team players in the broader AI landscape.

In practical terms, you might have a Conductor agent that not only invokes Salesforce-hosted agents (Supervisor, Action, etc.) but also calls out to a LangChain tool for an NLP task, and maybe triggers a CrewAI multi-agent brainstorming session for a creative problem, then consolidates all those results for a human decision facilitated by a Presenter agent. This kind of cross-platform orchestration is complex, but Conductor agents are conceptually equipped to handle it. By understanding how other ecosystems approach orchestration, you as an architect can design your Conductors to integrate or at least coexist with them, leveraging the best tool for each part of a complex workflow.

CONDUCTOR IN MULTI-PATTERN WORKFLOWS

In a comprehensive AI solution, agent patterns rarely operate in isolation. A single complex use case might involve multiple types of agents collaborating, each pattern handling a facet of the problem. The Conductor pattern often serves as the central hub in these multi-agent constellations, orchestrating and mediating between Sentinel, Companion, Supervisor, Curator, Action, and Coach agents. Let's illustrate how a Conductor can work in concert with other patterns through a few combined scenarios:

Sentinel → Conductor → Supervisor → Action (Automated Incident Resolution): Imagine an IT monitoring system where a Sentinel agent (Chapter 2) keeps watch for system incidents. One night, the Sentinel detects a critical server outage – an event triggers that agent to raise an alert. Instead of just sending an email, the Sentinel hands off to an Incident Response Conductor agent (the Conductor pattern) to handle the situation. The Conductor springs into action: first, it calls an Action agent (maybe via an Apex job) to attempt an automatic server reboot and gather diagnostic info (log files, CPU/memory stats). Next, the Conductor checks if the server came back online – let's say it didn't, indicating a deeper issue. The Conductor then invokes a Supervisor pattern: it pings the on-call human engineer via a notification, effectively saying "I tried the basic fix, it didn't work – please intervene." While waiting for a human, the Conductor might also call a Curator/analysis agent to parse the logs and highlight what might be wrong (to assist the human). The on-call engineer responds through a mobile app (approving a more invasive restart sequence). The Conductor receives this approval (Supervisor step done) and then calls another Action agent to execute the approved recovery steps (for example, failover to a backup system). Once the incident is resolved, the Conductor might use a Presenter agent to post an incident summary in the IT team's Slack channel (so everyone knows what happened and what was done). In this chain, the Sentinel detected the issue, the Conductor orchestrated the diagnosis and fix, the Supervisor (human) provided judgment at a key decision, Action agents performed the remediation, and a Presenter communicated the result. The multi-pattern dance ensured a 24/7 autonomous response with human oversight at the right point – all coordinated by the Conductor.

Companion + Conductor (Personal Assistant with Back-End Automation): Consider a sales executive using a Companion agent (Chapter 5) through a chat interface like Slack. The exec asks, "Can you prepare a weekly summary of my team's pipeline and schedule a review meeting?" The Companion agent (a user proxy) is great at the conversational part – it understands the request and knows the user's context (which team, which pipeline). But fulfilling the request involves many steps: querying Salesforce for pipeline data, generating a summary report, finding a meeting time when everyone is free, sending invites. The Companion itself isn't internally doing all that – instead, it invokes a Sales Pipeline Conductor agent to handle the heavy lifting. The Conductor goes to work: it first calls a Curator agent to collect and summarize the latest pipeline metrics (maybe an Apex action that runs some SOQL queries and uses an Einstein AI to draft key insights). Next, it calls a calendar integration (an Action agent or External

Service) to look at calendars and propose a meeting slot for the team review, then automatically books the meeting. Then the Conductor might call a Presenter agent to draft an email to the team: "Pipeline Review scheduled for Monday 10am. Attached is the pipeline summary – please review beforehand." Finally, the Conductor returns control to the Companion agent, perhaps with a structured result like: meeting confirmed, summary document link, email sent to team. The Companion agent then tells the executive in human-friendly form: "I've scheduled the pipeline review for Monday at 10 AM and sent the team a summary of our pipeline status." In this scenario, the Companion provided the personal, conversational interface and delegated the complex multi-system orchestration to a Conductor. The Conductor coordinated multiple patterns (Curator for data summary, Action for scheduling, Presenter for communication), then fed the result back to the Companion. Together, they delivered a seamless personal assistant experience backed by rigorous process execution.

Coach + Conductor (Proactive Insight to Action): A Coach agent (Chapter 8) is designed to analyze data and provide proactive advice or alerts. Suppose there's a Customer Success Coach agent observing customer support trends. It identifies that a particular product is seeing a spike in support tickets and, based on its internal knowledge, suspects an emerging product issue. The Coach agent's role is to alert the relevant team with this insight (e.g., "We've had a 40% increase in tickets on Product X in the last week"). But to fully address the situation, more work is needed – that's where it hands off to a Conductor. The Coach triggers a Product Issue Response Conductor. This Conductor orchestrates a response: it first calls a Curator/analysis agent to deep-dive into the support tickets and extract common themes or root causes (maybe an NLP analysis of ticket texts). It then uses a Presenter agent to draft a report on the findings and perhaps an internal knowledge base article if a workaround is found. Simultaneously, it might call a Supervisor agent to notify the product manager (human) and ask if they want to, say, initiate a formal incident or send an apology to customers – essentially getting human approval for next steps. With the product manager's go-ahead, the Conductor then calls an Action agent to execute the decided step (for example, send a service notification to all customers using that product with the workaround information). Here, the Coach pattern provided situational awareness ("Hey, something's wrong"), and the Conductor pattern took over to coordinate the multi-step investigation and response across support, documentation, and customer communication. The combination ensures that insight turns into action. Without the Conductor, the Coach's alert might sit idle or rely on humans to coordinate the response. With the

Conductor, the moment the Coach agent raises a flag, a whole orchestrated workflow kicks off to address the issue, with humans looped in appropriately for decisions and final approval.

These scenarios show that the Conductor pattern truly is the glue among agent patterns. A Sentinel agent can detect an event or anomaly, but handing off to a Conductor is what turns detection into resolution. A Companion agent can elegantly interface with a user, but delegating tasks to a Conductor is how it actually fulfills complex user requests. A Coach agent can identify opportunities or risks, but partnering with a Conductor means those insights lead to concrete interventions. Meanwhile, Supervisor agents (human-in-the-loop checkpoints) and Action agents (automated executors) naturally plug into Conductor-orchestrated flows wherever needed.

A real-world end-to-end example that uses many patterns could be a "Quote to Order" process in sales. Imagine: a Sentinel agent watches for a signed quote coming in from a customer. When it sees one, it triggers a Quote Conversion Conductor. That Conductor orchestrates converting the quote to an official order: it invokes an Action agent to create the Order record and related provisioning tasks; it checks with a Supervisor agent (maybe requiring the sales manager to approve if the discount was high); it might call a Companion agent to notify the sales rep that their order is being processed; and it engages a Presenter agent to send an order confirmation to the customer. The entire "Quote to Order" journey, from signature to confirmation, is handled by a team of agents led by the Conductor. Each agent pattern does what it's best at – the Presenter crafts a clear message to the customer, the Supervisor ensures policy compliance, the Action updates records quickly – and the Conductor ensures they all play in harmony to achieve the business outcome.

By combining multiple patterns in this way, organizations can design AI-driven processes that are both intelligent and reliable. The Conductor pattern provides the structured framework that allows other agents to interoperate effectively. In these multi-pattern workflows, the whole is greater than the sum of the parts: the Sentinel extends the Conductor's reach into real-time detection, the Companion and Presenter extend it into user-facing interaction, the Coach feeds it analysis, and the Supervisor and Action agents integrate human judgment and concrete effects. The Conductor is the choreographer making sure all these dance together correctly. This is the ultimate promise of Agentforce – an ecosystem of specialized AI agents, each with a defined role, collaborating to handle complex, end-to-end business processes autonomously under the gentle guidance of a Conductor.

SUMMARY

In this chapter, we explored the Conductor pattern and saw how it elevates AI agents from isolated problem-solvers to coordinated, enterprise-grade solutions. The Conductor agent serves as the strategic orchestrator, breaking down complex, multi-step jobs, delegating subtasks to the right agents or services, and reassembling the results into a meaningful outcome. We began by understanding when to apply the Conductor pattern – typically for workflows that are multi-step, cross-functional, or span multiple systems – and contrasted it with simpler single-agent automation. We then learned how to build a Conductor agent using Agentforce and Salesforce tools, seeing how to combine Flow Orchestration, Invocable Apex, and metadata-driven logic to implement an orchestrator. We also covered how to design for scale, observability, and resilience: planning for retries, fallbacks, and detailed logging. Orchestration, as we emphasized, is what makes AI agents truly scalable – it connects their narrow individual intelligences into an integrated intelligent system.

We also ventured beyond Salesforce, comparing the Conductor pattern to orchestration approaches in other ecosystems. We looked at how frameworks like LangChain and CrewAI implement agent orchestration, and how Salesforce's approach can interoperate with external platforms via APIs and emerging standards like MCP. These comparisons highlighted that while the technology may differ, the core need for orchestration is universal in complex AI workflows.

Finally, we saw how the Conductor pattern works in concert with other agent patterns. Through multi-pattern scenarios, we demonstrated that Conductors often act as the central hub in a network of agents – receiving signals from Sentinel agents, invoking specialized Action or Curator agents, involving Supervisor (human) agents for judgment, and delivering outcomes via Presenter or Companion agents. This multi-agent choreography is where the power of Agentforce really comes to life: each pattern plays its role, and the Conductor ensures the right pieces come together at the right time to drive a process to completion.

In short, Conductor agents unify and orchestrate the efforts of other agents to solve complex, multi-faceted problems. They bring order, reliability, and scalability to AI-driven workflows. With Conductors in place, you can trust that your autonomous agents won't work in silos, but in harmony as part of a larger process that serves your business goals.

Next, we zoom in from orchestration to personalization. In Chapter 5, the Companion pattern (User Proxy Agent), we'll explore how agents act on behalf of individuals. This most human-facing of patterns is all about learning user preferences, maintaining context, and providing proactive assistance to make each user more effective. It's a very different perspective – from coordinating systems to directly supporting a single person – and it builds on many concepts we've covered, connecting orchestration with user-centric design. Let's dive into the world of Companion agents and see how they become our trusted digital teammates.

5

THE COMPANION PATTERN (USER PROXY AGENT)

The Companion pattern is the most human-facing of all the agent designs in an enterprise AI system. Unlike orchestrators or task-specific bots that operate behind the scenes, a Companion agent is built around an individual user – effectively becoming that person's AI-augmented partner or proxy. This pattern centers on personalization: a Companion learns the user's preferences and habits, maintains context across sessions, offers timely assistance in the flow of work, and, over time, evolves into a trusted digital proxy acting on the user's behalf. It is not mere automation of routine tasks; rather, it is an intelligent assistant that anticipates needs, streamlines daily workflows, and provides insights or reminders before the user even has to ask. In other words, a well-designed Companion agent does more than execute commands – it observes and adapts to the user's context, acting almost like a digital colleague. (Indeed, Microsoft explicitly markets its Copilot assistant as a "digital companion" – "like having a smart, helpful friend at your fingertips!", capturing the essence of what Companion agents aim to be.)

Consider a few hypothetical examples across different roles and industries. An HR manager's Companion might track the onboarding progress of new hires and nudge the manager when paperwork is pending or orientation sessions haven't been completed. It could even draft a personalized welcome email for each new hire based on their role. A lawyer's Companion could monitor contract negotiations in progress – comparing each new document version to previous ones and highlighting clause changes or potential risks for the lawyer to review. For a field service technician, a mobile Companion agent can prepare a job-site brief while the technician is en route: pulling up past service history on the equipment, listing safety checklists relevant to the site, and even queuing up any troubleshooting guides if sensors report anomalies. Meanwhile, a finance director traveling for business might have a Companion that keeps an eye on expense reports and budget limits – if travel expenses start to approach a policy threshold, the agent flags the risk and offers suggestions (for example, recommending a less expensive hotel or noting that a colleague's trip spending was lower for a similar journey). In each of these scenarios, the Companion isn't performing a generic task in isolation; it's working in tandem with one person, tailoring its actions to that individual's goals and the context at hand.

Behind the scenes, several Salesforce Agentforce tools and design elements enable this level of personalization. Persistent user profiles and context stores (for example, a custom Salesforce object or Data Cloud record for each user) allow the agent to remember key details about the individual – such as their communication preferences, frequent tasks, or recent interactions – and recall that information later. A declarative UI layer built with Lightning Web Components (LWC) or embedded in an Experience Cloud page provides the front-end through which the Companion interacts with the user. This might be a sidebar widget showing the agent's suggestions, or a chat-style interface where the user can converse with the agent naturally. Under the hood, business logic is implemented using Salesforce Flows and Invocable Apex classes to handle the agent's decision-making and actions. These automate what the Companion should do when certain events occur or conditions are met – for instance, "if an escalation flag is set on a task, then alert the user with a suggested next step." Additionally, large language model capabilities (such as Salesforce Einstein GPT or other GPT-powered services) are woven in to give the Companion its language generation and understanding skills. The agent can use an LLM to draft a friendly message in the user's own tone, summarize a complex report into a brief update, or interpret a user's free-text request. All of these pieces are tied together on the Agentforce platform: using the Agent Builder tool, teams can encapsulate profile data, UI components, automation logic, and prompt templates into a reusable, user-bound agent definition. In effect, you design a Companion agent as a personalized app feature – one that's always by the user's side (across Salesforce apps or devices), working to make them more effective in their daily tasks.

In the rest of this chapter, we will explore the Companion pattern in depth – from its internal anatomy and behaviors, to when it's most useful, to how to build and scale one using Salesforce's tools. By the end, you should understand not only how to implement a Companion agent, but also how it fits into a broader ecosystem of AI agents. In the next section, we begin with the fundamentals: the anatomy and core behaviors that define a Companion agent in action.

ANATOMY OF A COMPANION AGENT

At its core, a Companion agent follows a continuous lifecycle in its interaction with a user: Identify → Personalize → Assist → Evolve. It begins by identifying the context and user (who is the user and what are they doing right now?), then personalizing its approach (adjusting to the user's history, preferences, or role), then assisting by performing an action or providing information, and finally evolving by learning from the interaction (updating its memory or adjusting its behavior for next time). This loop repeats as the agent and user work together. For example, when a user opens a sales opportunity record, the Companion might identify the user and record, personalize its response by recalling that this user prefers brief bullet-point updates, assist by generating a short summary of recent related customer communications, and then evolve by noting which summary items the user clicked (learning what the user found useful).

To support such a lifecycle, Companion agents exhibit a few key features and capabilities:

Memory of prior interactions and preferences: A Companion agent remembers important things from past sessions. This could include facts (e.g. "last week I gave this manager a summary of Project X"), user preferences (e.g. "the manager likes reports in PDF and a formal tone"), and outcomes (e.g. "my last recommendation to delegate a task was accepted, so the user might value similar suggestions"). This memory prevents the agent from treating each request as isolated – instead, it builds on what it has learned about the individual.

Awareness of the user's current context: At any given time, the agent stays aware of what the user is doing or what state they're in. Are they in the middle of composing an email? Viewing a particular record? On a mobile device in the field versus at a desktop? The Companion uses such context to tailor its actions. For instance, if it knows the user is on their phone between meetings, it might proactively read out a brief update instead of showing a long textual report.

Adaptive outputs based on role and behavior: The Companion adjusts how it delivers help. The content and format of its outputs might change depending on whether the user is a salesperson, an engineer, or a customer service rep, and based on the user's behavior patterns. If the agent knows the user has a tendency to skip long explanations, it will keep its suggestions concise. If it knows the user's job involves regulated data, it will use more caution and formality. This adaptiveness makes the agent's assistance feel relevant and personalized rather than generic.

From a technical perspective, a Companion agent processes inputs and produces outputs in a way that reflects those features. Typical inputs include the user's identity (who is the user and what are their attributes?), the session context (what page or process are they in, what time is it, perhaps what device?), any stored preferences or profile data for that user (past interactions, configured settings), and the active business data context (like the record currently open, or the content of an email being composed). Using those inputs, the agent generates outputs such as alerts (e.g. a notification: "Reminder: Your next meeting starts in 10 minutes"), drafts (e.g. a pre-written response email the user can send), suggestions (e.g. "Shall I create a follow-up task for this opportunity?"), summaries (e.g. a digest of what happened while the user was out of office), or step-by-step guidance (e.g. "Next, update the project status field since the deadline changed"). Each output is tailored – a summary delivered to an executive might highlight high-level metrics, whereas the same summary delivered to an operations lead might include more granular details.

To implement these capabilities on the Salesforce platform, a variety of tools and design elements are used in concert:

Lightning Web Components (LWC) – These provide the user interface for the Companion agent. For example, you might build an LWC that sits on a Salesforce record page or utility bar as a widget where the agent can display messages or accept input. The LWC could render a chat window, a list of recommended actions, or an icon that glows when a new suggestion is available. By using LWCs, the Companion's presence can be embedded seamlessly into the apps where the user already works, ensuring minimal friction for interaction.

Custom Metadata / Custom Objects – These are used to store the agent's long-term memory and configuration. A custom object (say, User_Preference__c) might store each user's agent profile: their preferences, an activity log, key context data like "last briefing time" or known goals. Custom Metadata Types can hold organization-wide or type-wide settings (for instance, what constitutes a "high priority" task for alerting purposes). By reading and writing to these data stores, the Companion agent can persist its knowledge safely between sessions and across devices. For example, after assisting with a task delegation, the agent could log an entry like "Delegated Task A to User Y on Oct 10" in a custom object. Next time, it can retrieve that and avoid suggesting the same delegation again.

Flow and Invocable Apex – These are the logic engines of the Companion. Salesforce Flow (especially record-triggered flows or scheduled flows) can handle many decision branches declaratively. For instance, a Flow could be set up to trigger whenever a case is marked "Escalated" and then call the Companion agent's subroutine to handle it (perhaps by composing an alert for the case owner). Invocable Apex is used when more complex logic or integrations are needed. You might write an Apex method to analyze a set of tasks and decide which ones are at risk, or to interface with an external system (like pulling in weather data for that field technician's route). The Flow can invoke this Apex, get the results, and then pass them to the LWC or to an LLM prompt. By combining Flows and Apex, you get a balance of ease-of-configuration and coding power: straightforward logic stays in Flow for admins to maintain, and rich branching or computations go into Apex code. (For example, a Flow could loop through all projects nearing deadline and then call an Apex findEscalations() method to pinpoint which tasks within those projects are overdue – returning a list that the agent will include in a user alert.)

GPT-powered prompts and language generation – This layer gives the Companion its fluent communication ability. Through Einstein GPT or another integrated large language model, the agent can turn raw data into natural language and vice versa. Teams can define prompt templates (using Salesforce Prompt Builder or code) that frame what the agent should say. For instance, a prompt template might be: "You are an assistant helping a project manager. Summarize the following project issues in a friendly, concise manner: {List_of_Issues}." At runtime, the agent fills in that template with real data and sends it to the LLM, then gets back a nicely phrased summary to present to the user. Similarly, when the user asks a free-form question ("Hey, what's the status of Project X?"), the agent can feed that query plus relevant context to the LLM to interpret it and formulate a useful answer. This GPT integration ensures the Companion's outputs are not only factually relevant but also polished and contextually appropriate in tone.

Pro Tip: Design Companion agents to degrade gracefully. If personalization data is missing or the context is incomplete, the agent should still function by falling back to default behavior. For example, if a user has no stored preferences yet, the Companion might use a generic interaction style rather than showing an error. Similarly, if an external system needed for context is down, the agent can apologize or defer an action. The goal is to never "break" the user experience – even with minimal information, a Companion agent should offer some help (albeit less personalized), rather than doing nothing. This ensures the agent remains useful and trustworthy at all times.

With the anatomy in mind, we can now consider when a Companion agent is the right solution. In the next section, we'll look at the scenarios and roles where the Companion pattern delivers the most value.

WHEN AND WHY TO USE THE COMPANION PATTERN

Not every situation calls for a personal AI proxy. The Companion pattern shines in certain roles and environments – typically those involving complex, dynamic work where personalized assistance can make a real difference. Here we outline a few key scenarios where deploying a Companion agent pays off:

Roles with high complexity or multitasking: Some jobs require juggling many threads at once – think project managers balancing multiple projects, sales executives handling many clients, or support agents dealing with numerous cases. In these roles, a Companion agent helps keep track of the moving pieces and reduces cognitive load. It can monitor different work streams and ensure nothing important falls through the cracks. For example, a sales representative often has to switch between prospecting, follow-ups, internal meetings, and data entry. A Companion can act as a personal coordinator: reminding them to follow up with a lead they haven't contacted in two weeks, auto-dialing into the next meeting and providing a quick briefing beforehand, or updating CRM records in the background while the rep focuses on the conversation. By offloading these auxiliary tasks and timing reminders optimally, the Companion lets the user concentrate on higher-value work (closing deals, building relationships) rather than on remembering schedules or shuffling through systems.

Situations where context improves outcomes: In many activities, having more context at hand leads to better decisions or better output. A Companion agent is ideal when the how or when of a task should change based on surrounding conditions. For instance, consider an approval workflow. If a manager is asked to approve a budget request, the optimal timing and manner of that approval could depend on context: Is the manager traveling? Are we near quarter-end? Has a similar request been approved recently? A Companion agent, acting on behalf of the manager, could recognize that context and, say, hold off on presenting a low-priority approval request if the manager is currently in back-to-back meetings (thus improving the likelihood of a thoughtful approval later). Or take communication tone – an agent crafting a draft email might adjust its tone depending on whom the email is addressed to and past interactions. If it's going to a long-time client, the Companion might make it more informal and warm; if it's going to an executive, more formal and concise. These context-aware adjustments can significantly improve effectiveness (e.g. approvals processed at optimal times, emails that resonate better with recipients). The Companion pattern excels here because it's privy to both the user's intent and the situational context, allowing it to do things like "send this as an SMS now because it's urgent and 7 PM" versus "schedule this as an email tomorrow morning because it's non-urgent."

Environments with frequent interruptions or context switching: Modern professionals often suffer from constant context switching – jumping between apps, meetings, and tasks. Studies have shown that frequent context switching can decrease human productivity by around 40% due to the mental reset time required. In such environments, a Companion agent can act as a stabilizing force that manages and preserves context for the user. For example, a customer support agent might handle live chats, emails, and phone calls all in the same hour. A Companion can help by maintaining a short-term memory of what the support agent was doing before the last interruption: "You were drafting a response to Case #123; here is where you left off." As soon as the interruption is over, the agent gently reminds the user what they were working on and even suggests the next step to pick back up. It can also buffer less urgent tasks – if the user is pulled into a meeting, the Companion might hold any non-critical alerts and then present them once the user is free, rather than distracting them mid-meeting. In essence, the Companion becomes a guardian of the user's focus, mitigating the productivity loss that comes from constant interruptions.

Workflows that benefit from proactive nudges or micro-insights: In many processes, there are opportunities for small improvements that humans often overlook due to busy schedules or cognitive overload. The Companion pattern is valuable when continuous, proactive assistance can cumulatively yield significant benefits. For instance, consider a field technician performing maintenance throughout the day. A Companion agent on a wearable device could give "micro-insights" before each job: "This machine had a sensor alert 2 days ago on temperature – double-check cooling." Or for a marketing manager, a Companion might gently nudge: "It's Thursday afternoon – that's typically the best time to send out the weekly newsletter, shall I prepare it now?" These little prompts and insights, based on patterns and data, help users take action at just the right moments. Over time, these proactive nudges can improve outcomes like faster response times, higher quality work (since issues are caught early), or simply reduced stress (because the user isn't solely responsible for remembering every minor to-do). The Companion agent basically serves as a second pair of eyes, always on the lookout for the next small improvement or timely action.

It's also important to clarify how the Companion pattern differs from some other agent patterns. Notably, one contrast is Companion vs. Supervisor (another pattern covered elsewhere): the Companion helps the user act, whereas a Supervisor agent reviews or checks actions (often for compliance or correctness). In practice these can complement each other. For example, a Companion might help draft a sales quote for a customer, doing the heavy lifting of data gathering and initial wording. A Supervisor-type agent (or simply a supervisory step) might then review that draft quote for any errors or policy violations. Finally, the Companion could help refine the quote based on that feedback. In this way, the Companion is like the proactive assistant on the user's side, and the Supervisor is like the safety net verifying things. Many teams find that using both patterns together – a Companion to accelerate work and a Supervisor to double-check it – yields both speed and safety. However, if you have to choose, use a Companion when the primary need is personal productivity and convenience for the user, and use a Supervisor when the primary need is oversight, compliance, or error-checking. (They are by no means mutually exclusive – as we will see later, you can chain agents so that a Companion and Supervisor work in tandem on a process.)

To summarize these considerations and illustrate the benefits in different roles, the list below maps a few example user roles to the key benefits a Companion agent can provide:

Sales Representative

- **Speed benefit:** Automatically fetches relevant data and drafts responses, enabling faster customer replies.
- **Accuracy benefit:** Cross-checks CRM data when preparing quotes or proposals to reduce errors.
- **Comfort benefit:** Handles activity logging and routine updates, reducing administrative burden.
- **Proactivity benefit:** Reminds the rep of follow-ups, renewals, and potential upsell opportunities.

Customer Support Agent

- **Speed benefit:** Suggests ready-to-use responses that accelerate case resolution.
- **Accuracy benefit:** Ensures required troubleshooting steps and policies are followed consistently.
- **Comfort benefit:** Automatically records case notes and updates, minimizing manual paperwork.
- **Proactivity benefit:** Alerts the agent to approaching SLA breaches before they occur.

Project Manager

- **Speed benefit:** Consolidates status updates and inputs from multiple sources to reduce planning overhead.
- **Accuracy benefit:** Cross-verifies schedules, dependencies, and budgets to surface conflicts early.
- **Comfort benefit:** Tracks tasks and commitments so nothing slips through the cracks.
- **Proactivity benefit:** Flags risks, delays, or scope issues before they escalate.

Field Technician

- **Speed benefit:** Delivers on-site information instantly without manual lookup.
- **Accuracy benefit:** Pulls the correct procedures and specifications from the knowledge base.

- **Comfort benefit:** Supports hands-free note-taking and updates through voice interaction.
- **Proactivity benefit:** Notifies the technician of upcoming maintenance needs or likely failures in advance.

In the list above, we can see how a Companion agent accelerates work (speed), improves quality (accuracy), reduces cognitive load (comfort), and increases proactiveness across very different jobs. A sales rep gets to respond to customers faster and with fewer mistakes (since the agent fills in CRM info correctly), and they experience less clerical burden. A support agent similarly benefits from quicker responses and consistent process adherence, with the agent quietly taking care of documentation. A project manager gains foresight into potential issues and relief from constant manual checking, while a field technician gets timely knowledge and reminders that prevent issues and save effort. These are precisely the kinds of advantages that justify using the Companion pattern.

Now that we've identified where Companion agents are most useful, the next section will dive into concrete examples across various departments. We'll see hypothetical Companion agents in HR, legal, finance, IT, and marketing, demonstrating how they function in real-world contexts.

CROSS-FUNCTIONAL EXAMPLES OF COMPANION AGENTS

Companion agents are broadly applicable across many business functions – anywhere an individual can benefit from a personalized assistant. Let's explore a series of hypothetical (but plausible) Companion agents in different domains to see how they operate. Each example will highlight the agent's use case, the signals or data it watches, and how it assists the user in that role:

Human Resources (HR) – Onboarding & Compliance Assistant: Imagine an HR manager who oversees hiring and onboarding. A Companion agent could be dedicated to tracking all the moving parts of the onboarding process. Its job: keep the HR manager informed and ahead of schedule. It monitors signals like open job requisitions (how many positions are currently being filled), new hire start dates, and required onboarding tasks or deadlines (training completion, form submissions such as I-9 or tax forms, etc.). As candidates move through the pipeline and become new hires, the agent observes feedback from interviews or orientation sessions as well. The assistive behaviors of the HR Companion might include daily or weekly summaries of hiring status (e.g. "3 positions remain open, 2 offers pending acceptance"), reminders of upcoming onboarding milestones ("Reminder: Alice's 30-day feedback session is due next week"), and even generating drafts – for instance, drafting a welcome email for a new hire's first day that the HR manager can review. It could also flag compliance issues, like if a new hire hasn't signed a policy document within the required timeframe, the agent alerts the manager or even pings the new hire with a gentle reminder. By personalizing these alerts to the manager's style (maybe the manager likes them as a checklist every Monday), the Companion ensures the HR manager never misses a step, and that new employees have a smooth, well-documented onboarding experience.

Legal – Contract Monitoring Assistant: Consider a legal counsel or contract manager who has numerous contracts in progress with clients or vendors. A Companion agent for legal could act as a diligent contract analyst. It keeps an eye on signals such as the current status of each contract (draft, under review, awaiting approval, etc.), deadlines for renewals or terminations, and especially any changes in language between contract versions. For every new document revision that comes in from the counterparty, the agent automatically compares it to the previous version and assists by highlighting what changed (e.g. "Clause 5.2 – liability cap amount changed from $1M to $500k"). It might also have knowledge of playbook standards – so if a risky or non-standard clause appears, the Companion flags it for the lawyer's attention ("Alert: the indemnification clause was removed – this deviates from our standard contract"). The agent could compile a brief summary of all outstanding issues on a contract and even suggest fallback language from the company's clause library. Through a simple chat interface, the legal counsel might ask, "Have any important terms changed in Acme Corp's contract since yesterday?" and the Companion would respond with a concise report of changes or confirm nothing significant changed. By acting as a tireless, context-aware reviewer, the Companion frees the legal professional from manually combing through documents line by line, and reduces the risk of overlooking a subtle but crucial edit from the other side.

Finance – Budget Advisor Companion: In a finance department scenario, imagine a finance manager or budget owner responsible for keeping spending under control. A finance Companion agent could continuously monitor company financial data and user-specific budgets. The signals it watches might include real-time expense reports being submitted, purchases orders in the system, travel bookings, and budget versus actual spend for various categories. The agent's assistive behavior is to advise the user on the financial impact of decisions in the moment. For example, if the manager is approving a new software subscription purchase, the Companion might interject: "This $50k annual subscription will push the Q4 IT budget 5% over its limit." It can suggest options ("Consider deferring the start to next quarter, or find $50k to cut elsewhere – shall I scan for underutilized services?"). If the manager is traveling, the agent might proactively alert them: "You've spent $4,000 of your $5,000 travel budget this month. At your current rate, you'll exceed it – consider moderating expenses or increasing the budget." The agent can also crunch numbers: if a new sales forecast comes in, the Companion can project end-of-quarter revenue and advise the manager on adjusting department budgets accordingly. Essentially, the finance Companion acts like a personalized financial analyst, giving the user timely warnings and recommendations that keep finances aligned with targets. This reduces the chance of nasty surprises (like finding out a budget was blown after it's too late) and helps the user make informed decisions backed by data in real time.

IT (Information Technology) – Technician Helper Companion: In an IT support or operations context, picture a support engineer or an on-call IT technician. Their Companion agent focuses on technical signals: system alerts, support ticket updates, knowledge base articles, and scripts or commands that could resolve common issues. When the engineer is working on a problem, the agent automatically pulls relevant information – if a server alarm comes in, the agent might retrieve the last 5 similar incidents and how they were resolved, presenting a quick summary ("Similar outage on 2023-09-10 was fixed by restarting the X service"). It also logs activity for the engineer: as the engineer runs commands or makes changes, the agent notes them down in the ticket or in a running log (so the engineer doesn't have to write as much documentation later). A particularly useful behavior is recommendation: based on the current issue context (log files, error codes), the Companion can recommend scripts or solutions ("It looks like a memory leak – you have a cleanup script Y, would you like me to run it?"). It might even have a library of approved automation actions that it can execute upon the engineer's confirmation. Additionally, for a field IT technician servicing equipment, the Companion can gather service history for that device, and maybe overlay IoT sensor readings, giving the technician a one-glance briefing through a mobile app or AR display. By doing all of this, the IT Companion not only speeds up problem resolution (less time hunting for answers or documentation), but also ensures nothing the technician does gets lost (because it's all captured in logs). It's like having a co-pilot that knows the systems as well as the veteran engineer, and is always ready to help troubleshoot and document.

Marketing – Campaign Assistant: In a marketing department, consider a marketing manager running multiple campaigns. A Companion agent could function as a campaign planning and content assistant. It monitors signals such as campaign schedules (when each campaign or social media post is planned), engagement metrics (opens, clicks, conversions coming in live), and even competitor activities (through news or social feeds). The Companion's assistive behaviors would include suggesting optimal timing and channel for content – for instance, "Your newsletter engagement is highest on Thursdays around 3 PM. It's 1 PM now, shall I prepare the send for 3 PM today with the latest content?" It can also help in content creation: the agent might review a draft of a marketing email and compare it against past high-performing emails, then suggest edits ("Emails with shorter subject lines had 10% higher open rates. Consider simplifying the subject line."). If the company's main competitor just launched a new product (a piece of data it gleaned from a news feed), the Companion can alert the marketing manager and perhaps recommend a responsive action (like a quick social media post or an internal strategy meeting). Essentially, the marketing Companion keeps the manager informed of both internal campaign status and external market context, and provides creative support. It may even track the tone or brand compliance of content – flagging if a draft social post doesn't fit the company's approved messaging style. By personalizing its guidance to the specific campaigns and the manager's goals (e.g. focusing on lead generation vs. brand awareness), the Companion helps the marketer maximize impact with minimal oversights.

We can summarize these cross-functional scenarios in a persona list:

HR Manager

- **Use case:** Onboarding new hires and ensuring compliance deadlines are met.
- **Signals observed:** Open requisitions; new hire start dates; completion status of onboarding tasks such as forms and training; HRIS feedback data.
- **Assistive behaviors:** Sends task reminders (for example, background check completion); compiles new hire feedback summaries; alerts when compliance steps such as policy acknowledgments are overdue.

Legal Counsel

- **Use case:** Managing contract negotiations and reviews.
- **Signals observed:** Draft versus redline contract versions; clause changes; approval status; key dates such as renewals and expirations.
- **Assistive behaviors:** Highlights clause edits between versions; flags risky or non-standard language; summarizes contract status; suggests approved replacement clause text.

Finance Manager

- **Use case:** Overseeing departmental budgets and spend approvals.
- **Signals observed:** Live expense reports and purchase orders; budget versus actual figures; financial thresholds and policy rules.
- **Assistive behaviors:** Advises on spend requests with over-budget warnings; suggests budget reallocations; alerts when run-rate indicates potential overspend; generates budget status reports.

IT Support Engineer

- **Use case:** Troubleshooting incidents and maintaining systems.
- **Signals observed:** System alerts and logs; support ticket updates; knowledge base articles; script libraries.
- **Assistive behaviors:** Automatically logs actions taken; surfaces similar past incidents and resolutions; recommends diagnostic or remediation scripts; flags patterns indicating a broader systemic issue.

Marketing Manager

- **Use case:** Running multi-channel marketing campaigns.
- **Signals observed:** Campaign calendars and deadlines; live engagement metrics; competitor media activity; content drafts.
- **Assistive behaviors:** Suggests optimal send times or channels; reviews and edits content for tone, length, and SEO; alerts on competitor campaign launches; tracks performance and recommends adjustments such as reallocating spend.

Each of these examples shows a Companion agent tuned to the needs of a specific domain, yet the pattern remains consistent: the agent observes the user's environment and actions, processes relevant data in the background, and proactively supports the user with timely, contextual assistance. Whether it's ensuring an HR task isn't forgotten, a contract change isn't missed, a budget stays on track, an IT issue is resolved efficiently, or a marketing campaign hits its marks, the Companion acts as an ever-vigilant, personalized aide-de-camp.

Having seen how Companion agents might function across various roles, the next question is: how do we actually build one of these within Salesforce's Agentforce framework? In the next section, we'll walk through the process of constructing a Companion agent – covering everything from defining its persona and memory to implementing its logic and UI.

BUILDING A COMPANION AGENT IN AGENTFORCE

Let's now shift from concept to implementation and explore how to build a Companion agent using Salesforce's Agentforce platform and tools. We will illustrate the process with a concrete example: a Companion agent designed for a Project Manager, whose job is to track project escalations and nudge the manager to delegate or address tasks as needed. This "Project Companion" will serve as our running example, and through it we'll touch on Agentforce components like Agent Builder, custom metadata, Apex, LWC, and GPT integration.

1. Define the Agent's Persona and Scope (Agent Builder): We start in Salesforce Agent Builder, which provides a low-code interface to configure the new agent. In Agent Builder, you would create a new agent (let's call it "Project Companion") and define its purpose and persona. For our example, we describe its job in natural language: "Assist a project manager by monitoring project issues and team workload, alerting about escalations, and suggesting task reassignments." Agent Builder lets us break this into topics or goals – for instance, one topic could be "Escalation Monitoring" and another "Workload Balancing". Under each topic, we write instructions the agent should follow. This essentially forms the agent's initial "brain". Agent Builder encourages thinking in terms of jobs to be done and actions: we might add instructions like, "If a task is marked high priority and is overdue, alert the user and recommend possible delegation." According to Salesforce's documentation, Agent Builder allows you to "Define Jobs" for the agent and specify the actions it can take. In practice,

this means after describing the agent's role, we move to configuring an Action Library for the Project Companion. Here, we list what actions the agent can perform or request. For example, actions might include: "Summarize Project Status" (maybe implemented via a Flow that queries all tasks due this week and compiles a summary), "Notify Escalation" (a simple action to send the user an alert about an overdue item), or "Reassign Task" (a more complex action that changes a task's owner field). Agent Builder lets us tie each of these actions to actual functionality – some actions could invoke Flows, some could call Apex, others might involve GPT prompts. Under the hood, what we're doing is building the menu of capabilities the Companion can choose from when assisting the user. For instance, the Create Action Libraries step in Agent Builder might reference an existing Flow called "Delegate Task Flow" and an Apex method "Find_Escalations" (we will discuss this Apex next). By defining the persona (topics/instructions) and actions here, we effectively encapsulate the Companion agent's role in a modular way.

2. Store User Preferences and Context (Custom Metadata/Objects): Next, we set up where the agent will keep its memory and any user-specific data. For the Project Companion, we decide to use a custom object Project_Agent_-Context__c. Each Project Manager (user) will have one context record, identified by their User ID. In that record, we can store fields like "Last Briefing Time", "Preferred Alert Channel" (maybe the user prefers notifications via Slack vs. email), or "Delegation Threshold" (e.g. number of tasks per person that triggers a suggestion to delegate). This custom object acts as persistent storage so that the agent remembers things beyond a single session. We might also use a Custom Metadata Type for org-wide settings, such as a list of what constitutes an "escalation" (e.g. task priority = High and status = Open for > 5 days could be defined in metadata). Storing such criteria in metadata means administrators can tweak the agent's sensitivity without changing code. At runtime, when the agent is about to perform its logic, it will query the relevant records: e.g., get the user's Project_Agent_Context__c to see their preferences, and get the Escalation_Criteria__mdt metadata to know the rules. By persisting memory safely here, we ensure the agent can retrieve historical info (like which tasks were escalated last week, to avoid duplicate alerts) and that it can do so in a governed way (Salesforce data access controls apply, keeping it secure). If any of this data is sensitive (like maybe performance feedback notes in HR use-case), we could leverage Platform Encryption on those fields as an extra safety measure. In summary, setting up these data stores is about giving the Companion a place to "think and remember" that is queryable with SOQL and maintainable by admins.

3. Design the User Interface (LWC for inline engagement): Now we focus on how the user will interact with this Companion agent. We decide to create a Lightning Web Component called projectCompanionPanel. This LWC could be embedded, for example, on the Project Manager's dashboard in Lightning Experience or as a utility bar component available globally. The UI might look like a small console where the agent posts messages or suggestions, and the user can click buttons or enter queries. For the Project Companion, the interface might have a section that says "Alerts & Suggestions" where the agent's latest alerts appear (e.g. "Task XYZ is overdue and high priority. You may want to reassign it." with a [Reassign] button next to it). It could also have an input area where the manager can ask questions like "Any updates on Project Alpha?". Building this in LWC allows us to use the full power of Salesforce's UI framework – we can reference Salesforce data in real time and also call Apex controllers from the LWC to perform actions when the user clicks something. The LWC will effectively serve as the front-end for our Companion's actions. For a chatty interface, we'd implement logic to handle a conversation history and maybe call an Apex method that interfaces with the LLM for responses. For a notifications interface, we'd implement a way for the agent (via Apex/Flow) to push new messages into the LWC (perhaps using a Lightning Message Channel or Pub/Sub pattern when an alert is generated). Additionally, this is where personalization touches the UI: because it's a user-specific agent, we might display the user's name or use their preferred theme. If one project manager manages projects A, B, C, we can contextually show suggestions relevant to whichever project record they're currently viewing (the LWC can detect the current record context and filter the agent's messages for that project).

4. Implement Core Logic with Flow and Apex: With the skeleton in place, we turn to constructing the agent's brains – the logic that decides when to do what. For the Project Companion, one core piece of logic is scanning for escalations and high workload situations. We can create a Scheduled Flow that runs, say, every morning for each project manager. This flow could query all tasks owned by that manager's team where status is open and due date is in the past (an initial filter for potential escalations). For each such task, the Flow invokes an Apex action to perform more nuanced checks (for instance, maybe ignore tasks that are only 1 day overdue but focus on those 5+ days overdue and high priority). Let's write a snippet of such an Apex method to illustrate:

```
public with sharing class ProjectAssistantActions {

  @InvocableMethod(label='Find Escalated Tasks')
```

```
  public static List<Id> findEscalatedTasks(List<Id> projectOrUserIds) {
      // This method finds tasks that meet escalation criteria for a given
project or user.
    List<Id> escalatedTaskIds = new List<Id>();
    for (Id recordId : projectOrUserIds) {
      // Example: if recordId is a User Id (project manager), find that user's
team's overdue High tasks
      List<Task> escalations = [
        SELECT Id, OwnerId, Priority, Status, CreatedDate
        FROM Task
        WHERE Priority = 'High' AND Status != 'Completed'
          AND Owner.ManagerId = :recordId /* tasks under this manager's
team */
         AND DueDate < TODAY
      ];
      for (Task t : escalations) {
        escalatedTaskIds.add(t.Id);
      }
    }
    return escalatedTaskIds;
  }
}
```

(The above Invocable Apex is a simplified example. In a real scenario, we would refine the SOQL, handle various criteria (like tasks specifically marked as "Escalation" via a checkbox), and possibly return not just Ids but also relevant info like task names or recommended delegates. But it illustrates how one might encapsulate logic that the Flow can't easily do on its own.)

The Flow would call ProjectAssistantActions.findEscalatedTasks (passing, say, the manager's user Id or relevant project Id) and get back a list of task Ids that need attention. The next steps in the Flow might loop through those task Ids and for each, create an Agent Alert record or directly invoke a notification action. We could, for instance, invoke another Apex method like SendAlert.create() that takes a task Id and composes a message for the LWC to display (or uses the Salesforce Notification Builder to send a push notification). Separately, we could have a Record-Triggered Flow on Task updates: if a task's status changes to "Escalated" by someone, that Flow immediately notifies the Companion agent to alert the project manager user in real-time (maybe via a platform event consumed by the LWC). Additionally, we implement the logic for nudging task delegation. This might involve monitoring if a particular team member has too many tasks. The agent could keep a count (which could be done in a nightly batch Apex or a Flow that runs when tasks are assigned) and if a single person exceeds, say, 10 high-priority tasks, the Companion will suggest to the manager: "John has 12 high-priority tasks — consider delegating some tasks to others." This suggestion generation can be done via Apex as well, or even an LLM prompt: "Draft a suggestion to delegate tasks given that John has 12 high-priority tasks, which is above threshold 10." The point is, by orchestrating Flows and Invocable Apex, we handle the Companion's decision-making in a structured way. Agent Builder would have references to these Flows/Apex actions, so the agent knows it can execute them (e.g. the "Notify Escalation" action in Agent Builder might map to an Apex that creates an alert record and pings the LWC).

5. Add GPT-Enhanced Generation for Messaging: Incorporating GPT capabilities will make our Companion's communication more natural and context-aware. In the Project Companion example, one use of GPT could be to generate the text of the alert or suggestion in a friendly tone. We might set up a Prompt in Prompt Builder such as: "You are an assistant helping a project manager. When a task is overdue by more than 5 days, you gently remind the manager and suggest considering delegation. Use a helpful and concise tone." Then we pass into this prompt the details of the specific task and the overburdened team member, and let the LLM output a nicely phrased suggestion. For instance, the raw data might be: Task = "Design Homepage", Assignee = "John Doe", Overdue by = 7 days. The LLM might produce: "Heads up – the task 'Design Homepage' is high priority and is now a week overdue under John Doe. It might help to reassign or redistribute some of John's workload to get this back on track." This message would then be delivered via the LWC to the manager. We can use Einstein

GPT's Apex SDK or an Invocable Action for text generation to integrate this step. Another area GPT can help is answering ad-hoc questions. If the project manager types into the Companion's UI, "Which tasks should I delegate from Project Alpha?", the agent can gather relevant data (maybe tasks sorted by how overloaded each owner is) and then prompt GPT to formulate a recommendation list in a polite manner. The result might be a short paragraph suggesting specific reassignments. Essentially, GPT becomes the language and advisory engine while our Apex/Flow logic provides the factual grounding (ensuring the LLM gets the correct context and data).

Bringing it all together, let's walk through the end-to-end flow of our example Project Companion agent in action:

Morning check: At 8 AM, a scheduled job (Flow/Apex) runs. The agent checks all projects and tasks for which our project manager is responsible. It finds two escalated tasks and one team member overloaded. It uses Apex logic to identify these and then GPT to draft two alert messages: one for each escalated task (with task name and suggestion to delegate), and one summary suggestion about the team member's workload.

User notification: The project manager sits down at 9 AM and sees a notification indicator on the Companion's LWC panel in their Salesforce homepage. Opening it, they see:

1. Alert: "Task Design Homepage is 7 days overdue (John Doe). Consider reassigning or getting extra help to meet the deadline." (With a button [Reassign] next to it.)

2. Alert: "Task Update Pricing Sheet is 5 days overdue (Jane Smith). This might need your attention or delegation."

3. Suggestion: "John Doe is handling a lot (12 high-priority tasks). You might redistribute some tasks to balance the load."

User action: The manager clicks [Reassign] on the first alert. That button is wired to either open a quick action or call a Flow that asks the Companion agent for a recommendation. Perhaps the agent quickly queries the team's availability and, via GPT, suggests: "Recommend reassigning to Alex (who has capacity). Proceed?" The manager confirms, and behind the scenes the agent triggers a Flow to update the task's owner to Alex and notifies John and Alex of the change (maybe even drafting a quick Chatter post explaining the reassign).

Continuous learning: Because the manager accepted the agent's suggestion, the Companion updates the Project_Agent_Context__c record (or an internal log) noting that "Task X was delegated from John to Alex on Oct 12 based on agent suggestion." This helps the agent learn which suggestions the manager finds helpful (if the manager never accepted delegation suggestions, the agent might tone them down or try a different approach over time). It also ensures the agent won't repeatedly suggest the same action (it won't bug the manager about that task anymore).

Ongoing use: Later in the day, the manager asks the agent via the LWC chat, "What's the status of Project Alpha?" The Companion agent calls a Flow that gathers key stats (milestones completed, any late tasks, upcoming deadlines) and then pipes that into a prompt. GPT returns a friendly paragraph summary. The agent displays: "Project Alpha update: 8 of 10 tasks are completed. The final deliverable is due Friday (2 days from now). One task is slightly behind (Design Homepage, now reassigned to Alex). Overall, we're on track but keep an eye on that last task."

User feels in control: The manager reviews this and feels informed. If something looked wrong, they could ask follow-ups or check the underlying data (transparency is important – maybe the agent provides links like "View task details" next to items). Over time, the manager grows to trust that the Companion agent will catch the urgent stuff and prep them with information, reducing the manual effort they spend in project tracking and team management.

This example illustrates how building a Companion agent involves configuring a blend of declarative and programmatic pieces: defining its purpose and actions in Agent Builder, giving it memory via Salesforce data, creating a user interface for interaction, writing flows/apex for decision logic, and integrating GPT for natural language generation. Salesforce's Agentforce is designed to support this modular approach – for instance, the topics and actions we set in Agent Builder align with using Flows and Apex (Agent Builder essentially can invoke Flows, Apex, etc., as we configured). We also see how important it is to test the agent's behavior: as we build, we'd use sandbox data to simulate scenarios (e.g. a project with many overdue tasks) and ensure the agent responds appropriately and not in an overwhelming or trivial way.

Pro Tip: During development, treat your Companion agent like a new team member joining the company. Give it a clear "job description" (the instructions we configure), ensure it has only the permissions it truly needs (data access limited to relevant objects, perhaps run it under a dedicated integration user if appropriate), and maintain a performance log of its actions (you can log key events, suggestions given, etc., to a custom object or the Salesforce Event Log). This practice not only helps in debugging and improving the agent (you can review what it did and why), but also builds trust with stakeholders – you can demonstrate that the agent operates within defined bounds and there's an audit trail of its decisions.

We have now seen how to build a Companion agent and give it form. However, building the agent is only part of the challenge – we also need to consider how it learns and how we keep it from going astray. In the next section, we'll look into how Companion agents handle memory, how they improve over time, and what guardrails are needed to ensure they remain helpful and safe.

MEMORY, LEARNING, AND BOUNDARIES

One of the defining qualities of a Companion agent is that it learns and adapts over time. But as we give agents the ability to "remember" and take initiative, we must carefully manage what they remember, how they learn, and where the boundaries of their autonomy lie. In this section, we discuss best practices for Companion agent memory and learning, ways to allow user control over the agent's knowledge, and the guardrails required to keep the agent's actions appropriate and safe.

Memory: What (and how) should a Companion remember? A well-designed Companion agent will maintain a memory of interactions and user-specific context that improves its usefulness over time. This memory can include concrete event history (e.g., what actions were taken and when, like "on Oct 10, the agent alerted the user about Task X"), recurring goals or patterns (e.g., "this user typically wants a weekly summary every Friday"), and user preferences for tone or format (e.g., "user likes brief bullet-point emails" or "user always schedules meetings for 30 minutes, not 1 hour"). Storing such information enables the agent to avoid repetition (not recommending something the user already did) and to personalize future outputs (using the user's preferred style of communication). Technically, as we saw earlier, this memory might be stored in custom objects or fields associated with the user. For example, a Companion might keep a list of recent items it recommended and whether the user accepted or ignored each suggestion. Over time, analyzing this could let the agent prioritize the types of suggestions the user tends to accept. However, it's crucial to scope the memory to what is necessary and relevant. A Companion agent shouldn't indiscriminately remember every single thing (that could raise privacy issues and even degrade performance). We choose what to remember based on what will help the agent help the user. For instance, remembering a user's last 10 questions to the agent can help it avoid giving redundant answers or allow it to follow up, but storing years of conversation history might be unnecessary. Additionally, memory can be temporal – some data might be kept for a session and then cleared (ephemeral memory), whereas other data is persistent across sessions. A good practice is to periodically prune or archive the agent's memory (maybe the last quarter's worth of interaction logs is enough to keep active; older stuff could be archived or deleted). The golden rule is: remember to help, not to spy. As long as what you store serves a user-benefiting function, it's likely appropriate.

Learning and evolution: Companion agents can employ simple learning strategies to improve over time. This doesn't necessarily mean full machine learning algorithms on user behavior (though that's possible in advanced cases); it can be simpler heuristic learning. For example, the agent can learn the optimal time to present information to the user by observing when the user actually reads or clicks its suggestions. If it notices the user usually dismisses notifications during certain hours (maybe when the user is in meetings) but responds in the early morning, the agent can adjust to deliver more suggestions in the morning. Another example: the agent can learn a user's writing style by analyzing emails or documents the user has written (with permission) – then mirror that style in drafts. This might cross into sophisticated ML territory (like fine-tuning a language model on the user's past writing for tone), which is powerful but should be done carefully. Importantly, any such learning must be transparent and under control. It's good practice for the agent to explain or confirm changes in behavior. For instance, the Companion could notify the user: "I've noticed you prefer shorter summaries. I will keep my daily reports brief moving forward. Let me know if you'd like more detail." This keeps the user in the loop and part of the learning process.

Safe persistence and retrieval of memory: With data being stored for memory, we need to ensure that this is done securely. That means leveraging Salesforce's robust security model: marking fields as encrypted or protected if they contain sensitive info, and respecting field-level security and sharing rules when the agent accesses information. The agent should only retrieve data that the user themselves is allowed to see. For example, if the Companion agent tries to pull in context about an account the user doesn't have access to, it should be prevented or at least handle that gracefully ("I'm sorry, I don't have details on that account"). Additionally, if we integrate external knowledge (say the Companion calls an external API to get data), we must handle that data carefully within Salesforce (maybe don't log it if it's sensitive, or store references instead of full data if not needed). In short: all the principles of data security and privacy that apply to building any Salesforce app apply equally to building the agent's memory. One might also implement an expiration policy: certain memory should be discarded after it's no longer useful. For example, if the Companion logs every user query and the user can retrieve it, consider auto-deleting or anonymizing entries after X months to reduce data clutter and risk.

User control over memory and behavior: It's essential that the human user feels in control of their Companion agent. This includes the ability to review what the agent has "learned" or stored, to correct it if it's wrong, and to reset or clear it if desired. A practical approach is to provide a "settings" or "insights" UI (perhaps a Lightning page or a command to the agent like "show me what you know about me"). For example, the user could ask, "What do you remember about my preferences?" and the agent might reply with something like, "You prefer morning summaries and concise emails. You often ignore notifications during 3-5pm. Shall I continue to adjust to these patterns?" This gives the user a chance to confirm or correct: "Actually, I do want notifications in the afternoon if urgent." Similarly, a reset command or button is important – maybe the user can click "Reset agent" which would clear stored preferences or conversation history. This might be used if a new person takes over the role (and inherits the same Companion agent setup), or if the user feels the agent's suggestions have gone off-track and wants a fresh start. Additionally, some form of audit log should be accessible, at least to an admin or the user, to see what actions the agent took on their behalf. This could be as simple as logging key events to a custom object "Agent_Action__c" (e.g. "Agent sent email draft for Task X at 10:00 on behalf of user"). Having an audit trail builds trust – if something unexpected happens, the user or support team can check the log to understand why the agent did what it did.

On the topic of trust, Microsoft's implementation of Copilot provides a good example of user control in practice: Copilot not only adapts to a user's working style (tone, role, etc.), but also allows the user to decide what it should remember and when to reset that memory. In other words, the user can instruct the AI to forget certain conversation history or not to use certain emails as context going forward. A Companion agent should offer similar controls – perhaps a simple command like "forget that" right after an interaction could instruct the agent to not retain that piece of information. Empowering the user in this way is crucial for long-term acceptance of these agents in an enterprise setting.

Guardrails and boundaries: While a Companion agent is meant to be proactive and helpful, it must operate within clear boundaries. By design, a Companion should never exceed its authorization or perform actions that the user themselves wouldn't or shouldn't do. Some guardrails to enforce:

Role-appropriate actions only: The agent's action library (as defined in Agent Builder or code) should explicitly list what it can do. It should not have free rein to execute random Apex or make unchecked changes. For example, if our Project Companion's scope is to suggest task delegation, we wouldn't include an action to delete projects or approve budget changes – that's outside its purview. Keeping a tight scope limits mischief.

Confirmation for sensitive actions: Even if an agent has the technical ability to do something potentially impactful (say send an email to a client or reassign a major task), it's wise to require user confirmation. The Companion might draft an email, but leave it to the user to hit "Send". Or it might recommend reassigning a task, but not actually do it until the user clicks "Confirm". This human-in-the-loop approach prevents a lot of possible errors or unintended consequences. Over time, as trust grows, some users might opt-in to let the agent auto-complete certain routine actions, but that should be a conscious choice.

Avoiding fabrication and maintaining accuracy: A common issue with AI (especially generative ones) is the tendency to hallucinate or make up information that sounds plausible. In a Salesforce Companion agent, we mitigate that by grounding the agent in actual Salesforce data and defined rules as much as possible. If the agent doesn't know something, a good guardrail is for it to say "I don't have that information" rather than guessing. Also, any content coming from an LLM should ideally be checked or validated if it's going to be used for a critical purpose. For instance, if the agent uses GPT to draft an answer to a client, a guardrail might involve scanning the draft for sensitive info or overly confident statements that aren't backed by data. You can implement a simple check: ensure that any numeric data in the GPT draft matches actual data from Salesforce (to catch if the model 'invented' a number). Ensuring accuracy also means setting up boundaries like not allowing the agent to access data it shouldn't. As mentioned, the agent should respect org security settings –

which it will if it runs in the user's context or a properly permissioned context.

No overreach in tone or scope: The Companion should remain an assistant, not a boss. Its suggestions should be framed as suggestions, not commands. For example, instead of the agent automatically rescheduling all of a user's meetings because it thinks they're too busy (overreach!), it should maybe point out "You have 5 meetings this afternoon, do you want to reschedule some?" and let the user decide. It's also wise to throttle how many suggestions or alerts it gives – even if there are 100 things it could tell the user, spamming them is counterproductive. A guardrail might be a maximum of, say, 3 proactive alerts per hour unless explicitly requested. This ensures the agent's helpfulness doesn't become a distraction itself.

Finally, let's revisit the analogy of treating the Companion like a coworker. Just as a human teammate has defined responsibilities, limited access permissions, and performance evaluations, we set up our agent similarly. We gave it a "job description" (the defined pattern and goals), we ensured it only has the data access needed (perhaps via a Salesforce profile or a careful design of queries), and we keep a log (performance log) of what it's doing. Periodically, the development team or admin can review this log to spot any odd behavior – effectively a performance review for the agent. If the agent is doing something outside its scope, that's like a human employee operating out of bounds and it needs correction (which might mean adjusting instructions or fixing a bug). By instilling these practices, we treat the Companion agent as an accountable digital colleague, which fosters a safer and more reliable deployment.

Pro Tip: Don't "set and forget" your Companion agents. Continuously monitor their outputs and gather user feedback, especially early on. Encourage users to use feedback commands or buttons (like "👍 Helpful" or "👎 Off-target" on suggestions) to give the agent guidance. This feedback loop, combined with guardrails, helps the agent stay on track. In essence, manage your Companion agent as you would a new team member during their probation: check their work, coach them with clear rules, and gradually grant more autonomy as they earn trust.

Our Companion agent now has memory and safety nets to guide its evolution. We've established how it learns and how we keep it from misbehaving. Next, we will step back and look at where Companion agents fit in the broader AI ecosystem – including how other platforms implement similar ideas and the emerging standards for cross-application agents. The next section will place Companion agents in context alongside tools like OpenAgents, CrewAI, Microsoft Copilot, and others.

COMPANION AGENTS IN THE AI ECOSYSTEM

The idea of a personal "user proxy" agent isn't unique to Salesforce – it's part of a broader movement in AI towards agents that are tailored to individuals. In this section, we'll explore how similar patterns are showing up in other platforms and ecosystems, and what that means for designing Companion agents that might need to interoperate with those systems. We'll discuss open-source agent frameworks, big tech offerings like Microsoft's Copilot and Apple's proactive intelligence, Meta's push into personal assistants, and the emerging Model Context Protocol (MCP) that could allow a Companion agent's identity and context to travel with a user across applications.

OpenAgents and CrewAI – user-assigned agents in open frameworks: In the open-source world, there are frameworks such as OpenAgents and CrewAI that allow developers to build and orchestrate AI agents. While these frameworks might not use the term "Companion," they do support patterns where certain agents are dedicated to interfacing with a user. For example, CrewAI is known for enabling collaborative teams of agents with specific roles. In a CrewAI setup, you might have multiple agents working on subtasks (one for web browsing, one for code generation, etc.), and you could designate one agent as the "user liaison" – effectively playing a Companion role that communicates with the human while the others toil in the background. CrewAI emphasizes flexible delegation between agents, and you can imagine a scenario where a CrewAI "team" includes an agent that specializes in understanding the user's requests and returning answers in a personalized way. OpenAgents, on the other hand, provides out-of-the-box agents for certain tasks (like data analysis or web research) and requires coding to customize them. In an OpenAgents scenario, a developer could compose these into a personal assistant package: one agent handles looking up info, another handles performing calculations, etc., and a central agent interacts with the user. The key takeaway is that open frameworks are converging on architectures where one agent is effectively assigned to the user. It orchestrates or queries specialized agents (similar to how a Salesforce Companion might query a Sentinel or Conductor agent, which we'll discuss later), but it remains the user's point of contact. From a design perspective, if you're aware that an organization uses such frameworks alongside Salesforce, you might consider how your Companion agent could integrate or at least co-exist. For instance, if a company already has a CrewAI setup where a "Chat

Agent" answers employee questions by pulling data from various sources, your Salesforce Companion agent for that user could focus on Salesforce-specific context and possibly hand off questions it can't answer to the CrewAI system. Standards like APIs or common protocols would facilitate that.

Microsoft Copilot's user-aware productivity layer: Microsoft 365 Copilot (and related "Copilot" products in Windows, GitHub, etc.) exemplify the Companion pattern on a huge scale. Copilot is designed to accompany the user through their work in Office apps, emails, meetings, and more, providing assistance that is heavily personalized to the user's content and context. It leverages the Microsoft Graph – essentially the user's emails, files, calendar, chats – to inject personal context into its prompts. This means when you ask Copilot a question, it's not answering with generic knowledge; it's answering based on your data (assuming you have permission to that data). In enterprise terms, Microsoft has basically rolled out a Companion agent that sits across their productivity suite. For example, in Outlook, Copilot can summarize an email thread you were CC'd on, because it knows what's in your inbox. In Teams, it can remind you of what happened in a meeting you missed, because it has access to the transcript. These behaviors mirror what we aim for with a Salesforce Companion – being contextually aware of user-specific information to help them. One difference is that Microsoft's Copilot is deeply integrated into the fabric of their applications. Salesforce's Companion would live within Salesforce (and perhaps on Salesforce-integrated channels like Slack or mobile apps). But a user doesn't care about these boundaries – they just want help wherever they are. We might expect, in the near future, that Salesforce Companions and Microsoft Copilots coordinate. Imagine you're in Outlook and Copilot notices an email from a customer about a deal – Copilot might fetch Salesforce info via Graph APIs to present context. Conversely, a Salesforce Companion agent might use Microsoft's APIs to, say, draft an email response for you in Outlook. In fact, Microsoft is enabling a kind of agent interoperability by allowing developers to create custom "Copilot plugins" or even their own agents within Teams that connect to outside systems. As AI ecosystems mature, your Salesforce Companion could potentially register as one of the user's known assistants in the Microsoft ecosystem, so that when the user asks Windows Copilot a question about Salesforce, it can defer to the Salesforce Companion. It's a fascinating cross-talk scenario that leads into standards like MCP.

Apple's intelligence and proactive suggestions: Apple doesn't (as of 2025) have a single anthropomorphized "assistant agent" beyond Siri, but what they do have is a suite of proactive features that effectively act as a quiet Companion agent on Apple devices. They call this Siri's Proactive Intelligence, and it manifests as suggestions like "Leaving for home? Open Maps" or auto-suggesting a meeting based on an email. These are built on-device through machine learning, looking at signals like location, time of day, app usage patterns, etc., to predict what the user might want to do next. For example, iPhones might learn a user's daily routine and then at 5pm show a suggestion to message your spouse if you usually do that after work. This is very much in line with the Companion ethos – assist the user preemptively based on personal context. The difference is Apple's approach is largely implicit (the user doesn't converse with the agent; they just get suggestions in the UI), whereas our Salesforce Companion is more explicit (with a visible UI and interactive prompts). Nonetheless, it's easy to see how these could converge. One could imagine our Salesforce Companion agent sending data to Apple's proactive engine (with user permission) – for instance, if the user has an iOS app for Salesforce, the agent could integrate with Siri Suggestions: "You have 3 urgent cases unresolved, perhaps you should check Salesforce app now." Conversely, the Apple system might inform our agent about device context: if the user just says "Remind me later," maybe the agent could schedule to bring something up when the user is next using their laptop. As Apple pushes more into on-device AI, including possibly an AI assistant that can summarize content on screen or do multi-step tasks, a Salesforce Companion could be one of the sources that assistant taps. For example, Apple could allow third-party "knowledge domains" for its assistant – our agent might register as the domain for "Salesforce data and tasks" for that user. It's speculative, but the trend is clear: these big ecosystems are moving toward ambient, personalized assistance as a core feature.

Meta's generative agents in social and wearable platforms: Meta (Facebook) is aggressively rolling out AI personas and assistants across its products. For instance, Meta has introduced various AI chatbots with distinct "personalities" on Instagram and Messenger. More relevant to the Companion pattern is Meta AI, a general assistant they are integrating into platforms – including their new Ray-Ban Meta smart glasses. The Ray-Ban Meta glasses allow you to interact with a personalized Meta AI assistant via voice, getting answers and performing tasks hands-free. This is literally a Companion agent riding on your face, accessible anywhere. It's personalized in the sense that it can access your Facebook content or maybe your preferences (and likely will become more so over time as they connect it to your data). Meta's vision is to have an AI companion in the physical world with you – answering "What kind of plant is that?" or "Take a picture and send it to Alice" just by you asking aloud. In their demo, Meta showed the assistant on glasses doing things like real-time translation or reminding you of calendar events. This strongly parallels what our enterprise Companion does, just in a consumer life context and through AR. What does this mean for our Salesforce agents? If employees adopt such devices or Meta's AI app (they launched a Meta AI smartphone app too), there could be opportunities to integrate enterprise tasks. Meta might allow connecting workplace systems to their assistant. Perhaps a field technician wearing Meta glasses could query "Meta AI, how many open tickets do I have in Salesforce for this client?" If our Companion agent can interface through an API, Meta AI could relay the question to Salesforce's agent and then speak out the answer to the user. Also, the popularity of these tools underscores the importance of the user experience – these assistants work in very natural, conversational ways. Enterprise companions should aspire to the same level of ease (even if they operate in a more focused domain). Another angle: the sheer usage of Meta's AI shows appetite – Meta reported hundreds of millions of interactions per month with its assistant. People are getting accustomed to interacting with AI personas regularly. That means employees will increasingly expect similar convenience at work. The Salesforce Companion pattern is our way of meeting that expectation within the enterprise context.

Interoperability and the Model Context Protocol (MCP): As all these ecosystems (open-source crews, Microsoft, Apple, Meta, and others like Google's Bard or OpenAI's ChatGPT plugins) introduce personal agents, a big question emerges: Will our personal AI companions be siloed, or will they be able to work together and maintain continuity? The Model Context Protocol (MCP) is an early attempt to address this by establishing an open standard for connecting AI assistants with the data and context they need across systems. MCP essentially proposes a way for an agent to retrieve relevant context from various sources through standardized connectors – almost like giving each AI agent a universal "USB port" to plug into other software. If widely adopted, MCP could allow a Salesforce Companion agent to carry a user's core context to another environment or vice versa. For example, say a user's Companion agent in Salesforce has built up a context of the user's pending tasks and preferences. Using MCP, if that user engages with an AI assistant in a different app (maybe a Slack AI or a car voice assistant), that assistant could query the MCP server (which might aggregate the user's context from multiple systems) and retrieve the Salesforce context to inform its answer. One could even imagine a future where the user has a single persistent AI companion that transcends platforms – it might live partly on their device, partly in cloud services – using protocols like MCP to talk to whichever system is currently in use (Salesforce, Office, Slack, etc.) and acting on the user's behalf across all of them. In such a scenario, what we are building now as the "Salesforce Companion agent" might become the Salesforce-specific skillset or module of a person's broader AI companion.

From a practical perspective, what can we do today? We can design our Companion agents with interoperability in mind. That could mean using APIs and webhooks so that external systems can trigger or query the agent (with proper auth). For example, perhaps expose a secured endpoint that, when hit with a user ID and query, will return a natural language answer from the Companion (this essentially turns the Companion into an API service – with all necessary permission checks). Or if MCP matures, implement an MCP client in our agent that can accept requests from an MCP server to perform certain tasks or provide certain info. Early adoption of standards can ensure our agents aren't isolated. It's analogous to making sure your app's data can be exported or integrated easily; for AI agents, making sure they can participate in a multi-agent, multi-platform conversation will be key to long-term relevance.

In summary, the Companion pattern we're implementing in Salesforce is part of a larger wave: personalized AI agents are appearing in various forms across the tech landscape. Each platform might have its own flavor – open frameworks emphasize customizability, Microsoft focuses on work productivity, Apple on seamless device integration, Meta on ubiquitous assistants – but the core idea is the same: AI that works for you personally. For us as Salesforce designers, this means two things. First, we should leverage the familiarity users will develop with these agents: if a user is comfortable saying "Hey AI, schedule a meeting," they'll likely be comfortable asking their Salesforce Companion "Find the latest opportunity updates." We should strive for that same natural, conversational interaction style (where appropriate) and integrate with the channels users like (voice, chat, AR, etc.). Second, we should prepare our Companion agents to collaborate – whether that's collaborating with other Salesforce agents (topic of the next section) or with external ecosystem agents. The AI ecosystem is heading towards networks of specialized agents working together, rather than one monolithic AI doing everything. Salesforce Companions will be one species in that ecosystem, ideally a well-behaved one that plays nicely with others via standards like MCP and robust APIs.

Having situated Companion agents in the broader AI world, let's turn our focus back inward for the final section of this chapter: How do Companion agents interact with the other agent patterns within an enterprise? We'll explore how a Companion coordinates with Sentinels, Curators, Conductors, Supervisors, and so on – essentially the "teamwork" of agents in an Agentforce deployment.

COMPANION AND THE AGENT PATTERN NETWORK

Within an enterprise, a Companion agent rarely operates completely alone. In Salesforce's Agentforce framework, we have a spectrum of agent patterns (Sentinel, Supervisor, Conductor, Curator, Action, Coach, Presenter, etc.), each with its role. The Companion pattern is about the user-facing proxy, so naturally it often serves as the last mile between the user and the rest of the agent network. In this section, we'll examine how Companion agents can integrate and coordinate with other types of agents to deliver a seamless experience. We'll look at a few pairings and combinations: Sentinel → Companion, Curator → Companion, Supervisor + Companion, Conductor + Companion, and we'll end with a narrative example tying many of these together in a field scenario. The theme is that a Companion agent can be thought of as the front-end or spokesperson of a larger multi-agent system, translating and tailoring what the behind-the-scenes agents do into something the user can consume and act on.

Sentinel → Companion: Sentinel agents, recall, are those focused on monitoring events and detecting noteworthy conditions (they "watch" and alert). A classic use of a Sentinel is to detect anomalies or triggers like "a case that has been open > 48 hours without response" or "a temperature sensor reading above threshold". On their own, Sentinel agents might create alerts in a queue or trigger some automated action. But the Companion agent is the ideal delivery mechanism for Sentinel findings to reach a human user in a meaningful way. Essentially, the Sentinel raises a flag, and the Companion catches it and presents it to the user with context. For example, imagine a Sentinel agent that scans all incoming customer support cases for certain keywords ("urgent", "escalation") or sentiment indicators. The Sentinel finds a case that looks like a serious escalation (maybe sentiment analysis says the customer is very unhappy). Instead of just auto-creating a high priority task (which might go unnoticed for a while), the Sentinel can invoke the user's Companion agent: "Hey, surface this to the user ASAP." In implementation, that could be done via a platform event or an invocable action – the

Sentinel, upon detecting the event, calls a Companion agent's alert action with details of the case. The Companion then formats that into a user-friendly message: "Alert: A new case (12345) contains escalation keywords and high customer frustration. Please review immediately." and maybe even attaches the relevant case link or summary (the Companion might even leverage a Curator agent here to summarize the case text, see below). The Companion ensures the user actually sees the output of the Sentinel in real-time, rather than it languishing in a report or queue. As another example, suppose a Sentinel agent in a manufacturing context detects an IoT sensor anomaly (machine overheating). Instead of just logging it, it triggers the field technician's Companion agent, which then speaks into the technician's earpiece or phone: "Sensor 7 on Line B shows an overheating condition beyond threshold. This needs immediate attention." In short, Sentinel + Companion = proactive alerting system where Sentinel is the detector and Companion is the messenger. This pairing prevents alert fatigue, too, because the Companion, being user-aware, can prioritize or throttle alerts from multiple Sentinels if needed (e.g., the Companion can consolidate 5 low-level alerts into a single summary for the user instead of spamming 5 separate notifications).

Curator → Companion: Curator agents are those that gather, filter, or summarize information – they "curate" content for usefulness. For instance, a Curator might compile a daily summary of key metrics or aggregate news articles about a company. When a Curator has done its job, the question is: who or what consumes that curated output? Often, the answer is a human needs to see the summary or synthesized information. The Companion agent is perfect for delivering a summary tailored for individual consumption. For example, say there's a Curator agent that each evening compiles updates across all projects in a department (like a brief status snippet from each project). That summary could be quite extensive in raw form. The Companion can take that and trim it down to what this particular user cares about. If the user is only actively involved in two of those projects, the Companion might highlight those and collapse the rest. Or it could learn from what the user tends to click on and prioritize similar info. Essentially, the Companion personalizes curated content. Technically, how does this look? Perhaps the Curator writes its daily summary to a record (or generates a PDF or email draft). The Companion agent has an action (or is triggered) when a new curated summary is available. It then might use a Presenter pattern logic (which is about formatting output optimally) to tailor the summary. For instance, it might break it into a bulleted list in the user's dashboard, or if the user is on mobile, it might only send the top 3 bullet points via a notification. Another scenario: a Curator agent might gather all relevant knowledge base articles when a user opens a case, essentially curating solutions. Instead of dumping ten article links, the Companion could step in and say, "I see you're working on case 1001 about Login Issues. Here are two knowledge articles that seem most relevant," picking the top two from the Curator's list based on context (maybe using what it knows about the user's technical skill to choose articles of appropriate depth). So, Curator provides the raw material, Companion personalizes and delivers it in context. This increases the likelihood that the curated info is actually useful to the user, because it's presented at the right time, in the right format, with the right emphasis.

Supervisor + Companion: The Supervisor pattern refers to agents that review or double-check work (for quality, compliance, or policy adherence). A Supervisor agent might, for example, scan an expense report for policy violations or review an AI-generated email draft for tone and accuracy. When a Supervisor agent finds an issue or suggests a correction, how do we loop the user into that process smoothly? Enter the Companion agent as a facilitator of a human-in-the-loop review cycle. One way to view it: the Companion and Supervisor can act in tandem like a pair of editors – the Companion helps the user create a draft, the Supervisor checks it, then the Companion conveys the needed fixes back to the user for finalization. For instance, let's say our Companion agent helped a manager draft a response to a customer using GPT. Before sending it out, a Supervisor agent (with a compliance focus) reviews the draft and flags that it accidentally included a non-public piece of info (maybe the draft mentioned an upcoming product release date that's not yet public, which is against policy). The Supervisor agent would generate an alert or suggested edit: "Remove the reference to the product release date as it's not public." The Companion can catch that feedback (since it's tied into the workflow of drafting the email) and present it to the user: "Supervisor Suggestion: Please remove confidential info (product release date) from your message before sending." If needed, the Companion can even help do the refinement (maybe offering to automatically remove that sentence if the user clicks "Apply suggestion"). Here, the Companion ensures the user is aware of the Supervisor's input in a friendly, guided way, and helps implement it. Another scenario is quality control: maybe the Companion drafts a sales proposal and a Supervisor agent (with an AI focusing on factual accuracy) reviews it and finds an error in a pricing table. The Supervisor agent could either fix it or annotate it. The Companion then notifies the user, "I've adjusted the pricing in the proposal based on latest approved figures (per our Supervisor check). Please review the final version." This triad – Companion drafting/presenting, Supervisor checking – can significantly boost trust because the user knows there's a safety net on the agent's output. The Companion acts as the liaison: it takes the Supervisor's possibly technical or stern feedback and translates it into a polite recommendation the user can act on. Without a Companion, a Supervisor agent might simply block an action or mark something as rejected without context. With the Companion in the loop, the user gets a conversational explanation and possibly assistance in resolving the issue. In essence, Supervisor + Companion yields high-quality outcomes with user awareness and control.

Conductor + Companion: The Conductor pattern involves orchestrating multi-step processes and coordinating multiple agents or systems to accomplish a complex task. Think of a Conductor agent as the project manager of the AI world – it doesn't directly do each task, but it delegates and composes tasks to achieve an end goal. Now, a Conductor might operate largely behind the scenes. For example, a Conductor agent could handle a multi-step process like "When a new hire joins, create accounts in system A, B, and C, set up a welcome email, and schedule orientation." This might involve multiple action agents or APIs. Once the Conductor has done its job, however, it's often the case that a human (like an HR manager or the new hire's manager) should be informed or might need to take a final step. This is where the Companion comes in to tailor the orchestration outcome for a specific user. Using that onboarding example: The Conductor agent orchestrates creation of accounts and scheduling of training. The Companion agent for the hiring manager could then provide a personalized summary: "New hire onboarding is 75% complete: network account created, email set up, orientation scheduled for Monday. Pending: assign a buddy (please choose a buddy) and building access card (awaiting facilities)." This summary is pulling from various outputs of the Conductor's actions and putting it into the hiring manager's perspective. Perhaps it even presents it as a checklist in the manager's Companion UI, where the manager can click "Assign Buddy" and that triggers another part of the Conductor or a separate Action agent. Without the Companion, the manager might have to go to three different systems to verify these things are done, or the Conductor would send multiple notifications that are not consolidated. The Companion gives a coherent interface for multi-agent outcomes. Another case: imagine a Conductor orchestrates a complex customer order fulfillment (checking inventory via one agent, scheduling delivery via another, updating billing via another). The user – say a sales rep – doesn't need or want to see all those intermediate steps in detail, but they do want to know the end result or if any exceptions occurred. The Companion can receive a final report from the Conductor and then tell the sales rep, for example, "Order 1001 for customer ABC is confirmed and scheduled for delivery on 20th Oct. [Details]" or if something went wrong in the orchestration: "Order 1001 processing hit a snag: the warehouse is out of stock for Item X. I've flagged this to procurement (Conductor handled alternate actions). You may want to inform the customer of a slight delay." The Companion thus humanizes the Conductor's automated processes, informing the user in plain language and highlighting if there's anything the user needs to do. In a sense, the Companion serves as the status dashboard and exception handler for orchestrations that otherwise run in the background. This ensures that automation doesn't happen in a black box – the relevant user is kept in the loop via their proxy agent.

To cement these ideas, let's walk through a visual example that was hinted in the outline: a field service rep's Companion interacting with Sentinel and Conductor agents to manage the user's schedule.

Scenario: A field service rep (we'll call him Alex) is out on the road servicing customer sites. He has a Companion agent on his mobile device (maybe through the Salesforce Field Service mobile app with an AI assistant). In the background, a Sentinel agent is monitoring various data streams – say urgent customer service cases that come in, as well as IoT alerts from devices in the field. Meanwhile, a Conductor agent in the operations center orchestrates scheduling logistics – if a new urgent job comes in, it tries to slot it into the right field rep's route by coordinating with the scheduling system.

Step 1 (Sentinel triggers): At 10 AM, an important customer ("Acme Corp") reports a critical outage on their equipment. A case is created and flagged urgent. A Sentinel agent detects this and identifies it as something requiring field service today. It sends an alert event to the system: "Urgent field task needed for Acme Corp, location X, estimated 1-hour fix, must happen by EOD."

Step 2 (Conductor orchestrates): The Conductor agent receives this and kicks into gear: it checks the locations and schedules of all field reps. It finds that Alex (our rep) is the closest and can potentially squeeze this in if his current 4 PM appointment is moved slightly later. The Conductor coordinates: it contacts the scheduling system (perhaps via API or an Action agent) to tentatively move Alex's 4 PM to 5 PM. It also liaises with another internal system to prepare the replacement part needed for the Acme fix and arrange for pick-up at a nearby depot.

Step 3 (Companion updates user): Now it's 10:15 AM and Alex just finished a job. His Companion agent pops up a notification (or voice alert through his smart earpiece): "Update: A new urgent job for Acme Corp has been added to your schedule today. I've moved your 4 PM appointment to 5 PM to accommodate this. The urgent job is at Location X and requires part #123 (ready for pickup at Depot 7). Your updated route is in your calendar." In a single update, the Companion combined info from the Conductor (schedule change, part pickup) and the Sentinel's alert content (the urgency and location), and delivered it in a digestible form. Alex can tap to see details or even converse: "Why was this added?" and the Companion can explain, "Acme Corp reported a critical outage. You are the nearest qualified technician. We didn't want to leave it unattended. Your manager approved the schedule change."

During execution: As Alex drives, the Companion might give a reminder when approaching Depot 7: "Arriving at Depot 7 in 1 mile. Don't forget to pick up part #123 for Acme job." (This could be triggered by geolocation – a Sentinel of another kind, or logic in the Companion reacting to calendar route info.) Alex services the Acme site. After completion, he notes in the app that the job is done at 3:30 PM.

Wrap-up (Supervisor/Curator involvement): Suppose a Supervisor agent or QA process checks Alex's work log and everything is fine, or maybe a Curator compiles a summary of his day. At day's end, Alex's Companion might say: "All done! Today you completed 5 jobs (1 was added emergency – great work handling that). All customers reported satisfaction. Drive safe home!" This final message might be pulling from both the Conductor (which tracked that an emergency was done) and maybe a feedback Sentinel that noticed customer survey responses, etc.

In this story, multiple agents (Sentinel, Conductor, maybe Supervisor for QA) worked in concert, but Alex primarily interacted with one interface – his Companion agent. The Companion took care of letting him know what the other agents decided, getting his acknowledgment or additional input if needed (if he could not accept the schedule change, he could tell the Companion "I can't do that" and the Companion would relay to Conductor to find plan B). It managed the human interface to a swarm of automated decisions, ensuring Alex felt informed and in control, even though much of the heavy lifting was automated behind the scenes. Visually, one could draw a swimlane diagram: Sentinel and Conductor in their lanes automating detection and orchestration; the Companion in the user's lane receiving triggers from them and interacting with Alex; Alex's actions (acknowledging, doing work) feeding back (through the Companion or directly through system updates) to the Conductor and other agents. Such a diagram would show arrows from Sentinel to Companion ("New alert"), Conductor to Companion ("Schedule updated"), and Companion to Alex ("notified user"), as well as Alex to Companion ("user confirms"), and then Companion back to Conductor ("user confirmed schedule change"). It illustrates a harmonious loop of agent-agent and agent-user interactions.

To conclude, in an enterprise with multiple AI agents deployed, the Companion agent often serves as the bridge between human and AI network. It listens to other agents (like Sentinel, Curator, Conductor) and translates their outputs into human-centric messages; it also voices the human's intentions or decisions back to those agents or initiates further actions (like telling the Conductor "user can't do task, find another resource"). By designing clear interaction protocols between Companion and other agent types (much like defining APIs or events between software modules), we ensure that the multi-agent system operates as a cohesive whole rather than isolated silos. Ultimately, the user should feel like they have one unified AI assistant that can tap into various specialized intelligences as needed – which is achieved by these agents working together behind the scenes. The Companion pattern is what makes the whole system feel unified to the user, by being their consistent point of contact across all the smart automation happening in the background.

SUMMARY

In this chapter, we introduced the Companion pattern – AI agents that act as personalized proxies for individual users. Unlike task-specific bots or orchestrator agents that work on system processes, Companion agents are user-centered. They learn a person's preferences and context, maintain continuity across sessions, and provide timely, tailored assistance in the user's daily workflow. We explored why these user proxy agents matter: they help prevent information overload, reduce context-switching penalties, and ensure that the outputs of other AI and automation processes are delivered in a human-friendly way to the right person at the right time.

We began by defining the Companion's role and anatomy, noting key features like memory, contextual awareness, and adaptive responses. We saw that a successful Companion agent remembers past interactions (so it can build on them), watches what the user is currently doing (so it can be relevant), and continuously adapts its help to fit the user's role and behavior. We also emphasized designing fallback behaviors – ensuring the agent remains helpful even if it has sparse data – which keeps user trust. Next, we discussed when to deploy the Companion pattern. It shines in complex, interrupt-driven roles (a product manager juggling tasks, a salesperson managing many leads), in scenarios where personalization greatly improves outcomes (like tailoring a message's tone to a client), and in environments where being proactive (with reminders or micro-suggestions) can prevent issues. We provided cross-functional examples, from HR to IT to Finance, illustrating how a Companion agent can be tuned to different domains while following the same core principles. Each example reinforced that the Companion acts as a smart assistant – handling routine observations and empowering the human to focus on higher-level work.

We then dove into building a Companion agent on Salesforce. Using the Agentforce toolkit, we saw how to define the agent's persona and allowed actions in Agent Builder, store its memory and preferences in custom metadata/objects, create a user-facing interface via LWC, implement logic with Flows and Invocable Apex, and incorporate Einstein GPT for natural language generation. The step-by-step walkthrough (framed around a Project Manager's Companion agent) demonstrated how these pieces come together: for instance, how an Invocable Apex method can detect overdue tasks, how the agent could prompt the user to delegate, and how GPT can help draft the actual messages. Along the way, we stressed the importance of governance – giving the agent only the permissions it needs and logging its actions ("performance log") so that the team can monitor and refine its behavior. The "Pro Tip" of treating the agent like a new team member encapsulates this: give it clear duties, limit its authority appropriately, and track its performance.

We also addressed memory, learning, and boundaries for Companion agents. The agent should definitely learn from its interactions (e.g. what suggestions a user ignores vs. uses), but this must be done transparently and with user control. We described providing users with insight into the agent's memory ("Here's what I've learned about you – is this correct?") and the ability to reset or adjust it. This ensures the user remains in control of their digital proxy, which is vital for trust and compliance. We highlighted guardrails: a Companion agent should not fabricate information or take actions without approval if those actions carry risk. It should stay within its lane of helping the user, not, say, changing system settings or sending communications on its own without sign-off (unless explicitly allowed). By implementing confirmations for significant actions and using safety checks (like Supervisor pattern agents or policy checks) on the Companion's outputs, we create a trustworthy agent that augments the user rather than becoming a loose cannon. The chapter's examples, including how Microsoft's Copilot allows memory resets, reinforced that major industry players are setting precedents for user control that enterprise agents should follow.

Crucially, we placed Companion agents in the context of the broader AI ecosystem. We compared them to analogs like open-source multi-agent frameworks (OpenAgents, CrewAI) and other big-tech offerings (Microsoft 365 Copilot, Apple's proactive Siri suggestions, Meta's AI assistant on smart glasses). This illustrated that Salesforce's Companion pattern is part of a larger trend: AI helpers that are personalized and context-aware are becoming standard. We discussed emerging standards like the Model Context Protocol (MCP) which could allow a user's Companion agent to share context with other agents across platforms – hinting that future enterprise agents might need to interoperate with personal assistants in other apps. The key message: while our focus is on Salesforce, we design with an eye to interoperability and user expectations shaped by these other experiences. In practice, that might mean enabling our Companion to receive or send information to, say, a Microsoft Teams bot or a Slack AI feature, ensuring the user's experience is cohesive across tools.

Finally, we explored how Companion agents coordinate with other agent patterns within the Salesforce/Agentforce environment. Through examples like Sentinel → Companion (for alerting), Curator → Companion (for delivering summaries), Supervisor + Companion (for a check-and-refine loop), and Conductor + Companion (for communicating orchestrated outcomes to users), we saw that the Companion often serves as the front-end for a whole network of backend AI processes. In the field service scenario, for instance, a Companion worked hand-in-hand with Sentinel and Conductor agents to reprioritize a technician's day – a real demonstration of multi-agent synergy with the Companion as the user's single point of contact. This modular, pattern-driven design means our AI system is scalable and maintainable: each agent has a clear role, and the Companion brings it all together for the human.

In summary, Companion agents are the personable, user-facing side of enterprise AI. They operate on the principle that even in an age of automation, the user's experience and context matter immensely. By acting as personalized proxies, they ensure that AI augments each individual's abilities in a way that feels intuitive and supportive, rather than overwhelming or impersonal. We've learned how to design them to be helpful, not intrusive – guiding users with timely assistance, learning and evolving responsibly, and respecting both user autonomy and organizational policies. When deployed effectively, Companion agents can measurably boost productivity, consistency, and user satisfaction across many roles in a company. They become, in essence, digital team-mates that individuals come to rely on daily.

As we move to the next chapter, we'll shift focus from the personalization aspect to the presentation aspect of agent outputs. The Presenter pattern (the topic of Chapter 6) deals with how AI agents communicate information to humans in the most clear, context-aware, and trust-building way. If Companion agents and others produce results or decisions, Presenter agents ensure those results are delivered in forms that humans can easily understand and act upon. In other words, if the Companion is what we present to a user (a friendly proxy), the Presenter is about how we present any agent's output (the format, tone, and medium). Together, these patterns – Companion and Presenter – form the human-interface layer of our agent ecosystem. So next up, we'll dive into the Presenter pattern and learn how to make all these AI-driven insights and actions not only personalized (thanks to the Companion) but also usable and trustworthy to the end user, which is the final step in ensuring AI agents truly empower people. (Stay tuned for Chapter 6: The Presenter Pattern, where we tackle that challenge of optimal AI-to-human communication.)

6

THE PRESENTER PATTERN (UX OPTIMIZATION AGENT)

In the complex choreography of enterprise AI, Presenter agents play a critical role: translating raw AI output into clear, contextual, and trustworthy communication for the end user. No matter how advanced an AI system's predictions or recommendations are, if the recipient can't understand or trust the output – or doesn't know what to do next – then the agent has failed. A Presenter agent takes the outputs of other agents or models and turns them into information that makes sense to the audience. It is the last-mile translator between AI logic and human understanding. Presenter agents form the UX layer of AI systems, ensuring that complex analyses become simple, actionable insights.

This pattern is essential for user adoption, clarity, and action. People ignore what they don't understand and mistrust what feels like a black box. Presenter agents bridge this gap so users of varied roles and skill levels can readily absorb AI-driven outcomes. When a Presenter agent does its job well, complex analysis turns into simple, actionable insight. This is especially important in high-stakes or high-volume environments. A front-line service rep might get an explanation in plain language during a customer call, whereas an executive might see a single graphic with key takeaways. Presenter agents don't change the underlying facts – they shape how those facts are communicated to best fit the situation and the audience.

It helps to contrast this with the Companion pattern from the previous chapter. Companion agents personalize assistance around an individual, focusing on what information a user needs. Presenter agents focus on how to deliver information so it's clear and credible. The same raw data may be presented very differently depending on who it's for, through which channel (screen, voice, wearable), and even what the user is doing at that moment. For example, an AI-generated system health metric might appear as a simple colored icon with a one-line caption for an executive, but as a detailed trend graph with notes for an engineer. The information is the same; the packaging changes with context. If a user is at a desk, a Presenter might show a subtle on-screen notification or email summary. If the user is on the go, the Presenter might send a push notification with a brief voice alert or a haptic buzz on a smartwatch to ensure the message gets through.

Consider a few scenarios:

- Field technician: Wearing augmented-reality glasses, a technician sees color-coded work order highlights floating in view instead of a text list. The Presenter agent formats job updates into a visual overlay – green for normal metrics, red for alarms – so the tech can grasp the situation at a glance, hands-free.
- Compliance manager: When a new regulation update needs attention, the manager's AI assistant reads out a one-sentence alert ("Policy XYZ changes next week"). The Presenter agent distills the bulletin to its key point and delivers it via a quick voice note, avoiding a lengthy memo.
- Visually impaired analyst: For a blind user, a Presenter agent outputs urgent issues as a distinct vibration pattern on a smart band along with a short audio summary. The vibrations signal urgency, and the speech provides details, ensuring critical updates aren't missed.
- Inventory supervisor: A smartwatch not only buzzes but also releases a subtle scent when inventory falls below a threshold. This multi-sensory notification – a special buzz pattern plus a scent cue – is orchestrated by a Presenter agent to make the alert unignorable during a busy day.

These examples highlight the mission of Presenter agents: adapt the format, tone, and channel of information so it truly reaches the recipient. Whether through visual cues, sound, touch, or even smell, the Presenter chooses the medium and style that will be most effective and context-appropriate. Salesforce's platform provides tools to build this adaptive layer. Flow Screens can display dynamic text and graphics in Salesforce apps or processes. Lightning

Web Components (LWCs) let developers create custom UI elements – for example, a component to show a risk score with colored badges or a progress bar. Invocable Apex methods can transform raw data into human-friendly messages (and be invoked from Flows whenever a polished output is needed). On the AI side, Einstein GPT (Salesforce's generative AI) can produce fluent summaries or explanations tailored to a user's reading level or preferred tone. Using custom metadata and context, a Presenter agent can decide on wording (formal vs. casual), language, or modality (text vs. speech) appropriate for each audience.

In the sections that follow, we'll break down the anatomy of a Presenter agent, discuss when to apply this pattern, and walk through how to design and build one with Salesforce's Agentforce toolkit. Let's start with the anatomy of a Presenter agent – its lifecycle, inputs, outputs, and core skills – to see how it turns raw outputs into clear communication.

ANATOMY OF A PRESENTER AGENT

What exactly does a Presenter agent do under the hood? At its core, a Presenter agent has a lifecycle with four stages: Collect → Format → Frame → Deliver. In the Collect phase, the Presenter gathers the raw material it needs to communicate. This often means pulling together outputs from other agents or systems – for example, ingesting a risk score and recommendation generated by a Conductor agent, a summary produced by a Curator agent, an alert from a Sentinel agent, or even a draft explanation written by a Supervisor (oversight) agent. The Presenter aggregates all relevant pieces of information and the context around them. Next comes Format, where the agent decides on the structural layout of the message: should this information be a bullet list, a chart, a highlighted sentence, an audio alert? Here the Presenter applies templates or formatting rules to convert raw data into a chosen structure or visual. Then in the Frame stage, the Presenter agent adjusts wording and emphasis to make the output clear and meaningful. This might involve adding a short intro sentence to give context ("Summary of last quarter's sales performance:"), choosing a polite or urgent tone, or including explanatory labels (like "High Priority" tags) based on the content. Framing is about providing the right context, tone, and nuance so that the user immediately understands the significance. Finally, in the Deliver phase, the Presenter sends out the formatted, framed result through the appropriate channel or interface. That could mean rendering a component in the Salesforce UI, pushing a notification to a mobile app, posting a message in Slack, or speaking through a voice interface – whatever delivery method suits the user's environment.

Because Presenter agents sit at the end of the processing pipeline, they typically consume inputs from other agents. They don't generate new raw insights from scratch; instead, they take the outputs of Sentinel, Curator, Conductor, Supervisor, and others and polish them for presentation. For example, a Presenter might receive a JSON payload of analytics results from a Conductor Orchestrator agent, along with a short summary from a Curator agent. It then merges those into a human-readable report. Or it might take a Sentinel's simple "threshold exceeded" event and combine it with contextual data (what threshold, by how much, why it matters) to construct a meaningful alert for the user. This means a Presenter agent is often the last link in an AI chain – it needs to interface with many types of upstream inputs and make sense of whatever it's given.

The output channels available to Presenter agents are diverse. Unlike a traditional single-mode app, a Presenter agent can decide to deliver information in any modality that the situation calls for. Common channels include:

- In-app UI components: e.g. updating a Salesforce Lightning dashboard card, a record page component, or a pop-up on a console screen with the formatted info.
- Messaging and notifications: e.g. sending an email summary, a Slack or Microsoft Teams message, or a push notification via the Salesforce mobile app.
- Voice or audio: e.g. using text-to-speech to read out an alert on a smart speaker or phone call, or playing a notification sound.
- Wearables and IoT: e.g. triggering a smartwatch notification (vibration + on-screen text), an AR headset highlight, or another connected device signal.
- Other modalities: in experimental setups, possibly outputting to things like a braille display or even triggering a scent or ambient light change for an alert.

No matter the channel, the goal is the same: deliver the content in the manner most likely to grab the user's attention and convey meaning in that context.

Given this role, Presenter agents must develop several core skills:

- Formatting complexity into simplicity: They excel at distilling complicated, cluttered outputs into concise, easy-to-digest forms. For instance, if given a 10-paragraph technical analysis, a Presenter agent might output a three-bullet summary or a simple chart highlighting the key points.
- Adapting tone and clarity to the user: They adjust language and detail based on the audience's role and preferences. The agent might use different phrasing when addressing an engineer ("CPU utilization exceeded 85% for 5 minutes") versus a non-technical manager ("The system was under heavy load briefly, but is stable now"). This includes handling jargon, reading level, and even cultural tone differences appropriately.
- Enhancing interpretability of AI outputs: Often Presenter agents have to take the sometimes uncertain or inscrutable outputs from AI models (like an LLM that says "The pattern is likely significant") and make them clearer. A Presenter might add explanatory context ("likely significant – confidence about 80%") or convert a raw probability into a more intuitive statement ("high confidence"). They act as an editor, smoothing out any ambiguity or rough edges left by the generative AI.
- Delivering outputs in multimodal formats: Presenters are comfortable mixing text, visuals, and other media. For example, an agent could present a performance report as a combination of an infographic (rendered via LWC) alongside a textual bullet list summary generated by GPT. Or it might accompany an on-screen alert with an audible chime and a vibration, covering multiple senses.

To enable these skills, Salesforce's Agentforce toolkit provides a range of supportive tools. Agent Builder allows architects to define an agent's persona and capabilities – for a Presenter agent, this means you can encapsulate all its formatting and delivery rules in one place, separate from the business logic. Flow Screens (part of Salesforce Flow) let you design guided screen interactions; a Presenter agent can use these to insert rich UI steps into a workflow (for example, a flow screen that shows an AI-generated recommendation with approval buttons). Lightning Web Components (LWCs) allow for custom, reusable UI elements – a Presenter might leverage an LWC to visualize data (like a gauge, chart, or dynamic text block) in a way that standard components cannot. When logic needs to get more advanced, Invocable Apex can be written to perform custom formatting or decision-making about how to present data. For instance, an Apex invocable method could take a complex object and return a short summary string or a set of display fields; the Presenter agent calls this as a step before output. And of course, Einstein GPT (Salesforce's generative AI) can be used by Presenter agents for natural language generation tasks – such as rewriting a block of text in simpler language, generating a friendly explanation for a prediction, or translating an output into another language for a multilingual audience. By combining these tools, developers can build Presenter agents that dynamically choose presentation strategies.

Pro tip: A good Presenter agent never just regurgitates raw data or the exact text it was given. Avoid simply repeating what the system already knows or what earlier agents produced verbatim. Instead, reframe it in a way that's immediately useful to the end user – that's what unlocks user understanding and confidence in the AI. In practice, this means adding that bit of context, choosing a clearer phrase, or highlighting the one anomaly that matters rather than showing a blur of numbers.

Now that we've dissected the makeup of a Presenter agent and its toolkit, we can turn to a strategic question: when should you use the Presenter pattern?

WHEN TO USE THE PRESENTER PATTERN

Not every AI agent needs a dedicated Presenter. Many simple automations can get by with direct outputs (like a field being updated or a basic notification). The Presenter pattern shines in scenarios where how information is delivered can make or break its usefulness. Consider using a Presenter agent in situations like these:

- When outputs require human validation or decision-making: If the AI's output isn't an end in itself but something a person must review or act on (approve a recommendation, interpret an insight), a Presenter agent helps ensure the person understands exactly what the AI is saying and feels confident making that choice.
- When insights need to stand out amid noise: In data-dense environments (dashboards with dozens of metrics, or logs full of events), a Presenter can highlight the truly significant pieces. It can surface the needle in the haystack – for example, flagging "the one anomaly among thousands of log lines" in red with a succinct note, so a user doesn't overlook it.

- When users are non-technical or multitasking: If the audience might struggle with technical jargon or can't devote full attention, Presenter agents become crucial. They translate complex terms into plain language, and they format information for quick absorption. Picture a busy call center agent who needs an AI summary of customer sentiment: the Presenter provides it as a simple emoji and one-liner rather than a verbose analysis, because the agent is simultaneously talking and clicking through screens.
- When decisions involve risk, ambiguity, or emotion: In cases like medical advice, legal risk assessment, or critical business strategy, how the information is communicated can influence whether it's trusted or understood correctly. Presenter agents can add necessary disclaimers ("Prediction – 70% confidence"), use a reassuring tone for sensitive topics, or otherwise frame outputs to respect the stakes. This reduces the chance of misinterpretation in high-impact scenarios.
- When the delivery context varies widely: If the same AI outcome might be delivered in a boardroom, on a factory floor, or to a phone lock screen, a Presenter ensures it's packaged appropriately for each. It will choose the right format for a slide deck versus a smartwatch ping, or for a user who's hands-free driving versus a user who's at a desk. Consistency of core message, delivered through the appropriate channel, is key.

In essence, the Presenter pattern is your go-to when raw AI output needs an extra layer of curation and presentation before it's ready for humans. It's especially common to pair Presenter agents with other patterns that produce complex or large outputs – for instance, after a Conductor orchestrates a multi-step process, a Presenter might disseminate a tailored summary of the results to stakeholders.

To help decide between using a Companion agent, a Presenter agent, or both, it's useful to consider the primary needs of your use case. The list below provides a decision framework:

Personalized user assistance over time

- **Companion pattern?:** Yes – focuses on user context, continuity, and ongoing support.
- **Presenter pattern?:** No – not primarily concerned with formatting or distilling outputs.

- **Notes:** An executive's daily AI assistant benefits most from a Companion, with presentation handled implicitly within the interaction context.

Complex output that needs simplification

- **Companion pattern?:** No – a companion alone does not clarify or restructure complex content.
- **Presenter pattern?:** Yes – a core use case for the Presenter pattern.
- **Notes:** Large analytics reports or machine learning outputs should be distilled and explained by a Presenter to ensure clarity and usability.

Non-technical or busy end users

- **Companion pattern?:** Maybe – a Companion can proactively filter and surface relevant information.
- **Presenter pattern?:** Yes – essential for translating outputs into accessible language or visuals.
- **Notes:** A field worker may rely on a Companion to retrieve information and a Presenter to convey it in a simple, consumable form.

High-stakes decision requiring user trust

- **Companion pattern?:** Maybe – a Companion can provide timely prompts or reminders.
- **Presenter pattern?:** Yes – critical for clear framing and transparent presentation of facts.
- **Notes:** In compliance approvals, a Presenter structures the facts clearly while a Companion nudges the user at the appropriate moment.

One-off AI feature embedded in an application

- **Companion pattern?:** No – a persistent personal agent is unnecessary.
- **Presenter pattern?:** Yes – ideal for presenting the feature's output cleanly.

- **Notes:** An auto-summarize button in a CRM can use a Presenter to generate a polished summary without requiring a Companion.

In summary, use Companion agents when the challenge is guiding or helping a specific user through varying tasks over time. Use Presenter agents when the challenge is making an AI's output understandable and actionable for any user who needs to consume it. And in many cases, the two patterns complement each other – a Companion agent might internally call on Presenter-style logic to format its responses, or you might design a solution where a user's personal Companion agent fetches results and then hands them off to a Presenter agent for the polished output.

One area where Presenter agents are especially important is regulated or high-trust environments. In industries like healthcare, finance, or government, simply showing an AI's raw recommendation may not fly – users need clear explanations, provenance of data, and appropriately cautious language. A Presenter agent can incorporate these elements (like citing sources of data in the output, or using carefully worded statements) to build the necessary trust. In high-trust scenarios, this pattern isn't just nice-to-have; it becomes essential to meet compliance and user acceptance criteria.

Having considered when to deploy Presenter agents, let's explore some concrete examples. In the next section, we'll look at use cases across various departments and how Presenter agents add value in each.

CROSS-FUNCTIONAL USE CASES FOR PRESENTER AGENTS

Presenter agents can add value in virtually every domain of an organization. Below are several hypothetical use cases across different departments, illustrating how a Presenter pattern might be applied in each:

HR – Feedback Themes

- **Agent input (from AI/agent):** Curator agent's summary of anonymous employee feedback data.
- **Presenter output:** Consolidated themes report for HR leadership, with tone adjusted for the intended audience.
- **Channel or medium:** Executive dashboard and email briefing.
- **Tools used:** Einstein GPT for summarization; Lightning Web Components for charts and visuals.

Finance – Forecast Anomaly

- **Agent input (from AI/agent):** Forecasting model output highlighting an anomaly, such as an unexpected revenue dip.
- **Presenter output:** Executive-ready talking points explaining the anomaly, drivers, and potential implications.
- **Channel or medium:** Email to executives and a slide-deck snippet for leadership reviews.
- **Tools used:** Apex-based formatting logic; Einstein GPT for narrative explanation.

Legal – Case Briefing

- **Agent input (from AI/agent):** Auto-generated case notes produced by a Curator summarizing legal documents.
- **Presenter output:** One-page briefing or escalation report with key risks and decisions highlighted.
- **Channel or medium:** Internal legal portal page and downloadable PDF report.
- **Tools used:** Salesforce Flow for a guided briefing screen; GPT for simplification and summarization.

Field Service – Diagnostics

- **Agent input (from AI/agent):** Sentinel alert containing equipment diagnostics and error codes.
- **Presenter output:** Tiered recommendations distinguishing immediate fixes from scheduled maintenance, supported by visuals.
- **Channel or medium:** Technician mobile app using notifications or AR overlays, with optional voice readout.
- **Tools used:** Lightning Web Components for AR or mobile cards; invocable Apex for logic; text-to-speech services.

Supply Chain – Risk Alert

- **Agent input (from AI/agent):** Conductor agent output aggregating delivery delay risks such as weather or supplier disruptions.
- **Presenter output:** Interactive map showing risk zones with a concise summary for warehouse and operations leads.
- **Channel or medium:** Operations dashboard map with push alerts.

- **Tools used:** Lightning Web Components for map visualization; Einstein GPT for summary text generation.

Each scenario shows the Presenter pattern tailoring AI outputs to specific needs. In HR, a Presenter agent takes aggregated sentiment data and frames it for leadership – perhaps softening the tone or anonymizing examples – so leaders get actionable themes rather than raw complaints.

In Finance, the Presenter turns a statistical anomaly into a set of plain-English talking points that a CFO can use in a meeting, complete with a chart generated from Salesforce data and a succinct explanation generated by GPT.

In Legal, a Presenter can condense a lengthy case file into a brief, highlighting risk areas in a format that busy attorneys or executives can digest at a glance.

For Field Service, the Presenter agent bridges IoT analytics and the technician: it visualizes diagnostics on an AR display or mobile screen and also provides a spoken summary if the tech is working hands-free – ensuring the critical info isn't missed on the job.

In Supply Chain, the Presenter combines geospatial data and narrative: warehouse leads see a live map of shipments, with red markers where delays are likely, and a GPT-crafted summary that calls out "Storm-related delays expected for Routes A and B, consider re-routing." The content is the same data from the AI predictions, but each Presenter delivers it in the language and format of the end user.

Notice the mix of Salesforce tools and AI components used: Lightning Web Components enable rich visual context (charts, maps, overlays), while Einstein GPT or similar LLM services provide fluent natural language summaries. Often, a Flow or Apex component coordinates these pieces – for example, invoking a GPT prompt to generate the explanation text, then embedding that text in a formatted LWC or screen. The Presenter agent pattern encourages this separation of concerns: let the AI models do what they do best (analysis, prediction, generation), and have the Presenter orchestrate the final mile by composing the outputs into an intuitive user experience.

By exploring these varied use cases, we see a common thread: Presenter agents translate and tailor AI outputs so that each stakeholder – whether an HR executive, a finance leader, a lawyer, a field technician, or an operations manager – gets the information in the way they can best understand and act on it. Next, we'll shift from what a Presenter does to how you can build one on Salesforce's platform.

BUILDING A PRESENTER AGENT IN AGENTFORCE

Designing and implementing a Presenter agent involves weaving together Salesforce's declarative tools and custom code in a thoughtful way. A key principle is separation of concerns: keep the presentation logic (how to format and deliver information) separate from the core business logic that produces the information. Salesforce's Agent Builder (a conceptual toolkit for defining AI-driven agents on the platform) helps enforce this separation. When you create a Presenter agent with Agent Builder, you primarily configure:

- Inputs it will receive (for example, the data structures or events coming from other agents like Curator or Sentinel).
- Presentation rules or persona (e.g. "This agent delivers compliance alerts with a formal tone and high visibility").
- Authorized channels it can use (maybe this agent is allowed to post to Slack and update a dashboard, but not send emails, depending on governance).

Using Agent Builder's metadata-driven approach, you might define a Presenter agent configuration in a metadata file or UI form, specifying things like: if Urgency__c field on input is "High", use Template X and Channel Y.

With the agent defined, the next step is implementing the formatting logic. Often, you'll use a combination of Flow and Invocable Apex for this. For example, you might build a Salesforce Flow that is triggered when a certain event or output record is created (say, a Curator agent writes a "ComplianceViolation__c" record). The Flow could then invoke an Apex action called "Format Compliance Alert" which encapsulates the presentation decisions. In Apex, you can handle complex logic:

```
public class ComplianceAlertFormatter {
  @InvocableMethod
  public static List<AlertOutput> formatAlerts(List<RawAlert__c> alerts) {
    List<AlertOutput> results = new List<AlertOutput>();
```

```
        for (RawAlert__c alert : alerts) {
            AlertOutput out = new AlertOutput();
            // Example: determine urgency and channel
            if(alert.Urgency__c == 'High') {
                out.Channel__c = 'Slack';
                out.Message__c = '[URGENT] ' + alert.Summary;
            } else {
                out.Channel__c = 'Dashboard';
                out.Message__c = alert.Summary;
            }
            // Add more formatting logic (tone adjustment, adding context, etc.)
            results.add(out);
        }
        return results;
    }
}
```

IN THIS PSEUDO-CODE, the Apex method checks an Urgency__c flag on the incoming alert and decides to either post an urgent Slack message or just update a dashboard, and it prefixes the message with an "[URGENT]" tag in the Slack case. In a real implementation, you could use this pattern to map various metadata attributes to presentation choices. For instance:

A low Confidence__c score could trigger the addition of a phrase like "(uncertain outcome)" in the message or choose a more cautious tone.

A specific Audience__c type (perhaps "Executive" vs "Technical") could toggle the verbosity of the explanation or the inclusion of technical details.

A Relevance__c or priority field might determine if the Presenter should interrupt the user (e.g. a push notification) or just quietly log the info for later review.

Flow Screens and Lightning Web Components come into play on the delivery side. Suppose our Compliance Alert Presenter needs to show a rich notification inside a Salesforce app for moderate alerts. We can create a Flow Screen that displays the alert message with a colored border (red for high urgency, yellow for medium, etc.) and perhaps buttons like "Acknowledge" or "Details". That Flow Screen can use conditional visibility: only pop it up for the relevant users or contexts. For more flexibility, an LWC can be embedded in a dashboard or record page, listening for new alerts (maybe via a Platform Event) and rendering them in a custom banner or feed component. The LWC could apply visual formatting logic – like using the Salesforce Lightning Design System classes to color-code, or adding an icon (e.g. a warning symbol for urgent compliance issues).

For channels outside the Salesforce UI, you can use integrations. Agentforce Presenter agents can call out to external services or use built-in connectors. In our example, to send a Slack alert, you might use Salesforce's Slack integration (perhaps an out-of-the-box Flow action "Send Slack Message" with the text and target channel coming from the Apex output). Likewise, for wearables or other devices, you could integrate with an API. For instance, a Presenter agent could call a custom Apex that sends a push notification to a mobile app, or triggers a vibration on a paired device (imagine using a custom IoT Cloud integration for a smart badge that vibrates on urgent alerts).

It's also important to prepare templates and multilingual support if needed. Einstein GPT (or OpenAI APIs via Apex) can be harnessed here. You might store a prompt template in Salesforce (or in code) that says: "Summarize the following alert for an executive audience in 2 sentences." The Presenter agent's Apex or Flow would feed the raw alert details into this prompt via an Einstein GPT action, and the result would be a nicely phrased summary that you then deliver. If supporting multiple languages, you could either prompt the LLM to output in the user's language or use Salesforce Translation Workbench/Custom Labels for static parts of the message.

Throughout the build, metadata is your friend. Define custom metadata types or custom settings for things like channel routing rules, templates, or threshold values. For example, a Custom Metadata Type could list "Urgency = High -> Slack + Mobile; Urgency = Medium -> Email; Urgency = Low -> Dashboard only". Your Presenter agent's logic can query this metadata so that changing the presentation policy is as easy as updating a config, not altering code. Similarly, store format strings or message templates in metadata: e.g., a template for an approval request vs. a template for an FYI update. This makes the Presenter agent easier to maintain and adjust as requirements evolve.

By following this layered approach – using declarative tools for orchestration, Apex for detailed logic, LWC/Flow for UI, and metadata for configuration – you ensure your Presenter agent is both powerful and flexible. The result in our compliance scenario is a full-stack workflow: a Sentinel detects a violation, a Curator compiles context, and our Presenter agent immediately delivers a clear, well-formatted alert to the compliance officer via the best channels. Now that we've walked through how to build a Presenter agent, we can explore some techniques to refine the user experience even further with sensory and UX optimizations, which is up next.

UX AND SENSORY OPTIMIZATION TECHNIQUES

Building a Presenter agent isn't just about content—it's also about delivery style. Beyond choosing the right channel or wording, advanced Presenter agents optimize the user experience by engaging multiple senses and following UI/UX best practices. Here are some categories of optimizations to consider:

Visual cues: Small design choices can make a big difference in clarity. Presenter agents can use badges or color-coded labels (e.g. a green "Approved" pill or a red "Overdue" tag), progress bars or sparklines (tiny trend graphs) to give instant context, and typography tweaks (larger or bold text for crucial numbers, muted gray for ancillary details). Even layout density matters: a Presenter might show a compact summary when screen space is tight (on a smartwatch or phone), versus a more expanded view with charts and tables on a desktop dashboard. These visual elements help users parse information at a glance.

Language and tone: The phrasing chosen by a Presenter agent can imply certainty, urgency, or politeness. For example, in uncertain situations it might use hedging words ("It looks like there could be a delay") whereas for a confident recommendation it will be direct ("A delay will occur unless we reroute"). The agent also adapts formality to the audience – using professional, succinct language for an executive update versus a more informal, detailed explanation for an analyst. By modulating tone (enthusiastic vs. matter-of-fact, persuasive vs. neutral) and including or omitting technical jargon as appropriate, the Presenter ensures the message lands well with its intended reader.

Audio elements: When delivering information via voice or sound, Presenter agents can go beyond a generic monotone reading. Using text-to-speech engines (with SSML, the Speech Synthesis Markup Language, for example), the agent can vary the pitch or emphasis of certain words (raising pitch at the end of a sentence to indicate a question, speaking more slowly for important parts). It might use distinct alert sounds – perhaps a gentle chime for an FYI notification versus a loud alarm tone for a critical alert. The timing of audio matters too; a Presenter might preface a spoken alert with a short beep to get attention, or insert a pause before delivering a crucial piece of data so the user can mentally prepare.

Tactile feedback: For wearables or devices that support haptics, Presenter agents can encode information through touch. A smartphone or smartwatch can produce different vibration patterns – e.g. two quick pulses for a low-priority notification, a long buzz for something urgent. Some accessibility-focused setups use braille displays or haptic belts that Presenter agents could leverage (for instance, vibrating in specific locations or patterns to convey directional information or categories of alerts). The goal is to provide a feel for the information, literally, which can be invaluable if the user can't look at a screen or hear audio at that moment.

Experimental modalities: Looking to the future (and some fringe present-day tech), Presenter agents might even employ unusual channels like scent or ambient temperature changes. Imagine an ambient office system that releases a subtle citrus scent when a sales target is met, or a calming lavender when an AI forecast predicts a stressful day ahead – reinforcing information in a subliminal way. While these are not mainstream interfaces, thinking in this way pushes us to design Presenter agents that are truly context-aware. For example, an autonomous car's AI might adjust the internal lighting or even seat vibration to get a driver's attention if an important navigation alert is being presented.

The overarching idea is that a great Presenter agent engages the appropriate human senses to maximize understanding and minimize annoyance. It will pick up on context like time of day, the user's current activity, or accessibility needs. A user in a noisy environment might benefit from a vibration or text visual instead of a voice alert; late at night, a soft notification (perhaps just a silent phone notification or a gentle blink of a nightstand device) is better than a loud alarm.

Pro tip: Sensory-aware design is the hallmark of advanced Presenter agents. The same insight might be best delivered as a smell at midnight but as a spoken alert at noon. Always consider the context – who, when, and where – and adjust the medium accordingly.

Equipped with these UX optimization techniques, your Presenter agents can truly meet users where they are. Next, we'll see how the Presenter pattern compares and connects with similar efforts in the wider AI ecosystem.

PRESENTER PATTERNS IN THE ECOSYSTEM

The idea of a Presenter-like agent isn't unique to Salesforce or Agentforce – it echoes across the AI world as developers grapple with how to make AI outputs consumable and useful. It's helpful to see parallels and related efforts:

LangChain and output formatting: LangChain, a popular LLM orchestration library, emphasizes structured outputs through constructs like output parsers and chains. For example, developers can specify a desired output schema (say JSON or a list of bullet points) and use a chain that formats the LLM's response accordingly. This ensures that raw model text is converted into a predictable format. In essence, it's a bit of Presenter logic embedded in the app – making sure the AI's output isn't just correct, but also well-structured for the next step or user consumption.

AutoGen and summarizer agents: Microsoft's AutoGen framework for multi-agent conversations allows for specialized agent roles. One common pattern is to have a dedicated "summarizer" agent in the mix that periodically takes the chat history or intermediate results and produces a concise summary for others to use. This is similar to a Presenter agent acting as an editorial assistant within an agent team – condensing and clarifying information so that the collective can proceed more effectively. In multi-agent research systems, one agent might explicitly be tasked with reporting findings in a human-readable form to a human overseer or to the next stage of processing.

Microsoft 365 Copilot Studio: Microsoft's Copilot (for Office 365 and other products) has to integrate AI outputs into familiar productivity tools like Word, Teams, and Outlook. That means formatting answers as ready-to-use content: for instance, generating an email draft with proper structure, or inserting an AI-generated summary slide in a PowerPoint deck complete with bullet points and even images. Microsoft's Copilot design guidelines note the importance of rendering content appropriately – the UI might include text, suggested action buttons, or adaptive cards as part of an AI response. This shows that beyond the AI logic, there's careful thought given to how the response is presented so users can immediately work with it (a chart, a to-do list, a formatted answer in a chat window, etc.).

Apple's on-device intelligence: Apple has been embedding AI-driven "intelligence" features in iOS/macOS that do Presenter-like tasks. A prime example is the automatic Notification Summary on iPhones, where the system summarizes a stack of notifications into a succinct overview to reduce distraction. This summary is generated on-device, phrased in a way to convey the gist (e.g. "3 new messages from Alice, Bob and 5 others") and delivered at appropriate times. Apple also adapts outputs contextually – for instance, Siri suggestions or Safari's "Highlights" use on-device models to present information in a concise form tailored to what you're doing. These features underscore the universal need for Presenter pattern: users everywhere benefit from clarity and brevity in AI-assisted interactions.

Beyond specific products, the multi-agent ecosystem increasingly recognizes the value of specialized presenter roles. In complex agent deployments, it's common to have one agent output be another agent's input. Defining a clear handoff to a Presenter agent at the end of an agent chain can ensure that no matter how messy or technical the intermediate steps, the final handoff to a human is polished. For example, one could design a pipeline where a Researcher agent focuses on finding facts, then hands facts to a Presenter agent which composes a human-friendly report out of them.

Efforts like the Model Context Protocol (MCP) aim to standardize how AI tools exchange information. Part of that involves agreeing on formats and context metadata. A Presenter agent can help here by enforcing those output formats before data is handed off to external systems. Think of it as the agent making sure, "I'm not just sending any text – I'm sending well-structured, labeled data that any tool following the MCP standard can understand."

In "swarm" or team-of-agents scenarios, a Presenter agent often acts as the narrator or spokesperson. Anthropic's research on multi-agent systems, for instance, included a dedicated agent to compile and present findings with citations for transparency. This narrator role means humans don't have to track dozens of agents' chatter – the Presenter/narrator consolidates it into an update or explanation. As AI systems scale, we can imagine an autonomous workforce where many worker agents do analysis and one Presenter agent summarizes their collective output to brief a human manager, very much like a team lead reporting to an executive.

The big picture: whether it's open-source frameworks, tech giants' products, or experimental AI swarms, the pattern of optimizing outputs for understanding is everywhere. Salesforce's Presenter agents are our particular implementation, but they stand on the shoulders of these broader trends. Knowing this helps you justify and design Presenter agents that play nicely not just in Salesforce, but in the wider AI ecosystem, ensuring that your solutions remain compatible and user-centric.

In the final section, we'll bring it back to the Salesforce world and look at how Presenter agents connect with the other Agentforce patterns in a full end-to-end scenario.

HOW PRESENTER AGENTS CONNECT WITH OTHER PATTERNS

Presenter agents rarely operate in isolation. They are typically the last mile in a network of AI agents, each with different responsibilities. Let's look at how a Presenter might slot into various pattern pairings:

Sentinel → Presenter: A Sentinel agent (which monitors events or thresholds) might detect something noteworthy – say an IoT sensor reading that exceeds a safe value or a social media mention spike. On its own, the Sentinel just raises a flag. Pairing it with a Presenter means that flag turns into an immediate, user-facing notification. For example, the Sentinel triggers the Presenter, which then sends a nicely formatted Slack message to the team ("Sensor 4 temperature critical at 95°C") and perhaps updates a dashboard card in Salesforce with a red status indicator (alert + context). The Presenter ensures the raw alert is delivered with context (which sensor? what threshold?) and via the channels people will see.

Curator → Presenter: A Curator agent (which we'll explore in the next chapter) specializes in synthesizing and structuring data – think of it as preparing the content. When a Curator produces a summary or report (e.g. it summarizes customer feedback from a survey), a Presenter agent can take that summary and decide how to deliver it. If the summary is meant for an upcoming meeting, the Presenter might embed it into a slide or email template. If it's for an interactive use, the Presenter could place it on a Screen Flow with "drill-down" buttons for details. The combination is powerful: the Curator distills information correctly, and the Presenter makes sure the right people actually see and understand that distilled insight (perhaps by highlighting key points or adding visual callouts in the report).

Conductor → Presenter: A Conductor agent (orchestration pattern) coordinates multiple steps or agents to complete a process. Once it finishes a complex task – imagine it orchestrated a customer onboarding across several systems – there is often a need to communicate the outcome to different stakeholders. A Presenter agent can take the aggregate result from the Conductor and tailor the messaging for each audience. The executive sponsor might get a brief high-level update ("Onboarding complete for 50 new clients this week, all checks passed"), while the operations team gets a detailed list of actions completed, and the new clients themselves receive a welcome email generated by the Presenter. Essentially, the Presenter becomes the post-process storyteller for the Conductor's orchestration, translating the multi-faceted results into the appropriate narrative for each constituency.

Supervisor → Presenter: A Supervisor agent (which handles oversight or human-in-the-loop approval) often works on draft outputs. For instance, a Supervisor might generate a draft response to a customer complaint or a proposed adjustment to a project plan, which then awaits human approval. A Presenter can step in after approval to polish and package that draft for final delivery. In a sales context, imagine a Supervisor agent drafted a contract amendment and a human legal officer approved it; a Presenter agent could then format the amendment into a client-ready PDF with cover page, summary of changes, and even a polite email body ready to send. The Presenter ensures that what the Supervisor agent and human agreed on is communicated out with professionalism and clarity – turning an internal draft into an external-ready artifact.

These patterns aren't mutually exclusive – in a single end-to-end workflow, you might see all of them play a role. To make this concrete, consider a high-priority customer case escalation:

1. Sentinel detects an issue: A Sentinel agent monitors social media and finds that a VIP customer just tweeted about a serious service outage. It raises an alert.

2. Supervisor triages and involves humans: A Supervisor agent (or simply a human in a supervisor role, augmented by AI) reviews the context of the issue and kicks off a response plan, perhaps approving an immediate action like granting the customer a service credit.

3. Curator compiles the details: A Curator agent gathers all relevant data about the outage and the customer – system logs, recent support tickets, the

customer's profile and history – and produces a concise summary of what happened and what was done to fix it.

4. Presenter delivers the summary pack: Now the Presenter agent takes over to close the loop. It prepares a "client-ready" communication: for example, a personalized email to the customer apologizing and summarizing the resolution, complete with a human-friendly explanation of the outage cause (sourced from the Curator's data) and a note about the credit offered. Simultaneously, the Presenter might post an internal summary in Slack for leadership, letting them know the issue was handled, and update a dashboard for tracking major escalations.

In this story, the Presenter is the final conveyor of trust and clarity. Each preceding agent did its specialized job – detecting, deciding, summarizing – and handed off to the Presenter to interface with the humans at the end. The value-add of the Presenter agent is that it ties the whole narrative together and delivers it in the right format to the right people (including the customer).

By connecting with all other patterns in this way, Presenter agents ensure that no matter which intelligent agents are involved behind the scenes, the outcomes are presented in a coherent, user-friendly manner. This builds understanding and trust in the overall AI system. With this comprehensive look at the Presenter pattern, we can now summarize the key takeaways and prepare to transition to the next chapter on the Curator pattern.

SUMMARY

In this chapter, we explored the Presenter Pattern and its vital role in turning AI outputs into clear, contextual communication that humans can trust and act on. We began by defining what Presenter agents do – acting as the voice or UI for other agents' insights. They don't invent new decisions or data; instead, they ensure that the outcomes of AI processes are delivered in the right format, with the right tone, through the right channel. This pattern is essential for adoption because even the smartest AI system fails if its results aren't understood or trusted.

We then dove into the anatomy of a Presenter agent, including its lifecycle (Collect → Format → Frame → Deliver) and core skills like simplifying complexity, adjusting to the audience, and using multimodal outputs. You saw when and why to deploy Presenter agents (for example, when explaining complex or high-stakes outputs to non-experts, or when multiple delivery mediums are needed). Through cross-functional examples in HR, Finance, Legal, Ops, and Service, we illustrated how Presenter agents tailor AI outputs across contexts. On the implementation side, we discussed using Salesforce tools – from Flow and Invocable Apex to Lightning Web Components and Einstein GPT – to build these agents, and how to use metadata to keep presentation logic flexible. We also covered advanced UX techniques, from visual design tweaks to leveraging audio, haptic, and even scent cues, ensuring Presenter agents engage users' senses optimally. Finally, we positioned the Presenter pattern within the broader AI ecosystem and within Salesforce's own agent network, seeing how it connects with Sentinel, Supervisor, Curator, and other patterns to deliver a coherent end-to-end solution.

Presenter agents ultimately shape how humans receive and interpret AI-driven outcomes. With their help, AI systems become not only smarter, but also more transparent and user-friendly. In the next chapter, we will go one layer deeper: examining the Curator Pattern, which focuses on synthesizing and distilling raw data – often providing the very content that Presenter agents will convey next.

7

THE CURATOR PATTERN (DATA SYNTHESIZER AGENT)

In an AI-first enterprise, Curator agents have rapidly emerged as indispensable "synthesizers" that turn overwhelming data into actionable insight. Modern organizations are swimming in data—from CRM records and ERP transactions to custom app logs, external API feeds, and public web information. Yet simply hoarding data isn't value; the real value comes from transforming it into timely, contextualized knowledge. This is exactly the role of a Curator agent. A Curator ingests disparate signals, filters noise, clusters related pieces, and ultimately summarizes and frames information into coherent knowledge that other agents or humans can act upon. It's like having a digital research analyst combing through thousands of inputs and handing you the key findings.

The Curator pattern underpins an effective AI agent ecosystem. Other agent types—Sentinels that monitor and alert, Supervisors that validate decisions, Presenters that communicate results—are only as good as the information they work with. Without curated inputs, those agents would be reacting to raw, unrefined data streams that often contain noise or irrelevant details. In other words, Curators provide the knowledge foundation that makes the rest of the agent "team" smarter and more reliable. A Sentinel agent can raise meaningful alerts instead of false alarms if a Curator has pre-aggregated and ranked events by importance. A Supervisor agent can draft better decisions if a Curator has already synthesized the context. Even a Presenter agent benefits from Curator outputs, since it can focus on formatting insights that have been distilled, rather than dumping raw data on users. The Curator pattern is thus the connective tissue of an agent ecosystem—without it, we'd be stuck reacting to a torrent of unprocessed data instead of leveraging insight.

It's important to distinguish Curator agents from traditional data tools like ETL pipelines or static business intelligence dashboards. A Curator is an active synthesis agent, not a passive reporter. Traditional dashboards might show you heaps of metrics and charts, but they rely on a human to interpret them. Curators, by contrast, operate in real time and across varied data fabrics (internal databases, external APIs, data lakes, etc.), proactively deciding what information is relevant, how it should be grouped, and how to explain it given the current context. They don't just aggregate; they interpret. In essence, where a BI dashboard might say "here are 10 pages of charts," a Curator agent says "here are the three insights that matter right now, and why." This moves organizations from being data-rich but insight-poor to truly leveraging data for strategic advantage. As one observer noted, AI agents are shifting us "from passive dashboards and alerts to active, decision-making systems that interpret data and take action." Curators epitomize that shift – they're the agents specifically tasked with making sense of complexity.

Consider a few examples of Curator agents in action across domains: In HR, a Curator can analyze exit interview texts and HRIS data to identify emerging turnover themes across business units (e.g. many exits citing lack of growth in a particular department). In Finance, a Curator monitors ledgers and transactions across subsidiaries to surface spend anomalies – perhaps summarizing that "Q2 travel expenses in Region X were 30% higher than average, mainly due to a spike in last-minute flights," highlighting a potential policy issue. In Legal, a Curator scans incoming vendor contracts and clusters any clauses that deviate from standard terms, giving attorneys a synthesized view of risk areas (e.g. "5 NDAs include non-standard confidentiality clauses, all from vendors in Europe"). In Customer Operations, a Curator agent continuously synthesizes customer sentiment by combining call transcript analysis, chat interactions, and CSAT survey results, yielding an overall "pulse" report of customer satisfaction drivers each week. These diverse cases underscore a common thread: the Curator turns a deluge of data points into concise knowledge, whether it's guiding HR retention strategy, financial oversight, legal risk mitigation, or customer experience improvements.

To build Curator agents on the Salesforce platform (what we call Agentforce), we leverage a suite of tools designed for data processing and AI orchestration. Salesforce Agent Builder provides the scaffolding to define an agent's structure – what inputs it takes, how often it runs or is triggered, and where its outputs go. Within that structure, heavy data crunching or custom logic can be implemented via Invocable Apex (Apex methods exposed to flows), which is ideal for filtering records or clustering data in ways that clicks alone might not achieve. Flow Orchestration (Salesforce flows and the Orchestrator add-on) helps manage multi-step Curator logic, such as first gathering data from multiple sources, then invoking an Apex action to process it, then calling an AI service to summarize, and finally routing the results. Curators often pull in data from beyond Salesforce as well – for that, External Services (declaratively invoking external APIs) and integration tools like MuleSoft are invaluable for retrieving data from third-party systems or data lakes. A Curator might call an external analytics service or query a data lake via MuleSoft, blending external insights with CRM data.

AI is a key part of many Curators: we frequently incorporate GPT-based summarization to turn raw text or numbers into a natural-language summary. Salesforce's Einstein Copilot (the conversational AI assistant layer in the platform) can be configured to assist in these summaries or interpretations, ensuring they align with company context and security. In fact, Salesforce's low-code Einstein Copilot Studio allows admins to craft custom prompts and skills for AI, which a Curator agent can invoke to summarize content in a specific tone or format. We also remain aware of emerging standards like the Model Context Protocol (MCP), an open standard for connecting AI agents to tools and data. MCP can enable a Salesforce Curator agent to ingest multi-system context in a standardized way, making cross-platform data synthesis more seamless. Together, these tools and techniques let us design Curator agents that operate confidently across Salesforce data and beyond.

In the pages ahead, we'll dive into how to design and deploy Curator agents following a structured approach. First, we examine the anatomy and lifecycle of a Curator agent (what stages it goes through to turn raw data into insight). Then we'll discuss when and why to apply this pattern, followed by concrete examples in various business domains. We'll walk through building a Curator agent with Salesforce technologies step by step, touch on advanced multi-source curation and data fabric integration, and see how this pattern connects with both the broader AI ecosystem and other Agentforce patterns. By the end of this chapter, you should see clearly how Curator agents become the insight engines of your AI agent network, and why mastering this pattern is crucial before we move on to the Action pattern in the next chapter. Let's begin by understanding the structure and lifecycle of a Curator agent, from data ingestion to synthesized output.

ANATOMY OF A CURATOR AGENT

What does a Curator agent actually do under the hood? At a high level, the Curator's lifecycle can be thought of as a pipeline with distinct stages: Ingest → Filter → Cluster → Synthesize → Output. Each stage transforms the data en route to producing meaningful insight. Let's break down each step and the key design elements involved:

Ingest: The Curator begins by gathering data from various sources. Inputs can be internal (records from Salesforce CRM objects, event logs, platform metadata, etc.), external (data fetched from APIs, files, RSS feeds, or even scraped from web content), or federated (combined queries to a data lake or data warehouse via tools like MuleSoft or GraphQL adapters). A robust Curator often handles multiple input formats. For example, a Curator might ingest a mix of Salesforce case records, CSV files from an FTP server, and real-time IoT readings via a platform event. The agent needs connectors or services for each source. In Salesforce, this is enabled through External Services (for REST APIs), MuleSoft (for complex multi-system queries and orchestrations), and platform event subscriptions (for streaming data). The ingest stage is about pulling in a comprehensive data set for a given purpose.

Filter: Once data is collected, the Curator applies filtering and relevance scoring. Not all ingested data will matter for the current context, so the agent should triage what's noise and what's signal. This could involve rule-based filtering (e.g. ignore transactions below a certain amount, or only consider support cases from premium customers) and algorithmic scoring (e.g. rank social media mentions by sentiment score, or discard sensor readings within normal ranges). The goal is to whittle down the data to the portions that merit further analysis. Invocable Apex is commonly used here – one can write an Apex method that, say, iterates through records and calculates a relevance score or applies thresholds, then returns only the significant subset. For instance, Apex code might drop any log entries that aren't errors, or filter product reviews to those with negative sentiment > 0.8. By filtering early, the Curator ensures subsequent stages focus on data that has a high information yield. (This stage is also where we heed a key design principle: graceful handling of missing or partial data. If some expected data isn't available, the Curator should flag it or fill defaults, not simply fail.

Pro Tip: Design your Curator agents to fail gracefully when data is partial—build logic to distinguish truly "missing" data from data that's present but not meaningful. This avoids false conclusions when, say, one data source is down, as opposed to genuinely reporting "no issues found.")

Cluster: Next, the Curator performs clustering and grouping on the filtered data. Clustering means organizing data points into subsets that share something in common – by type, topic, time window, entity, etc., depending on what pattern we're looking for. This is where the Curator begins to impose structure on the chaos. For example, a Curator agent looking at customer feedback might cluster comments by topic (delivery issues vs. product quality vs. pricing feedback). One analyzing financial transactions might cluster anomalies by root cause or by region. Clustering can be achieved through various techniques: simple grouping rules (e.g. group support tickets by product line), statistical methods (k-means clustering on numerical data), or even embedding-based similarity for text (where an AI model groups similar textual feedback together). In Salesforce, you might implement clustering in Apex for complex logic, or you could use an AI service. For instance, you could call an Einstein AI or external ML service to categorize text records by theme. The clustering stage often produces intermediate structures – perhaps a map or JSON where each cluster has a label and a collection of data points.

Synthesize: This is the stage where the Curator agent turns those clusters of data into human or agent-ready summaries, insights, or recommendations. Synthesis often involves natural language generation or statistical summary. With modern AI at our disposal, GPT models are frequently called upon here. The agent might take a cluster of related items and prompt a large language model: "Summarize the following 20 datapoints in a few sentences." For example, after clustering exit interviews into themes, the Curator could use GPT to produce a summary sentence for each theme ("Theme: Career Growth – 12 of 30 exit interviews mentioned lack of advancement opportunities as a reason for leaving"). GPT excels at turning raw facts into coherent narrative, especially when given clear instructions (which we can manage via Einstein Copilot Studio prompt templates). In cases where using an LLM isn't desired (due to governance or cost), synthesis might be template-based – e.g., filling in a pre-written template: "X outliers detected in category Y, average value Z," etc. Or it could use embedding-based similarity to pick a representative example from the cluster (like quoting a quintessential feedback comment for each theme). The result of this stage is typically a set of summarized objects or insights. These could be Salesforce records themselves (like creating a Summary__c custom object for each insight), or a JSON payload, or a simple text blob – whatever format makes sense for downstream consumption. Sometimes the synthesis also produces recommendations: e.g., "anomaly detected – recommended action: review supplier contracts for category ABC." This goes beyond summarizing into prescriptive output, which some Curators do especially when combined with a bit of domain logic or an AI prompt designed for recommendations.

Output: Finally, the Curator delivers its output to where it's needed. The outputs of a Curator agent can take multiple forms. Often, we think of a summary report or digest (natural language text) that can be handed to a human or passed to a Presenter agent. But outputs can also be structured data feeds – for example, a Curator could output a cleaned dataset or a list of "priority alerts" that a Sentinel agent will monitor. In many cases, the Curator writes to a custom object or database table: this provides a persistence layer so that other agents (or users) can query the curated insights later. For instance, an "IncidentDigest__c" object might store daily summaries of field operations incidents, which a Presenter could then format into an email. Another output mechanism is publishing an event or message. A Curator could send a platform event like CuratedInsightEvent with the results, allowing multiple subscribers (maybe several other agents) to react. In terms of Salesforce tools, the Curator might use a Flow for output routing – e.g., a Flow could take the result of an Apex action and decide to create records, send notifications, call another agent, etc. The design should also attach metadata to outputs, indicating provenance and context. Fields like "Source Data Timestamp" or "Records Aggregated Count" or even a list of source record IDs help downstream processes know how to trust and use the curated insight.

Throughout this lifecycle, a variety of Salesforce and external tools come into play. To recap the key tools mapping: Agent Builder defines triggers and overall flow; Invocable Apex handles filtering, clustering, and any custom scoring or math; GPT (via Einstein GPT/Copilot or external API) handles summarization and language generation; External Services/MuleSoft bring in off-platform data; and Flows/Orchestrations handle sequencing and output dissemination. This combination allows Curator agents to be both comprehensive (looking across systems) and contextual (tailoring their output to the situation). By carefully engineering each stage, we ensure the Curator agent is reliable. For example, we include error handling at ingest (what if an API is down?), use metadata flags at filter (to mark incomplete data vs. no relevant data), and limit the length of summaries (maybe by instructing GPT to keep it under 100 words so that a Presenter can fit it on a dashboard). These are the kinds of design decisions that make a Curator robust in practice.

Before moving on, let's visualize this with a pseudo-code outline of a Curator agent's logic:

```
// Pseudocode for Curator agent logic

DataSet rawData = ingestFromSources(sources);

DataSet relevantData = filterData(rawData);      // apply rules, get relevant subset

Map<ClusterKey, DataSet> clusters = clusterData(relevantData); // group by key (e.g., theme or type)

List<Insight> insights = new List<Insight>();

for (ClusterKey key : clusters.keySet()) {

  DataSet cluster = clusters.get(key);

   String summaryText = summarizeCluster(cluster, key); // e.g., call GPT or use template

  Insight insight = new Insight(key, summaryText);

  insight.sourceIds = cluster.getIds();    // tag provenance

  insight.recordCount = cluster.size();

  insights.add(insight);

}

publishInsights(insights); // store in Salesforce, or emit events, etc.
```

In this snippet, summarizeCluster() could be an Apex callout to an LLM or a built-in summary function. We also see an example of metadata tagging (insight.sourceIds and recordCount), capturing provenance so that any consumer of these insights knows what they're based on. This kind of tagging builds trust – if a Supervisor agent or a human user wants to double-click on an insight, they could retrieve the original records via those IDs.

Designing for traceability and confidence is a big part of Curator agent anatomy. In the next section, we'll revisit metadata tagging and origin tracking as a pro tip to avoid duplication and maintain trust across agents.

Now that we have a clear picture of a Curator's internal stages and components, let's discuss when you should use this pattern and how to recognize problems that call for a Curator agent.

WHEN AND WHY TO USE THE CURATOR PATTERN

Not every situation warrants the overhead of a Curator agent. Often, a straightforward report or a single-purpose script will do. But there are telltale scenarios where introducing a Curator yields significant benefit. Here are some common triggers for the Curator pattern:

"Drowning in data" scenarios: You have too much data and not enough time or human capacity to review it all. This could be a security team receiving thousands of log alerts a day, or a research team with a 100-page report for each of 50 regions. When the volume or velocity of data overwhelms human analysis, a Curator agent can step in to triage and summarize. If users are routinely skipping to executive summaries or spending hours aggregating spreadsheets, that's a strong signal for automation. As one commentary put it, businesses often find themselves "drowning in data but starving for insights," and AI-driven synthesis is the way out.

Pattern over points: Your decisions depend on finding patterns, not individual facts. This is when the forest matters more than the trees. For instance, one customer complaint might not mean much, but 50 complaints about the same product issue is a pattern calling for action. If your use case demands understanding trends, clusters, or statistical outliers (as opposed to handling singular events one by one), a Curator is the right pattern. It will ensure that macro-level insights emerge from micro-level data.

Pre-processing for smarter actions: You want AI agents to build context before taking action. In a multi-agent workflow, often an Action agent or a Decision agent (Supervisor) will perform better if they're fed context. For example, an Action agent executing an incident resolution might benefit from a curated summary of related incidents to avoid duplicate work. If you find yourself chaining a lot of data retrieval and parsing steps before an agent can do its main job, consider offloading that to a dedicated Curator earlier in the flow. The Curator pattern is effectively a context builder for subsequent reasoning or action.

One knowledge layer, many consumers: You need to serve multiple downstream agents or processes from a unified knowledge layer. This is a system design consideration. Suppose you have several agents (or departments) that all need insights from the same raw data. Rather than each one pulling and processing data in parallel (duplicating effort and possibly getting inconsistent results), a single Curator can produce a "single source of truth" summary that everyone uses. For instance, a Curator might compile a daily risk report that is used by a Supervisor agent (for approving exceptions) and by a Presenter agent (for notifying leadership) and by a Conductor agent (to decide if a contingency process should kick off). If you see opportunities for reuse of analysis across functions, that's a prime case for a Curator to centralize the synthesis.

Now let's compare the Curator pattern briefly with a couple of other patterns to clarify its unique role:

Curator vs. Conductor: A Conductor agent (from an earlier chapter) focuses on workflow orchestration – sequencing tasks, calling the right agents or services in order, handling branching logic. A Curator focuses on data understanding. One builds flow, the other builds knowledge. They often complement each other: for example, a Conductor might invoke a Curator at step 1 to gather context, then proceed to orchestrate different actions based on the insights returned. If you find your Conductor agent doing a lot of data massaging or analysis as part of its logic, that's a hint you should carve that out into a Curator. Conductors say "what's the next step?", Curators say "what's the situation?" – both are crucial, but they address different problems. In practice, you might use both: a Curator to analyze data, feeding a Conductor that decides process flow based on that analysis.

Curator vs. Presenter: A Presenter agent (from the previous chapter) is all about how information is delivered to humans (UI, format, channel, tone). It doesn't generate new insights; it takes whatever input it's given (often from a Curator or Supervisor) and frames it nicely for the end-user. A Curator, on the other hand, generates the content of insights by analyzing raw data. So, one produces summaries, the other presents summaries. If you skip the Curator and go straight to a Presenter, you might end up presenting raw data which can overload or confuse the user. Conversely, if you have a Curator but no Presenter, you might have great insights that no one sees or understands because they aren't packaged well. Often, Curator and Presenter work in tandem: e.g., a Curator agent outputs "key findings" and a Presenter agent turns those findings into a visual dashboard or a narrative report. It's useful to insert a Curator step whenever the raw data isn't immediately human-friendly or when it's not in the ideal shape for decision-making. The Presenter will thank you, because it can trust that the input is already vetted and concise.

Curator vs. Sentinel/Supervisor (when to insert): Sentinel agents watch for specific conditions to alert on (they're like guards with a yes/no alarm), and Supervisor agents double-check or validate decisions. If either of these patterns would be dealing with complex or high-volume signals, it's wise to put a Curator in front of them. For instance, a Sentinel watching individual transactions for fraud might alert too often (false positives) – but a Curator could first aggregate suspicious patterns and let the Sentinel focus on "meta-alerts" (like "10 high-risk events occurred in an hour" as one alert). Similarly, a Supervisor drafting an approval decision might use a Curator's summary of related cases to ensure it doesn't approve something out-of-norm. A simple decision list can guide when to add a Curator:

Monitoring high-volume events (Sentinel usage)

- **Without Curator:** Sentinel generates alerts for every incoming event, including low-value noise, overwhelming users and reducing signal quality.
- **With Curator:** Curator pre-aggregates and groups related events so Sentinel triggers alerts only on meaningful, consolidated signals.

Automated decision or draft preparation (Supervisor usage)

- **Without Curator:** Supervisor operates with limited context, evaluating each request in isolation and potentially missing trends or precedent.
- **With Curator:** Curator supplies summarized context such as historical patterns or similar past cases, enabling more consistent and informed decisions or drafts.

User-facing dashboard or report (Presenter usage)

- **Without Curator:** Presenter exposes raw or overly granular data, forcing users to interpret and synthesize insights themselves.
- **With Curator:** Curator distills key insights that the Presenter formats into a concise, digestible report.

Multi-agent workflows requiring shared facts (Conductor or multiple consumers)

- **Without Curator:** Each agent independently retrieves and analyzes data, causing duplication and inconsistent views of truth.
- **With Curator:** A single Curator provides vetted insights to all downstream agents, ensuring consistency and reducing overall computation effort.

In summary, use a Curator agent when data complexity or volume is a barrier to effective action, when patterns need discovering, or when multiple parts of your system would benefit from a common distilled knowledge base. If a process feels like finding needles in haystacks, or if an outcome depends on synthesizing diverse inputs, that's the Curator's cue. On the other hand, if your use case deals with one record at a time or straightforward rule processing, you might not need a Curator – a simple Apex trigger or a single-step agent could suffice. The Curator pattern shines in the gray areas requiring analysis, summarization, or sense-making. It sets the stage so that by the time other agents (or users) engage, they're dealing with insights, not raw data. With the "when and why" in mind, let's explore concrete use cases across different enterprise functions, to see how Curators actually drive value in HR, Legal, Finance, and beyond.

USE CASES ACROSS THE ENTERPRISE

Curator agents have broad applicability across virtually every domain of business. Any function that grapples with data overload or complex information can benefit from a data synthesizer agent. Let's look at five hypothetical yet plausible scenarios – in HR, Legal, Finance, Procurement, and Field Operations – to illustrate how the Curator pattern can be applied. Each example will show what the Curator would do and how that helps the team make better decisions.

HR (Employee Retention Insights): Imagine a human resources team trying to improve retention. They have exit interviews (long-form text from surveys or transcripts of interviews), HRIS data on attrition (numbers, departments, tenure), and perhaps industry benchmarks. A Curator agent for HR could regularly ingest all exit interview comments and relevant HRIS fields for recent departures. It would filter out irrelevant chatter and focus on reasons for leaving. Then it would cluster the feedback by theme – for example, grouping comments related to career advancement, compensation, management, work-life balance, etc. Using GPT or an AI model, the Curator synthesizes each cluster into a succinct insight: "Theme: Career Advancement – 35% of recent exits mentioned lack of growth opportunities; sample quote: 'I didn't see a path upward in the organization.'" It might produce a list of the top 3–5 turnover drivers, complete with supporting stats or quotes. The output could be a summary report object that HR business partners receive monthly. This saves HR from reading through dozens of interviews and trying to manually tally themes. Instead, they get a clear, data-driven narrative of why people are leaving, helping them craft targeted retention plans. The Curator might use Agent Builder to schedule this analysis monthly, Apex for text clustering (perhaps using Salesforce's Einstein NLP to detect topics), and Einstein GPT for generating the summary sentences in a friendly yet factual tone.

Legal (Legislation and Contract Risk Digest): Consider a corporate legal department that must keep up with new regulations and manage contract risks. A Legal Curator agent could monitor public data sources (like government websites or legal databases via APIs) for new legislation or regulatory changes in each region the company operates. It also ingests the company's own contract repository to find any clauses that have been flagged by past reviews (like indemnity clauses or data privacy terms). The agent filters for relevance – perhaps only laws in the industries of interest, and contracts above a certain value. It then clusters information by risk category. For legislation: by region and topic (e.g., "Data Protection – EU", "Labor Law – APAC"). For contracts: by clause type (e.g., "Non-standard indemnities", "Arbitration clauses"). The synthesis stage summarizes each cluster: "New Data Protection Law (EU) – introduces stricter requirements on data handling, effective Jan 2026, potential impact on marketing practices." For contracts, perhaps: "Flagged Indemnity Clauses – 5 vendor contracts this quarter have unlimited liability clauses (deviation from standard)." These summaries, along with links or references to the specific laws or contracts, are output as a weekly legal risk digest. The Curator might leverage MuleSoft to integrate with an external legal info service, and use an External Services registration to call into a contract analysis API. Summarization could be done with GPT, guided by a prompt that includes the legal department's preferred risk rating scheme. The result: the legal team isn't blindsided by new laws or risky clauses – they have a synthesized briefing that they can quickly act on (e.g., schedule a review meeting for the flagged contracts, or update compliance training for the new law). It's an end-to-end example of turning unstructured legal texts into actionable knowledge.

Finance (Spend Anomaly Detection): In finance, suppose the CFO's office wants a handle on unusual spending patterns across a company's many departments and subsidiaries. A Finance Curator agent aggregates data from the ERP (expenses, invoices) and maybe corporate credit card systems. It filters for anomalies – transactions that are way outside expected ranges (e.g., a department's travel budget spiking 300% month-over-month) or that hit certain risk triggers (expenses without proper category coding, or repeated small transactions that might indicate splitting to avoid approval limits). The agent clusters anomalies by type and severity. One cluster might be "Travel Expenses Anomalies" with entries from multiple business units; another might be "Approval Policy Violations." The Curator uses statistical techniques (or an AI anomaly detection model) to identify what counts as outlier behavior. It then produces a summary: "Spending Anomalies: 3 departments exceeded travel budget by >50% this month (Sales, Consulting, Marketing – see details); 12 expense reports were flagged for policy violations (mostly missing receipts for items > $500)." The output could be a structured list of anomalies with explanations, perhaps written into a custom object Spend_Anomaly__c and also summarized in an email to the finance controllers. Tools used might include Salesforce Data Cloud (if consolidating finance data from multiple sources), with an integration of Einstein Discovery or a custom Apex for anomaly scoring, and GPT for turning the findings into a narrative. The curated output saves finance analysts days of combing through spreadsheets, allowing them to focus directly on investigating the flagged items. Over time, as the agent learns what anomalies were true issues versus false alarms (maybe through feedback logged by analysts), it could even refine its scoring thresholds – illustrating a learning Curator that improves its precision.

Procurement (Vendor Performance and Pricing): The procurement team deals with suppliers, purchase orders, and payments. Let's say they want to ensure they're getting the best prices and timely deliveries. A Procurement Curator agent could pull in data from the procurement system and accounts payable – prices paid for key commodities, and records of payment times and delivery delays. It filters for outliers such as price points that are significantly higher for one vendor vs others for the same item, or instances where payments were delayed (either by the vendor invoicing late or internal process). Clustering might separate Price Outliers and Payment Delays, and further group by vendor or category. The agent might find, for instance, that "Vendor X's components are 20% costlier than the average price of identical components from others" and "Vendor Y had 5 late deliveries last quarter, average 10 days late." The synthesis stage could output a summary table or bullets for the procurement managers, highlighting which vendor relationships need review. The agent could automatically suggest actions as well: "Consider renegotiating contract with Vendor X or shifting volume to others; Vendor Y's SLA adherence is below target, meet with them to discuss penalties." This Curator's output format might be both a report and a set of records that feed into a Supervisor agent for compliance (e.g., a Supervisor might auto-generate a draft email to Vendor Y about performance, using the Curator's findings as input). Implementing this might use External Services/MuleSoft if some data is in an external SAP or Oracle system, combined with Apex for computing averages and variance. The Curator's benefit here is giving procurement a clear view of exceptions in vendor performance, which translates to cost savings and supply stability.

Field Operations (Daily Operations Digest): In field operations or engineering, managers often need to know what happened in the last 24 hours across numerous job sites or service calls. A Field Ops Curator agent could ingest data from IoT sensors (machine readings, alerts), field technician logs entered in a mobile app, and customer incident reports. Given that these might be streaming continuously, the Curator could run on a schedule (nightly or hourly) or be event-triggered. It filters to focus on notable incidents – machines that reported critical faults, jobs that took significantly longer than expected, safety incidents logged, etc. Clustering might organize the info by geography or by issue type. For example: "Region West – 2 critical generator failures (Sites 14 and 16); Region East – no critical events." Or cluster by issue: "Power Fluctuation Events – 3 occurrences (likely due to voltage spikes); Maintenance Delays – 4 jobs exceeded SLA." The synthesizer could create a daily incident digest with sections per cluster, giving a concise narrative of the day's operations: e.g., "Equipment Failures: Two generators failed in the West region last night due to coolant leaks, teams dispatched. Safety Events: One minor injury reported (slip and fall, Site 9, worker recovering). Service SLAs: 4 jobs breached their SLA (details...)." This report could be delivered each morning via a Presenter agent to operations managers' devices (perhaps as a Slack message or on a dashboard). The Curator here uses a mix of data sources – possibly leveraging Platform Events or Change Data Capture to get real-time logs, and might integrate with a system like Salesforce Field Service records. An Apex class could handle computing which jobs breached SLA. GPT could be used to nicely summarize technical incidents for a general audience (e.g., translating a sensor error code into plain language). The value is that field ops leadership can grasp the day's key issues over coffee, instead of sifting through logs or waiting for manual reports from each site.

These scenarios demonstrate the flexibility of the Curator pattern. To further clarify how a Curator agent functions across such examples, the list below summarizes each use case with respect to the Curator's key aspects:

HR – Retention Insights

- **Data types ingested:** Exit interview text, HRIS attrition data, industry benchmark statistics.
- **Curator's purpose:** Identify common drivers of employee attrition and cluster feedback into consistent themes.
- **Output format:** Thematic summary report highlighting top reasons for leaving, with percentages and representative quotes.
- **Tools used:** Agent Builder scheduled runs; Apex for text clustering; GPT for summarization; Salesforce Survey Data APIs.

Legal – Regulatory and Contract Digest

- **Data types ingested:** External legislation feeds and internal contract clause records.
- **Curator's purpose:** Surface newly enacted or changed regulations by region and flag risky or non-standard clauses across vendor contracts.
- **Output format:** Weekly digest including a bulleted list of regulatory changes with impact summaries and a table of affected contracts.
- **Tools used:** MuleSoft integrations to government APIs; external legal data services; GPT for summarizing legal changes; Custom Metadata for clause risk tagging.

Finance – Spend Anomalies

- **Data types ingested:** ERP expense records, accounts payable invoices, and corporate card transactions.
- **Curator's purpose:** Detect and explain unusual spending patterns or potential fraud across departments or business units.
- **Output format:** Structured list of anomalies with contextual details such as department, amount, expected range, and brief recommendations.
- **Tools used:** Data Cloud for financial data consolidation; invocable Apex for anomaly scoring; Einstein Discovery or Analytics; Salesforce Flow for email alerts.

Procurement – Vendor Performance

- **Data types ingested:** Supplier master data, purchase order pricing, delivery logs, and payment timelines.
- **Curator's purpose:** Identify outlier vendor pricing and delivery or payment issues to support supplier management decisions.
- **Output format:** Bi-weekly vendor scorecard showing pricing deviations, late delivery counts, and suggested action notes.
- **Tools used:** Flow Orchestration pulling ERP data via MuleSoft; Apex for calculations; GPT for recommendation phrasing; custom VendorPerformance__c objects for output.

Field Operations – Daily Operations Digest

- **Data types ingested:** IoT sensor alerts, field service work orders, incident reports, and safety logs.
- **Curator's purpose:** Summarize daily critical incidents and SLA breaches to keep operations leadership informed and proactive.
- **Output format:** Daily narrative report segmented by issue type or region, combining text summaries with key metrics.
- **Tools used:** Platform Events for sensor feeds; Salesforce Field Service data; Apex for SLA evaluation; Einstein GPT for narrative generation; Presenter agent for multi-channel delivery.

Each row highlights how the Curator pattern adapts to different data and goals: whether it's text-heavy HR feedback or number-heavy finance data, the agent filters the noise and delivers insight in a format the business can use. The tools column shows that often multiple Salesforce technologies and sometimes external AI/ML are combined for a single Curator. For example, the HR case mixes Apex and GPT; the legal case uses integrations plus GPT; the finance case might lean on analytics tools.

One thread common to all is that Curators improve speed to insight. They automate what domain experts might do manually (scan, compile, summarize), freeing those experts to act on the insights instead of spending time gathering them. Another common point is trust via provenance – good Curators include enough detail or references so that users trust the summary. For instance, citing "35% of exits mentioned X" or listing which vendors had issues. This builds credibility that the AI isn't hallucinating; it's grounded in real data points. In the next section, we'll take a deep dive into actually building a Curator agent on Salesforce (Agentforce) step by step, using a scenario that ties some of these ideas together. We'll see how to implement the pattern with the tools and best practices we've discussed.

BUILDING A CURATOR AGENT IN AGENTFORCE

Now that we've seen what Curators do and where to use them, let's walk through how to build one on the Salesforce platform. We'll use a concrete example to anchor the discussion: suppose we want to build a Project Status Curator for a Project Management Office (PMO). This Curator will aggregate project updates from multiple systems and provide a synthesized status report. In our scenario, the Curator's output will then feed a Supervisor agent that flags project risks and a Presenter agent that displays a dashboard for executives. This will illustrate how a Curator can be the linchpin in a multi-agent workflow. We'll cover the key build steps: defining the agent, implementing data processing (filtering/clustering), invoking LLM for summarization, storing outputs, and exposing the Curator for others to use.

1. Define the use case and agent structure (Agent Builder): We start in Salesforce's Agent Builder (a hypothetical interface that lets us configure agent patterns declaratively). We create a new agent entry, give it a name ("Project Status Curator"), and define its inputs and triggers. For our PMO case, inputs might include: project task data from Salesforce (perhaps a custom object Project__c and related Task__c records), issue logs from an external system (maybe Jira tickets via API), and budget vs actuals data from an ERP (via MuleSoft). We set the agent to run on a schedule – say every Friday at 5 PM – to produce a weekly status synthesis, as well as on-demand (triggerable via a button if the PMO wants an up-to-the-minute report). In Agent Builder, we specify these sources and the cadence. We also outline the output: we plan to create a custom object Project_Status_Summary__c that holds the curated summary (with fields like Project_Id, Status_Text, Risk_Level, etc.), and we intend for the agent to also fire a platform event or send a notification once the summary is ready (so the Supervisor and Presenter know to pick it up). At this stage, we're essentially configuring the "wrapper" for our Curator agent – how it plugs into the environment.

2. Implement filtering & clustering logic (Invocable Apex): Next, we tackle the heart of the data processing. While some filtering could be done in a Salesforce Flow using criteria, our use case likely needs more complex logic (e.g., combining data from multiple objects, performing calculations to assess status). We create an Apex class ProjectStatusCuratorProcessor with an @InvocableMethod that Agent Builder (or a Flow) can call. This Apex

method will: query relevant Salesforce project records (those updated in the past week, or all active projects), call external services to fetch related Jira issues and budget data, then filter and cluster. For filtering, maybe we decide: only focus on projects that are in "yellow" or "red" status on any dimension (schedule, scope, budget) – because green projects are on track and need little attention in the summary. So the Apex might drop all-green projects from further analysis to keep the report focused. It might also filter Jira issues to just "high priority" ones, and budget data to entries where variance > some threshold. Clustering in this context could be by project (since ultimately we want one summary per project) – but perhaps also within a project, cluster by risk category (schedule vs scope vs budget issues). For simplicity, let's say the agent will produce one summary per project, highlighting any problem areas. The Apex code can loop through each project, compile its relevant data: count of overdue tasks, any critical issues from Jira, budget percentage overrun, etc. This builds a structured picture of project health.

Here's a pseudo-code snippet sketching part of this Apex logic:

```
public with sharing class ProjectStatusCuratorProcessor {

  @InvocableMethod

      public static List<Project_Status_Summary__c> runCurator(List<Id> projectIds) {

    // 1. Query projects and related data

      List<Project__c> projects = [SELECT Id, Name, Status__c, Budget__c, Actuals__c FROM Project__c WHERE Id IN :projectIds];

      // (In reality, we might not pass projectIds but rather query all active projects or those updated recently)


      // 2. Fetch external issues via HTTP callout (Jira API) and budget variances (ERP via MuleSoft)

    //... (pseudo-code for external data fetch, omitted for brevity)...


      List<Project_Status_Summary__c> summaries = new List<Project_Status_Summary__c>();

    for (Project__c proj : projects) {
```

```
// 3. Filter: decide if this project needs summarizing
    if (proj.Status__c == 'Green' && noCriticalIssues(proj) && onBudget(proj)) {
    continue; // skip projects with no notable flags
}
// 4. Compute cluster info (gather key points for this project)
Integer overdueTasks = countOverdueTasks(proj);
Integer criticalIssues = getCriticalIssueCount(proj);
Decimal budgetVariance = computeBudgetVariance(proj);
// 5. Prepare a draft summary text via template or placeholder
String draftSummary = 'Project ' + proj.Name + ': ';
if (overdueTasks > 0) draftSummary += overdueTasks + ' tasks overdue; ';
if (criticalIssues > 0) draftSummary += criticalIssues + ' critical issues; ';
    if (budgetVariance > 0) draftSummary += 'budget overrun of ' + budgetVariance + '%.';
// We'll refine this text with GPT later.


// 6. Create summary record (to be finalized after GPT call)
    Project_Status_Summary__c summary = new Project_Status_Summary__c();
summary.Project__c = proj.Id;
summary.Draft_Summary_Text__c = draftSummary;
summary.Status_Flags__c = (proj.Status__c != 'Green') ? proj.Status__c : null;
summary.Overdue_Tasks__c = overdueTasks;
summary.Critical_Issues__c = criticalIssues;
summary.Budget_Overrun__c = budgetVariance;
summaries.add(summary);
```

```
    }
    // 7. Save draft summaries (optionally)
    insert summaries;
    return summaries;
  }
}
```

IN PRACTICE, we might not insert draft records mid-way, but here we show capturing key fields. At this point, we have identified the projects of interest and collected the cluster data (overdue tasks, issues, etc.) for each. We have a rudimentary summary text concatenated, which leads us to the next step.

3. Invoke GPT for summarization and tone (GPT integration): The draft summary text in the code above is fairly plain and mechanical. We want to refine it into a well-phrased summary sentence or two for each project. This is where we integrate a GPT model. We have a few options: use Salesforce's Einstein GPT built-in (via a PromptTemplate and an Apex AI.generate() call, for example), or call out to an external LLM API (OpenAI, Anthropic, etc.) via an External Service or Apex HTTP. Einstein Copilot Studio allows us to define a custom prompt for this scenario. We might create a prompt template like:

"You are an AI assistant generating project status summaries for executives. Given the following project data: {Draft_Summary_Text__c}, produce a concise sentence or two summarizing the project status in a positive, clear manner. Omit internal jargon. "

We would pass in our draftSummary (which contains the key points) and let the LLM produce something like: "Project Alpha is experiencing minor delays (3 tasks overdue) and has 1 critical issue open. Budget is 5% over target, but mitigation plans are in place." This reads much better for an executive than a raw listing of stats. The GPT model can also infer a tone or add a connective narrative (like mentioning mitigation if we prompt it to consider improvements – possibly by telling it if a plan is there). We ensure the model stays factual by providing it only facts we computed (no open-ended "analyze raw data" without context, to reduce hallucination). The summarization call could be done for each summary in Apex after the initial processing loop. It might look like:

```
for (Project_Status_Summary__c summary : summaries) {
  String prompt = makePrompt(summary);
  String aiResponse = AI.generate(prompt, /* model params like maxTokens, etc. */);
  summary.Final_Summary_Text__c = aiResponse;
}
update summaries;
```

Where makePrompt(summary) inserts the draft stats into the template. If using an external API, we'd do an HTTP POST and parse the response. Either way, after this step, each summary record has a polished narrative text. We also use this opportunity for tone shaping – maybe instruct GPT to be neutral or cautiously optimistic (depending on audience). We could even use multilingual output if needed (e.g., generate in Japanese for a Japan team, using the same data but different prompt). The flexibility of GPT in the loop is powerful, but we maintain guardrails by prompting carefully and keeping the context focused.

4. Store curated outputs for reuse: We've been building towards having Project_Status_Summary__c records. We finalize those by updating them with the final summary text and any derived risk ratings. At this stage, the Curator agent writes its output to the Salesforce database. Each summary record might have fields like Project, Summary Text, and perhaps a calculated Risk_Level (we could set an overall status: Green/Yellow/Red for the project based on the findings). Storing these is crucial because it enables reuse: tomorrow, if another agent or a user wants to know project status, they can query these records instead of running the whole analysis again. We might also maintain history (maybe keep one summary per week per project, or always update the latest – design choice depending on needs). Additionally, storing results allows us to attach origin metadata. For example, we include a field for "Source data as of date" (so consumers know how fresh it is) and maybe a reference list of issue IDs or task IDs that were included (as a text field or child records). This metadata can be important for traceability – if someone questions an insight, they can drill down to the raw records. Recall our earlier Pro Tip about tagging: by tagging every summary with origin info (like which records and when), other agents or users can trust and, if needed, verify the curated output.

We also consider performance: if this agent is heavy, we wouldn't want to run it more often than needed, and by storing outputs we enable downstream processes to retrieve the latest summary without recomputing. We might even expose the summaries via a Salesforce API or Experience Cloud page to non-Salesforce users, if that's useful (the Curator agent could thus serve insights to an entire org, not just inside Agentforce).

5. Expose the Curator as a service for other agents: In our design, we know a Supervisor agent will use the output to flag project risks, and a Presenter will use it to display a dashboard. How do they get the data? There are a couple of ways. One is what we've done – store in a custom object that the others can query (the Supervisor agent can simply read the summary records and apply rules like "if any project is Red status, escalate risk"). Another way is to make our Curator itself callable. We could wrap the Curator's main Apex in an Invocable Flow or even an API endpoint (maybe using Salesforce's REST API to invoke the Apex). For example, we could create a Flow that does "Run ProjectStatusCuratorProcessor then pass results to next step", and then expose that flow as a sub-flow or as an autolaunched flow. If the Supervisor agent is orchestrated with Flow, it could call this Curator sub-flow whenever it needs up-to-date context. Alternatively, using Platform Events, the Curator could emit an event "Project Status Curated" with summary IDs, which subscribers (Supervisor, Presenter) listen for to do their part.

In our PMO case, let's say we schedule the Curator weekly, and upon completion it updates summary records and also posts a Slack message (via a Presenter agent) to PMO members: "Project status summaries are ready." The Supervisor agent, which handles risk, might be triggered right after the Curator finishes (Agent Builder might allow chaining: run Supervisor X when Curator Y completes). In that chain, because we stored the data, the Supervisor could retrieve, say, all projects with Red status and automatically generate a "risk alert" if any are found with no mitigation plan. We won't detail the Supervisor here, but it shows how Curator output flows into the next step.

Build example recap: So for our multi-source project status Curator, we used Agent Builder to define sources (Salesforce + Jira + ERP), schedule, and outputs. We coded an Invocable Apex to do filtering (skip healthy projects), clustering (by project, gathering issues/tasks/budget info), and basic summarization data prep. We integrated GPT via Einstein Copilot or API to turn stats into executive-friendly text. We stored the results in a custom object with metadata (project IDs, timestamps, counts). We possibly signaled to other agents that new insight is available. The result is a working Curator that the PMO can rely on every week to know which projects need attention and why.

From a tooling perspective, this build leveraged multiple Salesforce capabilities: Flow/Agent Builder for orchestration, Apex for logic, External Service/MuleSoft for integration, and Einstein GPT for NLP. This combination is typical in Curator agents – they are inherently multi-faceted. The key in building is to maintain a modular structure: each stage (ingest, filter, cluster, synthesize) can be isolated for testing. For example, test the Apex filtering logic separately with sample data to ensure it catches the right conditions. Test the GPT prompt on a variety of inputs to ensure the style is consistent. Also incorporate error handling: what if the Jira API is down? Our Apex should handle that (maybe mark those projects with a warning "external data unavailable"). What if GPT returns something unusable? Perhaps have a fallback template summary if AI fails, so the agent still produces output. These considerations make a Curator reliable in production.

Finally, we should mention that building a Curator is not a one-time task. Iteration is expected. You might deploy the Project Status Curator and find that it flags too many projects as "at risk" because your filtering was too lenient. You then adjust thresholds or improve the scoring (maybe incorporate trend data – a project slightly over budget for one week isn't a true risk if it was under budget for many weeks prior). You might enhance clustering: initially group by project, later notice patterns across projects (like multiple projects have the same blocker – which could be a higher-level issue to escalate). A Curator agent can thus evolve, and because it encapsulates the synthesis logic in one place, it's easier to update that one agent than to coordinate changes across many reports or teams. This reinforces the benefit of the pattern: it centralizes expertise about "how to make sense of X data" into a reusable component.

With the Curator now built, we'll explore some advanced aspects: connecting to multiple sources in real-time, leveraging the wider data fabric, and ensuring uniqueness and trust in outputs.

MULTI-SOURCE AND FABRIC-BASED CURATION

In many enterprises, valuable insights lie at the intersection of multiple systems. A Curator agent often needs to pull data from a variety of platforms – CRM, ERP, HR systems, external APIs, IoT feeds, and more – essentially creating a mini "data fabric" for its analysis. Designing Curators for multi-source curation introduces additional considerations and opportunities. In this section, we'll discuss strategies for integrating diverse data sources, normalizing and scoring mixed data, and ensuring our Curator outputs remain reliable and de-duplicated in such complex environments. We'll also highlight the use of Salesforce External Services, MuleSoft, event-driven triggers, and even Einstein Copilot Studio in managing multi-source inputs.

Connectors for external data: Salesforce's platform provides multiple ways to connect to external data in Curator agents. The simplest is often External Services, which allows an admin or developer to declaratively integrate a REST API by importing its definition (OpenAPI spec). For example, if our Curator needs to call a weather service or a stock price API as part of analysis, we can set that up as an invocable action with External Services and then call it from Flow or Apex. Another powerful approach is using MuleSoft for federated queries. MuleSoft, as an integration middleware, can aggregate data from numerous sources and present it via APIs. A Curator agent could call a MuleSoft endpoint that, say, returns a combined JSON of relevant info from SAP, a data warehouse, and Salesforce in one go, rather than making separate calls. This simplifies the Curator's Apex logic – MuleSoft effectively acts as an extension of the Curator, handling complex ETL. For instance, our finance anomaly Curator might query MuleSoft for "all transactions over $10k with no matching PO", which MuleSoft could compile from an Oracle ERP and Salesforce data, returning a unified result. Using connectors like these keeps the Curator focused on analysis, not low-level data plumbing.

Real-time ingestion with events: Thus far we've considered Curators that run on schedules or on-demand. But some scenarios call for near-real-time curation. Salesforce's Platform Events and Change Data Capture (CDC) can trigger a Curator agent the moment new data arrives. For example, a sensor feed or a transaction log could publish events. A Curator can subscribe (via a Platform Event-triggered Flow or Apex trigger) and immediately include that data in its knowledge base. One design is to have the Curator maintain a rolling summary that updates with each event. For a concrete case, imagine a Customer Support Curator that summarizes customer sentiment (combining chat sentiment, call sentiment scores, survey feedback). Using CDC, whenever a new support case or survey is completed, an event could trigger the Curator to re-run or update the sentiment summary. This event-driven approach ensures insights are fresh. However, it demands careful design: if events are very frequent, you might not want to recalc everything on every single event (could be costly). A pattern here is micro-batches – e.g., accumulate events for a few minutes then process. Or have the event handler just flag that "Curator needs to run for X customer" and an orchestrator flow picks it up. The key point is Salesforce can listen to streams and invoke Curators accordingly, which is crucial for use cases like fraud detection (synthesizing signals within seconds) or IT operations (aggregating logs in real-time to spot outages).

Normalization and metadata in a data fabric: When pulling data from multiple sources, a Curator must reconcile different formats and schemas. This is where a unified metadata model helps. Salesforce's platform can use Custom Metadata Types or Config objects to store mapping rules – for instance, define that "High" severity in Jira = "Critical" in our internal terms, or that one system's timestamp should be converted to GMT. A Curator can reference these metadata mappings during ingest, so that by the time it filters and clusters, all data is speaking the same language. Additionally, if combining say IoT numeric data with text data, normalization might include scaling or categorizing values (e.g., sensor temperature above X = "overheat"). We may also use Platform Events as a normalization layer: multiple systems publish events which the Curator subscribes to in a consistent event schema. For example, different monitoring tools might all publish a UnifiedAlertEvent with fields like "system", "severity", "message", allowing the Curator to treat them uniformly.

Critically, when merging sources, duplication can occur (the same underlying event might come from two places). A robust Curator should handle this – perhaps by keeping a cache or using a unique key to ignore duplicates, or by merging records referring to the same incident. This is where the earlier advice on tagging origin comes in handy. If each input data point carries a unique ID or source reference, the Curator can ensure it doesn't double-count.

Pro Tip: To avoid duplication and confusion, tag every piece of summary output with origin metadata (source identifiers, timestamps, etc.). This way, if two agents or two runs of the Curator process the same data, they can recognize overlap and not falsely amplify an insight. For example, a sales Curator summarizing deals might tag summary records with an array of Opportunity IDs it covered – if run again tomorrow, it can skip those already summarized unless they changed. Other agents can also use this metadata to decide trust: e.g., a Conductor agent could choose the latest summary among multiple if it sees one has newer source timestamps.

Custom scoring and prioritization: In multi-source contexts, not all data points are equal. A Curator should apply custom scoring algorithms to decide what to focus on. Perhaps a certain source is more authoritative (maybe an anomaly in financial data is more critical than one in a social media mention). We can assign weights: e.g., give financial anomalies a score multiplier of 2x versus social sentiment anomalies. Another example: in IT ops, an error rate spike on a customer-facing app might be scored higher than one on an internal tool, because the impact is larger. We can implement such scoring in Apex or even using Einstein AI. Salesforce Einstein could be trained (via Einstein Discovery) to evaluate risk of events considering multiple factors from different systems. The Curator then uses that model's output as a composite relevance score. A simpler approach is writing a formula or method that takes inputs from all sources and outputs a single priority value. The filtering stage would then use that score to keep top items. The bottom line is, multi-source Curators should unify data into a common scoring framework to compare apples to apples. This ensures that when the Curator says "Here are the top 5 insights," those are truly the top when considering everything together, not just the top from one system but minor from another.

Using Einstein Copilot Studio for consistency: We touched on prompt design before – with multi-source data, crafting the right prompt or interpretation framework is important. Einstein Copilot Studio (or generally prompt libraries) can be used to define how the AI summarizer should treat different information. For instance, we might create a prompt that instructs: "If budget variance > 20%, mention budget concerns first; if critical issues present, highlight those with urgency; otherwise, give a general status." This logic can be embedded in the prompt via conditionals or few-shot examples. Copilot Studio allows us to test prompts with examples and refine them. By defining an interpretation framework, we ensure the summarization stage is aware of multi-source context. For example, if our input includes data from three sources, we could structure the prompt like:

Data Summary:

Project Status: Green/Yellow/Red

Finance: (Budget 110% of plan)

Issues: 2 critical issues open

Generate a summary focusing on any Red flags (budget or issues) first, then overall status.

This kind of guided prompt ensures that the AI output is aligned with our priorities (maybe we care about budget and issues more than schedule status). Essentially, we're encoding some business rules into the AI's phrasing. The benefit of Studio is that admins (not just deep AI experts) can adjust these prompts over time as needed, without altering code.

Federated data feeds and MCP: For truly complex fabrics, an emerging approach is using the Model Context Protocol (MCP) as mentioned earlier. In practice, a Salesforce Curator could be an MCP client reaching out to multiple MCP servers that expose data/tools from other platforms. For example, an MCP server might expose a "database query" tool or a "CRM search" tool. The Curator (through an MCP integration library) could ask for what it needs in natural language and get results. This is cutting-edge and not yet common, but it's worth noting as the ecosystem moves towards standardized agent-tool interoperability. Imagine writing a Curator prompt: "Fetch all unresolved high-severity incidents from ServiceNow and summarize their common causes" and having underlying MCP wiring do that. While futuristic, Salesforce is already looking at interoperability, so designing Curators with openness in mind is smart.

In multi-source curation, maintaining trust is both more challenging and more crucial. Data coming from outside Salesforce might be wrong or incomplete. A Curator should ideally include confidence levels or mark sections of its summary as "unverified" if a source failed. Perhaps use a field like Confidence__c on summary records. For instance, if the ERP connection was down, our Curator might produce a partial summary and flag confidence low for budget info. A downstream Presenter could visually indicate that ("Budget data unavailable – summary incomplete"). This kind of graceful degradation keeps user trust: the system admits when it's not fully informed, rather than silently outputting a possibly misleading summary.

By implementing connectors, scoring, normalization, and clear metadata, we ensure Curator agents remain reliable as they scale across a "big data" environment. We saw our Project Status Curator already doing some of this with multiple sources. Now imagine scaling up to dozens of sources – the principles remain: connect, normalize, filter, score, synthesize, tag, and update. With these best practices, our Curators become the single pane of glass for insights across the enterprise's data fabric, breaking down silos in the process.

Before concluding this section, let's not forget the Pro Tip mentioned earlier: "To avoid duplication, tag every summary object with origin metadata. This helps other agents trust, deduplicate, or override when needed." In multi-source scenarios, this is non-negotiable. It's our safety net against confusion when many data lines converge.

Having covered multi-source patterns, we can now step back and look at where the Curator pattern sits in the broader AI ecosystem. How do Curator agents in Salesforce compare or connect with similar ideas in frameworks like LangChain, CrewAI, or Microsoft's tools? We'll explore that next.

CURATOR AGENTS IN THE ECOSYSTEM

The concept of a "data synthesizer" agent isn't unique to Salesforce. In the wider AI ecosystem, many frameworks and products implement similar ideas under different names. It's valuable to see how our Curator pattern aligns with those, both to validate the pattern and to understand integration points. We'll briefly tour a few prominent examples: open-source libraries like LangChain, multi-agent orchestration frameworks like CrewAI and AutoGen, and enterprise solutions like Microsoft's Copilot/Syntex. Each echoes the need for curated context in AI workflows. We'll highlight parallels—like LangChain's retrieval chains (which gather and summarize documents) or CrewAI's "Researcher" agent role (which sounds a lot like a Curator). We'll also touch on how Salesforce's approach can interoperate or take inspiration from these ecosystem patterns, all while staying focused on our platform's strengths (trust, integration, low-code plus code, etc.).

LangChain's retrieval and summary chains: LangChain (an open-source toolkit for LLM-powered applications) emphasizes constructing "chains" of actions, and one common use case is Retrieval-Augmented Generation (RAG). In RAG, an agent retrieves relevant documents and then an LLM generates an answer or summary using those documents. This is very much in spirit of the Curator pattern – retrieval is like ingest/filter, and the summarization is like synthesize. LangChain even provides built-in chain types like Retrieval QA (find top N docs and answer a question) and Map-Reduce Summarization (summarize chunks then summarize the summaries). These can be seen as specific algorithms that a Curator agent might use internally. For example, a Salesforce Curator could use a LangChain-like approach by integrating with a vector store: when asked to summarize customer feedback, it retrieves top relevant feedback pieces via embeddings (vector similarity) and then summarizes them. So you can think of LangChain's retrieval chains as a flavor of Curator implementation. If we ever integrate Salesforce Agentforce with LangChain, a Curator agent could directly leverage Lang-

Chain components for heavy lifting (like calling a vector database of documents). In practice, while Salesforce has its own tools (Einstein, etc.), it's quite possible to call LangChain from Apex (via an API or local integration) if needed. The pattern is the same: curate knowledge, then act or answer. It's worth noting LangChain and similar frameworks underscore the importance of separating knowledge gathering from output generation, which is exactly what Curators do. Our advantage in Salesforce is that we combine that with enterprise data governance. (As a side note, LangChain's approach to maintaining memory in conversations – summarizing past interactions to keep context concise – is another example of curation: it curates conversation history for downstream turns. Curator agents may do similar for long-running workflows in Salesforce, summarizing state to feed into the next step.)

CrewAI's researcher roles: CrewAI is a multi-agent framework that encourages teams of specialized agents (often called a "crew"). In CrewAI, agents can have roles like "Researcher", "Writer", "Critic", etc., which collaboratively solve tasks. The "Researcher" agent type in CrewAI is essentially responsible for gathering and analyzing information – that sounds just like our Curator. In their documentation, CrewAI suggests the Researcher might excel at finding relevant info and presenting it clearly, whereas a Writer might produce content from those findings. This division of labor maps to Curator vs Presenter or Curator vs Action in our pattern language. A CrewAI Researcher agent might, for instance, search the web and summarize findings for a Writer agent that then drafts an article. Within Salesforce, our Curator might gather and summarize internal data for a "Presenter" agent that then formats a report. The philosophy aligns: use specialized agents for synthesis. If integrating with CrewAI, one could imagine a scenario where a Salesforce Curator agent interfaces with a CrewAI "crew". Perhaps Salesforce handles internal data curation and passes it to an external CrewAI Writer agent to generate a long-form document. Conversely, CrewAI's output could be fed into Salesforce for additional curation or storage. The fact that CrewAI even has a visual Agent Builder and emphasizes role-based agents reinforces that the industry at large finds patterns (like Curator) useful abstractions. We can confidently say the Curator pattern is not an isolated Salesforce idea but part of a broader movement toward modular AI agents.

AutoGen's summarizers and reasoning agents: AutoGen (from Microsoft Research) is a framework for multi-agent conversations, where agents can be LLM-driven and coordinate on tasks. In some published examples, AutoGen sets up a scenario with, say, a "Solver" agent and a "Helper" agent. The Helper might do something like summarize context or validate interim answers – again, a form of curation. In particular, AutoGen highlights the idea of an agent that can summarize conversation history to keep context manageable, and agents that can break down tasks. A summarizer agent in AutoGen may periodically read the dialogue between other agents and produce a concise summary (to prevent context window overflow). This is akin to a Curator working in real-time on streaming data (the stream being the conversation). Also, AutoGen's concept of a "Reasoning" agent could correlate with Curator if we think of reasoning as synthesizing multiple facts. How does this tie back to Salesforce? If we ever had a complex scenario where multiple Agentforce agents needed to chat or collaborate, a Curator agent could serve as the running memory or log analyst. For example, in a long approval process (maybe Supervisor and Action agents interacting), a Curator might record key points or decisions and summarize them at checkpoints. The goal is better decision-making through distilled information, which is universal.

From an integration perspective, AutoGen and similar frameworks often communicate via natural language messages. Salesforce could integrate an Agentforce agent with them via APIs or even using MCP as a bridge. The main takeaway is that the pattern of summarization and context-building is prevalent. Our Curator is Salesforce's embodiment of that pattern, emphasizing structured enterprise data and trust.

Microsoft Copilot and Syntex (document curation): Microsoft's ecosystem has introduced Copilot across many apps (like Office, Dynamics, etc.) and specifically SharePoint Syntex for content AI. Syntex, as discussed, automatically reads and tags documents, and can generate summaries of content to distill key points. This is precisely what a Curator for documents would do. For example, Syntex might take a 30-page contract and summarize the key clauses, or extract important fields. Microsoft 365 Copilot goes further to allow users to ask questions in plain language and get answers synthesized from their documents and emails (combining retrieval and generation). If we map that to our world: a Salesforce Curator could be set up to summarize documents stored in Salesforce (maybe files or Knowledge articles) relevant to a topic, akin to what Copilot might do with SharePoint documents. The difference is Salesforce's advantage in business context – our Curator could marry document info with CRM data (e.g., summarizing both the contract text and the related account's data). But conceptually, Syntex's capability of turning raw content into knowledge validates the Curator pattern strongly. It shows that major enterprise players see the need for AI that curates content, not just generates or records it. In fact, Microsoft's term "Content AI" is essentially about curation – classify, extract, summarize, connect content to make it usable.

We should also mention Tableau GPT (from Salesforce's side, introduced as part of AI Cloud). Tableau GPT aims to let users ask questions of their data and get natural language answers plus visualizations. Behind the scenes, it likely uses a combination of Curator-like steps: figuring out which data is relevant to the question, aggregating it (maybe running a query), then summarizing it in words and charts. So within Salesforce's own ecosystem, even outside of Agentforce, the idea of synthesizing data into insight is appearing.

Salesforce Data Cloud + GPT: Another piece from the ecosystem list is the combo of Data Cloud with GPT. Data Cloud (Salesforce's unified customer data platform) can act as a giant pool of data. But having data is not enough; insights must be extracted. Salesforce is indeed integrating GPT into Data Cloud for AI-driven insights. For example, finding patterns in customer behavior across millions of data points is a task for a Curator-like AI. One could see Data Cloud + GPT producing something like: "Segment X has seen a 20% uptick in engagement since last campaign, primarily due to feature Y usage" – which is a synthesized insight from raw telemetry and marketing data. Our Curator agents could be the ones orchestrating those Data Cloud queries and feeding the results to GPT. The outline specifically listed "Salesforce Data Cloud + GPT combos" as an ecosystem element, highlighting that our internal tools are moving in this direction. A Curator agent might soon be essentially a configuration in Data Cloud where you define a recipe of data + prompt and get auto-generated insights periodically. But until products fully automate that, our pattern and this playbook chapter help architects design it manually using the building blocks available.

Curators as glue in multi-agent swarms: A unifying perspective offered is that Curator agents are the glue in so-called "swarm" networks of agents. If you have a swarm of specialized AI agents working together (something envisioned by many AI thought leaders), those agents need to share context and memory. Curators serve exactly that role: gathering information, condensing it, and handing it off so the collective can be smarter. For instance, imagine an AI swarm handling an end-to-end customer service: one agent monitors social media (Sentinel), another formulates responses (Action), another checks policy (Supervisor), etc. A Curator agent could sit in the middle, building a real-time knowledge board of what's happening (customer sentiment trend, current issues, relevant knowledge base articles summarized) that all agents consult. This prevents each agent from working with a narrow view and enables intelligent delegation. One agent could ask the Curator, "Summarize the customer's history and recent sentiment" and then decide if escalation is needed. In essence, Curators provide a form of collective memory and situational awareness for multi-agent systems.

When integrating with external frameworks, we should ensure our Curator outputs are in standard formats (JSON, etc.) or even adhere to emerging standards like MCP or others. That way, if an organization wants to mix Salesforce agents with, say, an AWS or Azure-based agent, the hand-off can be smooth. Already, things like Model Context Protocol aim to standardize how AI agents exchange information and invoke tools. Salesforce could eventually support that, meaning a Curator agent could publish its summary in a format that any MCP-compliant agent (external or internal) can understand and use.

In conclusion for this section, the Curator pattern is widely recognized outside of Salesforce, albeit under various names (retriever, researcher, analyzer, summarizer). This validates its importance. Salesforce's implementation (Agentforce Curators) emphasizes integration with enterprise systems, point-and-click tooling plus Apex for flexibility, and trust (security & provenance). By referencing LangChain, CrewAI, AutoGen, and Microsoft's solutions, we can take comfort that adopting Curator agents is not a risky, unproven idea – it's becoming table stakes for AI-driven organizations to cope with the data tsunami. The difference is we are implementing it on our terms with Salesforce's trusted AI principles (e.g., respecting data governance, maintaining auditable logs via summaries stored in Salesforce, etc.). So, while learning from the ecosystem, we keep focus: our Curators ultimately serve Salesforce users and agents in a cohesive way.

With the ecosystem context clear, let's bring it back home. How do Curator agents specifically interconnect with the other Agentforce patterns we've covered? The final section will illustrate the downstream integrations – how Curators feed or enhance Sentinel, Supervisor, Presenter, Conductor, Action agents in practical workflows.

DOWNSTREAM INTEGRATION WITH OTHER PATTERNS

Throughout this chapter, we've mentioned that Curator agents often work in concert with other agent patterns. Now we'll explicitly map those connections, showing how a Curator's output flows into (or enhances) the behavior of Sentinel, Supervisor, Presenter, Conductor, and Action agents. By understanding these integrations, you'll see how Curators elevate the whole agent ecosystem's performance. We'll then cap it off with an end-to-end example – a Legal AI Workflow – combining Curator with several agent types in sequence, to paint a concrete picture of multi-agent collaboration.

Sentinel ← Curator: Sentinel agents are like watchtowers, scanning for specific conditions or threshold breaches. A Curator can act as a powerful pre-processor for a Sentinel. Instead of a Sentinel monitoring raw event fire-hoses (which could cause either alert fatigue or missed signals), a Curator can summarize and prioritize events, then feed those as a streamlined input to the Sentinel. For example, a Sentinel might normally watch every login attempt for suspicious patterns. With a Curator in front, that Sentinel could instead watch a curated feed like "summarized anomalous login events by region/hour". Concretely: the Curator could output something like "120 failed logins from IP range X in last 10 min (vs normal 5)" as a single record or event. The Sentinel then evaluates that (maybe it has a rule: if any summary shows >100 fails, trigger alarm). By doing this, we drastically reduce noise and false positives. The Sentinel isn't reacting to each blip but to patterns that the Curator distilled. This is how in security ops or system monitoring, you build a layered defense: detection (Curator compiles data) and alerting (Sentinel triggers on the compiled insight). In Salesforce terms, the Sentinel could be a Flow or Apex that subscribes to a platform event that the Curator publishes (e.g., HighFailLoginsEvent). The Curator essentially acts as a Sentinel's data analyst, ensuring the Sentinel gets high-quality, contextual input.

Supervisor ← Curator: Supervisor agents validate and refine decisions – often generating draft outputs (like a draft approval or recommendation) and checking against policies or context. Curators can greatly enhance Supervisors by providing the background context those decisions should consider. Take a use case: a Supervisor agent is deciding whether to approve a customer refund beyond policy. If it acts alone, it might just follow a rule (refund if < $1000). But if we insert a Curator that, for instance, summarizes the customer's profile ("Customer has 3 past escalations, VIP status, high lifetime value") and the reason for refund request (compiled from case notes), the Supervisor can make a more informed decision or craft a better justification. Essentially, the Curator supplies a dossier of relevant info for the Supervisor's decision. This could be fed directly – e.g., the Curator writes a summary to a field that the Supervisor's flow reads. Or orchestrated – the Supervisor's process calls the Curator sub-flow first to gather context, then proceeds to decision logic. Even in generative scenarios like a Supervisor agent drafting an email reply or a policy, having curated context means the Supervisor's LLM prompt can include "Given the following background...". For example, a "Contract Supervisor" agent generating a contract clause approval might use a Curator's summary of the clause differences to decide or to explain its decision. Without the Curator, the Supervisor might miss nuances or require human-provided context.

Presenter ← Curator: This pairing is one of the most direct. Presenter agents are the face of insights to end-users. When a Presenter is backed by a Curator, users get information that's both well-crafted (thanks to Presenter formatting) and substantive (thanks to Curator analysis). Consider a scenario: a Presenter agent is responsible for showing a sales manager a daily dashboard. If fed raw data, the Presenter might just show a bunch of charts and tables. But if a Curator first filters and highlights, the Presenter can instead display a crisp narrative: "Today's sales are 20% above average, driven by Region West (30% above target) while Region East is lagging." Perhaps with charts for each region attached. The Curator essentially provides the content that the Presenter turns into a final product. Technically, this might mean the Presenter's component (could be a Lightning Web Component or a formatted Slack message) calls the Curator's output object. As an example, a Presenter might retrieve the top 3 insights from a Daily_Sales_Insight__c object (populated by a Curator each morning) and then render them with nice icons and styling. The user doesn't even have to know there were two agents involved – they just see a great result. Another benefit: if the Presenter allows interactions (say a user clicks "Tell me more" on an insight), the Presenter could invoke the Curator to drill down and then display that. In a way, the Presenter and Curator can form a tight loop: Curator generates insights, Presenter delivers; user asks a follow-up, Presenter queries Curator for a deeper insight, and so on. This dynamic is reminiscent of Q&A systems like Copilot – the Curator is the knowledge provider, Presenter the conversational interface.

Conductor + Curator: The Conductor pattern coordinates multi-step workflows. When a Conductor has access to curated data, it can make smarter routing decisions. Imagine a Conductor agent managing an IT incident resolution process with multiple branches (like does it require a network specialist or a database specialist?). A Curator agent could analyze the incident details (logs, alerts) and determine the likely domain of the problem (e.g., "this looks similar to past database outages"). The Conductor then uses that info to route the flow down the "Database issue" branch automatically. Without the Curator, the Conductor might have to either default to a generic path or require a human classification. So Curator empowers autonomy in orchestration. In Salesforce, this could be implemented by having the Conductor's Flow call a Curator sub-flow at a decision point. The Curator returns a recommendation or classification, which the Flow evaluates in a Decision element to choose the next subflow. Another scenario is a Conductor orchestrating customer onboarding across departments. A Curator might summarize the customer's profile and needs after initial data collection, and the Conductor uses that to decide which teams (agents) to involve (e.g., if profile says "Large Enterprise with custom needs", branch to a more hands-on onboarding sequence). Essentially, the Curator injects "understanding" into what might otherwise be a static flow, making the Conductor more adaptive. This partnership highlights how patterns combine: Conductor (process logic) + Curator (data logic) yields a workflow that is both well-structured and context-aware.

Action agents and others: While not explicitly in the outline bullets, it's worth noting that Action agents (task executors) may also interface with Curators indirectly. For example, an Action agent that creates follow-up tasks based on analysis could take a Curator's output (insight) and then generate tasks from it. Think of a Customer Service Curator that finds "5 customers had repeat issues this week"; an Action agent might read that and create 5 proactive outreach tasks assigned to service reps. The Curator doesn't create tasks (that's Action's job), but it provides the reasoning for those tasks. Similarly, a Coach agent (pattern likely covered in a later chapter) that guides users might rely on curated knowledge to give advice. For instance, a Sales Coach agent telling a rep how to close a deal could use a Curator's win/loss analysis of similar deals to suggest best practices.

Let's bring it all together with the promised end-to-end journey example: a Legal AI Workflow. We'll string multiple agents in a sequence to see the interplay:

Curator (Legal Document Summarizer): This agent kicks off the process by reading new NDAs (nondisclosure agreements) that the company received from various partners. Suppose each NDA is slightly different. The Curator compares each to the standard NDA template and summarizes any non-standard clauses or risks. It clusters these by type (e.g., jurisdiction clauses, IP ownership clauses) and produces an output like: "NDA from Vendor X – non-standard jurisdiction (courts of Albania), no mutual indemnity (risk flag). NDA from Vendor Y – includes IP reuse clause not in template (risk flag)." Essentially, the Curator provides a digest of what's unusual in each document.

Supervisor (Legal Approval Agent): Now a Supervisor agent takes those Curator outputs and validates or decides what to do. For instance, this Supervisor's job is to decide if an NDA can be approved as-is or needs legal review. It reads the Curator's summary of Vendor X's NDA which has a risk flag on indemnity. The Supervisor has rules: any indemnity issues require review by a senior counsel. So it marks that NDA as "needs review" (maybe even drafts an email to the legal team highlighting the clause, using the Curator's text as a starting quote). For Vendor Y's IP clause, maybe the Supervisor knows the company stance on IP reuse is strict, so it also flags that. If an NDA had no flags from Curator, the Supervisor might auto-approve it or at least not escalate it. In effect, the Supervisor uses the background context from the Curator to apply policy intelligently. If we imagine this as a Flow: the Flow looped through each NDA, called Curator (maybe as an Apex action) to get summary, then in a Decision shape decided "if summary contains 'risk flag' then route for manual review, else e-sign automatically via an Action agent".

Presenter (Legal Escalation Summarizer): For those NDAs flagged by the Supervisor, a Presenter agent steps in to frame an escalation summary to the legal counsel or management. It might compile the two flagged NDAs into one report or message. For example, the Presenter sends a Slack message to the Chief Legal Officer: "2 NDAs need review: Vendor X (jurisdiction = Albania, indemnity clause missing), Vendor Y (IP reuse clause). Details attached." The "details" could be a nicely formatted table or embedded images of the clause text. The Presenter didn't discover these issues – it's simply packaging what the Curator and Supervisor identified, in a digestible way for a busy executive. The executive can quickly see the key issues without reading all documents.

Action (Automated Routing Agent): Finally, suppose once the NDA is approved (after legal review), some follow-up actions are needed – like storing the signed NDA in a repository, updating the vendor record, notifying the requestor. An Action agent can handle that. If the Supervisor agent approved some NDAs automatically, the Action agent might proactively route those to e-signature and archive them. For the escalated ones, after a human eventually approves them, a trigger could similarly call the Action agent to do the routing. This Action agent is more peripheral in the "insight" process, but it's important for closing the loop: ensuring the insights and decisions actually result in proper execution (documents stored, people notified). In our workflow, once legal gives the green light, the Action agent uses the info from Curator/Supervisor (like which clauses were modified) to maybe fill in metadata in the contract management system, then sends it off to DocuSign and updates Salesforce that NDA is in effect.

This scenario shows how multiple pattern-agents hand off to each other: the Curator provides the raw insight (document differences), the Supervisor provides judgement and decision based on that insight, the Presenter communicates it to a human stakeholder, and the Action carries out the final tasks (routing signed docs). The result is a semi-autonomous legal process: routine NDAs get handled without much human effort, and non-routine ones are surfaced with clear analysis for swift human decision. Trust is maintained because the human sees exactly what the AI flagged (transparency via the Curator's summary), and efficiency is gained by eliminating tedious reading for lawyers.

We can generalize from this: in many multi-agent systems, Curator agents feed information into decision or action loops, ensuring that each agent down the line isn't working blind. They reduce duplication (each agent doesn't need to gather context separately) and increase consistency (everyone uses the same synthesized truth). Whether it's a Sentinel reacting to curated alerts, a Supervisor making policy calls on curated facts, or a Presenter explaining curated findings, the Curator is an enabler and amplifier of value for the whole pattern network.

With these integrations understood, we have a full perspective on the Curator pattern: why it matters, how to build it, how it's applied in various domains, and how it meshes with other AI agent patterns in Salesforce and beyond. We can now summarize the key takeaways of the chapter and prepare to move from the realm of insight (Curator) to the realm of action.

SUMMARY

In this chapter, we introduced the Curator pattern, depicting agents that sift, structure, and synthesize data from multiple sources into actionable knowledge. We explored why Curator agents are rising in importance: they address the modern challenge of information overload by turning raw data into timely, contextual insights – enabling businesses to be insight-driven rather than data-blinded. We broke down the Curator's lifecycle (ingest → filter → cluster → synthesize → output) and saw how each stage can be implemented with Salesforce Agentforce tools (Agent Builder, Apex, Flow, External Services, etc.), often augmented with GPT for summarization. Key design principles like relevance scoring, metadata tagging for provenance, and graceful handling of partial data were highlighted to ensure Curators produce reliable and trustworthy outputs.

Crucially, we demonstrated that the Curator pattern is a force-multiplier for other agent patterns. Nearly every other AI agent – from Sentinels to Supervisors to Presenters – performs more intelligently and effectively when fueled by curated input. Curators serve as the insight layer that informs decision agents and focuses communication agents on what matters. Through examples in HR, Legal, Finance, Field Ops, and Procurement, we saw how Curators empower teams to uncover patterns (be it turnover causes, contract risks, spending anomalies, or operational incidents) that would have been hard to spot manually. Each use case reinforced the adaptable nature of the pattern across domains, as well as its consistent value: speed to insight, consistency, and context for action.

We also placed Curators in the context of the broader AI ecosystem. The pattern aligns with techniques in open frameworks like LangChain (retrieval + summary chains), multi-agent systems like CrewAI and AutoGen (researcher and summarizer roles), and enterprise AI offerings like Microsoft's Copilot and Syntex (content summarization). This context assures us that investing in Curator agents is part of a forward-looking AI strategy, not an isolated experiment. Salesforce's approach leverages our platform strengths – security, integration, low-code orchestration – to deliver Curators that are enterprise-ready.

By following the guidance in this chapter, you should be equipped to design Curator agents that act as your organization's "connective tissue" for knowledge. They gather and relate information that was previously siloed or overwhelming, and convert it into insights that drive smarter decisions and automations. In doing so, Curator agents help ensure that your AI solutions are not just automated, but intelligently automated, always starting from a foundation of understanding.

As we conclude, we transition from insight to execution. Now that we have mechanisms to produce high-quality insights (thanks to the Curator), the next step is to act on those insights safely and effectively. In the next chapter,

The Action Pattern, we'll see how Task Executor agents carry out work across systems and processes, closing the loop by turning curated knowledge and decisions into real-world changes. The Action agents will leverage the groundwork laid by Curators to ensure every automated action is informed and context-aware. Together, these patterns – Curator and Action – enable a powerful cycle of "understand, then act" that is at the heart of autonomous enterprise operations. Let's move on to Chapter 8 to explore how agents take action.

8

THE ACTION PATTERN (TASK EXECUTOR AGENT)

AI agents can fulfill many roles, but in the Salesforce Agentforce ecosystem one pattern serves as the bedrock for getting things done: the Action agent. While other agent patterns like the Conductor, Supervisor, or Curator are designed to orchestrate processes, provide oversight, or summarize information, the Action pattern is all about execution. An Action agent takes a defined intent and turns it into a concrete change in the system – it might update a record, send a notification, provision a user account, or log an event. Crucially, it does so within strict guardrails, ensuring safety and consistency. In essence, if other agents plan what to do or why, the Action agent focuses on doing the task within governed boundaries.

The Action pattern is often the most accessible starting point for teams beginning to build AI agents. It's conceptually straightforward and highly scalable, making it a great candidate for early automation wins. Many routine tasks in an organization – from escalating a support case, to adding a new hire to all the right systems – can be offloaded to an Action agent. These agents excel at handling repeatable steps that have clear instructions and don't require creative judgment. Importantly, every Action agent operates in a permission-aware manner: it respects Salesforce's security model and any business rules in place, so it only performs actions it's allowed to perform. This means you can deploy Action agents confidently in environments where data access and compliance matter, knowing that they won't overstep their privileges.

Several key traits make Action agents stand out relative to other patterns:

Bounded: An Action agent works within predefined logic and guardrails. It will never stray beyond the tasks and rules it was given. This bounded scope prevents "rogue" behavior – the agent can't suddenly decide to perform an unrelated action or exceed the limits set by its designers.

Auditable: Every step an Action agent takes is traceable. These agents produce clear execution logs or records of what they did, when they did it, and with which inputs. This audit trail makes it easy to review an agent's work after the fact or even replay its actions in testing. In regulated industries, such audibility is crucial – Action agents leave the kind of footprint compliance officers love to see.

Stackable: Action agents are modular building blocks. You can combine many small Action agents to accomplish a larger process. For example, a Conductor (orchestrator) agent might call a series of Action agents in sequence to fulfill a multi-step workflow. Because Action agents focus on discrete tasks, they stack neatly – the output of one can feed into the next. This composability means teams can reuse Action agents across different processes (one agent might handle "Send an email notification," reusable by many higher-level flows).

Testable: Given their deterministic and focused nature, Action agents are easy to unit test and integration test. There are no complex decision branches to simulate – you feed the agent an input and verify it produces the expected outcome. Teams can create robust automated tests for each Action agent (for instance, using Apex tests or Flow test plans) to ensure it handles both happy paths and error conditions. This testability leads to high confidence in deploying Action agents to production, since their behavior is well-understood and verified.

To support the Action pattern, Salesforce provides a rich toolkit. Agent Builder allows you to declaratively define an agent's purpose, its inputs and outputs, and even some guardrails, without writing much code. Under the hood, an Action agent's work is usually implemented with either an Invocable Apex class or a declarative Flow – these are the mechanisms that carry out the actual task. Teams often use Flow Builder for straightforward logic (point-and-click automation) and turn to Invocable Apex when more complex or external operations are needed. Action agents also leverage Custom Metadata for configuration: you might store allowable parameters, toggles, or limits in metadata to avoid hard-coding them. This way, administrators can adjust an agent's behavior (like turning an action on/off or changing a threshold) without modifying code. Finally, once deployed, all agent activities can be monitored through the Agentforce Command Center or similar logging dashboards. The Command Center provides a real-time view of what agents are doing – successful completions, any errors, execution times, and so on – giving ops teams the oversight needed to manage automation at scale.

In summary, the Action pattern gives us "safe automation building blocks." These agents carry out defined tasks reliably, enforce permissions at every step, and generate logs for accountability. They are simple by design – which is exactly why they scale so well across an enterprise. Many organizations start their agent journey with a few Action agents tackling low-hanging fruit in automation (for example, auto-closing resolved tickets or syncing data between systems) and then combine these into larger flows over time. As we move into the next section, we'll define more formally what makes a task executor agent tick and how to recognize the Action pattern in practice, distinguishing it from the other agent patterns in the Agentforce playbook.

DEFINING THE ACTION PATTERN

What exactly qualifies as an "Action" agent in Salesforce Agentforce? At its core, an Action agent is an autonomous task executor: it takes a specific input or command and carries out a single well-defined operation in response. Unlike more complex agents, it isn't expected to engage in extended dialogues, make nuanced decisions, or generate elaborate content – its job is to do the thing requested, then report back. To understand an Action agent's nature, it helps to break down its core lifecycle into a few succinct stages: Receive → Validate → Execute → Log → Respond.

Receive: The agent receives a task request or instruction. This could be triggered by another agent, initiated by a user action (like clicking a button that invokes the agent), or kicked off by an event (for example, a record change or a scheduled time trigger). The key at this stage is that the agent has a clear, structured input that tells it what to do – for instance, "Create a task for employee ID 123 with these details" or "Send an email to customer X using template Y."

Validate: Before doing any work, the Action agent validates the request. It checks that all required inputs are present and well-formed (e.g. if a record ID or an email address is provided, that they are in the correct format). It also checks permissions and business rules: should this agent run this action right now and for this data? For example, if the agent is supposed to update a record, it might verify that the running user or context has edit rights on that record, or consult a custom setting to ensure the action is currently enabled. This step acts as the agent's safety net – if anything is off (missing data, failed a safeguard, etc.), the agent will typically stop here and respond with an error or no-op, rather than attempting an unsafe execution.

Execute: If validation passes, the agent proceeds to execute the task. This is the primary work the agent was designed to do. In our examples, this might mean actually creating the new Task record in Salesforce for the onboarding checklist, or sending out the email via a Salesforce email action, or calling an external API through Apex to provision a user in a third-party system. The execution is done within the confines of Salesforce's transaction model (or according to whatever context the agent runs under). Notably, this step is deterministic – given the same inputs and state, the agent's execution should follow the same path and produce the same result. There's no randomness or complex AI reasoning here; it's often straightforward procedural logic.

Log: After attempting the execution, a well-designed Action agent logs the outcome. "Logging" could range from writing a record to a custom Log object (e.g. an Agent Execution Log custom object capturing agent name, time, success/failure, and details) to simply using the built-in platform event logs or debug logs. The purpose is to ensure that there is a record of this agent's actions for later review. If the agent hit an error or exception, this log is where it would note what went wrong (and often, the agent would also handle the exception gracefully so that the error can be surfaced without causing downstream chaos). Logging is part of what makes the Action pattern auditable – anyone with access can later answer "what happened and why" for each execution.

Respond: Finally, the Action agent returns a response or otherwise signals completion. In Salesforce terms, if the agent was invoked by another process (say a Flow or another agent), it might return output variables – for example, "success = true" or an ID of a record it created, or an error message if something failed. If the Action was triggered by a platform event or user action, the "response" might simply be that it updated the necessary records and maybe sent a confirmation (like posting a Slack message or updating a field to indicate completion). In some cases, the response could trigger downstream processes – for instance, the Action agent might fire a platform event or call another agent as a next step if it's part of a chain. But it does not linger around making further decisions: once its task is done, the Action agent's job is complete until the next time it's called.

This lifecycle ensures that Action agents remain predictable and safe. They always double-check conditions before doing anything irreversible, and they always leave behind information about what they did.

We can also describe the Action pattern in terms of a few important characteristics:

Deterministic: An Action agent's behavior is deterministic, meaning it's governed by predefined logic that produces expected results. Given the same inputs and system state, an Action agent should reliably perform the same steps and yield the same outcome every time. There's no open-ended reasoning or on-the-fly learning happening in an Action agent. This is important for trust – teams know that an Action agent won't suddenly change its behavior or output unpredictably. For example, if you have an Action agent for "deactivate user account," it will only perform that function following the script you gave it – nothing more, nothing less. This determinism makes it much easier to test and trust these agents in production.

Permission-bound: Action agents respect user roles, permissions, and system limits at all times. They run with a specific Salesforce user context (or integration context), and they are typically designed to honor the sharing rules and profile/permission set constraints of that context. If an Action agent is asked to do something that the initiating context isn't allowed to do, it should detect that and refuse or fail gracefully. For instance, if an Action agent tries to access a record type that the running user has no access to, it shouldn't magically bypass that – it's bound by the same data security model as any manual user or Apex code would be. Additionally, "system limits" means it's aware of governance limits (like API call limits, SOQL query limits, etc.) and any business-imposed limits (like "don't delete more than 50 records at once"). Designing Action agents with these boundaries in mind ensures they don't become a loophole that circumvents security or a runaway process that consumes too many resources.

Lightweight: By design, Action agents are kept lightweight. They don't maintain long-term state or memory between runs, and they don't engage in multi-step decision trees internally. Each invocation of an Action agent is independent – it does its one unit of work and ends. There's no session or context carried over (aside from what info you explicitly pass in or log out). This statelessness simplifies their design and scaling: you can run many instances of the same Action agent in parallel (for different tasks) without them conflicting. "Lightweight" also refers to the fact that they are meant to do a bounded piece of work quickly. If a piece of logic grows too heavy – for example, if what you're attempting stops being a single step and starts involving numerous conditional sub-steps – that might be a sign you actually need a different pattern (like a Conductor for orchestration). In practice, being lightweight means an Action agent's implementation (whether Flow or Apex) is typically concise and focused, often without complex branching logic.

In terms of inputs and outputs, Action agents deal with very concrete information. The input to an Action agent is usually a specific task definition or command. For example: "Create a follow-up task for case 00012345 assigned to the billing team," or "Generate a PDF of Contract 98765 and post it to the Documents library," or "Provision a new developer sandbox for user U12345." The input will often include identifiers (record IDs, user IDs), parameters (like template names, field values), or references to content. Because the input format is usually known in advance (indeed, defined when you set up the agent in Agent Builder), the agent can validate and parse it easily in the Validate stage. On the output side, the Action agent typically provides a simple confirmation or error status. If everything went well, the agent might return a success flag or a result object (e.g. the ID of the new record it created, or a message "Email sent to X"). If something went wrong, the output could be an error flag and an error message detailing the issue (which might be logged or displayed to a user). In some designs, an Action agent might not need to return anything if it's triggering further steps – for instance, if it emits a platform event or calls another process, the fact that it did so might be the "output." But generally, think of Action agent outputs as transaction receipts – they say "I did X, and here's the outcome."

Depending on the use case, Action agents can run in different execution modes in Salesforce. Some actions are best done synchronously: for example, if a user clicks a button in a Lightning page to perform an action and expects an immediate result, the Action agent's logic might run real-time in a Flow (synchronous Flow) or as part of the button's controller action. Other tasks might be better suited to queued or scheduled execution – especially long-running or bulk tasks. Salesforce Flow supports scheduled paths (e.g. "run this daily" or "run 10 minutes from now") which an Action agent can leverage for delayed jobs. And for programmatic control, you might implement an Action agent with a Queueable Apex class or a future method, to run asynchronously in the background (for example, processing a batch of records or calling an external service without making the user wait). The Agentforce framework doesn't mandate one or the other; it provides flexibility. A single Action agent defined in Agent Builder could have multiple implementations behind the scenes for different contexts (though usually you'll pick one). The key is that whether it runs in real-time or async, the agent still follows the same lifecycle and principles outlined above. It's often a good practice to keep the execution time of an Action agent short – if something will take a long time, offload it to an async process – so that each Action remains a quick, contained operation.

Now, let's talk about the tools that make all this possible in Salesforce. When building an Action agent, you'll typically use:

Agent Builder: This is Salesforce's declarative interface for creating and managing agents (part of the Agentforce suite). In Agent Builder, you define the agent's metadata: give it a name, description, define its role or purpose, specify what inputs it expects and what outputs it produces, and outline any guardrails (like requiring certain conditions). For an Action agent, this is where you set up the scaffold – essentially telling Salesforce "we have an agent that will perform X kind of task." Agent Builder might also allow you to select the underlying mechanism (Flow or Apex) that the agent will invoke for execution.

Flow Builder: Many Action agents can be implemented as Salesforce Flows. A Flow is a click-and-configure process automation tool that can update records, send emails, call Apex code, and more. For simple to moderately complex tasks, a Flow is often ideal because it's easier to maintain visually and can be modified without deploying code. For example, an Action agent that "creates an onboarding checklist record" could be a Flow that takes in a new hire's ID and then creates a set of Task records linked to that hire. You would build that logic in Flow Builder and then register the flow as the implementation for your agent. Flows can also include fault paths (to catch exceptions) which align nicely with the agent's logging and error response needs.

Invocable Apex: Sometimes the task is too complex for a plain Flow, or requires operations not supported in Flow (like calling an external web service, performing complex calculations, or handling large data sets with finer control). In those cases, developers create an Apex class annotated with @InvocableMethod to handle the logic. Invocable Apex methods can be called from Flows or Agent Builder as reusable actions. For our Action agent, an invocable Apex might encapsulate a chunk of logic like "deactivate user in Salesforce and also disable their Single Sign-On in the external system." Apex gives you the full power of code to do these things, including transaction control, error handling, and integration capabilities. When using Apex, you still keep the spirit of the Action pattern – the Apex method should do one focused task. Notably, if an Action agent uses Apex, that Apex can be invoked by other flows or even other agents, making the Action agent a kind of API endpoint inside your org for that functionality.

Custom Metadata: This is a powerful feature for making your Action agents flexible and admin-configurable. Custom Metadata Types allow you to store custom records that are deployable and packageable (unlike List Custom Settings, they are metadata rather than data). You might use custom metadata to define, for example, categories of tasks and what an Action agent is allowed to do for each category. Suppose you have an Action agent that can "generate a report" – you might have a metadata table of report types it can generate, and maybe which user profiles are allowed to trigger which reports. The Action agent's logic (in Apex or Flow) would reference this metadata at runtime to decide whether to proceed or how to execute. By using metadata for such rules, you avoid hard-coding critical controls into the agent. This means if a business admin needs to adjust a limit or add a new allowed value, they can do so via a metadata record rather than asking a developer to change code. In short, metadata turns your Action agent into a governed service – the logic is fixed, but the configuration is flexible.

Pro tip: Use Custom Metadata to define task categories and execution constraints for your Action agents. This makes it easy to delegate execution of tasks without exposing the underlying controls. For example, an agent might read a "Task Configuration" metadata entry to decide what it's permitted to do. By adjusting metadata, you can enable or disable certain actions, set thresholds (like maximum records to process), or switch the agent's behavior per environment – all without altering the agent's code.

Bringing these elements together, a well-defined Action pattern implementation might look like this: you create an Agent Definition in Agent Builder (say "Onboarding Checklist Creator" agent). You implement its logic with an Apex invocable method that creates checklist records, and you use a Custom Metadata type called "Onboarding Task Template" to drive what tasks get created for which role. The Apex method reads from that metadata to know that, for example, a Sales new hire gets a set of sales training tasks, while an Engineer new hire gets a different set. The agent validates the input (ensure the new hire Id exists and is active), executes by creating the tasks from the template, logs its actions in a custom "Onboarding_Log__c" object, and responds back (perhaps returning the list of tasks created or a success message). This entire agent can be invoked on-demand – maybe a Conductor agent calls it after a hiring approval.

By now, you should have a clear picture of what the Action pattern entails: a focused, reliable agent that executes one task at a time, under tight control. Next, we'll explore when to use this pattern (it's not for every situation) and how to recognize the appropriate scenarios. In the next section, we'll look at the ideal use cases for Action agents as well as situations where another pattern (like Supervisor or Conductor) would be a better choice, complete with a handy decision tree to guide your design choices.

WHEN AND WHY TO USE ACTION AGENTS

Even though Action agents are incredibly useful, it's important to deploy them in the right contexts. This section discusses where the Action pattern shines and where another agent pattern might be more suitable. In other words: when should a task be executed autonomously by an Action agent, and when should you involve humans, more complex orchestration, or analytical logic?

Ideal use cases for Action agents include "quick win" automations and well-bounded backend tasks. Because Action agents are straightforward and safe, they are perfect for low-hanging fruit automation – those tasks in your business that are clearly defined, frequent, and time-consuming for humans. For example, if every time a customer's contract is signed you need to create 3 follow-up tasks and send a welcome email, that's a repeatable process an Action agent could handle easily. Teams often start by identifying such opportunities: What are we doing over and over that a script could do for us? With Agentforce, an admin or developer can encapsulate that repetitive step in an Action agent and schedule or trigger it to run automatically, saving time and reducing errors. These quick wins not only improve efficiency but also build trust in AI agents within the organization – since Action agents are safe and auditable, stakeholders see that automation doesn't have to be a black box.

Another ideal scenario is replacing simple trigger logic or button-click routines with Action agents. In Salesforce today, many orgs have Flow triggers, Process Builder rules, or even Apex Trigger code that performs automatic updates based on certain conditions (for instance, "when an Opportunity is marked Closed-Won, create a renewal Opportunity" or "when a Case is escalated, notify the supervisor via email"). These are essentially hard-coded automations. By migrating such logic into an Action agent, you gain a few advantages. First, you can manage and version that logic more systematically via Agentforce tooling. Second, you can expose that action for reuse in other contexts (maybe that "create renewal" action should also be callable by a bot or from an external system – an Action agent can serve that need, whereas a trigger is internal-only). Third, wrapping the logic in an agent means you automatically get the logging, permission checks, and testing framework benefits we discussed. In sum, if you find yourself writing a bit of backend logic to do something simple, consider making it an Action agent instead – it could make the functionality more modular and maintainable.

Perhaps the most strategic use of Action agents is encapsulating backend execution for multi-agent workflows. In a complex AI agent system, you might have high-level agents that plan and converse (like a Conductor that decides a sequence of steps, or a Companion that chats with a user to collect input). These higher-level agents shouldn't themselves do the dirty work of updating databases or calling APIs – that would mix concerns and make them less general. Instead, they should delegate those tasks to Action agents. For example, imagine a Conductor agent orchestrating an employee onboarding: it might have steps like "setup IT accounts", "notify facilities for desk prep", "send welcome email". Each of those steps can be an Action agent (one for IT account setup, one for facilities ticket creation, one for sending email). The Conductor simply invokes them in order. This separation is good architecture: it means each Action agent can be developed and tested in isolation, and potentially reused in other processes (the IT account setup Action might also be used when someone changes roles or leaves the company, not just hiring). Thus, whenever you're building a workflow that has distinct tasks, it's a sign to implement each task as an Action agent and have a higher pattern coordinate them. We'll see more of this composition later in this chapter, but it's worth noting here as a "why Action agents matter" point – they enable complex automations by doing the individual steps reliably.

Now, knowing when not to use an Action agent is just as important. There are scenarios where the Action pattern is not the best fit:

If the task requires human judgment or discretion, don't automate it fully with an Action agent. In cases where a decision needs a person's approval, intuition, or domain expertise, the Supervisor pattern is more appropriate. A Supervisor agent is designed to involve humans in the loop – for example, an AI could draft a recommendation and a human supervisor approves or adjusts it. If you tried to force such a scenario into an Action agent, you'd either end up bypassing a needed approval (risky!) or you'd essentially build a check that halts for manual input, which an Action agent alone isn't equipped to handle elegantly. A concrete example: expense report processing. If an expense is above $5,000, maybe a human manager must approve it. It would be unwise to have an Action agent automatically pay out $10,000 because that needs discretion. Instead, you'd use a Supervisor agent to handle the approval workflow, and once approved, that agent (or a Conductor) would call an Action agent to actually issue the payment. In summary, Action agents thrive on clear-cut, no-human-needed tasks. The moment you need human sign-off or subjective judgment, bring in a Supervisor pattern to complement or replace the Action at that decision point. (Remember: an Action agent can still be part of the flow after approval – it's just not deciding anything, only executing the post-approval steps.)

If the process involves multiple steps, branching logic, or complex sequencing, an Action agent by itself is not sufficient – use a Conductor. The Conductor pattern (which we cover in another chapter) is essentially an orchestrator or workflow manager agent. If you find your "simple" task is actually not so simple – perhaps it involves calling several sub-tasks in order, handling different outcomes, or rolling back if something fails – then you're dealing with a multi-step process. That's beyond the scope of a single Action agent, which should ideally just do one of those steps. Trying to cram an entire process into one Action agent would lead to a bloated, hard-to-maintain piece of automation with lots of conditional code (breaking the "lightweight" principle). Instead, you would break it down: let a Conductor agent figure out the sequence and invoke a series of Action agents (or even other patterns like Supervisor or Curator if needed at certain steps). For instance, a customer onboarding might need to create an account, set initial preferences, send a welcome package, and schedule a follow-up call. Rather than one agent doing all of that, it's cleaner to have a Conductor call four Action agents in turn. Each Action does its piece, and the Conductor ensures they all happen in the right order, handling any branches (if account creation fails, maybe skip other steps, etc.). So, when coordination is complex, favor the Conductor pattern – use Action agents as the worker bees, not as the whole hive.

If the problem at hand requires data understanding, analysis, or summarization, the Action pattern is not the right approach – consider a Curator or Presenter agent. Action agents don't "think" or analyze; they execute known instructions. But many AI use cases involve interpreting data or generating insight (like reading a document and summarizing key points, or analyzing a customer's sentiment from their interactions). Those fall under patterns like the Curator (which synthesizes and structures information) or the Presenter (which formats and presents information to humans). If you have a task such as "summarize the last 100 support cases to identify common issues," that's not a straightforward deterministic action – that's an analytical job perfect for a Curator agent, possibly using an LLM under the hood. Similarly, if you need to take raw data and present it in a user-friendly way (perhaps an agent that creates a brief report for an end-user), that's where a Presenter agent shines. An Action agent in those scenarios would not be intelligent enough to do the summarization or presentation; it would either do nothing useful or you'd end up embedding an LLM call inside it which drifts from the Action pattern's philosophy. To put it simply: use the right tool for the job. Action agents are the doers, not the thinkers or explainers. When the task calls for understanding content or interacting with a user's request in a nuanced way, look to the other patterns.

To help decide between these patterns, it's useful to visualize a quick decision process. The following decision tree illustrates when you might choose an Action agent versus a Supervisor or Conductor:

Decision tree: Choosing the right agent pattern for a task. If a task requires human judgment or approval, prefer a Supervisor agent (involving a human-in-the-loop for oversight). If a task requires multiple coordinated steps or complex branching, use a Conductor agent to orchestrate (with possibly many Actions under it). If neither of those conditions apply – the task is a single, self-contained step that can be automated end-to-end – then an Action agent is likely the appropriate choice for full automation. This diagram helps teams quickly scope a new automation request: by asking a couple of key questions about the nature of the task, you can narrow in on the right pattern.

In practice, these patterns can also work together. It's not always "choose one and that's it." You might have a Supervisor + Action combination (for example, a Supervisor agent gets human approval on a recommended action, then calls an Action agent to execute it). Or a Conductor + Action relationship as discussed. The decision tree's main purpose is to prevent misuse of the Action pattern – such as trying to force a human workflow or multi-step saga into a lone Action agent – which would lead to brittle or unsafe automations.

As a general guideline, start by implementing tasks with Action agents when you can. They are the simplest to build and deploy, and you can always integrate them into larger flows later. Many organizations accumulate a library of Action agents for common tasks (create record, send email, update permission, etc.) across departments. Then, when higher-level processes are being automated, those building blocks are ready to plug in. On the flip side, recognize when not to push an Action agent too far. If stakeholders are uncomfortable fully automating a particular decision, that's a sign to use a human approval (Supervisor pattern) before the Action. If a single Action agent play is turning into a spaghetti of "if this then do that then the other," it's time to refactor that into a Conductor with multiple Action steps.

By wisely choosing where to apply the Action pattern, you ensure that your AI agents deliver value quickly and safely. In the next section, we'll explore concrete examples of Action agents deployed across various business functions. This will ground the discussion in reality – seeing how Action agents can automate tasks in HR, Finance, IT, Legal, Operations, and beyond, and how those use cases map to our pattern guidelines. These examples will also highlight the kinds of triggers and controls that go into real-world Action agents.

USE CASES ACROSS THE ENTERPRISE

One of the strengths of the Action pattern is its broad applicability. Virtually every department in an enterprise has repetitive tasks that follow rules – ripe opportunities for automation. In this section, we look at how Action agents can be applied in different functional areas like HR, Finance, IT, Legal, and Operations. Each example is hypothetical but reflective of common needs in that domain. We'll also illustrate these examples in a tabular format to show the key elements: the function, the specific task being automated, what triggers the agent, how the Action agent executes it, which Salesforce tools are involved, and what risk controls or guardrails are in place (since enterprise tasks often require oversight).

Consider the following cross-functional use cases for Action agents:

HR (Human Resources): When an employee leaves the company, HR and IT have to deactivate that person's access across numerous systems (Salesforce, email, VPN, building access, etc.). Often this is a manual process or handled by a combination of IT scripts and human follow-up, which can be slow or prone to misses. An Action agent can take a "user termination" event and automatically deactivate the user's accounts in integrated systems. For example, as soon as HR marks an employee record as terminated effective today, an Action agent could fire that night to deactivate the user in Salesforce (set their login inactive), call a script or API to disable their Active Directory account, remove their Slack access, and so on – all within seconds and with complete logging. This ensures no lag between someone leaving and their access being revoked, improving security.

Finance: In many companies, budget adjustments or expense approvals, once decided, have to be entered into an ERP or financial system. Suppose the finance team uses Salesforce to approve a budget increase for a project. Instead of relying on a financial analyst to then manually update the ERP, an Action agent could automatically submit the approved budget adjustment into the ERP system via an integration. The trigger might be the approval record reaching a "Approved" status. The agent (with proper integration credentials) could call a MuleSoft API or direct integration to the ERP, passing the relevant data. By doing this as an automated action, you remove a manual step, and because it's an Action agent, it will check that all required fields (cost center, approval IDs, etc.) are present and log the transaction ID from the ERP for audit. It essentially acts like a diligent accounting clerk who never types the wrong number.

IT (Information Technology): IT departments handle lots of service requests that are actually very standard, like provisioning a new software license for a user, resetting a password, or spinning up a development environment. These tasks have clear procedures. An Action agent in IT could be set up to handle, say, "Provision new developer sandbox" for a user. The trigger could be a Service Cloud case or a request in an IT portal; once approved (if approval is needed), an Action agent can take over. It might use the Salesforce Metadata API or SFDX (Salesforce DX) through an Apex call to actually create a sandbox for that user, assign them appropriate permissions, and maybe send them an email when ready. Another Action agent could handle simpler tasks like "unlock user account" or "generate VPN credentials" by interfacing with the appropriate systems via API. By automating these, IT can respond 24/7 and faster to common requests. Of course, each Action agent here must obey policies – e.g., only provision a sandbox if the user is in the allowed group, only generate VPN access for certain roles, etc., which can be enforced via metadata and checks.

Legal: Legal operations often involve moving documents and updating statuses across systems. For instance, once the legal team has reviewed a contract and marked it as "risk-approved," that contract might need to be docketed (filed) in a legal repository or sent to a monitoring system. An Action agent can watch for a "Risk Review Completed" field on a Contract record. When it flips to true (maybe set by a Curator or Supervisor agent that helped with the review), the Action agent kicks in to assign that contract to the next stage: perhaps creating a record in a docketing system with key metadata, or uploading the PDF to an archive, or even emailing a copy to external counsel. The agent ensures the contract is properly handed off without paralegals doing those routine steps. It would log, of course, the time and place it filed the contract. Risk controls here might include verifying that the contract indeed has a risk rating and approval attached before moving it – ensuring nothing slips through incomplete.

Operations: Think of a manufacturing or logistics context where sensors and devices emit signals. A warehouse might have IoT sensors counting items or noting equipment status. A Sentinel agent might detect an anomaly (like "conveyor belt motor overheating"). But an Action agent can handle routine logging of these events into Salesforce. For example, every hour, a sensor feed comes in with counts of packages processed. An Action agent could take those readings (maybe coming via an API or platform event) and log them into a custom Salesforce object for operational metrics. This replaces a manual data entry or separate ETL process. Or, if a threshold is passed (e.g., temperature too high), a Sentinel flags it and directly triggers an Action agent to, say, shut down the machine via an API call to the control system. In all such cases, the Action agent is doing a direct, physical or record update action in response to a signal. The benefit is real-time responsiveness and elimination of human error (no one forgets to log an event or turn off the machine). Naturally, you'd build in safety checks – the agent might check "if temperature > X and last shutdown action was > 10 minutes ago" before sending a second shutdown command, etc., to avoid spamming or overreacting.

These examples show how versatile Action agents can be. Let's compile them in a list for clarity, listing the function, task, trigger, the Action agent's role, the tools/implementation, and how we make sure each agent operates safely:

HR

- **Task (example use case):** Deactivate a terminated user across systems.
- **Trigger event or condition:** Employee termination finalized in the HR system, such as status set to "Terminated."
- **Action agent (role):** User Access Revoker, responsible for disabling the user in Salesforce and connected systems.
- **Tools used:** Salesforce Flow with invocable Apex calling external APIs such as Active Directory.

- **Risk controls and guardrails:** Executes only for confirmed terminations; uses administrator-level integration credentials; logs all changes for audit purposes.

Finance

- **Task (example use case):** Post an approved budget adjustment to the ERP system.
- **Trigger event or condition:** Finance approval record marked as "Approved."
- **Action agent (role):** Budget Sync Agent, responsible for updating ERP budget figures.
- **Tools used:** Apex invoking ERP APIs through MuleSoft.
- **Risk controls and guardrails:** Verifies approval signatures before submission; restricts execution to specific record types; records ERP transaction IDs and status.

IT

- **Task (example use case):** Provision new hire accounts such as email, CRM access, and VPN.
- **Trigger event or condition:** New hire onboarding case closed or an approved provisioning request.
- **Action agent (role):** IT Provisioner, responsible for creating user accounts and assigning licenses.
- **Tools used:** Multi-step Salesforce Flow calling Apex for external system integration.
- **Risk controls and guardrails:** Triggers only for new employees with HR approval; uses predefined provisioning templates; includes error handling that alerts IT if any step fails.

Legal

- **Task (example use case):** Docket a reviewed contract in the legal archive system.
- **Trigger event or condition:** Contract record marked with "Risk-Reviewed = Yes."
- **Action agent (role):** Legal Docketing Agent, responsible for archiving the contract and updating its status.

- **Tools used:** Invocable Apex integrating with a docketing database or API.
- **Risk controls and guardrails:** Confirms required approvals and risk ratings; restricts access to Legal Operations roles; writes a timestamped entry to a contract log object.

Operations

- **Task (example use case):** Log warehouse sensor readings on a recurring basis.
- **Trigger event or condition:** Scheduled execution or incoming IoT event stream.
- **Action agent (role):** Operations Event Logger, responsible for recording sensor data for reporting and analysis.
- **Tools used:** Scheduled Salesforce Flow with Apex for processing sensor JSON payloads.
- **Risk controls and guardrails:** Flags or skips anomalous readings outside expected ranges; applies rate limiting to prevent overload; records each execution in a logging object.

In this list, the Trigger could be a platform event, a record change, a scheduled job, or an API call – whatever initiates the Action agent. The Action Agent (Role) column gives a friendly name to the agent and a brief of what it does. Tools Used shows the mix of Salesforce tech (Flow, Apex, etc.) employed. And importantly, Risk Controls & Guardrails note how we ensure each automation doesn't go off the rails. You'll notice patterns like requiring a prior approval (human or otherwise), limiting scope (e.g., only certain record types or once per user), and thorough logging.

By deploying Action agents in scenarios like these, organizations can increase efficiency and consistency dramatically. HR accounts get deactivated on time every time, finance entries never wait in backlog, IT services are delivered faster, legal filings don't get forgotten, and operational data is always up to date. Moreover, because of the guardrails, these automations don't introduce undue risk – they're actually reducing risk by removing delays and errors, and by providing detailed records of every action.

Another benefit is that many of these Action agents can be reused or adapted across departments. For example, the "User Access Revoker" in HR might be very similar to a process in IT security; the two teams could collaborate on a single agent that serves both needs. Or the "Ops Event Logger" mechanism could be reused to log other kinds of IoT events with minimal changes. This reuse is exactly what the Agentforce patterns encourage – rather than every team building their own ad-hoc scripts or flows, you create a stable of well-designed Action agents that become internal services.

With these examples in mind, you can probably identify analogous opportunities in your own organization. The key is to start with processes that are well understood and rule-driven. Automation success breeds more automation: once one team sees HR or Finance having success with Action agents, they'll look for their own wins.

Having explored the what and where through use cases, we will now turn our attention to how to actually build an Action agent in Salesforce. In the next section, we'll go step-by-step through the development of an Action agent using Agentforce tools. We'll use an example (creating an onboarding checklist for a new hire) to illustrate the process end-to-end – from defining the agent in Agent Builder, to writing the logic (with Apex/Flow), to testing and deploying it.

BUILDING ACTION AGENTS IN AGENTFORCE

Designing an Action agent involves both declarative setup and programmatic logic, leveraging Salesforce's platform capabilities. In this section, we'll outline a general step-by-step approach to create a Task Executor agent and then walk through a concrete example. By the end, you should have a blueprint for building your own Action agents systematically.

Step 1: Define the Agent in Agent Builder – Every agent in Agentforce starts with a clear definition of its role. Using Salesforce's Agent Builder interface, you create a new agent entry (for example, "Onboarding Checklist Creator"). In this step, you provide metadata like the agent's purpose/description, its input parameters, and expected outputs. For an Action agent, you'd describe something like "This agent creates a standard onboarding task checklist for a new employee." You'd define inputs such as Employee ID (to know for whom to create the tasks, likely a text or record ID type) and maybe Start Date or Role if those influence the tasks. Outputs might be something like Success flag and List of Tasks Created. Agent Builder might also ask you to specify which tool will implement the logic – you could choose a Flow or an Apex class here (or sometimes you first create them and then link). Essentially, this step is about declaring what the agent will do and what it needs to do it. It's important to also set any guardrails available at this level: for instance, you might tag the agent with a category ("HR Automation") or a risk level, and indicate if it requires certain conditions (Agent Builder might allow setting a permission or context that can invoke it).

Step 2: Implement the Task Logic (Invocable Apex or Flow) – Once the agent is defined, you build the actual logic that executes when the agent is invoked. Depending on the complexity, you have a choice: Flow or Apex (or a combination). Salesforce Flow is great for straightforward record operations and sending emails or posting messages. You could create a Flow (perhaps a Screen Flow if it were user-initiated, or an Autolaunched Flow with no UI if fully automated) that takes the defined inputs and contains elements to perform the actions. In our onboarding checklist example, a Flow might have a Get Records element to fetch the new hire's details, a Decision element to branch based on role, and multiple Create Records elements to add tasks (like "Complete HR Orientation" task, "Configure Laptop" task, etc.). Each of those tasks might be defined in a template (which could even be stored in Custom Metadata that the flow queries). Alternatively, if the logic needs to loop or perform complex data manipulations, an Apex class might be more suitable. You would write an Apex class with a public static method annotated with @InvocableMethod so it can be called by Agentforce. The method would accept as input a list of requests (maybe a custom inner class with fields matching the inputs, like EmployeeId, Role, etc.), and then in code you'd perform the operations: query templates, insert tasks, gather results. Below is a simplified example of what such an Apex class could look like:

```
public class OnboardingChecklistAction {
  // Input class matching agent inputs
  public class OnboardingInput {
    @InvocableVariable(label='Employee ID')
    public Id employeeId;
    @InvocableVariable(label='Role')
    public String role;
  }
  // Output class matching agent outputs
  public class OnboardingResult {
    @InvocableVariable public Boolean success;
```

```
    @InvocableVariable public String message;
    @InvocableVariable public List<Id> createdTaskIds;
  }
  @InvocableMethod(label='Create Onboarding Tasks')
  public static List<OnboardingResult> createChecklist(List<OnboardingIn-
put> requests) {
    List<OnboardingResult> results = new List<OnboardingResult>();
    for (OnboardingInput req : requests) {
      OnboardingResult res = new OnboardingResult();
      try {
        // Validate input
        if (req.employeeId == null) {
          throw new ActionException('No Employee Id provided');
        }
        // Fetch employee record (ensure it exists and is active)
          Employee__c emp = [SELECT Id, Name, Status__c FROM Employ-
ee__c WHERE Id = :req.employeeId];
        if (emp.Status__c != 'Active') {
          throw new ActionException('Employee is not active');
        }
          // Determine tasks to create based on role (could query Custom
Metadata)
        List<Task__c> tasksToCreate = new List<Task__c>();
            for (Onboarding_Template__mdt tmpl : Onboarding_Tem-
plate__mdt.getAll().values()) {
          if (tmpl.Role__c == req.role) {
            Task__c t = new Task__c();
            t.OwnerId = emp.Manager__c;
```

```
                t.Subject = tmpl.Task_Name__c;
                t.Employee__c = emp.Id;
                //... set other fields...
                tasksToCreate.add(t);
            }
        }
        // Execute: create tasks
        insert tasksToCreate;
        // Log (could also insert a custom log record, omitted for brevity)
        res.success = true;
        res.message = tasksToCreate.size() + ' tasks created for ' + emp.Name;
        res.createdTaskIds = new List<Id>();
        for (Task__c t : tasksToCreate) res.createdTaskIds.add(t.Id);
      } catch(Exception e) {
        // Handle errors
        res.success = false;
        res.message = 'Error: ' + e.getMessage();
        res.createdTaskIds = new List<Id>();
      }
      results.add(res);
    }
    return results;
  }
  // Custom exception for clarity
  public class ActionException extends Exception {}
}
```

In the above code, we define input and output data structures, validate the input (employee exists and is active), then use a Custom Metadata type Onboarding_Template__mdt to fetch the list of tasks templates for that employee's role. We create Task records accordingly and insert them, capturing their IDs. We catch any exceptions to mark the result as failed with a message. We also noted how logging might occur (in a real case, you might insert into a Log object or use a platform event for logging, but here it's commented for brevity).

Whether you use Flow or Apex, the key things to implement are: input validation, the core action, and error handling/logging. Keep the logic focused on the single task. If you find yourself wanting to do multiple distinct things in one agent, consider splitting them into multiple Action agents or using a Conductor to sequence them.

Step 3: Add Validation and Guardrails – We touched on validation in the logic, but beyond that, think of any guardrails you can enforce declaratively or via metadata. For example, you might use a Custom Permission or a Protected Custom Setting that the Apex code checks – e.g., a boolean "Allow_Onboarding_Agent" that an admin can toggle off in case you need to pause the automation. Or use a Custom Metadata to list which profiles or roles are allowed to trigger the agent; then at the start of your flow/Apex, verify the invoking user is in that allowed list. Another guardrail is setting limits: if the action involves processing records, maybe limit to, say, 50 records at a time to prevent misuse (and then enforce that by code). These measures ensure that even if someone mistakenly triggers the agent in an unexpected way, it won't run wild. Agent Builder might allow some of these rules to be configured as well (for instance, linking the agent to a permission set or requiring a certain license). Use all available avenues to make the Action agent safe by default.

Step 4: Configure Metadata and Permissions – Make sure the agent can only be invoked by the appropriate users or other agents. In Salesforce, you might create a Permission Set like "Onboarding Automation Access" and only give it to the HR integration user or the one or two personas that are allowed to run this agent. If the agent is invoked by other agents (like a Conductor), you ensure those agents run in a context that has access. Also consider the execution context: should the agent run as a specific user (system context vs user context)? Flows have options for running as the user or system; Apex can be with sharing or without sharing. For task automation, you might typically run without sharing but manually enforce permissions in logic – this way the agent can do what an admin can do, but you explicitly check anything sensitive. Or you run with sharing to naturally respect record access. It depends on use case. The point is, decide and configure it deliberately. Additionally, set up any Custom Metadata records needed (like our task templates) so that the agent logic has something to reference. By the end of this step, the agent is essentially fully specified: it knows who can call it, when it can run, and what it will do.

Step 5: Test the Agent – Before unleashing the Action agent in a live environment, it must be tested thoroughly. Create a variety of test scenarios: valid input, missing input, edge cases (e.g., what if the employee already had tasks, or what if the ERP is down – can your agent handle that gracefully?). In Salesforce, write Apex unit tests for your Invocable method (you can call it like any other method, supplying dummy data, and then assert the expected results and that records were created or not created accordingly). If you used Flows, leverage Flow test features or build a small Apex test that calls the flow via the automation API. Testing isn't just for correctness – it's for safety. You want to ensure that if something's wrong, the agent doesn't, say, delete something it shouldn't or throw an unhandled exception that could disrupt a transaction. Also test the integration points: if your Action agent calls an external API, simulate that in a test or a sandbox (maybe using a mock service) to see how it behaves when the API is slow, or returns an error. Integration testing in a full sandbox or scratch org is also wise: trigger the agent in as realistic a way as possible (for example, change a record to fire the flow) and see end-to-end if it performs as expected. Salesforce's agent framework might also allow simulations through Agent Builder or a Command Center test mode. Use those if available – for instance, some orgs allow you to run an agent with dry-run to see logs.

Step 6: Deploy and Monitor – Once it's built and tested, deploy the Action agent to production (likely via metadata deployment for the Apex/Flow and via a change set or unlocked package for any metadata and the agent config). On deployment, immediately start monitoring its behavior in the Command Center or relevant dashboards. A best practice is to have dashboards or reports built on the agent's log data – for instance, a report of all "Onboarding Checklist" agent runs in the last week, with status and any error messages. This allows your team to spot if it's failing frequently or if it maybe created duplicate tasks by accident. In Command Center, you might set up an alert if the agent's failure rate goes above X%, so you can investigate quickly. Early monitoring is crucial especially when you first roll out; after a while, if an Action agent proves rock-solid, you can simply periodically audit its logs.

Let's tie this all together with our example: Onboarding Checklist Creator. Imagine we have a Conductor agent in HR that manages the new hire onboarding process (perhaps it coordinates paperwork, equipment, system access, etc.). One of its steps is to ensure an onboarding task checklist is created for each new hire. Instead of the Conductor doing that directly, it delegates to our Action agent "Onboarding Checklist Creator." Here's how we built it following the steps:

In Agent Builder, we created OnboardingChecklistAgent with inputs: EmployeeId (Id of the new hire's record) and StartDate (when the employee starts, just in case tasks are dated from that). Output: CreatedTasks (number of tasks created). We note in description that it creates a set of tasks for the employee's first week.

We chose to implement with Apex (named class OnboardingChecklistAction) because we want to use a custom metadata for templates and we have some complex logic deciding tasks by role. We wrote an Apex invocable method (like the one sketched above) that: validates the input, queries the employee and templates, creates tasks, handles errors. We also wrote an accompanying Apex test class to cover this logic.

We added guardrails: the Apex code checks that the employee's status is Active and that their role is one we have templates for. We also added a check: if an onboarding task checklist already exists for that employee (say we track a field "OnboardingTasksCreated = true"), the agent will not create duplicate tasks – it will instead log a message that tasks already exist, and set success = false or maybe success = true but zero tasks. This prevents accidental double runs. We enforced that by a SOQL query or by using an UPSERT with external ID to avoid duplicates. That's a guardrail for idempotency (important in automation to not do the same thing twice if not needed).

In metadata, we created custom metadata records under Onboarding_Template__mdt: for Role = Engineer, list tasks A, B, C; for Role = Sales, list tasks D, E, F, etc. This drives the agent's behavior. We also added an org-wide custom setting "EnableOnboardingAutomation = true". In the Apex, we wrap logic with if(EnableOnboardingAutomation) so that if needed, we can switch off all such agents quickly by flipping one flag (a big red button for the org if something goes wrong).

We set up permissions: only the HR Integration user (which the Conductor runs as) has the permission set that allows invoking OnboardingChecklistAgent. Normal end-users cannot directly call it (they don't even know it exists). This way, even if someone found the invocable action, they wouldn't be authorized to run it in isolation.

Testing in a full sandbox showed it created tasks correctly. We simulated an error by creating a metadata template with a missing required field to see if the error was caught and logged (it was). We also tested what happens if two hires are processed at nearly the same time (to ensure no conflict – it worked fine, as separate transactions).

After deployment, when the first real new hires were onboarded, we watched the Command Center which displayed the run of our agent. We saw "Success = true" for each, with, say, "3 tasks created for John Doe" in the log message. In one case, we saw a failure: the agent reported "Employee is not active." Investigating, it turned out HR had triggered it for an intern who wasn't marked active in the system yet. The agent correctly did nothing. We followed up with HR to adjust their process (they should mark active first or include interns in templates differently). This kind of immediate feedback loop was possible thanks to our logs and Command Center monitoring.

By following a structured approach like this, building Action agents becomes a repeatable practice. For each new task automation, you go through define → implement → secure → test → deploy. Salesforce's mix of declarative and programmatic tools really shines here: non-developers can configure the high-level agent and perhaps even build simpler flows, while developers can extend with Apex for tougher parts. And because we're using Agentforce patterns, everyone on the team has a common framework and vocabulary. An admin might say, "We need an Action agent for deactivating users," and a developer immediately knows what that entails and how to go about it.

With our agent built and running, the next consideration is how to manage a growing fleet of Action agents across an org. As you scale up automation, governance and maintenance become critical. In the next section, we will discuss strategies for governing Action agents at scale – controlling who can invoke them, tracking their usage, managing versions and changes, and ensuring they remain compliant with organizational policies as your Salesforce org and business evolve.

GOVERNING ACTION AGENTS AT SCALE

Implementing a single Action agent is straightforward; managing dozens or hundreds of them across an enterprise is the next challenge. Without proper governance, you risk "agent sprawl" (too many agents doing overlapping things or running unchecked). This section focuses on governance practices for Action agents: how to control access, monitor activity, version your automations, and generally keep the system tidy and safe as it grows.

Access Control: One fundamental governance question is: who or what is allowed to trigger each Action agent? In Salesforce, this ties back to profiles, permission sets, and potentially sharing rules. A good practice is to create a permission set for each critical agent or for groups of agents and assign it only to the roles or integration users that need it. For example, if you have an Action agent that can delete records (a potentially dangerous power), you might restrict it so that only a specific "Automation Admin" profile can invoke it, or only a particular integration user (maybe the user associated with a Conductor agent that calls it). By using permission sets, you can decouple it from general admin rights – you don't have to be a full Salesforce admin to run the agent, but you do need that specific permission. This way, if someone tries to call the agent (say via an API or Flow) without the permission, it won't execute. Additionally, consider leveraging the running user context: many Action agents might run as "System" (without sharing), which is fine, but you can simulate a sort of access check by coding it to respect a certain user's permissions or ownership. Another layer is Org-Wide Defaults and sharing settings: if your agent creates or modifies records, think about ownership and visibility of those records afterwards. Should they be owned by a generic user? Should they be private or public? For instance, the HR onboarding tasks might all be owned by an HR service user to centralize them. The goal is to prevent unauthorized or unintended use of these powerful little bots.

Invocation Tracking and Logging: Earlier we talked about logging each agent's actions for auditing. When you have many Action agents, it's wise to implement a unified logging strategy. One approach is to create a custom object in Salesforce, say "Agent_Execution__c", where each record represents one run of any agent. The record could store fields like Agent Name, Timestamp, Triggering User, Input parameters (maybe in a JSON or a related child record for details), Outcome (success/failure), and any message or error info. Your Action agents can create one of these records at the end of their run. (You might do this in Apex, or if using Flow, in a subflow or via a generic "Log Action" invocable you create.) By centralizing logs, you enable organization-wide reporting: you can have dashboards showing all agent activity today, or how many times each agent ran this month, etc. This helps in understanding usage patterns and also in spotting anomalies (like, why did the "User Deactivation" agent suddenly run 50 times today – was there a mass termination or is something misfiring?). It's also invaluable for compliance – if an auditor asks "who accessed or changed these records?", you can show that it was an automated agent and produce the log of its actions. Some companies integrate this with their SIEM (Security Information and Event Management) systems by exporting these logs or sending platform events so security teams know an automated action occurred.

Versioning and Change Management: Over time, you'll need to update your Action agents – perhaps to enhance their logic or adapt to new business rules. A naïve approach would be to just edit the Flow or Apex in place. But that can be risky if other processes depend on a certain behavior (plus, Salesforce flows changes might be hard to roll back). A better approach is to use versioning. Salesforce Flow natively supports versioning: you can create a new version of a Flow while the old one remains active, then switch which version is active when ready. This is great for testing a new version in the background. For Apex, you can version by class names or custom metadata. One pattern is to include a version number in the agent's API name or use a custom metadata to point to the active class. For example, you might have OnboardingChecklistAction_V1 and later deploy OnboardingChecklistAction_V2. The Agent Builder could have a setting (or you manage in code) to decide which class to call. More simply, since Agentforce is new, you might not have built-in support for multiple versions of an agent's implementation, so you might just deploy over the old logic – which makes thorough testing and a rollback plan important. Feature flagging can help: if you introduce a big change, put it behind a feature flag (maybe a custom metadata field "UseNewLogic" true/false). Deploy the new code which checks the flag, but leave it off initially – the code runs old logic. When you're ready, flip the flag to true (no code deployment needed at that moment) and voila, it uses the new path. If something goes wrong, flip it back. This technique, combined with maintaining older Flow versions, ensures you're not stuck if a new deployment has issues. In summary, treat your Action agent logic like any API or software component: manage versions, don't break backward compatibility without a plan, and document changes.

Deployment and Feature Rollout: Related to versioning is how you roll out agents across orgs. Many companies have multiple Salesforce orgs (dev, test, UAT, prod). You should move your agent definitions and logic through a proper pipeline. Because Agentforce might involve both metadata and data, consider using Unlocked Packages or change sets for moving the agent configuration and related Apex/Flow. Keep track of which version is in which environment. Some teams establish a "Feature Flag Org Preference" (could be a Custom Metadata or Custom Setting at org level) to enable an agent in prod only when ready. For instance, you might deploy an Action agent to production but not advertise or trigger it until a certain date when you enable its flag. This controlled rollout is especially useful if the agent's actions have user-facing impact. And always have a contingency: how to disable the agent quickly if it misbehaves. The simplest is often to include in the agent logic a check against a global org setting (like a custom setting "Agentforce Master Switch" or per-agent switch). That way, you can turn it "off" by making it simply exit without doing anything. Another method is to pause the agent via Agent Builder if supported (some systems allow marking an agent inactive). In the worst case, you can remove its permission or rename something to break it temporarily, but those are last resorts. It's better to build a deliberate kill-switch into each important agent.

External Checks and Balances: Sometimes an Action agent may need to incorporate external information to decide if it should proceed. This is where patterns can interplay – for example, a Curator agent might provide a risk score for an action. Suppose you have an Action agent that sends out an email to a customer whenever a case is closed. Normally that's fine, but what if the case closure has some sensitive content? You might want to scan it. A Curator agent (or even an AI service) could analyze the case text for sentiment or sensitive info. In a governed setup, your Action agent could call the Curator first or check a field set by the Curator (like "SafeToEmail = true"). Only if the score is below a risk threshold does the Action agent actually send the email. This layering ensures that your fast-moving Action agent doesn't inadvertently do something against policy. Another external check could be a simple lookup: e.g., an Action agent that issues a refund might check an "Outstanding Risk Flag" on the account via a quick SOQL query – if the customer is flagged for potential fraud, maybe the agent should not auto-refund without human review. Essentially, defense in depth: even though the agent itself is coded to do X, have it double-check context before final execution. This can often be achieved with one extra query or method call in the agent logic.

Monitoring and KPIs: At scale, you should treat your agents like a fleet of workers. Define some Key Performance Indicators: How many tasks are agents executing per day? What's the success rate vs failure rate? How much time saved? The Salesforce Command Center likely provides some metrics, but you can augment that. By logging execution times in your log object (maybe a field for duration), you can see if an agent is getting slower (maybe an API it calls is slowing down). By tracking count of failures, you can set up alerts. For example, if the "Provision Sandbox" Action agent fails 3 times in a row, maybe it's an API outage – have it notify the IT admin. These governance metrics help in two ways: operational awareness (keeping things running smoothly) and demonstrating value. You could show leadership that "Our Action agents executed 5,000 tasks this quarter with a 99% success rate, saving approximately 500 hours of manual work." That kind of reporting both justifies the initial investment and can secure future resources for expanding the program.

Lifecycle Ownership: Determine who "owns" each Action agent. In a small team it might be obvious, but in a big org, you should have a clear map: e.g., the HR systems team owns the user deactivation agent, the Finance team owns the budget sync agent, etc. They are responsible for updating requirements, testing changes, and responding if an issue arises with that agent. Often, this is documented in an internal wiki or even in the agent's metadata (maybe a field "Owner Team" or contact person). Why is this governance? Because when something goes wrong at 2 AM, ops needs to know who to call or which runbook to follow for that specific agent. If an agent triggers an alert ("Supervisor Approval Agent is failing repeatedly"), having pre-defined ownership means faster resolution.

To summarize the governance practices:

- Limit access to who/what can run Action agents (principle of least privilege).
- Log everything an Action agent does and centralize those logs for oversight.
- Version control your agent logic and use feature flags or metadata for safe rollouts.
- Establish kill-switches and toggles to disable agents quickly if needed.
- Incorporate external checks (other agents or data signals) for high-risk actions.
- Monitor actively and set up alerting for abnormal behavior.
- Assign ownership and maintain documentation for each agent.

Pro tip: Treat Action agents as you would treat internal APIs or microservices. They may not be exposed to external parties, but they are critical pieces of your systems. Govern them with the same rigor you apply to integrations or APIs. This means access control, documentation, versioning, monitoring, and lifecycle management. If you wouldn't deploy an API to production without those safeguards, don't do it for an Action agent either.

With solid governance in place, your organization can confidently scale up the use of Action agents. Instead of a chaotic proliferation of automations, you get a well-managed portfolio of "digital workers" each with a clear job and controlled entry points. This sets the stage for expanding into more complex agent patterns, knowing that the foundation (the Action agents) is strong.

Now that we've focused on Salesforce and internal governance, let's zoom out and see how Action agents relate to the broader AI and automation ecosystem. In the next section, we will compare the Action pattern with similar concepts in other platforms (like how other AI frameworks handle tool execution), and discuss why Salesforce's approach offers unique benefits in terms of governance and integration. We'll also touch on the emerging standards and how Action agents can participate in cross-system agent workflows, ensuring your Salesforce agents aren't an island but part of a larger AI strategy.

ACTION AGENTS IN THE AI ECOSYSTEM

Salesforce Agentforce is not the only player in town when it comes to AI agents executing tasks. It's helpful to understand how the Action pattern compares to similar ideas in other AI frameworks and products. In this section, we'll look at a few prominent examples – LangChain, Microsoft's AutoGen, Crew (CrewAI), and Microsoft Copilot – which all, in their own ways, have agents or components that execute actions. We'll also discuss the concept of a cross-platform agent protocol (like the Model Context Protocol) and how Action agents can fit into a multi-platform world. Finally, we'll consider the overlap with traditional RPA (Robotic Process Automation) and why a Salesforce-native Action agent can be a more governed and maintainable approach for many cases.

LangChain and Tool Executors: LangChain is a popular open-source framework (particularly in the Python community) for building LLM-driven agents. One key concept in LangChain is that of "tools" – functions that an AI agent can call to perform specific tasks (like a calculator, a web search, a database query, etc.). In a LangChain setup, the LLM acts as a reasoning engine that decides when to call a tool and how to use its output. The actual execution of the tool is done by code. You can see a strong parallel here: a "tool" in LangChain is essentially the analog of an Action agent in Agentforce. It's a predefined action that can be executed as part of a bigger chain. For example, if you have a LangChain agent that answers questions, it might have a tool called "SalesforceQuery" that, given an SOQL query string, returns data from Salesforce. The LLM might decide to use that tool when needed. The tool itself is deterministic and permission-bound (because it's coded to only do that query). The difference is that LangChain tools are often used transiently in one agent's context, whereas Salesforce Action agents are first-class citizens in your org, reusable by many flows and agents. However, conceptually we can say: Action agents = Salesforce-flavored tools. They contribute to structured agent chains by handling the actual task execution. The benefit of doing this in Salesforce is that each "tool" (Action agent) comes with Salesforce's security, logging, and integration into the CRM data model. In LangChain, you have to implement and enforce those aspects yourself for each tool.

Microsoft AutoGen (and similar multi-agent orchestration frameworks): Microsoft's AutoGen (from their research or Azure OpenAI examples) is about orchestrating multiple agents, often with roles like Solver agent, Tool agent, Evaluator, etc., working together. In those scenarios, they often designate certain agents to perform tool-like duties – for instance, an agent that can execute code or look up information. These could be considered "low-risk execution" agents because they do what they're told in a limited domain. An Action agent in Salesforce fills that niche within a larger Agentforce deployment: it's the reliable specialist that will carry out a command. You might imagine an AutoGen system where one agent is an LLM that figures out a plan and another agent is specifically there to perform an action in Salesforce via API. Rather than building that from scratch, if that external system can call a Salesforce Action agent (e.g., through a REST API or Apex endpoint), you basically have a ready-made execution agent. One might integrate an Action agent with AutoGen by exposing the Action agent as a RESTful service (perhaps using Salesforce's Apex REST or by having a small wrapper that AutoGen calls). The Action agent would receive the request, do the task in Salesforce, and return the result – acting as AutoGen's "tool operator" within the CRM context.

Crew (CrewAI operators): The term "Crew" might refer to an approach where you have a team (crew) of specialized smaller agents or operators each doing a piece of work (somewhat akin to the concept of a human crew where each member has a role). CrewAI could be an internal concept or another platform's idea of multi-agent collaboration. The outline mentions "operators who perform delegated, atomic steps." That sounds exactly like Action agents! In a crew of AI, an Action agent is like the reliable crew member who, when handed a specific task, will get it done without fuss. For example, if you had a "Crew" of agents handling a complex customer request: one agent parses the request (NLP), one agent decides on a solution (Planner), and one agent executes changes in systems (the Doer) – that Doer is analogous to our Action agent. The difference with Salesforce's approach is that Action agents are integrated into the platform and can leverage all the Salesforce functionality, whereas a generic "crew operator" might be more freeform but also more unwieldy without a platform. Salesforce's advantage here is giving you the scaffolding (Agent Builder, flows, etc.) to make building those operators easier and ensuring they operate within enterprise constraints (as we hammered in governance).

Microsoft Copilot (in-app task execution): Microsoft's Copilot, especially in contexts like GitHub Copilot or the announced Copilot for Windows/Office, often works alongside a user to help accomplish tasks. For instance, Outlook's Copilot might draft an email for you and even offer to send it, or Windows Copilot might adjust settings on your machine via some automation. These Copilot execution agents always have a notion of user confirmation or oversight for significant actions. For example, Copilot might say, "Shall I go ahead and schedule this meeting for you?" requiring you to confirm. This is a design choice to maintain user trust and safety. In the Salesforce world, you might incorporate similar patterns: a Presenter agent could show a user what an Action agent is about to do ("I can create these five tasks for you – do you want to proceed?" with a button that triggers the Action agent). That's akin to Copilot's confirmation gates. Action agents themselves, as we've described, don't usually ask permission at runtime (they either run or they don't based on trigger). But in a user-facing scenario, you might combine a Presenter (for the UI/confirmation) with an Action agent that actually executes once the user clicks confirm – effectively mimicking the Copilot style. The point here is that Salesforce's ecosystem allows you to implement Copilot-like experiences (through things like Einstein Bots, Lightning Components, etc.) but powered by our underlying Action agents to do the heavy lifting after the user's okay. Copilot and similar assistants show that even as AI gets more powerful, having an explicit confirmation step for actions increases user comfort. Salesforce customers might do the same: e.g., an Action agent can have a mode where it only prepares changes and waits for someone to hit "Apply."

Model Context Protocol (MCP) and cross-platform agents: As enterprises embrace multiple AI platforms, there's a need for a standardized way for agents to talk to each other and delegate tasks across systems. The Model Context Protocol (MCP) is hinted as an emerging standard for cross-platform agent reasoning. Without getting into deep technical detail (since MCP might be hypothetical or evolving), think of it as a way where one agent can package up a request, send it to another agent possibly running on a different system, and get back results, all with shared context. In such a scenario, Salesforce Action agents could be exposed as services or endpoints that other agents (external to Salesforce) can call upon. For example, an AI agent running in a cloud data platform might determine "I need to update a customer's info in Salesforce." If both systems speak MCP, the external agent could formulate a request in the MCP format saying "please execute action X for customer Y with data Z" and the Salesforce agent (Action agent) would receive that, verify it, execute it, and return a standardized response. Essentially, MCP or similar standards could make Action agents part of a federated multi-agent system. The Action agent becomes the Salesforce representative in that wider network, responsible for any changes on the CRM side. This is powerful because it means your Salesforce automation isn't siloed; you can coordinate with AI agents handling other domains (like a data science pipeline or an e-commerce system) in a common language. We already do something analogous with APIs, but MCP could allow more semantic and context-rich exchanges (like including the reasoning context or state of conversation between agents).

Task Bots and RPA vs. Action Agents: It's worth comparing Action agents to the world of RPA (Robotic Process Automation). RPA tools (like UiPath, Automation Anywhere, Blue Prism) are designed to automate tasks usually by mimicking user interactions (clicking UI, copying data between systems). They're often used when an official integration or API is not available – essentially, they're a layer on top of existing interfaces. Action agents, on the other hand, operate within Salesforce (or via official integration points from Salesforce). If you had to automate "take data from Salesforce and input into legacy system X which has no API," an RPA bot might do that by controlling a browser or desktop app. An Action agent would typically tackle tasks that can be done with Salesforce's capabilities or APIs. The benefit of Action agents is governance and reliability: they use supported methods (like Apex, Flows, APIs) and run on Salesforce's cloud with transaction management. They are less brittle than RPA, because they're not scraping screens – they're calling functions. Additionally, Action agents are inherently aware of Salesforce context (user permissions, record relationships, etc.) which an external RPA might not be. That said, RPA has its place, especially for integrating non-Salesforce systems. One could even imagine a combo: an Action agent that, when needed, calls an RPA bot for a step (though usually we try to avoid that if we can integrate directly). But if we consider something like task bots (small bots that do one thing, sometimes used in chat tools or RPA schedulers), those are conceptually similar to Action agents. The difference: Agentforce's Action agents are declarative and part of your metadata. You can manage them like code/configuration, they're part of your Salesforce deployments, and you get all the benefits of the platform (like rollback, monitoring in Salesforce UI, etc.). In contrast, a script sitting in an RPA tool might not have that tight integration or oversight from Salesforce's side.

Salesforce emphasizes trust, governance, and integration. The Action pattern embodies those principles – it's a way to do automation with guardrails, in a manner that's deeply integrated into the data and processes of your CRM. Competing frameworks might let you go faster in some cases (e.g., quickly scripting something in an AI agent), but they might do so at the cost of security or maintainability. By aligning with the Action pattern, you're essentially saying, "We want automation, but not at the expense of losing control or clarity." This resonates with Salesforce's philosophy of delivering AI with enterprise trust (e.g., Einstein GPT's focus on not exposing customer data, etc.).

To be clear, Salesforce isn't operating in a vacuum – the mention of LangChain, AutoGen, etc., shows that Agentforce patterns were not conceived in isolation but rather in dialogue with the broader AI community. The difference is how they're executed: Salesforce is bringing these concepts into a low-code platform that businesses already use, rather than requiring Python code or external services. Also, Salesforce is likely working on ways to allow interoperability – for example, allowing a LangChain agent to call an Agentforce agent easily, or vice versa. The mention of MuleSoft earlier in outline hints that, yes, through MuleSoft or APIs, you can hook these together.

In summary, the Action pattern maps to the "execution component" of many AI systems:

- In LangChain, tools = Action agents.
- In multi-agent orchestration (AutoGen, CrewAI), operator agents = Action agents.
- In user-facing copilots, the behind-the-scenes doer (with user confirmation) = Action agent.
- In RPA, a bot script automating a step = Action agent (but Salesforce's is more controlled).

- Emerging standards like MCP could make Action agents nodes in a larger web of AI.

Understanding this bigger picture can help architects justify using Agentforce: you're not doing something completely proprietary or strange – you're implementing industry best practices (task-specific agents) but doing it within a platform that offers enterprise-grade governance.

With that perspective, let's proceed to the next section, where we'll see how Action agents don't live in isolation even within Salesforce. They are often used in combination with other Agentforce patterns to deliver end-to-end solutions. We will walk through a full example of multiple patterns working together (including Sentinel, Supervisor, etc.) with the Action agent performing the critical execution step. This will solidify how the Action pattern fits into the broader agent ecosystem inside Salesforce, complementing what we just discussed about the external ecosystem.

COMPOSING WITH OTHER PATTERNS

No agent is an island. In complex workflows, multiple Agentforce patterns collaborate, each playing its role. The Action pattern, as the execution workhorse, often appears as a component in larger pattern combinations. In this section, we explore how Action agents pair with other patterns like Sentinel, Companion, Supervisor, Conductor, and Presenter to form end-to-end solutions. We'll outline a few common pattern pairings and then dive into a detailed scenario illustrating a chain of agents culminating in an Action agent doing the final task.

Sentinel → Action: A Sentinel agent is designed to monitor events or changes (think of it as an AI lookout or alert system). When a Sentinel detects a notable event, sometimes the appropriate response is immediate and can be automated – that's where an Action agent comes in. For example, imagine a Sentinel agent watching streaming data from a server farm for any critical alerts (CPU overheating, intrusion detection, etc.). The moment it flags a serious issue, it could directly trigger an Action agent to take a predefined step, like "reset the server" or "flip on a backup system." In Salesforce terms, a Sentinel might be monitoring data inputs (maybe a spike in customer cases tagged as urgent). If it detects a threshold (say 100 urgent cases in an hour), it could invoke an Action agent to automatically create a high-priority Ops ticket or send notifications to a team. The key is that the Sentinel's job is detection, and it hands off to an Action agent for execution.

This combo creates real-time responsiveness: detection followed by action. The benefit of separating them is you can evolve detection logic independently from what actions are taken, and vice versa.

Companion → Action: A Companion agent (discussed in another chapter) typically acts as a user's assistant or proxy – often a conversational or interactive agent that a user can instruct in natural language. When a Companion agent figures out that the user wants to do something concrete (like "please generate a quarterly report for client X"), it can rely on an Action agent to fulfill that request. The Companion is great at the interface (understanding the user, clarifying intent, perhaps applying some personalization or context from the user's profile), but it might not have direct access to perform system changes – nor should it, because we want a controlled execution. So, the Companion essentially translates the user's request into a structured command for an Action agent. For example, in Slack, you might chat with a Salesforce Companion agent: "Bot, update the status of Opportunity 123 to Closed Won and set close date to today." The Companion agent confirms the request, maybe does a quick sanity check ("are you sure, did the customer sign?"). Once confirmed, it calls the OpportunityUpdater Action agent with the specific record ID and new values. The Action agent then performs the update in Salesforce safely (perhaps also writing who requested it into a field or log). This way, the user got a conversational experience, but the actual database update happened through a tightly governed agent. This pattern shows how user-facing AI (Companion) and system-facing AI (Action) work hand in hand.

Supervisor → Action: We've touched on this earlier – a Supervisor agent involves humans for validation or approval. The typical flow is that an AI (or rule) suggests something, a human approves it, then it gets executed. The execution part is perfect for an Action agent. Consider a legal use case: A Curator agent drafts a contract amendment, a Supervisor agent presents it to a legal officer for approval. Once the officer clicks "Approve," a series of things need to happen – the contract document needs to be updated in the system, a notification sent to the client, and the status changed to "Active". Rather than expecting the Supervisor agent to do all that (its focus was on the approval workflow), a dedicated Contract Activator Action agent can be triggered to carry out the post-approval steps. The Supervisor agent simply passes along the needed context (contract ID, etc.) and maybe logs that the approval was given, then the Action agent takes over: it updates fields, generates a PDF of the final contract, sends emails, etc. This separation of concerns ensures that the human-involved part and the automation part are modular. Another example: an Expense Approval Supervisor agent gets a manager's approval on a large expense. After approval, an Action agent creates a payment record in Finance system or marks the expense as paid. By using an Action agent, we maintain that the execution is standardized and audited separately from the approval process. In summary: Supervisor handles "Should we do this?"; Action handles "Now it's done."

Conductor → Action: The Conductor pattern is about orchestration – multi-step processes possibly involving logic and branches. Almost by definition, Conductors will use Action agents as the steps in the process. If you think of a Conductor agent as a project manager, then Action agents are the team members carrying out tasks. For instance, a Customer Onboarding Conductor might have steps: (1) create the account in CRM, (2) set up billing in billing system, (3) send welcome email, (4) schedule follow-up call. Each of those could be a separate Action agent:

- Account Creator (Action) – to create account and contact records in Salesforce.
- Billing Integrator (Action) – to call an API and set up billing, return an account number.
- Email Dispatcher (Action) – to send the welcome email using a template.
- Follow-up Scheduler (Action) – to create a task for sales rep or a calendar event.

The Conductor agent would handle the sequence and any dependencies (maybe it waits for the account number from step 2 before composing the email in step 3, etc.). If any step fails, the Conductor could decide to roll back or notify someone. Using Action agents for each step means each unit is isolated and can be reused or tested individually. If the billing system changes, you update the Billing Integrator Action agent, without touching the overall flow orchestration. This pattern highlights how Action agents enable scalable complexity – you can build very complex flows (the Conductor's logic) out of simple blocks (the Actions). We saw a mini version of this where a Conductor (the hiring process) would call an onboarding tasks Action. In practice, most Conductor designs will have a mix of Action, Supervisor, maybe even Curator or Presenter calls at different points (some steps might need a human decision or a data summary). But whenever it comes to executing an actual change in a system, you'll likely delegate to an Action agent.

Presenter + Action: A Presenter agent's role is to deliver information to a user in a useful way (it might compile results and show them in a dashboard or message). Sometimes, while presenting information, there's a need for a quick action. Think of a scenario: a Presenter agent shows a customer service agent a synthesized summary of a case ("Here's what happened, and I suggest offering a 10% refund. [Offer Refund]"). The text summary is Presenter's job, but that little "[Offer Refund]" button is essentially a hook to an Action agent. If the human clicks it, that triggers, say, a Refund Processor Action agent that actually creates a refund record, emails the customer, etc. The Presenter can then even update its display ("Refund offered on 2023-07-04, confirmation #12345"). This synergy means users can take direct actions from within an AI-generated insight interface, but safely – because a vetted Action agent performs the change. We see analogs in everyday software: you get a notification (presenter) with a button to "Apply Change" which then runs some script (action). The difference in Agentforce is that this is built with these agent patterns, not just hardcoded UI logic. Another example: a Presenter agent for a sales manager generates a list of at-risk opportunities and includes a "Close Opportunity as Lost" quick action next to each one if the manager decides it's no longer viable. That action calls an Action agent to perform the closure steps (update status, log a reason, maybe notify the team). Presenter + Action basically enables a seamless bridge from insight to action, with the human as the mediator who chooses to invoke the action.

To cement these ideas, let's walk through a full end-to-end interaction involving multiple patterns, where the Action agent is the final executor:

Scenario: Field Service Incident Response

Imagine a company that maintains equipment (say, HVAC units) for clients. They have IoT sensors and also customer calls that can indicate equipment failures. We'll see how a chain of agents handles an incident from detection to resolution:

Sentinel: An IoT sensor on an HVAC unit detects an anomaly – the temperature is far beyond normal range, indicating a possible failure. A Sentinel agent in Salesforce is subscribed to these sensor events (perhaps via a platform event or API feed). It spots this anomaly because it crosses a threshold defined in its logic (maybe it's looking for temperature > 100°C). The Sentinel agent creates an "Incident" record in Salesforce and flags it as high priority. It then triggers the next agent in line, passing along incident details.

Supervisor: Before dispatching a field technician automatically, the company wants a human to verify the incident (maybe remote check or call the site). A Supervisor agent is invoked with the incident data. This agent might route a notification to an on-call engineer or even use an AI to attempt a quick diagnosis but ultimately awaits human confirmation. Let's say it sends an alert to a human supervisor: "Sensor X reports high temp on Unit Y at Location Z. Do you confirm this is a real incident requiring action?" The on-call engineer checks some camera feed or secondary data and clicks "Confirm Incident". The Supervisor agent records this confirmation (or if the human said "False alarm," it might cancel the process here). In our case, it's confirmed real.

Conductor: Now that it's confirmed, a Conductor agent takes over to orchestrate the response. This Field Service Conductor has a plan: (a) create a case in the Service Cloud or work order in Field Service Lightning, (b) schedule a field technician visit, (c) order any replacement parts if needed, (d) notify the client's facility manager, and (e) after resolution, follow up with a report. That's a lot of steps! The Conductor agent breaks these into tasks and will execute them in sequence (with some conditional logic perhaps, e.g., if scheduling fails, escalate to a manager). To execute each step, it invokes appropriate agents:

For step (a), it might call an Action agent "Case Creator" to open a new Case record with all relevant info (equipment id, issue, priority).

For step (b), scheduling might actually use an external optimization service. Possibly a Curator agent is used here to pick an optimal technician and time (or it calls Salesforce's Field Service scheduling API, which might be wrapped in an Action agent itself). Let's assume there's an Action agent "Schedule Technician" that interfaces with the Field Service module to book an appointment and returns an appointment ID.

For step (c), an Action agent "Order Part" places an order for a replacement part through an integration (maybe a MuleSoft connector to an inventory system). It might only do this if the initial diagnostics (maybe from the Curator or from the sensor data) suggested a specific component failure. If not needed, Conductor can skip it.

For step (d), an Action agent "Notify Client" sends an email or text to the facility manager: "We detected an issue with your HVAC, a technician has been scheduled at 3pm." This could also be a Presenter agent if we wanted a fancy message, but an Action sending a templated notification suffices.

The Conductor monitors each of these calls. Suppose the "Schedule Technician" action returns an error (no technician available today). The Conductor has logic to handle that – maybe invoke a Supervisor agent to alert a human dispatcher to manually intervene, or try scheduling for next day and notify differently. This demonstrates how patterns can loop: the Conductor might temporarily hand off to a Supervisor for a human decision at a branch, then continue.

After steps a-d are done (case created, tech scheduled, part ordered, client notified), the Conductor waits for the outcome of the field visit. This could be an hours-long or days-long gap. Perhaps it listens for an update (maybe a technician marks the case as resolved in Salesforce).

Once the incident is resolved, the Conductor triggers final step (e): generate a summary report. It might call a Presenter agent to compile a report of what happened (using data from case, sensor, etc., possibly with an LLM to narrativize it) and send that report to stakeholders. Or it could use an Action agent to simply close the case and send a closure email.

The Conductor then completes its process and closes out the Incident as handled.

Action: We already saw multiple Action agents in the above Conductor steps (Case Creator, Schedule Technician, Order Part, Notify Client, etc.). The final resolution likely also involves an Action agent, for example closing the case or updating maintenance records. One specific Action agent in this chain could be a Maintenance Logger that writes the incident details to a maintenance history object, for future analytics.

Presenter: Though not explicitly needed, a Presenter agent might have been used at the supervisor alert step (e.g., showing the human a nice dashboard of sensor readings to help decide confirm/deny). Also, at the very end, a Presenter agent could be used to display a summary in a command center dashboard: "Incident #123 resolved – replaced Compressor – downtime 3 hours" in a nice format for managers. The Presenter doesn't effect change here, just communicates the results.

Let's recount this flow in simpler form:

- Sentinel detects and triggers.
- Supervisor validates with human.
- Conductor orchestrates multi-step response using several Action agents (and possibly another Supervisor or Curator internally).
- Presenter (optionally) informs humans along the way or at the end.

- Action agents throughout ensure each tangible step is executed properly: creating records, scheduling, integrating with external systems, sending notifications.

This example shows all eight patterns could play a part (we had Sentinel, Supervisor, Conductor, Curator possibly for scheduling, Companion not in this scenario, Presenter for report, Action of course, and Coach pattern maybe not applicable here). It's a bit of an "Avengers assemble" scenario, but it highlights how the Action agent is often the last mile executor. It's the agent that physically does things – all others either decide, describe, or delegate.

From a design perspective, when crafting such a flow, architects explicitly decide what each part does:

- "Who detects the issue?" – Sentinel.
- "Who confirms it?" – Supervisor.
- "Who runs the show to fix it?" – Conductor.
- "What actual tasks need doing?" – define those and assign to Action agents.
- "Do we need to show info to people at some point?" – Presenter if yes.
- "Is there any learning/guidance aspect?" – Coach pattern would come in if, say, after the incident, a Coach agent gives advice to technician or suggests preventive steps next time (that could be Chapter 9's domain).

By using the Action pattern for all execution steps, you ensure that every change is governed and modular. If tomorrow the company gets a new scheduling system, you just replace that one Action agent (Schedule Technician) with one that calls the new system's API, without overhauling the rest of the logic.

Hopefully, this walkthrough gives you a concrete sense of how an Action agent lives within a larger solution. It's rarely acting completely alone for mission-critical processes; instead, it's embedded in a network of agents, each doing what they do best. This modular, pattern-oriented design is powerful – it makes the whole architecture more resilient to change and easier to scale.

We've now covered what Action agents are, when to use them, how to build them, how to govern them, how they relate to other tech, and how they combine with other agents. We'll conclude with a summary of the key points of the Action pattern and prepare to move on to the next chapter, which shifts focus from getting tasks done to providing guidance – the Coach pattern.

SUMMARY

In this chapter, we explored The Action Pattern, Salesforce Agentforce's blueprint for task execution agents. Action agents are the simplest type of AI agents – they don't deliberate or converse; they just execute predefined tasks in a safe, controlled manner. We began by highlighting their core traits: they operate within set boundaries (respecting permissions and business rules), produce clear audit trails of what they do, and are easy to stack and test as modular building blocks. These qualities make Action agents a natural starting point for organizations implementing AI-powered automation.

We examined the lifecycle of an Action agent (Receive → Validate → Execute → Log → Respond) and saw how every step reinforces reliability and trustworthiness. Through various enterprise use cases – from HR offboarding to IT provisioning – we demonstrated how Action agents can streamline repetitive processes across departments, all while enforcing guardrails like approvals and limits. The chapter provided a step-by-step guide to building Action agents with Salesforce tools: using Agent Builder for setup, Flow or Invocable Apex for logic, Custom Metadata for configuration, and Command Center for monitoring. We even dove into a concrete example of an onboarding checklist agent, complete with a sample Apex snippet, to illustrate the implementation details.

Governance emerged as a critical theme: as you deploy more Action agents, you must control who can invoke them, track their activity (e.g., via logging objects), manage changes via versioning and feature flags, and interlock them with any necessary human oversight or risk checks. We offered best practices to treat Action agents like internal APIs – meaning they should be documented, secured, and monitored with the same rigor.

Zooming out, we related the Action pattern to the broader AI agent ecosystem. Concepts like LangChain tools, AutoGen operators, or RPA bots map closely to what Action agents do, though Salesforce's approach embeds these "tools" natively into your trusted CRM platform. We discussed how Action agents can integrate into multi-agent workflows both within Salesforce and across systems (hinting at standards like Model Context Protocol for cross-platform agent communication). The takeaway is that Action agents bring the value of quick, autonomous task completion without compromising on enterprise requirements for safety and maintainability – a balance that many standalone AI solutions struggle to achieve.

Finally, we saw how Action agents compose with other Agentforce patterns. In multi-step scenarios, the Action agent is often the finisher – whether it's triggered by a Sentinel alert, carrying out a Supervisor-approved decision, executing a step in a Conductor's orchestration, or responding to a user's request relayed by a Companion/Presenter. A full example of a field service incident showed multiple patterns in action, with the Action agents diligently performing the concrete fixes and updates amid a swarm of coordinating agents. This reinforces that while Action agents on their own are simple, their real power is unlocked when they are combined with the intelligence and orchestration of the other patterns.

In summary, Action agents are your "doers." They turn intents into outcomes in a transparent and repeatable way. By implementing the Action pattern, you lay the groundwork for tangible business value – automating tasks that save users time and eliminate errors, all under a framework that your IT and compliance teams can trust. Whether used standalone for quick automations or woven into complex agent ecosystems, Action agents offer a scalable and testable path to real results.

Next, we transition from agents that act to agents that advise. Chapter 9 will introduce the Coach Pattern (Insight Advisor Agent), where AI agents don't execute transactions directly but instead guide and educate users with insights and recommendations. In that chapter, you'll discover how Coach agents complement the doers like Action agents by enhancing human decision-making and skill development in the flow of work. The journey continues as we explore how agents can not only automate work, but also elevate the people performing it.

9

THE COACH PATTERN (INSIGHT ADVISOR AGENT)

In an AI-powered workplace, not every digital assistant exists to do the work for you – some exist to help you do the work better. The Coach pattern's essential mission is not to automate work, but to elevate people. Unlike Action or Conductor agents that carry out tasks or orchestrate processes on your behalf, Coach agents deliver insight, reflection, and contextual advice that improves how humans perform. These agents are less about taking over duties and more about making you better at your duties. They act as a personalized advisor in your corner, analyzing what you do and guiding you to up your game next time.

Think of Coach agents as the advisors, tutors, mentors, and nudgers of the AI agent world. Instead of simply answering questions or executing commands, a Coach agent observes your actions, interprets patterns in your behavior, and offers data-backed suggestions or feedback just in time to drive personal or team improvement. They are always-on, aware of your role and context, and focused on helping you grow. A Coach might notice that you tend to rush through a particular step in a process and gently remind you of a best practice, much like a friendly mentor who's perpetually by your side, keeping an eye on your performance. The goal isn't to do your job, but to help you do your job better – whether that means refining a skill, adopting a best practice, or avoiding a mistake you made in the past.

Consider a few examples of Coach agents in action across different roles: A sales manager's Coach agent might monitor call transcripts and customer sentiment, then suggest "coaching moments" – for instance, flagging that when call sentiment drops, it's a good time to ask open-ended questions or offer a discount. A warehouse team lead's Coach could watch operational data and highlight process deviations on the shop floor, offering quick workflow tips to improve safety or efficiency (like reminding a team about proper scan procedures if inventory mismatches spike). In healthcare, a compliance Coach for physicians could scan patient notes and politely flag documentation gaps, guiding a doctor to add required details to meet regulatory standards. For a project manager, a Coach agent could summarize the "health" of the current sprint at the end of each week – noting patterns like rollover tasks or imbalances in workload – and then suggest backlog grooming strategies or resource adjustments for the next sprint. Each of these coaches is deeply context-aware, focusing on the person's unique activities and goals.

While Coach agents are highly personalized (in that sense, they may feel similar to Companion agents covered in earlier chapters), the key difference is focus. A Companion agent helps you execute tasks or find information in the moment, acting like an extra pair of hands or an assistant. A Coach agent, by contrast, helps you improve your approach to tasks over time – more like a skilled trainer or tutor. For example, a Companion might help a sales rep draft an email, whereas a Coach will quietly observe a series of emails or calls and later suggest how the rep could communicate more effectively or prioritize leads differently next time. Coach agents also differ from Presenter agents: a Presenter is concerned with translating or visualizing information you already have (for instance, turning raw data into a chart or narrative), while a Coach uses information to provide judicious advice on what you could do better in the future. In short, Companion helps get something done, Presenter helps interpret what's been done, and Coach helps you do it better next time.

This chapter explores how to design and deploy Coach agents across a variety of use cases and platforms using Salesforce's Agentforce toolkit. We'll break down the anatomy and lifecycle of a Coach agent, discuss when to use the Coach pattern (and when not to), and walk through cross-functional examples from HR to IT. We'll dive into how you can build Coach agents with Salesforce tools like Agent Builder, Flow, Apex, and Lightning Web Components, and how to incorporate feedback loops and behavioral design so your agents truly help (and don't annoy) your users. By the end, you'll see how Coach agents fit into the broader ecosystem of AI patterns – and be prepared for the next chapter's focus on multi-agent systems. Next, let's start by defining the architecture and lifecycle of a Coach agent.

ANATOMY OF A COACH AGENT

What makes a Coach agent tick? At its core, a Coach agent follows a continuous lifecycle of Observe → Interpret → Advise → Refine. Each stage in this loop corresponds to a distinct capability of the agent, and together they form a feedback cycle that enables the agent to guide users toward improvement:

Observe: The Coach agent monitors relevant actions and outcomes. It "listens" to what the human or team is doing in the workflow. This could mean capturing event logs (e.g. how a sales rep fills out opportunity fields or the outcomes of support tickets), tracking performance metrics (like call lengths, error rates, or task completion times), or receiving signals from other agents (perhaps a Sentinel agent's alerts). The observation phase builds the raw input data the Coach will need for analysis. Good Coach agents cast a wide but purposeful net – they gather enough data to see patterns, but focus on signals that truly matter for performance.

Interpret: Next, the agent analyzes the collected data to spot patterns, anomalies, or opportunities for improvement. This interpretation might involve analytic logic or AI models – for example, an Apex class computing that a customer support agent's average chat handle time is creeping upward, or an Einstein AI model detecting sentiment trends in call transcripts. The Coach compares observations against benchmarks, best practices, or past performance. Essentially, the agent is asking: what's going well, and what could be better? This step often produces a scored assessment or identified insight (e.g. "calls where the agent asks < 2 questions have 30% lower satisfaction").

Advise: Once a Coach agent has an insight, it formulates advice or feedback tailored to the user. The output could be a nudge – a subtle suggestion delivered via Slack or Microsoft Teams ("Heads up: Calls shorter than 3 minutes tend to end poorly. Consider spending a bit more time with the customer."). It might be a concise summary with improvement tips shown in a dashboard or sent by email ("Weekly Sales Debrief: You closed 8 deals, great work! Two stalled – perhaps re-engage those leads with a promo as your peers did successfully."). Or it could be an in-app prompt in a Salesforce Lightning page, like a popup in a case management console that says, "You've resolved 5 cases today. Here's one suggestion to improve CSAT based on today's patterns...". The advice is contextual (relevant to what the user is doing), role-aware (a senior manager might get a different kind of tip than a junior rep), and actionable (it suggests a next step or a behavior change). This is where the Coach's guidance is actually delivered to the human in a helpful way.

Refine: The cycle doesn't end after giving advice. A good Coach agent refines its understanding and approach based on what happens next. It observes how the user reacts – did they follow the advice, ignore it, dismiss it? Did performance metrics subsequently improve? This feedback allows the agent to adjust future recommendations. If the user keeps ignoring a certain suggestion, maybe the agent tries a different approach or backs off that topic. Refinement ensures the Coach agent becomes more personalized and effective over time, honing in on what truly helps the individual or team.

This lifecycle relies on several key inputs and outputs. Inputs to a Coach agent typically include: (1) Historical actions and outcomes – data about what the user/team did and what results were achieved (e.g. past quarter's sales metrics, or a log of code deployment failures in an engineering org); (2) Behavior patterns – trends or habits in how work is performed (for instance, noticing a certain support agent consistently forgets to follow up with customers, or that a manufacturing line's output dips on Fridays); and (3) Benchmarks, rules, and best practices – external standards the agent can use as reference (such as company policy that "emails should be responded to within 24 hours" or industry benchmarks like an average deal conversion rate). These inputs feed the Observe and Interpret phases. On the other side, outputs from a Coach agent manifest as guidance and insights delivered to the user: (a) Nudges, like real-time suggestions or reminders (often via chat or notification – for example, a Slack message that pops up saying "Try mentioning feature X, it's been effective in similar deals" right after a sales call ends); (b) Feedback summaries with improvement tips, perhaps sent in a weekly report or shown on a dashboard ("Your coding commit frequency dropped this month, maybe schedule focus time for coding"); and (c) Role-based insights embedded in the workflow, such as a custom Lightning Web Component (LWC) on a manager's homepage that highlights "Top 3 coaching opportunities for your team this week" based on aggregated data. The medium can vary – some Coach agents communicate via email, some inside Salesforce apps, others through collaboration tools – but the common thread is delivering timely, useful coaching in a place the user will see it.

Under the hood, a Coach agent's architecture in Salesforce Agentforce can be thought of in layered components. First is the data interpretation layer, where the heavy analysis happens. This could be implemented with an Invocable Apex class that crunches numbers or applies rules to incoming data streams. It might also leverage Einstein AI models or even integrate an external Large Language Model (LLM) like GPT for more nuanced interpretation (for example, using GPT to read open-ended survey feedback and extract themes for coaching). Next is the personalization layer, which uses information about the user and context to tailor the advice. Here, Salesforce metadata and user profile data play a big role – the agent might check a custom metadata setting for the user's role and preferred coaching style, or reference the user's past interactions (e.g. if the user previously said a tip was not relevant, the agent remembers this). This layer ensures the Coach agent's outputs aren't one-size-fits-all, but rather adapted to the individual's needs, seniority, and even their openness to feedback. Above that is the recommendation logic layer, which applies decision rules, scoring models, or behavioral templates to decide what to advise and when. This might involve a scoring formula (like computing a "focus score" for how well a person stays on top of tasks, and triggering a nudge if it falls below a threshold) or pattern templates ("if new employee + first project delayed, then suggest time management resources"). Finally, we have the delivery or interaction layer, using Salesforce tools to actually reach the user. Agentforce's Agent Builder can orchestrate these pieces declaratively, and Salesforce Flow can be used to sequence the observation-to-advice pipeline (for example, a scheduled Flow might run every Monday, calling an Apex action to analyze last week's data, then posting results to a Slack channel). Apex provides the custom logic where needed (such as complex calculations or external API calls to a GPT service for summarization). Experience Cloud or Lightning Experience pages can host the coaching UI components (like an LWC showing a personalized coaching dashboard). And of course, generative AI (GPT prompt chains) might be employed to phrase the advice in a friendly, clear manner, or to adjust tone. Salesforce's toolkit thus allows a mix of no-code, low-code, and pro-code elements to build a robust Coach agent.

Pro Tip: Always separate insight generation from recommendation delivery. In practice, this means design your Coach agent so that the analysis part (what the agent thinks is happening) is decoupled from the messaging part (how the agent tells the user). This makes it easier to adjust the guidance style based on the audience's role, experience level, or even mood. A junior employee might appreciate very explicit step-by-step coaching, whereas a veteran might prefer high-level pointers – the underlying insight might be the same, but the delivery should differ. By separating the layers, your Coach agent can flex its communication (tone, detail, timing) without having to rework the core logic each time.

With the anatomy of a Coach agent laid out – its lifecycle, key components, and tools – we have a blueprint for how these insight advisors function. Next, we'll discuss when and why to deploy a Coach agent. Not every situation calls for one, and understanding the ideal use cases for the Coach pattern (versus other agent patterns) is crucial.

WHEN AND WHY TO USE THE COACH PATTERN

How do you know when a Coach agent is the right solution? The Coach pattern shines in scenarios where the primary goal is to improve human performance over time rather than automate a process outright. If you find yourself saying, "We don't just want this task done – we want it done better (and consistently better) by our people," that's a signal a Coach agent could add value. Some common motivations for using the Coach pattern include:

Driving Continuous Improvement: Perhaps your sales team has a wide variance in how deals are handled – some reps excel, others struggle, and you want to lift the overall performance by sharing insights and best practices. A Coach agent can observe those patterns of success and failure and provide tailored tips to each rep, turning individual lessons learned into organization-wide improvement.

Role-Tailored Guidance Without Replacing Judgment: In fields like healthcare, legal, or customer service, you often want to support human judgment, not replace it. A Coach agent can be deployed to give suggestions that are specific to a role (e.g. a legal contract review coach that points out clauses that usually cause delays) while leaving the final decisions to the human expert. If you need an AI that respects human autonomy and expertise but still guides behavior, the Coach pattern is appropriate.

Addressing Variability and Drift: Over time, even experienced individuals or teams can drift from best practices – maybe due to bad habits forming or changes in the work context. For instance, an IT operations team might gradually start missing more change management steps as pressure mounts. A Coach agent is useful when you're solving for this drift in execution quality. It can catch those deviations (like "you skipped the QA step in 3 of 5 deployments this week") and gently course-correct before those habits solidify or cause major issues.

Enablement vs. Automation: There are situations where automating a task entirely is either impossible or undesirable, but providing better enablement for the human doing that task is valuable. For example, you might not automate a CEO's strategic decision-making, but a Coach agent could help enable better decisions by summarizing lessons from past projects or prompting the CEO to consider factors they often overlook. If your aim is to support learning and development rather than just efficiency, a Coach fits the bill. In short, you want an agent that acts like a tutor or trainer, not a doer – focusing on building human capability.

It's also important to know when not to use a Coach agent. If a process is highly repetitive, well-defined, and doesn't benefit from human judgment or variation, an Action agent or Conductor might be better to simply automate it and ensure consistency. Likewise, if users primarily need information presented clearly but not necessarily advice (for instance, a dashboard that aggregates KPIs for review), a Presenter agent could suffice without the complexity of adaptive coaching.

A helpful way to decide is to compare the Coach pattern side-by-side with the Companion and Presenter patterns, which are adjacent in purpose:

Companion Agent: Helps the user get something done in the moment. It focuses on execution assistance. Use Case: A sales rep uses a Companion agent to find relevant product info and draft an email on the fly. The agent's value is in speeding up or simplifying the task at hand.

Presenter Agent: Helps interpret or explain something that's been done or is known. It focuses on clarity and understanding. Use Case: After a quarter ends, a Presenter agent generates a clear report or presentation of sales results and insights for the team. The value is turning raw data into actionable information.

Coach Agent: Helps the user do it better next time. It focuses on improvement and learning. Use Case: Throughout the quarter (and especially at the end), a Coach agent gives each sales rep personalized tips on how to improve their technique or focus on certain leads, based on that rep's performance patterns. The value is improved future outcomes through behavior change.

To illustrate these choices, consider a few scenarios and which pattern is the best fit:

Team members are forgetting steps in a complex workflow and making avoidable mistakes

- Most fitting agent pattern: Coach (Insight Advisor)
- Rationale: The objective is to improve execution quality by reinforcing best practices and providing timely guidance, not to fully automate the work or take control away from the team.

A manager wants a daily brief of key metrics and events in a project

- Most fitting agent pattern: Presenter (Reporter)
- Rationale: The need is to summarize and clearly present existing information in a consumable format, without coaching behavior or task execution.

An employee has an overwhelming list of tasks to get through each day

- Most fitting agent pattern: Companion (Assistant)
- Rationale: The primary goal is hands-on assistance to reduce cognitive load, automate routine tasks, and help prioritize and schedule work efficiently.

A new customer service agent is struggling with call quality even though they follow the script

- Most fitting agent pattern: Coach (Insight Advisor)
- Rationale: The issue is not procedural compliance but skill development, such as tone, judgment, and problem-solving, which a Coach can address through analysis and targeted feedback.

In general, if you find yourself looking for a solution that guides and teaches rather than does or tells, the Coach pattern is likely what you need. It's an investment in human capital via AI – using an agent to multiply the impact of your training and coaching efforts continuously. Organizations often deploy Coach agents when scaling personalized coaching is otherwise hard (you can't assign every employee a human coach, but you can give them a digital one), or when the cost of inconsistent performance is high.

Having determined when the Coach pattern is most beneficial, we can move from the abstract to the concrete. In the next section, we'll explore cross-functional use cases for Coach agents across different business domains – seeing exactly how these agents can help in HR, Sales, Manufacturing, Healthcare, IT, and Legal scenarios.

CROSS-FUNCTIONAL USE CASES FOR COACH AGENTS

One of the strengths of the Coach pattern is its broad applicability. Virtually any domain where people are performing complex tasks or making decisions can benefit from a Coach agent providing insight and guidance. Let's tour a range of hypothetical (but very plausible) use cases across various functions – demonstrating how Coach agents can be tailored to different needs but follow the same core pattern of observe-analyze-advise. We'll look at six domains: Sales, Human Resources (HR), Manufacturing, Healthcare, Information Technology (IT), and Legal. For each, we'll describe how a Coach agent might work, and then summarize the scenario in a list of signals and responses.

Sales Enablement Coach: In a sales organization, a Coach agent can act like an ever-vigilant sales trainer for each rep. Suppose we have Momentum, a Coach agent that monitors a sales rep's activities and outcomes. Momentum observes signals like the rep's call durations, the sentiment of those calls (perhaps using sentiment analysis on call transcripts), and win/loss patterns in the CRM. It notices, for example, that the rep tends to talk 80% of the time on calls that eventually lead nowhere, whereas successful calls (especially among top-performing peers) involve more customer interaction. The Coach agent interprets this pattern and at the end of the week sends the rep a Slack message: "I noticed in your last few prospect calls you did a lot of the talking. Try asking at least 3 open-ended questions in your next call – our data shows successful deals have more prospect engagement. :thumbsup:" The output is a nudge that's friendly and data-backed. It could also provide resources, like linking to a short internal video on effective questioning techniques. The medium might be Slack, email, or even a pop-up in the sales app after each call summary. Salesforce tools at play here could include Einstein Conversation Insights (to get call sentiment and transcript analysis), an Apex job that compiles the stats, and a Flow that triggers the outbound message or creates a Task for the rep to review coaching feedback. Over time, as the rep improves (or if they ignore the advice), the Coach adjusts its tips – perhaps suggesting more advanced techniques or backing off if the rep consistently exceeds targets (no need to nag a top performer!).

HR Manager Coach: Imagine an HR department that wants to ensure managers give timely and quality feedback to their team members. Managers often get busy and may postpone giving feedback or conducting 1:1 meetings, which can hurt team development. A Coach agent, let's call it FeedbackGuru, is deployed for people managers. FeedbackGuru observes signals such as: how frequently a manager submits performance feedback forms, whether they complete employee review meetings on schedule, and even sentiment in employee survey comments about management support. Let's say a particular manager, Alice, has skipped the last two quarterly feedback sessions with her direct reports. The Coach agent notices this (maybe via Salesforce HR system data or a plug-in to the performance review app) and sends Alice a gentle prompt via email or a Teams chat: "It's been 3 months since your last check-in with John Doe. Regular feedback is key to engagement – consider scheduling a quick 1:1 this week. Need help? Here's a 5-point checklist for effective feedback conversations." The Coach output is a nudge with resources. Medium could be an in-app notification on the manager's HR portal dashboard and an email. Tools used might involve Salesforce Flow scheduling (triggered after a quarter ends with no feedback logged), integration with Calendar APIs to even propose a meeting time, and an LWC component in the HR app that shows a "manager coaching tips" panel. This Coach agent essentially serves as a personal leadership coach, nudging managers to complete feedback loops consistently and offering just-in-time training material (like how to give constructive feedback). Over time, if Alice starts doing this regularly, the agent might shift to more advanced coaching (e.g., "Your team's engagement survey scores suggest recognition is low – maybe try giving more shout-outs, here's how...").

Manufacturing Floor Coach: On a factory floor, consistency and safety are paramount. Consider a manufacturing company where technicians follow a standard operating procedure (SOP) for machine maintenance. A Coach agent (call it SOP Sentinel, blending a bit of sentinel monitoring with coaching) keeps an eye on how maintenance tasks are performed. It takes signals from IoT sensors or maintenance logs – for example, the time taken for each step, whether any steps were skipped, and outcomes like machine downtime incidents. Suppose a particular technician deviates from the SOP frequently – maybe they skip a cleaning step to save time. The Coach agent detects this pattern (interpretation could be done via an Apex routine processing maintenance records) and when it happens, it triggers a prompt on the technician's handheld device: "Reminder: Don't forget the nozzle cleaning step. Skipping it has led to 3 faults last month. Following the full SOP keeps our machines running smoothly!" This is delivered as a real-time nudge (perhaps via a mobile push notification or a message in the maintenance app interface). The agent might also escalate a pattern to a shift supervisor's dashboard if multiple techs are skipping the same step, suggesting that maybe the SOP needs clarity or additional training. Tools used here could include Salesforce Field Service data (to know task completion details), custom Apex to evaluate compliance rates, and a Lightning component that logs when the coach had to intervene. The output can also be a weekly summary to each technician: "Your maintenance compliance: 92%. Great job following procedures! Here are areas to watch...". Over time, SOP Sentinel helps reduce errors and downtime by ensuring process adherence and quick correction of bad habits.

Healthcare Compliance Coach: Healthcare providers deal with extensive documentation and strict compliance requirements. A Coach agent (let's name it MediMentor) assists doctors or nurses in keeping their documentation accurate and complete. MediMentor might integrate with an Electronic Health Record (EHR) system data (using Salesforce Health Cloud, for instance). It observes signals like patient note completion rates, missing fields (e.g., a doctor often forgets to fill the "follow-up plan" section), or even warning signs that documentation might not meet billing or legal requirements. When the agent notices a gap – say Dr. Smith consistently doesn't record a patient's consent discussion – it can flag this shortly after the patient encounter. The Coach could pop up in the EHR interface with a message: "Before you close this patient's record, note that the 'Informed Consent' field is empty. It's important to document consent for any procedure – consider adding a note now to stay compliant." The medium is likely an on-screen alert or a notification in the provider's task list. The tone is crucial here: it should come across as supportive ("to stay compliant") rather than accusatory. Tools: Salesforce's platform can host Health Cloud flows where an Apex trigger checks records after saving and if key fields are blank, invokes a prompt (perhaps leveraging a GPT-based text generator to suggest wording for the missing info). The Coach output might even provide an example snippet: "E.g., 'Discussed risks and patient gave consent.'" For longer-term coaching, MediMentor could send monthly compliance scorecards to each clinician, highlighting improvement (or decline) and offering targeted tips (like "You've improved documentation on follow-ups! Next, focus on recording medication changes."). This agent reduces the load on compliance officers by proactively guiding clinicians, which can improve patient safety and reduce audit findings.

IT Configuration Coach: In an IT context, especially within a Salesforce org or any large system, admins and developers often struggle with org health – things like too many deprecated fields, automation scripts that conflict, or security settings that need tightening. A Coach agent for an IT admin (let's dub it OrgCoach) could continuously analyze the system configuration and usage patterns. Signals it watches might include: number of unused fields or workflows, Apex error logs, user permission anomalies, or performance metrics in the org. Suppose OrgCoach identifies that there are 50 custom fields on the Account object that haven't been populated in over a year (a sign of "configuration sprawl"), and also notices the page load times are creeping up. The agent would interpret this as an opportunity to clean up and improve performance. It might surface an insight on the admin's dashboard or via email: "Your Salesforce org has a lot of unused or redundant fields (50+ on Account). This can slow down performance and confuse users. Consider reviewing and removing or repurposing these fields. Need help? Here's a link to a cleanup guide and a list of the top unused fields." This output is part nudge, part actionable report. The medium could be an Experience Cloud portal for IT where OrgCoach posts weekly "Org Health Tips," or simply a PDF report emailed monthly with color-coded health indicators. Tools involved: likely a combination of Apex (for org metadata analysis), maybe Salesforce Optimizer (Salesforce's own tool for org health) data feeding into the agent, and an LWC that presents the tips interactively (perhaps even with buttons to trigger cleanup scripts). OrgCoach can also coach on best practices: if an admin creates a new workflow rule where a newer Flow feature would be preferable, the agent might catch that and advise, "We noticed you added a Workflow Rule. Did you know Salesforce is deprecating these in favor of Flow? Consider using a Flow for future automation to stay up-to-date." Over time, this Coach agent helps IT maintain a cleaner, more efficient, and compliant environment, acting like an ever-watchful senior architect giving advice.

Legal Contracting Coach: In a corporate legal department, processing contracts involves negotiation back-and-forth, redlines, and approvals. Let's envision a Coach agent named Lexi for legal operations. Lexi monitors the contract review process data: how long drafts sit waiting for review, which clauses get heavily redlined by counterparties, and how often certain playbook guidelines are ignored. For instance, Lexi might notice that "Clause 5.2 – Liability Cap" in vendor contracts is almost always negotiated, causing delays, and that the legal team's own lawyers often end up manually adjusting it to a standard fallback. The Coach agent could suggest a process improvement: it might send a suggestion to the legal team lead, "The liability cap clause in our standard contract template has been redlined in 90% of recent contracts, adding ~1 week on average to deal closure. Consider updating the template language or creating a pre-approved fallback clause to streamline negotiations." This is higher-level coaching aimed at process improvement. On an individual level, Lexi could coach an in-house attorney by noting, for example, that they tend to delay sending out initial contract drafts until the last minute, and nudge them: "You have 3 contracts in queue awaiting initial draft. Our records show contracts initiated early in the quarter close 20% faster. Try to get those drafts out sooner – maybe block some time this week to tackle them." Medium for these might be a dashboard for legal ops and email alerts. Tools: Salesforce could be managing the contract workflow (perhaps integrated with a CLM – Contract Lifecycle Management – system), and an

Apex analytics job could crunch the numbers on cycle times and redline frequencies. An LLM (GPT) might even be used by Lexi to analyze common redline edits and suggest improved wording that could preempt those edits. By implementing Lexi, the legal team benefits from an agent that not only tracks their work but advises them on how to reduce bottlenecks and adhere to best practices (like always using the latest approved clause language, etc.).

Each of these scenarios is hypothetical, but they demonstrate how versatile Coach agents can be. Despite differences in domain, notice the consistent pattern: each Coach agent looks for signals (behavior or outcomes that matter), interprets them against some benchmark or rule, and then produces a Coach output (nudge, recommendation, or insight) delivered through an appropriate medium (Slack, email, in-app, report) using various tools (Salesforce platform features, possibly AI for analysis or message phrasing). The tone is always supportive and geared toward improvement, not punishment. Below is a list of these examples:

Sales

- **Key signal observed:** Call sentiment patterns, win or loss rates, and talk-to-listen ratios.
- **Coach output (advice):** Suggests asking more open-ended questions when engagement is low, supported by data such as "calls with more than three questions show a 20 percent higher close rate."
- **Delivery medium:** Slack direct message after calls and a weekly email summary.
- **Salesforce tools used:** Einstein Conversation Insights, Apex for analysis, Flow to send Slack messages, GPT for tone and phrasing of the tip.

HR (Management)

- **Key signal observed:** Missed feedback cycles and employee survey comments.
- **Coach output (advice):** Nudges managers to complete pending one-on-one feedback with a checklist for effective conversations; later suggests recognition actions if engagement trends downward.
- **Delivery medium:** Email notifications and in-app prompts within the HR portal.

- **Salesforce tools used:** Flow scheduler, Apex trigger on feedback objects, Lightning Web Components in the manager dashboard, calendar API integration.

Manufacturing

- **Key signal observed:** Skipped standard operating procedure steps and machine error incidents.
- **Coach output (advice):** Sends real-time reminders to follow missed steps to prevent faults, along with a weekly compliance scorecard.
- **Delivery medium:** Mobile push notifications and a supervisor dashboard report.
- **Salesforce tools used:** Salesforce Field Service logs, Apex rules engine, push notifications via Salesforce Mobile SDK, analytics dashboards.

Healthcare

- **Key signal observed:** Missing documentation fields and compliance flags.
- **Coach output (advice):** On-screen reminders to complete required fields before closing records and a monthly compliance report with personalized documentation tips.
- **Delivery medium:** In-application prompts within the EHR and email reports.
- **Salesforce tools used:** Health Cloud data, Apex trigger on record save, Einstein GPT for suggested wording, Salesforce email services.

IT (Administration)

- **Key signal observed:** Orphaned configuration elements such as unused fields and performance degradation indicators.
- **Coach output (advice):** Organization health tips recommending removal of unused fields, warnings about deprecated features, and an optional auto-generated cleanup task list.
- **Delivery medium:** Admin home page component and email summary.
- **Salesforce tools used:** Salesforce Optimizer outputs, Custom Metadata for best-practice rules, Apex for org analysis, Lightning Web Components for the health dashboard.

Legal

- **Key signal observed:** Contract negotiation delays and recurring redline clauses.
- **Coach output (advice):** Recommends updating contract templates to address common redlines and nudges counsel to send drafts earlier to avoid end-of-quarter bottlenecks.
- **Delivery medium:** Slack messages to the legal team for template suggestions and personal email reminders to counsel.
- **Salesforce tools used:** Contract data stored in Salesforce, Apex analytics on turnaround times, GPT to summarize redline patterns, Slack integration.

As shown, Coach agents can be introduced in nearly any business function where guidance would help. They are especially powerful in cross-functional scenarios – for example, a Sales Coach might team up with a Legal Coach, where the Sales Coach tells a salesperson "this deal is stuck awaiting legal approval" while the Legal Coach nudges the legal team "this sales deal is high-value and waiting on you, prioritize it." By standardizing on the Coach pattern, an organization can create a whole suite of specialized mentors: one for every department or even multiple per department (performance coach, compliance coach, wellness coach, etc.), all working in concert to uplift the human workforce.

Each use case above is hypothetical but grounded in real challenges organizations face. The implementation details would vary, but with Salesforce's rich platform (from Agentforce Agent Builder to Apex to Slack integrations), these Coach agents are entirely within reach. Now that we've explored what Coach agents can do across different domains, let's turn our attention to how to build such agents using Salesforce Agentforce, step by step.

BUILDING COACH AGENTS IN AGENTFORCE

Designing a Coach agent conceptually is one thing – building it in a robust way on Salesforce is another. Fortunately, Agentforce provides a collection of tools that make it feasible to implement the Coach pattern through a mix of declarative and programmatic development. In this section, we'll outline a practical approach to building a Coach agent, using Salesforce technologies like Agent Builder, Flow, Apex, Lightning Web Components (LWC), and even integrations with LLMs for advanced insight generation. We'll also walk through a concrete example: an "Agile

Sprint Coach" for a project management scenario, to illustrate the steps end-to-end.

1. Define the Observation Logic (Signals and Tracking): The first step is deciding what signals your Coach agent should pay attention to and setting up the mechanism to capture them. In Salesforce, this often means identifying the objects, fields, or events that will serve as inputs. For example, in our Agile Sprint Coach scenario, key signals might include: how many story points were completed vs. committed in a sprint (to gauge if the team overcommitted), how many bugs were reported, and whether retrospectives were filled out. These could be stored in custom objects like Sprint__c, Work_Item__c, or captured via Agile tooling integrated with Salesforce. Using Platform Events or Change Data Capture is a great way to have your Coach agent "listen" for certain events (e.g., a Sprint is closed, or a work item is marked done). You might create a Trigger or Flow that runs when these events occur, writing relevant info to a "Coaching Logs" object for later analysis. Additionally, if some signals come from outside Salesforce (say Jira or an external system), consider using MuleSoft or APIs to bring that data into Salesforce or directly call from Apex. The goal is to have a stream of data points that represent user or team behavior which the agent will analyze. If the observation needs to be continuous, a scheduled Flow or batch Apex might run daily/weekly to gather the latest stats.

2. Implement the Data Pipeline: Once you know what to track, implement the pipeline that moves this data through the system. This might involve creating custom metadata to configure what good vs. bad looks like. For example, you might have a custom metadata type Coaching_Benchmark__mdt with fields like MetricName, WarningThreshold, IdealRange etc., which defines targets for various metrics (e.g., "Sprint Completion % ideal >80%"). Your Apex or Flow can reference these benchmarks. It's also wise to store historical data for trend analysis – maybe a custom object Sprint_Performance__c that captures each sprint's outcomes for each team. By having a history, your Coach agent can identify improvement or decline over time, not just a snapshot. In practice, implementing the data pipeline could be as simple as a nightly scheduled Apex batch that reads the day's events and updates a summary table, or as sophisticated as streaming events processed in near-real-time. If using Agent Builder, you could configure Topics (types of inputs) and have Agentforce automatically route them to an agent logic function. But under the hood, often an Invocable Apex action is doing the crunching.

For our Agile Sprint Coach example, suppose we create an Apex class SprintCoachAnalyzer that has a method to evaluate a sprint. It might aggregate all work items of the sprint, calculate completion ratio, count how many carried over, check if a retrospective note exists, etc. Here's a very simplified pseudocode for such an Apex logic:

```
public class SprintCoachAnalyzer {

  @InvocableMethod

  public static List<Advice__c> analyzeSprint(List<Id> sprintIds) {

    List<Advice__c> adviceList = new List<Advice__c>();

    for (Id sprintId : sprintIds) {

        Sprint__c sprint = [SELECT Id, Team__c, CommittedPoints__c,
CompletedPoints__c, RetrospectiveNotes__c

                FROM Sprint__c WHERE Id = :sprintId];

      Decimal completionRate = sprint.CompletedPoints__c / sprint.Com-
mittedPoints__c;

      String guidance;

      if (completionRate < 0.8) {

            guidance = 'Your team completed only ' + (completion-
Rate*100).round() + '% of planned work. Consider improving estimation or
reducing scope for next sprint.';

      }

      if (sprint.RetrospectiveNotes__c == null) {

        guidance += ' (No retrospective notes found. Don't skip the retro – it's
key to continuous improvement!)';

      }

      // Create an Advice record with the compiled guidance

       Advice__c rec = new Advice__c(Team__c = sprint.Team__c, Sprint__c =
sprint.Id, Message__c = guidance);

      adviceList.add(rec);

    }
```

```
        return adviceList;
    }
}
```

IN THIS SNIPPET, the Apex method generates an Advice__c record (imagine we have a custom object for pieces of coaching advice) for each sprint analyzed. It checks two simple rules: sprint completion under 80% triggers a suggestion, and missing retrospective notes triggers another reminder. In a real implementation, you'd use custom metadata for the 0.8 threshold and have more nuanced text (possibly via a template or GPT for nicer wording). But this illustrates how Invocable Apex can encapsulate the interpretation logic.

3. Configure Insight Generation with AI (if needed): In many Coach agents, especially those giving written feedback or summarizing patterns, you may want to employ an LLM to enhance the insight generation. Salesforce's Einstein GPT (or connecting to OpenAI's API) can be used to turn raw analysis into a more natural-language explanation. For instance, after the Apex logic determines what the issue is (low completion rate, missing retrospectives), you might feed a prompt to GPT like: "You are an Agile Coach. The team completed 60% of their sprint commitment and did not hold a retrospective. Provide a brief, encouraging suggestion addressing these points." The model's response could then be stored as the Message__c in Advice__c. This step is about phrasing and tone modulation – ensuring the advice is delivered in a constructive, possibly even upbeat tone ("Keep an eye on sprint scope – aiming for around 80% completion is a good target. Also, try not to skip retrospectives; they help the team learn from last sprint!"). Einstein Copilot (Salesforce's term for built-in generative assistance) can also integrate in Flow, where you use a "Generate Text" action with a prompt that includes dynamic fields (like the calculated completion rate). The benefit of using GPT is that the advice can feel more human and context-aware in phrasing, possibly even adjusting language based on the audience (e.g., more formal for a senior manager vs. more casual for an intern, if you include role info in the prompt).

4. Routing and Delivery via Salesforce Flow and Channels: After generating the advice or coaching insight, the next step is to deliver it through the appropriate channel. Salesforce Flow Builder can orchestrate this. For our example, we could have a Record-Triggered Flow on the Sprint__c object

that fires when a sprint is closed (Status = Completed). The flow would call the SprintCoachAnalyzer.analyzeSprint Apex action (or an Einstein GPT action) to generate advice, then route that advice. Perhaps we decide to post it to the team's Slack channel and also log it in Salesforce. Salesforce has a Slack integration where you can use a Slack alert element in Flow (or Apex using the Slack API) to send a message. The Flow might create a nicely formatted Slack message like: ":robot_face: Agile Coach: Great sprint! Here's some feedback – Your completion rate was 60%. Consider adjusting scope next time. And don't forget to run a retrospective. :calendar: I'm here to help you continuously improve!" Similarly, the flow could create a Chatter post or send an email if Slack isn't used. If using Experience Cloud, maybe the team has a project portal where a Lightning Web Component displays current coaching tips; in that case, the advice record saved by the flow would be queried by the LWC. The key is to meet users where they work – if your company lives in email, deliver via email; if they're always on a Salesforce app, use in-app notifications or a Home Page component; if they love Slack or Teams, integrate there. Salesforce Flow can also handle decision logic: for example, don't send the Slack if the team's completion rate is 100% and everything is perfect (no one wants a needless pat on the back from a robot every time). Perhaps only send when there's constructive feedback or big kudos to share.

To illustrate the front-end piece, consider a simple LWC that could be embedded on a team's dashboard to show the latest coaching insights for that team. The LWC might use Apex to fetch any Advice__c records for that team's last sprint and display them. Additionally, it might have an action button "Mark as Read" or "Got it!" which lets the user acknowledge the advice (this could feed back into our system as a reaction). Here's a snippet of what the JavaScript for such an LWC might do when initialized:

```
// Pseudo-code for LWC JS controller

import getAdvice from '@salesforce/apex/AdviceController.getLatestAdvice';

export default class TeamCoachPanel extends LightningElement {

  adviceMessage;

  connectedCallback() {

    getAdvice({ teamId: this.teamId })

    .then(result => {

        this.adviceMessage = result;
```

```
        })
      .catch(error => {
          console.error('Error fetching advice', error);
        });
  }
  handleAcknowledge() {
    // Possibly call Apex to record that user acknowledged the advice
    this.adviceMessage = null;
  }
}
```

In this example, AdviceController.getLatestAdvice would be an Apex method that returns the latest advice text for the given team. The LWC displays it (in the HTML template we'd bind {adviceMessage} maybe inside a nice, formatted box with an icon). There's also a method to handle when the user clicks an acknowledge button – this could simply hide the message and call an Apex method to log the acknowledgment (useful for the feedback loop).

5. Build Example – Sprint Coach in Action: Let's put it all together in our scenario. Team Alpha completes Sprint 5. They close the sprint record in Salesforce (either manually or via integration with an external Agile tool). This triggers our automation: a Flow (or Platform Event subscriber) kicks off the Coach agent logic. The SprintCoachAnalyzer Apex class runs, computes that Team Alpha completed 60% of their committed work and skipped the retro meeting. It creates an Advice__c record with a message (potentially enriched by GPT). The Flow then takes that message and posts it to Team Alpha's Slack channel using the Slack Connectors. Team members see the message in Slack: it's concise, encouraging, and has an emoji or two to feel less formal. One team member clicks a reaction emoji "👍" which our bot notices (this could be another Flow or bot user configured to listen for reactions – if sophistication allows). Separately, the Scrum Master goes to the Salesforce project portal where a "Sprint Coach Insights" LWC component shows the same message and maybe a link: "Learn more about sprint planning best practices." The Scrum Master takes the advice to heart and adjusts

the next sprint's scope accordingly. In the next sprint, they hit 85% completion. The Coach agent notices the improvement and the next Slack message it sends starts with a positive note: "Nice work improving your completion rate! 📈 Here's some insight from Sprint 6: ...". This positive reinforcement is also crucial – a Coach agent should recognize improvement, not just nag about shortcomings.

By using Agentforce's combination of declarative and programmatic tools, building this Sprint Coach agent involved: setting up data capture (possibly using Flows and Triggers), writing Apex for analysis (with optional GPT integration for narrative), and using Flow and LWCs for output delivery. We also leveraged standard Salesforce integration capabilities (Slack in this case). If we wanted to adjust the coach's behavior, much of it could be driven by metadata – for instance, an admin could update the Coaching_Benchmark__mdt to change the 80% threshold to 90% if standards rise, without touching the code. The Agent Builder interface could package this logic, maybe allowing an admin to deploy a similar Coach agent to other teams or modify the channels used (e.g., toggle a setting to use Email instead of Slack).

Building a Coach agent, as we see, is an exercise in combining analytics (to generate insights), workflow (to trigger at the right time), communication (to deliver advice in context), and personalization (to tailor the message). Salesforce provides building blocks for each of these. The heavy lifting of analysis can be done in Apex or with Einstein AI; the timing and orchestration via Flows; the delivery via a host of channels (Email alerts, Slack, in-app components, mobile push, etc.); and personalization via metadata and the flexibility of LLM-generated text.

With our Coach agent built and deployed, the journey isn't over – arguably the most important part is ensuring it actually helps users and continues to learn. In the next section, we'll discuss designing feedback loops and behavioral adjustments into Coach agents, so they remain effective coaches (and not annoying nags) over the long run.

FEEDBACK LOOPS AND BEHAVIORAL DESIGN

A Coach agent's success isn't just measured by the quality of its initial advice – it depends on how users respond and how the agent adapts. Just like a human coach adjusts their approach based on the trainee's progress and feedback, a digital Coach agent should have built-in feedback loops and thoughtful behavior design to refine its guidance. In this section, we explore how Coach agents can collect user reactions, adjust the frequency and tone of advice, and maintain trust through transparency. We'll also highlight strategies (and a pro tip) to keep the coaching relationship positive and effective, rather than cloying or counterproductive.

Collecting User Reactions: The moment a Coach agent delivers advice is actually the beginning of a two-way interaction. Users might explicitly react – for instance, by clicking "Thanks" or "Dismiss" on a prompt, giving a thumbs-up/thumbs-down on a tip, or selecting a reason "This wasn't helpful." They might also respond implicitly through their behavior – e.g., following the advice (or not) in subsequent actions. It's crucial to capture these reactions. Salesforce allows multiple ways to do so: if using Slack or Teams, you can monitor emoji reactions or replies to the bot's messages; in a Salesforce UI (like an LWC), you can provide buttons like "✅ Applied this tip" or "❌ Not relevant" and handle those with an Apex controller to record feedback. Even just tracking whether the user clicks a link in the advice (like a "Learn more" link) can serve as a proxy for interest. These reactions should feed into a feedback data store. For example, you might have a custom object AdviceFeedback__c with fields for Advice Id, User, Reaction (applied/ignored/dismissed), maybe a rating, and timestamp. Over time, this builds a dataset of what advice resonates or gets ignored.

Closing the Loop – Adaptive Coaching: Once you have feedback data, put it to use to adapt the agent's behavior. If a user routinely dismisses a certain type of suggestion, the agent should either present it differently or less frequently. This could be implemented with fairly simple logic. For instance, store a count of dismissals in a custom field on the user's profile or a related CoachPreferences__c record. Pseudocode example in Apex might look like:

```
Integer dismissCount = feedbackList.size(); // number of recent dismissals of similar advice

CoachPreferences__c prefs = CoachPreferences__c.getInstance(userId);

if (dismissCount >= 3) {

  prefs.OptOutOfAdviceType__c = true; // user clearly doesn't want this type of advice

  update prefs;

}
```

. . .

In a more nuanced design, instead of a binary opt-out, you might implement a cool-down period. For example, if the user ignored the last two weekly tips, perhaps skip the next week to avoid annoyance, effectively throttling down. This can be done by maintaining a "last advised date" and spacing out future advice if needed. Using Flow or Apex Scheduler, you can add conditions like "only send advice if at least X days have passed since last advice or since last positive interaction." Storing the desired frequency in metadata helps too: maybe your Coach agent normally gives weekly tips, but for users who haven't engaged, you switch them to monthly. In fact, Microsoft's Viva Insights (an employee coaching tool) automatically unsubscribes users who repeatedly ignore its suggestions – an approach worth considering to avoid spam. You could mirror this by having a rule: if user ignores 5 consecutive tips, pause advice for a while and perhaps send a check-in later like "We haven't sent you tips in a while – would you like to resume coaching?" rather than endlessly pinging an uninterested user.

Tone and Personalization Adjustments: Feedback isn't only about frequency – it's also about tone and content relevance. If a user often clicks "Not relevant" on advice, that indicates a mismatch in context. It might mean the agent's signals aren't precise enough or the personalization is off (e.g., giving novice tips to an expert user). In Salesforce, you might use a Custom Permission or profile attribute to mark certain users as "Expert – minimal coaching" which your logic checks before offering basic tips. Or maintain a "tone preference" field (some users might prefer a very formal tone, others a casual one – perhaps gleaned from a user survey or default by role). An advanced technique: incorporate the user's feedback into the GPT prompt. For example, if the user previously responded negatively to an overly cheerful tone, adjust the prompt to: "Use a professional and concise tone" for that user. Over time, the agent can learn the user's style. This crosses into a bit of reinforcement learning concept – though even without complex ML, simple rules and metadata can achieve a lot of personalization.

Maintaining Trust through Transparency: Trust is paramount for a Coach agent. If the user doesn't trust the agent's advice, they will ignore or even resent it. One way to build trust is to surface the "why" behind suggestions. Instead of a mysterious statement like "You should update your approach," a trustworthy Coach agent provides rationale: "I suggest trying X because I noticed Y (and perhaps cite a benchmark or data)." For instance, "I recommend reducing scope – your last 3 sprints saw ~50% rollover of work, which is above the company's 20% benchmark." This way, the user understands the advice is based on facts or standards, not just a random nag. In Salesforce, this could mean including data points in the message (the Apex analysis should output not just "do X" but "because Y"). If using GPT to generate text, include the key data in the prompt so it naturally weaves in: e.g., "...the team's completion rate was only 60%, which is below the 80% target. Suggest how to improve this and mention the 60% vs 80%." The resulting advice likely contains the numbers.

Another powerful tool for transparency is offering an "Audit" or "Explain" option next to advice. Imagine each piece of advice in an LWC or message has a small "Why am I seeing this?" link. Clicking it could reveal a brief explanation: "This recommendation is based on the last three calls which had an average sentiment of -0.5 (negative). The Coach agent looks at call sentiment to identify coaching opportunities." This turns the agent into a bit of a teacher – showing the user the patterns it sees. If the user disagrees ("Actually those calls were outliers because...."), it opens a door: maybe they can provide that feedback back ("These calls were special cases"). This bi-directional understanding greatly enhances credibility.

Pro Tip: Include an "Audit this advice" or "Feedback" button with your Coach agent's outputs. Allow the user to challenge or contextualize the advice. For example, a sales rep might click "This doesn't apply because that deal was unusual" – the agent can then acknowledge and learn from that input (perhaps ignore that data point in future or prompt for more details). This not only builds user trust (they feel heard and in control), but also gathers precious information to refine the agent's logic. Users are more likely to trust a coach that's willing to show its reasoning and admit when it might not have the full picture.

Throttling and Timing: We touched on frequency throttling; let's elaborate on timing. The when of delivering advice matters for receptivity. A well-designed Coach agent considers the user's schedule and context. Salesforce can help here too – for instance, if the user has an upcoming big meeting (perhaps detectable via calendar integration), maybe don't interrupt them with a non-urgent tip. Or if a user typically starts work at 9am and hates morning interruptions (perhaps they always dismiss morning notifications), schedule the coaching nudges for midday. Utilizing Salesforce Scheduler or even Einstein Prediction Builder, you could find an optimal time per user. Admittedly, that's advanced; simpler: just give the user control. Maybe in a settings LWC, let them choose "Preferred coaching time: Afternoon/End of day/Real-time". Store this in a CoachPreference__c custom setting and have your flow respect it (e.g., only send Slack messages after 3pm if that's what they prefer).

Monitoring Effectiveness: It's worth setting up some telemetry on the Coach agent itself. Salesforce's monitoring tools (or a simple custom dashboard) can track metrics like: advice acceptance rate (how often users follow a suggestion or positively acknowledge), performance improvement (did the metrics the agent aimed to improve actually move in the right direction over time?), and user sentiment (perhaps via periodic surveys or analyzing feedback comments). This is analogous to A/B testing a human coaching program – you want to ensure the agent is delivering value. For example, if after 6 months, a Coach agent's target metric (say, average call sentiment) hasn't improved across users, maybe the advice isn't effective and needs tweaking. Or if one type of advice is frequently ignored, maybe it's not useful or needs reframing.

By incorporating these feedback loops and design considerations, you transform your Coach agent from a static advice dispenser into a dynamic, evolving mentor. Users will feel like the agent "gets them" more and more, instead of being a broken record. They'll also trust that the agent isn't just lecturing – it's partnering with them in improving, listening to their input too.

To summarize the design implications: (a) Always gather user feedback, explicit or implicit. (b) Use that feedback to adjust how often and how you coach each user. Over time, ideally each user has a tailored coaching plan – some might get frequent nudges, others only big-ticket advice occasionally. (c) Keep the agent's advice transparent and grounded in observable facts or rules. (d) Provide mechanisms for users to correct or clarify the agent's understanding. If these principles are followed, your Coach agent will be less Clippy-from-the-90s (annoying paperclip assistant) and more like a trusted colleague who has your best interests at heart.

Having fine-tuned our approach to individual Coach agents, let's zoom out. How do Coach agents relate to the broader ecosystem of AI tools and agents out there? Are there analogs or complementary patterns in other platforms? In the next section, we'll compare Coach agents to similar concepts emerging in the AI ecosystem, from LangChain's reflection agents to Microsoft's Viva Insights, to see how the idea of AI "coaches" is taking shape beyond Salesforce.

COACH AGENTS IN THE ECOSYSTEM

The Coach pattern we've explored is not unique to Salesforce – it resonates with concepts in the wider AI and software ecosystem. As AI agents become more common, different platforms have independently developed patterns for evaluation, feedback, and insight generation that parallel what the Coach agent does for humans. Understanding these helps put Coach agents in context and can inspire improvements to our implementations. Let's look at a few notable ecosystem patterns and how they compare or connect to Coach agents: LangChain reflection agents, Microsoft's AutoGen feedback loops, Microsoft Viva Insights (and Copilot), and some thoughts on Salesforce Data Cloud with GPT for pattern detection.

LangChain's Reflection Agents and Evaluators: LangChain, a popular framework for building LLM-driven applications, has a concept called reflection agents which is strikingly similar to a coach – except the "trainee" is another AI agent (or the agent itself). A reflection agent evaluates and critiques an AI's past actions or outputs to improve subsequent performance. In essence, it's an AI coach for the AI. For example, imagine an LLM-based agent that solved a math problem incorrectly; a reflection agent could analyze the solution, find the mistake, and guide the original agent to fix it. This is analogous to how our Coach agent might review a human's task and suggest improvements. The key principles overlap: look at past performance, identify mistakes or suboptimal choices, and feedback suggestions. LangChain also includes evaluators (sometimes separate from the main agent) that score or critique outputs, which can trigger a refine step. Our Coach pattern in Salesforce could similarly incorporate an evaluator – for instance, using an AI to evaluate the quality of a customer service email and give it a score, which the Coach agent then uses to advise the agent on writing better emails. The cross-over here is conceptual: the reflection agent does for AI behaviors what a Coach agent does for human behaviors. Both rely on the loop of output → critique → improved output. The difference is the end user (one is improving an AI model's answers, the other a person's actions), but the philosophy of continuous improvement via feedback is identical. This means techniques from that domain (like how to phrase critiques constructively, or how to use chain-of-thought to pinpoint errors) can inform how we build Coach agents for people.

Microsoft AutoGen's Feedback Loops: Microsoft's AutoGen platform is designed for multi-agent collaboration among LLMs, and one of its notable features is auto feedback loops, where agents can give each other suggestions and corrections mid-task. For example, an AutoGen system might have a "Coder" agent and a "Reviewer" agent – the Reviewer checks the Coder's output and provides feedback, which the Coder then uses to improve the code. This dynamic is very much like a Coach agent embedded in a multi-agent workflow. The feedback loop is automatic and conversational: agents talk to each other to refine results. In our context, consider multi-agent scenarios where a Coach agent might be one of the agents in an Agentforce solution – perhaps a Conductor agent is doing the main work (like planning a task list) and the Coach agent interjects with "hey, I see a potential issue with the plan, maybe we should add a contingency step." The idea of dynamic prompt tuning is also key in AutoGen – agents adjust their prompts based on feedback. A Coach agent in Salesforce could similarly adjust the prompts it sends to GPT for advice generation based on past success (e.g., if a certain phrasing got better user response, use it more). Moreover, in human terms, AutoGen's approach reminds us of the power of peer feedback: it's like having AI agents act as coaches to each other. A Coach agent working with humans can take inspiration from this by facilitating peer learning – e.g., sharing anonymized success stories ("Your peer Jane consistently hits her targets; one thing she does differently is...") which is a kind of feedback loop leveraging team data. In summary, AutoGen's feedback loops highlight how iterative refinement through agent collaboration can lead to better outcomes. For us, it reinforces the value of iterative coaching and suggests that sometimes the Coach might even orchestrate a mini feedback loop: the agent might propose an action, then evaluate the result and adjust the advice in a few rounds (sort of a back-and-forth with the user if possible).

Microsoft Viva Insights and Copilot (Employee Nudges): Microsoft Viva, particularly Viva Insights, is explicitly an employee-focused insight and coaching platform integrated into M365. It provides personalized recommendations or "nudges" to users and managers based on their work patterns – exactly the kind of thing our Coach pattern encompasses. For instance, Viva might notice you have had no 1:1 time scheduled with a key team member recently and nudge you to set one up. It might remind you to take focus time if your calendar is full of meetings, or suggest tasks that you promised in emails but haven't logged elsewhere. These are delivered in Outlook or Teams as gentle prompts, much like our Coach agent's Slack or email nudges. Viva even has features where managers get insights about their team's well-being (like too many after-hours emails) and nudges to address it. And as noted earlier, Viva will taper off suggestions if you continually ignore them, to avoid overwhelming you. Microsoft is also integrating Copilot into Viva, which means more natural language capabilities – e.g., a manager could ask, "Copilot, summarize my team's feedback engagement this quarter" and get insights that a Coach agent might proactively have given. The existence of Viva validates the Coach pattern as something companies are actively pursuing. For us building on Salesforce, it means we might draw inspiration or even integrate with Viva for customers who use both platforms. It's also a reminder to design with a similar ethos: privacy, personalization, and not crossing the line into creepy. Viva aggregates data and often only shows insights that maintain anonymity (for example, not pointing out a single person's behavior in a public report). Our Coach agents should also respect data sensitivity – e.g., a Coach for managers should aggregate team patterns without exposing an individual's weakness in front of peers.

One more angle: Microsoft's GitHub Copilot has an emerging feature called "Copilot for Business" which offers prompts based on project context – for instance, suggesting a developer write tests if they haven't in a while, or prompting a comment if committing code. This is again a Coach-like nudge but in context of coding. Salesforce could similarly integrate its Code Builder or DevOps Center with a Coach agent to nudge developers in a Salesforce org ("It's been awhile since a code review was done on that trigger – maybe run a static code analysis."). We see a convergence: whether it's writing code, managing a team, or selling to customers, AI-driven nudges and coaching are being embedded to improve outcomes.

Salesforce Data Cloud + GPT for Behavioral Patterns: Salesforce's Data Cloud (formerly known as Customer Data Platform) lets an organization unify and analyze vast amounts of data in real-time. Marrying this with GPT or AI pattern recognition opens doors for very advanced Coach agents. For example, a large enterprise could feed Data Cloud with performance data from across departments – sales numbers, support ticket resolution times, employee satisfaction surveys – and then use AI to detect behavioral drift or anomalies. Maybe the AI finds that in a certain region, sales teams have gradually stopped using a certain discount approval process, leading to margin erosion. A Coach agent can be informed by these high-level patterns and then deliver targeted advice at the team or individual level ("Your team in Europe is discounting more heavily than others – retrain on value-selling techniques."). Essentially, Data Cloud could act as the "Sentinel + Curator" combo on big data, and feed insights to Coach agents at scale. The mention of "behavioral drift" in our outline suggests using AI to catch when someone's performance or behavior shifts in a potentially negative direction: imagine a normally stellar customer support agent whose CSAT is declining month-over-month – a pattern matching algorithm flags this and triggers a Coach agent to intervene and help before it becomes a crisis. Integrating GPT here might allow understanding why that drift is happening (e.g., analyzing text of interactions for signs of burnout). So, while earlier sections focused on building one Coach for one purpose, Data Cloud implies the possibility of enterprise-level coaching, where macro trends are identified and then personalized micro-coaching is delivered via many Coach agents. It's like giving your AI coach a bird's-eye view so it knows not just the user's own history, but how it compares to broader trends or best performers.

Swarm and Multi-Agent Ecosystems: Finally, consider the role of Coach agents in systems where many agents work together (often called agent swarms). We touched on how an Action agent or Conductor might do the heavy automation, but a Coach agent provides reflection and course correction without "blocking" the process. In a swarm, you might have some agents producing outputs and others checking or optimizing those outputs (Coach falls in latter category). For example, in a customer service scenario, you could have an Action agent drafting a response to a customer, and a Coach agent reviewing the draft for tone and accuracy before it's sent – akin to a junior writing an email and a senior reviewing it. This feedback doesn't halt the entire system; it's part of the system's internal quality control. In human terms, the Coach agent in a multi-agent team ensures the whole operation improves over time. A multi-agent sales system might have agents finding leads, scheduling meetings, and a Coach agent analyzing outcomes of those meetings to update the strategy of the lead-finding agent. The Coach pattern thus is critical in these complex ecosystems as the role that keeps the system from going off-track (course correction) and drives continuous learning. It's much like in sports: you have players (action agents) and a coach on the sidelines (insight agent) calling time-outs, adjusting plays, motivating – but not physically playing the game, and not stopping the game unless needed.

In summary, the Coach pattern aligns with a broader shift in AI from just automating or informing, to collaborating and improving. Whether it's an LLM reflecting on its own answers, two AI agents giving each other feedback, or a corporate tool nudging employees to build better habits, the essence is the same: use AI to make either AI or humans better over time. Our Salesforce Coach agents are part of this zeitgeist. They can learn from these external analogues (for instance, adopting proven techniques from Viva nudges or ensuring they have a reflection mechanism like LangChain's agents). And importantly, because Salesforce Agentforce is extensible, we might even integrate these external systems. Perhaps a Salesforce Coach agent could call a LangChain evaluator as part of its logic (for example, to rate a piece of content), or ingest Viva Insights data if a company uses both Salesforce and Microsoft ecosystems, consolidating coaching messages.

Having situated the Coach pattern in the wider world, we can now look at how Coach agents interact with other agent patterns within Salesforce. In the next section, we'll connect the Coach pattern with Sentinel, Supervisor, Curator, and others – painting a picture of a multi-agent symphony where each pattern plays a role, and the Coach ensures the melody stays sweet.

CONNECTING THE COACH PATTERN WITH OTHERS

No agent is an island. In a sophisticated Agentforce deployment, multiple agent patterns often work in tandem to deliver end-to-end solutions. The Coach agent, with its focus on improvement and guidance, frequently relies on or supports other types of agents. Let's explore how the Coach pattern connects with the others we've discussed in this playbook – such as Sentinel, Conductor, Curator, Companion, Supervisor – and walk through a full journey example that highlights these interactions. By understanding these combinations, you'll see how a Coach agent can be woven into larger workflows and multi-agent systems to amplify its impact.

Sentinel + Coach: The Sentinel pattern is about monitoring and detecting notable events or anomalies (think of it as the eyes and ears). It makes a natural partner for the Coach. A Sentinel agent can watch a stream of activity and, upon detecting a potential issue or trend, hand it off to a Coach agent to provide feedback. For instance, a Sentinel agent in a call center might continuously monitor support call metrics and flag when an agent's average call handling time exceeds a threshold or when customer sentiment drops significantly on a call. However, the Sentinel's role ends at detection. This is where the Coach agent picks up: it takes that signal ("Agent's sentiment score dropped on 3 calls today") and delivers feedback to the human ("Those last calls seemed tough. Consider taking a brief pause or using empathy statements – it can help reset the tone."). In this combo, Sentinel is the trigger mechanism, and Coach is the advisory mechanism. The synergy ensures that observations translate into actionable guidance. Technically, this could be implemented by having the Sentinel (maybe as an Apex job or Einstein Analytics dashboard) create a record or event that the Coach agent (via a Flow) subscribes to. The Coach then contextually enriches that with advice. Together, they form a continuous loop: signal observed → feedback delivered to the team.

Conductor + Coach: The Conductor pattern orchestrates multi-step processes or multi-agent workflows. After a Conductor agent finishes running a complex playbook (say it coordinated a customer onboarding process across several departments via different agents), a Coach agent can come in to do a retrospective or after-action review. Think of it like this: the Conductor ensures the job gets done, the Coach ensures that next time the job gets done even better. For example, imagine a Conductor agent automates the process of completing an insurance claim with steps involving data gathering (via Curator), approvals (via Supervisor), and final communication (via Presenter). The process completes, but maybe it took longer than expected or there were hiccups (like multiple back-and-forth for approval). A Coach agent can review the execution log of the Conductor (many Conductors will produce a log or summary of what happened) and flag areas for improvement: "The claim process for Case 1234 took 5 days due to 2 rework cycles in the approval step. Suggestion: clarify the approval criteria upfront to avoid rework." This could be delivered to a process owner or admin as an improvement recommendation. In effect, after the process complete → retrospective flagged. The Coach here acts almost like a process improvement consultant, driven by data from the Conductor. This interplay is valuable in complex operations where learning and iterating on processes is key to efficiency gains.

Curator → Coach: The Curator pattern deals with gathering, filtering, and summarizing information – effectively curating knowledge or data so that it's useful. A Coach agent can leverage Curator outputs to drive its insights. For instance, suppose you have a Curator agent that compiles weekly sales win/loss reasons from Salesforce data and customer feedback. The Curator might produce a summary like: "Wins are commonly due to product fit; losses often due to price." A Coach agent targeting salespeople could take this curated insight and convert it into a nudge: "This week's trend: We're losing deals mainly on price. Make sure to highlight ROI and value to defend our pricing." Essentially, insights summarized by a Curator → behavioral nudges offered by the Coach. Another scenario: a Curator agent gathers all the recent technical support cases and finds a cluster around a certain product feature. It passes this info to a Coach agent which then advises the support team, "There's a spike in issues on feature X; perhaps review the troubleshooting guide for that feature or escalate a bug if needed." The Curator distills the raw data, and the Coach translates that into a recommendation or learning moment for the team. In building such a system, you might have the Curator write to a "Insights__c" object, which triggers the Coach agent to read those and produce coaching alerts. It's a separation of concerns that works well: Curators answer "What's happening?" and Coaches answer "What should we do about it (to improve)?".

Companion + Coach: A Companion agent (a friendly assistant that helps a user accomplish tasks) often works closely with a human in real-time. A Coach agent, as we know, tends to intervene around tasks to suggest improvements. These two can complement each other in a user's workflow. Imagine a scenario with both: a Companion agent might help an employee fill out a complex form by fetching information and auto-filling fields (taking workload off the user), while a Coach agent monitors how the user interacts with the form and afterwards gives pointers to reduce errors or speed things up ("I noticed it took a while to find the client ID – next time, try using the search feature at the top; it's faster."). So the personal action → improvement suggestions sequence could be: the user completes an action with the Companion's help, then the Coach comes in to suggest how that action could be done even more smoothly next time (maybe even how to better utilize the Companion's capabilities!). In another example, consider a software developer: a Companion coding agent suggests code snippets and helps write code (like a smart autocompletion), and a Coach agent later analyzes the code the developer wrote to suggest how to improve code quality or adhere to best practices (sort of like a proactive code review coach). The interplay needs to be well-timed to avoid overlap. Usually, the Companion operates during the task, the Coach after the task or between tasks, so as not to confuse the user with simultaneous assistance and advice. If orchestrated correctly, the user experiences a continuum of support: help while doing (Companion) and guidance after doing (Coach). Salesforce could facilitate this by having, say, a global Companion agent in the UI (perhaps a chat sidebar that can do things for the user), and a Coach mechanism that triggers on record save or at end of day to review what happened.

Coach → Supervisor: The Supervisor pattern involves oversight and gated approvals – ensuring compliance, risk management, or policy adherence typically by involving a human or higher authority for final decisions. How does a Coach relate to that? In some cases, a Coach agent might detect something that's not just a learning opportunity but a potential risk or rule violation. In those situations, the Coach can escalate to a Supervisor agent or process. For example, suppose a Coach agent in Finance notices that an employee's expense reports are increasingly borderline or contain potential policy breaches (maybe the employee is expensing unusually high amounts for meals). The Coach might normally advise the employee "Your recent expenses seem higher than the norm; remember the meal limit is $X." But if the behavior continues or the amounts exceed a certain threshold, the Coach agent might kick it up to a Supervisor pattern: flagging the issue for a manager or compliance officer to review formally. Thus, risk-flagged guidance queued for review – the Coach essentially says "I tried nudging, but this might need actual intervention." In implementation, the Coach agent could create a Supervisor task or case when its internal logic crosses a severity level. Another angle: The Coach could feed into Supervisor workflows by providing recommendations to the Supervisor. Imagine a Supervisor agent that must approve or reject content. A Coach agent could analyze the content first and attach a recommended action ("Coach suggests to approve because it meets all criteria" or "Coach recommends caution: some language might be sensitive"). This speeds up the Supervisor's decision and provides rationale. In that sense, the Coach supports the Supervisor by adding an AI second opinion to the mix.

To cement these connections, let's walk through a full journey example that brings several patterns together:

Full Journey Example – Help Desk Improvement: Consider a scenario in a company's IT help desk:

A Sentinel agent keeps an eye on support metrics and notices that one help desk rep, Alice, has missed the SLA (service-level agreement) targets on 5 out of 10 of her cases this week. The allowed response time was 2 hours, but she's averaging 4 hours. The Sentinel flags this trend as noteworthy.

A Curator agent retrieves and clusters Alice's case data to find commonalities. It finds that many of her delayed cases are related to a specific product area and came in during the evening shift. It summarizes that information: perhaps the product area is one she's less familiar with, and working late shift means fewer colleagues online to ask for help, leading to delays.

Now the Coach agent comes into play. Using the Sentinel's alert and the Curator's analysis, the Coach agent composes an improvement guide for Alice. It might say: "Hey Alice, I noticed many of your after-hours cases about Product X ran past SLA. It might be due to difficulty in that area. Here are two knowledge articles on Product X that could help for next time. Also, consider using our internal expert forum – even after hours, someone from the product team might see it. You're doing a great job handling tough tickets; these resources could help reduce wait time for customers. 👍" This message is delivered via email or a ping in the help desk app, privately to Alice. It likely includes peer examples – maybe highlighting that Bob, another support rep, had similar issues but improved after following those tips (if Bob consents to share, or it could be anonymized like "another colleague").

1. Alice reads the guide, appreciates the tips, and follows the links to refresh her Product X knowledge. The next week, her SLA stats improve.

2. The Coach agent tracks this improvement (since it's observing metrics too). It sends a follow-up maybe: "Great improvement this week on Product X cases! 👏 Your average response time is down to 1.5 hours. Keep it up, and don't hesitate to ask the product team if you get stuck."

Now, suppose Alice's SLA performance was not improving or the issue indicated something systemic. The Supervisor pattern might come in if, say, multiple agents are struggling with Product X, raising a risk of customer dissatisfaction. A Supervisor agent (or simply a manager alerted by these insights) might decide to mandate a training or update a process. But because the Coach intervened early, ideally it doesn't need escalation.

In the above journey: Sentinel did the monitoring and flagging, Curator organized the data and context, Coach provided personalized guidance with resources and peer examples, and Supervisor could have been invoked if needed for escalation. It showcases how the Coach is interlinked – it receives inputs from patterns like Sentinel/Curator and feeds outputs to patterns like Supervisor (if higher-level action is needed).

Multi-pattern interplay is a hallmark of sophisticated AI systems. The Coach pattern's role among them is somewhat unique: it's the one explicitly oriented toward human growth and adaptation. Other agents focus on tasks and control, while the Coach focuses on people and performance. Together, they form a complementary team – some agents doing the work or controlling the flow, others ensuring the work is done right and gets better every cycle.

By connecting the Coach pattern with others, we not only enhance individual outcomes but also create a robust multi-agent ecosystem where continuous improvement is baked in at both the micro (individual) and macro (process) levels. This sets the stage for the next part of the book, where we move beyond individual patterns to designing entire multi-agent systems that leverage combinations of these patterns for large-scale impact.

SUMMARY

In this chapter, we explored the Coach pattern, an AI agent design focused on delivering insight-driven guidance to help people and teams get better. Unlike agents that execute tasks or simply present information, Coach agents play the role of mentors and advisors – observing what humans do, interpreting how it could be improved, and offering timely, personalized feedback. We began by defining what makes a Coach agent tick (its observe → interpret → advise → refine loop, key inputs and outputs, and internal architecture using Salesforce tools). We then discussed when to use the Coach pattern, highlighting scenarios where improving human performance is the goal (as opposed to pure automation), and we contrasted Coach agents with Companion and Presenter agents to clarify those differences.

Through cross-functional use cases in Sales, HR, Manufacturing, Healthcare, IT, and Legal, you saw how versatile Coach agents can be – from nudging sales reps with better techniques to guiding managers on giving feedback, to helping IT admins maintain org health. We detailed how to build Coach agents on Salesforce's Agentforce platform, combining declarative Flow, Apex logic, Lightning Web Components, and even GPT-based natural language generation to implement a practical Coach (our Sprint Coach example). Crucially, we emphasized feedback loops and behavioral design: a great Coach agent listens to the user's responses and adapts, throttling its advice when needed and being transparent about its suggestions to build trust. We provided tips for keeping users engaged (and not annoyed), such as offering "why" explanations and giving users control over the coaching process.

Comparing the Coach pattern to ecosystem patterns like LangChain's reflection agents and Microsoft's Viva Insights, we found that the idea of AI-facilitated improvement is a common theme – our Salesforce Coach agents are part of a broader movement towards AI systems that not only solve problems, but also help humans (and other AIs) learn and improve. Finally, we connected the Coach with other Agentforce patterns: we saw that Coach agents often work hand-in-hand with Sentinels (turning alerts into advice), with Curators (turning insights into actions), with Companions (enhancing assisted tasks with post-task feedback), and others – acting as a key piece in multi-agent workflows to ensure continuous improvement and alignment with best practices.

Ultimately, the Coach pattern adds enormous value by creating a feedback-rich environment in the enterprise. It's like giving everyone a personalized trainer or consultant that's always watching out for them – at scale. When implemented thoughtfully, Coach agents can boost productivity, accelerate skill development, and help maintain consistency and quality across the organization. They enable your human workforce to evolve alongside your automation, ensuring that as AI handles more routine work, your people are simultaneously growing into more skilled, informed, and efficient contributors.

As we move forward, we transition from focusing on individual agent patterns to looking at multi-agent systems as a whole. In the next chapter, we'll dive into designing and orchestrating groups of agents working together – essentially composing patterns like Coach, Sentinel, Supervisor, etc., into larger solutions. This will involve considerations of architecture, governance, and how to make these diverse agents collaborate effectively. The journey continues as we step into the world of agent teamwork in Chapter 10, bringing everything we've learned about individual patterns into a unified, powerful agent ecosystem.

10

DESIGNING MULTI-AGENT SYSTEMS

The evolution from single-agent solutions to multi-agent systems marks a shift in both complexity and capability. An individual AI agent can excel at a narrow task, but modern enterprise challenges – from answering multifaceted queries to automating cross-department processes – often exceed the scope of any lone agent. Multi-agent systems offer a way forward, consisting of multiple specialized agents working together on tasks that would overwhelm one agent. Instead of a monolithic "godlike" AI trying to do everything, responsibilities are distributed among distinct agents, each an expert in a specific domain or function. This modular team-of-agents approach echoes human organizations: just as a company has departments with defined roles, an AI system can have dedicated agents (for example, a Data Retrieval Agent, a Reasoning Agent, a Presentation Agent, etc.), collaborating to solve complex problems.

Shifting to a multi-agent design brings notable benefits. For one, it enables distributed reasoning – each agent can contribute unique knowledge or skills, and collectively they tackle problems no single agent could handle alone. One agent might gather information, another draws inferences, and another makes recommendations, combining their outputs into a more comprehensive solution. This kind of collaborative reasoning often yields more accurate and creative outcomes than a solitary model's effort. At the same time, multi-agent setups inherently improve fault tolerance. Because intelligence is distributed, the overall system can be more resilient: if one agent fails or reaches its limits, others can continue the work or provide redundancy so that the entire workflow doesn't collapse. For example, if a data-fetching agent encounters an API error, a downstream analysis agent might still proceed with cached or partial data, or a backup agent could step in – resulting in graceful degradation of service rather than a full stop. This distributed nature creates more robust systems for critical applications.

Of course, introducing multiple autonomous agents means coordination becomes paramount. Without structured interaction, a team of agents could degenerate into a chaotic swarm of conflicting actions. Designing effective multi-agent systems requires careful definition of how agents communicate, synchronize, and delegate tasks. Fortunately, established collaboration patterns have emerged – from simple linear chains of agents handing off outputs, to hub-and-spoke models with a coordinating agent, to dynamic feedback loops where agents iteratively refine each other's results. We'll explore these patterns in detail in this chapter. Alongside task coordination, shared context is a key consideration: agents need mechanisms to share knowledge or state so they can work toward a common goal without each needing complete information. Achieving this might involve a shared memory, a common knowledge base, or an orchestrator agent that passes along relevant context. The challenge is to enable information flow among agents without overwhelming them – often solved by passing succinct summaries or using a central datastore that agents can read/write in turn.

Another motivation for multi-agent systems is the need for scale and specialization in enterprise AI applications. As organizations apply AI across diverse functions (customer service, marketing, IT, finance, etc.), a single all-purpose agent becomes a bottleneck in terms of expertise and capacity. By deploying multiple specialized agents, each can focus on what it does best, and tasks can be processed in parallel or in a segmented pipeline – dramatically improving throughput. For instance, an enterprise virtual assistant might employ separate agents for handling product inquiries, legal compliance checks, and pricing calculations, coordinated so that a complex customer request is addressed by the right expert agent at each step. This specialization not only improves the quality of each subtask (since each agent is a master of its narrow domain) but also makes the overall system more adaptable: new capabilities can be added by introducing new agents rather than retraining or reconfiguring one giant model. In short, multi-agent architecture allows AI solutions to scale across functions and handle complexity by dividing and conquering.

It's important to note that multi-agent systems introduce design and management complexity that must be addressed with robust tools and practices. Monitoring the interactions of many agents, troubleshooting their errors, and governing their behaviors require careful planning – topics we will cover in depth. Industry trends underscore this need: enterprises are beginning to demand AI systems that are modular, collaborative, and traceable by design to cope with increasing model complexity and data volume. Throughout this chapter, we'll examine how to design multi-agent systems thoughtfully – from defining each agent's role and boundaries, to choosing collaboration models, enabling distributed reasoning, implementing agents on Salesforce's platform, and instituting proper observability and governance. By the end, you'll see how individual AI "talents" can be orchestrated into an AI "team" that is greater than the sum of its parts.

In the next section, we begin with the fundamentals: defining clear responsibilities and boundaries for each agent to ensure a harmonious and effective multi-agent ensemble.

DEFINING AGENT RESPONSIBILITIES AND BOUNDARIES

Designing a multi-agent system starts with a deliberate definition of each agent's role. Just as employees have job descriptions, AI agents need well-scoped responsibilities to prevent overlap and confusion. A multi-agent architecture thrives on the single-responsibility principle – each agent should focus on one primary function or area of expertise. If an agent's task becomes too broad, its performance and manageability suffer. Instead, it's better to partition the problem and introduce multiple agents with tighter scopes. As one engineer quipped, this is like applying the "single responsibility principle" from software design to AI agents: rather than having one agent handle both information retrieval and result generation, you can have a dedicated retrieval agent and a separate answer-generation agent. The result is a cleaner division of labor – and often a more efficient problem-solving process.

When defining agent responsibilities, think in terms of distinct skills or subtasks of your overall workflow. For example, in an AI-driven document processing system, you might have one agent whose sole job is to extract data from documents, another agent that analyzes or interprets that data, and a third that composes a report or updates records based on the analysis. Each agent addresses a different question ("How do I get the data?", "What does the data mean?", "How to present or act on the insights?"). Crucially, each agent should have a clear boundary: a defined set of inputs it will handle and outputs it will produce, and explicitly what it will not do (i.e. anything outside its scope should be left to other agents). By giving agents non-overlapping charters, we avoid situations where multiple agents accidentally duplicate work or, worse, make contradictory decisions. This clarity also makes it easier to reason about and test the system – you can validate each agent's functionality in isolation, confident that it won't stray beyond its intended domain.

To illustrate, consider a simple multi-agent pipeline and how responsibilities can be divided:

Agent A: DataFetcher. Its responsibility is to fetch or retrieve raw data from sources (databases, APIs, etc.) relevant to a query or task. It does not do any interpretation of that data. If any analysis or decision is needed, Agent A hands the data off.

Agent B: Analyzer. This agent takes data (possibly provided by Agent A) and performs analysis or reasoning to produce insights. It focuses on decision-making or inference. It does not concern itself with how to fetch data (that's Agent A's job), nor with presenting results to a user.

- Agent C: Presenter. This agent's role is to take insights or answers (perhaps from Agent B) and format them for end users – generating a report, crafting a response message, updating a dashboard, etc. It doesn't do heavy analysis itself; it relies on Agent B for the logic and ensures the final output is human-friendly and actionable.

Each agent's "job description" is distinct. We can summarize this example in a responsibility list:

DataFetcher A

- **Primary responsibility:** Retrieve required data from internal and external sources.
- **Boundaries (delegates/excludes):** Does not perform analysis or make decisions; passes all retrieved data to Analyzer B.

Analyzer B

- **Primary responsibility:** Derive insights, classifications, or decisions from the data provided.

- **Boundaries (delegates/excludes):** Does not fetch raw data (relies entirely on DataFetcher A); does not handle user-facing presentation or formatting.

Presenter C

- **Primary responsibility:** Format and communicate results for end-user consumption.
- **Boundaries (delegates/excludes):** Does not analyze data or generate insights; trusts outputs from Analyzer B and focuses solely on clarity, framing, and delivery.

This approach follows the separation of concerns that makes multi-agent systems manageable. Notably, each agent can often be developed and improved independently as long as the input/output contracts remain the same. In practice, you might implement DataFetcher A and Analyzer B as completely separate modules or services – or even different underlying AI models – connected only by the defined interface (e.g., Agent A outputs a structured dataset which Agent B knows how to consume). Microsoft's research on multi-agent systems highlights that optimally allocating tasks to specialized agents (leveraging each agent's unique skills) is key to effective collaboration. Put simply, let each agent do what it's best at, and nothing more.

When designing agent boundaries, also consider tools and permissions. Each agent should only have access to the data and APIs it needs for its role. For example, a PricingAgent might be allowed to query pricing databases but have no authority to send emails (that might be the job of a CommunicationAgent). Isolating permissions in this way enhances security and prevents an agent from accidentally or maliciously acting outside its purview. In Salesforce's Agentforce platform, you could enforce this by assigning each agent (or the Apex code running it) a distinct integration user with a minimal permission set. This aligns with guidance to treat AI agents like specialized microservices or bots within your system.

Salesforce's own documentation for Agentforce provides concrete examples of agent specializations by business domain. For instance, it defines types like Healthcare Agent (scheduling appointments, retrieving medical records), Retail Agent (checking inventory and processing orders), HR Agent (handling onboarding queries), and so on. Each agent type comes with clearly delineated functions and use cases, reinforcing how important scoping is. Whether you partition agents by business function (as Salesforce's types suggest) or by technical function (as in our fetch/analyze/present pipeline), the goal is the same: clarity of responsibility.

Finally, explicitly document each agent's boundaries during design. It can be helpful to write a short "charter" for each agent – its goal, its inputs/outputs, and a list of tasks it will delegate to others. This not only guides development but also aids governance (team members or stakeholders can review and agree that agent X is only responsible for Y). It becomes part of your "agent registry" (which we'll discuss later) – a catalog of what agents exist in the system and what each is meant to do. That registry approach pays dividends as your system grows, ensuring you don't unintentionally create two agents that overlap in function or miss a gap where no agent is handling an important subtask.

Pro Tip: When assigning responsibilities, aim for reusability. If an agent is designed with a very clear, generic role, you can reuse it across multiple workflows. For example, an "OCR Extraction Agent" (scans documents for text) or a "Translation Agent" can be invoked in different business processes wherever that capability is needed. Well-defined, modular agents act like building blocks that can be composed and recomposed without rewriting logic.

Pro Tip: Just as important as defining what an agent does is defining what it doesn't do. Be explicit about out-of-scope activities. This will help you identify when a new agent is needed to handle something and prevent agents from gradually accumulating unintended duties. If you find an agent has started doing tasks outside its original scope, consider refactoring – that might be a signal to spin off another agent.

COMMON COLLABORATION MODELS (CHAIN, HUB-SPOKE, FEEDBACK LOOP)

With agents' individual roles defined, the next design challenge is how those agents will work together. Multi-agent systems can be organized in different collaboration models, each suited to particular types of workflows and coordination needs. In this section, we'll cover three of the most common patterns of agent collaboration: Chain, Hub-and-Spoke, and Feedback Loop models. Think of these as architectural blueprints for agent interactions. Choosing the right model (or combination of models) is crucial – it affects the system's efficiency, complexity, and fault tolerance.

Chain (Sequential Workflow)

In a chain model, agents are organized in a linear sequence where each agent's output is passed as input to the next agent in line. This pattern is essentially an assembly line of AI agents, each performing one step of a process. It's a natural choice when a task can be broken into a well-defined series of stages, each building on the result of the previous stage. The chain model is conceptually simple and aligns with many business workflows that have a clear start and end with sequential steps in between.

In a chain, there is typically an initial trigger or input that goes to the first agent. That agent does its part and hands off to the second, and so forth, until the final agent produces the end result. No central coordinator is needed because the flow of control is implicit in the sequence. Each agent in the chain just needs to know who the "next" agent is and what format of input that next agent expects.

Example – Sequential Onboarding Process: Imagine a new employee onboarding workflow in an enterprise automated by AI agents. This is a multi-step process that fits a chain well. For instance:

HR Policy Agent – Step 1: The first agent (triggered when a new hire joins) gathers all relevant HR policies and orientation materials for the new employee's role. It compiles documents like company policies, benefits information, etc.

IT Setup Agent – Step 2: The next agent takes the employee's details and the context of their department, then provisions necessary IT resources. It might create accounts, assign hardware, or fetch documentation specific to the employee's department (e.g. engineering onboarding guidelines). This agent receives input from the HR Policy Agent (like the employee's role/department) and produces technical setup outputs.

Summary Agent – Step 3: Finally, a summary agent collates the outputs of the previous steps – the HR info and IT setup details – and generates a personalized onboarding summary for the new hire. This could be an email or portal page that welcomes the employee, lists their accounts/access, provides links to policies, and so on.

Each agent in this chain has a clearly defined stage of the process, and the output cleanly flows into the next step. The HR Policy Agent doesn't worry about IT setup or summarization; the IT Setup Agent doesn't revisit policy docs; the Summary Agent trusts that needed inputs were prepared by prior steps. This one-directional handoff minimizes complexity. Notably, if something goes wrong mid-chain (say, the IT setup fails to create an account), that failure will typically halt the chain at that point – one of the considerations we'll address in failover design. For straightforward processes, however, chains are very efficient.

Benefits: The chain pattern shines in its simplicity. It's easy to trace the flow of information and debug where a breakdown occurs, since there's a single path. There's also a natural modularity – you can insert or remove agents from the chain as requirements change (e.g., add a background-check agent as a new step 2 in the onboarding chain). Many initial multi-agent prototypes use a chain because it's conceptually similar to a linear workflow or pipeline that developers and architects are already familiar with.

Trade-offs: On the flip side, chains can become brittle if not managed carefully. The whole process is only as strong as its weakest link – if one agent fails or produces poor output, downstream agents might receive no data or garbage data. Error handling needs to be incorporated (we'll discuss strategies later in this chapter. Also, chains are inherently sequential; they may not take full advantage of opportunities for parallelism. If certain steps could be done concurrently, a pure chain won't exploit that, potentially leading to longer end-to-end execution times. Finally, because each agent only sees the output of its immediate predecessor, no agent (except perhaps the last one) has a global view of the process. That can be fine for simple flows, but for more complex coordination, a different model might be more appropriate.

Pro Tip: Keep your agent chain as streamlined as possible. Each additional step introduces latency and another potential point of failure. If you find a chain becoming very long, consider whether some steps can be combined or executed in parallel. For example, if two agents in sequence don't actually depend on each other's output, those might not belong in a single chain – they could be executed by a coordinator simultaneously (enter the hub-and-spoke model) or perhaps merged into one multi-functional agent if the tasks are small. Simplicity contributes to reliability.

Hub-and-Spoke (Central Orchestrator)

The hub-and-spoke model centers around a coordinator agent (the "hub") that delegates tasks to one or more worker agents (the "spokes") and then collects their results. This is analogous to a project manager who assigns work to various specialists and then synthesizes their contributions. In multi-agent terms, the hub agent receives the initial problem or goal, then decides which specialized agents need to be invoked, in what order (or even in parallel), and how to integrate their outputs. The hub may also handle contingencies – if one agent's result indicates more work is needed or another agent should be consulted, the hub can facilitate that. Because of this central brain, hub-and-spoke architectures are also referred to as manager-worker or orchestrator patterns.

This model is well-suited when the overall task can be naturally split into parts that do not strictly flow in a single sequence, or when some tasks can proceed concurrently. It's also useful if you need a dynamic decision point: the orchestrator can adjust which agents to call based on conditions. For example, consider an AI system handling a complex customer request in a telecom company: a customer asks to upgrade their service plan, check for discounts, and report a network issue at the same time. A hub agent could parse this request and realize it involves multiple domains – billing, sales promotions, and technical support. It could then dispatch subtasks to a Billing Agent (to handle the upgrade), a Promotion Agent (to find applicable discounts), and a Network Diagnostics Agent (to log and analyze the network issue). These might be done in parallel since they are independent. Once each returns its output, the hub agent compiles a unified response to the customer that addresses all aspects.

In a hub-and-spoke setup, the orchestrator often maintains the overall state and context, and worker agents may only communicate with the orchestrator, not directly with each other (hence the "spoke" analogy: information radiates out from and back to the hub). The orchestrator essentially routes tasks to the right agent and can make higher-level decisions. In terms of implementation, you might literally have one agent designated as the "manager." In practice, this orchestrator might be an Apex class or a Flow (on Salesforce) or a dedicated coordination script – but conceptually, it's playing the role of an agent making meta-decisions about other agents.

Example – AI Service Orchestration: Consider a Deal Coordinator Agent in an enterprise sales context – this would be a hub orchestrator. When a big sales deal comes in, there are several parallel tasks: a legal review of the contract, a financial credit check on the customer, and a pricing approval. In a hub model, the Deal Coordinator (hub) agent receives the new deal request. It then:

Delegates the contract document to a Legal Agent for clause-by-clause analysis.

Delegates the customer's financials to a Risk Assessment Agent for creditworthiness evaluation.

Delegates the pricing details to a Pricing Agent for margin analysis and approval workflow.

Each of these specialist agents works independently on their piece. The Legal Agent might take some time to scan through terms (perhaps using an LLM to flag risky clauses), the Risk Agent pulls credit data, and the Pricing Agent computes profitability. As each finishes, they report back to the Deal Coordinator agent. The coordinator then synthesizes the results: if all three are green-lit, it compiles a summary "deal approval" for sales with notes from each department. If one of the spokes raises an issue (say, Legal finds a non-standard clause), the coordinator might integrate that feedback (e.g., instruct a revision via the sales team or escalate to a human legal officer) and hold off on final approval. The orchestrator is actively making sure all necessary components are completed and combined.

In this pattern, the orchestrator agent often contains the logic of the workflow (order of operations, what to do on certain results, etc.). Salesforce Flow Orchestration is a great analog here – it can serve as the hub, calling various sub-flows or agents (spokes) and merging outcomes. In fact, implementing a hub-and-spoke often means building a flow or script that embodies the "manager" behavior.

Diagrammatically, it looks like a star: one central node connected to multiple peripheral nodes. For instance:

```
                User Request
                     ↓
              [ Coordinator Agent ]
               /     |       \
   [Agent X]    [Agent Y]    [Agent Z]
       ↓            ↓            ↓
   (result X)   (result Y)   (result Z)
         \          |          /
          [ Coordinator Agent ]
                    ↓
          Combined Result to User
```

Here, the Coordinator receives a request, fans out tasks to Agent X, Y, Z (the spokes) – potentially in parallel – then waits for their results. Once gathered, it might do post-processing and then output the final result.

Benefits: The hub-and-spoke model excels in scenarios requiring coordination of multiple inputs or decisions. It's powerful for parallelism – many agents can work at the same time, reducing overall latency (in the above example, legal, risk, and pricing checks can happen simultaneously, speeding up the deal review). It also centralizes the "game plan" in the orchestrator, which can make complex workflows easier to manage in code: instead of a fixed rigid sequence, the orchestrator can include conditional logic (e.g., "if pricing fails, skip legal and go straight to a rejection"). Another benefit is that the orchestrator (hub) can maintain a broader view of the task's state than individual agents could. This can enable more dynamic behavior; for instance, the orchestrator can decide to run an additional agent mid-process if needed ("Hmm, the network diagnostic agent found an outage; I should also invoke a Messaging Agent to draft an apology email to the customer"). Many real-world multi-agent systems, especially in enterprise settings, effectively use an orchestrator pattern – sometimes not even framed as an "agent" but just as the flow logic connecting services.

Trade-offs: The presence of a central hub means the orchestrator can become a single point of failure or a bottleneck if not designed well. The orchestrator agent itself must be robust – it has to handle partial failures of workers gracefully (e.g., if one spoke agent doesn't respond, how long does the hub wait and what does it do?). The logic in the hub can also become complex if there are many conditional branches. In terms of maintenance, you need to ensure the orchestrator's logic stays in sync with the capabilities of the agents it oversees; adding a new agent or altering an agent's interface means updating the orchestrator's logic. Performance-wise, while spokes can run in parallel, the hub itself might introduce overhead, especially if it waits for all responses or needs to merge them. Additionally, debugging a hub-and-spoke system can be slightly more involved than a simple chain – you might need to inspect interactions going out and coming back to the orchestrator, which can be more complex than a straight-through trace. However, good logging (discussed later) can mitigate this.

Pro Tip: Keep the orchestrator (hub agent) as lightweight as possible. The hub should ideally not perform heavy computations itself – let the specialist agents do the heavy lifting. The hub's job is to route, not to reinvent what a specialist agent could do. This prevents the hub from becoming a performance bottleneck and keeps responsibilities separated. In practice, this means if you find your orchestrator doing significant data processing, consider delegating that to a new agent. The hub should mostly contain decision logic ("who should do what, when") rather than business logic of the task itself.

Feedback Loop (Iterative Collaboration)

Not all multi-agent interactions are one-and-done handoffs; some involve agents engaging in an iterative back-and-forth to refine a solution. The feedback loop model is characterized by a cycle where one agent's output is evaluated or used by another agent, which in turn provides feedback (or a modified output) that the first agent (or a third agent) uses for improvement. This continues for a few iterations until some criterion is met (e.g., quality threshold or max rounds reached). This pattern is common when solving open-ended problems where an initial attempt may be improved through critique or additional insight – effectively letting agents "think together" through a problem via multiple rounds.

A classic example of a feedback loop is a generator–critic pair of agents. Imagine Agent A produces a draft answer to a complex question, and Agent B acts as a critic or checker, examining A's output for errors or improvements. Agent B then feeds back suggestions: "I think you missed considering X, maybe refine these parts." Agent A then takes that feedback, revises its answer, and the cycle repeats. After one or two iterations, the answer might be far superior to the initial attempt. This is analogous to a writer (Agent A) and an editor (Agent B) collaborating on an article – the editor's feedback loop leads to a better final product than the first draft alone.

Example – QA refinement loop: Suppose we have a multi-agent system handling customer Q&A. One agent, AnswerAgent, generates answers to customer questions using an LLM. Another agent, ReviewAgent, specializes in checking those answers against a knowledge base for accuracy and policy compliance. When a question comes in, the AnswerAgent drafts a response. The ReviewAgent then inspects this response: it might catch factual errors or flag wording that doesn't align with company policy ("This answer might be too verbose, and it didn't mention the premium plan option"). The ReviewAgent provides structured feedback to the AnswerAgent, for instance: "Your answer overlooked the premium plan details and contains an outdated interest rate, please correct these." The AnswerAgent then uses this feedback to generate a corrected answer. This loop could run again if needed, or stop once the ReviewAgent has no further critique. In the end, the customer receives a more accurate, refined answer than the AnswerAgent's first attempt. Essentially, the agents engage in a mini dialogue, improving the result step by step.

Under the hood, implementing a feedback loop can be done with an orchestrator (hub) that facilitates the turn-taking, or by having agents directly call each other in turns (though care must be taken to avoid infinite loops). Some frameworks allow agents to be in a "group chat" where each agent sees the others' messages and can respond – a configuration naturally enabling iterative dialogue. For example, Microsoft's AutoGen framework supports group conversations among agents and even allows them to reflect or debate, which is an advanced form of the feedback loop pattern. Research has shown that letting agents engage in debate or iterative critique can significantly improve reasoning quality, as errors are caught and ideas refined through multiple perspectives.

Benefits: The feedback loop pattern can dramatically increase the quality of outcomes in tasks where evaluation and revision are important. It injects a form of quality control into the agent ecosystem – one agent's second opinion can catch mistakes that the first agent made. This is especially valuable in generative AI scenarios (where an answer might need fact-checking or ethical review) and in complex planning (where one agent might propose a plan and another checks feasibility or risks). It's akin to having a built-in peer review system. Additionally, this pattern can help in situations where no single agent is "smart" enough to solve a problem in one go; through iterative improvement, the agents together converge on a solution. From a design standpoint, it allows specialization in a different dimension: you might have one agent specialized as a Creator and another as a Critic – leveraging different skill sets (creative generation vs. analytical verification). The interplay of these roles can yield results that neither could achieve alone.

Trade-offs: The obvious cost of feedback loops is time/efficiency. Iteration means multiple rounds of processing, which can be slower and more resource-intensive (more API calls, more compute) than a one-pass approach. In a worst-case scenario, agents could get stuck in a loop – continuously finding issues with each other's output without converging (think of two agents endlessly nitpicking each other's work). To mitigate that, one should enforce limits (e.g., at most 3 iterations) or convergence criteria. Another challenge is complexity: the logic to handle iterative interaction is more involved than a simple chain or hub dispatch. If you're using flows or orchestrator code, you need looping constructs and perhaps state memory of what happened in previous rounds. Debugging can also be trickier, since the final outcome is the product of several revisions – you'll want logs of each step to understand how a particular answer was arrived at. Fortunately, techniques like logging every agent message in the loop or assigning iteration counters can help.

There is also a design consideration around diminishing returns: often the first or second iteration yields big improvements, but beyond that, agents might not add much new value. The system should be designed to recognize when to stop. For example, if the ReviewAgent finds no new issues, or if the AnswerAgent's output changes only minimally, it's probably time to conclude the loop. Additionally, one must ensure that feedback is constructive – the reviewer agent should ideally know how to phrase feedback in a way the generator agent can use. This sometimes requires careful prompt design so that Agent B's output is formatted as actionable advice rather than vague criticism.

Use Cases: Feedback loops are common in content generation (as described), complex problem solving (where agents take turns making incremental progress or exploring solutions), and scenarios requiring high assurance. An enterprise example: a Compliance Agent might loop with a Drafting Agent when generating a legal document, iteratively removing any non-compliant language. Another: two planning agents could debate the best approach to allocate a budget until they reach an agreement (or a superior agent chooses the best plan from their discussion). This pattern aligns with emerging AI safety techniques too – like "chain-of-thought" with self-critique, where an agent effectively reviews its own reasoning. In multi-agent terms, you can externalize that self-critique to a dedicated critic agent.

Diagram (Feedback Loop between two agents):

Agent A (Proposer) --[proposal]--> Agent B (Checker)

Agent A (Proposer) <--[feedback]-- Agent B (Checker)

(cycle repeats N times)

Agent A (Proposer) --[final output]--> (to user or next process)

Here Agent A and Agent B might swap messages a few times before a final output emerges. If more than two agents are in the loop, it could be a round-robin or free-for-all discussion moderated by a hub.

Pro Tip: Implement iteration limits and exit criteria for feedback loops. It's important to prevent endless cycling. For instance, configure your system such that agents will revise at most two times unless a clear improvement is being made. You can also give the reviewing agent the power to decide "looks good enough" and break the loop. This ensures that you gain the quality improvements of iterative refinement without incurring unbounded cost or time delays. In practice, many systems use a counter or a confidence threshold from the critic agent (e.g., "I'm 95% satisfied with this answer now") to know when to stop iterating.

Pro Tip: Use structured feedback between agents. If Agent B is providing feedback to Agent A, consider a format that Agent A can reliably parse, such as a list of issues or instructions. For example, Agent B might reply with a JSON listing errors found, or a numbered list of required changes. This reduces the chance of misunderstanding in the loop. Clear, structured feedback makes the iterative process more efficient and predictable.

DESIGNING FOR DISTRIBUTED REASONING

One of the most powerful aspects of multi-agent systems is their ability to reason in a distributed manner – effectively partitioning a complex cognitive task across multiple agents and then synthesizing the result. To harness this capability, you must design how knowledge and intermediate reasoning results are shared among agents. Distributed reasoning doesn't happen automatically; it emerges from careful planning of the information flow and division of labor in your agent ecosystem.

A central question is: How will agents share context and partial results with each other? Too little context shared, and agents operate in silos, possibly duplicating work or missing the bigger picture. Too much context indiscriminately shared, and you risk overwhelming agents with irrelevant details (not to mention increasing the token usage if using LLMs). Striking the right balance often involves creating a structured memory or blackboard that agents can contribute to and consult. In classical AI, the blackboard architecture was a model where multiple specialist processes write to and read from a common data store (the "blackboard"), gradually solving a problem. The same concept can be applied in modern multi-agent setups. For instance, you might have a shared object or knowledge base in Salesforce that all agents reference: Agent A writes the raw data it gathered to this store, Agent B reads that plus adds its analysis, Agent C later reads all accumulated info to produce a final outcome. In effect, the knowledge is built up collaboratively.

Modern implementations use various means for shared context. One approach is maintaining a shared state in memory that agents can access concurrently (if your platform supports it). LangChain's framework, for example, allows agents to update a graph state – essentially a shared memory space – which other agents can query. This could hold facts uncovered, decisions made, or any variable that agents should know about the others' work. Another approach is using shared message lists or chat history accessible to multiple agents. For example, in a group chat setting, all agents see each message (question, intermediate reasoning, answers) and can condition their next action on the collective conversation history. This can be very effective: one agent can "think out loud" by posting its reasoning, and another agent can pick up those thoughts and continue or correct them. A less tightly coupled method is to use a vector database or knowledge graph: agents contribute knowledge (e.g., embeddings of findings) to a common store. Other agents can then query this store as needed (for instance, a later agent might do a similarity search to see if a piece of information was already found by an earlier agent). In an enterprise context, this could be a Salesforce Knowledge article or a custom object that agents update with notes as they run.

Design principle: decide early what information needs to be shared globally among agents versus kept local. For example, if multiple agents are working on parts of a customer support case, it might make sense to use a single "Case Context" record where each agent posts its findings (one posts "Customer is asking about billing error," another posts "Previous tickets show a related issue last month," etc.). That record then represents the aggregate reasoning that any agent can look at. On the other hand, an agent's internal step-by-step reasoning (like an LLM's chain-of-thought) might be unnecessary or even harmful to share beyond the agent – it could confuse other agents or violate least privilege of information. So you might keep that internal.

Task allocation for distributed reasoning is another facet – deciding which sub-problem each agent addresses (which we did earlier in this chapter) and ensuring each sub-problem's solution can integrate into a whole. Often, an orchestrator or a planning agent is used at the outset to break a complex goal into sub-tasks assigned to different agents. This is a form of reasoning distribution: one agent (planner) reasons about the task structure, while others reason about task execution. Research suggests that optimizing this task allocation – matching each sub-task to the agent best suited for it – is vital to overall performance. So when architecting, consider an initial "decomposition" step. In Salesforce, this could be a Flow that, given a user request, makes a decision (via formula or Apex or an AI classification) on which agents to invoke. Or you might have a dedicated Agent, say a CoordinatorAgent, that has a prompt like "Analyze the request and delegate to the appropriate agents." This coordinator could output a plan (e.g., "Agent X do task 1, Agent Y do task 2") that the system then follows. Designing such a planner agent can dramatically improve efficiency by ensuring each part of a problem is handled by the most appropriate agent.

Communication mechanisms: if not using a single shared memory, agents may pass messages through the orchestrator or directly. In Salesforce terms, if using Flow Orchestration, the orchestration can collect outputs from one agent and feed them as inputs to another (effectively the flow acting as the communication bus). Alternatively, if agents are implemented as Apex services or external microservices, they might call each other's APIs. There's also the event-driven approach: one agent can fire a Platform Event when it's done, carrying its result, and another agent is subscribed to that event type and picks up the baton. For example, a DataGatheredEvent could wake up an AnalysisAgent. This decouples the agents and is a Salesforce-friendly way to do asynchronous multi-agent coordination.

Another strategy is employing a common data structure that multiple agents update. We touched on the blackboard concept – on Salesforce, a realistic implementation could be a Custom Object record that represents the "current state of the problem." All agents read from and write to that record. Consider a multi-agent trouble ticket resolution: the record might have fields like "Root Cause Hypothesis," "Customer Info Verified," "Proposed Solution," etc., and different agents fill in different fields as they complete their specialized tasks. The final agent or orchestrator then reads all fields to finalize the resolution. This approach ensures persistence and traceability of the reasoning process (and conveniently leverages Salesforce data model for sharing).

Example – Distributed Diagnosis: Imagine an IT incident within a company – multiple factors could be at play (network, server, software bug). You deploy a set of agents to collaboratively diagnose the issue. One agent (NetworkAgent) checks network logs, another (ServerAgent) checks server performance data, and a third (AppAgent) reviews recent software deployments. Each agent writes its findings to a shared "Incident Analysis Board" (say, a record or a file). The combined evidence on this board provides a fuller picture: NetworkAgent might note high latency at certain times, ServerAgent might post "CPU spikes on Server3 at 2am," and AppAgent notes "New release deployed at 1:50am on Server3." Reading the board, an orchestrator agent or simply the agents themselves can now connect dots – the deployment likely caused a performance issue on Server3 affecting the network. None of the agents alone had the full story, but through shared notes they achieved a holistic diagnosis. This scenario showcases distributed reasoning in action: parallel specialized analysis, followed by synthesis.

Implementing such a system requires your agents to agree on data formats and protocols for sharing information. This is where standards like MCP (Model Context Protocol) are emerging. MCP provides a structured way for agents (and tools) to exchange context, so that even if they're built on different platforms, they can interoperate. An agent might package its output and context in an MCP-defined JSON, for example, which another agent can parse to incorporate those results into its own context. By adhering to a protocol, you ensure that your distributed reasoning isn't hampered by miscommunication. In practical terms, if you design your own multi-agent system, define a clear schema for any shared context: it could be as simple as "Agent outputs will be stored as records with Type and Data fields," or a more complex contract like "Agent outputs a list of facts in format X, which become inputs for the next agent." In our Salesforce environment, this could mean using custom metadata or a static schema (e.g., fixed fields on an object) to structure inter-agent info.

A noteworthy benefit of designing for distributed reasoning is scalability. If each agent handles a portion of reasoning, you can scale the system by scaling agents individually. Need more performance in data fetching? Scale out that agent (run multiple in parallel or beef it up) without altering the analysis agent. In Salesforce, you might run certain agents in batch or as asynchronous parallel flows if needed. The architecture can handle increasing complexity by adding more agents or subdividing tasks further.

Caution: When multiple agents share and update context, guard against conflicts and inconsistencies. If two agents might update the same piece of information, you need a rule for whose input wins or how to merge them. For example, if two agents both post a "Root cause" hypothesis and they differ, will you have a mechanism to reconcile that (maybe a third agent to decide, or a weight given to one agent's confidence)? In many cases, careful scoping avoids this (each piece of info is owned by one agent), but overlapping domains can occur. Having an orchestrator mediate updates (like only the orchestrator writes the final fields based on agents' contributions) is one solution.

Security and privacy are also considerations in context sharing. In a corporate setting, you wouldn't want an agent sharing sensitive data with another agent that isn't authorized to see it. This ties into governance, but from a design perspective you might enforce that certain data remains siloed. For instance, perhaps a HR Agent dealing with personal info never writes full SSNs or salaries to the shared context – instead it could provide a redacted or conclusion-based output ("Verified eligibility = Yes") so other agents get only what they need. Designing these boundaries into the context-sharing model is prudent.

To sum up, designing for distributed reasoning means establishing how agents decompose problems, how they communicate intermediate results, and how they aggregate their knowledge to form solutions. It's about creating an information architecture for your multi-agent system. Done right, it allows your AI agents to collectively solve problems that none could solve alone, effectively sharing the thinking load. As one framework's documentation notes, a shared memory or state can allow agents to access and modify information relevant to the overall goals, enabling truly collaborative thinking. This is a core advantage of multi-agent systems – you create an emergent intelligence from multiple narrow intelligences.

Pro Tip: Be deliberate about what context to share versus keep local. A good rule of thumb: share conclusions, not raw thought processes. Let each agent do its internal reasoning in private, but have it publish key findings or decisions to the common context that others truly need. This keeps the shared knowledge base concise and focused. For instance, an agent might run through a 100-step internal chain-of-thought to come to an answer; only the final answer (and perhaps a rationale summary) goes into the shared memory for others, rather than the entire 100-step log.

Pro Tip: Use a common schema or format for inter-agent communication. Unstructured text can lead to misinterpretation between agents. If possible, define a simple schema: e.g., "When posting to the shared board, always use the format: {AgentName}: FINDING - <short summary>". Or for more complex data, use JSON or fielded records. This way, if one agent is reading another's output, it can reliably parse it. Standardizing communication (even informally) is a backbone of successful distributed reasoning, ensuring all agents speak the same "language" when sharing knowledge.

IMPLEMENTATION IN SALESFORCE (AGENT BUILDER, FLOW ORCHESTRATION, APEX, METADATA)

Translating multi-agent designs into a working system on the Salesforce platform involves weaving together several tools. Salesforce's ecosystem – with its low-code capabilities and robust Apex programming – is well-suited to host multi-agent patterns, especially with the introduction of Agentforce. In this section, we discuss how to implement multi-agent systems using Salesforce Agent Builder for defining agents, Flow Orchestration for coordinating them, Apex for extending logic and integrations, and metadata for configuration and scalability. The key is to leverage Salesforce's strengths (declarative workflows, security model, integration endpoints) while maintaining the modular, reusable nature of your agents.

Agent Builder and Multi-Agent Setup

Agent Builder (part of Salesforce's Agentforce platform) is a low-code tool that allows creators to define AI agents by specifying their behavior, knowledge sources, and actions in a declarative way. Using Agent Builder, you typically start by creating individual agents – for example, a "Customer Support Agent" or "Invoice Analysis Agent" – providing a description of its role and maybe some conversational prompts or rules. Agent Builder then helps scaffold the agent's logic (potentially even using AI to assist, given a description). For multi-agent systems, you would use Agent Builder to configure each agent independently according to its responsibility, and then later link them via orchestration. This means when building an agent, you focus on its specific tasks and outputs.

In Agent Builder, you define topics and actions the agent can handle. For a multi-agent scenario, you might create fewer topics per agent, each very focused. For example, if building a Finance Report Agent (whose job is to generate financial summaries), you might have a topic like "GenerateQuarterlyReport" with actions to retrieve financial metrics and produce a summary. Separately, a Compliance Agent might have an "CheckRegulatoryCompliance" topic with actions to scan a document for prohibited terms. Each agent is built and tested in isolation with Agent Builder's conversation preview – you ensure it does what it's supposed to do on its own.

Now, Agentforce's architecture is designed to integrate these agents into larger workflows. When you define an agent in Agent Builder, you effectively create an "endpoint" (think of it like an AI service that can be invoked). According to Salesforce's guidance, Agentforce agents can be exposed as invocable actions in Flow or callable via Apex. This is crucial: it means once you have multiple agents defined, you can orchestrate their execution using other Salesforce tools. Each agent's definition (prompts, tools it can use, etc.) is stored as metadata and configuration in the platform, often in an Agent Definition object behind the scenes. You don't need to hard-code agent logic; you configure it, which fits the Salesforce ethos of declarative setup.

Designing multiple agents: When implementing, ensure each agent's name and description clearly reflect its duty, because you'll be selecting these agents by name in flows or Apex. For instance, you might register agents like "LegalReviewAgent", "PricingApprovalAgent", etc. (Salesforce Agentforce likely registers them with unique names or IDs). It's also wise to implement any guardrails or knowledge limits at the agent level using Agent Builder. If an agent shouldn't answer questions outside its domain, you can bake that into its prompt or intents. This way, the agent won't stray when later orchestrated.

Agent Builder provides testing for each agent (via chat simulation) – do this before orchestration. In a multi-agent system, debugging is far easier if you know each component agent works properly on its own given expected inputs. For example, test that your "DataFetcher Agent" indeed returns data in the format your "Analyzer Agent" expects. If using Agent Builder's preview, you might simulate by giving it representative input and ensuring the output matches the contract.

A practical consideration: if your multi-agent system will involve agents talking to each other (feedback loops or hub broadcasting to multiple agents), Agentforce doesn't yet automatically set up agents to chat amongst themselves (the way AutoGen or other frameworks do). You'll typically orchestrate them via flows or Apex (see the next sections). However, conceptually you could configure an agent to act as a proxy for another – though that likely complicates things. It's more straightforward to use flows/Apex to manage multi-agent conversations rather than trying to nest agents within Agent Builder definitions.

Agent Builder is used to define the behavior of each agent; it's the foundation. Once those agents are defined and active in your org (Agentforce registers them, possibly listing them in an Agent registry visible in Setup or via metadata), you move to orchestrating their interaction.

Flow Orchestration for Agent Workflows

Flow Orchestration on Salesforce is a powerful tool to coordinate multi-step, multi-user (or multi-system) processes. In the context of multi-agent systems, Flow Orchestration can serve as the "conversation conductor" – controlling which agent runs when, passing outputs from one to another, and applying decision logic. Even if you think of your orchestrator agent as a conceptual entity, implementing it as a Flow (with possibly some subflows) can be very effective and maintainable by admins.

Using Flow Orchestration, you can create an Orchestration Flow that encapsulates a multi-agent workflow from start to finish. Salesforce flows now support calling Apex actions and even other flows, meaning each agent can be invoked as an action. For example, suppose we have two Agentforce agents defined: DataAgent and AnalysisAgent. In a flow, you can add an "Action" element that corresponds to calling DataAgent. Agentforce likely provides an invocable action or global method to invoke an agent by name (if not out-of-the-box, one can be created in Apex; we'll cover that in the Apex section). The flow passes in whatever input the agent needs (perhaps in a record field or variable), and the agent returns its output which you store in a flow variable. Then you add another Action to call AnalysisAgent, feeding it the output from the first agent. This is essentially building a chain via Flow.

Flow Orchestration specifically allows for stages and steps with potentially parallel branches. This aligns well with the hub-and-spoke pattern. You could create a stage where multiple agents are invoked in parallel steps. For instance, a Flow Orchestration for a contract review might have a stage "Gather Approvals" with three parallel actions: one calls LegalAgent, one calls FinanceAgent, one calls VPApprovalAgent. The orchestration waits until all three are complete (or whichever logic you choose) before moving to the next stage where perhaps a CombineResults action (maybe an Apex action) compiles the responses. This visual layout is intuitive and powerful – you get a diagram of your multi-agent interaction in the Flow Builder, which is great for documentation and updates.

Decision elements in flows allow branching logic based on agent outputs. Say the RiskAssessmentAgent returns a risk score. In the flow, you can have a Decision: if risk > X, invoke a ManualReviewAgent (or just create a Case for a human). If risk is low, proceed to the next automated step. This kind of logic is straightforward in Flow and spares you from writing a bunch of Apex if-else.

Another handy aspect is using subflows as agent wrappers. You might create a Flow (or Subflow) for each agent invocation that includes any pre/post processing. For instance, perhaps the raw output of an agent is JSON or needs parsing – you could handle that in a subflow. The main orchestration flow then just calls that subflow. This fosters reuse: if multiple orchestrations use the same agent, encapsulate the invocation in a subflow once.

Error handling in flows: It's wise to use fault paths on your agent call actions. If an agent invocation fails (maybe the agent ran into an error or an unhandled exception), the flow can catch it. You could route to a clean-up or fallback path (for example, notify an admin, or call a fallback agent). This way the orchestration doesn't just crash invisibly. Salesforce flows also allow setting up roll-back or commit behaviors if using transactions – relevant if your agents update database records as part of actions.

From a deployment perspective, flows are metadata, meaning you can deploy and version them as part of your org's configuration. That's great for multi-agent logic which might evolve. One could have a flow per environment or easily propagate improvements to orchestrations.

Invoking flows vs. Apex: Note that flows themselves can be triggered by platform events, schedules, or UI actions. So, you can connect a multi-agent orchestration flow to real business triggers. For example, when a new opportunity is marked "Needs complex approval", you trigger a flow that runs a multi-agent approval orchestration. Or an Omni-Channel input from a chat could trigger a flow that engages different agents (perhaps one agent to classify the request, then others to fulfill, etc.). This integration into Salesforce's event model is a big advantage of using Flow Orchestration – your AI agents can be naturally inserted into existing business processes.

Finally, consider permissions: flows run in a certain context (either system or user depending on settings). If your agents need to perform data actions, ensure the flow (and underlying Apex actions) have access. Often, a system context is used so that agents aren't limited by a single user's permissions – but governance might require that you do limit what they do. You can also incorporate checks within flows (like using a Login Flow or some intermediate approval if needed for sensitive actions).

In sum, Flow Orchestration acts as the central nervous system of a multi-agent solution on Salesforce, especially for those chain or hub patterns. It provides a high-level map of interactions, leveraging the declarative power of the platform. Many multi-agent processes that in other ecosystems require writing a coordinator script can be built with clicks, decisions, and invocable actions in Flow – making the system more transparent to maintain and adjust by admins. Salesforce even envisions orchestrator agents (sometimes called "Conductor" pattern) being implemented largely with flows and invocable calls.

Extending with Apex and Custom Code

While low-code tools handle a lot of the orchestration, Apex (Salesforce's Java-like programming language) remains a crucial part of implementing multi-agent systems, especially for fine-grained control, complex logic, or integration with external systems. There are several roles Apex can play in a multi-agent architecture:

1. Invoking Agents Programmatically: If Agentforce exposes agents via an Apex SDK or global methods, you can use Apex to run an agent and fetch its output. For example, Agentforce might provide a class like AgentService with a method runAgent(agentName, input). In Apex you'd do something like:

```
String agentOutput = AgentService.runAgent('DataAgent', someInput);
```

If such an API doesn't exist yet, you can often create it using Apex callouts or wrapper classes. For instance, if Agentforce's Agent Builder ultimately uses Einstein GPT behind the scenes, there might be a REST API to call the agent; Apex can invoke that (with proper auth) and get the response. Having an Apex method to call each agent allows more flexibility than relying solely on Flow – you can loop, handle errors, transform inputs, etc., in code.

2. Complex Orchestration Logic: Some coordination might be easier in code, especially feedback loops or conditional retries. Apex can implement a Conductor Agent pattern entirely in code if needed: receiving a request, then in a loop calling an agent, evaluating output, calling another, and so on. Pseudocode for an Apex-based orchestrator might look like:

```
// Pseudo-Apex example for orchestrating two agents in a loop
String draftAnswer = AgentService.runAgent('AnswerAgent', userQuestion);
Integer attempts = 0;
Boolean approved = false;
while(attempts < 2 && !approved) {
  String feedback = AgentService.runAgent('ReviewAgent', draftAnswer);
  if(feedback.contains('Approved')) {
    approved = true;
  } else {
```

```
        draftAnswer = AgentService.runAgent('AnswerAgent', feedback);
        attempts++;
    }
}
String finalAnswer = draftAnswer;
```

THIS SNIPPET IMAGINES a reviewer agent giving either an "Approved" message or feedback, and the answer agent revises if not approved. Such logic – a feedback loop with break conditions – is currently easier to implement in Apex than Flow (since flow loops are possible but less flexible, and until recently, flow couldn't easily handle arbitrary loops or complex conditions). Apex gives you full control over data structures, loop counts, and error handling in these scenarios.

3. Integration with External Tools or Data: Apex is your go-to for calling external services (via HTTP callouts) if agents need to fetch or post data outside Salesforce. For example, an agent might need to query an external knowledge base – Apex can call that API, then feed results to the agent. Or you might integrate with non-Salesforce agent frameworks: suppose you have a Python service running LangChain agents. Apex could make REST calls to that service to trigger those external agents as part of an orchestration (effectively treating them as part of your multi-agent system). Salesforce's MuleSoft or Platform Events could also be involved, but Apex is a straightforward way to glue such pieces together, especially if the integration logic is simple. (Note that if doing heavy integration, consider using MuleSoft or an External Service for a more config-driven approach; but Apex is fine for moderate needs).

4. Custom Data Processing: Sometimes agents will output data that requires processing not easily done in Flow or by the agents themselves. Apex can parse JSON, perform calculations, or manipulate records extensively. For instance, if an agent returns a detailed JSON with multiple sections of a report, Apex could parse it and create multiple Salesforce records out of it (like creating Task records for follow-ups mentioned in the agent's output). Or an Apex trigger might further process agent outputs in real-time. Essentially, Apex can take the "raw intelligence" from agents and apply business rules or data transformations before finalizing outcomes.

5. Utility and Reuse via Apex Services: You can wrap common sequences in Apex classes for reuse. If multiple flows or parts of the system need to call the same combination of agents, writing an Apex service class method for it avoids duplication. For example, a method runBackgroundCheck(customerId) might internally orchestrate a KYC agent and a credit agent and return a combined result. This can then be called from flows or other Apex contexts easily. By consolidating such logic in code, you ensure consistency and make maintenance easier (update in one place).

Invocable Apex for Flow: To marry Apex and Flow, you can expose Apex methods as Invocable Actions. This is a best-of-both-worlds strategy: use Apex to do heavy logic, but call it from a flow so you still have the high-level orchestration visible declaratively. For example, you might write an Apex invocable method invokeAgents(List<String> agentNames, String input) that runs a series of agents sequentially and returns a combined result. The flow can then use this single action instead of stringing multiple steps. Or an invocable that specifically implements a mini feedback loop as above. The outline for the Agentforce playbook suggests using invocable Apex for agent delegation and complex steps. This approach also encapsulates complexity: non-developers can drag-and-drop the invocable into flows without worrying about the code inside, and developers can version and test that Apex independently.

Example Apex Snippet: Let's illustrate a simple use case with pseudo-Apex code. Suppose we want to implement a chain of two agents (like DataAgent then AnalysisAgent) via Apex:

```
public with sharing class AgentOrchestrator {

  @InvocableMethod

  public static List<Output> runDataAnalysis(List<Input> requests) {

    List<Output> results = new List<Output>();

    for(Input req : requests) {

      // Call DataAgent (assume AgentService.run returns JSON string)

      String dataJson = AgentService.runAgent('DataAgent', req.query);

      // Optionally parse or process dataJson here...

      // Call AnalysisAgent with the data

      String analysis = AgentService.runAgent('AnalysisAgent', dataJson);
```

```
        // Prepare output
        Output o = new Output();
        o.result = analysis;
        results.add(o);
      }
      return results;
    }

    public class Input { @InvocableVariable public String query; }
    public class Output { @InvocableVariable public String result; }
}
```

IN THIS PSEUDO-CODE, AgentService.runAgent is an imagined utility that would call the actual agent (maybe via an HTTP to Salesforce's AI endpoints or an internal mechanism). The invocable method runDataAnalysis orchestrates the two-agent pipeline for each input request. We define inner classes Input and Output to use Salesforce's invocable method structure. This Apex could be invoked from a Flow, passing the query, and it would return the analysis result. The use of with sharing or not would depend on whether agent actions are permitted to see data as system or user – a governance decision.

Apex and Metadata Config: Apex can also leverage custom metadata (discussed next) to drive behavior. For instance, you could store agent names or parameters in metadata and have Apex read from it. That way, you don't hard-code agent identifiers. If tomorrow you want to swap out which agent is called first, you could change the metadata instead of editing code. This is a pattern commonly used for flexibility.

One more aspect: Asynchronous Apex. Multi-agent flows might benefit from running some agents in parallel or outside of the transaction context (especially if calling external services which might hit timeouts). You can use Queueable or Future Apex to run agents asynchronously. For example, after a record is saved, you enqueue a job that orchestrates several agents and then updates the record with results when done. This avoids hitting governor limits in a synchronous process and can improve user experience (the user doesn't wait for the AI to finish on save). Just ensure you handle the callback/updates properly and consider using Platform Events or status fields to report when async processes complete.

In summary, Apex provides the muscle and flexibility under the hood of a Salesforce multi-agent system. It's the tool of choice when you need to go beyond what Flow can easily do – implementing loops, complex decisions, error recovery, or external integration. By combining Apex and Flow, you often get an optimal solution: high-level orchestration and visibility via flows, with heavy lifting and intricate logic encapsulated in Apex actions. Salesforce's multi-agent support acknowledges this combination – for instance, calling invocable Apex from flows is explicitly recommended for delegation and custom tool integration. Remember to write unit tests for your Apex orchestrations (simulate agent responses if possible) to ensure your multi-agent logic is solid.

Metadata-Driven Configuration (Agents and Registries)

As your multi-agent system grows, you'll want to avoid hardcoding details like agent names, prompts, or process logic. Metadata-driven design means using Salesforce's metadata (custom metadata types, custom settings, or records) to store configuration, so that the system can be adjusted without code changes. In multi-agent systems, this approach dramatically improves maintainability and governance.

Consider establishing an Agent Registry as a central catalog of all agents in your org – effectively a custom metadata type or custom object where each record represents an agent. Fields might include: Agent Name (unique key to call it), Description, Status (active/inactive), Version or Last Update, and perhaps metadata like "Permitted Actions" or "Owner (business owner of the agent)". This registry serves multiple purposes. From a governance view, it lets administrators see all defined agents in one place. From a technical view, your orchestration logic can reference this registry to discover agents or check if an agent is allowed to be invoked.

For example, instead of coding AgentService.runAgent('PricingAgent', input) directly, your Apex could look up the registry: find the record where Name = 'PricingAgent' and check if Active = true. If not active, perhaps skip or throw an error (so a rogue agent can be turned off via metadata flip). You could also store in that record what implementation method to use – e.g., a field "InvocationType" with values like "OpenAI API" or "On-platform" or

"ExternalLangChain" to indicate how to call it. Your AgentService.runAgent could then branch accordingly without you writing separate code paths for each agent type. Essentially, metadata entries can drive the dynamic behavior of a generic agent invoker.

Prompts and configurations: Custom Metadata is a great place to store agent prompts, system messages, or tool configurations. For instance, if you have a KnowledgeBaseAgent that answers from a knowledge base, you might have a metadata record with a field for "PromptTemplate" like "You are a KnowledgeBaseAgent. Use article snippets to answer user questions." If the knowledge base or guidelines update, an admin can tweak this text in metadata rather than a developer editing code or an agent builder config. Some orgs store entire prompts or few-shot examples in metadata for quick iteration. Keep in mind custom metadata has size limits (a few hundred characters per field unless marked as large text), but it's typically sufficient for reasonably sized prompts. Alternatively, static resources or even records in a protected custom object can be used if very large content must be stored.

Flow and Apex reading metadata: Flows can use Custom Settings and Custom Metadata via "Get Records" elements, and Apex can query them like regular sObjects (with the benefit that custom metadata queries are cached for efficiency). This means you can design flows that adapt based on metadata. For example, you could have a custom metadata type that defines a sequence of agents to run for certain scenarios. Perhaps a ProcessDefinition metadata where one field is Process Name (e.g., "OrderFulfillment") and then fields like Step1Agent, Step2Agent, etc. A flow could query ProcessDefinition where Name = "OrderFulfillment" and then, rather than having static calls, it could loop through the steps defined in metadata, calling each agent in turn. If tomorrow the business decides to add a third step (say a FraudCheckAgent) in the fulfillment process, you update the metadata (add a Step3Agent field to that record with "FraudCheckAgent") and the flow automatically will include that on next runs because it's data-driven. This is a more advanced use of flows, but feasible with some creativity (using collection loops or maybe a generic subflow that takes an agent name and executes it).

Using Metadata for tool integration and keys: It's also wise to use custom settings/metadata for storing things like external API endpoints, agent API keys, or version flags. For example, if some agents use OpenAI GPT-4 and others GPT-3.5, you might have a metadata field on the agent record specifying model or provider. This way switching models is a metadata deploy, not a code change. Or if you decide to route all AnalysisAgent calls to a new microservice instead of an internal method, you change a URL or type field in metadata.

Enterprise governance via metadata: One particularly valuable use of metadata is implementing feature toggles and guardrails. For instance, a custom setting "EnableMultiAgentAutomation" (true/false) could globally turn on/off the automated multi-agent flows (maybe default off in case something goes awry, you can disable automation quickly). Another idea: a Confidence-Threshold metadata that says if an agent's confidence score is below X, require human review – this threshold can be tuned by admins over time as they see fit.

The outline in the Agentforce playbook explicitly mentions metadata-driven agent registries and orchestration logic. This underscores how Salesforce expects customers to use metadata to configure which agents to call and how. In practice, you might have multiple multi-agent workflows across an enterprise, and metadata provides a uniform way to manage them. It also facilitates compliance: an auditor could review a report of all agent definitions and their statuses from metadata (which is easier to interpret than scanning code).

Example – Agent Registry Metadata: Suppose we define a Custom Metadata Type AI_Agent__mdt with fields: Agent_API_Name, Active, Invocation_Method, Model_Type, Max_Retries, Owner_Team. An example record might be:

- Agent_API_Name = "LegalReviewAgent"
- Active = true
- Invocation_Method = "OpenAI-ChatCompletions" (meaning use OpenAI API)
- Model_Type = "gpt-4" (the model to use)
- Max_Retries = 1 (if this agent fails, try once more at most)
- Owner_Team = "Legal Dept"

Your Apex AgentService.runAgent(name,input) function could do:

```
AI_Agent__mdt agentConfig = AI_Agent__mdt.getInstance(name);

if(agentConfig == null) throw new AgentNotFoundException(name);

if(!agentConfig.Active__c) throw new AgentDisabledException(name);

String method = agentConfig.Invocation_Method__c;
```

```
if(method == 'OpenAI-ChatCompletions') {
  // Use OpenAI API (maybe with model type)
  String model = agentConfig.Model_Type__c;
  return OpenAIService.callChatCompletion(model, input);
} else if(method == 'Salesforce-EinsteinAPI') {
  // Call internal Salesforce AI endpoint
  return EinsteinService.invokeAgent(name, input);
}
//... other methods
```

THIS WAY, adding new agent methods or switching one agent's method doesn't require code rewriting, just adjusting metadata or extending the AgentService logic slightly.

Process Metadata: Similarly, you could have a type Agent_Workflow__mdt to define sequences or relationships: e.g., a record where Workflow_Name = "DealApprovalProcess", Step_Order = 1, Agent_API_Name = "PricingAgent", Next_Step_On_Success = 2 (just conceptual fields). Multiple records for the same Workflow define the chain or graph of agent calls. At runtime, you query all steps for "DealApprovalProcess", sort by Step_Order, then loop through them calling each agent. Or define branching by having conditions fields. This can get elaborate, essentially making a state machine out of metadata – which is doable but one has to weigh complexity vs. using Flow. Sometimes a simpler compromise: metadata can list which agents to run in parallel at a certain stage, but the flow controls the overall structure.

Storing Prompts/Instructions: A Custom Metadata Type Agent_Prompt__mdt might map an agent to its system prompt or sample conversation. E.g., fields: Agent_API_Name, System_Message, Temperature, etc. Then your invocation logic (especially for external LLM calls) can fetch those and apply them. Imagine being able to tweak an agent's "personality" or strictness by editing a metadata record instead of redeploying code – extremely useful for iterative improvement in production. Admins or product managers could even adjust those with appropriate access.

Security for metadata: Keep in mind custom metadata can be protected or not. Protected means only code from the same package (in a managed package scenario) can read it, which is more relevant for ISV packages. For in-house, all Apex can see it. Custom settings are mostly deprecated in favor of custom metadata (for app config), but settings allow easier editing in setup UI for admins (unless you build a custom UI for metadata, which is possible). Decide what makes sense – if you want admins to quickly toggle a flag, a Hierarchy Custom Setting might be simplest.

Audit and Versioning: Because metadata is deployed, you get a version history via deployment tracking (or using source control if you have SFDX). If an agent's config changes, you'll see a diff in the metadata, providing a record of changes. Additionally, you could create an Agent Log custom object where each agent invocation records which version of config it used (maybe store a config version or timestamp in the log). That might be overkill, but for highly regulated contexts it's an idea (similar to logging model version used for each decision).

Example scenario tying it together: Let's say your multi-agent system needs to adapt on the fly – maybe if volume is high, you want to swap one agent's implementation to a simpler method to save cost. You could have a custom metadata "SwitchToLiteVersion" flag that your AgentService checks: if true, it calls a simpler agent variant. Flipping that flag (perhaps via a quick metadata deploy or through a custom UI that updates a setting) would reroute logic without downtime.

In practice, many Salesforce multi-agent deployments will likely rely on a combination of flow and metadata, with Apex bridging where needed. The upshot is flexibility – multi-agent systems are novel and will evolve, so building in configurability from day one is a wise investment. As a final note, treat your metadata with the same rigor as code: plan the schema, add descriptions to each field (so others know what they control), and keep documentation of how changing values affects the system.

Pro Tip: Use Custom Metadata Types to externalize magic values and agent configurations. If you find any "hardcoded" agent name, endpoint, threshold, or prompt in your flow or code, ask: can this be in a custom metadata instead? Externalizing these allows administrators (or your future self) to fine-tune the system in minutes rather than hours or days. A small metadata table for agents and their properties can make a huge difference in agility – you can disable an agent by flipping a flag, or increase an agent's allowed runtime by changing a setting, all without redeploying or stopping the system.

Pro Tip: Maintain an Agent Registry (even if it's just a spreadsheet for human reference in early stages) in parallel to building your system, then implement it as a metadata object in Salesforce. This ensures no agent is "unknown" or forgotten. Each entry should capture who is responsible for the agent's logic (business owner), what data it can access, and when it was last reviewed. This not only aids governance and compliance, but also helps new team members understand the constellation of agents in your org. By implementing the registry in the org's data, you can even build admin-facing Lightning pages to display agent statuses or a dashboard of agent activity, supporting transparency and trust in the multi-agent ecosystem.

OBSERVABILITY, DEBUGGING, AND FAILOVER

When multiple agents are operating and making autonomous decisions, observability becomes critical. You need to be able to peer inside the system to understand what each agent did, how they interacted, and where things might have gone wrong. In a multi-agent system, debugging can't be an afterthought – it must be baked into the design so that when something unexpected happens (and it will), you have the data and tools to diagnose it. Likewise, failover mechanisms (gracefully handling agent errors or outages) are essential for a robust deployment. In this section, we cover strategies to monitor agent behavior, debug issues, and design for fault tolerance.

Centralized Logging: A first step is to set up comprehensive logging of agent activity. At minimum, every time an agent is invoked, log the event: which agent, what input (perhaps truncated if large or sensitive), and the outcome. If the agent returns a result, log a summary of that result; if it errors or produces no answer, log that as well. In Salesforce, you have a few options for logging: platform events, custom objects, or even the standard debug log (though that's more for developers and harder to analyze at scale). A good approach is to create a Custom Object like Agent_Run__c with fields such as Agent Name, Start Time, End Time, Success (checkbox), and maybe text fields for Input Summary, Output Summary, and Error Message if any. Every agent invocation creates one record. Over time, this becomes an audit trail and a dataset for analysis (you could track, for example, average execution time per agent or success rates).

Salesforce's Event Monitoring could also capture some aspects, but since these are custom AI processes, it's better you instrument it yourself. By logging in a structured way, you can build reports and dashboards. For example, you might have a dashboard of "Agent Errors in the Last 24 Hours" to quickly alert you if an agent started failing frequently. Or a report per agent of their average response length or time, to spot anomalies.

Agent Transcripts: For debugging content issues (like "why did the agent give this answer?"), you may need more than just inputs and outputs – you might need the intermediate chain-of-thought or the conversation between agents if feedback loops are involved. If using an LLM that provides reasoning (some frameworks allow capturing the model's reasoning steps or you can prompt it to show them), consider logging that reasoning to a secure location. This can, however, raise information security issues (the chain-of-thought might contain snippets of data). One compromise is to log reasoning in a secure data store accessible only to admins and for a limited time. Alternatively, you could enable verbose logging only when a debug mode is on (we'll talk about toggling debug).

For multi-agent interactions, consider logging the message exchange. If Agent A and Agent B are in a loop, log each message with a sequence ID. Essentially, you're creating a transcript. This is invaluable when analyzing a problematic outcome – you can see what each agent said to each other. It's analogous to having server logs in microservice architecture. Some frameworks (like LangChain with LangSmith) provide such trace logging out of the box. If you roll your own in Salesforce, you might store these in a related object (e.g., Agent_Run__c has children Agent_Message__c records with content and sender).

Monitoring Tools: Salesforce doesn't (as of 2025) have a native UI specifically for AI agent monitoring (that might come with Einstein analytics or "AI Cloud" dashboards). In absence of that, you can integrate with external monitoring: for instance, send critical logs to an external system via a callout or use a service like Splunk or New Relic if you have connectors. However, building a simple Lightning App page for agent logs is quite achievable. For example, a Lightning datatable of recent agent runs, filterable by agent or success/failure, could be put in an admin console.

Also remember, if your orchestration is via Flow, you can leverage Flow's debug logs and Platform Debugger. Each flow run can log its path (especially if you include "Log" elements or fault connectors with screens). Flow doesn't log by default every action's output in an easily readable way, so adding your own logging steps or using Apex that logs, is helpful.

Error Alerts: It's wise to set up alerting for failures. This could be as simple as an email alert when an Agent_Run__c record is created with Success = false. Or a more advanced option: use Salesforce's Platform Events. You could define an AgentErrorEvent platform event, fire it whenever an agent fails critically, and have a trigger or an external subscriber handle notifications (for example, ping an admin on Slack or create a Case for IT to investigate). The right mechanism depends on the volume – if failures are rare, an immediate email might be fine; if frequent, you might aggregate.

Failover Strategies: Now on failover – what do we do when an agent fails? Failures might include technical errors (exception thrown, API callout failed, timeout) or functional failures (agent couldn't come up with an answer or produced a low-confidence result). You should design for both.

Retry Logic: On technical hiccups, a simple retry can resolve transient issues (like a momentary API timeout). If you have a Max Retries setting (perhaps in metadata per agent, as described earlier), implement that. For example, if an OpenAI call times out, try once more after a brief pause. Salesforce Apex callouts have limits, so perhaps queue a retry asynchronously if needed. Do log retries as well (maybe mark in log "retry 1"). But avoid endless retries – usually 1 or 2 is enough; otherwise, escalate.

Fallback Agents: You might have a backup method or agent if one fails. For instance, if the advanced AI Summarizer Agent fails to return a summary, you could fall back to a simpler rules-based summary or a template ("We're sorry, we can't summarize at this time"). Or even route to a human (like create a Task for a person to do it). This ensures the overall process doesn't grind to a halt. In flows, you can implement fallback by using Decision branches after an agent call: if the output is empty or indicates failure, then call an alternate agent or flow. In Apex, it's straightforward try-catch: in catch, call AlternativeAgent. Designating fallback agents can be part of your planning – maybe noted in metadata ("AlternateAgentName" field for an agent). Example: if AnswerAgent fails, use FallbackAnswerAgent (which maybe uses a simpler model or returns a canned message).

Human-in-the-loop: Not exactly failover in the traditional sense, but a controlled pass to human review. If an agent outputs something with low confidence or an error, you can escalate to a human. For instance, a Supervisor Pattern (as referenced in earlier chapters) can wrap around: the agent proposes something, but a human must approve or edit if the agent was unsure. This is more of a design choice than a runtime failover, but it is a way to handle agent shortcomings gracefully. If using Salesforce, this could mean creating a record in a queue or sending a chatbot message to a human agent to intervene.

System Safeguards: Multi-agent systems should be protected from runaway behaviors. If two agents start feeding each other in a loop incorrectly (maybe due to a bug), you need a circuit breaker. One guard could be a loop counter were we ensure only N iterations max. Another guard is timeouts – if an agent normally responds in 5 seconds but 60 seconds have passed, assume it's hung and stop that thread. In Flow, long-running callouts will eventually hit limits, but you can also use a combination of scheduled path or asynchronous processes to enforce time constraints.

Salesforce doesn't allow infinite loops in flows; in Apex, you have control to break them. Use those controls. If using external agent processes, implement a timeout on waiting for their response.

Debug Mode: Introduce a debug mode toggle in your system. This could be a custom setting "DebugMode" (true/false). When true, your agents or orchestrator could log much more detail, maybe even include sensitive intermediate data, and possibly skip some optimizations. This mode is used only in sandboxes or when investigating an issue. When false (normal operation), you log only essentials (to reduce noise and protect info). For example, debug mode might log full prompts and responses, whereas normal mode logs just "Agent succeeded" or only the final answer. Having this switch is extremely useful – you can dynamically turn it on (if it's a custom setting, you could even turn it on in production briefly to capture data about an ongoing issue, then turn it off). Just be cautious: ensure that any detailed logs in debug mode are stored securely and wiped or archived appropriately, since they might contain sensitive content. A practice could be: if DebugMode is on in production, direct logs to an encrypted custom object or to a secure external log store, and automatically turn off debug after some time.

Example of Observability Implementation: Consider a scenario: an agent produced a nonsensical answer to a customer. To debug, you go to your "AI Agent Runs" tab (a custom Lightning page). You find the log for that interaction by timestamp or case ID. You open it and see: Agent = QnAAgent, Input = "Customer asked about pricing options", Output = "(some weird answer)", plus a child log line: "ReviewAgent feedback: incoherent response flagged, but QnAAgent output used anyway." Aha – perhaps the orchestrator didn't handle the feedback loop properly. You then see in the transcript messages that the QnAAgent mentioned a pricing that's outdated. With this information, you know to retrain or reconfigure the QnAAgent's knowledge source, and to fix the orchestrator logic to not use an answer that the ReviewAgent flagged. Without logs, this scenario would be a black box – you'd just have an unhappy customer with a bad answer and no clue why.

Integration with Salesforce Command Center: If your organization uses a monitoring dashboard or the Salesforce Einstein Analytics (Tableau CRM) for operations, consider feeding your log data there. The outline hints at using "Command Center for end-to-end telemetry". This could mean having a live dashboard showing agent activity and status. For instance, you might display: "20 agent tasks completed in the last hour, 2 failures (90% success rate)." You could integrate this with IT incident management – e.g., if agent failure rate > X%, automatically create a high-priority incident in Service Cloud to investigate. These are advanced but very useful for running AI systems in production reliably.

Failover Example: Suppose an agent that writes back to a record fails to do so. A failover plan might be: catch that error, create a Case or Task for a human to complete that record update later, and notify an admin that the agent couldn't do it. The system thereby ensures the task isn't dropped entirely. Another example: if an agent normally handles customer chat autonomously but fails (maybe can't answer a query), failover might route the chat to a human live agent ("Sorry, I'm transferring you to a specialist"). This kind of fail-safe maintains user experience. In Salesforce's Omni-Channel, you could programmatically transfer the session if your bot agent signals confusion.

Testing failovers: It's not enough to plan them; simulate agent failures in a test environment to ensure your detection and fallback works. For instance, deliberately disable an agent via metadata and see if the orchestrator uses the alternate path. Or have an agent throw a custom exception in a test context and verify the retry or human escalation triggers.

In conclusion, robust observability and graceful failover are what turn a cool multi-agent demo into a production-grade system. Borrow best practices from microservices and distributed systems: log extensively, monitor continuously, set up alerts on anomalies, and always have a Plan B (or C) when parts of the system misbehave. Multi-agent AI systems can be unpredictable, so assume things will go wrong and instrument accordingly. As a result, when an issue arises, you'll be equipped with the insights to fix it quickly and the controls to mitigate it in the moment.

Pro Tip: Implement a trace ID or correlation ID for each multi-agent transaction. Assign a unique ID when a process starts (e.g., a customer request), and pass it through all agent calls and logs. This way, all log entries related to a single flow can be easily aggregated even if multiple agents and orchestrator steps are involved. You can store the trace ID in the Agent_Run__c records or include it in log lines. It makes debugging across many interwoven activities much easier – akin to how distributed tracing in microservices works.

Pro Tip: Regularly review and replay failure scenarios as part of your testing regimen. Don't wait for real incidents to test your failover. Use a sandbox to simulate agent outages or errors (for example, point an agent to an invalid endpoint or force a timeout) and ensure the system responds as designed – perhaps the flow should catch that exception and invoke the backup agent. This practice not only validates your fallback paths but also keeps the team familiar with how the system behaves under stress, building confidence that if something goes wrong in production, it's not the first time you're seeing that failure mode.

GOVERNANCE – PERMISSIONS, REGISTRIES, AND COMPLIANCE

As organizations deploy AI agents more widely, governance becomes a top priority. This includes controlling what agents are allowed to do (permissions), maintaining an inventory of agents and their configurations (registries), and ensuring compliance with regulations and company policies (data handling, ethical guidelines, etc.). A multi-agent system should be designed not just for functionality, but for accountability and control. In this section, we discuss how to put guardrails around your agents and manage them in an enterprise environment.

Agent Permissions and Access Control: Just as human users are granted permissions on a need-to-know and least-privilege basis, AI agents should operate under the principle of least privilege. This means each agent gets only the minimum data access and system privileges necessary for its role. In Salesforce, this can be implemented by running agents under specific user contexts or integration credentials. For example, you might create a dedicated Salesforce user (or better, a Named Credential or External Credential if calling external services) for a particular agent or group of agents. That user would have a tailored profile or permission set limiting what objects and fields it can read or write. If an agent like HR Onboarding Agent only needs access to Employee records and sending welcome emails, it should not have permission to view financial records or modify security settings. By constraining the agent's operating user, even if the agent tries to do something out-of-scope, the platform would prevent it.

Salesforce's field-level security and object permissions apply to any actions the agent performs through Apex or flows if executed in user context. When using Flow, you can choose to run a flow in system context or user context. For governance, consider running agent actions in user context tied to an "AI Agent" user profile. This adds overhead (you must manage that user's permissions), but it creates an audit trail and safety net. Every data modification by an agent will show up as done by that integration user, which is useful in logs and helps with compliance audits.

If an agent needs to call an external API or service, apply similar API key management. Don't give one agent a key that has broader access than necessary. For instance, if an agent uses a cloud storage API only to fetch certain files, its API token should be scoped to read-only on the specific bucket or directory, not full admin of the storage account.

Agent Registry and Lifecycle Management: In previous sections, we touched on maintaining an Agent Registry (potentially via custom metadata or objects). From a governance perspective, this registry is a source of truth for oversight. It should list all active agents, who approved/created them, what purpose they serve, and when they were last reviewed. Many organizations might set up an AI Governance Board or similar body that reviews any new AI agent before deployment. By consulting the registry, one can ensure no agent goes unaccounted. The registry can also hold metadata like "Compliance Rating" or "Risk Level" for each agent. For example, an agent that merely summarizes public knowledge might be low-risk, whereas an agent that handles customer personally identifiable information (PII) or makes financial recommendations would be tagged high-risk and require more stringent controls.

You might integrate the registry with Salesforce's change management process. If using DevOps Center or changesets, treat agent definitions as first-class metadata. Perhaps even write a script that exports the registry to a document for quarterly compliance review meetings. Additionally, consider automating notifications when certain changes happen: e.g., if someone marks a new agent as "Active" in metadata, send an email to the governance team for awareness.

Approval Workflow for Agent Changes: Implement a policy that significant changes to agents (like enabling a new agent, granting it broader data access, or updating its core prompt with compliance ramifications) require approval. This could be managed outside the system (via meetings or a JIRA ticket) or within Salesforce (for instance, an approver could have to mark an

"Approved" checkbox in the Agent registry metadata before an agent can be activated). This ensures oversight. In some industries, you might even need compliance officer sign-off and documentation showing you evaluated the agent for biases, etc., before going live.

Data Compliance (Privacy & Security): Multi-agent systems often process sensitive data. Ensure your design adheres to data protection laws (like GDPR, HIPAA, etc. depending on your domain). Key strategies:

Minimize Data Exposure: If an agent doesn't need a certain piece of personal data, do not include it in the prompt or context. For example, a sales analysis agent likely doesn't need customer phone numbers – so don't fetch or pass those along. Mask or anonymize where feasible. If using an external LLM service, be extra cautious – any data sent could be stored outside your environment, so only send what's necessary and consider using anonymization (e.g., refer to customers by an ID rather than name in prompts if possible).

PII Detection: You could implement a check where certain types of data (like SSNs, credit card numbers) are stripped from agent inputs automatically. For instance, before an agent sees case description text, run it through a simple pattern mask to redact digits that look like SSNs or credit cards. Or utilize Salesforce's Einstein Data Detect or third-party libraries to scrub PII from unstructured text fed to agents.

Audit Trails: For compliance, log not just what agents do, but what they saw. If an agent accessed a record with sensitive info, you may need an audit log of that access (especially in regulated sectors). Normally user access logs handle that, but if agents run as a special user, make sure that user's data access logs are retained. Salesforce Shield's Field Audit Trail and Event Monitoring might help track data access at a high level – but custom logging might be needed for fine detail.

Retention Policies: Determine how long you keep agent-related logs, especially those containing reconstructed content or intermediate reasoning that could contain sensitive info. You may need to purge logs after X days or anonymize them. For example, you might keep full verbose logs for 7 days for debugging, then delete or aggregate them, keeping only high-level stats. Align this with company policy on log retention.

Ethical Guardrails: On top of data issues, consider the ethical behaviors of your agents. Governance might require that agents do not generate disallowed content (hate speech, harassment, etc.), maintain fairness (avoid biased decisions), and comply with industry-specific rules (e.g., financial advice agent must include disclaimers). To enforce this:

Content Filtering: Use built-in or custom content filters on outputs. For instance, if using OpenAI, use their moderation API on the agent's response before using it. Or have a Sentinel Agent whose job is to scan other agents' outputs for compliance and either sanitize or block if issues are found (this is related to the Supervisor/Review agent concept, but specifically for compliance).

Pre-defined Responses: In certain sensitive cases, restrict the agent to choose from vetted responses. For example, an agent responding to customer complaints might be constrained to use company-approved apology phrasing. This can be done by including those as guidelines in the prompt or by post-processing the agent's answer to ensure it contains required elements.

Testing for Bias: Periodically test your agents with a variety of inputs, including edge cases or inputs that could reveal bias (e.g., varying demographic details in a request to see if recommendations differ unjustifiably). This is more a process outside the system, but results might lead you to adjust training data or prompts. Document these tests as part of governance to show proactive bias mitigation.

Compliance with Regulatory Mandates: If you're in finance, healthcare, etc., there may be rules about automated decision-making. For instance, GDPR gives individuals the right not to be subject to decisions based solely on automated processing if those decisions have legal effects. If an agent is making such decisions (like approving a loan), you may need to implement an option for human review or an explanation mechanism. This ties to the Supervisor pattern – you might require a human in the loop for certain high-impact decisions, effectively making the AI an advisor rather than final authority.

In Salesforce, implementing a human approval step is straightforward with Approval Processes or a simple flow that assigns a task to a user. For example, an agent prepares a draft contract, but a human legal counsel must click "OK" before it's sent out. Your governance policy can dictate thresholds when this is needed (often based on risk or amount).

Agent Identity and Scope Clarity: Each agent should have a clearly defined scope to prevent "scope creep." This is partly technical (ensuring they only have permissions for their role) and partly prompt-level. In the agent's definition, reinforce its boundaries. E.g., "You are a Pricing Agent. You do not access customer personal data or make recommendations beyond pricing." This reduces chance of an agent stepping into another's lane. Also, in any multi-agent discussions, include an identity prefix so agents don't blur roles. Like Agent A always states "As the Compliance Agent, I think...". This can be done via system prompts or conversation structuring.

Emergency Stop: Consider implementing a "kill switch" or global off toggle for the AI system in case something goes seriously wrong (perhaps an agent starts giving harmful advice unexpectedly, etc.). This could be as simple as a global custom setting "AgentsEnabled = false" that your orchestration checks and will bypass agent calls if false (maybe default to a safe fallback or message). That way, with one config change, you can halt all autonomous actions and revert to manual or rule-based processes until issues are resolved. It's like having a big red button for the AI. Not every scenario requires this, but in high-stakes contexts it might be prudent.

Training and Awareness: Governance isn't only technical – ensure your teams (including non-developers who work with these agents) understand what the agents do and don't do. Document the system's boundaries and share that with stakeholders. For example, customer support managers should know that "Agent X can draft responses, but it never sends without human approval" or "Agent Y can automatically adjust a customer's billing plan up to $100 credit but anything beyond requires human input." By setting these expectations, you align operational processes with agent capabilities. Also, provide a channel for staff or users to report if an agent does something odd or against policy, so you can feed that back into system improvements.

Finally, tie this back into the next chapter's theme (Trust and Guardrails). Governance measures like permissions, oversight, and compliance checks directly contribute to building trust in AI systems. Guardrails (technical and procedural) ensure agents act within acceptable bounds, which increases user and stakeholder confidence. In Chapter 11, those trust mechanisms – some of which we've previewed through governance and logging – will be explored in depth, presumably focusing on designing agents to be transparent, controllable, and aligned with human and organizational values.

Pro Tip: Treat each AI agent as a virtual employee when it comes to governance. That means giving it an employee-like identity (role, department), a manager (the person or team responsible for its output), permissions like you would in an org chart, and performance reviews (regularly evaluating its outputs). This mindset helps enforce structure. For example, if you wouldn't let a junior analyst directly email a client without review, you probably shouldn't let an AI agent do so either without a safeguard. Assign an "owner" to each agent who is accountable for reviewing its behavior and updating it as policies change.

Pro Tip: Maintain a compliance log for agents that handle regulated tasks. This could be a simple custom object that records, "Agent X gave advice Y on date Z." Include any disclaimer or reference that shows compliance. For instance, if an agent gives investment advice, log the exact advice and that a disclaimer was appended. This kind of record can be invaluable if auditors come knocking or if a decision made by an agent is ever legally challenged – you have the evidence of what was done and why. Tie these entries to case IDs or customer IDs so you can trace the AI's involvement in any customer interaction end-to-end.

REAL-WORLD EXAMPLES AND ECOSYSTEM INTEGRATION (LANGCHAIN, AUTOGEN, MCP)

To ground our discussion, let's explore how multi-agent patterns manifest in real-world enterprise scenarios, and how they connect with the broader AI agent ecosystem. Organizations across industries are beginning to deploy multi-agent systems to streamline complex workflows. Meanwhile, open-source and commercial frameworks – like LangChain, Microsoft's AutoGen, and emerging protocols like MCP (Model Context Protocol) – provide tools to build and connect these agents beyond the Salesforce platform. By looking at examples and these ecosystem links, we can better envision how the Agentforce approach fits into the larger picture.

Enterprise Example 1: Customer Support Augmentation – Industry: E-commerce.

A large e-commerce company implemented a multi-agent system to improve its customer support efficiency. When a customer inquiry comes in (via email or chat), it triggers a trio of agents working in concert:

A Classifier Agent first analyzes the message to determine the issue category (billing, product info, return request, etc.).

Based on the category, an Action Agent is engaged. For example, for billing issues, a BillingAgent can pull up the customer's order and payment history; for product questions, a ProductInfoAgent fetches details from the catalog.

Finally, a Responder Agent drafts a reply to the customer, incorporating the information gathered by the Action Agent (and possibly following a template or style guide).

These agents operate under a hub orchestrator (which could be implemented in Salesforce Flow). The classifier's output directs the orchestrator which specialist agent to invoke next. Once the data is gathered by the specialist agent, it's passed to the responder agent for final message construction. In practice, this reduced average handling time significantly – straightforward queries never even needed a human, yet responses were accurate and rich because the agents tapped into real data. The company maintained governance by keeping a human supervisor in the loop for certain sensitive categories (e.g., complaints about policy triggered an agent to draft a response but wait for human approval). This is a real-world pattern many companies are now trying, essentially combining triage, automation, and content generation.

Notably, parts of this solution leveraged external frameworks: the company used LangChain to build the Responder Agent's natural language capabilities. LangChain provided a convenient way to integrate a large language model and define prompt templates for the reply (including customer context and the Action Agent's findings). Because LangChain's LangGraph supports multi-agent orchestration with tools and memory, it was relatively straightforward to connect it: Salesforce passed the necessary context (customer info, classification) to a LangChain agent which then composed the answer and returned it to Salesforce to send out. This highlights how Salesforce Agentforce can interoperate with external agent frameworks – you don't have to reinvent the NLP wheel on the platform if a specialized library can do it, as long as you integrate via API.

Enterprise Example 2: Financial Research Co-Pilot – Industry: Investment Banking.

A bank built an internal research assistant for analysts, which is essentially a multi-agent research workflow. The user can ask a question like "Analyze the impact of oil prices on our energy sector portfolio." Behind the scenes, multiple agents activate:

A Query Planner Agent (akin to a manager) breaks this request into subtasks: (1) retrieve relevant data (oil price trends, portfolio composition), (2) perform analysis (correlation or regression), (3) draft a summary of findings.

For data retrieval, it calls a Data Agent that's integrated with the bank's data warehouse (via APIs). That agent might itself consist of sub-steps: it runs an SQL query or calls a data API to get price and performance data.

An Analysis Agent then takes the raw data and maybe uses Python tools (via an API or a service like an AutoGen tool runner) to calculate correlations or other statistics. This agent could be realized with Microsoft's AutoGen framework, since AutoGen excels at enabling agents to generate and execute code dynamically for analysis.

Finally, a Report Agent (a LangChain or Salesforce agent) writes up the insights in a human-readable form, perhaps including charts or bullet points.

This example shows multi-agent and multi-tool usage. The bank might use AutoGen for the Analysis Agent because AutoGen supports agents that can generate code (like Python) and run it in an isolated environment to crunch numbers. In fact, Microsoft's AutoGen has patterns for an AssistantAgent working with a Python execution agent to do exactly that. By using AutoGen, the bank's AI team didn't have to build code-execution ability from scratch – they leveraged open-source. The Model Context Protocol (MCP) comes into play as they stitch everything together: they adopted MCP as a standardized way for these diverse agents (Salesforce-oriented ones, LangChain ones, AutoGen ones) to share context. MCP acted like a common language or interchange format: the Query Planner in Salesforce could package the subtask instructions in an MCP-defined format, which the AutoGen agent understood and responded to in kind. Essentially, MCP allowed the Salesforce Flow orchestrator (hub) to call out to external agents in a structured way and then reintegrate their results. One LinkedIn case study demonstrated AutoGen + MCP enabling such coordination, where agents built in different frameworks conversed seamlessly via MCP as a bridge.

The result for the bank: a powerful research co-pilot that significantly sped up analysis. What used to take an analyst a day of number-crunching and writing, the AI co-pilot could assist in doing within minutes – with the analyst now validating and fine-tuning the output rather than doing all grunt work. And because they used open frameworks, the solution is flexible: they can upgrade the LangChain or AutoGen components independently as those evolve, and MCP ensures interoperability. As one tech lead put it, "AutoGen and MCP together make this vision practical" for enterprise-grade multi-agent systems.

Enterprise Example 3: Cross-Department Process Orchestration – Industry: Manufacturing.

A manufacturing firm implemented a multi-agent system to streamline new product introduction, which touches multiple departments. The process goes like this: when a new product idea is proposed, an orchestrator agent kicks off to coordinate:

An Engineering Agent reads the proposal and generates a draft spec (bill of materials, design notes) using past similar product data as reference.

A Market Research Agent (leveraging an LLM via LangChain) conducts a quick analysis of market trends for the product category – it might query external market data APIs or internal sales databases to forecast demand.

A Compliance Agent (built on Salesforce) checks the draft spec against regulatory requirements (for safety, environmental regulations, etc.), using a rules database.

Then a Project Planning Agent compiles inputs from engineering, marketing, and compliance to create a high-level project plan: timeline, cost estimate, identified risks. This agent might actually be powered by something like Microsoft Project or an internal tool – the AI agent populates a template project plan document.

Finally, a Summary Agent (perhaps Salesforce Einstein or an AutoGen agent) writes an executive summary for decision-makers, highlighting key points: market opportunity, estimated cost, compliance flags, etc.

This all happens in a coordinated fashion orchestrated by Salesforce Flow and Apex. They integrated external analysis via LangChain (for market research) and internal rule checking via an engine in Salesforce for compliance. Notably, they used Crew (a hypothetical example akin to LangChain or a newer framework) for agent collaboration: a CrewAI coordinator helped different agents built in different languages talk to each other. To ensure everything stayed in sync, they again used a protocol like MCP or a custom JSON-based context passing. The Model Context Protocol (MCP) in particular allowed their Salesforce orchestrator to treat an external market analysis agent (running on a Python server) and an internal Apex compliance agent uniformly – it would send a structured context containing the product info and required outputs, and each agent would fill its part and return context updates.

From an ecosystem perspective, this example shows how multiple frameworks and services can be knitted together: Salesforce for orchestration and internal data, LangChain for heavy NLP and external data queries, possibly AutoGen or similar for dynamic planning/coding tasks, and a protocol like MCP to glue them. The alternative would have been to build everything on one platform, which might not leverage each component's strength. By integrating, the firm achieved a robust system relatively quickly. One engineer noted that using LangChain and AutoGen shaved months off development, because they could use pre-built agents for common tasks (like web research or code execution).

LangChain vs AutoGen in practice: In these examples, we see a pattern: LangChain tends to be used where flexible integration of LLMs and tools is needed with a lot of customization – e.g., crafting the exact prompts for summarizing market data or doing a Q&A. It offers that flexibility and the ability to maintain state or multiple agents in a graph, which enterprises used to tailor to their domain. AutoGen, by contrast, shines in letting agents create and execute code or in setting up multi-agent conversations easily (like an assistant agent and a user proxy agent chatting). Enterprises experimenting with it found it valuable for scenarios like the financial analysis, where the agent might need to compute something on the fly (which essentially means writing a bit of Python or using a tool). Both frameworks, as a Medium article notes, have complementary strengths: LangChain for flexible control and varied communication channels, AutoGen for modular agent patterns and event-driven interactions.

Integration with Salesforce Agentforce: Salesforce's AI Cloud (Agentforce) is positioned to incorporate these advances. Through Apex and external services, Salesforce can call LangChain or AutoGen processes. Conversely, Salesforce's data and process strengths can complement them (providing the CRM data or workflow triggers). We already see Salesforce enabling such connections; for instance, there are demo integrations where a LangChain agent is invoked from a Salesforce Flow to handle a complex query, then the result is brought back into Salesforce to take action (like update records or post a chatter message). Similarly, MCP being an open protocol means if Salesforce adopts it or at least aligns to it, agents running on Salesforce could participate in a multi-platform agent society. In one demo, an agent in Salesforce and an agent running externally were able to coordinate because they adhered to the same MCP message format (the external one was decorated to understand MCP messages, making it plug-and-play).

MCP's promise: Model Context Protocol aims to be for AI agents what HTTP is for web servers – a standard way to communicate. In our enterprise examples, MCP allowed an AutoGen agent and a LangChain agent to share a "context" including tools and memory. Imagine in the future a Salesforce agent could invoke any third-party agent that speaks MCP just by sending a context packet (e.g., "Here is the user request, here are available tools, proceed."). The receiving agent, regardless of framework, can parse it and act, then return an MCP context update with its results. This interoperability means enterprises aren't locked in – they can mix and match best-of-breed agents from different vendors. We see early signs: the integration of AutoGen + MCP mentioned earlier led to a seamless workflow where developers combined Microsoft and OpenAI tech with their own APIs.

One can foresee ecosystem links growing: LangChain might integrate connectors to Salesforce (indeed, there are community tools for that), AutoGen might offer Salesforce-specific patterns (like an agent that can act through the Salesforce Metadata API or do SOQL queries directly). Meanwhile, Salesforce could incorporate open-source adapters to call out to LangChain agents as invocable actions.

Real-world outcome: Enterprises that have piloted multi-agent systems often report a jump in productivity or capability – but also note the need for careful oversight. For example, the bank's co-pilot saved analysts hours, but they still require a human check for any recommendations to clients (trust but verify). The e-commerce support reduced human involvement for simple queries by 50%, freeing agents to handle complex issues. These examples underscore that multi-agent systems are not theoretical; they're being applied and bringing value now. They also highlight the synergy between Salesforce's platform and the wider AI ecosystem: using Salesforce for what it excels at (data integrity, user interface, business process) while offloading some heavy AI reasoning to specialized frameworks, all coordinated in one harmonious system.

To wrap up, as we integrate these frameworks:

LangChain provides that flexible orchestration of LLMs and tools, which an enterprise can use within or alongside Salesforce to implement sophisticated reasoning chains.

AutoGen offers a ready way to spin up multi-agent conversations and even let agents write code for tasks, which can supercharge automation in domains like data analysis or code generation.

MCP and similar standards will increasingly ensure these pieces can talk to each other, meaning your Salesforce agents can be part of a larger agent ecosystem – you could have, say, an Einstein GPT agent in Salesforce collaborate with an Azure AutoGen agent and a Google PaLM agent in real time, each bringing unique strengths, to solve enterprise problems.

As one publication summarized: "Multi-agent AI systems represent the next evolution of enterprise AI — moving beyond single-purpose tools to coordinated networks of specialized agents that think collaboratively and scale across functions". Our journey through examples and ecosystem tools reinforces that: the future (in fact, the present) is a rich tapestry of cooperating AI agents, and with the design principles we've discussed, you're equipped to weave these into your own enterprise solutions.

Pro Tip: Stay updated on open standards and frameworks for multi-agent systems. The landscape is evolving quickly (what's cutting-edge today – LangChain, AutoGen, MCP – might be joined by new players soon). By modularizing your system and using protocols like MCP, you make it easier to plug in improvements. Today's experimental library could be tomorrow's enterprise workhorse, so design with interchangeability in mind. For instance, you might abstract your agent calls behind Apex interfaces; if you decide to swap out a LangChain agent for an updated MCP-compliant service from another vendor, you can do so with minimal disruption. Embracing standards and loose coupling to specific tools will "future-proof" your multi-agent architecture amid the ecosystem's rapid innovation.

Pro Tip: Leverage the community and pre-built agents when possible. Frameworks like LangChain come with a zoo of ready-made agents (for web search, SQL query, etc.), and Microsoft's AutoGen provides preset agent classes (like an AssistantAgent vs. a UserProxyAgent). Before coding an agent from scratch, check if the ecosystem has something you can adapt. For example, if you need an agent to answer questions over documents, LangChain has QA chains that might fulfill much of your requirement. Using these can drastically cut development time and benefit from collective testing by the community. Just be sure to validate and fine-tune them for your enterprise context (security and accuracy), but don't reinvent the wheel if a solid one is freely available.

Summary

Multi-agent systems usher in a new paradigm of AI in the enterprise, where multiple specialized agents collaborate to deliver outcomes that were once beyond reach. In this chapter, we journeyed from the foundational steps of multi-agent design to the complexities of orchestration in the real world. We saw how defining clear agent roles and boundaries (often guided by the single-responsibility principle) is the bedrock for modular, maintainable systems. Building on that, we explored collaboration patterns – whether a simple linear chain of agents, a central hub orchestrating many spokes, or iterative feedback loops for refinement. Each pattern offers tools to tackle complexity, from distributed reasoning across agents to fault tolerance when one component falters.

Crucially, we translated these patterns into practical implementation on Salesforce. By marrying Salesforce's Agent Builder and Flow Orchestration with Apex extensibility and metadata-driven configs, we can deploy multi-agent workflows that are both powerful and governed. We emphasized observability – implementing logging, monitoring, and graceful failover strategies so that these AI systems can be trusted in production. Governance, permissions, and compliance formed another key theme: multi-agent intelligence must operate within the guardrails of enterprise policy and ethics. Through careful permission scopes, agent registries, and oversight mechanisms, we ensure our AI teammates are reliable and accountable, not rogue free agents. These guardrails – technical and procedural – reinforce stakeholder trust in AI outcomes.

Finally, looking outward, we connected our Salesforce-centric approach with the broader ecosystem. We illustrated with real-world examples how frameworks like LangChain and AutoGen, and protocols like MCP, integrate with enterprise workflows. The takeaway is that Salesforce's multi-agent capabilities do not exist in a silo; they complement and interoperate with a growing AI landscape. This means an enterprise can leverage the best of all worlds: orchestrating secure, compliant processes in Salesforce while tapping external AI services and libraries for their strengths. We saw multi-agent systems applied to customer support, financial analysis, product development – and in each case, the combination of specialized agents working in concert led to breakthroughs in efficiency and insight.

As we conclude this chapter, a few themes stand out. Modularity and reusability have proven critical – by designing agents as interchangeable parts with well-defined roles, we built systems that can scale and adapt. Coordination and communication were the glue – patterns and protocols ensure that agents don't work at cross purposes but rather as a team. And underpinning all of this is a strong layer of trust and governance – the knowledge that we can monitor what agents do, set limits on their actions, and align them with human and organizational values. This alignment is where we transition next.

In Chapter 11: Trust and Guardrails, we will dive deeper into how to maintain control and confidence as AI agents take on greater responsibilities. We'll examine techniques to ensure agents remain aligned with their intended goals and constraints, methods for explaining and validating their decisions, and how to handle the ethical and risk dimensions of autonomous systems. In many ways, trust is the sum total of everything we've discussed – from clear design to rigorous monitoring – and it deserves its own focused discussion. Chapter 11 will equip you with strategies to implement robust guardrails, so that the multi-agent systems you build not only achieve performance, but do so safely, transparently, and in a manner that earns the trust of users and regulators alike. The journey to harnessing multi-agent intelligence in the enterprise continues, with trust as our guiding principle. Let's ensure our AI agents remain responsible partners as we venture into this exciting future of collaborative AI.

11

BUILDING AGENTS WITH TRUST AND GUARDRAILS

In enterprise AI, trust is the foundation – without it, even the most capable agent will never leave the lab. Salesforce's Agentforce platform was built with the conviction that AI agents must be secure, transparent, auditable, and aligned with core ethical principles from day one. Enterprise teams need to know exactly what their AI agents are doing, why they're doing it, and how to control them. In fact, early AI agent deployments revealed a clear blocker: lack of visibility and governance made organizations hesitant to scale up autonomous agents. Agents operating without guardrails could inadvertently expose sensitive data or make harmful decisions, jeopardizing customer trust and violating regulations. To harness AI's benefits in business, we have to design for trust by default.

Salesforce responds to this challenge by baking in Trusted AI principles at every layer of Agentforce. "It is not enough to deliver only the technological capabilities of AI – we also have an important responsibility to ensure that AI is safe and inclusive for all," Salesforce's Office of Ethical and Humane Use declared. Trusted AI principles like responsibility, accountability, transparency, empowerment, and inclusivity are not just lofty ideals – they directly inform how we build and deploy agents. For example, Agentforce agents are required to respect data security and user permissions, explaining their actions and sourcing answers from verifiable data where possible. They come with built-in safeguards against bias and toxicity (via the Einstein Trust Layer) to filter harmful outputs before any content reaches users. They even follow transparency patterns like automatic AI disclosure –

clearly indicating when an agent-generated content or recommendation is AI-created – so there's no confusion between human and machine guidance. In short, trust isn't an afterthought; it's architected into the agent's very role.

In this chapter, we explore how to build Agentforce agents with robust guardrails to meet enterprise trust requirements. We'll look at how to design agents that are secure in accessing data and taking actions, transparent in their reasoning and outputs, and auditable in their decisions – all aligned with Salesforce's Trusted AI guidelines for accuracy, safety, honesty, and empowerment. We'll dive into specific implementation strategies using Salesforce-native tools: the Agent Builder for declaratively defining what an agent can (and cannot) do, Topics and Actions as built-in permission scaffolds, and techniques like Invocable Apex and Flow Orchestration to enforce business logic guardrails. We'll see how permission sets and user context act as security sandboxes for agents, how metadata-driven policies (like the Einstein Trust Layer configuration) can mask sensitive information and enforce compliance, and how the new Agentforce Command Center provides end-to-end observability – a "single pane of glass" to monitor and audit agent activities in real time.

Crucially, we will map these guardrail techniques to the Agentforce pattern catalog introduced earlier in this playbook. Each agent pattern – whether an Action agent executing tasks, a Supervisor agent enforcing policy, a Coach agent guiding users, a Presenter agent delivering information, a Conductor agent orchestrating workflows, or other patterns – faces unique trust challenges. For each, we'll discuss pattern-specific guardrail strategies. How do we prevent an Action Agent from running wild with destructive changes? How can a Supervisor Agent remain fair and explain its decisions? In what ways should a Coach Agent be constrained to give helpful yet compliant advice? What makes a Presenter Agent credible and factually correct in what it shows? How does a Conductor Agent safely coordinate multiple systems or even multiple sub-agents without losing control? We'll address all these questions with concrete techniques and real Salesforce platform features.

Throughout, we'll also contrast Salesforce's enterprise-centric approach to trust with other tools in the AI ecosystem. Open frameworks like LangChain or multi-agent systems like CrewAI give developers flexibility but often require hand-built guardrails for safety – essentially, you're on your own to implement filtering, permissions, and logging. Microsoft's Copilot Studio provides a managed way to build AI assistants in the M365 environment, but its guardrails are mostly tied to Microsoft's ecosystem (e.g. relying on Azure OpenAI's content filters and Microsoft Graph permissions). In Agentforce, by comparison, trust and governance are first-class citizens: every agent action passes through Salesforce's secure architecture and is governed by platform rules and audit trails. Agentforce "pairs open connectivity with enterprise-grade trust," delivering interoperability without compromising on control. We will highlight these differences not to disparage other approaches, but to illuminate how Agentforce's patterns and toolset uniquely empower architects to deploy AI agents that earn the trust of security teams, end users, and regulators alike.

By the end of this chapter, you will understand how to embed guardrails at each stage of an AI agent's life cycle – from design-time restrictions in Agent Builder, to runtime oversight via Command Center, to post-run auditing and feedback loops. The following sections each focus on a major Agentforce pattern or use-case category, detailing how to apply Salesforce-native safety mechanisms and governance best practices for that pattern. As we step through these patterns (Action, Supervisor, Coach, Presenter, Conductor, Curator, and Companion), watch for the recurring theme: trusted agents marry capability with control. With the right guardrails in place, an AI agent can be as autonomous as you want, while staying firmly within the boundaries you set – thus delivering business value "with clarity and control". Let's dive into the specifics of building agents you and your stakeholders can trust.

GUARDRAILS FOR THE ACTION PATTERN: SAFE AUTONOMY IN ENTERPRISE TASKS

Action agents are AI agents empowered to execute tasks on our behalf – creating or updating records, sending communications, escalating issues, and so on. They are the "doers" of the agent world, turning decisions into tangible outcomes. Unsurprisingly, the Action pattern carries the highest immediate risk if misconfigured. An unchecked Action agent could, for example, send out incorrect invoices, delete critical data, or make unauthorized changes at scale. Designing a trustworthy Action agent means enabling useful autonomy without giving it free rein over the enterprise. We achieve this by enforcing strict boundaries on what the agent can do, requiring approvals or checkpoints for sensitive actions, and maintaining an audit trail of every step.

In Salesforce's Agentforce, the first line of defense is the Agent Builder configuration itself. When you define an agent's Topics and Actions, you are essentially programming its permissions and skills in a declarative way.

Topics delineate the scope of the agent's knowledge and operations – in other words, the domains in which it's allowed to act. Each topic comes with an explicit set of Action definitions (which are often implemented as Flows, Apex invocable methods, or external API calls) that the agent can execute. Anything outside those topics and actions is off-limits. If a user asks an Action agent to do something it doesn't have a topic for, the agent will politely refuse or report it cannot help – this is by design. In fact, during early demos, Agentforce agents simply could not fulfill requests that fell outside their assigned topics, and Salesforce highlights this as a guardrail: the agent's inability to perform unassigned tasks is a feature, not a bug. By carefully scoping topics, you prevent an Action agent from straying into areas it shouldn't touch.

Whitelisting allowed actions is a critical guardrail. In Agentforce, every action the agent might take (e.g. "Create Case", "Update Opportunity Stage", "Send Contract for Signature") must be explicitly attached to a topic and thereby explicitly granted. Under the hood, these actions are backed by trusted automation like Salesforce Flows or Apex routines that you (the developer/architect) control. Because you build or vet those flows/Apex, you can bake in additional safety logic – for example, a Flow could include decision elements to check conditions ("only proceed if Opportunity Amount < $100,000") or an Apex invocable method might validate inputs and abort if something looks off. This means the agent never directly writes to the database or calls an API; it invokes a predefined piece of business logic that has all the necessary checks. Guardrails are thus applied at two levels: first at the capability level (the agent can only call allowed actions), and second at the action implementation level (each action has internal safeguards).

Let's illustrate with a scenario. Suppose we have an Action agent for customer support that can open cases, reset passwords, or send a follow-up email. In Agent Builder, we'd create topics like "Account Support" or "Password Reset" and assign actions such as OpenSupportCase (Flow), ResetPassword (Flow), SendEmail (Flow). Each of those flows is built with guardrails: ResetPassword Flow might require the agent to provide a reason code and log the event to an audit object, and maybe even call an approval if a high-privilege account is involved. The SendEmail Flow could be limited to using approved email templates and will CC a supervisor for any customer-facing messages. By pre-defining these flows, we ensure the agent cannot generate a completely arbitrary email or execute a password reset without proper logging. The agent is powerful but constrained – it has the tools to solve the customer's problem, but only within the sandbox we've designed.

Another key aspect is using the Salesforce security model to our advantage. An Action agent should operate under a dedicated integration user or running user context with minimal permissions. Even though the agent's allowed actions are gated via topics, using Salesforce's standard permission sets and profiles provides a belt-and-suspenders approach. For example, you might create an "Agent User" profile that only permits read/write on specific objects and fields the agent truly needs, and no access to high-risk objects. If the agent somehow tries to access something outside its zone, platform security will stop it. This leverages Salesforce's proven role-based access controls as an additional guardrail. In essence, the agent gets a virtual driver's license with clear endorsements: it can drive certain vehicles (perform certain actions) but is not allowed on others. It is also prudent to utilize field-level security and object CRUD settings to ensure the agent cannot see or modify sensitive fields (like salary, SSN, etc.) even if a buggy action tried to. These layers align with the principle of least privilege – a cornerstone of enterprise security.

Human oversight is another consideration for Action agents. Not every agent-initiated action should happen silently. For high-impact transactions, a human-in-the-loop checkpoint can provide a critical fail-safe. Salesforce Flow offers elements like Approval Processes or Screen Flows that can pause for human confirmation. One pattern is to let the agent prepare an action but require a user click "Accept" before it's executed. For instance, an agent could draft a contract amendment and route it to a salesperson for review before sending. This approach aligns with Salesforce's empowerment principle – AI should augment, not fully replace, especially where judgment is required. You wouldn't want an AI unilaterally offering a discount to a customer without a salesperson's sign-off, for example. By designing these checkpoints (perhaps configurable by a risk threshold), you combine automation with human governance.

Alongside proactive controls, monitoring and logging form the reactive guardrails that catch any issues and enable auditing. The Agentforce Command Center and underlying telemetry give us deep visibility into every action the agent takes. Each agent session can be recorded, with timestamps of each step, the prompts, the chosen actions, and the outcomes – all stored in a session tracing log in Data Cloud. This means if an agent does something unexpected, you have a forensic trail to investigate. In practice, you should also consider building custom logs for critical actions: e.g., a custom "Agent Action Log" object where your flows write an entry for any case created or email sent by the agent, capturing fields like Agent Name,

Action, Target Record, and a status. This redundancy ensures that even outside the Command Center UI, your org has a permanent record of agent activity (useful for compliance and auditing). Many compliance regimes (like SOX in finance or HIPAA in healthcare) require auditable records of system actions – by logging agent actions just like user actions, you satisfy this requirement. Agentforce's native audit metadata (every prompt and response can be recorded as metadata events) further bolsters this, simplifying compliance reporting.

Finally, there's the question of error handling and fail-safe modes. A trustworthy Action agent should be built to fail safely. If the agent encounters a situation outside its knowledge or permissions, it should not attempt a risky workaround; it should either defer to a human or fail gracefully. For example, if a customer asks our support agent to perform a task it doesn't know, the agent might respond, "I'm sorry, I can't assist with that request," rather than attempting something unpredictable. From a design perspective, this is achieved by ensuring the agent's LLM prompt instructions include guidance to not act outside its scope, and by not assigning any "catch-all" action that could be abused. It's better for the agent to do nothing than to do the wrong thing. In testing, make sure to simulate out-of-scope requests and verify the agent responds with a safe fallback. Salesforce's Testing Center (part of Agentforce Studio) can simulate various scenarios to see how the agent handles them. Use those tools to pressure-test your Action agents under edge conditions.

Pro Tip: When first deploying an Action agent, run it in a "shadow mode" before giving it free rein. Let the agent make recommendations or draft actions (e.g., log its intended changes or post them to a private Chatter group) without actually executing them for a period of time. Observe its decisions and get human experts to review them. This trial phase builds confidence and uncovers any logic gaps while a human can still intervene. Only once the agent consistently makes good choices should you allow it to act autonomously. This phased rollout ensures you tune the guardrails under real-world conditions, catching missteps early.

GUARDRAILS FOR THE SUPERVISOR PATTERN: POLICY ENFORCEMENT AND OVERSIGHT

If Action agents are the doers, Supervisor agents are the watchers and enforcers. A Supervisor agent's role is to monitor activities (by users, systems, or other agents) and ensure compliance with policies, standards, or best practices. Examples include an agent that monitors customer chats for offensive language and intervenes, or one that reviews field updates for potential data quality issues, or an agent that oversees sales discount approvals to flag any that violate policy. These agents operate as a kind of AI auditor or moderator. Trust and guardrails for Supervisor agents focus on consistency, fairness, explainability, and restraint – the Supervisor must enforce rules accurately and without bias, and it must not overstep its authority (e.g. taking punitive action without human review, unless explicitly allowed).

To build a trusted Supervisor agent, start by clearly defining the policies or rulesets it is meant to uphold. Salesforce provides multiple ways to encode policies: you might use Decision Tables in Flow, custom Metadata Types for rules, or even an external policy engine. The key is to have an explicit source of truth for the rules the agent should enforce. For instance, if the agent monitors chat for harassment, define what "harassment" means (perhaps a list of forbidden words or phrases, or a toxicity score threshold). If it's watching for GDPR violations, maybe a rule is "no customer PII should be shared in Slack" – define PII (emails, phone numbers, etc.) in a data table or detection algorithm. By externalizing policy definitions, you make the Supervisor agent's job transparent and adjustable. This also makes audits easier: compliance officers can review the rule definitions directly, rather than the inscrutable weights of an ML model. In Agentforce, you might implement this by creating a Supervisor Topic with associated actions that perform checks. For example, a "Compliance Supervisor" topic might have an action "ScanMessageForPII" which is backed by an Apex class that uses regex or Einstein Data Detect APIs to identify sensitive data in text.

One powerful guardrail for Supervisor agents is to run them in a monitor-only mode initially. That is, let the agent observe and flag issues, but not actually prevent or change anything in the early stages. Salesforce's platform events and Einstein Trust Layer can assist here. For instance, the Einstein Trust Layer can be configured to scan prompts or outputs for toxicity and simply flag them (score them) without blocking. Your Supervisor agent could subscribe to these events or scores and log a finding whenever something crosses a threshold. By monitoring first, you gather data on how often real violations occur and how accurate the agent's detection is, before empowering it to take action. This is analogous to a new security guard who first reports incidents to a supervisor rather than directly reprimanding employees. Over time, if the agent's judgments prove sound, you might grant it more autonomy (e.g. automatically hiding a message that's certainly toxic, while still notifying a human).

Even when a Supervisor agent is allowed to act, human override and review should be built in for most scenarios. Think of how Salesforce's standard approval processes allow for auto-approval criteria but always have a human chain for exceptions – similarly, a Supervisor agent might auto-approve or auto-reject routine cases but escalate edge cases. For example, if a sales rep gives a 5% discount (within policy), the agent auto-approves it; if they try 50%, the agent can automatically reject it but also notify a sales manager or log it for review. Having a "second pair of eyes" on significant enforcement actions ensures that if the agent errs, a human can correct it before harm is done. This aligns with the accountability principle: the organization remains accountable, and thus a human should be in the loop for anything high-stakes. It's also good for user trust – employees will accept an AI supervisor if they know there's an appeal process or that a human has final say on contentious calls.

For a Supervisor agent to be trusted, it must be impartial and explainable. Bias in enforcement can be a big concern (e.g., does an AI supervisor flag certain employees or certain phrases more often due to training data bias?). To mitigate this, leverage diverse training data and ethical assessments if using ML for detection (Salesforce's guidelines emphasize bias testing and red-teaming for safety). Moreover, design the agent to explain its reasoning whenever it flags something. In Agentforce, you can achieve this by including the rationale in the agent's response or log. If the agent closes a case for non-compliance, have it add a note: "Closed by AI Supervisor because: The case description contained a credit card number, violating policy ABC." This level of transparency (the why behind the decision) is crucial. It not only helps humans understand and trust the agent's decisions, but also helps in auditing – you can later review if the rationale was valid. Supervisor agents should ideally provide evidence: if it flagged an outbound email as sensitive, it might highlight the exact snippet of text that triggered it (much like how track changes work). All this reflects Salesforce's honesty and transparency values in AI.

From an implementation standpoint, Salesforce offers several native tools to support Supervisor patterns. Einstein Data Detect can find PII or sensitive info in text fields, and could be part of an agent's toolkit. Apex can utilize the Content Detector or Einstein OCR to scan documents for keywords (for example, scanning uploaded contracts for forbidden clauses). Flow Orchestration might be used to run periodic checks – e.g., nightly run a flow that has the agent review all cases closed that day for quality issues. The Omni-Supervisor for Agentforce, as noted at Dreamforce '24, provides a UI to see agents and recent interactions – this can be repurposed so human supervisors can also supervise the AI supervisors! The Agentforce Command Center itself is a huge boon: it can trigger real-time alerts when an agent's metrics go out of bounds. For instance, if our Supervisor agent starts flagging an unusually high number of messages (maybe due to a bug causing false positives), Command Center analytics would show a spike in that agent's intervention rate, prompting the team to investigate.

Let's not forget regulatory compliance guardrails. Supervisor agents often directly intersect with regulations: monitoring communications touches privacy laws, enforcing financial controls touches SOX, etc. A best practice is to consult with compliance officers to formalize the agent's role. For example, under GDPR, if an agent is monitoring user-generated content for personal data, you must ensure this processing is covered in your data privacy agreements (since it's effectively an automated processing of personal data). Fortunately, Salesforce's platform is built with compliance in mind – data processed by Agentforce stays within the Salesforce Trust Boundary and isn't used to train models outside your instance. Features like Field Audit Trail and Event Monitoring can store evidence of what data was accessed or changed by the agent. If a regulator asks, "how do you ensure no one shares health info improperly?" you can demonstrate: our Supervisor agent scans all messages and we keep a log of any detections along with outcomes. Moreover, if the agent itself makes a mistake (false positive or false negative), you have the logs to trace it. In sensitive areas like healthcare (HIPAA), you might add an extra guardrail: have the Supervisor agent not only block something but also notify a compliance officer when a HIPAA keyword appears, ensuring the incident is reviewed and properly reported if needed.

One pattern that often emerges is using Supervisor agents in tandem with Action agents or others: a checks-and-balances system. For instance, you might have an Action agent proposing resolutions to cases, and a Supervisor agent that evaluates those resolutions for tone and accuracy before they are sent to the customer. This "two agents are better than one" approach can significantly reduce risk. It mirrors the real world where a colleague reviews another's work. In Agentforce, you can implement this by chaining topics: the Action agent generates an answer (say to a customer query) but doesn't directly send it; instead, it hands it off internally to a Supervisor agent (perhaps via an internal event or a hidden field) that runs a check (like toxicity score or validation against knowledge base). Only if the Supervisor gives a green light does an Action (send message) occur. This essentially creates a human-in-the-loop scenario without a human, using two AI agents to cross-verify. It's worth noting, however, that complexity grows with such designs – you need to carefully manage the interplay to avoid deadlocks or conflicting agents. Agentforce's upcoming MCP (Model Context Protocol) support could facilitate multi-agent orchestration with governance, as it's meant to standardize such hand-offs with security and identity in mind. The Conductor pattern (discussed later) might also be relevant here to coordinate multi-agent workflows.

In summary, a Supervisor agent is like an AI compliance officer or moderator embedded in your processes. To trust it, you give it clear laws to enforce, tools to enforce them fairly, and oversight to ensure it doesn't become overzealous. You use Salesforce tech – from flows and Apex for rule enforcement to Command Center for watching the watchers – to implement these guardrails. The goal is a Supervisor agent that reliably catches issues before they cause damage but does so in a way that users find fair and leaders can audit.

Pro Tip: Use scoring and thresholds to tune your Supervisor agents' sensitivity. Many detection algorithms (toxicity, spam, anomaly detection) produce a risk score. Instead of a binary yes/no, leverage a tiered approach: e.g., if toxicity score is mild, the agent simply warns or highlights the content; if it's high, the agent might block the content or escalate to HR. Store these threshold values in Custom Metadata (e.g., "ToxicityWarnThreshold=0.5, ToxicityBlockThreshold=0.9") so they can be adjusted without code. This way, you can calibrate the agent over time – avoiding both false negatives and false positives. A well-tuned Supervisor agent that strikes the right balance will gain the trust of the user community far faster than one that's too strict or too lax.

GUARDRAILS FOR THE CONDUCTOR PATTERN: CONTROLLED ORCHESTRATION AT SCALE

The Conductor pattern refers to agents that orchestrate complex workflows, processes, or even multiple other agents – much like an orchestra conductor coordinating different musicians. Conductor agents shine in scenarios that span multiple departments or systems (e.g., onboarding a new employee involves HR, IT, Facilities; a Conductor agent could coordinate the tasks across all). They can also manage multi-step processes with dependencies (for example, a "Sales Deal Conductor" agent that, once a deal is closed, triggers provisioning, notifies finance, schedules training for the client, etc.). The trust concerns for Conductor agents revolve around maintaining control and consistency across these many moving parts. When you let an AI handle an end-to-end process, you need assurance that it won't get off track, miss a step, or cause a cascade of errors. Essentially, the Conductor must not turn into a rogue symphony – it should follow the score as written.

One fundamental guardrail is to design Conductor agents with a deterministic backbone. While an LLM might be used for flexibility (e.g. to interpret an open-ended request into a series of steps), the actual orchestration logic should be encoded in a structured way. Salesforce Flow Orchestration is an ideal tool here. You can think of a Conductor agent as a Flow Orchestrator that calls sub-flows or agents and makes decisions based on their outputs. By using Flow's declarative logic, you gain all of Flow's safety features: transaction control, error handling, rollback on failure, and audit logs of each step (the Flow interview logs). For instance, if step 3 fails, you can have the flow automatically rollback steps 1-2 if needed, or mark the whole orchestration as incomplete and alert a human. This ensures that partial automation doesn't leave the business in a weird state. If our onboarding Conductor agent fails to create a laptop provisioning request in IT's system, it can roll back creating the employee's account, or at least flag the HR system that manual follow-up is needed. The orchestration flow effectively acts as a guardrail against incomplete transactions, preserving the integrity of multi-step processes.

Another important aspect is idempotency and duplicate handling. Conductor agents may be triggered by events or requests, and there's a risk that the same process gets started twice (e.g., two agents or two triggers initiate overlapping processes). To guard against this, design your Conductor's triggers and flows to detect duplicates. This could be as simple as checking "is there already an active process for this record?" using a custom status field or a record in a "Process Instance" custom object. If yes, the agent should not start a new one or should merge the intent. This prevents conflicts like two agents trying to do the same thing or performing steps out of order. Salesforce metadata can help here too – for example, define a unique external ID for processes (like using the employee ID for onboarding process) so any duplicate attempt hits a uniqueness check. The Conductor should also maintain state – perhaps using a custom object to track workflow state – so that if it stops and restarts, it knows where it left off. All these are classic workflow design considerations, now applied to autonomous agents.

Concurrency control is likewise vital. If a Conductor agent coordinates multiple parallel tasks (say, provisioning accounts in different systems), ensure that if those tasks have a dependency on each other, the agent waits or synchronizes properly. Salesforce Flow provides features like "Pause" elements and "Wait" events (e.g., waiting for a platform event or an outcome). A well-guarded Conductor agent will use these to avoid race conditions. For example, our sales deal conductor might wait for a "ProvisioningCompleted" event from the product team's system before triggering the customer training scheduling. Without that wait, it might schedule training before the product is ready – leading to a poor customer experience. By orchestrating with explicit wait conditions, the agent behaves more predictably, and stakeholders can trust it to do things in the right order.

Because Conductor agents often touch many systems, integration security is a big part of the guardrail strategy. Salesforce's Agentforce 3 update introduced the concept of MCP (Model Context Protocol) and Agent-to-Agent (A2A) support which basically allow agents to connect to external tools and other agents in a standardized, governed way. When using MCP or any integration (MuleSoft, external APIs), treat those connections with the same scrutiny as any integration: use secure credentials stored in Named Credentials, enforce OAuth scopes so the agent can only perform designated actions in the external system, and ensure all data exchange is encrypted (TLS). The Agentforce platform's "Shared Trust Boundary" means that when an agent uses an external AI service via Salesforce, data masking and zero-retention policies apply. But if your Conductor is calling, say, a third-party project management API, you must ensure only necessary data is sent and fetched. A guardrail here is to use field filtering – maybe your agent doesn't need full records from the external system, just a status field. Only retrieve and process what's needed, reducing both risk and complexity.

Error handling in orchestration warrants extra attention. A misstep by a Conductor agent can have ripple effects across systems. Thus, design your Conductor flows with compensating actions where possible. If step 4 fails after steps 1-3 succeeded, ideally automate a rollback: e.g., if step 2 created a record in System A, have a "Undo Step 2" action defined (maybe a deletion or status mark) and call it. If full automatic rollback isn't feasible, at least have the agent notify responsible owners for manual cleanup. For instance, if the final step of onboarding (creating building access badge) fails, the agent might send an email to Facilities: "Badge creation failed for Jane Doe, please handle manually." It sounds mundane, but these guardrails ensure the business process doesn't silently break. Additionally, log the error in a persistent way – e.g., update the process record to "Failed" with error details, and maybe have a dashboard of currently failed agent processes. The Command Center can aggregate agent error rates and alert you in real time if something is off. If our Conductor starts encountering errors in 30% of runs, an ops team should know immediately from a spike in error metrics, and they can investigate the cause (maybe an external API changed). This ties into observability as a guardrail: treat your agents like you treat microservices – monitor their health and set up alerts.

We should also consider guardrails against misuse or malicious triggers. If the Conductor agent can be invoked by user input (say, a user can ask "Agent, kick off X process"), ensure that only authorized users can do so and only with valid parameters. This might involve permission checks at the start of the process. For example, only managers can ask the "Onboarding Agent" to onboard a new hire; if a regular employee tries, the agent should refuse. Use the user's context and Permission Sets to enforce this (Agentforce can pass along who the requesting user is). Similarly, validate the input: if the user says "onboard John Smith", the agent should verify John Smith is indeed in the new hires list or that all required info is provided. This prevents an agent from starting a nonsense or harmful process (imagine someone prank-triggering an "offboarding" process for a colleague – the agent should not comply without proper authorization).

Interestingly, Conductor agents sometimes orchestrate not just systems but other agents – a concept emerging in multi-agent systems (where one agent may delegate sub-tasks to specialized agents). If you employ this, the guardrails multiply: you need to trust each sub-agent and also the "manager" agent. Best practice would be to limit the number of sub-agents and define clear contracts: e.g., Conductor calls a Presenter agent to generate a summary, and then an Action agent to send it. Ensure the Conductor verifies the Presenter's output (maybe checks it's not empty or not too large) before passing it on. The Conductor should also handle if a sub-agent fails or returns an error (maybe try a fallback agent or notify a human). Essentially, the Conductor becomes a Supervisor of agents in these cases, so apply similar oversight principles as above.

One more guardrail: performance and scaling limits. Orchestration can be heavy. If a Conductor agent tries to perform 100 tasks in parallel, can your org handle it? Check Salesforce governor limits, API call limits, etc. You may need to stagger or queue certain actions. For example, if onboarding 50 new hires at once, instead of hitting an external system with 50 simultaneous requests, the agent could process them in batches of 5 to avoid denial-of-service triggers. Use Platform Events or Queueable Apex for such staging. And always guard against infinite loops – since agents can trigger agents, put timeouts or max step counts. Agentforce's Atlas engine likely has protections (it won't loop infinitely on its own reasoning steps), but if you've wired up external triggers, be careful. For instance, a Conductor updates a record that inadvertently triggers the Conductor again via a trigger – that recursion must be avoided (perhaps with a custom field "ProcessInProgress" to prevent re-entry).

Pro Tip: Leverage Agentforce's testing tools and sandboxes extensively for Conductor agents. Because these agents span many systems, a full integration test is crucial. Use the Agentforce Testing Center with state injection to simulate various conditions (e.g., external system down, partial data available, user inputs missing). Also, consider creating a digital twin of the process in a lower environment: if you have a staging or UAT sandbox with integrated systems, run the Conductor agent through a complex scenario there first. This not only validates the happy path but also lets you tweak the guardrails when you find edge cases. Many orchestration issues only surface under load or unexpected sequences – better to catch them in test. A well-tested Conductor agent, with robust error handling and clear fallbacks, will be trusted by your IT and business teams to autonomously run even mission-critical processes.

GUARDRAILS FOR THE CURATOR PATTERN: FILTERING INFORMATION WITH ACCURACY

The Curator pattern is applied to agents that specialize in handling information overload – sifting through large volumes of data, curating relevant insights, and delivering just the information that a user or system needs. These agents act like intelligent research assistants or data librarians. For example, a Curator agent might scan all customer feedback and surface the top pain points, or comb through knowledge base articles to answer a specific question. Trust in Curator agents boils down to accuracy, completeness, and confidentiality. We need confidence that the agent is picking the right data (not missing something important or including something irrelevant/wrong), that it's not hallucinating answers out of thin air, and that in doing its job it's not exposing data it shouldn't (especially when dealing with lots of raw information, some could be sensitive).

A primary guardrail for Curator agents is implementing Retrieval-Augmented Generation (RAG) techniques with controls. Salesforce's Agentforce uses the Atlas Reasoning Engine which incorporates RAG – meaning the agent will query relevant data from Data Cloud or CRM before answering. To ensure accuracy, you want your Curator agent to rely on actual data rather than model memory as much as possible. This involves setting up the knowledge sources correctly: e.g., indexing your knowledge base, enabling Einstein Article Recommendations or using the Vector Database in Data Cloud for semantic search. The guardrail part is twofold: limit the agent's answers to the retrieved data (so it doesn't wander beyond evidence), and ensure the retrieval itself is scoped and filtered.

For the first, you can craft the agent's prompt or use Agentforce's settings to instruct the model to only use provided context. There's often a parameter like "If you are not sure, say you don't know" – enforce that. Salesforce's principle of accuracy calls out that if there's uncertainty, the agent should enable validation, e.g., through citations or asking a follow-up. This is why a good Curator agent might present sources or at least easily allow a user to drill down into where info came from. In implementation, you might use an Agentforce Presenter action to show a snippet of a document (we'll discuss Presenter pattern next) or simply have the agent include a reference ID from the database.

For the second part (scoping retrieval): use data category filters, queries, and security predicates. If the agent is answering a question about, say, a product, maybe restrict it to search only the product documentation and not everything. You can tag the data by topic. Additionally, respect data visibility – the agent's retrieval mechanism should run under a user context or with filters that exclude data the requesting user shouldn't see. For instance, if a manager asks a Curator agent for "employee satisfaction issues", perhaps it can pull from an HR feedback database – but if a regular employee asks, maybe it should not have access to certain HR data. This can be managed by setting up separate "knowledge indexes" with different permission scopes, or by encoding user roles in the query. Salesforce's platform allows attaching permissions to data sets (like Data Cloud uses data streams with policies). A well-guarded Curator agent will have multiple layers of filtering: by relevance (so the answer is on-point) and by permission (so the answer is appropriate for the user).

The quality of data used by a Curator agent is also a guardrail concern. Outdated or incorrect data can lead to incorrect answers. Establish a process to keep the agent's knowledge updated – whether it's scheduling re-indexing of documents or nightly syncing of data into the vector DB. If the agent is using cached knowledge (embeddings) from Data Cloud, ensure those are refreshed when source data changes. Metadata can help: mark each data entry with a last-updated timestamp and have the agent verify freshness. If data might be stale, a cautious agent should either fetch an update or alert the user that information is as of a certain date. This aligns with transparency: users should know if the curated info is potentially outdated.

Bias and completeness are subtle issues for Curators. If the underlying data has biases or gaps, the agent's curation will too. To guard against this, you might want to incorporate multiple sources and even multiple viewpoints. For example, if summarizing employee feedback, maybe ensure the agent clusters both positive and negative feedback, not just focusing on one. Tools like Einstein Discovery could be invoked to statistically verify a trend the agent spots (e.g., "is it really true that many customers mentioned pricing?" – maybe run a quick keyword frequency check via a Data Cloud query). Essentially, consider augmenting the LLM's selection with some data analytics for critical questions. That's a guardrail to avoid over-reliance on the language model's judgment of relevance.

Privacy is a huge factor for Curator agents because they may be combing through raw data that contains sensitive info. Guardrails here include data masking and anonymization. Einstein Trust Layer's Data Masking feature is particularly relevant: it can mask PII like names, emails, etc., before sending data to the LLM. If your agent will be summarizing customer support chats, you should enable masking so that if someone's credit card or phone number is in those logs, the LLM doesn't see it raw (it might see **** or a token instead). This prevents the model from accidentally leaking that info in its summary. Additionally, consider aggregating data before feeding to the agent when possible. For instance, instead of giving the agent 100 raw customer transcripts, you might pre-run an analytics query: "count of mentions of Issue X per month" and have the agent interpret those counts. By reducing exposure of raw data, you reduce risk. It's a balance – too much pre-aggregation and you lose detail, but find a sweet spot. You can also employ pseudonymization: replace real names with placeholders like "Customer A, Customer B" in the data you feed the agent, if identities aren't needed for the task.

A trustworthy Curator agent should also acknowledge uncertainty. If the agent isn't sure it found everything, it should say so. It's better an agent says "Based on the files I have, it looks like X, but I did not find information on Y" rather than giving false completeness. This behavior can be encouraged via prompt engineering: e.g., "If relevant data might be missing, include a note about it." It might also proactively suggest where to look next ("I answered from our internal knowledge base. For a more detailed answer, you might consult the engineering wiki."). Encouraging the agent to provide citations or references is one of the best guardrails for transparency. Salesforce's guideline of verifiable sources is apt – if your agent can output a list of document titles or record links it used, the user can double-check. In Agentforce, you might incorporate an action where the agent, after formulating an answer, calls a function to retrieve the URLs of the top 3 records it used, and appends those as reference links.

When integrating Curator agents with other Salesforce tech: consider using Einstein Search or Salesforce Graph APIs for structured retrieval. For example, if the agent is to retrieve customer data, a SOQL query might be more precise than an open-ended vector search. You could have the agent decide: "for this kind of query, use a direct database search vs use a knowledge vector search." That decision itself can be encoded or constrained. It's a guardrail to avoid misusing the wrong tool (LLMs sometimes try to answer from memory even when exact data exists – instead, force it to call a search action). Some developers even implement a pattern where the LLM must call a search action for certain question types, and only after search will it form an answer. This ensures the answer is grounded in actual records. In Salesforce, you can define an Invocable Action that runs a SOSL or searches an index, and in the agent prompt, make it part of the chain.

For highly regulated contexts (like legal or medical information curation), you may need an additional layer: expert review or sign-off on curated outputs. A Curator agent that summarizes legal documents should ideally have its summary reviewed by a legal counsel agent (or human lawyer) before being used. At minimum, disclaimers should be added ("This summary is AI-generated and for informational purposes, not legal advice."). In fact, Salesforce's Acceptable Use Policy disallows fully autonomous legal or medical advice generation. If your agent ventures near those areas, be very conservative: lean on retrieval of official statements rather than any generative interpretation.

One more guardrail: time-bound context. If the agent is mixing information from different time periods, it could cause confusion. Imagine a Curator agent summarizing "trends in sales over the last 5 years" – ensure it notes the timeline. Or if part of the data is pre-merger and part is post-merger, the agent should separate those. Including metadata like dates, regions, categories in the feed and instructing the agent to respect them is wise. For example, feed ": " lines to the agent and ask it to group by year in the output. Without that, an agent might combine unrelated info incorrectly.

Pro Tip: Instrument your Curator agent with feedback hooks. A great feature for info retrieval agents is to allow users to easily say "this wasn't correct" or "show me more like this". Implement a quick feedback mechanism: if the user finds the curated answer lacking or wrong, they can click a button or prompt the agent further. Capture this feedback (even if informal) as data to improve the agent. For instance, log when users ask follow-up questions indicating the first answer wasn't sufficient. Over time, analyze those logs: you might discover the agent frequently misses a particular data source or misinterprets a type of query. Then refine the retrieval process or training with those insights. By closing the loop – from user feedback back to agent improvement – you continuously sharpen the curator's accuracy. Remember, a Curator agent's trust is earned gradually by consistent correct answers, and learning from mistakes is the best path to consistency.

GUARDRAILS FOR THE COACH PATTERN: RESPONSIBLE GUIDANCE AND FEEDBACK

The Coach pattern describes agents that provide guidance, mentorship, or feedback to humans. These agents act like personal coaches, trainers, or advisors – for example, a sales coach agent that gives reps tips on their opportunities, a code review agent that offers developers suggestions, or a wellness coach agent that prompts employees to take breaks and manage stress. Coach agents often deal with behavioral and qualitative guidance, which is tricky territory: advice can impact decisions, morale, and compliance. Therefore, trust for Coach agents hinges on credibility, positivity (non-harmful motivation), personalization within appropriate bounds, and alignment with company policies and values. We want Coach agents that truly help users improve while never straying into inappropriate or biased commentary.

First and foremost, a Coach agent's guidance must be grounded in sound knowledge or policy. If a sales coach agent suggests next steps to close a deal, those suggestions should reflect proven best practices (perhaps drawn from past win/loss data or official training materials). One effective guardrail is to equip the Coach agent with a knowledge base of coaching guidelines. For example, provide it a curated set of "sales playbook" points or a model answer for certain situations. In Salesforce, this could be done by giving the agent access to a custom object or dataset of tips keyed by context (industry, stage, etc.), and having the agent retrieve relevant entries. Essentially, treat it partially like a Curator: rather than generating free-form advice, it's assembling advice from a vetted library plus some generative polish. This ensures consistency – all sales reps get advice aligned with the official methodology, rather than whatever the AI dreams up.

Tone management is crucial. A Coach agent must be encouraging and constructive, not overly critical or negative (even when pointing out mistakes). We can enforce this via prompt settings and perhaps sentiment checks. For instance, instruct the agent: "Always use a supportive tone. Never use derogatory or discouraging language." The Einstein Trust Layer's toxicity filter can catch obviously harsh output, but more subtle tone issues might require fine-tuning or example-based training. It's wise to test the agent's feedback on some edge cases (like what if a rep completely missed quota – does the agent shame them or motivate them?). You may deliberately include style examples in the agent's training (few-shot prompts) that demonstrate the desired coaching style. A Pro Tip in style: many successful coaching bots use the "Praise-Question-Suggest" framework – first praise something that was done well, then ask a question to promote reflection, then suggest an improvement. Structuring the feedback this way can be baked into the agent's logic or prompt as a guardrail to keep feedback balanced and helpful.

Another critical guardrail is ensuring factual correctness in feedback that refers to data. If the coach agent says, "You have only contacted this customer 2 times this month," it must pull that fact from Salesforce data (like Activities on that account). False or outdated facts will quickly erode trust. So connect the Coach agent to live data via actions: an action to get interaction count, an action to fetch pipeline history, etc. Then have the agent incorporate those facts. In code review context, if it says "Function X is never used," it should have actually checked references (maybe integrate with a static code analyzer). The theme is: whenever possible, back the agent's advice with real data points. This not only makes the advice more credible, it also keeps the agent from hallucinating critiques (LLMs might sometimes "invent" a flaw to discuss). An example implementation: a "Deal Coach" agent might call a custom Apex getDealHealthMetrics(OpportunityId) which returns days since last contact, number of stakeholder roles filled, product usage stats, etc., and the agent's prompt includes those metrics to comment on. This ensures the coach's advice ("Engage with the economic buyer since you haven't met them yet") is anchored in actual CRM status.

Privacy and boundaries are also a concern for coach agents, especially ones dealing with personal or sensitive topics (like an agent coaching on work-life balance or handling employee issues). The agent should never overstep confidentiality. For instance, if a wellness coach knows an employee's health data (maybe their step count or stress level from a wellness app integration), it must handle that carefully and not reveal it to others. Likely, such an agent would be a one-on-one private bot for the employee. But in any case, store personal data securely (Platform Shield encryption for health data, etc.), and give the user clear control – possibly an opt-in for an agent to access certain data. Align with regulations: a wellness coach might cross into health advice, so it must avoid actual medical advice territory (that would breach Salesforce's acceptable use and possibly HIPAA). A guardrail could be explicit: if the conversation veers to medical (e.g., "I feel depressed"), the agent should not handle it alone but suggest speaking to a professional or escalate to HR's provided resources. Essentially, program the agent with escalation protocols for out-of-scope issues, just like a human coach would know when to refer someone to a specialist.

Bias mitigation is essential, because a coach agent might inadvertently reinforce biases (e.g., giving different feedback to individuals based on gender or using stereotyped assumptions). Train and test the agent for fairness. If it's a career coach agent reviewing performance, ensure it focuses on objective criteria and not anything that could be discriminatory. Use the guidelines to avoid protected attributes – the agent should not mention or factor in things like gender, age, etc., unless explicitly relevant and appropriate (which is rare). For safety, you might run the agent's outputs through a bias detector or have a Supervisor agent audit a sample of its feedback for bias patterns.

One interesting guardrail approach is user feedback and control. Empower the user to rate or react to the coach agent's suggestions. A simple thumbs-up/thumbs-down after advice can signal if it was useful. If a user disagrees with the advice, maybe they can say "Why do you suggest that?" and the agent should be able to explain its reasoning ("Because last quarter deals with 3+ meetings closed 30% faster, I suggest more meetings"). This again ties to transparency: an agent that can justify its advice is more trusted. Technically, you could implement a feedback loop where low-rated advice triggers a retraining or refining of the agent's prompt over time. At minimum, logs of feedback can be reviewed by the program team.

Another guardrail is scope limitation: the agent should stick to its coaching domain. If it's a sales coach, it should not start giving advice on personal life or on completely unrelated work topics. LLMs can sometimes wander if the user asks something off-topic. So include in the agent's instructions what it should or shouldn't talk about. If user asks a sales coach "How do I fix my laptop issue?", the agent should ideally defer ("I'm here to help with sales techniques; for IT issues, you should contact support."). This avoids the coach giving possibly incorrect guidance in areas it's not designed for.

Salesforce-specific implementation for a coach might involve tools like Einstein Behavior Scoring or Next Best Action rules as inputs. For example, a service coach agent might take Einstein Article Recommendations (suggested knowledge articles) and frame them as advice for an agent ("The system suggests these articles might help resolve the case faster."). Combining AI insights with the agent's conversational guidance yields a more robust coach. But make sure the agent acknowledges the source of such insight ("Based on similar cases, I recommend...") to maintain honesty.

Consider also the impact on morale and culture. If a coach agent constantly pushes workers to do more (close more deals, fix more bugs), it could cause stress or be counterproductive. Program the agent to also recognize and celebrate successes. Maybe if metrics are all green, the agent says "Great job! You're doing well – keep it up and maybe share your tactics with the team." Positive reinforcement is as important as constructive critique in coaching. This can be codified: e.g., if a rep is above quota, advice agent should not say "sell even more!" but rather "congrats, maybe focus on upselling existing customers gently to further boost revenue". It's a nuanced thing – essentially, align with your company's coaching culture. If your culture values work-life balance, ensure the agent's suggestions reflect that (e.g., "It's 7pm, consider wrapping up for the day – fresh mind tomorrow closes deals better."). This might be weird for an AI to say, but if that's a value, encode it! In doing so, you reinforce that the AI is an extension of the company's ethos, which builds trust with users that it's not just some robot boss.

Pro Tip: Personalize within policy. A coach agent can be much more effective if it personalizes its advice to the individual – referencing their goals, past performance, or style. Use Salesforce data to your advantage: for a sales coach, know the user's past deals or learning preferences (perhaps stored in a custom "Rep Profile"). However, draw the line at what's appropriate: personalization should never turn into creepiness or favoritism. For example, it's fine for a code review coach to note "I see you struggled with NullPointer exceptions last sprint, watch out for those here," but not fine to say "Unlike your peers, you often make mistakes in X" – that comparison could demotivate or cause friction. Implement rules for the agent to focus feedback on the user's actions, not in relation to others, and certainly not on personal attributes. By carefully tuning personalization, the agent's advice feels relevant and helpful ("It remembers my context!") while still being fair and respectful.

GUARDRAILS FOR THE PRESENTER PATTERN: TRANSPARENT AND ACCURATE INFORMATION DELIVERY

Presenter agents are those that take information and present it to users in a synthesized, often visual or report-like format. Think of an agent that generates a slide deck of quarterly results, a bot that produces a customer briefing document, or even an AI that responds to an executive's question with a formatted report or dashboard. This pattern focuses on communication and explanation. The biggest trust factors here are accuracy of content, clarity of presentation, and completeness of context. Unlike Curator agents that might give a conversational answer, Presenter agents often create artifacts (summaries, charts, emails) that might be directly used for decision-making or shared with others. So the tolerance for error is extremely low – a beautifully formatted but incorrect report is worse than no report at all.

To guard against inaccuracies, data binding is a must. A Presenter agent should incorporate actual enterprise data dynamically rather than relying on the language model to generate figures. If the agent is preparing a sales performance summary, have it pull the numbers from Salesforce (Opportunities, forecasts) using SOQL queries or Analytics API. This can be achieved by defining actions for data retrieval (like GetTotalSales(currentQuarter) that returns a figure) and template the results. In fact, Agentforce can use prompt templates with variables – one pattern is to fill those variables with query results and let the LLM do the narrative part. For instance, supply: "Total sales = $X (up Y% from last quarter)" into the prompt, and the model will generate commentary around it. This way the hard numbers are guaranteed correct (since they came straight from the source). It's akin to mail merge but with AI-generated prose around the merged fields. Additionally, if creating graphs or tables, use the actual data points. If your agent can output Markdown or an embedded chart via an integration, feed it the data points explicitly.

Review and approval workflows are a wise guardrail for Presenter outputs, especially if the output is going to a wide audience (like a customer or an executive). You might have the agent prepare the report and then require a human (maybe the analyst or manager) to approve it before it's sent out.

This could be facilitated by an Agentforce integration with Salesforce Quip (now Slack Canvas) or Files: the agent drafts a document and saves it, then pings the owner to review. Only after approval does it distribute or publish. This ensures no embarrassingly wrong or sensitive info accidentally goes out. It's similar to how you wouldn't send a board slide deck without someone double-checking the numbers – same here, but accelerated by AI. Over time, as trust grows, some routine reports might go out directly, but initial deployments should err on the side of caution.

Presenter agents should also be transparent about their sources and confidence. A good practice is to include footnotes or an appendix in an AI-generated report indicating where data came from (e.g., "Data source: Salesforce Opportunity records as of 2025-06-30" or "Knowledge source: Customer Satisfaction Survey 2024"). This allows readers to verify the info or at least know it's based on authoritative data. The agent can either pull references via IDs/URLs or at least name the objects. If the agent makes any assumptions or if something wasn't found, it should note it. For example, "Note: Data for APAC Q4 is not yet available, so projections are used." That level of candor might be unusual for an automated report, but it will greatly increase trust from savvy users. They need to know the limits of the content.

Visual fidelity and correctness is another aspect: if the agent presents a chart or any visualization, ensure the labeling and scaling are correct. If using something like Tableau or CRM Analytics via the agent (maybe the agent fetches an existing dashboard snapshot), that's safer because those tools have been configured by humans. But if the agent itself is generating a chart (some advanced multi-modal outputs allow AI to assemble a chart), double-check that the chart matches the data. Sometimes AI might flip axes or mislabel categories. You can guardrail this by using templated chart frameworks where you plug in data and the chart is drawn by a library rather than by the AI's imagination. In the current Salesforce ecosystem, an agent might leverage Tableau CRM (Einstein Analytics) – e.g., call an API to render a chart image from a known lens. That approach ensures corporate-approved visuals.

Completeness of context is key too. A Presenter agent should avoid oversimplifying to the point of misrepresentation. If it's summarizing a complex topic, it should mention key caveats or minority data points if relevant. For instance, "Overall customer satisfaction is 4.5/5, however we saw a drop in APAC region this month." Without that nuance, leadership might think everything is great and miss a brewing issue. Encourage the agent to cover both highlights and lowlights. This can be guided by instructing it to include an "Insights" or "Exceptions" section if any. One could implement an action that checks the dataset for outliers or significant changes and feed that to the agent so it definitely knows about them. Perhaps a small piece of Apex or a SAQL query that finds any region more than 10% below average, and if found, the agent is prompted with: "Important: APAC satisfaction fell by 7 points, include a note on this."

Because Presenter agents often aggregate info, data privacy by aggregation is a natural guardrail. Still, be mindful: if there are only one or two data points in a category, "aggregated" might effectively reveal individual info. E.g., an HR report by department where one department has 1 employee – the average salary for that department basically reveals that person's salary. The agent should be aware of such situations. You might enforce a rule: don't display metrics for groups smaller than N. This is similar to how some analytics tools have a "minimum n" for privacy. If needed, combine small groups or anonymize them ("Departments with <5 employees are combined under 'Other'"). These are choices a human analyst might make; the agent can be taught them too.

For implementing these ideas on Salesforce: Use Salesforce Reports and Dashboards as building blocks. A Presenter agent could literally run a saved report and then summarize it. There is an API to run a report and get JSON results. The agent could take that JSON, maybe apply a formula, and then produce a narrative. Using existing reports as data sources ensures the numbers align with what users see elsewhere (single source of truth). Additionally, consider Einstein GPT for Tableau (if available) – Salesforce has teased conversational analytics in Tableau ("Explain this dashboard" features). Those might be parallel to what an Agentforce Presenter agent does. Possibly integrate such explanation engines if available, but even then put a guardrail that the explanation is double-checked.

Model containment policies (part of Einstein Trust Layer) also apply here: instruct the model that certain topics are off-limits. For instance, if generating a financial summary, the agent should not speculate beyond the data (like it shouldn't give financial advice or forward-looking statements not in the data). If an executive asks "Should we invest more in product X?", the agent (as a Presenter) should not present a definitive recommendation as if it's factual – that crosses into decision-making. Instead, maybe it presents scenario data ("In the past, investment of Y led to Z outcome"). Essentially, keep the agent in the lane of informing, not deciding for humans. That is a philosophical guardrail but can be implemented by prompt: "Do not provide prescriptive advice beyond the provided data. Your role is to inform, not decide." And if needed, the agent might politely suggest who to consult for decisions ("You may consider discussing with the Finance team for investment decisions.").

One more thing: Presenter agents might automate communications (like drafting an email to a client recapping a meeting). Ensure that any such draft is reviewed by the account owner. And include disclaimers if needed, or ensure tone is professional. Similar to the Coach's tone, but in a customer-facing context. Possibly integrate Compliance Email policies if in place (Salesforce has an email relay where compliance can copy emails – if agent sends emails, that should apply too).

Pro Tip: Maintain an audit copy of all AI-generated reports or communications. When a Presenter agent produces something – be it a PDF report, an email, a slide deck – store a version of it in Salesforce (e.g., as an Attachment or Content document, or a Note on a record). This serves two purposes: (1) If there's ever a dispute or question ("Where did this number come from?" or "The client claims the briefing had an error"), you can retrieve exactly what the agent provided and analyze it. (2) It allows comparison over time; as you improve the agent, you can review old outputs vs new outputs to ensure changes are positive (kind of regression testing for the agent's content). This archival is basically an AI output audit trail – extremely useful for compliance in regulated industries (some laws might even mandate retaining communications records). By keeping these copies, you enhance accountability: it's clear what the agent said, and that's a basis for trust (no ephemeral, untraceable answers). Users and auditors alike will feel more comfortable knowing that everything the AI presents is recorded for future reference.

SUMMARY AND KEY TAKEAWAYS

Designing and deploying AI agents with trust and guardrails is not just a nice-to-have in the enterprise – it's absolutely essential. In this chapter, we introduced the mindset that trust must be engineered into every aspect of an AI agent, from its initial design in Agent Builder to its day-to-day operations under Command Center's watchful eye. We explored seven major agent patterns (Action, Supervisor, Conductor, Curator, Coach, Companion, Presenter) and learned that while each has unique challenges, they all share common trust principles: be secure with data and actions, be transparent about what's happening, stay accountable with auditability, and remain aligned with business policies and ethical principles at all times.

A recurring theme is that Salesforce's platform provides many native tools to implement these guardrails – we are not building trust from scratch. Topics and Actions in Agentforce act as a permission whitelist, naturally limiting what an agent can do or access. The Einstein Trust Layer gives us out-of-the-box capabilities like data masking, toxicity filtering, and zero-retention assurance with third-party LLMs. Features like Agentforce Command Center and the underlying OpenTelemetry-based trace logs let us monitor agents in real time and analyze every decision they make. And Salesforce's core security (identity, OAuth, permission sets, field-level security) remains a steadfast guardrail underlying everything – by running agents in the Salesforce Trusted Cloud, we inherit those enterprise-grade protections.

Each pattern we examined demonstrated specific guardrail strategies:

Action agents: We constrain their scope with least-privilege permissions, require human confirmation for critical actions, and log every change for audit. They deliver automation with oversight, never operating in the dark.

Supervisor agents: We codify clear policies for them to enforce, tune their sensitivity, and always keep a human appeal path. They increase compliance and quality, but the organization stays in control of the rules they enforce.

Conductor agents: Through orchestrations in Flow/Apex, we ensure multi-step processes either complete correctly or not at all – preventing half-done work. With careful error handling, transaction control, and integration security, they coordinate complexity without chaos.

Curator agents: By grounding them in real data (RAG) and filtering that data by relevance and permissions, we trust their answers because we know exactly what it's based on. They don't fabricate knowledge – they fetch and filter it, and stay within the lanes we set.

Coach agents: We align their advice with official best practices and positive tone. They personalize feedback but avoid bias and negativity. In effect, they amplify good coaching practices consistently to every user, while respecting personal and ethical boundaries.

Companion agents (from our discussion on coaches and beyond): They act as helpful assistants tuned to individual needs, yet never crossing lines of privacy or propriety. They're empathetic but also programmed to escalate or step back when something is out of scope (like personal crises or medical issues).

Presenter agents: They stick to the facts – using live data, citing sources, and refraining from conjecture. We treat their outputs as we would any official report: double-checked and approved if going public. In doing so, they save tons of time preparing materials, without sacrificing accuracy or consistency.

We also contrasted Salesforce's Agentforce approach to trust with other ecosystem players. Open frameworks like LangChain and CrewAI offer flexibility, but developers must assemble their own guardrails (often using additional libraries or manual checks) to reach the level of security and governance Agentforce provides out-of-the-box. Microsoft's Copilot Studio integrates with its enterprise ecosystem, but if you're in the Salesforce world, Agentforce's native trust layer – from CRM data permissions to built-in audit trails – gives you a more seamless governance story. The bottom line is that Agentforce was built for enterprise trust from day one, leveraging Salesforce's decades of experience in security and enterprise software. By using its native tools and patterns, you can achieve in weeks what might take months to harden if starting from scratch with a generic AI framework.

As you design your own AI agents, keep these guiding questions in mind: "Can I explain what my agent is allowed to do and why?", "If something goes wrong, will I know and be able to intervene?", "Does this agent's behavior align with our company's values and policies?". If you can answer yes, you likely have the right guardrails in place. It's all about balancing innovation with intention – empowering agents to drive efficiency and insights, while ensuring humans remain in control and informed. Salesforce's Trusted AI principles – responsibility, accountability, transparency, empowerment, and inclusivity – aren't just slogans; they can be translated into concrete design elements as we've done in this chapter.

In closing, a trusted AI agent is one that augments your workforce, not alienates it. When employees see that an agent reliably follows rules, respects their role, and actually makes their job easier, they will embrace it. When leaders see that agents can be monitored and audited just like any other business process, they will scale it. By building agents with robust guardrails, we unlock the tremendous potential of agentic AI safely – turning sci-fi concepts into productive reality in the enterprise, with Salesforce's trust-first architecture as our compass. As you move forward to deploy Agentforce agents in your organization, remember: trust isn't a hurdle, it's the highway. Build on it, and your AI agents will drive far.

12

MANAGING AGENT MEMORY, CONTEXT, AND PERSONALIZATION

Personalization and contextual awareness are the heart of human-like AI. An agent that recalls past interactions, understands who it's helping, and adapts to the situation will always feel more "intelligent" than one that doesn't. In fact, without some form of memory, AI agents are just glorified wizards – always starting from scratch, repeatedly asking for context they should already know. In this chapter, we tackle that fundamental truth of agent design: how memory, context, and personalization make your AI agents truly user-aware and effective. We'll explore how to give Salesforce-based agents a sense of continuity and personality, safely and respectfully across users and sessions.

The goal here is not merely adding a first name to a greeting or remembering a trivial detail. It's about engineering memory-aware performance. We'll teach you how to manage session history, user preferences, and contextual signals so your agents become adaptive, relevant, and trustworthy companions. Personalization doesn't mean overstepping bounds or becoming creepy – it means precision, empathy, and continuity in what the agent delivers. The pay-off is huge: less friction for users, more trust in AI assistance, and smarter automation that feels like it "gets" the nuances of the task at hand.

Consider a few examples of what's possible with thoughtful memory design. A Companion agent can remember a manager's approval patterns, learning when to offer a quick one-click approve versus when to ask for confirmation. A Presenter agent might adjust its language and visual format based on the audience's reading level or locale, ensuring complex analytics are explained simply to a new analyst but with depth for an expert. A Coach agent could detect repeated mistakes a user makes (like always forgetting a field on a form) and proactively provide tailored tips or even gentle reminders to correct habits. These aren't static behaviors coded once – they emerge from agents tapping into memories of past interactions and preferences.

At a high level, agent memory in Salesforce exists in three scopes or levels, each with different purpose and persistence:

Session memory – Temporary context that's scoped to the current workflow or conversation. This includes things like recent actions taken, the current record or case being worked, or even the open tabs and selections a user has made in a single session. Session memory resets or expires when the interaction ends (or after a short time of inactivity), but while it's active it provides immediate continuity so the agent doesn't lose track of what's going on right now.

User memory – Persistent context about a specific end-user, lasting across sessions. This encompasses personal preferences (preferred language, communication tone, which types of alerts they like or ignore), prior interaction history with the agent, and learned behaviors (e.g. the user tends to always choose the second option in a list of recommendations). User memory makes the agent personalized: it can greet the user with relevant info, avoid repeating advice the user has already seen, and align with that person's working style. It's longer-term but scoped per individual.

Global (system-wide) memory – Broad context and insights that span across users and the entire organization or system. Think of business rules, company-wide policies, common product knowledge, or risk thresholds that apply to everyone. Global memory might include patterns learned from all users (for example, an agent noticing that "end-of-quarter" is always chaotic in Sales and adjusting its behavior accordingly), or organizational guidelines like branding voice and compliance rules that every agent interaction should respect. This is the memory that encodes the environment and norms in which the agent operates.

Throughout this chapter, we'll learn how to define, implement, and govern memory at all three levels inside Salesforce's Agentforce framework. We will dive into the practical techniques – from using Agent Builder settings and

Salesforce Flow variables for session memory, to storing user preferences in Custom Metadata and designing global knowledge bases. We'll also highlight the importance of doing all this ethically and transparently. Users should feel the benefits of a smarter agent without feeling spied on. That means obtaining consent for personalization, explaining what's being remembered and why, and giving users control (like resetting their profile or entering an "incognito" mode when needed).

By the end of this chapter, you'll know how to make your AI agents contextually adaptive, memory-aware, and personalized – all while respecting privacy and organizational policies. We'll start by breaking down the types of memory and context an agent can use and how to scope them correctly for different agent patterns. From there, we'll build up through strategy, technical implementation, prompt design, multi-user considerations, pattern-specific personalization, and even compare how other AI ecosystems (like LangChain, CrewAI, and Microsoft's Copilot) handle memory. Let's begin by defining the foundations: what kinds of memory exist in an agent system, and where does all that context actually live?

TYPES OF MEMORY AND CONTEXT IN AGENT SYSTEMS

Designing an agent's memory starts with understanding its scope and format. Not all information should be treated the same – some context is fleeting and relevant only within a single interaction, while other knowledge must persist for months and across devices. In Salesforce's Agentforce (and AI systems in general), we classify memory into the three scopes introduced above: session, user, and global. Each serves a different purpose:

Session memory is short-term and context-specific. It includes things like the user's recent actions, the current Salesforce record or object in focus, and even UI context such as tab or page history. For instance, if an agent is helping a service rep during a call, session memory might contain the case details, the last customer query, and the fact that the rep already tried two solutions that failed. Session memory typically lives in ephemeral stores – e.g. variables in a Flow or state held by a Lightning web component – and it evaporates when the session ends. It's all about giving the agent immediate awareness: what just happened and what is the user doing right now?

User memory is longer-lived and tied to a specific person. This covers preferences and profile data (like language choice, preferred communication channel, notification settings), as well as interaction history (the issues they've asked the agent about before, how they responded to advice, etc.). In Salesforce, user-level memory might be stored in a Custom Metadata record or a Custom Setting object keyed to the user, or even in the standard User record (for example, fields or a related "User Preferences" object). This memory persists between sessions – when the user comes back tomorrow, the agent still remembers these details. A well-designed user memory means a sales rep's assistant agent can recall that the rep hates verbose output and always wants bullet points, whereas a different user's agent might know they prefer thorough explanations. User memory makes personalization possible on an individual level.

Global memory spans the whole org or agent ecosystem. It isn't about any one user, but rather the collective context and rules under which the agent operates. Think of it as the institutional knowledge and configuration: product catalogs and pricing rules, compliance policies, escalation paths, common Q&A pairs from your knowledge base, or even machine learning insights gleaned from aggregate data. Global memory in Salesforce could live in custom objects (like a knowledge object or a "Playbook" record that agents reference) or in Salesforce Data Cloud where unified profiles and segments reside. It might also be partially stored in external systems (an enterprise wiki, a vector database of common queries, etc.). Global memory ensures that when an agent gives advice or takes action, it's consistent with the organization's wisdom and constraints. For example, an agent with global memory knows the company's refund policy without needing a user to tell it each time.

Beyond scope, we also consider different memory formats and storage mechanisms:

Some memory is best kept as simple key-value pairs or JSON blobs (for quick lookups like "user123:preferredTone = casual"). Salesforce's Platform Cache or even Custom Settings can serve this need for fast, transient key-value storage.

Other memory might be modeled as metadata records or custom objects – structured data that can be versioned, audited, and leveraged declaratively. Storing an agent's configuration or a user's preferences as Custom Metadata means it's easy to manage in the setup UI and deploy between orgs. For example, you might have a Custom Metadata Type called "Agent_User_Preferences__mdt" with fields for each personalization lever (tone, default report format, etc.), and one record per user or per persona.

For unstructured or semantic memory (like remembering past conversations or large knowledge bases), vector stores come into play. These allow encoding textual information (e.g. chat transcripts, documents) as embeddings and retrieving related context via similarity search. While Salesforce doesn't natively provide a vector DB, you can integrate external ones (Pinecone, Redis with vector support, etc.) or use Salesforce Data Cloud which can act as a big data store for profile traits. Vector memory is useful when agents need to recall things like "what was the gist of the last 10 customer calls?" beyond exact keyword matching – essentially giving a form of semantic long-term memory. Many advanced AI systems use a combination of summary text plus vector search to manage large histories.

It's also critical to note where these memories live. In a Salesforce-centric agent:

Session memory might live in the running Flow (using Flow variables or the Flow's output variables to pass context along), or in the Lightning Web Component (LWC) state if the agent interacts through a UI component. For example, an LWC that hosts a chatbot could store the conversation ID and recent messages in the browser memory or component state so that if the user navigates to a new screen, the conversation can continue without confusion. Session memory can also be kept in an Apex Cache.Session for a server-side store that persists during the user's login session.

User memory can be stored server-side in Salesforce. You might use Custom Metadata for relatively static preferences (because it's easy to package and deploy defaults) or Custom Settings (especially Hierarchy Custom Settings, which allow per-user values overriding an org default). There's also the newer concept of a User Profile object or the standard User record where certain "UserPreferences" fields exist (Salesforce provides some out-of-the-box preferences, like locale and time zone, which agents should respect as well). In some cases, a simple custom object related to the User (like a child object "Agent_Interaction__c" logging key events or storing JSON of last session summary) works, especially if you need to query this info in Apex or reports.

Global memory often lives in data and metadata that Salesforce already houses. For instance, an agent can query standard objects like Product information, or a Custom Metadata type that lists approved escalation procedures. Additionally, Salesforce Data Cloud (formerly known as Customer 360 Audiences / CDP) can act as an external but integrated source of truth for things like customer segments and attributes, which an agent might use as part of its context. If an agent knows a user belongs to the "Field Service Technicians" segment via Data Cloud, it could adjust its suggestions to focus on maintenance schedule updates rather than sales leads, for example. External stores (like a Redis cache or external knowledge base) can be linked via Apex connectors or MuleSoft if truly needed for system-wide memory that isn't stored in Salesforce.

Whatever the scope or storage, a guiding principle is: Agents should remember the right things – and forget the rest. Memory is not a log of everything; it's a curated cache of what's likely to be relevant. Pro tip: Memory ≠ history. Not every detail from the past is worth recalling. Designing an effective agent means deciding what to remember, how long to keep it, and what format to keep it in so that it can be retrieved quickly and safely. A session might only need the last few interactions, whereas global memory might need quarterly retraining. Curate memory with purpose: the agent's decisions should only be influenced by information that you, as the designer, deem useful and allowable for it to use.

Having defined these types of memory and context, we can now move on to using them intelligently. It's one thing to store data; it's another to leverage it for personalization in a way that users appreciate. In the next section, we'll develop a personalization strategy – understanding use cases for tailoring agent behavior and how to gather and use personal data with user consent and clarity, so that our memory design translates into truly helpful (and welcomed) agent actions.

PERSONALIZATION STRATEGY AND CONSENT

Memory is the raw capability; personalization is how we apply it to make an agent's behavior more useful and user-centric. A solid personalization strategy answers the question: Given what the agent knows (or can know) about the user and context, how should it modify its behavior to serve them better? In a business setting, good personalization reduces friction, builds trust, and improves efficiency – but it must be done thoughtfully, with respect for user consent and privacy.

First, let's identify some common use cases for personalization in enterprise agents. Broadly, we can categorize them as:

Role-based personalization: Tailoring the agent's behavior based on a user's role or job function. A field service technician and a financial analyst have very different needs. For example, an agent assisting a field tech might prioritize voice interactions on mobile and offer concise checklists (because the user is hands-on at a job site), whereas for an analyst sitting at a desk, the same agent could provide detailed data exports or charts. In Salesforce, you might implement role-based variations by checking the user's profile or a custom "Role" attribute and then switching prompts or recommended actions accordingly.

Goal-based personalization: Adjusting to the user's immediate goals or priorities. Some users value speed and convenience, others might prioritize compliance or thoroughness. Imagine a sales agent that can operate in "speed mode" for a rep who wants quick, automated logging of activities versus a "compliance mode" for a finance user where every step is double-checked. This can be an explicit setting the user chooses ("Focus on speed vs. accuracy") or inferred from context (e.g. if it's end-of-quarter crunch time, assume speed is paramount for sales closing tasks).

History-based personalization: Learning from the user's past choices or corrections. If the agent offered three suggestions in the past and the user always picked the second one, the agent can start highlighting that option or even defaulting to it. If the user consistently corrects the agent's tone or output (e.g. they always rephrase a draft email to be shorter), the agent should take the hint and adjust future outputs. This is where pattern recognition in a specific user's interaction history becomes gold – it can eliminate repetitive micro-frustrations and make the agent feel proactive. A Coach agent might notice a user never follows certain tips, so it stops nagging about them and tries a different approach.

To enable these kinds of personalization, we need to gather personal data – but do it in a way that's transparent and comfortable for the user:

Some preferences can be gathered explicitly via surveys or settings panels. Salesforce could expose a Preference Center (perhaps a Lightning Component or Experience Cloud page) where users check what they want the agent to remember. For instance, a user might toggle "Remember my preferred dashboard layout" or select a preferred language or content style. This upfront approach is clear and opt-in.

Other personalization points might be prompted in context. The first time an agent interacts with a user, it could ask something like, "Do you prefer a brief summary or detailed explanations?" – effectively setting a preference on the fly. Agent Builder can help script these initial onboarding questions.

The key is not to overwhelm with too many questions; pick one or two high-impact ones to ask early, and perhaps let the agent discover the rest gradually.

A lot of personalization can also be inferred over time with user consent. For example, you might not ask a user "Do you want me to use metric units?" – instead, the agent can notice the user always converts Fahrenheit to Celsius in responses, and infer that metric is preferred. These inferences should ideally be confirmed (the agent could say: "I've noticed you seem to prefer metric units – shall I use those by default going forward?"). This kind of learning builds a sense of a relationship between user and agent.

Crucially, with great memory comes great responsibility: we must respect privacy and consent at every step. Here are some principles and practices to embed into your personalization strategy:

Opt-in and transparency: Always allow users to opt in to personal data being stored. Salesforce gives tools like the Consent Management Object for handling customer consents; for internal user-facing agents, you can simply respect a user's decision in settings. For example, maybe an agent has an "Enable personalization" master switch. If off, the agent operates in a stateless, generic mode (and possibly gently reminds the user that turning it on can enhance their experience). When on, make it clear what the agent is remembering. You might even provide a short summary: "Enabled: This agent will remember your last 5 requests and your preferred output style for future sessions."

Explain the why: Users are more comfortable if they know why the agent is asking for or storing something. If a Companion agent says, "Mind if I remember your favorite escalation option for next time? It will save you a step in urgent moments," the user sees the benefit and can agree knowingly. In contrast, if the agent quietly stores that info without telling and then surprises the user later ("I went ahead and escalated via your favorite method!"), it might feel uncanny or even alarming.

Give control – reset and pause: Provide a way for users to reset their personalization or go "incognito." Maybe a user had a bad quarter and doesn't want their performance companion agent to reference it – they might wipe the slate clean for that data. Or perhaps during a sensitive project, they want the agent to operate without using any stored memory (to avoid any accidental mention of prior confidential info). You can implement a simple "Forget my history" button or a mode toggle. Technically, this could clear certain Custom Metadata records tied to the user or instruct the agent (via a context variable) to ignore stored preferences temporarily. The user should feel in control of their data footprint with the agent.

Data minimization and expiration: Not all personal data should live forever. Define an expiration logic for memory. For example, session memories obviously expire quickly (end of session), but what about user preferences? If a user hasn't engaged with the agent in 6 months, should we purge their interaction logs to be safe? Also, some preferences change – perhaps store a timestamp and have the agent occasionally reconfirm long-held assumptions ("Your notification preferences were set a year ago to daily summaries. Still okay, or update them?"). This practice not only is good for data hygiene but reminds the user that these preferences exist (and that they have agency to change them).

One helpful approach is to create a decision matrix for personalization data – basically a table or chart that maps out: Type of Personalization vs. How it's Stored vs. Retention Policy. For instance, you might map: "Locale/Units Preference – stored in User.CustomFields – no expiry (user can change anytime)"; "Recent 10 questions asked – stored in Agent Interaction custom object – auto-delete after 30 days"; "Favorite dashboard – stored in Custom Metadata – review every 6 months with user". Such a matrix, even if informal, ensures the team building the agent has thought through each bit of memory: why it exists, how it's used, and how it's controlled.

To sum up this strategy: Personalization matters because it can turn an agent from a generic bot into a truly helpful aide that feels tailored to each user. Done right, it saves time, builds user trust (ironically, by being predictable in understanding what the user wants), and can even drive adoption of the agent. But it must always be the user's choice to be known, and the user's right to be forgotten.

Now that we have a strategy blueprint and ethical guardrails for personalization, let's get practical. Next, we'll explore the concrete techniques for managing memory in Salesforce – the tools and methods to implement these ideas (session memory, user preferences storage, etc.) using Agentforce's builder, flows, Apex, and more. We'll also walk through a detailed example to see how it all comes together in a working agent.

TECHNIQUES FOR MANAGING MEMORY IN SALESFORCE

Salesforce provides a rich toolkit to implement the memory and personalization strategies we've discussed. It's time to translate theory into design and code. We'll look at how to use Agentforce Agent Builder, Flows, Invocable Apex, Lightning Web Components (LWC), and Custom Metadata/Settings to give our agents a working memory. The focus is on three scopes – session, user, global – and ensuring the agent can seamlessly pull in context at each of those levels when needed.

Annotating memory needs in Agent Builder: Salesforce's Agent Builder (the low-code interface for configuring AI agents) is a great starting point. It allows you to define an agent's "memory usage" in a declarative way. For example, when creating an agent, you might have options or flags to indicate that the agent will use session memory, or require certain user data. Perhaps you'll tag certain Topics or prompts with the type of memory they rely on. By annotating memory needs, Agent Builder can automatically handle some of the plumbing – e.g. ensuring a Flow passes along the right variables or that an agent has access to the user's ID to fetch preferences. Always start by explicitly marking where your agent touches memory: this improves transparency and maintainability. Future admins looking at the agent configuration should be able to tell "Ah, this agent stores something at user-level" without digging through code.

Now, let's break down implementation by memory scope:

1. Implementing Session Memory: In Salesforce, Flow is often the engine behind an agent's decision logic and actions. Flows come with input and output variables that you can use to carry data through the agent's execution path. For example, imagine a chatbot agent built with a Screen Flow – you can have a variable that accumulates the conversation history or the last user utterance. Each time the flow is invoked (say, each message exchange), you feed it the latest state. If using an Apex-based agent logic, you might maintain a Map<Id,Object> cache in memory keyed by session or conversation ID (though Platform Cache is a better place for cross-transaction session persistence). Salesforce also has a feature called Platform Cache, which includes a Session cache segment – you can store small bits of info (like "case 1234 already acknowledged by user") that persist for the user's session across transactions. Use Flow fault paths and exit conditions wisely to clear or update session variables when appropriate, preventing stale data from lingering longer than it should.

For UI-based agents (like a sidebar component that helps fill out a form), Lightning Web Components can manage short-term state on the client side. For example, an LWC could keep track of which records a user has opened in that session, and feed that to the agent (perhaps through an Apex call or directly via the Agent API) so the agent knows, say, the user already looked at three related cases before asking the agent for a summary – context that might affect the answer.

2. Implementing User Memory: User-specific memory often ends up in Salesforce's database in one form or another. A straightforward approach is to use a Custom Setting (Hierarchy) or Custom Metadata for each user's preferences. Suppose we want to remember each manager's preferred "escalation pathway" (e.g. escalate to email vs. Slack, or which manager to notify first). We could create a custom metadata type called Escalation_Preference__mdt with fields like User__c (lookup to User), Preferred_Method__c (picklist: Email/Slack/Phone), Last_Updated__c, etc. When the agent (maybe a Supervisor agent pattern) faces a decision of how to escalate an issue, it can query this metadata. In Apex, that's as easy as a SOQL query on the metadata, or using the Runtime APIs for custom metadata. In Flow, you can use a Get Records element on the Custom Metadata (they're queryable just like custom objects via Flow now) filtered by the running user's ID.

Another method is the User object's built-in fields or a related custom object for preferences. Salesforce has a "UserPreferences" set of fields (mostly for standard features), but you can also create something like a User_Preferences__c custom object that has one record per user for agent-specific settings (tone = casual, detailLevel = high, etc.). The advantage of a custom object is you can update it easily from Apex or Flow and track history of changes.

Additionally, consider using Invocable Apex for more complex memory updates. For example, after each agent interaction, you might want to log what happened (success, failure, user overridden suggestion, etc.) to a "Feedback" custom object. You can write an Invocable Apex action LogFeedbackAction that takes in details and inserts a record. This becomes part of the agent's memory too – a log the agent (or at least those maintaining it) can review to adjust behavior. It's not memory the agent actively queries, but it's memory in the sense of learning from the past (perhaps for an admin or data scientist to analyze later and tweak the agent's rules).

3. Implementing Global Memory: Global context often involves connecting to data that is outside the immediate agent logic. One powerful resource

here is Salesforce Data Cloud. Data Cloud can act as an org-wide memory by storing unified customer profiles, segments, and even calculated insights. An agent could query Data Cloud (via an API or an Apex connector) to pull traits like "Customer Lifetime Value tier" or "Preferred Language" (which might be aggregated from multiple systems). In the context of Agentforce, Data Cloud can feed the agent real-time relevant data at runtime – ensuring the agent's global knowledge is up-to-date. For example, an agent might use Data Cloud to know that a given account is flagged as high risk by the finance system, so it should behave more cautiously or involve a human earlier.

Other global memory implementations include using Custom Metadata as a knowledge base (like a list of standard steps for a procedure that any agent can reference) or external knowledge stores. If using an external vector database for long-term knowledge, you'd likely use Apex to call out (maybe via an HTTP callout to an AWS Lambda, etc.) to perform a query and get results, which then become part of the agent's context. This is more advanced, but it mirrors what frameworks like LangChain do under the hood for knowledge retrieval.

Ephemeral data and caches: Sometimes the agent needs a short-term memory that isn't tied to a user or a session but still shouldn't be permanent. For example, during a long multi-step Flow, you might accumulate a list of records processed. Or an agent might store intermediate results while orchestrating multiple sub-tasks (like a Conductor agent pattern coordinating several Action agents). For these cases, Salesforce's Platform Cache (Org Cache) or even static Apex variables (careful with scope!) can be useful. Platform Cache's org partition could hold something like an "Agent Scratchpad" – e.g. map of Conversation ID to summary – which you manually purge or set to expire after X hours. It's faster than database writes and avoids hitting storage for truly transient info. Just be mindful that Platform Cache is not guaranteed (it can evict entries under pressure), so critical data should still land in a persistent store if it can't be reconstructed.

Let's bring these techniques together with a concrete walkthrough example to see memory in action:

Walkthrough Example – Memory-aware Escalation Agent:

Imagine we're building a Supervisor-type agent for a customer support scenario. This agent's job is to monitor ongoing support cases and escalate them to a manager when certain conditions are met (high priority, breaching SLA, customer sentiment negative, etc.). We want the agent to be smart about how it escalates, personalized to each support manager's preference.

Requirement: Some managers prefer escalations via Slack (real-time ping), others via email (for a paper trail), and perhaps some want a phone call for top issues. Also, if a particular manager tends to always reassign escalations to a deputy when they're on vacation, the agent should remember that pattern.

Design: We introduce a User-level memory for managers called "Escalation Preference". We create a Custom Metadata type Escalation_Preference__mdt with fields: Manager_User__c, Preferred_Channel__c (Slack/Email/Call), Use_Deputy__c (Boolean), Deputy_User__c (Lookup to User as the deputy). We populate this metadata for each support manager in the org (this could also be done via a simple setup UI where managers fill their preferences, which then saves to metadata or a custom object – but we'll assume an admin pre-filled it for now).

Agent Builder Setup: In Agent Builder, when configuring the Supervisor agent, we mark that it will use "user memory" and specifically note it pulls from Escalation_Preference__mdt (perhaps Agent Builder lets us document or link the metadata). We also give it access to an Invocable Action called "SendSlackMessage" and one called "SendEmail" and so on, which it will use to perform the escalation.

Flow Logic (Session memory): The agent is triggered (maybe by a Platform Event when a Case is marked "escalate") and a Flow is executed. This Flow gathers context: it pulls the Case details (case ID, severity, etc.) – this is session context. It then determines who the on-call manager is (maybe from a custom object or just the Case.Owner's manager field). Let's say it gets Manager = Alice (User Id 005…). The Flow then does a Get Records on Escalation_Preference__mdt where Manager_User__c = Alice. It finds that Alice prefers Slack and has Use_Deputy = true with Deputy = Bob.

Using that memory (User & Global): Now the Flow's decision diamond can branch: since Slack is preferred, it calls an Apex action to send a Slack message. Also, it sees Use_Deputy is true and maybe it's during off-hours, so it actually messages Bob (the deputy) instead of Alice, saying "Escalation: Case 1234 needs attention" with a link. If no preferences were found, maybe it falls back to a global default (global memory might be "Company default escalation = Email to Case Owner's manager").

Learning (updating memory): Suppose Alice manually changes an escalation's outcome – like she reassigns it to a different team or always adds a note "Please call customer first". The agent could log that in a Feedback object: e.g. Agent_Feedback__c record with fields for Case Id, what the agent did, what the manager did after. Over time, we might spot a pattern that Alice always adds a certain note. At that point an admin or the agent designer might update Alice's preferences (or even the agent could be designed to suggest an update) – but doing that automatically is advanced and would require high confidence. At minimum, the feedback log is there for a human to improve the system.

Result: Next time an escalation for Alice happens, the agent remembers to Slack Bob (deputy) immediately with a concise message, because it knows that's the preferred method. For another manager, say Carlos, who has no special record, the agent might use the default email path. Each manager feels like the AI knows how they want to be engaged, which increases their trust in it (and they're more likely to let the AI run without intervening).

This example showcases how Custom Metadata + Flow + Invocable Apex come together: metadata for persistent user prefs, flow to orchestrate logic using that data, and Apex actions to do the work (sending messages). Importantly, the agent's memory was segmented properly: it checked user-level memory for preferences, used session context (case details) in the message, and fell back on a global default. This pattern can be reused for countless scenarios (approval assistants, recommendation adjusters, etc.).

As a Salesforce practitioner, whenever you implement memory, consider: How will I debug or monitor this? It's often helpful to include the current memory context in agent logs or responses for transparency. For instance, the agent could attach a note "(Using Alice's escalation settings: Slack to Bob)" in a private log. That way, when testing or if something goes awry, you can trace decisions back to memory references.

We've now covered building blocks for memory in Salesforce. Next, we'll look at how to leverage that memory when interacting with language models – essentially, how to do prompt engineering for contextual awareness so that all this stored knowledge actually influences the AI's output effectively.

PROMPT ENGINEERING FOR CONTEXTUAL AWARENESS

Storing memory is only half the battle – the other half is getting your AI models to use it. This is where prompt engineering meets memory management. The goal is to inject the right context into your prompts (or other API calls to LLMs) so that the model's responses are relevant to the user's situation and preferences. However, we must do this efficiently and safely, because large prompts can hit token limits or inadvertently leak information. Let's explore techniques for weaving context into prompts in a Salesforce agent scenario, and how to optimize it.

Include session context directly in prompts: A simple but powerful approach is to explicitly include recent context in the LLM prompt. For example, if an agent is summarizing a case, the prompt might say: "You are helping with Case 1234. The last thing the user did was reset the password. The user now asks for account unlock." In a conversational agent, a common pattern is prepending a summary of the conversation so far. Agentforce's integration with GPT might allow you to provide a system message or context field – there you can inject lines like "Last user request was X. Agent already provided Y." If the user told the agent, "Give me the short version," and it's a follow-up interaction, put that note in the prompt: "(Context: Last time, this user asked for the short version of the report.)" This signals the model to be concise now. Similarly, you might include facts like "(Context: The user has overridden auto-routing twice today)", which could influence the model to maybe ask if they want to disable auto-routing going forward.

The key is to identify what session facts are relevant. You wouldn't dump everything – just the highlights or recent critical actions. This is where a Curator agent pattern can help (more on that in a moment).

Chained or two-step prompting: Sometimes it's inefficient to throw all context at the model every time. A technique is to use a chain of prompts – first have one prompt condense or filter context, then feed that condensed context into the final prompt for answer generation. For example, suppose a user had a 100-message long Slack thread that the agent has access to. Instead of sending all 100 messages to GPT when asking for a summary, you might first have a Curator sub-agent or even a pre-prompt step that says: "Here are the last 100 messages. Summarize the key points in 5 bullet points." Then take those 5 bullets and include that in the actual question prompt to get the final answer. In Agentforce, you might implement this by having an agent composed of multiple "topics" or steps: one to prepare context, another to answer. This separation ensures the heavy lifting of digesting context is done in a controlled way, and the decision-making LLM call sees a focused summary, reducing noise and token usage.

Memory stubs and references: If an agent has a known piece of user memory, you can sometimes reference it in the prompt in a shorthand way that the model has been trained to understand. For example, instead of injecting a full paragraph about the user's style, you might use a simple tag like "[Tone: Casual]" at the start of the user prompt to the model. If you have control over the prompting logic, you could format it like: "User's preferred tone is casual. User's request:." The LLM can then factor that in. In some systems, developers create a convention in system prompts, such as: "The assistant has the following profile of the user: {profile data}. Use this profile to tailor your response." A concrete instance could be "(Note: manager prefers bullet points in responses)" – a short statement that guides the model's style without a lengthy explanation.

Salesforce's Prompt Template builder can help maintain these "memory stubs." For instance, you define a prompt template with placeholders for {userTonePreference} or {recentActionsSummary}, and at runtime the agent's code fills those in from memory stores.

System message vs. user message for context: Many LLM APIs (like OpenAI's) allow a system-level message that sets behavior context separate from the user query. This is often a great place to put contextual memory. For example, the system message might be: "You are a helpful assistant. The organization's policy is X. The user's role is Y. Keep responses under 200 words." By putting memory in the system message, you differentiate it from the user's prompt. The model is more likely to treat it as ground truth or rules to follow, rather than part of the query. Agentforce's GPT integration likely supports some form of system or context message – use it to preload memory like user preferences, global rules, etc.. Alternatively, if no dedicated field is available, prepend it to the user prompt with a clear delimiter.

Caching and reuse: If your agent frequently uses the same context in prompts, consider caching the LLM's output for that context to avoid redundant calls. For instance, if at login an agent generates a summary of "What has this user done in the last week that I should remember?", store that summary (maybe in a Custom Object or Platform Cache) and reuse it in prompts during that session rather than recalculating each time. Another scenario: if you have an expensive operation like vector search for relevant knowledge articles, do it once and reuse the results for subsequent related queries in the same session. You could even cache partial LLM completions: e.g. you asked GPT to summarize a policy, store that summary for future use so you don't ask for it again unless the policy changes.

One word of caution: cached info can become stale or irrelevant if the context shifts, so implement invalidation rules or context keys (cache per record ID or user ID appropriately, so you don't mix things up).

Now, about that Curator agent for summarization – this is a recommended pro tip in multi-agent setups. If an agent has to handle very large histories or data (like a customer's full case history), use a specialized agent or component to condense large histories into brief, salient summaries. For example, a "Conversation Curator" could use an LLM to compress 50 chat messages into a 3-sentence summary, which the main agent then uses in its actual decision-making prompt. This aligns with the principle of chained prompting above, and keeps the main agent focused.

Prompt safety and memory: When injecting memory into prompts, be mindful of not violating privacy or policy. Only include data that the model is allowed to use or reveal. For example, if a global memory includes sensitive internal codes or raw customer data, perhaps don't feed those directly – have them processed into a safer form first. The Model Context Protocol (MCP), which we'll touch on later, is looking at ways to tag and control context metadata so that such constraints can be standardized (e.g., marking a piece of memory as "not to be revealed verbatim").

In summary, prompt engineering for context is about balancing completeness with conciseness. You want the model to have all the relevant memory at its fingertips, but not be drowned in superfluous details or run out of capacity. Use direct inclusion for immediate recent context, summaries for long histories, placeholders for style prefs, and system prompts for rules and profiles. By constructing prompts artfully, your agents' responses will reflect the rich memory you've built without you having to write complex conditional code for every scenario – the model naturally adapts its output.

We've now enabled our agents to remember and to use that memory in generation. The next challenge: ensuring agents adapt to different users and scenarios on the fly, especially in multi-user environments. In the following section, we'll discuss how to design agents for adaptive behavior and supporting multiple users or teams simultaneously, building on the memory concepts we have so far.

ADAPTIVE BEHAVIOR AND MULTI-USER SUPPORT

Every user is different, and often our agents serve not just one person but many, sometimes all at once. An agent might be assisting an entire team or jumping between contexts (a Slack channel here, a CRM screen there). To succeed, the agent must adapt its behavior based on who it's dealing with, through what channel, and even group dynamics. This section is about using memory and context to make an agent flexible and context-aware in multi-user, multi-channel environments, without leaking information where it shouldn't.

Let's break down a few axes of adaptation:

Persona-based adaptation: We touched on role-based personalization earlier; persona is a broader concept. Within a company, you might categorize user personas like Executive, Manager, Front-line Employee, IT Admin, New Hire, etc. An agent can adjust its depth or tone accordingly. For example, an executive persona might trigger the agent to be extra concise and focus on KPIs, whereas an IT admin persona might get more technical detail in responses. You can implement this by storing a "Persona" field on the User (or in a preference object) and having the agent reference it. Perhaps in the system prompt or logic: if persona == Executive, use summary style; if == IT Admin, include troubleshooting data. One could also maintain separate prompt templates keyed by persona. The idea is the agent essentially shapeshifts its communication style to match the user – like a chameleon agent that knows how to talk to different audiences.

Channel-based adaptation: The medium is part of the context. Agents might operate in Slack, Email, Salesforce Console, or mobile SMS – each has constraints and opportunities. In Slack (or Microsoft Teams, etc.), messages are often brief and conversational, and there may be multiple participants in a channel. In email, more formality and structure might be expected. In a Salesforce UI, the agent might have modals or side panels to show info. Your agent should detect or be told the channel and adapt output format. For instance, if channel is Slack, maybe it uses more bullet points or code block formatting for clarity; if it's voice via Einstein Voice or a phone assistant, it might speak more verbosely to be clear (and obviously not output a text table). One practical approach: use separate prompt templates per channel, or include channel cues in the prompt like "[Format: Slack message]" vs "[Format: Email]". Also, adjust content – e.g. in a public Slack channel with multiple people, the agent should avoid personal sensitive info and maybe be more general, whereas in a private one-on-one chat it can reference the user's personal data freely.

Interaction style adaptation: Some users are chatty and want detail, others type "TL;DR" the moment the agent responds too long. The agent can adapt its interaction style (verbose vs concise, formal vs informal, proactive vs only-on-demand) based on either known user preference or live signals. Known preferences we've covered (store "verbosity=high/low" in user memory). Live signals could be things like sentiment or feedback during the conversation – if the user keeps interrupting or not responding to long outputs, the agent might shorten future outputs automatically. You could implement a simple heuristic: after each message, if the user's next message is "okay, got it" with no other input, maybe you're overwriting them – try less next time for that session.

Now, enabling these adaptations often means storing some logic or data in a way that's easy to update as you learn. Custom Metadata can be a great place to externalize adaptation rules. For example, have a Metadata type Agent_-Tone_Config__mdt with fields for Persona, Tone, Formality, etc., which your agent's prompt builder references. This way, tweaking how an "Analyst" persona should behave is a metadata change, not a code change.

Let's talk about multi-user memory. Sometimes an agent isn't just dealing with one user in isolation – it's working with a team or on records that involve multiple stakeholders. A classic scenario: a team assistant agent in a group Slack channel. It might be helping an entire project team coordinate. In such cases, there may be a concept of shared or team memory in addition to individual memory:

You could create a Project-wide memory object (custom object) that stores things like "Project Goals", "Last Key Decision", "Team Preferences". The agent can reference this to answer questions like "What's our last agreed deadline?" or to remember that the team decided "no meetings on Fridays" so it avoids scheduling one.

The agent might log the last team decision in that object. E.g., after a lengthy discussion the team agreed on approach A – the agent notes that. If later someone asks the agent "What did we decide about X?", it can retrieve that and answer.

For coaching scenarios, if an agent is coaching a whole team (let's say a sales team agent that gives tips to the group), it might maintain memory of common coaching moments – e.g., it noticed multiple team members are struggling with the same new product pitch, so it can offer a group training or mention "3 of you asked about product XYZ details this week, here's a summary cheat sheet."

In Salesforce, enabling team memory might mean a memory store keyed not by User but by Team or Project. This could be a custom object with a look up to a Team (if you have a Team object or use public groups, etc.), or even using something like a Slack channel ID as key if bridging Slack.

Safe multi-user design: The flip side of sharing is making sure the agent doesn't leak personal info where it shouldn't. If our agent serves multiple users, it must wall off private memories unless explicitly allowed. For example, a companion agent that helps two different sales reps should not say "Hey Alice, you might handle this like Bob did yesterday with his customer," unless Bob and Alice are in a context where sharing is okay (maybe same team and non-confidential). This is mostly a matter of careful context use: always scope queries to memory by user unless a shared context is intended. If you use a vector store for memory, consider including user or team identifiers in the metadata/tags for embeddings, so you can query "give me similar past conversations for this user" rather than the whole company, unless desired.

A practical tip: implement an "instance context isolation" flag. In Agent Builder or your agent code, mark which memories are global vs per-user vs per-team. Then enforce that logic. For example, if a global memory fetch finds something highly relevant but it belongs to a different user and isn't marked shareable, maybe the agent intentionally filters it out or generalizes it ("In a past case, someone resolved this by... [anonymous]").

To illustrate adaptation in a multi-user scenario, consider this walkthrough:

Walkthrough – Team Slack Companion Agent Adapting Tone:

Suppose we have a "Companion" agent in a Slack channel for a project team. This agent posts reminders and answers questions. The twist: sometimes the CIO is tagged in the channel, sometimes it's just the engineers.

We give our agent a bit of social intelligence: if certain high-profile users (like CIO or VP) are present in the conversation (e.g., they're CC'd or they recently posted), the agent will switch to a more formal tone and maybe be less jokey or speculative. If it's just the core team of peers, the agent can be more informal and quick.

Implementation: We maintain a list (Custom Metadata perhaps) of "VIP Users" or just key off their roles (Executive persona). The agent, when formulating a response, checks via Slack API or context which users are in the thread. If any user in the thread matches the VIP list, the agent sets a flag highAudienceSensitivity=true.

In the prompt or agent logic, we incorporate that: maybe we have two versions of the answer, or simply an if/else on tone. Pseudocode: tone = highAudienceSensitivity ? "formal" : userPreferredTone. So if the CIO is around, even if the user who asked is normally fine with casual tone, the agent errs on formality out of respect to the larger audience. It might also avoid referencing internal nicknames or unverified info in that case.

Additionally, our agent might adapt content: If a question is asked and multiple people are listening, the agent might give a bit more background than usual for clarity. If one engineer asks privately, the agent might assume a lot of technical context.

Finally, the agent always respects boundaries: If one team member privately asked it to track something (like "remind me about X later"), it won't blurt that out in the group channel unless that user triggers it, etc. Essentially, it tags any memory with the context of where it was gathered (private vs group).

This scenario shows how an agent can dynamically adapt to not just the direct user but the audience. It's like how a human might speak differently in a team meeting versus a 1:1 conversation.

The overarching principle is that an adaptive agent uses all available context – who, where, how – to modulate its behavior, all within the guardrails of privacy. Technically, this means merging multiple context sources: user profile, channel info, perhaps device info (if it knows the user is on mobile, maybe it keeps things short and actionable vs if on desktop).

With adaptive, memory-rich agents in place, we should also consider how these practices differ across various types of agents. A pattern that works for a Companion might not apply to a straightforward Action bot. In the next section, we'll examine personalization across different agent patterns (Companion, Coach, Supervisor, etc.), highlighting which memory types matter most for each and what unique risks or considerations come with them. We'll also summarize this in a handy comparison list to see it all at a glance.

PERSONALIZATION ACROSS AGENT PATTERNS

Not all agents are alike. In the Agentforce playbook, we have several agent patterns – such as Companion, Coach, Supervisor, Curator, Presenter, etc. Each pattern has a distinct role, and consequently, different needs and opportunities for memory and personalization. Let's discuss how personalization manifests in each pattern and what memory scope they lean on. We'll also consider the Salesforce tooling that supports those needs and any particular risks to watch out for.

To make this crystal clear, we'll use a list to compare these patterns side by side. First, some context on each:

Companion agents (personal digital assistants for users) are the most memory-intensive. They follow a user through various tasks and over time, which means they accumulate lots of preferences and history. A Companion might remember everything from the user's working hours (so it doesn't send alerts on weekends) to the fact they always skip a particular step in a process (maybe auto-handle that next time). It uses session memory to track what the user is doing at the moment, heavy user memory to personalize suggestions, and even global memory to incorporate company news or policy changes relevant to the user's work.

Coach agents (providing guidance or training) rely on memory to avoid being a broken record. A Coach logs prior advice given, the user's progress, and which tips were taken or ignored. It might keep a score or status for the user (are they improving? where do they need reinforcement?). User memory is key (progress history), session memory too (context of what they're working on right now that needs coaching), and maybe some global memory for benchmark comparisons (e.g. team average performance, so it can say "you're in the top 10%!" or similar).

Supervisor agents (governing or approving) use memory in a somewhat different way – often to adjust thresholds or catch patterns of overrides. If a Supervisor agent notices that a particular rule is overridden by a human manager frequently, it might learn and adjust its strictness for that case or at least highlight the recurring issue. It could store user-specific trust levels ("Manager Alice has overridden me 3 times, I'll be less aggressive with auto-blocking for her") which is user memory, but also could log globally which rules are most overridden to possibly suggest policy changes (global memory). Supervisors must be careful – their "personalization" might mean being more permissive with experienced users versus very strict with new users, etc., so they combine user memory (experience level, past interactions) with global business rules.

Curator agents (aggregating and summarizing data) typically deal with a lot of information. They might personalize by understanding what a particular user cares about in a report. For example, a Curator generating a sales summary for a salesperson might remember that this person is interested in pipeline changes and not so much in closed won deals (because they track those separately). So it emphasizes pipeline. It might also recall the user's past queries to tailor what data it fetches (if they always ask about product X, include that proactively). Much of Curator's memory might be global (knowledge base, data sources) but user memory helps decide emphasis and format.

Presenter agents (delivering outputs, explaining results) focus on how to communicate. Personalization here often means tone and format adjustments. A Presenter might know that an executive audience prefers a short paragraph with key points, whereas a technical audience wants a detailed table of numbers. It could use user memory (if presenting directly to a known user with preferences) or adapt on the fly if it knows the audience type. Presenter agents should avoid redundancy – if the underlying data was already seen by the user, maybe frame it differently rather than repeat. So they might keep memory of what knowledge the user already has, perhaps gleaned from earlier parts of the interaction.

To consolidate these ideas, here's a comparison list of key aspects for each pattern:

Companion

- **Primary memory scope:** Session, user, and global context.
- **Personalization focus:** Remembers user habits such as frequent tasks and schedules; adapts to preferred timing and medium (for example, Slack versus email); maintains continuity across tasks by carrying context between CRM, email, and calendar.
- **Key Salesforce tooling:** Agent Builder for user-context entry points; Custom Metadata for user preferences such as tone and notification settings; Flow and Apex for cross-application integration; Lightning Web Components for on-screen assistance.
- **Unique risks:** Over-personalization that feels invasive; privacy issues if personal data appears in public channels; staleness if user roles or preferences change and memory is not refreshed.

Coach

- **Primary memory scope:** Session and user.
- **Personalization focus:** Tailors advice to user history to avoid repetition; tracks improvement over time and adjusts guidance depth; may benchmark against team norms to contextualize feedback.
- **Key Salesforce tooling:** Custom Coaching Log object per user; Flow logic using user skill or stage fields; prompt templates that adapt tone based on user sensitivity.
- **Unique risks:** Nagging if reminders are too frequent; misjudging skill level due to incomplete or incorrect memory; accidental disclosure of one employee's performance to another if data is not properly siloed.

Supervisor

- **Primary memory scope:** Session, user, and global.
- **Personalization focus:** Remembers past approvals and overrides by each approver to calibrate trust; enforces global policies while learning common exceptions; personalizes escalation paths and notification timing.
- **Key Salesforce tooling:** Approval Processes with AI checks driven by metadata; Custom Settings for manager-specific thresholds and notification channels; invocable Apex within Flow for dynamic rule application.
- **Unique risks:** Becoming overly lenient if it learns the wrong lessons from overrides; compliance violations if personal bias overrides policy; auditability challenges if personalized decisions are not clearly logged and explainable.

Curator

- **Primary memory scope:** Global and user.
- **Personalization focus:** Highlights data relevant to the user's role or prior interests; summarizes in preferred formats such as visual versus text; avoids repeating information the user has already seen.
- **Key Salesforce tooling:** Salesforce Reports and Dashboards as global data sources; Einstein GPT or query tools for data selection;

Custom Metadata for report and format preferences; Agent Builder topics for role-based summarization.

- **Unique risks:** Omitting critical information due to incorrect assumptions about user knowledge; information overload if personalization fails; biased summaries that overemphasize favored topics while underreporting issues.

Presenter

- **Primary memory scope:** Session, user, and global.
- **Personalization focus:** Adapts tone and formality to the audience; selects output format such as slides, text, or charts based on device or preference; structures content according to what the user values, such as "bottom line first."
- **Key Salesforce tooling:** Lightning Email Templates or Lightning Web Components for dynamic assembly; prompt templates with style guidelines stored in Custom Metadata; Data Cloud segments for audience- or industry-specific phrasing.
- **Unique risks:** Tone misalignment that erodes trust; challenges presenting to mixed audiences with differing preferences; overfitting to user expectations and failing to surface uncomfortable or alternative perspectives.

As we see, each agent pattern leverages memory differently. Companions and Presenters heavily use user-specific memory; Supervisors lean on global rules but tweak per user; Coaches and Curators sit somewhat in between. Salesforce gives us the tools (metadata, objects, flows, etc.) to implement all these, but it's up to us to configure them correctly for each pattern's needs.

One common risk across all patterns is that personalization and memory can introduce bias or errors if not monitored. For instance, if a Coach agent's memory incorrectly flags something as repeated when it wasn't, the user might get no advice where they needed some. Or if a Companion agent "inherits" a preference from someone else due to a data mix-up, it could behave inappropriately. Thus, testing and validation of memory-driven behavior is crucial – ideally each pattern has test cases like "with fresh memory vs with learned memory" to ensure it behaves logically.

Having contrasted in-platform patterns, it's valuable to also look beyond Salesforce and see how other AI agent ecosystems approach memory and context. In the final section of this chapter, we'll compare Salesforce's approach to those of LangChain, CrewAI, AutoGen, Microsoft's Copilot Studio, and even how Salesforce Data Cloud intersects with these. This will highlight where Salesforce shines and where it differs, preparing you to integrate or draw inspiration from outside practices.

EXTERNAL ECOSYSTEM APPROACHES TO MEMORY AND CONTEXT

Salesforce Agentforce doesn't exist in a vacuum. In the wider AI world, several frameworks and platforms tackle the memory challenge in their own ways. By comparing notes, we can glean ideas and ensure our Salesforce agents can interoperate or at least measure up to the state of the art. Let's take a brief tour of some prominent ecosystems: LangChain, CrewAI, AutoGen, and Microsoft Copilot Studio, and also see how Salesforce's own Data Cloud + GPT fits into the picture. Finally, we'll mention the Model Context Protocol (MCP) – an emerging standard aiming to make context sharing easier across platforms.

LangChain (Open-source LLM framework): LangChain is known for providing building blocks to create LLM-powered applications, and one of its strengths is a variety of memory modules. These include simple buffer memory (which just keeps a running log of conversation), summary memory (which condenses past interactions into a summary to save tokens), and even vector store-backed memory for long-term knowledge. For example, LangChain's ConversationBufferMemory will feed the entire conversation history into the prompt until it gets too large, whereas ConversationSummaryMemory uses an LLM to summarize old messages once the history grows, keeping the prompt size manageable. In Salesforce, we don't have these as built-in abstractions, but we can mimic them: e.g. use a Flow or Apex to concatenate recent chat messages (buffer memory), or invoke an Einstein GPT prompt to summarize and store it in a custom object (summary memory). The big difference is that LangChain gives these to developers out-of-the-box, whereas in Salesforce you'd implement the pattern yourself with available tools. The similarity is that both recognize short-term vs long-term context is a thing – Salesforce practitioners might explicitly integrate a vector database for semantic memory, akin to how LangChain would hook one up with a few lines of code. One area Salesforce is more cautious about is data governance – LangChain will happily connect to Pinecone or any DB you point it to; in Salesforce, you'd ensure any external memory store meets your security standards (and maybe use Salesforce's native stores where possible for compliance).

CrewAI (Multi-agent orchestration framework): CrewAI approaches memory with the concept of a "crew" (a group of agents working together). It often implements memory at the crew level rather than individual agent level. That means all agents in a crew might share a common contextual memory space, which is great for collaboration but could limit per-agent uniqueness. CrewAI also supports specialized "persona memory" for each agent role in the crew. For instance, if you have a "Researcher" agent and a "Writer" agent in a crew, each might remember different things relevant to their role. CrewAI's documentation notes that user-specific memory used to be handled via an external service (Memo) as a somewhat legacy approach – meaning if you needed each agent to remember separate info for separate users, you'd integrate a separate memory store. In Salesforce, because each agent typically runs within a user context or an org context, it's naturally isolated or shared as needed: e.g., one agent per user (Companions) won't share memory unless you program it, whereas a single multi-user agent (like a Conductor) could share everything globally unless you add user context checks. In practice, if we want Salesforce agents to work in a CrewAI-like swarm, we'd likely need to implement a shared memory layer ourselves (maybe a custom object that agents read/write to as a message board). The Model Context Protocol (MCP) could facilitate this by providing a standard way to package an agent's memory and state so another agent (possibly on another platform) can understand it. CrewAI's benefit is making multiple agents memory-coherent. Salesforce could achieve similar by, say, using Platform Events or a common Custom Metadata as the "crew memory" to which all relevant Agentforce agents subscribe.

AutoGen (Microsoft's multi-agent framework): AutoGen allows multiple LLM agents and tools to work together, and it emphasizes continuous conversations and tool use. A key aspect is how it handles tool-call memory and session continuity. AutoGen agents can carry over working memory across tool invocations and even between separate agent interactions, largely by using Python objects to persist state or by logging events. For example, AutoGen might have an agent that, after calling a code execution tool, stores the result in a memory variable to use in the next prompt. In Salesforce, tool use (like calling a Flow or Apex from an agent) can also return data that you store – maybe in the Flow's context or in a hidden field in the UI. The challenge is that Salesforce agents typically run per transaction (especially if invoked via Flow), so to maintain continuity, you have to explicitly save and retrieve state between invocations. AutoGen provides more of a continuous runtime (especially if you run it as a long-lived process). Salesforce is working within a stateless web request model mostly, so our strategies often involve saving state to the database or cache between turns. AutoGen also categorizes memory into things like "short-term vs long-term" and even procedural memory (knowledge of how to use tools). Procedural memory in Salesforce could be analogous to the agent knowing which Flow to run for which task – something we might implement via metadata (capability mappings). The bottom line: AutoGen gives developers explicit memory objects (like the ListMemory and VectorMemory classes) and events for memory retrieval, whereas in Salesforce we design around platform features (cache, objects, etc.) to get similar results. The two can complement: one could imagine an AutoGen agent calling a Salesforce agent via MCP, handing off context.

Microsoft Copilot Studio: Microsoft's Copilot Studio is aimed at building custom copilots (agents) within the M365 and Azure ecosystem. It inherently has access to the user's content and context in Microsoft 365 – emails, documents, calendar, etc. In other words, a lot of "memory" is automatically there via Microsoft Graph (the unified API for user's data). Copilot Studio allows designers to create adaptive flows (workflows that the copilot can carry out) and to specify what user data the copilot can use. For example, you might create a copilot that, when given a task "Prepare for meeting X," automatically pulls the relevant emails, the meeting agenda from your calendar, previous meeting notes from OneNote, etc. This is effectively using the user's digital footprint as memory without the designer coding all those retrievals – Microsoft provides connectors and the platform handles context injection. Salesforce's equivalent is the combination of Data Cloud and MuleSoft/External Services – connecting the agent to various data with prebuilt connectors. However, out-of-the-box, Salesforce agents might not automatically know a user's files or emails (unless those are in Salesforce records). You'd integrate those deliberately.

Where Copilot Studio does allow custom memory is in defining conversational context and actions. It might not call it "memory," but if you create a bot that has multi-turn dialogs, it will maintain context within that dialog by design. Also, Copilot can leverage "user memory" like preferences if they're part of the Microsoft 365 profile or set in Azure Cognitive Service's bot configuration. For instance, Azure Bot Service historically let you store user state in a state service – Copilot likely abstracts that, but it's there.

One thing Copilot focuses on is user-by-user deployment – you enable it per tenant, and it respects each user's permissions on data. This is similar to Salesforce's approach of running as a user and checking field/org permissions. An area Copilot might be less flexible is fine-grained memory control:

as a developer, you don't get to code how it stores context beyond what the platform does, whereas in Salesforce you could custom-tailor memory storage. The flip side is Copilot might do a lot for you (like auto-summarize a document if needed) with minimal prompt engineering.

Salesforce Data Cloud + GPT: We've discussed Data Cloud a bit already – it's Salesforce's way to unify data and provide real-time context. For AI agents, Data Cloud can act as a global memory reservoir. Imagine an agent that when asked about a customer, can pull up not just CRM data but also recent e-commerce interactions, support cases, marketing email engagement – all from Data Cloud unified profile. This is incredibly powerful for personalization and context: you essentially have a 360° memory of the customer. Data Cloud also allows segmentation (grouping users by traits) which can feed behavior targeting. For example, your agent could detect "User is in segment 'Frequent Flyer'" and adjust its responses to assume more product knowledge, or if "Customer is high-value", the agent might take extra steps or route differently. Integrating Data Cloud with GPT means you might generate dynamic prompts that include segment attributes: "This customer is in Segment: VIP; they prefer premium support." Already, Salesforce has been demoing GPT using Data Cloud to tailor outputs like marketing copy for specific segments. It's akin to giving the AI a cheat sheet about the user or entity it's dealing with.

One must be careful though: if Data Cloud has a ton of data, you don't dump it all in the prompt. Instead, likely you'll select key attributes or use it to retrieve the most relevant info (like last purchase, most used product category, etc.). Setting up those mappings (which Data Cloud fields influence which agent behavior) is a design exercise that can differ per use case.

Model Context Protocol (MCP): Now, tying these all together is MCP – an open standard from Anthropic and others to allow different AI tools to exchange context seamlessly. The idea is an agent can package its state (memory, capabilities, intent) in a standardized JSON or message format and send it to another agent or system, which can then incorporate that context without custom integration. In our terms, MCP could let a Salesforce agent hand off to, say, a LangChain agent running in Python by including memory payloads and descriptors in the call, so the LangChain side knows the user is an executive, with these 3 preferences, and here's the conversation history summary. Or vice versa: a Copilot could invoke a Salesforce agent through MCP, providing the relevant Microsoft context (doc summary, user profile) in a structured way, which our Salesforce agent could map to its own memory model. MCP is still emerging, but it's basically aiming to solve the

"N×M integration problem" of every AI needing custom connectors. Instead, any MCP-compliant server (Salesforce could be one, with an MCP interface to Agentforce) can talk to any MCP-compliant client (maybe a future version of LangChain or Copilot supports MCP out of the box).

Salesforce is already conceptually on board with composability and orchestration across platforms (recall earlier chapters about swarms). Embracing MCP would mean designing our agents to produce and consume standardized context packets. For instance, an Agentforce agent might output a JSON like: { user_context: {...}, conversation_history: "summary text...", pending_task: "need approval for X" } and label it as MCP format, so an external orchestrator can pick it up. While MCP details are beyond our scope here, it's worth noting that future-proofing your agent design might involve keeping context in well-defined data structures, making it easier to transform into whatever standard wins out.

Cross-ecosystem example: Consider a scenario – a user asks Microsoft 365 Copilot (in Teams) to initiate a complex deal process. Copilot might not have all CRM data, so it reaches out to a Salesforce Agent (via an integration) to handle CRM-specific subtasks. Using something like MCP, Copilot could send the Salesforce agent a context package: "User is asking to create a new sales opportunity for ACME Corp, here's a summary of their last Teams meeting notes about ACME." The Salesforce agent uses this as session memory, creates the opportunity with relevant fields (through Flow/Apex), maybe even runs an Agentforce Conductor agent that calls a pricing service. Then it responds back with results and any questions. The memory flows back to Copilot, which then presents the combined outcome to the user. In that chain, we had cross-platform memory sharing – Teams meeting notes (external context) injected into Salesforce process, and Salesforce's outcome (e.g. opp ID, next steps) fed back into the Teams context. This kind of interoperability is exactly what's envisioned with MCP and similar efforts.

As a Salesforce agent designer, keep an eye on how memory is handled by others: LangChain teaches us modular memory patterns; CrewAI shows the importance of shared context in multi-agent systems; AutoGen demonstrates maintaining continuity through tool usage; Copilot underscores leveraging existing user data and adaptive workflow integration; Data Cloud within Salesforce itself offers a treasure trove of context for personalization at scale. By understanding these, you can build agents that are not only strong in isolation but also play well in the broader AI ecosystem.

And hey, if all else fails, you can always cheekily tell your stakeholders: "Our Salesforce agent has a better memory than ChatGPT – because we designed it that way!"

Having journeyed through internal designs and external comparisons, we've built up a comprehensive view of managing agent memory, context, and personalization. From session tidbits to long-term user profiles to cross-platform context hand-offs, we've covered how to make AI agents in Salesforce truly contextually adaptive. In the next chapter, we'll shift gears from design to operations: taking these smart agents and deploying, monitoring, and governing them in the real world. But as you turn the page, remember – an agent that remembers is an agent that can learn, adapt, and ultimately deliver far more value than one that forgets every interaction. With that design superpower in hand, you're ready to tackle the practical realities of bringing these agents to life at scale.

13

DEPLOYMENT, OBSERVABILITY, AND LIFECYCLE MANAGEMENT

Releasing AI agents into production is a team sport that goes far beyond writing clever prompts or automation flows. The simple truth is that even the best-designed agent is only as useful as its deployment, monitoring, and iteration strategy. This chapter is where agent theory becomes operational reality. You've built intelligent agents – now you need to roll them out safely, watch what they do, and evolve them with confidence.

We will focus on three critical areas in the agent lifecycle: Deployment, Observability, and Lifecycle Management. First, we'll explore deployment strategies to ensure agents move from development to production reliably and without disrupting your org. Next, we'll cover observability – how to track what agents are doing in the wild, detect when they misfire, and glean insights to improve them. Finally, we'll tackle lifecycle management – how to version, pause, update, or retire agents as your ecosystem of AI teammates matures over time.

Why invest in these operational disciplines? Consider that many CIOs are still unsure if AI agents can truly deliver at enterprise scale; there are open questions about agent reliability, governance, and measurable ROI. Salesforce's response has been to bake in robust deployment and monitoring tools (like Agentforce's new Command Center) to give teams better visibility and control. In fact, without clear insight into how AI agents perform, business leaders are unlikely to trust or expand their use. The takeaway: treat your agents like production software – with proper environments, telemetry, and rollback plans – or risk unwelcome surprises in production.

Agentforce provides several features to support safe deployments. Salesforce Agent Builder allows you to configure agents in a sandbox, mark their readiness status, and only expose them to users when appropriate. Standard Salesforce DevOps tools like Change Sets and Unlocked Packages let you promote agent components (flows, Apex classes, etc.) between orgs in a governed way. The Agentforce Command Center, introduced in Agentforce 3, adds an "observability layer" – a unified Command Center dashboard inside Agentforce Studio where you can monitor agent health, performance, and outcomes in real time. These tools work together to ensure that a small change in one agent doesn't ripple out of control across a swarm of agents. In a multi-agent system, one tweak can affect others, so governance and monitoring are not optional.

In the sections ahead, we'll dive into how to prepare agents for deployment, set up observability with Salesforce Command Center, establish metrics and logging patterns for different agent types, manage versioning and changes, plan for rollbacks or sunsets, coordinate multi-agent releases, and leverage broader ecosystem tools (like LangChain, Microsoft's AutoGen, crewAI, and the emerging Model Context Protocol). By the end of this chapter, you will have a playbook for launching, monitoring, and evolving Agentforce agents in a way that is scalable, auditable, and safe – setting the stage for the next chapter on designing great UX for human-AI interaction. Let's begin with getting your agents deployment-ready.

PREPARING AGENTS FOR DEPLOYMENT

Launching an AI agent into production requires the same diligence as releasing any mission-critical app. Before you push that "Activate" or "Deploy" button, ensure your agent passes a deployment-readiness checklist:

Robust input validation & error handling: Agents must handle unexpected inputs or failures gracefully. Validate all inputs (from users or systems) and include error-handling paths (e.g. a Flow fault connector or a try/catch in Apex) so the agent doesn't crash or produce unsafe outputs if something goes wrong. For example, if an external API call fails, the agent should log the error and perhaps notify a human supervisor rather than silently failing.

Metadata tagging: Leverage metadata to tag each agent with key attributes like environment (sandbox, UAT, production), version, and pattern (Sentinel, Supervisor, etc.). These tags make it easier to manage deployments and later analyze agent behavior. For instance, you might use a custom metadata type or fields in the agent's configuration object to indicate "version 1.3 – Prod" vs "v2.0 – Beta" as well as the agent pattern. Consistent tagging allows you to quickly filter logs or telemetry by version or team ownership.

Audit trail fields: Ensure each agent's actions are stamped with an audit trail. If your agent invokes actions in Salesforce (like creating a case or updating records), include fields such as "InvokedBy (AgentName)", timestamps, and a status or outcome code on those records. Similarly, log who or what triggered the agent (e.g. user ID or process) and the agent's decision or result. This audit data will be invaluable for debugging and compliance reviews.

Agent Builder visibility status: Salesforce's Agent Builder provides status controls (such as Draft, Testing, Production) to manage agent availability. Use these status fields to control who can interact with the agent. For example, keep a new agent in Draft or Test mode so that only admins or specific users can invoke it (perhaps via a preview panel) until it's fully vetted. Once it's ready, switch to Production status for general availability. This avoids exposing unproven agents to end-users too early. (If such granular statuses aren't built-in, you can simulate this by using permission sets or feature flags to limit access during testing.)

Deployment via Change Set or Unlocked Package: Plan how you will migrate the agent and its related components from a development org to production. For simple setups, a Change Set can capture the Flow, Apex classes, custom objects, and metadata related to your agent. Remember that when deploying flows with change sets, the flow may arrive inactive by default, so you'll need to activate it in the target org (and include all referenced subflows or components in the change set). For a more systematic approach, consider using Salesforce DX unlocked packages. Unlocked packages allow you to treat your metadata as versioned, modular units of deployment, with a source-of-truth in version control. Using an unlocked package for your agent means you can push updates with version numbers, roll back to prior versions by installing an older package version, and even release the same agent to multiple orgs consistently. Pro tip: Always include automated tests (for Apex code or even manual scripts for flows) in your deployment process. A deployment isn't ready unless you've validated that the agent's logic works in a fresh environment.

Launch criteria and gating: Decouple the act of deploying an agent from the decision to "turn it on" for end users. Use feature flags or other gating mechanisms to control the rollout. Feature flags are configuration toggles (often in Custom Metadata or a Hierarchy Custom Setting in Salesforce) that your agent's code or flows check before actually executing their core logic. This allows you to deploy the agent in an "off" state, then flip the flag to on when you're ready (or gradually enable it for a subset of users or context). For example, you might deploy a new Assistant Agent to production but have a flag AgentEnabled=false. The UI component that would invoke the agent checks this flag and only shows the agent to admins initially. Once business stakeholders approve, you set AgentEnabled=true via metadata to launch it to users. Alongside feature flags, define explicit approval checkpoints: require sign-off from a business owner or product manager before an agent moves from testing to live. You can document this approval in the agent's metadata (e.g. a custom field "Business Approval Date") or in release notes. If the agent interacts with end customers or critical data, also ensure UAT (User Acceptance Testing) is completed and recorded. UAT sign-off can be captured by updating a metadata field or an annotation on the agent (for instance, a checkbox "UAT_Approved__c" on an Agent config object) once testers give the green light. By gating deployment in this way, you maintain control – the agent only truly goes live when all conditions are met.

Rollback readiness: Hope for the best, plan for the worst. Before deploying an agent (especially an update to an existing one), have a rollback plan. This could mean keeping the prior version of a Flow intact (not deleting old versions) so you can quickly reactivate the old version if needed. In Apex, it could mean retaining the old class (maybe suffix "_v1") and having a way to switch back to it (perhaps via that feature flag or a settings table that points agent requests to either the new or old class implementation). The goal is that if the new agent behaves badly in prod, you can quickly revert to a known-good state without a rushed hotfix. For example, if deploying InvoiceProcessingAgent v2, do not overwrite or destroy v1 logic. Instead, deploy v2 separately and use a flag CurrentInvoiceAgentVersion = 2. If issues arise, change that flag back to 1 to route processing back to v1 while you troubleshoot. In Salesforce, because deploying code or flows takes time, using configuration toggles for rollback provides near-instant reversion.

Finally, remember that deploying an AI agent is not just moving code – it's also deploying knowledge and visibility. Always bundle any necessary test data (for example, prompt/test cases, sample inputs the agent should handle) so you can validate the agent in the new environment. Additionally, deploy telemetry dashboards or reports alongside the agent. If you have a custom Report or Dashboard in Salesforce to monitor the agent's activity, include it in your change set or package. This ensures that from day one in production, you have eyes on the agent. In short: don't fly blind. A deployment isn't truly done until you can confirm the agent is working as expected in prod and you have the tools to observe it.

Pro tip: Consider creating a "Metadata checklist" for agent releases. This checklist might be a table listing all components and assets an agent needs: e.g. Flows, Apex classes, Prompt templates, Custom Objects (logs or config), Permission Sets, Dashboards, etc. Check off each item as you prepare the deployment. This reduces the chance of "oops, we forgot to deploy the custom permission that allows the agent to access Cases!" type mistakes.

With your agents thoroughly prepared and gated, let's turn to the next challenge: keeping an eye on them once they're running in the wild. In the next section, we set up Salesforce Command Center and other observability tools to monitor AI agents in action.

USING SALESFORCE COMMAND CENTER FOR AGENT MONITORING

Once your agents are live, you need to continuously monitor their health and performance. Salesforce's Agentforce Command Center is designed as the nerve center for AI operations – a "unified pane of glass" where you can see what all your agents are up to. Just as a DevOps team uses application performance dashboards and alerts for a website, your AI agents demand the same level of attention. In this section, we'll cover what to track in production, how to leverage Command Center for observability, and how to set up custom telemetry and alerts.

Salesforce's Agentforce Command Center provides a unified dashboard for monitoring AI agents. This observability layer lets teams track agent interactions, performance metrics, and anomalies in real time.

Key metrics to track: At minimum, configure Command Center to display the following for each agent or agent group:

Invocation counts: How often is each agent being invoked? This might be number of conversations handled (for a chat agent) or number of times the agent's Apex/Flow was called (for background agents) per hour/day. Spikes or drop-offs in usage can indicate adoption trends or potential issues (e.g., an abrupt drop to zero might mean something broke).

Success vs. failure rates: Define what "success" means for each agent and track its success rate. For a Service Agent, success might be "case resolved by the agent without human hand-off." For an Action Agent, success might be "completed the task (e.g. created the record) without errors." Monitor the failure rate too – errors, exceptions, or user escalations. A healthy agent should have a high success rate; if failures begin to climb, that's a red flag needing investigation. Command Center's analytics can show success/failure trends and outliers.

Latency and performance KPIs: How fast are your agents responding or completing tasks? Track end-to-end latency for each agent invocation (from trigger to completion). If an agent calls external APIs or performs heavy computations (like an LLM call), track those durations as well. Sudden increases in latency could degrade user experience or indicate an upstream service slowdown. Command Center's real-time health monitoring provides live analytics for latency and can trigger alerts if response times exceed a threshold. Other performance KPIs might include throughput (tasks per minute) or resource usage if applicable (like API callouts, etc.).

In Agentforce Command Center, you can group and filter agents to focus on relevant subsets. Use tags or naming conventions to group agents by their pattern or owning team. For example, tag each agent's metadata with Pattern=Supervisor or Team=HR AI and ensure those tags flow into the Command Center interface (Salesforce might automatically tag by agent type, but you can also maintain a lookup). This lets you quickly filter the dashboard: e.g., view all Supervisor agents across the org to compare their performance, or view all agents owned by the Finance department. Grouping by pattern is useful because each pattern might have different normal behavior profiles (a high error rate might be expected in an experimental Action agent but would be unacceptable for a Sentinel watchdog agent).

Alerting for anomalies: A good monitoring setup doesn't just passively display metrics – it actively alerts you when something's wrong (or about to go wrong). Leverage the Command Center's alerting features or Salesforce Event Monitoring to set up triggers for unusual events:

If an error spike occurs (e.g., a particular agent suddenly logs a surge of failures in a short time), have Command Center send a notification or create a

Salesforce Task/Case for the responsible team. You might even integrate this with a Supervisor agent pattern: for instance, configure a Supervisor Agent that watches error events and automatically pings the on-call engineer on Slack or posts an alert in a Chatter group when errors exceed X per hour. This way, an agent (Supervisor) oversees other agents' health – eating your own AI cooking!

If a critical agent goes silent or misses a "heartbeat," raise a Sentinel alert. A "heartbeat" could be a scheduled job or ping that the agent sends (or simply the expectation that it should do something periodically). For example, if you have a Sentinel Agent that monitors incoming data feeds, you expect it to fire at least once a day. Command Center can be set to flag if no invocations are recorded in 24 hours. Your incident playbook might involve a fallback process or a restart of the agent. Essentially, treat key agents like services – no heartbeat means something's stuck. A Sentinel pattern agent (true to its name) could be tasked to detect this and escalate, e.g. log an emergency event or notify a human operator.

Anomaly detection: Look for other anomalies like a sudden drop in usage (could indicate an integration broke or users found it unhelpful), or unusual output patterns (maybe an agent's responses became dramatically longer or shorter, signaling a possible regression in an LLM prompt). Salesforce Command Center provides AI-driven recommendations and can highlight anomalies in agent performance. You might integrate it with external monitoring tools as well – notably, Agentforce Command Center is built with support for the OpenTelemetry standard, meaning you can pipe these agent metrics into third-party systems like Datadog or Splunk. If your organization already has an observability platform, use that integration so ops teams have a unified view of traditional app metrics and AI agent metrics together.

Custom dashboards: Beyond the out-of-the-box panels, build custom reports or dashboards for specific stakeholders. For example, a dashboard for a Product Manager might compare usage of an Action Agent across different business units or regions. Did Sales in EMEA invoke the Quote Generator Agent more times than Sales in NA this quarter? Such insights can inform training or support – maybe one group needs more awareness of the agent. Another useful view is to monitor the impact of coaching or advisory agents: for a Coach Agent that provides guidance (say, a Legal compliance coach), you could track "guidance given vs. guidance followed." This might involve logging whenever the agent gives advice and whether the user followed that advice (e.g., if the user clicks "Apply Suggestion" or some outcome occurs). A dashboard could then show the percentage of agent suggestions accepted. Low adoption of suggestions could mean the advice isn't useful or the agent's interface needs improvement.

For more technical agents, create a telemetry log schema and corresponding report. Let's walk through a simple example telemetry schema using a custom object to store agent logs:

Example: Agent Telemetry Log Schema

Agent Name

- **Data type:** Text (Picklist or Lookup)
- **Description:** Identifies which agent generated the log (for example, "OrderConductor").

Timestamp

- **Data type:** DateTime
- **Description:** Records when the agent run or event occurred, stored in UTC.

Request ID

- **Data type:** Text (Unique)
- **Description:** Correlation identifier used to tie together all events from a single agent invocation or session.

Invoked By

- **Data type:** Text (Lookup/User)
- **Description:** Indicates who or what triggered the agent, such as a user ID or a system process name.

Outcome

- **Data type:** Text
- **Description:** Captures the result status of the agent run, for example "Success," "Failed: Validation Error," or "Escalated to Human."

DurationMs

- **Data type:** Number
- **Description:** Measures how long the agent execution took, in milliseconds, when applicable.

Key Metrics

- **Data type:** Text (JSON or structured fields)
- **Description:** Stores run-specific metrics such as number of records processed or LLM tokens consumed.

Error Details

- **Data type:** Text (Long)
- **Description:** Contains the error message or exception details when the outcome indicates a failure.

Version

- **Data type:** Text
- **Description:** Identifies the agent version or build information, such as "v2.0-beta."

Using a custom object like Agent_Log__c with fields as above, the agent (via Flow or Apex) can create a record each time it runs. This gives you a database of granular data to query. You can then build a Salesforce Report or SOQL queries to analyze, for instance: average DurationMs of ActionAgent by day, top 5 error messages for CuratorAgent this week, etc. It complements the aggregate view in Command Center with raw data you can slice and dice.

If implementing such logging, ensure to balance detail with volume – logging too much (like every single prompt and response) could be overkill in production or hit storage limits, whereas logging too little defeats the purpose. Identify a few key fields to log consistently across agents (like those in the schema above). Also, purge or archive old log records as needed (or better yet, export them to an external data warehouse for long-term analysis).

To illustrate, imagine a telemetry log entry for a Supervisor agent that approves discounts:

Agent Name: DealDeskSupervisor

Timestamp: 2025-07-04 16:30:00 UTC

Invoked By: User J.Smith (ID 005...)

Outcome: Success (Approved)

DurationMs: 845

Key Metrics: {RequestedDiscount: "15%", ApprovedDiscount: "10%"}

Version: 1.4-prod

Such entries let you later answer questions like: How often is DealDeskSupervisor approving vs rejecting? What's the average turnaround time? Are certain users invoking it more?

In summary, set up your Command Center as the mission control for agents. Track the essential metrics (invocations, successes/failures, latency), group agents logically, and configure alerts for anomalies. Use the power of Salesforce's integrated monitoring and external tools via OpenTelemetry to ensure you're never in the dark about agent behavior. In the next section, we'll drill down deeper into observability best practices for each agent pattern type, and how to log the right things and set the right alerts tailored to what each kind of agent does.

OBSERVABILITY PATTERNS FOR EACH AGENT TYPE

Not all agents are created equal – a Sentinel agent that monitors events will have different behaviors (and risks) than, say, an Action agent that performs transactions. Therefore, our observability approach should be tailored to each Agent Pattern. By tracking pattern-specific metrics and logs, you can better understand an agent's performance in context and set meaningful alert thresholds. The list below summarizes observability considerations for each of the eight core agent patterns:

Sentinel (event monitor)

- **Key metrics to monitor:** Rate of signals detected (events per hour); count of threshold breaches or alerts raised.

- **Recommended log fields:** Event type or signal detail; threshold values versus actual readings (for example, "CPU 95% > 90% limit"); follow-up action taken.
- **Alert triggers and thresholds:** No signals received within the expected interval (possible data feed failure); high burst of alerts such as five alerts within ten minutes, indicating a potential incident storm.

Supervisor (approval and oversight)

- **Key metrics to monitor:** Approval versus rejection rates; average decision latency from request to decision; escalation rate to humans.
- **Recommended log fields:** Decision outcome with reason code; requestor identity; auto versus manual handling indicator.
- **Alert triggers and thresholds:** High rejection rate (for example, more than 20 percent, suggesting policy mismatch); slow decisions exceeding SLA (such as latency over five minutes).

Conductor (orchestrator)

- **Key metrics to monitor:** Number of sub-tasks or agents coordinated per run; orchestration success rate; total orchestration time.
- **Recommended log fields:** List of agents or tools invoked; per-step success or failure summary; orchestration context ID linking all related logs.
- **Alert triggers and thresholds:** Any workflow failure where a critical step does not complete; excessive duration (for example, alert if a process that normally completes in two minutes exceeds five minutes).

Companion (user assistant)

- **Key metrics to monitor:** Session volume; user satisfaction or feedback scores; handoff rate to humans.
- **Recommended log fields:** Session or conversation ID; interaction count per session; handoff flag and escalation reason.
- **Alert triggers and thresholds:** High handoff rate (for example,

more than 30 percent of sessions); user frustration signals such as repeated low ratings or phrases indicating lack of help.

Presenter (content formatter)

- **Key metrics to monitor:** Average output length; format usage such as charts versus text; delivery success rate.
- **Recommended log fields:** Output format (HTML, PDF, etc.); output size; target delivery channel.
- **Alert triggers and thresholds:** Delivery failures such as email send errors or UI component failures; output size anomalies such as empty output or sizes far outside the normal range.

Curator (data gatherer)

- **Key metrics to monitor:** Number of sources accessed per request; retrieval success rate; cache hit rate if caching is used.
- **Recommended log fields:** Sources accessed; result size; miss indicator showing whether useful information was found.
- **Alert triggers and thresholds:** High miss rate indicating incomplete data or poor query tuning; source failures such as external API downtime.

Action (transaction executor)

- **Key metrics to monitor:** Task execution volume; success versus failure rates; rollback or compensation occurrences.
- **Recommended log fields:** Action details describing what was executed; error messages; rollback indicator.
- **Alert triggers and thresholds:** Sudden spike in execution errors affecting data integrity; any rollback invocation, signaling a significant failure requiring investigation.

Coach (advisor or guide)

- **Key metrics to monitor:** Number of suggestions delivered; suggestion acceptance rate; follow-up or clarification query rate.
- **Recommended log fields:** Suggestion category or content type; user response or feedback; session or user context reference.

- **Alert triggers and thresholds:** Low acceptance rate indicating off-target guidance; high clarification rate such as more than two follow-up questions per suggestion, suggesting confusion.

Each pattern has its own "shape" of data. By logging the recommended fields, you create a rich dataset for analysis. And by setting alert triggers appropriate to each, you avoid false alarms and catch true issues. For instance, a Sentinel agent might legitimately go quiet if no events occur – that's fine, but if it goes beyond a known interval, then alert. A Supervisor agent might reject 5% of requests normally (that might be fine, indicating it's catching invalid ones), but if rejection jumps to 50%, something's off either in the criteria or in the input quality.

A few best practices emerge across all patterns.

Use consistent log formats: If possible, have a common logging framework (like the custom object schema earlier in this chapter) that all agents use, with extensions for pattern-specific data. This makes it easier to build unified dashboards and do org-wide queries. For example, every log could have fields like AgentPattern, Outcome, Duration, plus some free-form JSON field Details that might contain pattern-specific info (like the list of sources for Curator or suggestion text for Coach).

Leverage Salesforce Event Monitoring and Field Audit Trail: Some agent actions might be observable via existing Salesforce logs. For instance, if an Action agent creates records, Salesforce's setup audit logs can track that. However, these won't have the rich context (like which agent did it) without your custom logging. Still, consider enabling Event Monitoring (which provides log events for Apex errors, etc.) to complement your agent's own logs.

Correlate across agents: In multi-agent workflows, correlating logs can help. Using a common Request ID or Session ID across an orchestration (e.g., Conductor passes an ID to all sub-agents) means later you can trace a whole story of what happened across agents. This is invaluable when debugging a complex scenario involving multiple patterns.

Finally, ensure you capture failure paths. Many Salesforce admins are familiar with setting up Flow Fault Paths for error handling. If your Agent is implemented as a Salesforce Flow (perhaps an Autolaunched Flow for an Action agent or part of a Conductor flow), always configure the Fault connectors on key elements to catch exceptions. Those fault paths can invoke an "Agent Fault Log" subflow or Apex that writes to your log object, capturing the exception details, the agent name, and context. This way, even if the agent hits an error, you get a log record before the flow terminates. You could even combine this with alerting: e.g., the fault-handling subflow not only logs the error but also sends an email alert to the support team or creates a high-priority Case. In Apex, similarly, use try-catch blocks to handle exceptions and log them (perhaps calling a common logging utility).

Pro tip: Build a simple Lightning dashboard for real-time "agent observability." For example, a Lightning Web Component that queries the Agent_Log__c object and displays recent errors or key metrics, perhaps with filters by pattern. Pin this in your Agentforce Studio or on an Operations Console. This complements the official Command Center with any custom data you track.

With robust observability in place, you can confidently deploy agents knowing you'll catch issues early. Next, we address how to manage changes over an agent's lifetime – versioning and change management, so you can improve agents without breaking existing functionality.

AGENT VERSIONING AND CHANGE MANAGEMENT

In a dynamic business environment, your AI agents will not be one-and-done; they'll evolve. You'll tweak prompts, upgrade models, refine flows, and add features. A sound versioning strategy ensures you can introduce changes in a controlled way, track what changed and why, and maintain compatibility. This section offers guidelines for versioning both declarative and programmatic agents (Flows and Apex), managing metadata around versions, and rolling out updates smoothly.

Version your agents explicitly. Salesforce provides some inherent versioning: Flows have version numbers, and you can create new versions of a flow while keeping the old one (only one version can be active at a time per flow). Apex classes don't have built-in versioning, so you manage that via naming conventions and multiple classes if needed. Embrace these patterns:

Apex invocable actions: If you have agents implemented in Apex (e.g., an Apex class that an Agent Builder topic calls), consider suffixing class names with version numbers for major changes. For example, you might have PaymentAgentAction_v1 and later create PaymentAgentAction_v2. The v2 class can be deployed alongside v1 without conflict. If you design the agent to call a specific class, you can switch which version it calls via a metadata setting. Alternatively, publish new Apex actions and mark older ones as deprecated. The key is to avoid a scenario where you modify a single class in place and inadvertently break the agent for existing users. By maintaining AgentTaskV1, AgentTaskV2, etc., you can even allow both versions to run concurrently for different contexts (perhaps V2 is used for a pilot group while everyone else still uses V1). This approach is akin to having API versioning – treat your agent's logic as an API that needs contract stability.

Flow versioning: When updating a Flow that powers an agent, you have two main choices: use the built-in version mechanism or create a new flow. For minor changes, you might simply save a new version of the existing Flow and activate it (Salesforce will then automatically start using the new version in all entry points). However, for major changes, especially those that might not be backward compatible, it can be safer to build a separate Flow (with a new API name, like MyAgentFlow_v2) and leave the original intact. This way, you could even run them in parallel (with some logic deciding which one to call). Using the Metadata API, you can retrieve and deploy flows and even script the creation of new versions, but conceptually, having separate Flow names for major revisions gives you more flexibility. Keep in mind that when you deploy a flow via metadata, the target org will see it as a new version if the API name matches an existing flow, or as a separate flow if you changed the name.

Custom metadata for versions: Maintain a registry of agent versions and their statuses. For example, a Custom Metadata Type or custom object Agent_Version__c could list each agent by name, with fields for "Current Version", "Deprecated Versions", "Beta Version Available" etc. This acts as documentation within Salesforce. You could even have the agent check this metadata at runtime: e.g., an agent might read a config that says "use Flow X v2 for logic, but still call Apex Y v1 for a sub-task because v2 of that sub-task isn't GA yet," etc. This might be more complexity than needed for small deployments, but in large orgs with many agents, a central version table helps keep track. At minimum, use descriptions and labels in your Flow/Apex metadata to note version info (e.g., put "v1.4 – Added new field validation" in the Flow description so anyone can see the history).

Document behavior changes and approvals: Each new version should come with notes on what changed, why, and who approved it (if governance is in place). For example, if Agent ContractCopilot v2.0 loosens some legal approval rules, note that the Legal team approved this change on X date. Custom metadata can store these notes (perhaps a long text field "Changelog__c"). Or you might use source control commit messages if you manage flows as XML. The point is to create an audit trail so that if someone asks, "Why did the agent start doing Y instead of X?", you can trace it to "Version 2.1 deployed on 2025-08-01, change approved by John Doe (Legal) to comply with new policy."

Deprecation schedules: Plan the retirement of old versions. It's tempting to keep v1, v2, v3 all running forever "just in case." But stale logic can confuse maintenance and pose risks (e.g., someone might accidentally invoke an outdated version). Instead, once a new version is stable, schedule the deprecation of the old. You might mark older versions as "Deprecated" in metadata and after, say, 90 days of running in parallel, remove or disable them. Communicate to any stakeholders that "v1 will be sunset on DATE; please switch to v2 endpoints or interfaces." In the context of Agentforce, if an agent's API is invoked internally (by flows or Apex), ensure all references are updated to the new version by that date. This is similar to how API deprecations are handled.

Feature flags for rollout: Earlier we discussed using feature flags to enable an agent. The same applies within an agent to enable new features or behaviors. Suppose AdvisorAgent v3 introduces a new suggestion algorithm, but you're not sure if it outperforms the old one. You could deploy v3 with a flag NewAlgoEnabled that is false by default, meaning it still behaves like v2. Then toggle it on for a subset of cases or users to test. This is a config-driven change management approach that Salesforce teams can implement with Custom Settings/Metadata easily. It allows progressive rollout of features without constant redeployment. If the new feature misbehaves, you flip the flag off – a quick mitigation.

Backward compatibility and grace periods: In multi-agent ecosystems, think about consumers of agent outputs or chained agents. If you upgrade a Conductor agent that calls two Action agents, ensure the new Conductor can still work if one of the Action agents is on an older version (maybe because that one hasn't been upgraded yet). One strategy is to build the new Conductor to support dual modes: e.g., if new Action v2 is present, use it, otherwise call Action v1. Alternatively, deploy the new Conductor in parallel, while the old Conductor continues with old actions, and gradually shift traffic. During transitions, monitor for any mismatches. Maintain backward compatibility for at least one cycle – for example, if external systems or processes call your agent's API (maybe via a named credential or something), don't remove fields or change contracts abruptly. Deprecate slowly: log a warning in old version that it's deprecated before turning it off.

To make this concrete, let's use the outline's example: deploying a new Conductor agent that supports both old and new Action agents for 90 days. Imagine we have an orchestrator agent OnboardingConductor that coordinates two sub-agents: HRAction (creates user accounts, etc.) and ITAction (sets up equipment). We have existing Action agents v1 for HR and IT. Now we developed improved versions of both sub-agents (v2) with more capabilities. We want to roll them out without disrupting onboarding.

Step 1: Deploy HRAction_v2 and ITAction_v2 alongside v1s. They might be inactive or gated initially.

Step 2: Deploy an updated OnboardingConductor that is aware of two modes: it has logic like "if version metadata says use v2, then call HRAction_v2, else call HRAction_v1." We set in metadata that only a small pilot department uses v2, everyone else uses v1. For instance, maybe a field HRActionVersionForDepartment__c custom metadata mapping department to version.

Step 3: For 90 days, both versions run: pilot users trigger the Conductor, which sees their department and uses v2 sub-agents, others continue with v1. We gather telemetry: Are v2 actions succeeding? Are they faster? Any errors not seen in v1?

Step 4: Gradually increase the % of usage of v2 (update the metadata to roll v2 out to more departments). Always keep an eye on logs (Comparative success rates). If any severe issue in v2 arises, the Conductor can be quickly flipped to route everyone back to v1 by changing the metadata mapping to "use v1 for all" – an instant rollback at the configuration level.

Step 5: After confidence in v2 (say after 60 days), we plan deprecation of v1. Announce that after Day 90, v1 will be turned off. On Day 90, update Conductor to remove the branching logic and always call v2 (or deploy a simplified Conductor v2 that doesn't even know about v1). Retire the v1 agents (deactivate them or remove their actions from the library).

Throughout this, version tagging in logs helped: every log entry from the Conductor and Actions noted which version was used, so we could compare performance. We also documented in the Agent Registry that HRAction_v2's differences from v1 included, say, a new field and were approved by HR department head.

This level of change management may seem heavy, but for agents handling critical business processes, it's worth the rigor. Agents, especially those powered by AI, can have unpredictable changes in behavior with even small tweaks (a single prompt change might alter outcomes). So controlled versioning and careful rollout is your safety net.

In summary, treat agent logic like versioned APIs or microservices: use semantic versioning ideas, isolate major changes, track metadata, and double-lane new and old versions during transitions when possible. That sets the stage for the next topic: what if despite careful deployment, something goes wrong and you need to rollback, or what about when an agent's time has come to an end? We'll handle rollback and sunset strategies next.

ROLLBACK AND SUNSET STRATEGIES

No matter how well you prepare, reality can bite back – maybe a new agent version has a critical bug, or business priorities change and an agent is no longer needed. Rollback strategies ensure you can gracefully back out a bad deployment, and sunset strategies provide a roadmap for retiring agents without chaos. This section covers both scenarios.

Rollback Strategies

When an agent deployment doesn't go as planned (e.g., causing errors or unintended outcomes), you need a quick way to revert to the last known good state:

Metadata toggles for quick switch: As discussed, feature flags or a metadata setting can act as an "on/off" switch or version selector. This is usually the fastest rollback method. Ensure your design includes such a toggle wherever feasible. For instance, a custom setting ActiveAgentVersion can be read by your agent's orchestration logic. If the new version misbehaves, changing that setting back to the old version instantly routes logic to the stable path. This avoids the delay of redeploying code in an emergency. Always test these toggles ahead of time – simulate a rollback in a staging environment to be confident it actually reverts everything needed.

Parallel run and redirection: Another approach is to keep the old agent running in parallel (as we did with v1 and v2 above) and simply redirect traffic. For example, if you launched a new CustomerSupport Chatbot Agent but find it giving incorrect answers, you might have left the older Einstein Bot in place. You can then change your chat entry point or chatbot routing to send users back to the Einstein Bot (or a simpler fallback script) while you diagnose the new agent. This could be as simple as toggling which Bot is active on your Digital Experience or chat channel configuration. The principle is: don't pull the rug from under the old solution until the new one proves itself, and if the new trips, divert users back.

Apex/Flow fallback branches: Build fallbacks into the agent's implementation where possible. For instance, in an Apex-based agent, you might catch exceptions or undesired outcomes and have a fallback method or class. Perhaps something like:

```
try {
  newAgent.process(request);
} catch(Exception e) {
  Log.error(e);
  LegacyAgent.process(request); // fallback to old logic
}
```

Similarly, in Flow, use Decision elements or Fault paths: if new step fails, route to alternative older subflow. This way the system "self-heals" in the moment by using a degraded but working path rather than just failing. Use this sparingly (you wouldn't want complex logic always double-processing), but for critical transactions, a fallback could save the day. Also log that a fallback was used so you can track how often it happens (if too often, that's essentially a silent rollback in progress).

Data and state rollback: Sometimes an agent's actions involve data changes that need undoing if we roll it back. For example, an Action agent might have created records with a new format or incomplete info. Part of rollback planning is knowing how to handle any partial outputs. Ideally, your agent transactions are atomic (complete success or no changes). But if not, consider building a "compensation" flow or script. For instance, if ContractGeneratorAgent v2 created 50 draft contracts in a new format before you caught a bug, you might need a script to clean up or convert those to v1 format. Keep such utilities handy, or at least documented, as part of your deployment plan ("if rollback, run XYZ to clean data").

Archive conversation or action logs for replay: When you rollback an AI agent, it's useful to have a record of what it did while it was live, both for root cause analysis and for possibly replaying with a fixed version. For conversational agents, save transcripts. For processing agents, save a list of transactions or inputs it handled. After fixing the issue, you might want to "replay" some of those through the new agent to verify it handles them correctly (this could be done in a sandbox with the logs as input). Archiving these also helps train future iterations (if the agent is LLM-based, transcripts of failures can be great training data for improvements).

Sunset (Decommissioning) Strategies

At some point, an agent might become obsolete or be replaced by a more advanced system. Sunsetting an agent should be done deliberately to avoid user confusion or broken integrations:

Communicate end-of-life: Just as you would announce the retirement of a software feature, inform users or stakeholders that an agent will be retired. If the agent has direct user interaction (like a chatbot or an assistant in Salesforce UI), consider using the agent itself or its UI to notify users. For example, a Companion agent could display a message like: "This assistant will be upgraded to a new version on [date]." or "Note: This agent will be discontinued soon, please use [NewAgentName] instead." If the agent works behind the scenes, send out communications to the business owners or log something notable. For internal agents, maybe a Slack announcement by a Supervisor agent or an email from the product team suffices. The key is to give advance notice.

Redirect or handoff on sunset date: On the day of sunset, implement a graceful handoff. If a new agent replaces the old, ensure any invocation of the old agent is forwarded or handled by the new agent. In Salesforce, that might mean if something tries to execute the old Flow, you modify that Flow to simply call the new Flow and then record a log "Redirected from old to new." If the agent is user-facing, perhaps keep a stub alive that only says "I've been replaced, please use [new agent]" or automatically transfers the user to a human. For example, if a customer tries to interact with a retired chatbot, it could respond: "Let me connect you to an agent, as I'm no longer active." The idea is to not leave users at a dead end.

Update or remove integrations: Check all places where the agent was referenced. This could include: Apex schedulers, Flow triggers, UI buttons, external API calls, etc. Update them to use the replacement or remove them entirely. A thorough search in your org's metadata (using VSCode or metadata search tools) for the agent's name can be helpful to catch all references. If you have an Agent Registry object listing where each agent is used, that's invaluable here (more on that registry soon).

Log last-used date & archive: It's good practice to log when an agent was last actively used, and by whom. This can be as simple as updating a "LastUsedDate" field in the agent's config each time it runs. When planning a sunset, review this: if something supposedly unused for 6 months is still running daily, that's a red flag! After sunsetting, keep an archive of essential info: final logs, knowledge bases or prompts it used, etc., in case you need to audit or revive any piece. You might export these to a document or repository. Then you can delete or deactivate the agent components from Salesforce (maybe after a buffer period of a few weeks of zero activity to be safe).

Fallback agents or default behavior: If the agent being retired leaves a gap, fill it. For instance, if you remove an automated Q&A agent and haven't yet got a replacement, make sure the user requests are routed to a human or an FAQ page instead, rather than just failing. In the Agentforce context, you might configure a Companion agent to catch queries that used to go to the old agent and present a helpful message or route. Or a Supervisor agent might detect a scenario and take manual input instead. Essentially, design a fallback so that the business process still continues, albeit in a more manual way, rather than just breaking.

One neat idea is to implement a "Paused" status in Agent Builder (if not already available). This would be akin to deactivating the agent without removing it. A paused agent remains in the system (so you can resume it if needed) but it does not respond or execute. Perhaps it returns a polite message "temporarily unavailable" or simply doesn't trigger. This status could be used during maintenance or as a soft-retirement step (maybe you pause it for a week to see if anyone complains, before fully deleting). The outline specifically suggests a paused status – check if Agentforce UI has such an option; if not, you can simulate it with a feature flag "Active=false" as mentioned.

Example: Let's say we have an agent TravelRecommender that employees barely use anymore (maybe they now use a new corporate travel tool). We decide to retire it. We'd announce "TravelRecommender will be discontinued on Aug 31." On that date, we set a flag so that if anyone invokes it (perhaps via a Slack command), it replies: "This agent is no longer available. Please contact the travel desk for assistance." It logs that interaction (so we know someone tried). After a month of seeing no one really needed it, we then remove its configuration from Slack and delete the agent's components from Salesforce. We update our Agent Registry to mark it "Retired on Aug 31, 2025".

In summary, plan rollback and sunsets as part of your deployment strategy. Rollback plans mean you're never stuck in a bad release; sunset plans mean you keep your AI ecosystem tidy and relevant over time. As your organization's roster of agents grows, you'll routinely cycle through updates and retirements – doing this cleanly maintains trust with users and keeps maintenance manageable.

Next, we will discuss how to coordinate when multiple agents need to be deployed or updated together (a scenario that's increasingly common as you adopt "swarms" of agents working in concert).

MULTI-AGENT RELEASE COORDINATION

In complex orgs, you won't just deploy one agent in isolation – you might deploy a team of interdependent agents. For example, a new product launch could involve updates to a Curator agent (to fetch new product info), a Presenter agent (to format it for sales reps), a Conductor agent (to orchestrate an end-to-end demo workflow), and a Companion agent (customer-facing assistant for FAQs). Coordinating such multi-agent releases is critical to avoid mismatches (one agent expecting another to have new capabilities when it doesn't yet). This section provides strategies for choreographing multi-agent releases, including manifests, dependency mapping, sequencing with Flow Orchestration, and using an Agent Registry.

Deployment manifests for swarms: When releasing a set of agents (sometimes called an "agent swarm" when they work together), create a deployment manifest – essentially a playbook of what agents and components are involved, and the order of operations. This manifest could be a simple document or spreadsheet that lists:

- All agents being updated or created (with versions).
- Entry points for each (e.g., "CuratorAgent – invoked by Apex class X, or via API Y").
- Exit points or outputs of each (e.g., "ActionAgent outputs a Record Id which is used by PresenterAgent").
- Dependencies (e.g., "Agent B must be deployed before Agent C" or "Agent A's new output will not be used until Agent D is live").
- Any config toggles (like feature flags) and their desired state through the rollout (e.g., "FeatureFlagNewProductFlow = true only after all agents updated").

- Rollback plan for each agent (maybe link to the section in the doc covering rollback).

Having this manifest ensures everyone (developers, QA, release managers) are on the same page about the moving parts. It's particularly useful if different teams own different agents – all teams can contribute to and review the manifest.

Define entry and exit points per agent: Clarify how each agent is triggered and what it produces that others may consume. For instance, CuratorAgent might be triggered when a user asks a question, and it outputs a list of knowledge articles. PresenterAgent takes that list to generate a response. Knowing this chain helps you understand that if Curator fails, Presenter has nothing to work with, etc. Documenting "Agent X starts when... and ends by doing..." for each agent in the release helps plan testing and identify weak links.

Include readiness checks and rollback plans: For each agent, define how you will verify it's working (readiness) and what to do if it isn't (rollback). In a multi-agent scenario, a readiness test might involve running a full scenario end-to-end. For example, for an open enrollment benefits release: readiness might be "simulate an employee enrolling in new benefits: the Companion agent greets them, the Curator agent fetches policy info, the Conductor orchestrates enrollment steps, Presenter agent confirms the summary. All steps should succeed in staging." Only when the entire chain passes do you proceed. If any fails, you rollback changes (perhaps revert to old agents in staging, fix, retry). Plan these gating tests before doing the production deployment.

Map dependencies: If Agent A calls Agent B's API or output, then Agent B must be updated before or at the same time as A (unless A can handle both old and new B). Mark such dependencies clearly. You might use a simple directed graph or list. This will influence deployment order. Maybe you deploy lower-level utility agents first (e.g., Action agents that do basic tasks) and verify them, then deploy higher-level orchestrators that use those outputs.

Use Flow Orchestration for rollout testing: This is a creative use of Salesforce Flow Orchestrator (which is typically for business processes, but here we use it for a test harness). You can build an orchestration flow that mimics a user journey or a sequence of events that involve multiple agents. For example, create an Orchestration with steps: (1) simulate event to trigger

Agent A, (2) call Agent B, (3) verify outcome, etc., possibly with human steps to verify outputs. By running this orchestration in a test environment (or even production as a dry run if it doesn't commit data), you automate the integration testing of your multi-agent system. Orchestration flows can sequence both automated steps (auto-launched flows) and manual steps (screen flows for a tester to validate something). This ensures that when you do a big, coordinated release, you have repeatedly tested the whole before flipping the switch.

Cross-team communication and dashboards: Multi-agent releases often involve multiple owners (e.g., Sales Cloud team owns one agent, Service Cloud team owns another). Establish a shared communication channel – maybe a Slack/Chatter group or a short daily stand-up during the release period – to coordinate. Also, utilize shared dashboards in Command Center that show all related agents' status. For instance, create a Command Center view filtered to just "Open Enrollment Agents" pattern or tags, so everyone can monitor that set during rollout. If one agent in the set starts erroring, the team will spot it and know it affects the others.

Agent Registry for tracking: Maintain a central Agent Registry (perhaps a custom object Agent__c with records for each agent in your org). This registry can include fields like Owner Team, Pattern, Current Version, Dependent Agents, Last Deployed Date, etc. Before a release, update the registry entries for all agents involved (e.g., bump their version, mark status "In Deployment"). You can also log the release event, e.g., have a related object Agent_Release__c that records "On 2025-09-01, Agents A, B, C were deployed as part of release R123 by Jane Doe. Change summary: ..." Keeping such data in Salesforce not only serves documentation, but you can use it for impact analysis. Say, 6 months later, someone asks "Our order processing seems slow, did we change anything?" – you could query Agent_Release records for that timeframe and see if any agent involved might be relevant.

Let's illustrate multi-agent coordination with the example given: an annual benefits open enrollment update. The scenario: every year, the company updates its benefits and you have several agents to help employees with enrollment:

- A Curator agent that gathers the latest benefits info (e.g., new health plan details from HR systems).
- A Presenter agent that presents personalized enrollment options to employees in a chat or portal.

- A Conductor agent that orchestrates the overall open enrollment workflow (perhaps coordinating between HR systems, sending notifications, collecting confirmations).
- A Companion agent that answers employees' FAQs about benefits and assists them through the process.

For the new year's enrollment, all four need updates (new data, updated rules, etc.).

Planning: You create a manifest listing each. For example, CuratorAgent v3 will now fetch new fields (like HSA options), PresenterAgent v2 will have new templates for those options, ConductorAgent v1.1 will include steps to handle a new verification requirement, CompanionAgent knowledge base updated with new FAQs. Dependencies: Curator must retrieve data that Presenter expects; if Curator fails or has old data, Presenter's output is wrong. Conductor uses Curator's data as well, and relies on Presenter for final confirmation. Companion is somewhat standalone but it shares the knowledge base content that Curator uses. So essentially, all should be updated before we turn on the feature.

Testing: In UAT, you run through an entire fake enrollment: The Companion greets a test user, user asks a question (Companion uses updated info – verify it's correct). Then user proceeds to enroll: Conductor kicks off, calls Curator to get plans (with new year data), then maybe calls some Action agents to record choices, then Presenter confirms. Use Flow Orchestration to automate this test: Stage 1 could call an autolaunched flow that triggers the Conductor (simulating an employee starting enrollment), Stage 2 could be a human step "Check that the presented summary is correct", Stage 3 could simulate finalizing and then verify records in HR system (or stub). This orchestration can be run as many times as needed to iron out issues.

Deployment: On deployment day, perhaps you deploy Curator and the updated knowledge data first (since others depend on data). Then deploy Conductor and Action sub-agents next, and Presenter and Companion updates last. Or all together if you're using a packaging mechanism, but ensure feature flags are off such that no one accidentally hits the half-deployed state. Only once all are confirmed deployed do you enable them (maybe via a master "OpenEnrollment2025Enabled" flag that multiple agents check). If an issue surfaces in one agent after go-live, you might toggle that flag off (pausing the whole feature) or revert that particular agent to previous version if possible, while communicating with teams.

Communication: All teams (HR IT, Salesforce devs, etc.) watch the Command Center where you've set up a dashboard showing: Curator invocations success rate, Presenter response times, etc., in real time as employees start using it. The first day, maybe have hourly check-ins to ensure everything is smooth. The Agent Registry is updated to reflect all these changes, so later analysis knows that these versions went live for Open Enrollment 2025.

This example underscores how multi-agent releases need orchestration much like multi-microservice releases in traditional IT. Flow Orchestration is a great tool not just for business processes, but also for coordinating and testing complex releases within Salesforce – treat the release itself as a business process!

With coordination strategies in place, we last turn to how Salesforce's AI agent ecosystem fits into the broader picture. There are external frameworks and standards evolving (LangChain, AutoGen, crewAI, MCP, etc.) – how do those mesh with Salesforce, and what deployment/monitoring considerations do they introduce? Let's explore that in the final section.

ECOSYSTEM STRATEGIES FOR DEPLOYMENT AND MONITORING

Salesforce Agentforce doesn't exist in a vacuum. Many organizations will complement their Salesforce-based agents with external AI services or frameworks. It's important to understand how to integrate those into your deployment and monitoring strategy. We'll look at a few popular frameworks – LangChain, Microsoft's AutoGen, crewAI – and the emerging Model Context Protocol (MCP) standard, as well as CI/CD considerations.

Continuous Integration/Continuous Delivery (CI/CD) for Agents: First, consider how you manage releases. Within Salesforce, you might use Salesforce DX, scratch orgs, and tools like Gearset or Jenkins for metadata deployments. This should include your agent components. For example, treat "Agent definitions" (if they are metadata) like code – pull them into source control. If an agent involves code (Apex, LWC for UI, etc.), that naturally goes in your repo. Even if an agent is mostly configuration (prompts, flows), you can capture those as metadata (Flows, Custom Metadata for prompts, etc.) in source control. External platforms might orchestrate deployments too – e.g., using GitHub Actions to spin up a scratch org, deploy the new agent pieces, run tests (maybe even run a headless browser to trigger a flow or agent in a UI for testing), then promote to staging and production.

Some teams integrate Salesforce deployment with broader pipelines: for instance, a Jenkins pipeline might deploy a Salesforce agent update and a Node.js service that the agent calls, in one go. Coordination is key so that if your agent relies on an external API, that API is deployed and ready first (or vice versa depending on coupling).

If using changesets manually, be extra careful with order and completeness (as we discussed in deployment prep). It's slower but can work for simple cases. Larger orgs should invest in DX and unlocked packages to manage agent releases, especially as number of components grows.

LangChain and chain-of-thought agents: LangChain is an open-source framework popular for building AI chains and agents (often in Python). Some companies might host LangChain-based agents outside of Salesforce but integrate them via API. If you use LangChain for complex reasoning or tool-using agents, you should still apply deployment rigor: version your chain definitions or prompts (store them in a Git repo), have a testing script to simulate conversations through the chain, and monitor it. LangChain provides callback hooks where you can capture each step in a chain. Use those to log into Salesforce or an external log when the agent is used. For instance, if a Salesforce Flow calls an AWS Lambda that runs a LangChain agent, that Lambda should log steps to CloudWatch and possibly return a summary back to Salesforce for logging (like "Agent used tool X, got result Y"). Ensure you also secure and govern the integration – a misconfigured LangChain agent might try to do things outside its scope.

For observability, you might not have Salesforce Command Center watching these directly (unless you pipe logs in). But you could leverage OpenTelemetry in your LangChain code to emit metrics/traces that tie into the same monitoring systems. The goal is to avoid having a blind spot: an agent is an agent, whether in Salesforce or off-platform, users won't care – they just see a solution. So instrument it similarly.

Microsoft AutoGen: Microsoft's AutoGen framework (from MSR) allows multi-agent conversations and workflows in a programmable way. If your architecture involves AutoGen (say you have an Azure Function orchestrating a set of agents including Salesforce Agentforce ones and external ones), treat the AutoGen config as code. Keep prompt definitions, tool configurations, etc., in source control and version them. AutoGen v0.4 and above emphasize observability – they have built-in tracing and even support

OpenTelemetry for standardized logging. This means if you use AutoGen to manage agent interactions, you can hook it into your monitoring stack so that, for example, a trace can show "Step 1: Salesforce Agent responded, Step 2: Python Agent responded" etc., complete with timings.

Deployment-wise, AutoGen agents are essentially code – likely deployed as containers or functions. Use your existing DevOps practice for those (Docker images versioned, etc.). The key interplay with Salesforce is that any changes in the external agent might need changes on Salesforce side (like if an API changes). So coordinate releases – possibly using the manifest approach across systems. For example, if AutoGen's agent will call a Salesforce Apex REST endpoint, deploy that Apex endpoint first, then the AutoGen update.

crewAI: crewAI is another framework for multi-agent orchestration, focusing on agents working as a "crew" with roles. Suppose you use crewAI for some complex processes and those agents interact with Salesforce (maybe via APIs or even embedded). crewAI emphasizes a simple management UI, integration with apps, and complete visibility into AI agent performance (quality, efficiency, ROI). In practice, if you deploy crewAI agents, you might self-host them or use their cloud. Deployment strategy should include how those agents connect to Salesforce and vice versa – e.g., do you register each crewAI agent as an external service in Salesforce? Observability-wise, if crewAI provides a dashboard for agent performance, you might not replicate all that in Salesforce. But do ensure any critical failures in those external agents surface to your Salesforce ops. Perhaps set up error webhooks: crewAI might be configured to call a Salesforce webhook or send an email that can create a Case when an agent fails. That way your Salesforce Command Center isn't oblivious to an external agent's status.

"Swarm-level control policies" likely refers to controlling the whole group of agents (like pausing an entire crew, rolling out an update to all). crewAI probably has features to roll out updates across agents or manage them collectively, which you'd use in tandem with Salesforce's controls for any integrated pieces.

Model Context Protocol (MCP) compatibility: MCP is an open standard (spearheaded by Anthropic) for connecting AI agents to external tools and data. Salesforce Agentforce 3 has native support for MCP, essentially making it easy for Agentforce agents to call out to MCP-compliant services or for external agents to call into Salesforce securely. In deployment terms, adopting MCP means your agents can be more plug-and-play with external capabilities. For example, instead of writing custom integration code, you might deploy an MCP server (maybe via MuleSoft, which can convert APIs to MCP services) and your agent just declares it needs "Service X" and uses MCP to invoke it.

When deploying agents that use MCP, ensure you declare their capabilities and requirements clearly – e.g., "this agent expects an MCP endpoint for 'DatabaseSearch'". The idea of "agents declaring version and capability metadata on instantiation" means an MCP client (the agent) can advertise what version it is and what tools it can use. This can assist in orchestrating multi-agent setups. Make sure to version those MCP interfaces too – if you update the schema of a tool's interface, consider it like an API version bump.

Monitoring MCP calls is also key. Since MCP runs over a standardized protocol (often JSON-RPC), you might capture logs at the MCP server or integrate into the agent's telemetry. Salesforce might log MCP usage via Command Center (especially if integrated with MuleSoft, maybe those calls show up in some dashboard). Regardless, treat an MCP service like a dependency: have monitoring on its availability and performance, so your agent doesn't silently suffer if the external tool is slow or down.

Comparing CI/CD approaches: It's worth noting differences between deploying in Salesforce and external platforms:

- Salesforce deployments (changesets, metadata API, unlocked packages) are declarative and atomic (you deploy a bunch of metadata and either it all goes or fails). External platforms (like a Node.js service for an agent) might use containerization or scripts, which can be more flexible in deployment ordering and partial deployments.
- Testing in Salesforce often requires a sandbox or scratch org; external agents can sometimes be tested locally or in isolation more easily. Plan your pipeline to include integration tests that span both (for example, run a script that hits your external agent then checks a Salesforce outcome).

Tools like MuleSoft or Airflow might be used to orchestrate across systems. You could have Airflow job that at midnight deploys a Salesforce metadata package and then triggers an update of an external AI service and then runs tests. This is fine; just ensure logging and error handling in that pipeline (so you know if step 3 failed and can rollback step 2, etc.).

In ecosystem terms, Salesforce Agentforce is becoming more open and interoperable – Command Center and OpenTelemetry let you plug into enterprise monitoring, MCP and standards like Google's Agent-to-Agent (A2A) allow cross-platform agent communication. Embrace these rather than doing one-off integrations. For instance, instead of writing a custom HTTP callout in Apex to some AI service, if that service supports MCP, use the standard – it will likely simplify future maintenance.

MCP example: Salesforce noted that Slack will offer a native MCP server – imagine you have an agent that needs to get Slack messages or post something. Via MCP, your Salesforce agent could connect to Slack's MCP interface with minimal fuss, as opposed to a bespoke Slack API call integration. Deployment of such an agent just means ensuring the MCP connection details (endpoint, auth) are configured. Monitoring means ensuring the MCP handshake works; maybe the agent logs "Connected to Slack MCP v1.2" on startup. If Slack updates to v1.3, you might need to update config – track these versions.

In conclusion, when extending beyond Salesforce:

- Apply the same rigor of versioning, testing, and logging to external agent frameworks.
- Use open standards (MCP, OpenTelemetry) to reduce integration friction – they are the "USB-C for AI" that make different components plug-compatible.
- Coordinate deployments across platforms (perhaps through a unified pipeline or at least a shared schedule/manifest).
- Centralize monitoring as much as possible – whether it's pulling external metrics into Salesforce's Command Center or vice versa, aim for one cohesive view of your agents' health.

By doing so, you avoid the trap of having a well-monitored Salesforce agent but an unknown black-box Python agent that could be failing silently. The strategies we covered – CI/CD pipelines, observability standards, feature flag rollouts – all can and should be extended to every part of your AI agent ecosystem.

We've now covered deployment, observability, and lifecycle from many angles. To wrap up, let's summarize the key takeaways and prepare for what's next in this playbook.

SUMMARY

In this chapter, you learned how to launch, monitor, version, and govern Agentforce agents in a way that's scalable, auditable, and safe. We began by stressing that operational excellence (deployment, observability, lifecycle management) is what turns a clever agent prototype into a reliable business solution. You now have a deployment readiness checklist to make sure agents go live with proper validation, metadata tagging, and rollback plans. We explored Salesforce's Agentforce Command Center and how to track crucial metrics – from invocation counts to success rates and latency – keeping you alerted to anomalies so no agent goes rogue without you knowing. We provided an observability blueprint for each agent pattern, including what to log and when to set off alarms, so you can tailor monitoring to an agent's role (e.g., watching reject rates for Supervisors or suggestion uptake for Coaches).

On the change management front, we covered strategies for versioning agents (using Flow versions, Apex classes per version, and metadata tags) and rolling out updates gradually with feature flags and parallel runs. You saw the importance of backward compatibility and how a Conductor agent might run old and new versions of sub-agents in tandem to ensure a smooth transition. We also tackled rollback and sunset strategies – having configuration toggles to instantly disable or revert an agent, archiving agent outputs for analysis, and gracefully retiring agents with announcements and fallbacks. For multi-agent releases, we introduced the idea of deployment manifests and using Flow Orchestration to test and coordinate complex rollouts, exemplified by a multi-agent benefits enrollment scenario. An Agent Registry can serve as your source of truth for all agent deployments and their interdependencies.

Finally, we stepped back to see how Agentforce fits into the broader ecosystem. We highlighted that modern AI systems often span platforms, and thus deployment and monitoring should extend to frameworks like LangChain, AutoGen, and crewAI. By leveraging standards like OpenTelemetry for observability and MCP for interoperability, you can manage Salesforce and non-Salesforce agents under a unified operational strategy. The common theme is consistency – treat every agent (no matter where it runs) with the same discipline of version control, automated testing, and performance monitoring. This ensures your "digital workforce" is reliable and accountable.

With your agents successfully deployed and under vigilant watch, you're ready to focus on the next piece of the puzzle: how these agents interact with people. Up next, Chapter 14 shifts focus to UX – designing human-AI interactions and embedding agents across Salesforce surfaces in ways that drive adoption and delight users. After all, a well-deployed agent is great, but we also need to ensure users embrace it. In the next chapter, we'll explore patterns and best practices for the user experience side of AI agents, completing our journey from the backend to the front-end of the agent-powered enterprise.

14

HUMAN-AI INTERACTION AND UX DESIGN

In the new era of AI, user experience (UX) is emerging as a critical differentiator for enterprise AI agents. Today's users are accustomed to getting instant answers from AI and expect the same seamless assistance in their workplace tools. Salesforce's Agentforce platform was introduced to meet this demand, enabling teams to build AI agents (for sales, service, commerce, etc.) that can proactively assist users by reasoning over data and taking action in context. But delivering these capabilities effectively isn't just about the AI's intelligence – it's about embedding AI into the flow of work in a thoughtful way that users trust and adopt. Salesforce emphasizes that building trust between humans and agents is paramount, guided by responsible AI principles in design and development. To earn that trust, AI agents must be accessible to users where they already work (whether in Salesforce apps, Slack, or customer-facing channels) and behave in ways that feel intuitive, helpful, and safe.

When done right, a well-designed AI agent can dramatically improve productivity and satisfaction – indeed, 80% of employees using AI report it's already improving their productivity. Salesforce Einstein Copilot (now part of Agentforce) exemplifies this by being natively embedded across Salesforce applications, delivering a consistent user experience that can answer questions, generate content, and automate actions in context. In this chapter, we will explore how to achieve such integration and design excellence. We begin with strategies for embedding AI agents directly into Salesforce experiences (from the CRM UI to Slack to customer sites) to meet users in the moment of need. Then we'll dive into human-centered interaction patterns that keep users in control and confident when collaborating with AI. We'll discuss crafting the agent's tone, voice, and personality to align with your brand and user expectations. Next, we examine designing multi-channel experiences – ensuring your agent provides cohesive help whether the user is on a desktop, mobile, or chat platform. We'll also cover accessibility and inclusion considerations (so every user can benefit), along with visual and interaction cues that foster transparency and trust. Finally, we'll look at measuring UX success through metrics and feedback loops to continuously improve your agent, and review common UX patterns in an agent ecosystem (when multiple AI agents or integrations coexist). Throughout, we'll highlight Salesforce-specific tooling (Agent Builder, Flows, Apex, Lightning Web Components, Slack SDK) and compare approaches with other ecosystems (like Microsoft's Copilot, the LangChain framework, CrewAI, and the emerging Model Context Protocol) to provide a well-rounded playbook for designing human-AI interactions that drive adoption, trust, and usability.

EMBEDDING AGENTS IN SALESFORCE EXPERIENCES

Successful AI agents meet users where they work. Embedding an agent into Salesforce experiences means integrating AI assistance seamlessly into the interfaces and workflows users already know. Rather than forcing users to context-switch to a separate AI app, the agent should surface within Sales Cloud, Service Cloud, Slack, or an Experience Cloud site so that interacting with the AI feels like a natural extension of normal work. This tight integration is key to adoption – when an AI helper is just one click or command away, users are far more likely to leverage it routinely.

Lightning Experience and Console Integration: In core Salesforce CRM (Lightning Experience), AI agents can be embedded as on-screen assistants or utilities. For example, Einstein Copilot (now part of Agentforce) appears as a user-facing assistant panel right on the Salesforce screen for sales, service, marketing, and other users. Users can open or hide the Copilot via a small Einstein icon in the UI, summoning the AI only when needed and dismissing it when not. This design keeps the AI "in reach" without overwhelming the interface – much like a smart sidekick that sits in the corner until called upon. Once opened, the Copilot panel can accept natural language questions or commands, and it can display answers or execute actions in the context of whatever record or page the user is on. For instance, on an Account record, a sales user might ask the Copilot, "Summarize recent activities with this account" and get an on-the-fly brief. Because the agent is embedded within Salesforce, it can deeply integrate with CRM data and take actions like updating records or creating tasks via predefined Copilot Actions. (Copilot Actions are units of work the AI can perform, like logging a call or creating an opportunity, implemented behind the scenes with Apex or Flow.) This native UI integration ensures that the agent's assistance is only a click away and leverages Salesforce's design conventions – it feels like just another part of the platform, which lowers user hesitation.

In a Service Cloud console, an agent (the human service agent, in this case) might get AI suggestions in a panel while working a case. By embedding an AI-driven knowledge search or reply suggestion component directly in the console, the service rep can seamlessly use AI to draft responses or find answers without switching context. Salesforce has designed Copilot such that it can be toggled on globally but will stay present across the apps – meaning a support agent in Cases, a sales rep in Leads, and a marketer in Campaigns all have access to an AI assistant in their respective workspaces. Moreover, because Copilot/Agentforce is part of the Salesforce Platform, you can use the same low-code and pro-code tools to extend it. For example, you might create a custom Lightning Web Component (LWC) to embed a mini chat interface or to display the AI's output (like recommended next best actions) in a record page. Using LWCs and the Lightning Design System styles will ensure your custom AI UI elements are accessible and consistent with Salesforce's look and feel. Many out-of-the-box components are already AI-enabled (for instance, the Einstein Next Best Action component, or dynamic forms that show AI-suggested fields), but with LWCs you have full flexibility to tailor how and where the agent interacts with users. An advanced example might be building a Lightning Utility Bar item that glows when the AI has a proactive insight (e.g., "The account you're viewing has an unresolved support issue – want me to summarize it?") – giving users a gentle nudge within the familiar UI.

Experience Cloud and External Sites: AI agents aren't just for internal users – Salesforce allows embedding them in Experience Cloud digital experiences (customer or partner portals, public sites) to support external users. In these contexts, an AI agent often takes the form of a chatbot or virtual assistant on the website. Using Agentforce's Service Agent capabilities, you can deploy an autonomous customer service bot on an Experience Cloud site to handle routine customer queries 24/7. This involves connecting the agent with the Service Cloud backend so it can create or update cases, retrieve knowledge articles, etc. A Salesforce developer workshop on Agentforce illustrates how a Service Agent can be distributed through Experience Cloud, by combining it with Omni-Channel routing in Service Cloud to route incoming chats from the site into the Agentforce agent for handling. In practice, this means a customer on your support site might click a "Chat with an agent" button and get the AI agent first; the AI can greet them, ask about their issue, and either resolve it (if it's something like "what's my order status?" which the agent can answer from CRM data) or escalate to a human agent via Omni-Channel if it's complex or if the user requests a human. The user should experience this hand-off smoothly – the chat window might indicate "Handing you to a human agent..." and the human picks up with full context of the AI's conversation so far. To implement such an embedded agent, Salesforce provides a Chatbot component in Experience Builder that you can configure to use an Agentforce agent as the bot engine. The design should follow your site's branding (so the chat widget skin is familiar) while also clearly indicating when the assistant is an AI. It's also critical to design the conversation flow (using tools like Flow Builder or Dialog Builder) so that the AI agent's prompts and responses on the site are user-friendly. For example, providing quick-reply buttons ("Check Order Status", "Reset Password", etc.) can guide users to effective interactions. By thoughtfully embedding an AI service agent in your Experience Cloud site, you create a first line of support that's always available. Done right, this improves customer satisfaction through instant answers and frees up human service reps for more complex issues – all without the customer ever leaving the website.

Slack and Collaboration Surfaces: Salesforce's acquisition of Slack means many employees live in Slack as much as in Salesforce's own UI. Agentforce recognizes this by bringing AI agents directly into Slack. In Slack, agents essentially become virtual teammates: you can interact with them in channels, direct messages, or threads just like you would with a human colleague. Salesforce notes that "Agents become teammates with Agentforce in Slack", leveraging relevant Slack conversations and enterprise data to suggest or take action right in the flow of work. For example, a sales rep could mention a deal-support agent in a channel (@DealSupport) and ask for help preparing a custom quote; the agent (a Slack app user) can respond in-thread with the information or even draft a document, all visible within Slack. Because Slack is a rich, interactive platform, these embedded agents can do more than just chat – they can present interactive elements. A Slack-based agent might post buttons, forms, or even canvases. In fact, Agentforce can automate Slack native actions: it's capable of creating or updating Slack canvases, opening channels, sending DMs, and more on behalf of users. This means an agent could not only tell a user "I've gathered the data you need," but also spin up a new channel with the relevant colleagues invited, or draft a Slack Canvas (which is an editable document in Slack) with a summary for the user to review. These actions are of course governed by rules and guardrails you set, to ensure the agent only performs appropriate actions under the right conditions.

Integrating agents into Slack requires setting up the Salesforce-Slack connection (using the Slack SDK for Salesforce and an OAuth app in Slack). Once connected, admins can deploy Slack Agent Templates or custom-built Slack bots powered by Agentforce. From a UX perspective, when designing an agent in Slack, you'll choose how users invoke it (e.g., via a slash command like /askSalesBot, or by mentioning the bot's username, or even the bot proactively listening for certain keywords). You also decide how it responds – ephemeral messages to just the requester for sensitive info, or public channel messages when collaborating. Pro Tip: Make the agent's presence and capabilities in Slack obvious to users. For example, give the bot a clear name and profile (with an avatar image and a description of what it can do in its Slack profile). Consider posting a pinned introductory message in relevant channels (or an onboarding DM when someone first interacts with the bot) listing sample commands or tasks it can help with. This encourages discovery and sets correct expectations about the agent's role.

By embedding agents into Slack, you bring AI to the place where cross-functional work already happens. A marketing manager who rarely logs into Salesforce can still benefit from a marketing content agent right from Slack – for instance, asking in a project channel, "@MarketingAgent draft a social post for this new campaign" and getting a proposal in seconds. The convenience of not having to switch to another app cannot be overstated. Early adopters of Slack-based agents have reported significant productivity gains, as employees can resolve issues or retrieve information within the conversational interface they use daily. In essence, Slack becomes an additional Salesforce UI – one where plain-language requests to an AI are instantly turned into real work outputs. As we design such experiences, we must ensure the agent's Slack interactions follow the platform's interaction norms (short messages, support for threading, using emojis or reactions where appropriate for feedback). This maintains a feeling that the agent "belongs" in Slack, rather than being an awkward foreign AI.

An example of an AI agent embedded in the Salesforce UI. Here, Einstein Copilot appears as a panel within a Salesforce app, responding to a user's prompt by taking action (updating a case record and confirming the escalation). Embedding the agent directly into the CRM interface allows users to invoke AI assistance in context without switching applications. The agent can interpret the user's intent (like routing a case for approval) and perform multi-step tasks through Salesforce flows and actions, all from a single conversational UI.

Extending and Customizing Embedded Agents: One advantage of deeply embedding agents in Salesforce experiences is that you can harness the full power of the Salesforce platform to extend those agents. Salesforce provides an Agent Builder and related tools to configure what an agent can do. Through the Agentforce builder UI (part of Salesforce Setup, similar to how you configure Einstein Bots historically), you can define the agent's capabilities: its underlying LLM model, its topics (areas of knowledge or conversation flows), and the actions it can take. Many actions will be Salesforce Flows or Apex methods exposed as invokable actions. For example, you might create a Flow that takes inputs (say a customer ID) and returns some result (customer's eligibility for an offer), and then allow the Agentforce agent to call that flow as needed. This low-code approach means you're not coding the entire agent logic; you're assembling building blocks and letting the AI reasoning engine orchestrate them. Administrators can outline the agent's purpose and constraints using natural language instructions in Prompt Builder, effectively guiding the agent's behavior and tone via prompts. The result is a tailored AI that knows your business context. As one review put it, "building the agent allows you to change certain features and approaches on a custom level – outline your needs, define the purpose of each agent, provide custom instructions, create workflows, and compile action libraries". With that done, embedding the agent into various channels (UI, Slack, etc.) is straightforward, since the core logic is centralized.

From a deployment standpoint, once an agent is configured, making it available in the UI or Slack may simply be a matter of toggling it on or assigning it to a channel. Salesforce has strived to make the deployment "quick once you know what you're doing" – but careful UX design is what ensures that after deployment, the agent is actually used and adds value. Always test the embedded experience in each channel: Does the Copilot panel obscure important screen real estate or is it unobtrusive? In Slack, does the agent accidentally spam channels or is it well-behaved and context-aware? The goal is an integrated AI assistant that feels like a natural part of the Salesforce ecosystem, helping users accomplish tasks faster and smarter without forcing them to learn a new system.

In summary, embedding agents in Salesforce experiences means weaving AI capabilities into the fabric of everyday tools – be it a Sales Cloud page, a Slack workspace, or a customer community. By using Salesforce's rich UI frameworks (Lightning, LWC), declarative tools (Flow, Omni-Channel, etc.), and platform integrations (Slack SDK), we can deliver AI help at the user's fingertips. The next sections will build on this by examining how to design the interactions themselves to be human-centered, ensuring that these embedded agents are not only present, but also pleasant and effective to work with.

HUMAN-CENTERED INTERACTION PATTERNS

Even the most well-embedded AI agent can fall flat if interacting with it is confusing, frustrating, or erodes user confidence. Human-centered interaction design focuses on making the AI agent a helpful partner that collaborates with the user on the user's terms. In practical terms, this involves adopting design patterns that keep the human in control, provide clarity and transparency in the AI's behavior, and gracefully handle errors or uncertainties. In this section, we'll outline key principles and patterns for designing AI-agent interactions that feel intuitive and trustworthy. Many of these principles echo general HCI (Human-Computer Interaction) best practices, but with twists unique to AI – such as dealing with AI unpredictability or learning from user feedback. Companies like Microsoft have published guidelines for Human-AI interaction, and Salesforce's own Responsible AI guidelines also reinforce several of these ideas. Let's translate these into concrete patterns you can apply when designing your Salesforce AI agents.

Design for Clarity, Control, and Context

Make the AI's capabilities and limits clear: When a user starts interacting with an AI agent, they should quickly grasp what the agent can and cannot do. An effective pattern is to provide a brief introduction or menu of suggestions at the start of a session. For instance, an onboarding chatbot might begin with, "Hi, I'm an AI assistant that can help with benefits, IT support, or time off requests. How can I assist you today?" This sets scope. If the agent only handles certain domains, say so up front, so users don't get frustrated asking unrelated questions. Clarity also means the agent shouldn't pretend to have authority it lacks – if it's not sure of an answer or unable to fulfill a request, it should say so in a helpful way (and perhaps offer to escalate to a human or find alternative info). Never design an agent that bluffs; honesty is essential to maintain trust. Salesforce's principles emphasize being transparent that content is AI-generated and ensuring users know the AI's outputs may need validation. Concretely, your agent's responses might include phrases like, "As an AI agent, I don't have access to that information," or "I'm not certain, but here's my best attempt...". These admissions are far better UX than confidently incorrect answers that mislead the user.

Keep the user in control at all times: A well-designed agent does not wrest control away or take actions without some form of user consent or undo capability, especially for high-impact operations. One pattern is the confirmation step for any non-trivial action. If an AI agent is about to perform a significant update (e.g., delete records, send out an email on the user's behalf), it should ask for confirmation: "Should I go ahead and send this email to the client?" – ideally with a summary of what it's sending. Another example: if an agent auto-generates a draft (say, a contract or a knowledge base article), present it to the user for review/edit rather than directly publishing it. This pattern of human-on-the-loop ensures the user remains the ultimate decision-maker, using the AI as a smart assistant rather than an unchecked automaton. In Salesforce, you can implement confirmations via UI elements (like a Lightning prompt modal or Slack message buttons "Approve ✅ / Edit ✏️"). The interaction shown below illustrates this principle:

An Agentforce IT support agent embedded in Slack asks a user to confirm an action before proceeding. The employee reported a lost phone, and the AI agent offers to order a replacement – but first presents a "Yes/No" choice to the user. This pattern of explicit confirmation ensures the human user stays in control of important decisions. The agent also provides context ("I found details on your lost phone and can order a new one") so the user understands what's happening and why.

In that Slack example, the agent not only asks permission, but also shows it understood the context (lost phone details) and offers a logical next step (ordering a new one). This builds confidence that the AI is acting appropriately. Always aim to design the interaction such that the user feels empowered by the AI, not overruled. Salesforce explicitly calls out human-AI partnership as a design goal: AI should supercharge human capabilities, and know when to step back and let a human decide. In practice, this might mean an Agentforce service bot can automatically resolve a low-tier issue but will offer to escalate to a human for anything sensitive, or an agent might do 90% of a task then hand off to the user for final touches (e.g., "I've drafted an analysis, would you like to review it?").

Provide context and explanations: AI agents often have access to a lot of data or perform complex reasoning, which can make their outputs seem like black boxes. A key interaction pattern is to have the agent show its work when appropriate. This doesn't mean overwhelming the user with technical details, but rather giving enough context so the user understands the output. For instance, if an agent recommends a product to a customer, it might add, "I suggest Product X because your purchase history shows similar items and it's highly rated (4.8/5) by similar customers." Such an explanation increases the user's trust in the recommendation. Similarly, if an agent answers a question using knowledge base articles or documentation, providing citations or reference links is an excellent practice. Salesforce's Agentforce encourages backing up generated content with verifiable data sources, allowing users to cross-check information. In a UI, this could be implemented as footnote numbers or "According to [Source Name]" hyperlinks in the agent's response. For example, an agent might respond: "Your current SLA is Gold, which guarantees a 4-hour response time." The reference might link to the SLA policy document. This pattern not only bolsters trust but also helps users learn from the AI (turning the interaction into a mini training moment).

Explanations are also critical when the AI cannot fulfill a request. Instead of a generic "I'm sorry, I can't help with that," a human-centered agent explains why and what's next: "I'm sorry, I don't have the financial data for 2019 because that's outside my data access. You might try asking FinanceBot, or I can connect you with a finance specialist." This approach treats the user respectfully and provides a path forward. Another pattern is clarification questions – when the AI isn't sure what the user means or needs more info, it should ask rather than guess incorrectly. For example, user says: "Schedule a meeting with Acme." The agent should clarify: "Sure. I found two contacts named Acme Corp in our system – one in London and one in New York. Which did you want to meet with?" This is far better UX than arbitrarily picking one or failing. Designing good clarification dialogues is an art: keep them brief, use simple language, and whenever possible present options as buttons to reduce user effort.

Guiding Interaction Flow and Error Handling

Use guided prompts and suggestions: A blank chat prompt can be intimidating or confusing to users unfamiliar with an AI's capabilities. A human-centered pattern is to guide the user proactively. In a Salesforce context, this might involve the agent presenting suggested questions or actions. For instance, when a support agent opens a case, an embedded AI assistant could display suggestions like "Summarize this case", "Draft an email to customer", or "Check knowledge base for similar issues". These serve both as affordances (teaching the user what the AI can do) and as quick actions that save time. Slack agents might periodically advertise their abilities: e.g., an onboarding bot could post, "Tip: you can ask me help me find my remaining PTO balance anytime." The key is to offer help without being too pushy or spammy – balance is needed so the AI doesn't come across as Clippy from the 90s. In UI terms, designing a small hint text in the input area (e.g., "Ask me to draft a follow-up task or type #help for examples...") can be effective. Also consider multi-turn guidance: if the user seems stuck or asks an overly broad question, the agent can break the task down. For example, user says "Help me with onboarding." The agent might respond: "Sure – I can help with several onboarding tasks like setting up accounts, sending welcome emails, or scheduling training. Which of these would you like to do?" This scaffolding makes the interaction more conversational and user-friendly.

Plan for hand-offs and graceful failure: No matter how advanced, AI agents will encounter queries they can't handle – and that's okay if you design a smooth fallback. A critical human-centered pattern is the AI-to-human hand-off. In customer service, this means if the AI cannot solve a customer's issue (due to lack of data, user frustration, or any reason), it should politely hand the conversation to a human agent, transferring all relevant context so the customer doesn't have to repeat themselves. Salesforce Agentforce Service Agents use Omni-Channel routing for exactly this: conversations can be triaged to the AI and then routed to a human if needed, with conversation transcripts attached. The design here should ensure the user is informed ("I'm going to connect you with a human agent for further help.") and maybe even empowered to trigger the hand-off themselves: e.g., provide a "Talk to a human" quick command. Internally facing agents (like in Slack or in CRM) also need failure plans. If an employee asks the sales AI something it can't do, maybe it routes the question to the sales operations team or at least provides a contact/link for help. Never design the agent to just give up with "I don't know" and end the chat – always offer an alternative (different query, human assistance, or a help document link). This way, even an "unsuccessful" AI interaction can leave the user feeling satisfied that they got to an answer or next step.

Error handling is closely related. Consider what the agent should do if an underlying action fails – say it tried to execute a Flow to update a record but an error occurred (perhaps missing permissions or bad data input). A raw error stack trace is obviously poor UX. Instead, catch errors and express them in human-friendly language, along with guidance. E.g., "Hmm, I wasn't able to update the contact's email – it looks like I don't have access to that record. You might need an administrator to grant me permission." This honesty combined with guidance turns a failure into a more tolerable experience. In development, you can build error-checking into the agent's action logic, and use prompt instructions to tell the AI how to respond if an action result indicates failure (the Agentforce reasoning engine allows handling exceptions via instructions). Pro Tip: Map out common error scenarios in advance and decide how the agent should respond. Do a few "negative tests" where you feed the agent bad inputs or trigger its limits, and refine its replies to be as helpful as possible in those cases. This preparation separates a frustrating bot from a reliable assistant that "owns" its limitations.

Personalization and remembering context: Humans appreciate when an assistant remembers details and preferences – it makes interactions more efficient and pleasant. Your AI agent should leverage context to avoid making the user repeat themselves. In Salesforce, context is rich: if a user has opened a case and then asks the agent, "update the status to priority," the agent should infer they mean the case they're viewing. This can be done by the agent's context engine (like Atlas) having access to the current record context. Also, across a multi-turn conversation, the agent should recall what was said earlier. If the user tells the agent their goal in one message, the next answer should not ignore that. Maintaining a conversational memory (for the duration of a session) is a default in most AI systems, but designers should test that the agent indeed carries information forward correctly. Beyond session context, consider personalization: could the agent remember user-specific preferences? For example, if a user always prefers formal language in email drafts, maybe allow them to set that preference ("Always draft formally."). This might be implemented via a profile attribute or simply the agent recognizing the user's edits over time and adapting. Human-centered design means the agent adapts to the human, not just the human adapting to the agent. However, be cautious with long-term memory of user data, especially under privacy considerations – always respect what data the agent is allowed to store or use.

Key Guidelines for AI Interaction Design

To summarize the human-centered patterns, let's list some essential guidelines to check against when designing your agent's interactions:

Be Transparent: Clearly signal that the agent is AI, what it can do, and when content is AI-generated. Use disclaimers or subtle cues where appropriate. Transparency builds trust.

Guide the User Gently: Provide suggestions, example commands, or UI hints to help users get started and understand the agent's scope. But avoid overwhelming the user with too many choices or messages at once.

Keep User in Charge: Require confirmation for critical actions. Allow users to cancel or override actions easily. Design the agent to ask when in doubt (clarify) rather than act on shaky assumptions.

Use Human Tone and Manners: We'll dive more into tone in the next section, but generally the agent should communicate politely, avoid jargon (unless the user uses it), and possibly apologize for errors or delays. Small courtesies ("Thanks for waiting, I found the info...") go a long way to making the interaction comfortable.

Provide Explanations and Sources: When giving answers or recommendations, include the rationale or source data succinctly. This not only instills confidence but also educates the user.

Handle Errors Gracefully: When the agent doesn't understand or can't comply, it should respond with helpful feedback or next steps, not a dead end. Design fallback paths (like escalation to humans or alternative queries).

Adapt to the User: Take advantage of context – use any relevant information from the current record, previous messages, or user profile to tailor responses. Don't force the user to repeat context that the system already knows. At the same time, don't overly personalize to the point of feeling creepy – stick to context that makes sense to recall.

Iterate with User Feedback: Treat the initial deployment as a learning phase. Provide ways for users to give feedback on the agent's helpfulness (a thumbs-up/down on answers, a short survey, or even analyzing user corrections).

Then refine the agent's prompts, knowledge, or actions based on common issues.

Salesforce's emphasis on empowerment and effective hand-offs in agent design aligns with these guidelines – the technology should empower people, and know when to yield to human judgment. As you craft conversation flows or design the agent's UI dialogs, continuously ask: "Is this the simplest, most intuitive way for a user to accomplish their goal with the agent's help? Are we respecting the user's intent and authority?" By following the patterns above, you'll avoid the common pitfalls of AI assistants (such as being seen as annoying, unreliable, or opaque) and instead create a solution that users welcome and rely on.

In the next section, we'll zoom in on one particular aspect of human-AI interaction design: the tone, voice, and personality of the agent. This is another key ingredient to user acceptance – after all, how an AI "speaks" to your users will shape their perception of it and willingness to engage.

TONE, VOICE, AND PERSONALITY

An AI agent's personality is conveyed through every message it outputs – its choice of words, tone, level of formality, use of humor (or lack thereof), and even how it refers to itself and the user. Designing the right voice and tone for your Salesforce AI agent is crucial for two reasons: consistency with your brand/user expectations, and establishing a rapport that users feel comfortable with. A haphazard or inappropriate tone can alienate users ("Why is our HR bot cracking jokes about payroll?"), while a well-crafted persona can make the interaction feel natural and even enjoyable ("The bot is polite and empathetic, it feels like our company's style"). In this section, we discuss strategies for defining your agent's personality and implementing it in practice, using Salesforce's tooling and some general best practices. We'll also compare how different ecosystems approach AI tone – from Microsoft's generally professional Copilot style to more playful assistants – to help you calibrate the right voice for your context.

Defining the Agent's Persona

Start by considering the role of your agent and the audience it serves. Is this agent assisting internal employees (and if so, in what department or job function?), or is it customer-facing? For instance, an agent that helps developers troubleshoot code (perhaps integrated in Slack or an IDE) might have a more technical, concise tone, whereas a customer service bot for a retail site should be friendly, patient, and use simpler language. Salesforce encourages aligning AI agents with the brand's values and style – an extension of "your company's voice." If your company is known for a fun, approachable brand, you might give the agent a mild sense of humor and a casual tone. Conversely, in a serious domain (say a banking or healthcare agent), you'd keep the tone formal, factual, and reassuring. It's helpful to write down a short persona statement for the agent. For example: "Our agent is a knowledgeable but friendly assistant. It speaks in clear, professional language, like a helpful colleague. It never uses slang, and it addresses users by name to personalize interactions. It remains calm and courteous, even if the user is frustrated." This sort of description sets guardrails for the tone.

Many conversational AI designers borrow techniques from character design or content design to flesh out the persona. Some teams even give the agent a name and backstory (though be careful not to over-humanize to the point users think it's a real person – transparency that it's AI is still required). In Salesforce's Prompt Builder for Agentforce, you have the ability to set system instructions that influence the agent's style. This is where you'd encode things like "You are a helpful CRM assistant that always responds in polite full sentences and uses a warm tone." Because large language models can vary style wildly based on prompt, giving these consistent instructions helps maintain the voice you want.

One convenient approach is to use examples – show the model a few sample Q&A pairs in the desired tone. For instance: User: "Hey, I need help with my sales pipeline." Agent: "Sure thing! Let's take a look. I can help analyze your pipeline stages or find any stalled deals. What would you like to do first?" By including such examples in the agent's prompt instructions (if using a prompt-based agent) or training data (if fine-tuning), you anchor the style. Salesforce's Agentforce allows topics and instructions to guide response formatting and tone. According to the Agentforce Guide, you should use instructions (rather than code) for things like defining the agent's conversational style, because the reasoning engine will then consistently apply that tone when formulating responses.

Matching Tone to Use Case and User

It's important that the agent's tone matches the context of the interaction. A single agent may even need to modulate its tone slightly depending on the situation. For example, a customer support agent might be generally upbeat and casual, but if a customer says "I'm really upset about this issue," the agent should respond with empathy and a more serious tone ("I'm sorry to hear that. Let me do everything I can to help.") – perhaps dropping any playful language at that moment. Designing this dynamic adaptability can be complex, but you can outline simple rules: detect sentiment or certain keywords and adjust style accordingly. Some AI frameworks or NLU (Natural Language Understanding) components can gauge user sentiment; Agentforce's underlying models might not do this explicitly for you yet, but you can instruct the agent, for example, "If the user sounds frustrated or uses words like 'angry' or punctuation like '!!!', respond with empathy and no jokes."

Consider also the medium: voice vs text. If your agent were to be used with a voice interface (say integrated with a phone IVR or via a speech-to-text in a mobile app), the tone needs to account for spoken language patterns (perhaps more conversational contractions, shorter sentences, and even audible cues like "Hmm" or a friendly intonation if synthesized). While most Salesforce agent deployments are text-based (chat or email), the principle remains: read the responses out loud to see if they sound natural for spoken delivery. Slack messages can be a bit more informal (throw in an emoji occasionally if it aligns with culture – e.g., a light bulb emoji when presenting an idea), whereas an email composed by the AI might need a more formal structure ("Dear [Name], ... Sincerely, [Agent Name]").

Consistency is crucial. If you have multiple agents in your ecosystem (which we'll cover later), each could have a distinct persona, but they should feel like they belong to the same family. For example, maybe all your company's AI agents introduce themselves in a similar way or follow the same etiquette guidelines. A sales agent and an IT support agent might have different expertise and slight tone differences (sales agent might be more enthusiastic, IT agent more straightforward), but if one uses emoji and the other is completely stoic, that might seem jarring under the same corporate umbrella. Often, companies develop a voice and tone guide for their AI similar to their brand style guide. This might include do's and don'ts (e.g., Do use active voice, don't use slang like "gotcha" or "LOL," do express gratitude, etc.).

Let's illustrate tone differences with a quick example. Suppose the scenario is a delayed shipment and the user (customer) is upset:

Friendly & Empathetic Tone (perhaps for a retail customer service agent): "I'm really sorry your order hasn't arrived, that must be frustrating. Let me check on the status right now... Thank you for your patience – I see it's in transit and should arrive by Tuesday. I'll keep an eye on it and update you if anything changes."

Formal & Reassuring Tone (perhaps for a financial services agent): "I apologize for the inconvenience caused by the delay. I am reviewing the shipment status now. Thank you for waiting. According to our system, the package is currently in transit and is scheduled to arrive by Tuesday. I will monitor its progress and ensure you are updated promptly with any changes."

Both convey similar info, but the style differs. The choice depends on brand and user expectations. Notice both are polite and apologetic, but the level of formality, use of contractions ("I'm" vs "I am"), and conversational fillers differ.

Here's a simple list comparing tone styles in an example response from an agent informing a user about an account issue:

Friendly and casual

- **Example agent response:** "Hi John! Just a heads up – I noticed your account needs a quick update. No biggie, we can sort it out in a minute. Ready to get started?"

Professional and formal

- **Example agent response:** "Hello John. I wanted to inform you that your account information requires an update. I can assist you with this process step by step. Shall we proceed?"

Empathetic and reassuring

- **Example agent response:** "Hi John, I understand updating your account can be a hassle. Don't worry, I'll help you through it. It will only take a moment. Let me know when you're ready."

Concise and technical

- **Example agent response:** "John, your account is missing required information (Field X). Please provide the updated details. I will then confirm the changes."

In a Salesforce context, an Agent Builder interface might allow setting a default tone (perhaps a dropdown like "friendly", "professional", etc., which internally adjusts prompts). Some platforms like Intercom's Fin or Gorgias AI customer service tools let you choose presets or train the tone on your FAQs and macros. Salesforce is moving toward giving admins similar control, where you could specify tonal preferences in the Agent's configuration.

Implementing Tone Programmatically

Once you've defined the desired personality, how do you ensure the agent sticks to it? As mentioned, the prompt instructions in Agentforce are your primary tool. In Prompt Builder or Agent Builder, include guidelines about style. For example: "Use a warm, conversational tone. Refer to the user by name if provided (e.g., 'Hi [Name]'). Use please/thank you when asking for input. Do not use emoji. Keep sentences short and easy to read." This explicit instruction guides the LLM's output format. According to Salesforce's guidance, instructions can shape formatting and tone of the agent's responses. You might need to iterate – if you find the agent is too verbose, tighten the instruction ("respond in 1-2 sentences when possible"). If it's too terse, maybe instruct it to be more explanatory.

Another technique is to utilize the Language Settings if provided. In the SalesforceBen article, it alludes to being able to select the tone of conversation for Copilot in Copilot Builder. This suggests Salesforce might provide built-in tone settings (perhaps "friendly", "formal", etc.). Under the hood, these likely adjust system prompts or parameters of the model. Keeping an eye on such features is worthwhile – they provide a shortcut to enforce tone without you crafting it all from scratch.

During development and testing, evaluate the agent's outputs thoroughly. Do a review of sample interactions and see if the tone aligns. It can help to have non-developers (like someone from content design or even a representative end-user) read the transcripts and give impressions: Does the agent sound on-brand? Is anything it said potentially off-putting or confusing in phrasing? Sometimes small tweaks make a big difference (e.g., deciding whether the agent says "I" or refers to itself in third person as "this assistant" – most go with "I" for a friendly vibe, and that's generally fine as long as it's clear it's an AI).

One must also consider language localization if your user base is international. If you plan to have the agent communicate in multiple languages, define the tone in each language context. A "professional" tone in English might look different in Japanese or French due to cultural differences in business communication. Salesforce Einstein Copilot was initially English-only, but as support for other languages comes, you'll need to ensure the personality carries over appropriately. This might involve translation of your prompt instructions or working with native speakers to craft the style.

Avoiding Anthropomorphism and Bias in Personality

While a bit of personality is good, it's wise not to overdo the anthropomorphism. The agent should not deceive or overly emote in ways that mislead the user into thinking it has human feelings. For example, an AI can express empathy ("I understand this issue is frustrating") but it shouldn't say "I feel happy that you like my answer" – that's oddly personal. Keep the persona focused on helping the user, not on the AI's pseudo-emotions. This is part of ethical design: being clear it's an AI, and not making the AI pretend to have human experiences. Salesforce's Honesty principle touches on this – design should make it clear when content is AI-created, which implicitly means don't mask the AI as a human.

Another consideration is bias and inclusion in language. Tone includes how the agent addresses people. Ensure the agent's training/instructions avoid stereotypes or biased language. For instance, if the agent uses examples or names, ensure diversity (the agent shouldn't always use "he" by default for an unspecified person, etc.). Also avoid colloquialisms that might not be understood by non-native speakers or that have cultural connotations. If your company has guidelines for inclusive language (many do), apply them to the AI's voice. A trivial example: instead of the agent saying "Thanks guys!" which is gendered and informal, have it say "Thanks everyone!" which is more inclusive.

Salesforce's default is to guide the LLM to avoid sensitive or inappropriate outputs (the Einstein Trust Layer and content filters handle a lot of this at runtime). In tone design, you align by not encouraging any edgy humor or commentary. Keep it "professional-friendly" unless there's a good reason to have a very distinctive quirky personality (some consumer chatbots go that route, but for enterprise contexts, err on the side of neutral-positive professionalism).

Pro Tip: Draft a short script of an ideal interaction with your agent, in the tone you envision, and use that as a reference. For example, write out 5-6 turns between a user and the agent showcasing the agent's voice. Share this with stakeholders (including marketing/comms folks) to get buy-in that this reflects the desired brand voice. Then use that script to fine-tune your prompts. This helps catch tone issues early.

To illustrate how persona might differ across ecosystems, consider Microsoft 365 Copilot: it's designed to be useful in Word, Excel, Teams, etc. Microsoft has generally given Copilot a polite, helpful, but fairly neutral personality. It doesn't crack jokes, it doesn't use slang; it comes off like a diligent assistant. That fits the Office suite context. On the other hand, CrewAI (an open source multi-agent framework) doesn't impose any personality by default – as a developer you'd have to define each agent's style. In CrewAI, since it's code-centric, you might not focus on tone as much unless you're building a user-facing chatbot. LangChain similarly leaves it to the developer to inject personality via prompts. So one advantage of Salesforce's higher-level approach is giving admins control over tone without deep coding, which encourages thinking about UX aspects like voice. Meanwhile, Anthropic's Model Context Protocol (MCP) doesn't directly handle tone – it's about providing context to models – but indirectly, it could allow pulling user or company style guidelines as context for the model, thereby shaping responses to match the desired voice across tools.

Maintaining Personality at Scale

Once your agent's voice is defined, ensure its documented and maintained. As you update the agent's knowledge or add new capabilities, consider if those changes affect tone. For example, if you integrate a new action from an external system, does the response coming from that action align with tone (you might need to post-process the text it returns)? If multiple people are working on the agent (admins, prompt engineers), have a shared checklist for tone consistency. One common pitfall is the agent sounding different in different channels – maybe in Slack it includes more exclamation marks than in the Salesforce UI. Try to harmonize this unless intentionally different personas.

Finally, always gather user feedback. If users comment that "the bot's replies sound rude" or "the bot is too verbose," treat that as gold for refinement. Sometimes adjusting the persona can dramatically improve user sentiment. The beauty of these AI agents is that they are malleable – unlike a static UI, you can tweak the style via prompt changes and instantly the next interaction is different. Use that to your advantage to fine-tune the voice over time until it hits the sweet spot.

With a clear, well-implemented personality, your AI agent will not only perform tasks but also connect with users in a way that feels engaging and on-brand. This contributes greatly to adoption – users are more likely to trust and use an assistant that "speaks their language." Now that we've covered embedding and interaction patterns and tone, our next focus is extending these principles across multiple channels. How do we ensure a great UX when the agent is accessible via web, mobile, Slack, and maybe other surfaces? We'll explore that in the following section on multi-channel experience design.

MULTI-CHANNEL EXPERIENCE DESIGN

Users today expect a seamless experience across all the channels and devices they use. Whether they're interacting with your AI agent via a web portal, a mobile app, an email thread, or a Slack conversation, they should feel like it's a consistent and continuous interaction. For Salesforce AI agents, multi-channel design is especially pertinent: Salesforce prides itself on enabling omnichannel customer service and unified customer experiences. Agentforce and Einstein Copilot follow this ethos by being deployable in multiple contexts – embedded in Salesforce apps, available in Slack, even potentially integrated into third-party channels via APIs or the emerging Model Context Protocol (MCP) which aims to standardize context sharing across systems. In this section, we discuss how to design your agent's UX to be effective and coherent across channels. We'll consider differences in UI constraints, how context is shared, and ensuring that if a user moves from one channel to another, the agent can follow (or at least pick up without missing a beat). We'll also contrast how Microsoft's Copilot handles multi-channel (e.g., different Office apps) and touch on standards like MCP which can enable cross-platform agent interactions.

Consistency vs. Adaptation Across Channels

One key design decision is how uniform the agent's interface and behavior should be across channels. On one hand, consistency is valuable: the agent's persona and core capabilities should remain the same no matter where it's used. If your sales AI is helpful and formal in Salesforce, it shouldn't become a goofy casual bot in Slack. Users should recognize it as the "same assistant" helping them, which builds trust and mental model accuracy. Consistency also applies to invocation methods – for example, if the agent in Salesforce responds to natural language queries, the Slack version shouldn't suddenly require slash commands with rigid syntax (unless necessary). Strive for users to be able to ask for things in a similar way across interfaces.

On the other hand, each channel has unique interaction patterns and UI elements that the agent should leverage (or constrain itself to) for best experience – this is adaptation. For instance, in a web chat on an Experience Cloud site, you might have a graphical interface with clickable suggestion chips, rich card responses (images, buttons), etc. In Slack, rich interaction can be through message buttons or Slack canvases. In email, responses might need to be plain text or HTML and the agent must be concise to fit an email format. In voice (if applicable), brevity and clarity is key since listening is slower than reading. So the agent's output format and sometimes tone may adapt to channel norms. As a simple example: Slack is often more casual and uses emojis, whereas an email response might be formatted as a formal letter. You can maintain a consistent persona while still adjusting formality to the medium.

The agent's name and identity should ideally carry over across channels. If it's called "Assist-O-Bot" in your CRM, call it that in Slack too, unless you intentionally differentiate (some companies might have different bots per channel for technical reasons). With Salesforce's approach, it's often one agent distributed to many channels. Slack integration allows multiple specialized agents (HR agent, IT agent, etc.), but even then those agents likely also exist in the core system as distinct Agentforce agents. Keep the naming clear so users know who they're dealing with. If a user sees "Acme Support Bot" on the website and later interacts with "Acme Support" via SMS, they should be able to tell it's the same helper.

Channel-Specific Design Considerations

Let's break down a few major channels and their UX design considerations for AI agents:

Salesforce Desktop UI (Lightning Experience): This is a rich, mouse-and-keyboard environment with ample screen space. The agent can appear as a side panel (as Einstein Copilot does) or as part of existing layouts (like suggestions inline). Design for quick interactions that complement the user's workflow – e.g., if a user is viewing an Opportunity record, the agent panel might proactively show "Need help with this opportunity? Ask me to update fields or summarize notes." The agent can utilize Salesforce UI elements like tabs within its panel if needed (maybe one tab for chat, another for history of commands, etc.), because desktop affords multi-pane views. However, be cautious not to overload; a clean chat interface is usually best, with an option to expand for more details. Also, since on desktop the user might do other work while the AI processes a request, ensure there's a visual indicator if the agent is working ("drafting response..." spinner).

Salesforce Mobile App (or Mobile Browser): Screen space is limited, so the agent UI might collapse to a small icon or bottom sheet when not actively used. When active, it likely takes the full screen or a large portion. Keep responses shorter; consider that typing is slower on mobile, so maybe provide more quick action buttons (the agent could present common options to tap). Multi-step flows on mobile should be broken into bite-size interactions. Also, mobile usage might imply on-the-go context – e.g., a field service agent using a mobile app might benefit from voice input. Salesforce's mobile SDK could allow integrating voice to text – imagine an agent where the user presses a mic, speaks "Find the latest case for ABC Corp," and the agent texts back the info. If implementing voice, make sure the agent's text responses are brief enough to be read out via text-to-speech if that's in scope.

Slack (or Microsoft Teams, etc.): Chat platforms have their own UI constraints and opportunities. In Slack, messages can be long, but it's often better to break things into multiple messages for readability. Slack threads are useful: the agent can thread its answer under the user's question to keep channel clutter down. Or, if the conversation should remain 1-1, it might DM the user. Slack also supports interactive message components (buttons, dropdowns) – use these for confirmations or option selections. For example, the agent might present a list of results with each having a "View Details" button. Slack's ephemeral messages (visible only to one user) can be used if the agent is posting in a public channel but something should be shown only to the requester (like a prompt to enter confidential info). From a design standpoint, Slack is very textual, so ensure the agent's text is formatted nicely: use bullet points if listing items, use code blocks if showing code or error logs, etc. Also consider Slack notifications – if an agent proactively notifies a user (perhaps via a scheduled job or trigger), that's powerful but can be intrusive, so use sparingly and allow users to configure them (maybe via a slash command to opt in/out of alerts).

Email or Collaboration Docs: It's possible your agent might output content that goes into emails or documents (Salesforce has Einstein for Outlook or could insert drafts). If an agent drafts an email, it must follow email etiquette (include a greeting, proper sign-off if required, etc.). The user will likely edit before sending, but the closer the draft is to a ready-to-send state, the better. If your agent interacts through Quip docs or Chatter posts, again adapt style: Chatter might allow a more conversational update, whereas a formal customer-facing email needs polish. Keep in mind email threads – if the AI is to understand context from previous emails, ensure your integration provides that context (like by summarizing the thread for the prompt). Designing the agent to operate in such asynchronous channels might require it to be more verbose in explaining itself, since there's more delay and formality in email.

Voice (Telephony or Virtual Assistant): While Salesforce's agent solutions are currently text-focused, integrating with voice (like a phone bot or Alexa-type interface) could be done via APIs. Voice demands extremely clear and concise prompts. Users can't skim or easily refer back to what was said. So the agent should confirm critical info ("You want to reset your password, correct?") and chunk information in a stepwise manner ("The first step is... Once done, say 'next'."). If designing for voice, also account for mishearing – maybe spell out critical info ("That code is C-7-K-2"). Multi-modal experiences (where a voice agent can send a text or link to the user's phone for complex info) are a great pattern. For instance, a voice bot could say "I've found several knowledge articles; I'll send a link to your email so you can read them." That uses each channel for what it's best at.

A useful pattern is channel hand-off or continuity: if a conversation starts in one channel, can it continue in another without losing context? Salesforce's omnichannel approach in Service Cloud tries to achieve this (cases capturing the whole interaction history). For an internal agent, you might not have a formal hand-off, but consider scenario: an employee asks Slack bot for help, it does some work and then advises checking a Salesforce record. Ideally, the Slack bot could provide a deep link to the Salesforce record, and when the user clicks it and perhaps opens Copilot in Salesforce, the context carries (maybe the same query is already there). Achieving this might involve storing conversation context in a session object that multiple channels can access. Model Context Protocol (MCP) is relevant here – it aims to let different AI clients share context by querying a server. In the future, MCP could allow a Salesforce agent to retrieve context from an email thread or Slack automatically. For now, design simpler: for example, after a Slack conversation, log the transcript to a Case so that when the user (or a support agent) goes into Salesforce, they see what transpired.

Salesforce UI (Desktop)

- **Interaction design highlights:** Side-panel assistant; leverage available screen space for rich information; non-intrusive icon when idle; use the Lightning Design System for visual and interaction consistency.

Salesforce Mobile

- **Interaction design highlights:** Compact interface; prioritize quick taps over typing; optional voice input; keep responses short and scannable.

Slack (Chat)

- **Interaction design highlights:** Conversational text style; use threads to preserve context; include interactive buttons for quick actions; keep messages polite and concise, splitting longer responses into multiple messages when needed.

Experience Site / Web Chat

- **Interaction design highlights:** Branded chat widget; guided prompts using buttons or carousels; smooth escalation and handoff to human agents; optional multilingual support.

Email

- **Interaction design highlights:** Formal tone; complete sentences; clear formatting with line breaks and greetings; include context from prior threads when summarizing or responding.

Voice (if applicable)

- **Interaction design highlights:** Extremely concise responses; explicit confirmation of understood intent; break complex tasks into small steps; provide a visual fallback such as a text link or email for detailed information.

Designing across channels also requires considering security and access differences. For example, an internal Slack agent might have access to internal data that a customer-facing web chatbot should not expose. So, ensure the agent's brain (the backend logic) knows which channel it's serving and applies appropriate filters. This is part of UX too – accidentally revealing info to a customer that was meant for employees is a huge trust breaker. Salesforce's trust layer and platform security models can help enforce this (different Agentforce agents or topics for different audiences).

Example: Microsoft Copilot's Multi-Surface Approach

It's instructive to compare Microsoft's approach with Copilot across Office apps. In Word, Copilot shows up as a pane that can insert text into the document. In Excel, it can create formulas or generate analyses with charts. In Teams, it can summarize meetings. Each is tailored to the app: e.g., Word Copilot might have a tone slider for writing style, Excel Copilot might present data bullet points or tables, and Teams Copilot uses live meeting transcript to produce a recap. Yet, Microsoft brands them all "Copilot" and uses a consistent icon and generally consistent UI styling (pane on the right). They focus on a single user experience embedded in each product, rather than one chat that spans all (though they demoed some cross-app capabilities like referencing a Word doc in an Outlook email draft via Copilot – showing context integration behind scenes). The takeaway for our Salesforce agents: similarly, we want a consistent presence (Einstein icon, etc.) across Salesforce apps, but the agent will use context of that app. Salesforce Copilot does this by being "embedded directly within Salesforce's #1 AI CRM applications" and having no silos between them. In practice, if you're in Sales Cloud, Copilot knows you likely mean sales data if you ask for "top accounts," while in Service Cloud it might assume you mean top support accounts. Design for such implicit context usage.

Ensuring Continuity and State Management

A tricky aspect of multi-channel UX is how to maintain continuity if the same user switches channels mid-conversation. Ideally, if a user says to the Slack bot "Summarize my last customer call" and then later in Salesforce Copilot they ask "Draft a follow-up email for that," the agent should know "that" refers to the call summary from Slack. This is advanced and typically requires a shared memory or linking the two interactions via a record (e.g., maybe the Slack bot actually created a note on the contact with the summary, and now in Salesforce the agent sees that note to draft the email). That kind of design – using the Salesforce database as the single source of truth to pass context – is often safer than trying to have cross-channel session memory. For example, train your agents: if a user asks for something in Slack that results in data (like a summary or an analysis), always offer to save it somewhere (log a Call Summary on the CRM record, or post it to Chatter). Then, when the user is in Salesforce UI, that info is available. This leverages Salesforce's strength: a unified data model that multiple interfaces tap into. It might not be real-time "the bot remembers what I said 5 minutes ago on a different platform," but it achieves a persistent context.

MCP might in the future allow a more direct sharing of session context between agent instances in different platforms through a standardized approach. Salesforce is piloting MCP support, which means your Agentforce agent could query an MCP server to get external context or share its own. For example, maybe an agent in Salesforce could query a Slack MCP server for recent conversation history about a customer. This would empower multi-channel experiences where context is not lost. While designing today, keep an eye on such developments – designing modularly (with clear context inputs and outputs) will make integrating new context sources easier later.

Testing Across Channels

Multi-channel design demands thorough testing in each channel. You might find, for instance, that a prompt that yields a great answer in the desktop UI comes out too verbose for Slack. You may need to adjust formatting logic by channel. One approach is to have channel-specific "post-processing" of the agent's response. For example, after the LLM provides an answer, if the channel is Slack, maybe truncate after 5 bullet points and say "...(truncated)" with a button to get more. Or if the channel is voice, maybe break one response into multiple pieces with prompts for user to say "continue" to hear more. These are design decisions that ensure usability per channel.

Also gather channel-specific feedback. Users might love the agent in Slack but find it not so useful in the CRM, or vice versa. That can highlight UX issues (maybe the Slack one is too limited because it can't show a rich UI, so users prefer CRM, or maybe users in Slack wanted more proactive suggestions). By monitoring usage metrics per channel (which we'll discuss in the next section on metrics), you can identify where the agent is shining or struggling and iterate the design for that context.

To conclude this section, let's imagine a user journey to illustrate multi-channel fluidity: A sales rep, Alice, starts her day on Salesforce desktop. She uses Einstein Copilot to ask: "Give me a summary of my open deals and any risks." The Copilot panel provides a nicely formatted summary of, say, 3 deals and flags one at risk (with a link to the Opportunity). She clicks the link, goes into that Opportunity, and asks Copilot to "Draft an update email to the customer about addressing the risk." Copilot drafts it right in Salesforce, she tweaks and sends. Later that day, Alice is in a meeting and gets a Slack message from her manager about that account. Alice quickly invokes the sales agent in Slack: "@SalesBot show recent activity for ABC Corp." The agent pulls the latest info (including that email she sent, perhaps logged as an activity, and maybe a case that was just escalated by service). It replies in Slack thread with key points. Alice sees something about a support escalation. She then uses Slack to ping the support agent: "@SupportBot what's the status of case 12345?" The support bot responds in Slack. All the while, if Alice goes back into Salesforce later, the record of the case and opportunity will reflect those activities. She could also open Copilot in Service Cloud to dig deeper if needed. This scenario shows multiple channels (Salesforce UI and Slack) working in concert. Achieving this requires careful planning of what each channel can do best, making sure context (like case statuses, email logs) are stored centrally, and giving the user a consistent mental model ("I can ask either bot about related info and they'll fetch it").

By designing for multi-channel experience, we aim to meet users wherever they are and provide a cohesive, convenient AI assistance experience. In the enterprise world, this is crucial – people use many tools, and AI should be an asset in all of them, not locked in one. Salesforce's platform advantage is that many of those tools (Salesforce apps, Slack, etc.) can be unified under Agentforce, and open standards like MCP point to even broader connectivity (e.g., connecting with Microsoft's ecosystem or others). The next section of our book will touch on ensuring that as we broaden our agent's reach, we don't leave anyone behind: we must consider accessibility, inclusion, and trust cues in the design, so the experience is equitable and users feel safe. Let's explore that next.

ACCESSIBILITY, INCLUSION, AND TRUST CUES

As we design AI agents for broad use, it's vital to ensure that everyone can use them comfortably and confidently. Accessibility means users with disabilities or different needs can interact with the agent effectively (e.g., via screen readers, keyboard navigation, high contrast visuals, etc.). Inclusion means the agent's design and behavior are welcoming and respectful to people of all backgrounds, languages, and abilities – avoiding biases or exclusionary practices. And trust cues are the visual and interaction elements that signal to users that the AI agent is trustworthy, secure, and acting with integrity. In enterprise settings especially, trust is paramount: users (and customers) need to know the AI isn't doing anything shady with their data and that they can rely on its outputs. Salesforce has heavily emphasized trust in its AI principles (accuracy, safety, transparency, etc. all feed into trust). In this section, we'll break down how to bake these considerations into your agent's UX design.

Designing for Accessibility

Salesforce's own design system (SLDS) and Lightning components come with accessibility standards (meeting WCAG 2.1 AA typically). When embedding your agent in Salesforce UIs, using standard Lightning Web Components or base components where possible will carry those benefits (like proper ARIA labels, keyboard support, and color contrast). Here are key accessibility points:

Visual Design: Ensure sufficient color contrast for any text the agent displays. For example, if your agent highlights code or data, the colors chosen must be readable by those with low vision or color blindness. Avoid relying solely on color to convey meaning (like "I marked the urgent issues in red" – a screen reader user or colorblind user might miss that). Instead, include an icon or text label ("[Urgent] Issue description").

Screen Reader Compatibility: All interactive elements (buttons, links) from the agent should have descriptive labels. If your agent's UI is custom, test it with a screen reader (like NVDA or VoiceOver). The agent's messages should be output in the DOM in a logical order. If using a chat interface, ensure that new messages are announced properly. Possibly use ARIA live regions to announce incoming messages from the agent. E.g., the Copilot panel can be set with aria-live="polite" so the screen reader reads out the agent's reply when it appears.

Keyboard Navigation: Some users don't use a mouse. So all features of the agent must be operable via keyboard (or alternative input). This means if the agent provides a list of options or buttons, a user should be able to tab through them and press Enter/Space to activate. If the agent is hidden behind an icon (like Einstein icon), that icon must be focusable and have an accessible name like "Open AI Assistant".

Timeouts and Interruptions: If your agent has any auto-refresh or auto-close behavior, be cautious. Users with certain disabilities may need more time to read or respond. Generally, don't impose short timeouts on agent interactions. If an agent is speaking (voice output), allow the user to interrupt or pause it because some may process slower.

Alternative Modalities: Think about users who cannot easily read text. If your agent outputs a chart or image (maybe via an integration that returns a graph), provide an equivalent textual summary (the agent itself can do this: e.g., "Here is a bar chart of sales; in summary, region A leads with $X, followed by region B..."). If voice is available, also provide text for those who are deaf or in quiet environments. Essentially, offer multiple ways to receive information.

Salesforce has guidance like "use semantic HTML and proper ARIA" when building Lightning components, which applies here. If you're using the out-of-box Copilot UI, Salesforce likely handled a lot. But if customizing, stick to known patterns (e.g., use lightning-button which is accessible vs. custom <div> that looks like a button).

Test with actual users or at least with personas: how would a low-vision user fare? how about someone using only keyboard? We want the agent to empower these users possibly even more – for example, an employee with a motor impairment might rely on voice commands to the AI to do tasks rather than many mouse clicks, which could be game-changing if implemented well.

Inclusive Design and Bias Mitigation

Inclusion goes beyond accessibility. It's about cultural and linguistic inclusivity and avoiding reinforcing biases. Language support is one aspect: if your workforce or customer base is multilingual, can the agent understand and respond in their languages? Salesforce is adding language support to its AI; if you operate in a single language environment you might not worry, but global companies likely want multi-language agents. Even if the agent only speaks English, ensure its language is simple enough for non-native speakers: avoid idioms, figurative language or complex vocabulary unnecessarily. Clarity trumps cleverness.

Avoiding bias: AI can inadvertently produce biased outputs (e.g., using gendered pronouns by assumption, or being less polite to certain names due to training data biases). Salesforce tries to mitigate this with toxicity and bias assessments. As a designer, you can reinforce it by instructing the agent to use neutral language. For example, if referring to a generic person, maybe use "they" instead of "he" by default. If the agent provides examples or analogies, ensure they're diverse (not always "ACME Corp sells shoes to women" type of stereotypes). This may seem subtle in a corporate agent context, but imagine an AI sales coach – if all its example leads are male-named, that sends a message. Instead, consciously use a mix ("John and Priya are both customers in the scenario...") or generic roles ("the customer", "the agent").

Another angle: ensure the agent is inclusive in content. Suppose it generates interview questions or customer outreach emails – verify those outputs don't include bias (like asking female candidates different questions than male, or making assumptions about someone's background). This is more on the AI model side, but your design can include instructions or filters to catch certain things. The Einstein Trust Layer filters attempts to use sensitive attributes – e.g. guiding the LLM to avoid using race, gender etc. inappropriately. So, an Agentforce prompt could include "Do not mention or assume attributes like gender or ethnicity of people unless it's explicitly relevant and provided in data."

Inclusive imagery and naming: If your agent has an avatar or icon (some companies use mascots like Salesforce has Astro, Codey etc.), consider representation. E.g., if using avatars for different specialized agents, Salesforce gave them icons (HR agent had a people icon, IT agent a computer icon, etc. in the Slack example). They avoided human faces which is wise to not imply a specific race/gender. If you do give it a persona name, be mindful of cultural implications – something neutral or that resonates positively across cultures.

User empowerment and privacy: Inclusion also means giving users control over their data and privacy – because feeling safe is part of being included. Agents should follow privacy guidelines (e.g., not exposing personal data unnecessarily) and possibly give users options: e.g., "This conversation will be logged for quality – would you like to opt out?" might be an option in customer support contexts. Salesforce's principles talk about respecting data provenance and consent – design can reflect that by perhaps letting a user know when the agent is using their personal data ("I see your profile says you prefer email communication; I'll draft an email accordingly." The user set that preference, so it's fine to use, but making it visible builds trust that agent isn't guessing or snooping).

Visual Trust Cues and Transparency

When a user interacts with the agent, certain visual cues can immediately set a tone of trust. One basic cue is branding: because the agent operates within your trusted Salesforce environment, carry over familiar branding. For external customers, ensure the chatbot has your company logo or colors so it's clear this is an official channel (not some scam). For employees, maybe incorporate your intranet's style.

Another cue is security indicators. For instance, on a web chatbot, you could include a small lock icon or text like "Securely connected" if appropriate, to reassure users that their conversation is protected. This is akin to how browsers show a lock for HTTPS. In Slack or internal, this might not be needed explicitly, but the agent could occasionally reassure in wording ("I can handle that request. Your data will remain within our secure systems.").

Disclosure of AI nature: One of the biggest trust factors is knowing it's AI. Users get uncomfortable if they suspect a human is actually reading or vice versa. Salesforce's guideline is to clearly disclose AI-generated content. Concretely, when an agent sends an outbound message to a customer (like an email or a chat reply that the customer might think is human), Salesforce ensures there's disclosure. Agentforce's out-of-the-box agents like the Sales Development Rep agent and Service Agent "clearly disclose when content is AI-generated to ensure transparency". How to do this in UX? Possibly a small footer line: "(This response was generated by an AI assistant)" on emails or chat. Or an initial intro, "Hi, I'm AgentName, a virtual assistant." After that, it might not repeat every time, but any formal communication should somewhere tag itself as virtual. Internally, employees should also know – with Slack, it's usually obvious because the bot has a bot icon or [Bot] label. In Salesforce UI, the Einstein icon and style differentiate it from chatter coming from a human. So use those conventions (like use the Einstein avatar or a custom robot icon for the agent's messages) so no one mistakes it for a colleague.

Reliability cues: Users also judge trust by how reliable and accurate the agent appears. You can't control the model's every output, but you can design confirmation mechanisms. For example, when the agent executes an action, show a confirmation message "✅ Case closed successfully" – this assures the user the task was done and they can trust the agent's action. If there's uncertainty, as recommended before, show sources or ask for validation. If the agent provides a critical answer, perhaps accompany it with citations or an "Verify" button. An interesting pattern could be a "Confidence meter":

some AI UIs have tried to show a confidence score. Salesforce hasn't exposed that directly in UI (and sometimes it's hard to compute accurately), but you might do a simpler version: If the agent's answer is potentially unsure, maybe it says "(I'm not 100% sure, please double-check the data.)". Being forthcoming about uncertainty paradoxically increases user trust overall, because they see the agent isn't blindly confident.

Einstein Trust Layer and Guardrails: Salesforce includes many guardrails, like toxicity filters and topic restrictions. When these triggers activate, how does the agent respond UX-wise? If a user asks the agent something out-of-policy (say, request for personal data or something abusive), the agent might refuse. The refusal message should be polite and explain without being too technical. E.g., "I'm sorry, I can't assist with that request." Possibly followed by a general reason if appropriate ("It may involve sensitive information that I'm not allowed to access."). Designing good refusal messages is part of trust cues – you don't want to leave the user confused why the agent isn't helping. Similarly, if content was filtered (maybe user said something with profanity), the agent can still handle gracefully ("I can help, but please refrain from offensive language." – or just ignore profanity and answer the core question). Maintaining a professional tone even in face of user anger will demonstrate the agent is a stable, safe entity.

Audit trails: In enterprise contexts, letting users know there is an audit trail can reassure them that AI actions are accountable. For instance, if an AI agent sends an email or changes a record, it might tag the entry "by AI Agent" and log that somewhere. If an end-user can see "AI Agent updated this record at 3pm" with maybe a link to details, it fosters trust because it's not hidden. People fear AI doing things behind the scenes – so make its actions visible and traceable. An admin or manager should be able to review what the agent did (Salesforce logs and analytics help with that). While this is more of a governance feature, it intersects UX when you think of a user noticing something changed and being able to find out it was the AI. Good UX: maybe have a subtle icon next to AI-made feed posts or updates.

Pro Tip: In any user communications about the new AI agent (training materials, announcement emails, onboarding tips), emphasize the measures taken to ensure responsible AI: mention the guardrails, the human oversight in place, and how data is handled (e.g., "The agent does not store any personal data outside Salesforce" if that's the case). Educating users on these builds trust before they even use the tool. This is outside the UI per se, but it's part of the holistic UX – trust is also shaped by what users are told about the system.

Building Trust Over Time

Trust is not established overnight; users will test the agent and see if it keeps confidence. Encourage and design for user feedback loops about trust issues. For example, allow users to flag an answer as possibly incorrect or inappropriate. If your agent's interface has a thumbs down or "Report issue" option, that provides a safety valve. Even if rarely used, just having it visible can reassure users that you care about quality and will review problems. Internally, you should have a process: those flags go to someone who can correct the knowledge base or adjust prompts.

In terms of inclusion and trust, also be mindful of user emotional state. Agents, especially in service roles, should express empathy appropriately (as discussed in tone section). Empathy is a trust cue – it shows the agent "cares" (in its AI way) about the user's situation. For instance, if a customer says "This is really frustrating," the agent acknowledging that ("I understand that you're frustrated, and I'm sorry about the inconvenience.") can reduce tension and increase willingness to continue working with the agent. Salesforce's Atlas engine even mentions "offer empathetic and human-like responses" as a goal. Just ensure empathy lines are sincere and not over the top or repetitive. We've all seen poorly programmed bots that say "I'm sorry" too often in a canned way – that can backfire. It's a fine line, but a well-designed agent will have a varied but genuine-sounding repertoire for such situations.

Another trust aspect is performance. If the agent is slow or frequently unavailable, trust erodes (people think "it's flaky"). So invest in making the user perceive it as responsive. If an action will take time (maybe it's doing a complex multi-step process), give a progress indicator or at least an acknowledgment ("Got it, let me work on that for you..."). Silence is the enemy of trust in interactive systems, because the user wonders if it's broken. A simple spinning icon or animated ellipsis can suffice for a short wait. If something fails (like the AI couldn't retrieve info), apologize and either retry or offer to try later. These UX touches show reliability.

Security and privacy factors visible to users: since the agent might handle sensitive data, think about where it displays info. Example: an agent might fetch some confidential data – ensure it doesn't accidentally post it in a public channel. If a Slack agent is about to output sensitive data, perhaps detect channel type (if not a DM, maybe respond with "I have that information; I'll message you privately for security."). That design decision protects data and signals to all in channel that the bot is following privacy rules.

Similarly, if multiple users are around (like screen sharing or an open office), maybe a voice agent shouldn't read out PII aloud. These situational things are hard to cover fully, but by analyzing typical use scenarios, you can add guardrails for obvious cases.

At Salesforce, the Einstein Trust Layer ensures things like zero data retention by the LLM and no PII leakage. While those are under-the-hood, if you have a way to inform users ("Powered by Einstein Trust Layer – your data isn't used to re-train models"), that could be a footnote or a tooltip somewhere.

In sum, designing for accessibility, inclusion, and trust is about being mindful of all your users and their concerns. If done right, it makes your AI agent not just a powerful tool, but one that users feel comfortable inviting into their daily work. They know: it will work for them (regardless of disability or language), it will treat them fairly and respectfully, and it will be transparent and secure in operation.

With these foundations of UX – embedding, interaction patterns, tone, multi-channel strategy, and trust/inclusion – we should also ensure we're measuring success. That's where UX metrics and feedback loops come into play, which we'll explore next. After all, you can design the most thoughtful experience, but you need to verify in the real world if it's effective and iterate accordingly.

UX METRICS AND FEEDBACK LOOPS

Designing and deploying an AI agent is not a one-and-done effort – it requires ongoing monitoring and refinement. To achieve that, we need to define metrics that indicate how the agent is performing from a user experience perspective, and establish feedback loops to gather insights from users (and from the agent's own operation) to drive continuous improvement. In this section, we'll discuss which metrics are useful to track the UX and adoption of your Salesforce AI agent, how Salesforce's platform helps with analytics, and how to collect and use feedback (both implicit and explicit) to refine the agent's design and behavior. We'll also touch on setting up governance processes (who reviews the metrics, how often, etc.) because mid-to-advanced Salesforce practitioners will likely be tasked with demonstrating the ROI and effectiveness of these agents. As the saying goes, "if you can't measure it, you can't improve it" – so let's ensure we're measuring the right things.

Defining Key UX Success Metrics

First, consider what success looks like for your agent. The metrics should tie to the goals you had when introducing the agent. Common high-level goals include improving productivity, reducing response times, increasing user satisfaction, and driving adoption of the feature. Here are some metrics and KPIs (Key Performance Indicators) that often apply:

Adoption Rate: How many target users are actually using the agent? For internal agents, this could be percentage of employees who have engaged with the agent at least once in a given period. For customer-facing, it could be percentage of website visitors or support queries handled by the AI. Salesforce likely provides usage counts – e.g., number of Copilot sessions, number of prompts executed. In fact, Agentforce provides analytics and reporting on usage and adoption right out of the box. Tracking unique users and session counts will tell you if the agent is gaining traction or if awareness/training needs boosting.

Engagement and Frequency: Beyond just who tried it, measure how often people use it. For instance, average number of queries per user per day/week. If users try it once and drop off, that signals issues (maybe they didn't get value or had a bad experience). Conversely, growth in queries per user suggests increasing trust and reliance. You can also look at session length (though with goal-oriented bots, shorter might be better if it means quick resolution).

Task Success/Automation Rate: This metric looks at outcomes. For support scenarios, what percentage of cases or chats are resolved by the AI agent without human intervention? For sales, maybe how many follow-up tasks or emails did the AI handle. Agentforce's analytics mention tracking things like case resolution time and whether the AI responded (Salesforce's agent reports show metrics like resolution rate, deflection rate, etc.). A high success rate indicates the agent is effectively doing its job; a low one might mean it often escalates to humans or users abandon it.

Time Savings: Measure the impact on time. If an agent handles tasks, how much faster are they completed versus before? For example, if before a support rep manually categorized cases in 5 minutes and now the AI does it in seconds, that's a quantifiable time save. On a macro scale, metrics like average handling time per case or average sales cycle time can be monitored to see if they improve post-agent. Agentforce is designed to reduce things like case handling time (they gave an example of 20% reduction by streamlining screens).

User Satisfaction Score: This can be captured via surveys or rating prompts. For instance, after an agent interaction, you might prompt the user "Was this helpful? (👍 or 👎)". Or a CSAT (customer satisfaction) question on a 1-5 scale. Internally, you could survey employees periodically about the tool. If integrated in UI, Salesforce might allow capturing thumbs-up/down on Copilot answers (some beta features were aiming to do that). Indeed, Salesforce has introduced Prompt Performance Metrics with user feedback (Beta) to track how users rate the outputs. A rising satisfaction trend indicates UX improvements are working; declining satisfaction would be a red flag.

Error/Failure Rates: Track how often the agent fails to fulfill a request. This could be measured as the frequency of fallback responses ("Sorry I can't help with that") or number of escalations to human. If those go down over time, great. If certain types spike, identify those issues. Also monitor technical errors (like if an integration fails causing the agent to error out).

Conversion or Business Impact Metrics: If applicable, tie to business outcomes. E.g., did the sales agent help increase pipeline or conversion? Did the service bot deflect enough cases to save X dollars? These might be longer-term, but they justify the agent's existence. Not purely UX, but relevant to proving value.

Many of these metrics Salesforce might aggregate in dashboards. For example, Agentforce provides analytics on key metrics like case resolution time, agent productivity, and customer satisfaction scores via reporting features. There's mention that Agentforce has reports to show adoption and success, and Copilot has admin dashboards for usage and success rate. As a designer, ensure those analytics are enabled and accessible to the team.

Gathering Feedback: Implicit and Explicit

Explicit user feedback is direct input from users about their experience. This can come from:

- In-app ratings (thumbs up/down, stars, etc. on responses).
- Surveys or forms (maybe a quarterly internal survey like "How helpful do you find the Sales AI assistant? Any suggestions?").
- Interviews or focus groups with a sample of users. Especially early on, talk to actual users: ask them what they like, what frustrates

them. Sometimes anecdotal feedback reveals things metrics can't (like "It always uses too formal language, which I find off-putting" – you might not catch that in numbers).

It's wise to incorporate an easy feedback mechanism. For instance, Slack bots can accept a command like feedback [message] to record user comments. Or the Salesforce UI Copilot could have a little feedback link. Salesforce's doc on Prompt Feedback suggests they are capturing thumbs and showing those in metrics, which is great.

One technique for explicit feedback is Wizard-of-Oz testing or pilot programs – earlier, maybe you manually monitor and intervene to see what users ask and how they react, then fine-tune. But once live, rely on ratings and comments.

Implicit feedback comes from observing user behavior:

- If a user rephrases their query multiple times, that implies the first answer was not satisfactory (because they had to try again). That can be logged. Some advanced systems use this to auto-tune – not sure if Agentforce does yet, but you can manually glean it. E.g., check conversation logs: did user ask something, agent answered, then user immediately asked the same or a similar question? Possibly the first answer missed the mark.
- If users are skipping the agent for certain tasks (e.g., even though they could ask the bot, they still do it manually in the UI), that indicates a trust or discoverability issue. You'd see that in process metrics (like if manual case escalations haven't decreased).
- Usage patterns: what topics or intents are most common? Are there frequently asked questions the agent struggles with? The logs can show common unanswered queries. That's an opportunity to expand the agent's knowledge or capabilities.
- Another implicit metric: time spent or drop-off in a session. If a user spends 10 minutes chatting and nothing gets resolved, likely frustrating. If they quit after the agent gives an answer and then immediately escalate to a human channel, it means the agent failed them. Try to correlate agent involvement with outcomes (did it actually solve or did user still create a ticket anyway).

Utilizing Salesforce Tools for Analytics

The nice part about Salesforce's platform is it often has built-in analytics or easily configurable ones for new features like Agentforce. As mentioned, Einstein Copilot has an Analytics section for admin with data points: total sessions, interactions per user, actions launched, success rate. It even specifically calls out an "action adoption" section with a dashboard for which Copilot Actions are being used and their success. That's gold for UX improvement: if some actions are never used, maybe users don't know about them or don't need them. If some have low success (maybe user tries but something fails often), that's a point to investigate.

Agentforce also provides something akin to "who's using your agents and how successful they are". So definitely leverage these out-of-the-box reports. An admin or analyst can create custom reports too, e.g., group by department or region to see if adoption differs.

One can also use standard Salesforce logging: e.g., each Agentforce invocation could be recorded as a record (maybe in a custom object or event log) with details like user, timestamp, intent, outcome, feedback rating. Then normal Salesforce reporting or Tableau CRM could slice and dice it.

Don't forget qualitative metrics too, though harder to track, they matter: things like user sentiment (if an agent logs sentiment from text, you could track average sentiment score at start vs end of conversations as a proxy for how well it resolves issues). Slack messages or emails might contain thanks or exasperation – maybe analyze a random sample of transcripts each month.

Iterative Improvement Process

Metrics and feedback are only useful if you act on them. Establish a feedback loop meaning a regular process:

Monitoring: Have a dashboard or report that stakeholders (product owner, support lead, etc.) can check. Possibly set alerts for certain thresholds (e.g., if satisfaction drops below X or if error rate spikes, notify the team).

Review Cadence: Perhaps weekly quick reviews of metrics, and monthly deeper dives to spot trends. Bring in cross-functional team – devs, support reps, business owners – to interpret results.

User Feedback Review: If you have user comments or thumbs-down reasons, categorize them. For example, many users might be complaining "Agent's answers are too generic" – that's something to address by giving the agent more context or improving prompt.

Continuous Prompt/Knowledge Tuning: With Agentforce, a lot can be tuned without heavy coding – adjusting instructions, adding new knowledge docs, tweaking thresholds. Use the data to justify those changes. For instance, if metrics show the agent often fails on queries about a certain product, maybe you need to feed it that product's FAQ.

Update and Validate: After changes, see if metrics move in the right direction. It's a bit like DevOps monitoring but for AI behavior. If you change the tone or output format based on feedback, does satisfaction go up?

Training and Communication Adjustments: The data might show not a flaw in AI, but in user understanding. E.g., low adoption might mean users aren't aware or not confident. Address that through more training sessions or internal comms: share success stories ("Agent helped reduce support backlog by 20%!") to encourage usage. Or embed a short how-to video in the UI for first-time users.

One must be careful to interpret metrics properly. For example, a decrease in average interactions per session might mean the agent is getting better (solving things faster, so users don't need as many back-and-forths), or it could mean users are giving up sooner. Correlate with other signals (did satisfaction rise? Did resolution rate improve? That would indicate positive cause).

Case study example: Suppose you find that the Service AI agent has a high deflection rate (it resolves 50% of chats fully) – great, but the other 50% still end up with a human. Dive into those transcripts or metadata: maybe 30% of those it escalated appropriately (complex issues it's not meant to solve, fine), but 20% it should have solved but didn't. Why? Possibly it failed to understand a certain phrasing. You can then expand its intent training. Or maybe it gave an answer but customer wasn't satisfied and asked for human – that might be a trust issue, maybe the answer lacked sources. So perhaps for those kinds of questions you implement a policy to include a knowledge base citation, to bolster trust so user doesn't feel need for human confirmation.

Owning the Agent's Evolution: Salesforce guidance (like from the Noltic guide) emphasizes you need a business owner continuously tuning the system, not just IT setting and forgetting. This is crucial: allocate responsibility for monitoring metrics and championing improvements. That person or team uses the feedback loop to keep the agent aligned with user needs. The quote from Noltic: "Agentforce is not a set-it-and-forget-it tool... someone needs to watch service metrics, gather feedback, adjust workflows... You need a business owner who understands service goals and agent challenges". Implement that advice: perhaps form an "AI Agent Steering Committee" that meets to go over the analytics and decide on changes or training needs.

Additionally, use metrics to demonstrate success to leadership. Show how key KPIs moved after deploying the agent (e.g., case resolution time dropped 15%, or sales reps report saving 5 hours/week). This can secure further investment or at least continued support for the initiative. It can also highlight if something's not working and needs a pivot (if adoption stays low for a long time, maybe the use case wasn't right or users prefer a different interface – better to find out and adjust strategy).

Closing the User Feedback Loop

When users give feedback, try to acknowledge it or let them know how it's being addressed. For internal users, you can publish a "We heard you" update: e.g., "Based on your feedback, we've improved the AI assistant. It will now provide more detailed context when summarizing cases, and we fixed an issue where it sometimes gave outdated data. Keep the feedback coming!" This encourages further feedback and shows the organization's commitment to making the tool better, which in turn improves adoption and trust.

For customer-facing bots, you might not individually respond to feedback, but if you have a persistent user base (like community members), you could announce improvements in release notes or a community post ("Our virtual agent is now smarter! It can handle billing questions – give it a try.").

Remember to also gather feedback from human agents or colleagues who work with the AI indirectly. For instance, support agents might say "The AI often assigns wrong case categories which I then have to fix." That's feedback to incorporate into retraining the categorization logic. Or sales managers might say "My team isn't using the AI email draft because it doesn't include our latest product info." That could prompt adding that info to the prompt knowledge.

In summary, building robust metrics and feedback loops turns your AI agent deployment into a living program that continuously adapts to deliver value. Salesforce provides many of the hooks (reports, dashboards, logs) to facilitate this, but the human side of analysis and iteration is what makes it effective. With proper metrics, you can move from intuition ("I think the bot is helping") to evidence ("CSAT is up 10 points since bot launch and agents are closing 20% more cases/day"). This not only validates the UX design decisions but also guides future enhancements systematically.

Finally, with all these aspects – from embedding and design patterns to tone and trust to metrics – under consideration, we can step back and see the bigger picture of UX patterns in the agent ecosystem. Many enterprises will not have just one agent but an ecosystem of multiple agents or integrated AI services. Ensuring consistency and synergy among them is our next and last major topic before we conclude the chapter.

UX PATTERNS IN THE AGENT ECOSYSTEM

As organizations adopt AI agents, they often proliferate into an ecosystem of agents serving different functions, departments, or even interacting with each other. Salesforce's Agentforce envisions a "digital labor" platform where multiple specialized agents (sales, service, marketing, IT, etc.) can all work in concert alongside humans. In such an ecosystem, maintaining a coherent user experience and effective coordination is a new design challenge. This section will outline UX patterns and best practices when you have multiple agents or complex agent environments. We'll cover patterns for discovery (how users find and invoke different agents), consistency across agents, hand-offs between agents, and interoperability facilitated by standards like the Model Context Protocol (MCP) and multi-agent frameworks (e.g., CrewAI). We'll also consider the perspective of scaling from one agent to many: how do you introduce new agents without confusion, and how do you ensure an overall governance so the "AI team" doesn't become the wild west.

Discoverability and Onboarding of Multiple Agents

When you have several agents available (like HR Agent, IT Agent, Sales Coach, etc.), how do users know which to use and when? One UX pattern is to provide a directory or launcher for agents. For instance, Slack's approach is to treat each agent as a Slack app that can be added to channels or DMed. Users discover them like they would Slack apps. Salesforce could incorporate an "Agents" panel or menu in the UI listing available assistants (maybe Agentforce Command Center, as hinted by an Agentforce 3 announcement, might centralize management). In absence of a built-in directory, consider documenting them on your intranet or training material: e.g., "Meet your AI Agents: SalesBot for pipeline help, KnowledgeBot for product info, DevOpsBot for release queries..." – give a one-liner for each, and perhaps the command to invoke (like the Slack slash command or where in Salesforce it lives).

A crucial element is clear naming and scope. If names are ambiguous, users won't recall which agent does what. Names can be functional ("Service Agent", "Finance Assistant") or branded but then clarify purpose in UI (maybe when you open it, it says "I can help with financial reports, expense approvals, and budget queries"). In the Slack UI snippet, they had labels like "HR Agent – Provide automated employee support..." which is good. Carry such descriptions wherever possible (tooltips, documentation).

Onboarding: The first time a user interacts with an agent, provide a mini-tutorial or example. For each agent, we might implement a help command that lists what it can do. Ensure consistency: all agents respond to help with a similarly formatted help message. That's an example of a cross-agent UX pattern. Maybe all your agents share some core commands (help, feedback, maybe switch context etc.). If you have a central orchestrator (like a Command Center UI), onboarding could happen there: e.g., "Looking for help? Try asking the IT Agent for tech support issues or the Sales Coach for tips – click an agent to start."

Consistency and Shared Design Language Across Agents

Even if agents have different personas (tone might differ slightly by department context), they should still feel like parts of a whole. This can be achieved by a shared design language:

Visual consistency: If you have avatars for agents, perhaps they all follow the same style (like Slack used simple line icons for each category). If you have one agent represented by, say, a robot icon, maybe all have variants of that icon (a robot with a briefcase for Sales, with a wrench for IT, etc.). This shows they are a family. Salesforce often uses its mascots (Astro, etc.) in various costumes for different contexts – you could do similar if it fits your culture.

Interaction patterns: Ensure similar triggers and response styles. If one agent uses a Q&A style, others shouldn't have completely different interaction paradigms (unless necessary). For example, if HR Bot always asks multiple-choice questions to drill down, but IT Bot is completely free-form, users may get confused. It's fine to have differences when the tasks differ, but keep underlying philosophy: all agents perhaps confirm actions before executing, all agents allow cancellation by typing "cancel", etc. These become standard UX patterns across your agent ecosystem.

Terminology: Use consistent terms for similar concepts. If one agent refers to "Knowledge Base" and another says "FAQ articles," unify that wording if they're the same thing. If the AI calls users by name or titles, ensure similar politeness levels across agents (you don't want one agent calling a customer "valued client" and another bluntly using first name in a scenario where that might be too casual).

Persona alignment: While agents can have distinct personalities (the IT agent might be a bit nerdy jokey, the legal agent more formal), they should share core values like politeness and helpfulness. They are all representatives of your brand. It helps to have a centralized AI persona guideline document (as discussed in Tone section) that sets the overall tone and then perhaps minor tweaks per agent.

Standard safety responses: All agents should handle sensitive or off-limits requests in a unified manner. If a user asks any agent for something out-of-policy, the refusal style should be consistent ("I'm sorry, I can't assist with that." maybe followed by a standard company policy statement). This uniformity signals that the agents are governed and trustworthy.

Orchestration patterns: If you have an orchestrator agent that can direct to other agents (imagine a user could ask a general "Assistant" which then determines that the HR agent should handle this query and passes it along), that's one way to simplify UX by offering one entry point. Microsoft sort of avoids multiple personalities by having one Copilot that works in contexts. Salesforce may head that way too – they talk about no silos and reasoning engine handling multi-step plans across systems. Possibly the Atlas engine or future updates might allow one agent to call upon another.

If you implement such a pattern manually: e.g., the main agent checks the question topic ("benefits" goes to HR agent, "technical issue" goes to IT agent) – be transparent to the user. The agent can say, "Sure, I'll have our IT virtual assistant help with that:" and then either internally switch persona or just route the user to the right agent. Alternatively, if each agent is separate, an error handling pattern could be: if user asked the wrong agent (like asked SalesBot a HR question), SalesBot replies "I'm not equipped for that, but let me ask the HR Agent..." and then either HR Agent joins the thread or instructs user how to contact it. This cross-agent politeness ensures the user doesn't hit dead ends. Slack's multi-agent environment benefits from being all in one platform, so possibly one bot can mention another or pass context (there might even be Slack workflows to route between bots).

Agent-to-Agent Interactions and Multi-Agent Orchestration

Beyond just multiple agents with a single user, in some advanced cases agents might work together on a task, either sequentially or collaboratively. For example, a sales agent and a marketing agent might coordinate: a sales agent finds an upsell opportunity and then asks the marketing agent to draft a custom brochure for that client. With frameworks like CrewAI, multi-agent systems run behind the scenes to achieve a goal. CrewAI and Lang-Chain AgentExecutor patterns often have one "manager" agent delegating to specialist tools (which could be seen as agents). In Salesforce's vision, we see hints of this with "Agent2Agent (A2A) support coming in the future" which implies agents could call each other or share tasks.

From a UX perspective, you usually won't expose the complexity of multiple agents talking to each other to the end user – you want to present one coherent answer or action. However, designing the system, you should ensure if multiple agents are involved, the handoff is smooth and doesn't require user intervention unless needed. If user does see it, make it comprehensible: e.g., "I'm collaborating with our Marketing AI on this. One moment..." then combined result is given.

Interoperability via MCP: The Model Context Protocol aims to let agents connect to various context providers or tools uniformly. Salesforce supporting MCP means your agent can leverage external AI services or data in a plug-and-play way, and even agents from partner ecosystems can interoperate. For UX, this means the user might not even realize when an external system is being tapped – which is fine if integrated seamlessly. But you might surface source info: e.g., if your agent used a Google Maps MCP server to fetch store locations, you might note "(via Google Maps)" in the answer to credit the source, which also adds trust. Another UX benefit of MCP could be that if the user has another MCP-compatible agent (maybe a personal AI assistant on their device), it could talk to Salesforce's agent in the background. In such cases, ensure security (the Salesforce agent should authenticate requests from external agents appropriately – trust cues might include confirming with the user if an external agent tries to do something on their behalf).

Agent Exchange and Marketplace: Salesforce launched AgentExchange, akin to AppExchange, for agents and components. If you adopt agent apps from marketplace, try to maintain UX consistency. It's like installing a third-party app in Salesforce – you ensure it aligns with your UI and processes. Possibly, you might have to reconfigure an Agentforce agent from a partner to match your tone and rules. The more you integrate them into your ecosystem, the less disjointed the experience.

Governance and the Human Element in an Ecosystem

When multiple agents are active, having a governance strategy is important to avoid chaos:

Policy Consistency: All agents should adhere to company policies (data handling, tone guidelines, escalation protocols). A central team (maybe your Center of Excellence for AI) can maintain these and audit agents. For example, check that each agent's prompt instructions include the necessary ethical guidelines.

Change Management: If you update one agent's behavior or fix an issue, consider if similar changes apply to others. E.g., if you learned users don't like too formal tone and you adjust SalesBot to be more casual, maybe also adjust ServiceBot similarly to keep style aligned.

Avoid Agent Overload: Too many bots can overwhelm users (analysis paralysis – which bot do I go to?). So scale deliberately. Perhaps start with one generalist and a couple of specialists, and add more only if needed. Alternatively, collapse overlapping ones. If IT and HR agents often get similar "how do I" queries, maybe a single "Employee Help" agent could cover both with internal branching. Always design with the user's mental model in mind – they likely don't want to memorize a dozen bot names for each nuance of work. Simplify the ecosystem where possible.

One interesting emerging pattern is having a unified conversation space where multiple agents can chime in if relevant. Some experimental UIs allow a user question to be visible to multiple agents and whichever has the best confidence or is domain-matched responds. That could be confusing if more than one responds, so perhaps a mediator chooses. As a pattern: you could have one primary agent that reaches out to others behind the scenes (like "skills" or "tools"). This is akin to the LangChain approach where one agent calls different tools (which could be thought of as silent sub-agents) – the user only sees the primary agent. Salesforce's reasoning engine works similarly: it picks which action (tool) to use. So likely, Salesforce encourages that pattern to avoid user juggling multiple assistants. But in Slack, separate personas per department might be more straightforward, since Slack's UI is channel-focused.

CrewAI style multi-agent: If you ever expose multi-agent reasoning to power users (maybe a dev who wants to see how the sausage is made), consider a mode where the conversation between agents is visible (some dev tools have an "AI thought process" toggle). But for general UX, keep it hidden to avoid confusion.

Real-World Example: The Salesforce Ecosystem Approach

Salesforce's open ecosystem approach with Agentforce 3 suggests that they want third-party agents and components to "build once, connect everywhere". They mention partners like Box, AWS providing MCP servers that Agentforce agents will use. From a UX perspective, that means your Salesforce agent can suddenly do a lot more – retrieving documents from Box, summarizing videos from AWS, etc., all within one agent's capabilities. The pattern is an extensible agent rather than multiple siloed agents. You may incorporate new abilities as needed (similar to adding new actions in Agent Builder). This is likely the direction for enterprise AI – a few core agents augmented by many specialized tools integrated.

Thus, the ecosystem UX might become less about user switching agents and more about the agent switching tools. If so, focus on making that seamless: ensure the agent uses each tool in a way that still yields a consistent style answer. For example, if it calls a Writer.com agent via MCP to generate content with specific tone guidelines, ensure it still matches your brand voice (maybe the call includes your style prompt). The user sees one unified agent delivering the outcome.

Pro Tip: Think of your multiple agents as an AI "team." Like any team, they need coordination, clear roles, and good communication to the rest of the organization. Create an AI agent playbook (literally this is what we're writing!) for your company that outlines each agent's responsibilities and how they complement each other. Share this with users so they understand the ecosystem too. This manages expectations and helps users appreciate the designed structure rather than feeling it's a random bunch of bots.

Summary of Ecosystem Patterns

To recap key patterns:

- Provide a clear way for users to discover and access multiple agents (directory, naming, documentation).
- Maintain consistency in design (visual and interaction) across agents – they should feel like part of one ecosystem/brand.
- Enable agents to seamlessly route or hand off tasks to each other when appropriate, without burdening the user (the user's problem gets solved even if it crosses agent domains).
- Utilize orchestrator patterns or unified agents where possible to avoid fragmentation of experience.
- Leverage interoperability standards (MCP) to enrich agent capabilities rather than adding user-facing agents. Keep complexity behind the scenes.
- Govern centrally to ensure all agents align with company standards and to monitor the overall user experience across the AI ecosystem.

As the number of agents grows, so does the importance of metrics and feedback (which we covered). You might have to track performance per agent and also collectively (are they together achieving the desired outcomes). There's also a human change management element – introducing multiple AI assistants might require cultural adoption efforts in your org. But with thoughtful UX design, you can make interacting with a fleet of AI helpers as natural as using different apps on your phone for different tasks – integrated, yet specialized where needed.

Having navigated through all these facets of human-AI interaction and UX design for Salesforce agents, we can now summarize the key takeaways of this chapter and how they prepare us for what comes next.

SUMMARY

Human-AI interaction and UX design are pivotal to the success of AI agents in Salesforce. In this chapter, we explored how thoughtful design can drive adoption, build user trust, and make AI agents truly useful partners in work. We began with the big picture: why UX matters for AI agents. Users will only embrace agent technology if it's seamlessly embedded in their flow of work and if interactions feel intuitive and reliable. Salesforce's approach with Agentforce and Einstein Copilot exemplifies this by integrating AI across the platform and focusing on trusted, grounded responses. The introduction underscored that as AI becomes pervasive, designing for a great experience is not a luxury – it's a necessity to fulfill AI's promise of productivity and empowerment.

We then dove into embedding agents in Salesforce experiences. The core idea is to meet users where they already spend time: inside Salesforce apps, Slack, or customer-facing sites. We saw how Einstein Copilot surfaces as a handy sidekick in the UI that can be toggled on demand, and how Slack integration turns agents into collaborative teammates. By using Salesforce's UI frameworks (Lightning Web Components, Experience Cloud chat) and tools (Flow, Apex actions, Slack SDK), we can weave AI capabilities directly into user workflows. The key is a frictionless experience – whether an agent is suggesting field updates in a record page or answering questions in a Slack channel, it should feel like a natural extension of the platform. Pro Tip: Integrate AI at points of user need. For example, embed a service agent into the support site so customers get instant help in context, or add Copilot to record pages so salespeople can query data without navigation. Well-embedded agents boost usage by eliminating context switches.

Next, we covered human-centered interaction patterns, essentially the dos and don'ts of designing the conversation and decision flow between humans and AI. We emphasized keeping users in control – through confirmations, the ability to correct AI, and transparent explanations (like providing sources for answers). Patterns such as guiding the user with suggestions, handling errors gracefully with fallbacks or human hand-off, and allowing natural dialog (clarifying when needed, remembering context) all contribute to an experience where the user feels the AI is a cooperative assistant, not a frustrating black box. By applying guidelines (e.g., Microsoft's Human-AI interaction principles and Salesforce's own Responsible AI tenets), we ensure the AI augments the human rather than causing annoyance or confusion. In short, effective agent UX should be intuitive (users can naturally express needs), forgiving (the agent helps resolve misunderstandings), and reliable (the agent communicates what it's doing and respects user decisions).

We then zoomed into tone, voice, and personality – giving the agent a consistent character that aligns with the company's brand and the users' expectations. We learned that we can configure an agent's persona via prompt instructions, and that the agent's style (formal, casual, enthusiastic, etc.) should be deliberately crafted. The tone must be appropriate for the context: maybe friendly and conversational for an internal helper, but more formal and reassuring for a customer-facing support agent. Crucially, consistency in voice builds familiarity and trust; an agent that one day sounds like a legal contract and the next like a buddy in chat could unsettle users. We discussed using examples and guidelines to teach the AI the desired style, and ensuring not to overstep into over-humanization – always maintaining that slight professional distance so users know it's an AI (with empathy, but not pretend emotions). The result of a well-designed persona is an AI agent that "sounds like us" – reflecting the organization's values and speaking the user's language, whether that means technical jargon for developers or simple language for end-customers. In practice: define your AI's voice and document it, just as you would for brand messaging, and implement it consistently across prompts.

Shifting to multi-channel experience design, we tackled the challenge of delivering a cohesive experience across Slack, Salesforce desktop, mobile, and beyond. The mantra here is consistency with context-appropriate adaptation. Users should recognize they're dealing with the same assistant, regardless of channel (through consistent naming, behavior, and core personality), but the agent should also leverage each channel's strengths. For example, in Slack it might utilize interactive buttons and thread conversations, whereas in the Salesforce UI it can present richer output with formatted text or even visuals. We highlighted the importance of maintaining continuity – ideally, a conversation's context can carry from one channel to another to avoid siloed experiences. Realistically, achieving perfect cross-channel memory is complex, but tools like Salesforce's unified data and upcoming standards like MCP help bridge those gaps. Design-wise, we ensure, at minimum, that each channel experience is optimized (mobile-friendly UIs, accessible web chat, etc.) and that if a user transitions channels (say from a chat to a phone call), the agent facilitates that handoff by logging context or summarizing progress. The multi-channel section underscored that our AI agent should be ubiquitous yet consistent – meeting users on email, voice, Slack, or CRM with equal competence and a unified purpose of helping them achieve their tasks.

No UX discussion is complete without accessibility, inclusion, and trust. We dedicated a section to ensuring everyone can use the agents and feel safe doing so. Accessibility means designing the agent interface to support screen readers, keyboard navigation, high contrast, and other needs – essentially following WCAG standards and Salesforce's own accessible component practices (e.g., using SLDS base components that are accessible out-of-the-box). Inclusion extends to avoiding bias in agent responses (thanks to guardrails like the Einstein Trust Layer limiting use of sensitive attributes) and making the agent culturally competent and respectful to all users. We saw that trust is built by transparency: the agent should disclose its AI-generated content, provide verifiable sources, and operate within clearly defined ethical bounds (accuracy, honesty, safety, empowerment, sustainability – Salesforce's five AI guidelines). Visual trust cues might include differentiating the agent's messages (so it's never mistaken for a human) and using branding or lock icons to signal it's official and secure. Ultimately, an accessible, inclusive design coupled with overt trust signals (like clear disclosures and user control options) ensures users, regardless of ability or background, can confidently engage with the agent. This fosters the adoption and positive sentiment critical to the agent's success.

We then turned to UX metrics and feedback loops, recognizing that deploying an agent is just the start. To continuously improve, we need to monitor usage and outcomes. We discussed tracking adoption rates, engagement frequency, resolution success rates, satisfaction scores, and more – many of which Salesforce provides via Agentforce analytics dashboards. By analyzing these metrics, we can spot friction points (e.g., low usage of a feature might imply discoverability issues) and quantitatively measure the agent's impact (e.g., reduction in case handling time or increase in first-contact resolution). Coupled with metrics, we set up feedback channels: explicit feedback like user ratings or comments on answers, and implicit feedback like observing rephrasing or escalation patterns. Salesforce's platform includes feedback capture mechanisms (for instance, Prompt Feedback in Beta), which we should leverage. Then comes the iteration: using data to refine prompt instructions, add new training data, adjust the UI, or even roll out additional training to users if needed. A key point made was the need for a human in the loop on improvement – a business owner for the agent who regularly reviews metrics and feedback and drives enhancements. This ensures the agent stays aligned with user needs and continues to deliver increasing value over time. In summary, a metrics-driven, user-informed approach allows the UX of the agent to evolve from good to great, and keeps stakeholders bought in by demonstrating ROI and responsiveness to user input.

Finally, we explored UX patterns in the agent ecosystem, zooming out to organizations that deploy multiple AI agents or integrate external AI services. As Agentforce enables a constellation of specialized agents (sales, service, marketing, etc.), we provided patterns to avoid user confusion and maintain coherence. This includes having a centralized directory or consistent invocation methods so users can easily find the right agent, ensuring all agents share a familial resemblance in interaction style (common guidelines for confirmations, error messages, tone formality levels), and designing hand-offs between agents such that the user's journey isn't disrupted (e.g., one agent can summon another expert agent as needed behind the scenes, as supported by upcoming Agent-to-Agent interoperability). We touched on advanced interoperability like the Model Context Protocol, which will allow Salesforce agents to plug into external data and even collaborate with agents from other ecosystems in a trusted way. From a UX perspective, this means more capability without more complexity for the user – ideally, users ask one agent and it figures out which tool or partner agent to leverage. We underscored governance: as more agents come online, a governance team should enforce consistency and compliance across them, preventing a disjointed "wild west" of bots. The agent ecosystem section essentially highlighted that scaling AI assistance in an organization should be done in a user-centric manner – providing breadth of help while preserving unity in design. When done right, a user can seamlessly interact with an entire team of AI specialists as easily as they would with one, because the experience feels unified (much like interacting with different departments of one well-coordinated company).

In conclusion, designing and deploying AI agents with Salesforce is as much about human experience as it is about technology. By embedding agents into the fabric of work, crafting interactions that honor human needs for clarity and control, giving the agents engaging yet appropriate personalities, and ensuring inclusivity and trust, we create solutions that people genuinely welcome. Measured improvement closes the loop, turning initial user curiosity into long-term reliance and appreciation. The patterns and practices discussed in this chapter equip mid-to-advanced Salesforce professionals – developers, architects, product owners – to not only build powerful agents, but to drive their adoption and effectiveness through superior UX.

As we move forward in this playbook, equipped with UX design strategies, we implicitly set the stage for the next chapter, which will likely venture into the deployment, management, or future outlook of AI agents. Having designed our agents for success with users, the next step is to consider how to operationalize them at scale and govern them within the enterprise's AI strategy. The principles of human-centric design we've covered will continue to underpin those advanced topics, ensuring that no matter how sophisticated our AI agents become, we remain anchored to delivering value to and earning trust from the people who use them every day.

15

AGENT GOVERNANCE AND OPERATIONAL RISK MANAGEMENT

AI agents built on Salesforce Agentforce promise unprecedented efficiency and autonomy – but without proper governance, they can just as easily introduce risk. Imagine a well-intentioned HR onboarding bot like "JoinForce" accidentally leaking personal data or making biased decisions. Such scenarios underscore why strong governance is non-negotiable in any AI agent ecosystem. A governance plan provides the guardrails and roadmap for safe AI adoption, defining policies, procedures, roles, and tools to keep agents on track. In fact, nearly half of IT leaders worry their data isn't ready for AI, and 55% lack confidence in implementing AI with appropriate guardrails. Their concerns center on ensuring compliance, protecting privacy, and maintaining trust – all fundamental to successful AI deployments.

Governing AI agents means more than preventing isolated errors; it's about shaping agent behavior to align with business values, regulatory requirements, and user expectations. Salesforce embeds trust into its platform via features like the Einstein Trust Layer (for data masking, retention control, toxicity filters) and Agentforce Guardrails – but human oversight and clear processes must complement these tools. This chapter dives into how hands-on Salesforce teams can implement a holistic governance framework around their AI agents. We'll begin by assembling the right governance team (from Agent Owners to Ethics Leads) and defining their responsibilities. Next, we'll craft a structured agent documentation template and link it to compliance obligations like GDPR and HIPAA. We'll then explore methods to score and monitor operational risk using Salesforce metadata and Command Center dashboards. From there, we'll outline a maturity-based lifecycle (from Draft to Retired) with governance "gates" at each stage to ensure no agent goes rogue during its development journey. We'll also tackle strategies for controlling cross-agent interactions – enforcing invocation rules, throttling runaway processes, and managing context propagation so agents collaborate safely. Finally, we'll expand governance across platforms via the emerging Model Context Protocol (MCP), enabling integration with external frameworks (Microsoft's Copilot, LangChain, etc.) without compromising on compliance or security.

Throughout, we'll favor Salesforce-native tooling – Agent Builder, Command Center, Flow, Apex, and metadata-driven policies – to implement these controls in a practical way. You'll see how fictional agents like JoinForce (HR onboarding) or LedgerGuard (finance approvals) can be kept in check through proactive design and oversight. By chapter's end, you'll have a clear, pragmatic understanding of how to balance agility and autonomy with the responsible AI practices that enterprise stakeholders demand. In the next chapter, we'll put these principles into action for a first-time agent deployment, but first, let's establish the governance roles that make it all possible.

ESTABLISHING GOVERNANCE ROLES AND RESPONSIBILITIES

Effective AI governance starts with people. Just as a successful Salesforce project has defined owners and architects, an AI agent initiative needs a clear cast of roles to guide it. Each role brings a unique perspective – from technical design to ethical oversight – ensuring that the agent is not only powerful, but also safe, compliant, and aligned with business goals. Here are the core governance roles for Agentforce and what they do:

Agent Owner

- **Key responsibilities:** Ultimately accountable for the agent's success and compliance. Defines the agent's purpose and KPIs, approves major changes, and ensures it delivers business value. Often acts as the product manager or business lead for the supported process, coordinating across teams and serving as the escalation point for decisions.

Pattern Architect

- **Key responsibilities:** Designs the agent's technical architecture and integration patterns. Determines how topics, instructions, and actions are structured in Agentforce, how the agent interfaces with Salesforce data and external systems, and how guardrails are enforced. Ensures adherence to best practices such as efficient reasoning loops, secure API usage, scalability, and evolvability.

Ethics Lead

- **Key responsibilities:** Oversees responsible AI behavior. Reviews agent design and outputs for bias, fairness, privacy compliance, and appropriateness of tone and content. Establishes policy constraints (for example, prohibiting medical advice or unencrypted personal data) and conducts periodic audits of agent interactions.

Business Sponsor

- **Key responsibilities:** Acts as the executive champion providing strategic direction and securing resources. Aligns the agent's objectives with organizational goals, tracks ROI, and often chairs the agent's governance board. Resolves conflicts, removes organizational blockers, and ensures adequate funding, staffing, and ownership are in place.

Other supporting roles may include a Salesforce Platform Owner (to manage technical environments and deployments), a Data Scientist or AI Specialist (to tune the LLM prompts and evaluate model performance), and a QA/Test Lead (to develop rigorous agent test cases). However, the four roles above form the core governance circle driving accountability. It's advisable to document each person's name and responsibilities in the agent's official record (more on documentation soon) so everyone knows "who's in charge of what."

Crucially, these roles must collaborate continuously. For example, if JoinForce (the HR onboarding agent) proposes an action that might violate a policy (like emailing sensitive info), the Ethics Lead and Pattern Architect should have a process to intercept and adjust the agent's instructions. The Agent Owner ensures such guardrails don't cripple productivity, mediating between innovation and caution. Regular governance meetings or stand-ups

– perhaps weekly during development and monthly in steady state – can facilitate this cross-role communication.

Pro Tip: Treat your AI agent governance team as a product team. Schedule design reviews, ethics check-ins, and stakeholder demos just as you would for any Salesforce feature. This keeps the agent's development transparent and inclusive, preventing a siloed build that misses key concerns. When every role engages early, you'll catch issues (like a potential GDPR conflict or a flawed reasoning approach) when they are cheapest to fix.

With a governance team in place, you're ready to define the "source of truth" for your agent: a living document that captures its design, purpose, and controls. In the next section, we'll draft a structured Agent Documentation Template and see how to bake compliance checkpoints right into the agent's blueprint.

DOCUMENTING THE AGENT AND ALIGNING WITH COMPLIANCE POLICIES

A well-documented agent is a well-governed agent. Before an AI agent like LedgerGuard ever writes its first line of Apex or executes an action, there should be a clear specification describing what the agent does, how it works, and which rules it must obey. This section presents a structured agent documentation template and shows how to use it to align agent behavior with critical compliance policies (think GDPR, CCPA, HIPAA, and beyond).

Agent Documentation Template: Every agent should have a comprehensive design record. Below is a suggested template structure that teams can adopt and tailor:

Agent Overview: Basic info – Agent Name, a one-line summary of its role (e.g. "Onboards new hires by gathering documents and answering policy questions"), and version or last updated date.

Business Rationale: The use case and intended value. What pain point does the agent address? Who are the end-users or beneficiaries? For instance, JoinForce might aim to reduce HR manual workload by 50% in onboarding.

Scope and Limitations: Clearly define what the agent will and won't do. This manages expectations and is crucial for compliance. For example, JoinForce handles general HR FAQs and form submissions but will not give legal or medical advice. LedgerGuard might process expense approvals under $5,000 but escalate anything above.

Core Team & Roles: List the governance roles (by name). E.g., "Agent Owner: Alice Morgan (HR Product Manager), Pattern Architect: Bob Chen (Salesforce Architect), Ethics Lead: Carol Gupta (Compliance Officer), Business Sponsor: Diana Lee (VP of HR)". This makes accountability explicit.

Design Components: Outline the agent's technical design in Salesforce terms. Document its Topics (the high-level tasks it can handle), Instructions/Prompts (key prompts or dialogues it uses), Actions (which Salesforce or external actions it can execute). For each, note any important parameters. For instance, LedgerGuard might have an "Approval" topic with an action that calls a Finance API – the doc should describe that integration and any guardrails on it.

Data Sources & Inputs: Catalog the data the agent can access. Which Salesforce objects, fields, or Data Cloud datasets are in play? Are there external MCP (Model Context Protocol) resources or APIs it uses? Mark any sensitive data elements here with a label (e.g. "contains PII" or "HIPAA data") so everyone is aware. Salesforce's Data Cloud governance tools allow tagging records as "GDPR", "HIPAA", etc., which should correspond to what's documented. For example, if JoinForce accesses employee contact info, mark those fields as personal data.

Compliance and Ethics Checklist: Embed a subsection explicitly for compliance requirements. List relevant regulations or policies (GDPR, HIPAA, company ethics guidelines) and how the agent addresses each. For GDPR, consider how the agent ensures data minimization (only using data truly needed for its tasks) and handles user requests like data deletion. For HIPAA, note that the agent runs in Salesforce's HIPAA-compliant environment (if applicable) and does not output protected health information in open text. Include any required consent or disclaimer messaging the agent will provide to users. This section basically translates legal requirements into agent design decisions.

Security & Access Controls: Document which Salesforce profiles or permission sets the agent runs under and what it's allowed to do. Does it use a dedicated integration user? Are its actions constrained by Apex security checks or Flow entry conditions? For instance, LedgerGuard might only operate on a restricted set of objects and cannot create new payees, etc. Note usage of platform security features: e.g., "Agent leverages Salesforce Shield encryption for field X" or "Einstein Trust Layer masks credit card numbers before sending prompt to LLM".

Operational Metrics: Define how you'll measure the agent's performance and risk (foreshadowing the next section). E.g., expected accuracy rate, average handle time, escalation rate, and any risk score (if assigned). Including this in the doc sets the stage for monitoring.

Lifecycle Status: Note the current stage of the agent (Draft, In Development, Pilot, Live, etc. – as defined in your lifecycle model). Also include upcoming governance gates: e.g., "Next review: Ethics Lead to sign off on bias testing before moving to Pilot stage."

By filling out this template, the team creates a single reference that not only guides development but also serves as evidence of due diligence. During audits or stakeholder reviews, you can pull out this document to show what safeguards were planned.

Aligning with compliance policies is not a one-time task done at go-live – it must be baked into the agent from day one. Salesforce provides powerful native capabilities to help align agents with regulations:

Salesforce Trust Layer: This is an out-of-the-box safety net that intercepts all prompts and actions between your agent and the LLM (Large Language Model). It automatically enforces certain compliance measures. For example, it can mask sensitive data (like names, emails, social security numbers) before that data ever leaves Salesforce for AI processing. It also ensures zero retention of sensitive data by the LLM provider and flags toxic or biased outputs for review. In practice, when JoinForce asks an LLM to draft a welcome email, the Trust Layer might strip out a person's SSN if it somehow ended up in the prompt – thus preventing an accidental privacy breach. As a governance team, you should configure these trust settings to match your policies (e.g., define which fields to mask).

Data Classification and Policy Management: Using Salesforce's metadata-driven governance in Data Cloud, you can tag data as sensitive and author policies that apply automatically. For instance, if you tag a field "EU_PersonData=Yes" (GDPR relevant), you could enforce via policy that no agent action can export that field's value outside the EU region or to any non-compliant service. These policies execute behind the scenes, but it's important to note in your documentation that such controls exist. It assures stakeholders that, say, any HIPAA data JoinForce handles is labeled and restricted consistently across the platform.

Consent and Logging: If regulations require user consent or logging of AI decisions, integrate that into the agent's flow. For example, GDPR might require informing users that an AI is involved in decision-making. LedgerGuard could be configured to note "Decision recommended by AI" in an approval record. Meanwhile, keeping logs of agent decisions (which Salesforce's Command Center will help with) ensures you can respond to compliance inquiries (like "why did the AI reject this request?").

Testing for Compliance: Before going live, the Ethics Lead and Pattern Architect should test the agent against negative scenarios: Does JoinForce accidentally reveal any private data when prompted in weird ways? Does LedgerGuard show bias in how it treats large expenses vs. small ones? This should be part of the QA plan, and the results (with any fixes) documented.

Reviewer Checklist – Compliance Alignment: As a final step in documentation, include a short checklist that the Ethics Lead or an auditor can use to verify compliance alignment:

- Have all data fields accessed by the agent been classified (e.g. PII, confidential) and handled according to policy?
- Is there a mechanism (automated or manual) for a user to correct or delete data the agent produced, if needed (data subject rights)?
- Does the agent avoid storing transcripts or outputs longer than necessary (data minimization)?
- Were bias testing and accessibility reviews completed? (E.g., does the agent work for users with disabilities and produce acceptable output for them?)
- For regulated industries, do we have documentation of compliance approval (e.g. a security officer signed off on the agent)?

Completing this documentation template might seem tedious, but it pays dividends. It forces clarity among the team and serves as insurance when questions inevitably arise about why the agent did X or whether it considered Y regulation. The document should be kept up to date as the agent evolves (especially the Compliance and Metrics sections). Storing it in a Salesforce knowledge repository or as an attachment to an "Agent" metadata entity is a good practice, ensuring it's versioned and accessible.

With the agent thoroughly documented and compliance considerations woven into its design, the groundwork is laid for responsible operation. Next, we shift from planning to active oversight: how to manage operational risks once the agent is running, using Salesforce metadata to score risk and Command Center dashboards to keep a watchful eye on agent performance.

OPERATIONAL RISK MANAGEMENT AND SCORING

Even a well-designed agent can encounter issues in the wild – perhaps a spike in errors when encountering edge cases, or user behavior that triggers unexpected outcomes. Operational risk management is about continuously tracking and mitigating these real-world hiccups. In this section, we discuss how to assign a risk score to AI agents using Salesforce metadata and how to monitor agents in real time through the Agentforce Command Center and other dashboards.

Defining Risk Factors: Start by identifying what "risky" behavior or conditions mean for your agent. Common risk factors for AI agents include: the sensitivity of data they handle, the financial or reputational impact of their actions, their level of autonomy (fully automated vs. requiring human approval), and their past performance record (error rates, incident counts). For example, LedgerGuard – which approves financial transactions – inherently carries higher risk than JoinForce answering common questions, because a mistake in LedgerGuard could result in financial loss. We can classify LedgerGuard as a High Impact agent. Meanwhile, an internal Q&A bot with no critical actions might be Low Impact.

Salesforce metadata can be used to encode these classifications. One approach is creating a custom Metadata Type or custom fields on the Agent definition (if Agentforce provides metadata for agents) to store attributes like "Data Sensitivity: High/Med/Low", "Criticality: High/Med/Low", "Requires Human Oversight: Yes/No". The combination of these attributes can roll up to an Agent Risk Score. For instance, you might assign numerical values (High = 3, Medium = 2, Low = 1) and calculate a weighted sum. An agent handling High sensitivity data (3) and high critical actions (3) that is fully autonomous (High autonomy = 3) might score a 9 out of 9 – a top risk agent. In contrast, a read-only knowledge agent might score a 3. Storing this score in metadata means it's visible and reportable across the Salesforce org.

This kind of risk scoring echoes classic risk assessment: consider severity (impact of something going wrong) and likelihood (chance it goes wrong). The "severity" maps to data sensitivity and business impact; "likelihood" might map to the agent's complexity or known error rate. If JoinForce failing to answer a question correctly is minor (low severity) and occasional (medium likelihood), its risk profile is mild. But if LedgerGuard misrouting an approval could violate compliance (high severity) and its operating in a complex environment it hasn't been fully trained on (higher likelihood of confusion), we have a serious risk to manage.

Operational Risk Dashboard: Once you've defined these risk attributes, you can create a dashboard (perhaps in Salesforce Analytics or even a simple report) listing all agents with their risk scores and statuses. This acts as a heat map for stakeholders – for example, highlighting that LedgerGuard is high risk and needs more frequent monitoring or stricter controls, whereas JoinForce is low risk and can be allowed more leeway.

However, risk scoring isn't a one-and-done exercise at design time. It must be informed by live performance data. This is where the Agentforce Command Center shines. Command Center, built into Agentforce Studio, provides deep observability into agent operations. It's essentially a central cockpit to manage and monitor all your AI agents in one place. Let's look at how Command Center and related tools help mitigate operational risk. At a glance, you can see each deployed agent, who owns it, its function, and key metrics like number of sessions, average latency (response time), and a "quality" score for its responses. Command Center essentially surfaces the KPIs we defined in the documentation: performance, usage, and any red flags. In practice, a governance team should define thresholds for these KPIs that would trigger investigation. For example, if an agent's error rate exceeds 5% in a day or if latency doubles unexpectedly, that might indicate the agent is struggling or something in the environment changed.

Salesforce has equipped Command Center with alerting capabilities. It can flag issues like high error or escalation rates in real time. An "escalation" in this context might mean the agent had to hand off to a human or could not complete a request – a possible sign of either a gap in capability or a policy block it hit. By monitoring escalations, you not only see where user frustration might build, but also where your governance guardrails might be repeatedly preventing the agent from doing something (which could indicate a need to adjust either the agent or the policy).

Quality monitoring is another facet. In the screenshot, there's a "Quality" column – how is that determined? Often it's through user feedback or an internal scoring of how well the agent followed instructions. For instance, Agentforce might use Instruction Adherence Checks to monitor if the agent strayed from its allowed actions. If LedgerGuard ever tries to perform an action outside its defined toolset, that would lower its quality score and raise an alert. As a governance mechanism, you should configure these adherence checks – basically, define what "bad behavior" looks like for your agent so the system can catch it. An example rule might be: "If agent response contains any unapproved external link, flag it" or "If agent calls an API more than 3 times in one session, flag a potential loop."

Beyond Command Center's built-in analytics, consider leveraging Salesforce Event Monitoring and logs for a finer grain view. Every agent session and action can produce log entries (potentially stored in Data Cloud or via OpenTelemetry streams). Your DevOps or security team could feed these into a SIEM (Security Information and Event Management) system to correlate with other events (for instance, to detect if an agent action coincided with a system error or a spike in user traffic). This is advanced, but for high-risk agents, it might be warranted. Salesforce's mention of OpenTelemetry suggests you can trace an agent's steps similar to tracing microservice calls – extremely useful for debugging complex issues.

How do we tie the metadata risk score with the live metrics? One way is to overlay them on a dashboard. Imagine a "Risk Matrix" chart: X-axis could be the agent's inherent risk score (from metadata), Y-axis could be current error rate or number of incidents. This would highlight, for example, an inherently high-risk agent that's currently performing poorly (danger zone), versus a high-risk agent performing well (needs watching but OK for now), versus a low-risk agent with high errors (perhaps the errors are less critical, but still an issue to address for user experience). This kind of visualization helps prioritize governance attention.

Consider also automated risk mitigation workflows. If an agent hits a critical threshold (say, it's making too many mistakes or there's a suspected security issue), you might want to automatically pause or disable it – essentially a kill switch for safety. You can implement this with Salesforce tools: for example, a Flow or Apex trigger subscribed to Command Center alerts or a custom platform event. If an alert comes in labeled "SEVERE", your Flow could flip a field on the agent's config to "Disabled" (assuming Agentforce supports that) or notify an admin to intervene. This is analogous to a circuit breaker pattern in software. LedgerGuard, for instance, might be set to disable itself if more than 3 high-value transactions are rejected erroneously in a short span, pending review.

Now, let's talk about using Command Center dashboards in practice. A best practice is to set up different views for different stakeholders:

The Agent Owner might have a dashboard focused on business outcomes (e.g. number of tasks completed by the agent, time saved, user satisfaction ratings).

The Pattern Architect and dev team get a technical dashboard (like the one above) showing performance stats, errors, and usage trends.

The Ethics Lead might have a specialized dashboard or report showing any content flags (toxic output flagged by the trust layer), any privacy incidents (like if the agent attempted to access a disallowed field), and perhaps transcripts of a random sample of sessions for spot-checking appropriateness.

Fortunately, Command Center allows drilling into session transcripts and tracing. This means for a given interaction, you can see step by step what the agent considered and did. As an Ethics or Compliance reviewer, this is gold – you can audit the agent's reasoning and ensure it wasn't making decisions based on forbidden criteria. It's akin to being able to peer into a human's thought process after the fact (something we rarely get!). Use this feature for periodic audits: for example, review 10 random sessions of JoinForce per month to ensure its responding accurately and respectfully to employees, or review all LedgerGuard sessions that were escalated to see if it made the right call.

Continuous Improvement: Risk management isn't just defensive; it feeds into improving the agent. Patterns uncovered in Command Center can guide training and tuning. If users keep asking JoinForce questions it can't answer, maybe it needs an expanded knowledge base (and you update its documentation and capabilities). If LedgerGuard frequently escalates a certain type of expense, perhaps policy could be adjusted or the agent's instructions refined to handle it. The governance team should set a cadence (e.g. quarterly) to formally reassess each agent's risk status and performance. Update the risk score if needed and archive the past metrics for historical analysis.

To conclude this section, Salesforce's deep observability tools let you trust, but verify your AI agents. By combining a proactive risk scoring framework with real-time monitoring, you gain confidence to deploy agents at scale. You know which ones need a tight leash and which can be given more autonomy, and you can catch small fires before they become infernos. With operational risks under watch, we can turn to governing the agent's journey over time – the lifecycle from inception to retirement, and the checkpoints that ensure an agent is ready for each next step.

Next, we'll examine the maturity lifecycle of an AI agent and how to enforce governance gates at each stage, ensuring our agents graduate from idea to production (and beyond) with flying colors.

LIFECYCLE GOVERNANCE: FROM DRAFT TO RETIRED (GATES AT EACH STAGE)

AI agents aren't a "set and forget" technology – they evolve through a lifecycle, much like any Salesforce implementation or software product. However, the agent lifecycle brings unique considerations: an agent's behavior can shift as models are updated or as it learns from new data, and governance must be applied continuously, not just at launch. In this section, we outline a maturity-based lifecycle model for agents, from initial Draft to eventual Retirement, and describe the governance gates at each stage that ensure quality and compliance before an agent progresses.

Let's define typical lifecycle stages for a Salesforce AI agent:

Draft (Ideation) – The agent concept is being formulated. At this stage, it exists as a proposal or design document (perhaps leveraging the documentation template from Section 2). It's not yet built; the focus is on brainstorming capabilities, assessing feasibility, and initial risk brainstorming. Governance gate: Idea Approval. The Business Sponsor and relevant stakeholders (e.g. the Ethics Lead) should sign off that the use case is worthwhile and appropriate. Key questions: Does this use case align with our AI usage policies? Is there a clearly identified Agent Owner and team? If the idea doesn't pass ethical or strategic muster, it shouldn't proceed to build. For example, a proposal for an agent to replace a sensitive human judgment (like firing decisions) might be stopped right here for ethical reasons.

Design & Prototype – The Pattern Architect and team design the agent's structure and possibly develop a small proof-of-concept (for example, a prototype in a sandbox using a subset of Topics/Actions). Here, the agent documentation is completed in detail. Governance gate: Design Review. This is a formal check where the Pattern Architect walks through the proposed agent logic, data usage, and compliance checklist with the broader governance team. The Ethics Lead evaluates the design against policies (e.g., are we collecting only necessary personal data? Have we built in necessary prompts for user consent?). The Agent Owner ensures the design still meets business goals. Often this stage includes a threat modeling or risk assessment workshop where worst-case scenarios are imagined and mitigations planned. Only after addressing any red flags (say, adding a filter to prevent a known risk) does the project move on. Salesforce's secure development practices should be enforced now: for instance, if the agent will use Apex actions, ensure code goes through a security review (no SOQL injection holes, etc.).

Build (Development) – The agent is actively being built in Agentforce. This could be a combination of low-code configurations (Agent Builder for topics/instructions) and pro-code (Apex, external MCP connectors). During build, developers and admins will be iterating and testing features. Governance in this stage is about guidance and incremental checks. Proactive steps include:

The Ethics Lead might provide ethical design input: e.g., crafting certain prompt wording to avoid bias, or specifying that the agent must explain its actions to users for transparency.

QA should include tests for "does the agent violate any rules when stressed?" akin to negative testing.

Gate: Pre-Test Check. Before moving to formal testing, ensure development is complete and key governance elements are in place. For example, verify that the Trust Layer is configured (masking turned on for PII fields), that any external integrations have security tokens stored in a secure manner, and that the agent's actions respect user permissions (perhaps test with a low-privilege user to see if it tries to do something it shouldn't). This check might be performed by the Salesforce Platform Owner or Security team in conjunction with the dev team. Essentially, it's like a code review but for compliance and security aspects. Salesforce's metadata can help here – e.g., running a scan with Security Center to confirm no sensitive fields are left unprotected.

Test (Validation) – Now the agent (in a sandbox or test environment) undergoes thorough testing. This includes functional testing (does it do the job?), performance testing, and importantly governance testing (does it stay within bounds?). Salesforce provides the Agentforce Testing Center for rigorous agent testing with realistic data. At this stage, you might run simulations of many conversations to see how the agent handles them. Governance gate: Go-Live Approval (Pilot Approval). Typically, this is the big checkpoint before an agent faces real users. The governance board – Agent Owner, Pattern Architect, Ethics Lead, Business Sponsor, plus possibly Security and IT Ops – convene to review test results and a readiness checklist. That checklist would include: All critical test cases passed? No high-severity bugs outstanding? All compliance checks (bias testing, privacy testing) completed with acceptable results documented? Incident response plan in place (e.g., if something goes wrong, do we know how to roll back the agent or inform users)? And is the business sponsor satisfied with the agent's output quality (maybe they reviewed some outputs for tone and accuracy)? If yes, the agent can move to a Pilot or Limited Production.

Often, prudent governance means doing a pilot deployment – release the agent to a small set of users or for a limited set of tasks. For example, LedgerGuard might only handle a subset of approvals or a single department initially, or JoinForce might be available to the HR team but not all employees as a test. This pilot phase is essentially an extended test in real conditions. It should have a defined duration or success criteria (like "if no major issues in 2 weeks, proceed to full launch"). A governance gate could be at the end of pilot, requiring another sign-off to proceed to full production.

Deploy (Production Live) – The agent is deployed broadly, available to its target end-users, and actively working. By this point, it should have passed all previous gates. Governance during production focuses on monitoring and control, which we addressed earlier in this chapter. The key here is having the right processes to continuously govern:

- Set up a schedule for the governance team to review Command Center metrics (say, a weekly report email to stakeholders with key stats and any alerts).
- Ensure someone (often the Agent Owner or a delegated analyst) is reviewing user feedback channels. For instance, users might have a way to rate or flag agent responses ("This answer was not helpful" button). Incorporate that feedback loop.

Gate: Periodic Audit. Establish a cadence (quarterly, or more frequently for high-risk agents) where the Ethics Lead and Pattern Architect do a mini-audit of the agent. They might sample conversation logs for compliance, verify no drift in performance, and check if any new regulatory changes might affect the agent. For example, if a new data privacy law comes out, does the agent need an update in how it stores logs? These audits ensure the agent stays in compliance over time, not just on day one.

Continuous Improvement: Production isn't static. New requirements might arise, or the LLM model might get updated (Salesforce might update the Atlas AI engine or you might switch to a newer model via BYOM). Any significant change should go through a governance review again. Think of it as re-entering the lifecycle at Draft or Design for that new feature, then testing, etc. In practice, treat each major agent update as a mini-project that passes through gates as appropriate.

Optimize (Maturity) – Over time, the agent might grow in capabilities or efficiency. This stage isn't separate from production but represents a mature phase where the agent is stable and you are fine-tuning. Governance here might loosen in some areas (perhaps less frequent meetings as confidence builds) but it also needs to ensure that complacency doesn't set in. Some organizations form an AI Governance Council that meets periodically to review all AI agents in this mature phase collectively, sharing lessons learned and updating standards. If you have multiple agents, this is valuable – e.g., ensure JoinForce and LedgerGuard are both following the latest corporate AI policy, and if one team found a great way to log data for audit, others adopt it.

Retire (Decommission) – Eventually, an agent may become obsolete (perhaps business processes changed or a new version is built from scratch). Retirement must be handled cleanly to avoid compliance issues. Governance gate: Retirement Review. Before turning an agent off, confirm several things: All data or knowledge base the agent generated is archived if needed (especially if any decisions need to be retained for regulatory reasons). Remove the agent's access to systems – for instance, revoke any API keys or credentials it used, to prevent any ghost usage. Update documentation to mark it retired (and maybe link to a successor if one exists). Notify users who were using it (transparency even in decommissioning is good practice: e.g., "The LedgerGuard agent will be sunset on X date and replaced by Y process"). Also, evaluate the agent's life: do a post-mortem to capture lessons. Did the governance process catch everything or were there surprises? Feed that back into improving how you govern future agents.

This lifecycle model introduces gates – decision points where the agent must meet certain criteria to proceed. These gates are essentially quality control checkpoints for governance:

- Early gates focus on doing the right thing (valid use case, ethical design).
- Later gates focus on doing it right (proper implementation, tested thoroughly).
- Ongoing gates ensure staying right (monitoring and adjustments in production).
- Final gate ensures retiring right (no loose ends).
- In Salesforce development terms, you might integrate these gates with existing processes:

- Leverage Salesforce DevOps Center or change sets for promotion between environments, and tie promotion to gate approvals. For example, require a Change Advisory Board (CAB)-style approval (with the Ethics Lead and Sponsor included) before deploying from UAT to Production – that approval serves as the go-live governance gate.
- Use checklists in Agile user stories: e.g., a story like "As an admin, I want to deploy JoinForce to all employees" should have acceptance criteria that "Compliance officer approved privacy controls" and "Performance met SLAs in pilot" etc.
- Maintain a simple RACI matrix for stages vs. roles. For instance, at "Design Review" stage: Pattern Architect = Responsible, Ethics Lead = Accountable (for policy compliance), Business Sponsor = Consulted, etc. At "Pilot Complete Review": Agent Owner = Responsible for gathering results, Business Sponsor = Accountable for decision to fully launch, etc. This ensures everyone knows their part at each gate.

Pro Tip: Don't rush the gates. It's tempting, under business pressure, to push an agent from test to prod quickly ("the demo at Dreamforce is next week!"). Resist skipping governance steps. A rushed AI deployment can lead to very public failures or compliance violations that are far costlier than a delayed launch. Use the gates to your advantage – they are your evidence to executives that due diligence is done. If pressed, you can say, "We cannot launch because it hasn't passed the ethical review gate yet – doing so would violate our AI policy." In most cases, higher-ups will understand the importance or at least take accountability if they insist on moving ahead (in which case, get that in writing!).

By managing the lifecycle with these structured stages and gates, you de-risk the path from an agent's conception to its daily operation. The maturity model also dovetails with change management – users get a better product when it's phased and reviewed, and you can gradually build trust in AI by expanding agents' scope in a controlled way.

Having covered internal lifecycle governance, we now turn to a new dimension: how do we govern when multiple agents start interacting with each other? Next, we'll explore cross-agent invocation, throttling, and propagation policies – essentially, the rules of engagement when agents team up or communicate, so that our growing "digital workforce" doesn't run amok.

GOVERNING CROSS-AGENT INTERACTIONS: INVOCATION, THROTTLING, AND CONTEXT PROPAGATION

As organizations adopt more AI agents, those agents will increasingly need to work together. For instance, your customer support agent might need to invoke a specialized inventory agent to get stock data, or our hypothetical JoinForce HR agent might call a separate "PayrollBot" agent to set up a new employee's payroll. Agent-to-agent collaboration can unlock powerful workflows, but it also introduces complexity and risk. Who oversees their conversation? Could two agents call each other in a loop? How do we ensure an agent doesn't exceed its authority when delegating a task? This section lays out policies for cross-agent invocation, throttling, and propagation of context, ensuring multi-agent systems remain safe and controllable.

Cross-Agent Invocation Policies: This defines when and how one agent is allowed to trigger another. In Salesforce's Agentforce ecosystem, agents can be invoked via platform mechanisms – for example, an Apex call or Flow can start an agent, so one agent could indirectly start another if allowed, by calling an invocable action. There's also the concept of Agent-2-Agent (A2A) communication being supported through things like MuleSoft's Flex Gateway, which can broker secure interactions between agents. Governance needs to decide:

Allowed Interactions: Make an explicit registry of which agents are permitted to talk to or trigger which other agents. This could be a simple matrix or list in your documentation: e.g., JoinForce is permitted to call PayrollBot for payroll setup, but JoinForce should never call LedgerGuard (because HR onboarding doesn't need financial approvals, and such a call could indicate misuse). By whitelisting valid pairings, you prevent an agent from straying into another's domain. Salesforce could facilitate this by metadata as well – perhaps tagging each agent with a scope or by using the upcoming MCP registry (discussed in next section) to control allowed connections.

Invocation Method: Determine how the hand-off happens. Ideally, use Salesforce Flow Orchestrator or subflow as an intermediary. For example, when JoinForce needs payroll info, it triggers a Flow that invokes PayrollBot and then returns results to JoinForce. This approach means the Flow can include checks or transformations (governance points) around that invocation. The Flow could check: is the request within certain bounds? Do we have user consent to fetch this info? If all clear, proceed; otherwise, maybe log an alert or require an approval. Essentially, Flows or Apex wrappers act like gatekeepers when bridging agents.

Auditing Cross-Calls: Ensure that any cross-agent call is logged with context – which agent requested what from whom, and when. This creates a trace in case something goes wrong ("Why did PayrollBot change an employee status? Oh, it was asked by JoinForce on 5/5 at 3PM, approved by HR policy X."). Command Center and OpenTelemetry traces should capture cross-agent workflows, but you might add custom logging in your Flow/Apex as well for clarity.

Throttling Policies: AI agents can potentially operate at machine speed, which is great for productivity but could overwhelm systems or run up usage costs if not checked. Throttling policies put limits on frequency and concurrency of agent actions, especially in multi-agent scenarios. Key aspects:

Rate Limits: Define how often an agent (or a group of agents collectively) can perform certain actions or invocations. For example, LedgerGuard might be limited to initiating at most 5 approval workflows per minute, to avoid spamming the approvers or the underlying ERP system. Similarly, if JoinForce is calling PayrollBot, you might restrict it to, say, one call per new hire to avoid looping. Salesforce's platform natively has limits (Apex governor limits, API call limits), but you can add functional limits at the design level. One way is to use a Platform Event or custom object as a counter. Each time JoinForce calls PayrollBot, record an event "J->P call". A Flow subscribed to that event can count events in the last hour and if above threshold, delay or block further calls.

Concurrent Sessions: You might also want to limit how many instances of an agent run in parallel. If dozens of different processes all call LedgerGuard at once, and it in turn calls others, you could end up with resource contention or unpredictable outcomes. If the agent uses external APIs, those APIs might have their own rate limits which you need to respect via throttling. Command Center can show active sessions; a governance policy could be "if more than X sessions at a time, queue new requests". Implementing a queue in Salesforce could involve an Apex scheduler or leveraging Salesforce Queueable jobs to process agent calls gradually. It's a bit advanced, but doable: for example, instead of calling LedgerGuard immediately, your Flow could post a job to a queue; a queueable Apex job picks it up if under limit, otherwise waits.

Emergency Stop: In throttling design, include a circuit-breaker for runaway situations. Suppose due to a bug, JoinForce keeps calling PayrollBot in a loop ("create payroll -> payroll says already exists -> JoinForce misinterprets and calls again"). Some anomaly detection can help: if the same invocation repeats too often, automatically disable that link. This could be as simple as "if more than 3 calls between Agent A and B occur within a minute for the same record/user, then block further calls and alert." Salesforce could implement that logic via a custom Apex trigger on a log object or using the upcoming MCP registry policies (MCP tools might allow setting a max calls per minute).

Cost Management: Remember that many AI services (LLM usage, etc.) cost per use. Throttling ensures you don't get bill shock. If one agent calling another triggers heavy computation, a policy might limit those calls after hours or require certain conditions to be met (like the user has a premium license). These business rules tie into throttling as well.

Context Propagation Policies: When agents call each other, they need to pass some context – e.g., the user's identity, the task at hand – so the receiving agent can do its job properly. But we must be careful: propagate only the necessary context, and ensure privilege does not accidentally escalate. Some guidelines:

Identity and Permissions: If JoinForce (running with HR permissions) calls PayrollBot, does PayrollBot run with JoinForce's permissions, the original user's permissions, or its own service account? This is crucial. The safest approach is usually that each agent has its own fixed permission set and they simply share a reference ID and perhaps the requesting user's ID for logging. That way, PayrollBot will still enforce its own access control (it will only do what its role allows). If you propagate a full user context, you might inadvertently give an agent more access through another agent than intended. For example, JoinForce might have access to certain data that PayrollBot normally wouldn't, and if JoinForce passes that data along, PayrollBot might do something outside policy. So governance might dictate: cross-agent calls should be treated as integration calls – each agent performs only what it could if it were called directly by a user or system, nothing more. Use the principle of least privilege for every agent involved.

Data Minimization in Handoffs: Only share data needed for the specific interaction. If JoinForce is asking PayrollBot to create a payroll record, it might pass employee ID and start date – it should not pass the employee's entire HR file. This reduces risk of data leakage or misuse. In practice, design your agent prompts or API calls between agents carefully to include just what's required. Document these interfaces in your template ("JoinForce -> PayrollBot call passes: EmployeeID, Name, StartDate").

Conversation Context Limits: If agents engage in a longer back-and-forth (less common in current agent designs, but possible as multi-step multi-agent flows evolve), set a limit on context accumulation. Two agents could theoretically start chatting in a loop (each reacting to the other). Policies can enforce that after a certain number of exchanges, either a human takes over or the conversation is reset. This prevents infinite loops and also ensures the conversation doesn't drift into unintended territory. It's analogous to how human escalation works: if a support chatbot and a scheduling bot keep handing off a customer without resolution, eventually a person should intervene.

Monitoring and Debugging Cross-Agent Flows: Ensure your observability covers the end-to-end flow. Tools like MuleSoft Flex Gateway support tracing these interactions with protocols like A2A and MCP. You might implement correlation IDs (a unique ID per request that is passed through all agent calls) so you can follow a chain. This is more technical, but it helps when something goes wrong – you can see the whole story: Agent A -> Agent B -> response, etc. If, say, LedgerGuard calls RiskAnalyzerAgent for a fraud score as part of approval, you'd want to know if a delay or error in RiskAnalyzerAgent caused LedgerGuard to stall.

Example Policy in Action: Let's illustrate a scenario. JoinForce needs to set up hardware for a new hire, which is handled by an IT agent called "TechSetup". Policy says JoinForce can invoke TechSetup via a Flow. The Flow ensures:

1. The new hire's ID is passed, but no sensitive personal data (TechSetup doesn't need their salary or medical info, for example).

2. TechSetup runs under an IT service account with access only to relevant systems.

3. Throttle: JoinForce will only call TechSetup once per new hire. If JoinForce is somehow asked twice for the same person, the Flow will ignore the second request.

4. Logging: Each call is recorded with the hire's ID and both agent names. If TechSetup fails or returns an error, that's logged too.

5. If TechSetup returns "hardware not in stock – waiting", JoinForce might be designed to not keep pinging TechSetup. Instead, it will wait for a callback or an event from TechSetup when ready. This prevents a loop and reduces load. This is an example of an async pattern for cross-agent comms, which is often safer.

With such a framework, multiple agents can form a composed workflow reliably. You essentially have a digital assembly line where each agent is a station with defined inputs/outputs and timing.

One more consideration: Propagation of accountability. When one agent triggers another, who is accountable for the result? In governance terms, make it clear that the original Agent Owner still owns the end-to-end outcome. If JoinForce delegates to TechSetup and TechSetup fails, ultimately the JoinForce owner should address that (perhaps by building in an escalation to a human when TechSetup fails). This clarity avoids scenarios where an issue falls through the cracks because each agent team says "not my problem, the other agent messed up." Essentially, treat the network of agents as a team with defined responsibilities, similar to microservices.

By enforcing these cross-agent invocation and throttling policies, you prevent many potential runaway scenarios. You won't have agents spamming each other or endlessly bouncing a task around. And by controlling context propagation, you ensure that information and permissions flow only as intended. This is vital for maintaining data security and proper conduct in an agent ecosystem.

Our focus so far has been on agents within the Salesforce Agentforce environment. But many enterprises operate in a heterogeneous AI landscape – Salesforce agents might need to interface with Microsoft's Copilot agents or a LangChain-based service. How do we extend governance across platforms and ensure a consistent trust fabric? In our next section, we'll explore the Model Context Protocol (MCP) as a bridge for cross-platform agent integration, and how to integrate Salesforce governance with other AI frameworks to maintain control over this wider agent network.

CROSS-PLATFORM GOVERNANCE: USING MCP FOR A UNIFIED TRUST FRAMEWORK

Modern enterprises often deploy AI agents across multiple platforms – what if your Salesforce Agentforce agent must pull data from a Microsoft 365 Copilot plugin, or coordinate with a LangChain orchestration that lives outside Salesforce? Without a plan, you'd have siloed agents each with their own rules, leading to inconsistency and security gaps. Model Context Protocol (MCP) emerges as a solution: it's an open standard handshake that lets disparate AI systems communicate in a common language. Salesforce calls it "USB-C for AI agents" because it provides a universal plug for connecting agents to tools and data anywhere. In this section, we'll discuss how to leverage MCP to enforce governance across platforms and what it means to integrate with frameworks like Microsoft Copilot and LangChain without losing control.

First, a quick primer on MCP in practice. MCP defines a client-server architecture for AI interactions :

An MCP client lives in the AI agent platform (Agentforce, Copilot, etc.) and connects to MCP servers.

An MCP server exposes tools, resources, or prompts that an agent can use. For example, a Salesforce data API, or a third-party service like a calendar app, could be wrapped as an MCP server. The agent (through the client) can query what actions ("tools") the server offers, then invoke them securely.

Tools/Resources/Prompts are standardized units in this protocol – each tool has a name, input/output schema, and typically some metadata about permissions.

How does this help governance? Because MCP is a formal interface, Salesforce is building an MCP Server Registry and policy layer into Agentforce. Authorized admins will have a registry of all MCP servers (i.e., external connections) that their agents can access, and they can enforce enterprise policies on these connections. Think of it as an allow-list and control panel for integrations:

- Only MCP servers that have been vetted and registered can be called by agents.
- For each server, you can define security requirements (maybe a certain auth method, or limiting which agents can use it) and rate limits (ensuring an agent doesn't overload an external system).
- The registry enforces identity – ensuring the agent authenticates properly to the external tool, and perhaps vice versa (the tool only accepts calls from your org's agents).

For example, let's say JoinForce needs to integrate with Microsoft's Azure OpenAI service via LangChain (maybe to use a specialized model). Using

MCP, JoinForce can call an MCP server that wraps the Azure OpenAI API. In the registry, you've specified: this server requires OAuth with specific credentials, and only JoinForce (Agent ID 123) is allowed to use it, at a max of 100 calls per hour. If JoinForce tries to exceed that or if another agent tries to use that server unapproved, Agentforce will block it – thereby upholding the governance policy automatically.

Now consider Microsoft 365 Copilot integration. Microsoft's Copilot also supports extending capabilities via something analogous to MCP (they sometimes call them plugins or "Teams messages extensions" etc., but conceptually similar). Through MCP, Agentforce agents and Copilot agents can talk. The Zenity security article noted: "Microsoft Copilot Studio or Agentforce integrates with cloud-hosted MCPs to access enterprise systems". So an enterprise could have a workflow where Salesforce's Agentforce agent triggers an action in Microsoft's world, or vice versa, using MCP as the bridge.

Governance across this boundary means:

Shared Context, Segregated Control: Ensure that when crossing platforms, the Salesforce trust and governance model is still applied on the Salesforce side, and Microsoft's on theirs. If a Microsoft Copilot agent calls into Salesforce (e.g., via an MCP server exposing Salesforce data), the Salesforce side should treat it like any external integration – enforce field-level security, audit the access, and apply the Einstein Trust Layer if the data goes into an AI model. You would configure the MCP connection such that Copilot only sees the data it's allowed to (for example, maybe it can fetch a customer's billing info but not their password or something).

End-to-End Identity: Use federated identity so that when Copilot requests something from Salesforce through MCP, it carries a user or application identity that Salesforce can log and verify. Salesforce's MCP client will support authentication methods like OAuth or mTLS for servers. That means if a Copilot agent (on behalf of user John Doe) tries to do something, it could authenticate as John (or a delegated service identity with John's permissions). Governance wise, you'd ensure a Business-to-business (B2B) trust is set: perhaps an Azure AD app registration corresponds to your Salesforce org's MCP trust. Setting this up might involve both the Salesforce admin and the Microsoft admin exchanging keys or tokens, which is a one-time heavy lift but ensures continuous secure ops.

Consistent Policy Enforcement: You don't want an external agent bypassing policies that an internal agent must follow. For instance, if Salesforce agents are configured not to show full credit card numbers, a Microsoft agent shouldn't be able to query and get them either. With MCP, the data still flows through Salesforce as the server, so Salesforce can apply the same data masking and filtering rules before handing it over. This is a big plus – the Trust Layer and guardrails in Salesforce will act on any prompt/result leaving Salesforce via MCP just like it would for internal agents. So in design, treat any cross-platform call as if it were a user request hitting Salesforce – meaning all your org's security & compliance configurations apply.

Cross-Platform Activity Monitoring: It's important to have visibility into these integrations. Salesforce's Command Center might not directly know about what a Copilot on the other side did with the data after. And Microsoft's monitoring might not see inside Salesforce. Therefore, it's wise to log interactions at the integration point. The MCP registry could log each request (tool used, which agent called it, timestamp, success/failure). Possibly pipe these logs to both monitoring systems. If there's a central enterprise monitoring (like Splunk or an Azure Sentinel), ensure logs from both sides converge. This way, if an incident occurs (e.g., data was mishandled), you can trace it across systems.

Integration with LangChain and other frameworks: LangChain is a popular framework for building agentic applications in Python. Many LangChain agents run outside Salesforce but might want to use Salesforce data or functions. With MCP, Salesforce can expose certain capabilities to LangChain agents. For example, you could have a Salesforce Hosted MCP Server (as Salesforce plans to offer) that allows querying Salesforce objects. A LangChain agent could connect to it and ask "get customer by email" as a tool. The benefit for governance: instead of giving a LangChain agent direct API access with a potentially broad token, you give it a specific MCP endpoint that perhaps only returns certain fields and logs all usage. Salesforce even indicated they plan to let customers build custom MCP servers for their own functions and host them on-platform, and that these will support identity and policy enforcement natively.

Another angle: Salesforce's MuleSoft Anypoint can turn existing APIs into MCP endpoints. This means if you have a library of enterprise APIs (SAP, ServiceNow, etc.), you can quickly make them available to any MCP-compliant agent (Agentforce, Copilot, etc.) with security and monitoring in place. From a governance perspective, you'd apply the same API management policies you have for standard integrations – rate limits, API keys, payload scanning – just now applied in an AI context.

One risk to highlight: MCP is new and still evolving, and by itself doesn't mandate security or audit – "the spec doesn't enforce audit or sandboxing; it's up to the enterprise to manage trust". So implementing MCP without governance could open holes. But Salesforce is aware: their approach is to build trust and governance into their MCP support (the registry and policies). Nonetheless, as a best practice, vet each MCP server integration like you would a third-party app. If you wouldn't install an AppExchange package from an untrusted vendor, similarly, don't connect to a random MCP server someone found on GitHub. Zenity's blog gives examples of rogue MCP tools causing leaks. So maintain a whitelist and require security review of each new MCP connection.

Keep your security team in the loop. They might need to update threat models: an attacker could attempt to exploit an MCP tool (e.g., prompt injection to get it to do something unintended). Ensure the team monitors AI agent activity as part of security operations. Salesforce's upcoming features and third-party solutions (like Zenity's platform) are focusing on exactly this: inventorying MCP usage, scanning configs, and allowing/blocking servers as needed.

Plan for cross-platform incident response. If your Salesforce agent misbehaves because an external service sent bad instructions, who handles it? Ideally, have a communication channel or runbook with the external platform's team. For example, if a Microsoft Copilot-based workflow did something wrong with Salesforce data, involve both Salesforce admins and Microsoft admins to diagnose. Establish that relationship early if possible.

Integration with Microsoft Copilot specifically could involve using Microsoft's Teams Toolkit or Copilot plugins to tie into Salesforce. Microsoft might have its own compliance settings (like not allowing Copilot to access certain SharePoint data). Ensure those settings align with your Salesforce agent's policies. It's wise to have a joint workshop between platform teams to map out responsibilities. The result might be a document akin to our agent template, but for the combined system: listing data flows, who approves what, and how governance is enforced on each side.

In summary, MCP and cross-platform governance allow you to extend your AI ecosystem without loosening the reins. Salesforce Agentforce can become one member of a larger agent society, speaking a common protocol – but thanks to the MCP registry and enterprise interoperability features, you as the Salesforce admin or architect maintain a single orchestration layer to govern which agents connect to what and how. This ensures that whether an action is taken by an agent in Salesforce, or triggered from a completely different AI system, the same corporate policies (security, privacy, throttling, audit) are uniformly applied.

As AI frameworks converge via standards like MCP, expect even more tooling to emerge – maybe a unified "Agent Control Tower" that spans platforms. Until then, focus on mirroring your governance practices across systems: maintain clear documentation of integrations, conduct joint risk assessments with other platform owners, and use technology like MCP to centralize control as much as possible.

We've now covered roles, documentation, compliance, risk monitoring, lifecycle management, multi-agent coordination, and cross-platform governance. The pieces of the puzzle are on the table. In our final section, let's bring them together with Salesforce-native tools and pragmatic best practices. We'll look at how Agentforce's own features (Agent Builder, Command Center, flows, metadata) can be used to implement these governance mechanisms effectively, and we'll present an implementation matrix that maps governance needs to specific Salesforce tools or configurations.

SALESFORCE-NATIVE TOOLS AND BEST PRACTICES FOR GOVERNANCE IMPLEMENTATION

Bridling an AI agent might sound abstract, but Salesforce provides an array of concrete tools to make governance actionable. In this section, we'll map the governance concepts we've discussed to specific Salesforce platform features and best practices, creating a playbook for hands-on implementation. Think of this as the "how to" section: how do we actually use Agent Builder, Command Center, Flow, Apex, and metadata configurations to enforce the roles, rules, and risk controls defined earlier? We'll also incorporate some field-tested tips and a responsibility matrix to clarify who does what in maintaining these controls.

Let's break down key governance needs and the Salesforce tools to meet them:

Agent Design and Documentation

- **Salesforce tool or feature and usage:** Use Agent Builder Studio to define Topics, Instructions, and Actions with clear names, descriptions, and help text. Treat description fields as embedded documentation by recording each action's purpose and guardrails.

Create a Custom Metadata Type such as "Agent Registry" to track agent owner, business sponsor, risk level, and status, and use this metadata to drive governance dashboards and reports.

Compliance Enforcement

- **Salesforce tool or feature and usage:** Enable and configure the Einstein Trust Layer for masking and retention controls. Use Salesforce Shield and Platform Encryption to protect sensitive fields while allowing agents to operate safely. Classify data in Setup using Salesforce Data Classification and apply Data Cloud Governance policies, such as restricting agent queries on fields tagged as "Restricted." Use Transaction Security Policies or Apex-based intercepts to block or alert on prohibited agent actions like deletes on sensitive objects.

Testing and Quality Control

- **Salesforce tool or feature and usage:** Use the Agentforce Testing Center to run bulk scenario tests, including governance-focused tests (for example, verifying that sensitive data is masked or refused). Write Apex test classes for invocable actions and simulate agent calls with different user profiles using System.runAs. Incorporate low-code and pro-code DevOps practices with sandboxes, scratch orgs, CI pipelines, and static analysis of prompt templates to prevent disallowed behavior before deployment.

Deployment and Change Management

- **Salesforce tool or feature and usage:** Treat agent configuration as metadata and deploy through Salesforce DevOps Center or change sets. Require peer reviews for Apex code and structured reviews for Flows and prompt configurations. Where possible, package agent components using Unlocked Packages to enable versioning. After deployment, use Org Monitor and Event Monitoring to detect post-release anomalies such as error spikes that may require rollback.

Real-Time Monitoring and Alerts

- **Salesforce tool or feature and usage:** Use Agentforce Command Center as the primary real-time monitoring interface. Configure dashboards with governance KPIs such as compliance violation counts populated from custom logs. Publish Platform Events for agent alerts and subscribe via Flow to notify Agent Owners or Ethics Leads when thresholds are exceeded, ensuring timely response without manual dashboard monitoring.

Throttling and Load Management

- **Salesforce tool or feature and usage:** Centralize agent invocation through Salesforce Flow or Flow Orchestrator rather than direct calls. Implement decision logic to enforce rate limits based on invocation history stored in a custom object. For advanced scenarios, use Apex schedulers and a queue object to manage deferred agent tasks. Funnel all agent calls through shared invocable actions to simplify throttling and load control.

MCP Integration and Security

- **Salesforce tool or feature and usage:** Use the MCP Registry in Agentforce to configure external tool connections with explicit authentication, IP allowlists, and usage policies. For custom MCP servers hosted externally, use Heroku Private Spaces and App Shield for network isolation, and MuleSoft API Manager to apply security policies such as token validation or mutual TLS. Apply the same governance rigor to MCP integrations as to any enterprise API surface.

This matrix shows that for virtually every governance aspect, Salesforce offers a tool or feature. The key is configuration and vigilance: the tools won't magically govern themselves, but they empower you to encode your policies into the platform.

Now, let's talk about responsibility mapping in practice. We identified roles (Agent Owner, Pattern Architect, Ethics Lead, Business Sponsor). Here's how they engage with these tools:

The Pattern Architect likely drives setup of Agent Builder, designs flows/Apex for throttling, configures the DevOps pipeline, and sets up Command Center dashboards for the team. They translate governance requirements into technical implementation (with help from admins/developers).

The Ethics Lead might not be hands-on with Flow or Apex, but they should be given access to the Command Center (perhaps in a read-only capacity) to monitor, and to the logs (maybe via Event Monitoring). They also should be involved in Data Classification setup – working with Salesforce Admin to label fields and define masking rules. In testing, the Ethics Lead defines the scenarios for bias or misuse that the team then automates.

The Agent Owner ensures that from a user perspective, throttling or invocation limits still meet business needs (they might say "if we throttle to 5 per min, is that okay for our volume?") and they coordinate responses when alerts come (if Command Center flags an issue, the Agent Owner likely decides whether to pause the agent or let it continue while fixes are made). They also verify that any changes (like new compliance rules) are integrated by the tech team.

The Business Sponsor often will not interact with these tools directly (they might get high-level reports). But they must champion and approve resources for governance tooling. For instance, if using Shield or advanced Event Monitoring (which may cost extra), the Sponsor should back those investments as part of the project budget to ensure robust governance.

Field-Tested Insight: Teams who've implemented Agentforce pilots note that a lot of governance happens in design and testing phases, not just in production oversight. In practice, allocating extra time in sprints for "governance tasks" (like writing that negative test or configuring that policy) is critical. A common mistake is treating agent development like a quick chatbot build – but an agent is more powerful and thus needs more checks. Build a governance checklist into your Definition of Done for each sprint or user story involving the agent:

- "Security review completed for new Action"
- "PII fields tagged and tested for masking in this feature"
- "Performance test run for new workflow – no major degradation"
- "Update documentation for any new data sources added"

This DevOps integration ensures governance is continuous.

Visual Walkthrough – Example: Consider LedgerGuard going through its lifecycle:

During Draft, the team uses a Confluence page (or Salesforce Quip/Notes) with the documentation template to brainstorm safely.

At the Design stage, the Pattern Architect creates a skeleton agent in Agent Builder (maybe a dummy Topic and one Action) just to see how it might fit, and simultaneously the Ethics Lead classifies all Finance data fields in Salesforce (mark account numbers as sensitive, etc.). They set up an org policy: "Mask all but last 4 digits of account numbers in AI outputs" using the Trust Layer config.

In Build, the developer creates an Apex action for "post transaction to ERP". They also create a corresponding Unit Test that verifies if a user without proper permission calls it (simulated), it throws an exception (thus the agent would be prevented from unauthorized use). This catches any permission leaks early.

When moving to UAT, the team uses a Sandbox with partial data. They run Agentforce Testing Center with a set of test cases including edge cases like "Large amount approval" expecting the agent to escalate. They find one case where it auto-approved beyond its limit – a bug in a rule. They fix the prompt instructions and document the change.

Go Live: They deploy via change set. The Business Sponsor is nervous (finance is high stakes), so they insist on a Command Center wallboard in their office. The Pattern Architect sets up a big screen that refreshes key stats. In the first week, they notice the agent's average latency is quite high and trace it to an external API being slow. The Sponsor decides that's acceptable for now but notes it.

Multi-agent: Later, when LedgerGuard needs to call a FraudCheck agent via MCP, the Architect registers the FraudCheck MCP server (provided by a third-party vendor) in the Agentforce MCP registry, setting it so LedgerGuard can only call the specific tool "runFraudScore" on that server. In testing, the Ethics Lead deliberately tries to prompt LedgerGuard to misuse FraudCheck (maybe by injecting a prompt to make FraudCheck return extra data). The Trust Layer catches and strips the malicious part, and they verify the integration is safe.

Maintenance: Over months, new regulatory requirements come (say a new SOX control for approvals). The Ethics Lead updates the agent's policies (maybe now every approval over a certain amount must be logged in a special audit file). The Architect updates the Flow to create those audit records, and updates the documentation. This agile response keeps the agent in compliance.

By favoring Salesforce-native solutions in each step, the team benefits from platform familiarity and robustness. For example, using Flow for orchestration means existing Salesforce admins can understand and adjust the process if needed (versus a black-box script). Storing config as metadata means they can use tools like Gearset or Copado to track changes (great for audit trails on the agent itself).

Light at the end of the tunnel: Implementing governance might seem like adding extra work, but it significantly lowers the chance of catastrophic failures and builds trust with stakeholders. When business owners see Command Center charts proving the agent is behaving – and when auditors see detailed documentation and logs – confidence in AI grows. In turn, this allows you to scale up agent adoption. It's much easier to get approval for a second or third agent if the first one was delivered with strong governance and faced no major issues.

Finally, always keep the human in the loop as a fallback. No matter how many guardrails we implement, there should be a clear path for a human to intervene. Salesforce Flow and Agentforce allow human approvals and escalations to be inserted at critical points (for instance, LedgerGuard can ask a manager for approval above a threshold via a simple Approval Process). These are your ultimate safety nets – design them in from the start.

With our toolbox laid out and responsibilities assigned, you have a concrete game plan to govern AI agents on Salesforce effectively. The combination of role clarity, process checkpoints (gates), and enabling technology is powerful. As you deploy these agents, governance will become second nature – a part of the development DNA rather than an afterthought. This not only prevents disasters but often improves the agents' quality (many guardrails like instruction checks actually make the agent more accurate and reliable).

We've traveled from high-level principles down to in-the-weeds configuration. Let's now recap the core lessons from this chapter and see how they prepare us for the journey of actually deploying an agent for the first time in production.

SUMMARY

Governance and risk management might not be the most glamorous aspects of AI agents, but this chapter has shown they are the bedrock of success for

Salesforce Agentforce deployments. We began by highlighting why governance is needed: AI agents wield tremendous power to act autonomously, so clear policies and oversight are essential to harness that power responsibly. By assembling a governance team – from the hands-on Agent Owner and Pattern Architect to the guiding voices of the Ethics Lead and Business Sponsor – you create accountability for every dimension of an agent's behavior. Each role has distinct duties, yet they collaborate to ensure the agent delivers value safely and in alignment with your organization's values.

We introduced a structured Agent Documentation Template as a single source of truth for an agent's design and obligations. This living document captures everything from the agent's purpose and technical specs to compliance checkpoints (GDPR, HIPAA, etc.) and risk classifications. By filling out this template, the team cements a shared understanding and anticipates challenges early. Aligning agent behavior with corporate and regulatory policies is not a hurdle but a prerequisite – through Salesforce's trust tools (like the Einstein Trust Layer's data masking and toxicity filters) and diligent design (e.g., limiting what data an agent sees), we can ensure privacy and ethics are baked in from day one.

Operationally, we learned how to score and monitor risk. Using Salesforce metadata to tag an agent's risk factors, and Command Center's rich observability to watch live performance, you can continuously gauge an agent's "health". The introduction of Command Center in Agentforce 3.0 addresses one of the biggest concerns early adopters had – lack of visibility. Now, with real-time dashboards, alerts for anomalies, and session traces, governing an agent in production is much more feasible. We emphasized setting thresholds and automations (like alerts or even auto-disabling an agent on critical failures) to proactively manage issues before they escalate.

The chapter also presented a maturity model from Draft to Retired, detailing governance "gates" at each stage. These gates function as quality and compliance checkpoints – a chance to say "Is this agent ready to graduate to the next phase?" By enforcing design reviews, testing sign-offs, and periodic audits, you drastically reduce the chance of unpleasant surprises after deployment. In effect, the lifecycle approach shifts governance left (into early design and testing) and also sustains it throughout the agent's life via monitoring and periodic reassessment. This is exactly how you strike the balance between speed and safety: you allow rapid innovation within a controlled, gated framework that catches problems early.

As multiple agents come into play, we tackled cross-agent governance. We established that agents should not operate in a vacuum – but when they interact, it must be by design, not by accident. Policies for cross-agent invocation ensure that if, say, JoinForce calls LedgerGuard, it's an intended, audited, and safe interaction. We discussed using Flows and orchestrations to implement these hand-offs with oversight, and applying throttling to avoid runaway scenarios (no infinite loops or system overloads). The concept of context propagation was introduced to remind us that an agent passing information to another is effectively extending trust – so only minimum necessary information and privileges should be shared. The MuleSoft gateway support for Agent-to-Agent (A2A) and the new Model Context Protocol are technical enablers that, when coupled with strong policy, provide a secure bridge for agents to collaborate.

Zooming out to cross-platform governance, we looked at the emerging Model Context Protocol as the lingua franca for AI agents across ecosystems. The exciting part is that Salesforce Agentforce and other frameworks like Microsoft's Copilot are converging on interoperability standards – meaning your Salesforce agents can one day seamlessly work with AI services elsewhere. But with that integration comes the responsibility to extend your governance framework accordingly. We saw how Salesforce's MCP support introduces an enterprise-grade layer of trust and control over these external connections, letting you integrate without ceding oversight. By treating external AI endpoints as managed services (with allow-lists, auth, and monitoring), you ensure a consistent compliance posture no matter where an agent is running or what it's interacting with. In short, MCP will let your governed Salesforce agents safely plug into a broader AI universe – a key capability as AI strategies become more multi-faceted.

Finally, we translated all these principles into practical steps on the Salesforce platform. Through an implementation matrix, we mapped needs to tools: Agent Builder for documentation and design, the Trust Layer and Shield for data protection, Testing Center for QA, DevOps Center for controlled releases, Command Center and custom alerts for monitoring, Flow/Apex for throttling, and the MCP registry for secure integrations. The message is clear – Salesforce provides the pieces; it's up to us to assemble them into a governance engine. The chapter's examples, from fictional agents like LedgerGuard and JoinForce to real Salesforce features, show that this is entirely achievable with today's technology.

In wrapping up, the tone to carry forward is one of pragmatic optimism. Yes, governing AI agents is a serious endeavor – we must be vigilant about ethical risks, compliant with laws, and prepared for technical glitches. But with the frameworks and tools discussed, you can approach agent development with confidence. Instead of fearing what an AI might do, you'll have the mechanisms to guide it, monitor it, and intervene if needed. As you involve stakeholders (security teams, compliance officers, business owners) in this governance process, you also build trust organizationally. People begin to see the AI agent not as a mysterious black box, but as another well-managed part of the Salesforce ecosystem – subject to checks and balances like any other mission-critical system.

This chapter laid out the governance playbook – from team roles to lifecycle gates, from single-agent controls to multi-agent and multi-platform strategy. With these foundations, you are now prepared to move to the hands-on deployment of your first AI agent. In the next chapter, we'll focus on exactly that: taking an agent from concept to production for the first time. We'll apply the governance principles in real-world steps – configuring Agentforce, building out instructions, testing with end-users, and doing a pilot launch. By following the guidelines we've established, your first deployment can be not just exciting, but smooth and uneventful in the best possible way. Governance will give your project the quiet confidence that everything is under control, even as you unveil cutting-edge AI capabilities.

Get ready to launch your first agent – with governance as your co-pilot – and set the stage for many more successful, responsible AI agents to come. The journey from theory to practice begins now, as we turn our focus to executing that inaugural Agentforce rollout with all the preparation and wisdom you've gained. Onward to deployment!

16

STARTING FROM ZERO – YOUR FIRST AGENT DEPLOYMENT

Starting from scratch with an AI agent project can feel overwhelming. If you've made it this far in the playbook, you've been introduced to a spectrum of Agentforce patterns and possibilities—from Sentinels that monitor events to Coaches that guide users. With so many options on the table, it's natural to wonder: Where do I begin? The truth is every sprawling multi-agent ecosystem you admire started with just one well-chosen, well-scoped agent. In this chapter, we'll focus on helping you plan and execute your very first Agentforce deployment. Our aim is to replace that initial overwhelm with a clear, confidence-building game plan.

This chapter is structured as a tactical blueprint for delivering a meaningful, safe, and maintainable win in just 90 days. Rather than trying to boil the ocean by launching a fleet of agents at once, you'll learn how to nail one high-impact agent end-to-end. We'll cover how to select the right first pattern, keep the scope manageable, bring the right stakeholders on board, and iterate in short sprints to avoid overengineering. By following a focused 90-day roadmap, you can demonstrate real value quickly while keeping risks low and learning as you go.

Think of your first deployment as an opportunity to build momentum and credibility. The goal isn't to automate everything on day one—it's to deploy something useful and trustworthy that earns buy-in from users and leadership. A small success can become a big story: one effective agent that addresses a real pain point will generate excitement, provide user feedback, and lay the groundwork for future projects. By capturing quick wins and learning what works in practice, you set your team up for long-term success without betting the farm on unproven ideas.

Fortunately, Salesforce's Agentforce platform makes this journey not just possible but practical. You have an arsenal of Salesforce-native tools at your disposal to streamline development and ensure safety. Agent Builder will help you define your agent's core parameters (purpose, inputs, outputs, and pattern) with clicks not code. Flow Builder lets you orchestrate the agent's logic declaratively, designing how it interacts with users or systems step by step. When you need custom logic or integration, Invocable Apex provides a trusted way to extend your agent's capabilities within Salesforce's governance framework. Throughout development and after go-live, the Agentforce Command Center offers telemetry dashboards to monitor agent activity, performance, and outcomes in real time. And as emphasized in Chapter 15, good governance is key—every agent should have a clear owner, documentation, proper approvals, and versioned metadata for safe iteration.

Over the next sections, we'll walk through each stage of the 90-day journey, from planning to deployment to reflection. We'll start by tackling the first crucial question: choosing the right agent pattern for your inaugural project. Selecting an appropriate pattern is half the battle, setting you up to deliver maximum value with minimal headache. Let's dive in.

CHOOSING THE RIGHT FIRST PATTERN

Every agent project begins with a fundamental choice: Which pattern should I implement first? Picking the right pattern is crucial because it determines the scope of work, the complexity you'll handle, and the kind of value you deliver. You have eight core agent patterns in your toolkit, but they're not all equally suited for a first outing. The key is to choose a pattern that meets a few essential criteria:

Clear Business Value: Your first agent should tackle a problem that people care about. Look for a use case where an AI agent can save time, reduce errors, or improve outcomes in a visible way. For example, an agent that automatically updates onboarding tasks or triages IT tickets has a tangible impact that stakeholders can appreciate.

Contained Scope and Dependencies: Aim for a project with limited moving parts. If your agent needs to pull data from five systems and coordinate across multiple departments, it's probably too ambitious for a first try.

Instead, favor an agent that can operate within one primary platform or dataset. Fewer dependencies mean fewer points of failure and easier testing.

Low to Moderate Risk: Steer toward a use case where mistakes are not catastrophic. Avoid scenarios where an agent could inadvertently expose sensitive data or make irreversible changes. The ideal first agent provides assistance or automates a minor process, but leaves critical decisions or approvals to humans (at least initially). This way, if something goes wrong, the blast radius is small.

Opportunity for Insight or Personalization: While keeping risk low, try to choose a project that isn't purely trivial. The best first agents offer a hint of the "AI magic" that gets users excited—perhaps by personalizing a response or offering a smart recommendation. It's a balancing act: you want a simple scope, but also a result that feels novel or intelligent so that the project earns attention and praise. For example, an internal help-desk agent that not only acknowledges a support ticket but also suggests a relevant knowledge base article adds an intelligent touch beyond pure automation.

With these criteria in mind, which pattern should you start with? Here are a few patterns from Act I that typically make good first-agent candidates, along with why they're beginner-friendly:

- Action Pattern: Action agents excel at performing well-defined tasks under strict guardrails. They operate like smart macros that only do what they're explicitly permitted to do. For a first deployment, an Action agent is attractive because it's predictable and easy to test. For example, you might build an Action agent that closes out IT support tickets that meet certain criteria or updates a checklist when a new hire completes an onboarding step. The agent's behavior is bounded and transactional, minimizing surprises.
- Presenter Pattern: Presenter agents focus on communicating information in a helpful way—like summarizing data or generating a draft message. They don't take irreversible actions on records; they just present insights or content to a user. This makes them low-risk. A Presenter could, for instance, read through an employee feedback dataset and produce a summary of key themes for an HR report. If the summary isn't perfect, no harm done—it can be improved iteratively. Meanwhile, users get immediate value from clearer information.
- Coach Pattern: Coach agents provide non-binding guidance or nudges to users. Think of a Coach as a friendly advisor living in the

system: it might suggest how to improve a sales pitch or remind an employee to follow a best practice, but the user ultimately decides what to do. This human-in-the-loop design means a Coach agent's "mistakes" are easily caught (the user can ignore bad advice). As a first pattern, a Coach shines in environments like HR or ops where slight improvements in behavior (e.g., healthier meeting habits, more consistent data entry) can add up.

- Companion Pattern (Lite): Full-fledged Companion agents are like digital assistants handling a wide range of user requests, which can be complex for a first project. However, a lite version of a Companion—one with a very scoped focus—can work well. For example, a Companion-lite might be a simple Q&A bot for internal policy questions or a helper that knows only how to fetch and display certain data on command. Because it's preference-aware, it can give a personalized touch ("Here are your pending tasks, and I highlighted the urgent ones for you"), yet it stays safely within a sandbox of predefined capabilities.
- On the other hand, some patterns are not ideal for your first deployment due to their complexity or risk profile:
- Conductor Pattern: Conductor agents orchestrate multiple steps, often coordinating other agents or complex workflows. Building a Conductor as your first project is like trying to conduct an orchestra before you've learned to play a single instrument. With many interdependencies and a need for robust error handling across processes, a Conductor agent can be overwhelming to implement from scratch. Save this pattern for when you have a bit more experience under your belt.
- Sentinel Pattern: Sentinel agents vigilantly monitor signals from various sources and react to important events. They're powerful—used for things like detecting anomalies or policy violations in real time—but that power comes with added complexity. A Sentinel often requires integrating event streams, defining nuanced rules for alerting, and handling potentially critical actions when something is detected. As a first agent, a fully autonomous watchdog might be too unpredictable. It's better to start with an agent you can trigger and control more directly.

If you're unsure which pattern to choose, try sketching a simple decision tree based on your use case. Ask yourself questions like: "Is my problem mostly about automating a straightforward task? Or is it about delivering information or recommendations to a user?" If it's the former, an Action agent might be the right call. If it's the latter, lean toward a Presenter or Coach. The goal is to match the pattern to the nature of the problem. By doing so, you leverage a blueprint that aligns with your needs instead of starting from a blank slate.

Pro Tip: You can't scale what you can't explain. Start with an agent pattern your team can easily document, demo to others, and iterate on confidently. Choosing a simple, well-understood pattern sets you up to learn fast and show tangible results.

SCOPING YOUR MVP AGENT

Once you've chosen a pattern for your first agent, the next step is to clearly define what that agent will actually do. This is where scoping comes in. In product development, we talk about a Minimum Viable Product (MVP)—the smallest functional version of a product that delivers value. Similarly, for AI agents we want a Minimal Viable Agent that accomplishes a useful task without unnecessary complexity. Scoping your MVP agent means pinning down three things up front:

Inputs: What does the agent need to know or receive in order to do its job? Define the data sources, triggers, or user inputs that will kick off the agent's process. It could be a record change in Salesforce, a prompt from a user (e.g., a Slack message), a scheduled time trigger, or any combination of these. Be explicit: list the fields, events, or context your agent will require. If something isn't directly available, consider simplifying—your first agent shouldn't depend on pulling data from a dozen places.

Outputs: What will the agent produce or change as a result of its work? This might be an action (like updating a field or creating a record), a message (such as posting a summary or recommendation to a user), or a decision (perhaps setting a status or triggering another process). Identify one primary output that signals the agent has done its job. Keeping the output focused will help everyone understand the agent's purpose and measure its success.

Surfaces: Where and how will humans interact with the agent? Determine the "surface" or interface through which users will experience the agent's functionality. Is it in the Salesforce UI (e.g., a component on a Lightning page, or a button that users click to invoke the agent)? Or is it in a chat interface like Slack or Microsoft Teams? Maybe it's triggered behind the scenes by a system event with no direct user interface at all. For the MVP, pick one primary interaction surface. Limiting to one channel (for example, only Slack, or only a Salesforce screen action) will make design and testing much easier.

A golden rule for scoping: don't build all the bells and whistles on day one. Focus your first agent on one outcome, delivered through one interface, for one target audience. By narrowing scope in this way, you reduce complexity and ensure the agent's value can be demonstrated quickly. Let's break down those three "ones":

One outcome: Identify the single most valuable thing this agent will accomplish. Maybe it completes a specific task (e.g., closing a service case after verifying certain criteria) or provides a specific answer (e.g., giving a summary of yesterday's sales figures on command). You might have a wish-list of ten things the agent could do eventually, but the MVP should nail one of them end-to-end.

One interface: Choose a primary way users will interact with the agent or see its output. It could be via a chat message, a Salesforce Lightning component, a mobile app notification, or even an email. By choosing one interface, you avoid the overhead of building and supporting multiple channels at once. You can always extend to other interfaces after the initial success.

One audience: Define who will use or benefit from this agent initially. Is it the HR onboarding team? Sales reps in the North America region? New hires at your company? Focusing on a specific user group helps tailor the agent's behavior and language to that audience, and it makes gathering feedback easier. You can expand to more users or departments later, once the kinks are worked out.

To aid in scoping, leverage Salesforce's tools early. The Agent Builder in Salesforce can act as your design canvas: as you fill in the agent's name, description, pattern type, and owner, you're effectively writing down its intent. Use Agent Builder's fields to document inputs and outputs – for example, you might specify that the agent will take a "Task ID" and a "Completion Status" as input, and its output is an "Updated Task record" plus a confirmation message. Planning this in Agent Builder creates metadata that scaffolds your project.

Next, map the flow of logic with Flow Builder. Even before you configure anything, it helps to sketch a simple flow diagram: When X happens, the agent does Y, then Z. Identify which parts of the logic can be done with declarative Flow elements (decisions, record updates, etc.), and which might need a bit of code or AI. This sets the stage for implementation. If there's complex data transformation or a call to an external AI model needed, note that as a spot where Invocable Apex or a generative AI step (like an Einstein GPT action) will play a role. The goal at the scoping phase isn't to build the Flow yet, but to understand its building blocks.

Let's consider an example of a well-scoped MVP agent: an Action-pattern agent that updates onboarding tasks from a Slack prompt. Imagine your company's HR team wants to streamline new-hire onboarding. Right now, new employees have a checklist of tasks in Salesforce (like completing training modules, submitting documents, etc.), and they often inform HR via Slack when something is done. We can introduce an agent to make this smoother:

Pattern: Action (the agent will perform an update in Salesforce).

Outcome: Mark an onboarding task as completed on behalf of the employee.

Interface: Slack – the new hire will send a Slack message to the agent (for example, "Task ABC123 done") and the agent will respond with a confirmation.

Audience: New hires (as the ones triggering it) and the HR coordinators (who get to see tasks auto-updated without manual effort).

Here's how this MVP agent would work at a high level: A new hire posts a message to a dedicated "Onboarding Bot" in Slack, saying something like, "I finished my security training." The agent (listening via a Slack integration) takes that input, matches it to the corresponding task record in Salesforce (e.g., finds the "Complete Security Training" task for that user), and updates the task status to "Completed." It then pings back in Slack: "Got it! Marked your Security Training as complete ✅."

Notice how this scope checks all our MVP boxes. There's one clear outcome (updating a task status), a single interface (Slack chat), and a defined user group (new hires and HR). The agent's inputs are simple (a text message plus the user's identity), and its outputs are clear (the task record update and a confirmation message). We're not trying to boil the ocean by having it handle every onboarding need or integrate with five different systems on day one.

By rigorously defining your agent's scope in this manner, you set yourself up for success in the build phase. A tightly-scoped agent is easier to explain to stakeholders, easier to test, and less likely to encounter unexpected edge cases. With a solid MVP definition in hand, you can now turn to aligning stakeholders and defining success metrics, which we'll cover next.

ALIGNING STAKEHOLDERS AND SUCCESS METRICS

With a clear pattern and scope in hand, it's time to get everyone on the same page. Early stakeholder alignment is critical for your 90-day agent project. Why? Because this isn't just a developer's solo mission – it's a cross-functional effort that needs buy-in, oversight, and feedback from various corners of the organization. In this phase, you'll rally the key people who have a stake in the agent's success, and you'll define what "success" actually looks like through metrics. Let's break down the game plan:

Identify Your Core Stakeholders

Assemble a small team or working group for the project kickoff. Typically, this includes:

Business Sponsor: This is the person who cares most about the problem the agent is solving – often a manager or executive in the department where the agent will be used. The sponsor champions the project's business value. They can help remove roadblocks and secure resources. For example, if you're building an HR onboarding agent, the Head of HR or an HR operations manager might be the sponsor.

Data/AI Lead: You'll want someone who understands the data and the AI components at a technical level. This could be a Salesforce architect, a developer, or a data scientist/analyst. Their role is to ensure the agent has the data it needs and that any AI (like an LLM or prediction model) is used correctly. They'll think about things like data quality, model prompts, and integration points.

End-User Representative: Don't build in a vacuum – include a representative (or a few) from the actual user base. If the agent is for new hires, maybe a recent hire or someone from the onboarding team can provide perspective. If it's for sales reps, get a salesperson involved. These reps will give practical insight, help with initial testing, and keep the solution grounded in reality. They are also likely to become the agent's advocates among their peers if it works well.

Governance or Compliance Rep: As discussed in Chapter 15, governance is essential. Have someone who's responsible for AI or IT governance, security, or compliance give input from the start. Their job is to ensure the agent meets any regulatory or policy requirements (for instance, making sure no sensitive data is used improperly) and follows internal guidelines. This person might be from the IT governance board, a security officer, or simply a senior admin who oversees change management. Early involvement of governance helps avoid red flags later and reinforces that you're doing this the right way.

Bringing these stakeholders together for a kickoff meeting is a great idea. In that meeting, you can present the agent's MVP scope and get everyone's questions and concerns on the table. Also decide how often the group will check in (weekly 15-minute stand-ups? bi-weekly demos?) to stay updated.

Define Success Metrics (Lightweight and Meaningful)

To know if your first agent is doing a good job, you need to measure something. But since this is new territory, keep metrics simple and directly tied to the agent's purpose. Here are a few metrics to consider:

Response Time: How fast does the agent complete its task or respond to a user? For example, if a user asks the agent a question or triggers it via Slack, is the reply nearly instant (a few seconds) or does it take minutes? Set an expectation (perhaps "under 5 seconds for a response" if using an LLM, or even faster if purely using Apex/Flow) and monitor this. A snappy agent experience will build user trust.

Accuracy/Relevance: How often does the agent get things right? This can be tricky to quantify, but you might use proxy measures. For a Presenter or Coach agent, you could have users rate the helpfulness of its output (thumbs-up/down or a 1-5 star scale). For an Action agent, accuracy might mean it updated the correct records and only when it was supposed to. You could review a sample of agent actions to see if any errors occurred. Aim for a high success rate but expect to iterate as you gather data.

User Engagement: Are people actually using the agent? Track usage stats such as number of agent invocations per week, or what percentage of the target audience has tried it at least once. If the agent posts recommendations or answers, do users click or act on them? For example, if your agent suggests knowledge articles to service reps, measure click-through on those suggestions. Early on, a qualitative metric (like anecdotal positive feedback) can supplement numbers. The key is to show that the agent is being adopted and not sitting idle.

You don't need dozens of metrics – pick 2 or 3 that best indicate the agent's value. It's okay if they are rough at first. You can refine how you measure success over time (Chapter 17 will dive deeper into value tracking). For now, having any agreed-upon targets or KPIs will give the team something concrete to aim for (e.g., "reduce response time to under 5 seconds," "achieve 90% accuracy in task updates," "at least 20 users actively use the agent in the first month").

Build a Communication Plan

Keeping stakeholders in the loop throughout the 90-day project keeps momentum up and prevents surprises. Develop a simple communication plan that includes:

An Internal Wiki or Page for the project: Set up a spot on Confluence, Google Docs, Salesforce Quip, or wherever your company keeps project notes. Use it to store the agent's design document, scope, metrics, and eventually user guides or FAQs. This becomes the single source of truth that anyone can check for updates.

Weekly Updates: Decide on a cadence and channel for brief status updates. Many teams use a dedicated Slack channel or an email thread. You might post every Friday a few bullets: what happened this week (e.g., "Flow built, initial testing done"), any blockers, and what's next. This keeps the sponsor and others aware of progress. It's also a chance to celebrate small wins ("Agent successfully updated a task in testing!") which builds confidence.

Milestone Demo Dates: Lock in the date for the first demo now. For instance, plan a demo around day 30 or 45 to showcase a working prototype to stakeholders. Having a date on the calendar creates urgency and also gives stakeholders something to look forward to. You may also schedule a second demo near day 60 (after the internal pilot) to show improvements. These demos are key for maintaining buy-in and excitement – everyone can see the agent in action and provide feedback.

To make sure you've covered all bases, it helps to create a quick stakeholder kickoff checklist. This list might include:

- Roles assigned (who is sponsor, lead, user rep, governance).
- Success metrics decided and documented.

- Approval or compliance steps identified (if any).
- Communication channels set (Slack channel or email list created; wiki page link shared).
- Meeting cadence agreed (e.g., weekly stand-up every Tuesday 10am).
- Demo date confirmed with everyone.

By aligning stakeholders and defining success early, you set a positive tone for the project. It's clear to everyone what you're doing, why you're doing it, and how you'll measure it. This alignment will pay off when it's time to pilot and deploy – your stakeholders will already be on board and ready to champion the agent if it meets the agreed goals.

With the team and targets in place, you're ready to actually plan the work. In the next section, we'll outline a 90-day sprint plan to build, test, and roll out your agent in manageable phases.

SPRINT PLAN – THE 90-DAY ROADMAP

Now that everyone is aligned and we know what we're building, it's time to execute – step by step. A 90-day project can feel like a marathon, but breaking it into shorter sprints or phases will make it manageable and keep progress visible. We'll divide the journey into roughly four two-week sprints (with one longer building sprint in the middle) to go from zero to deployment. Each phase has a focus and a concrete outcome. Here's an overview of the recommended timeline:

Days 1–15: Scope Lock and Design. In the first two weeks, nail down everything discussed so far. Finalize the agent's scope (no new features creeping in!), and design the solution architecture. By Day 15, you should have your Agent Builder metadata set up (agent record with key details), a draft Flow design on paper or in a dev org, and all stakeholders signed off on the plan. It's also a good time to set up project documentation (if you haven't already) and any tracking tools. Essentially, this phase turns the initial concept into a blueprint for development.

Days 16–45: First Build and Test. This roughly month-long sprint is where you build the MVP agent in Salesforce. Develop the Flow, write any necessary Apex, and integrate the LLM or external calls (if any). Since 30 days is a long span, aim to have a demo-able version by around Day 30. For example, by the halfway mark of this phase, the agent should be able to run through its basic use case in a test environment. Use the remaining time to refine and fix bugs. Simulate GPT calls or outputs during this phase if possible – instead of burning API calls or waiting on perfect prompts, feed the Flow some dummy responses to ensure the logic works. Also, set up Command Center logging and telemetry now, so you begin capturing data from the get-go. By Day 45, you want a working agent in a sandbox or dev environment, with initial tests passing.

Days 46–60: Internal Pilot. Now take your agent for a test drive with real users. In this two-week pilot, enable the agent for a small group of 2–5 friendly users or stakeholders (your end-user reps are perfect for this). Have them use the agent in their actual workflow, and gather feedback. Encourage them to note any confusion, errors, or unexpected behaviors. Capture logs and anecdotal notes: did the agent respond on time? Did it do something odd? What did users like or dislike? Also monitor telemetry from the Command Center – are there errors or slow responses showing up? By Day 60, you should have a list of improvement ideas and maybe some enthusiastic quotes ("This saved me 30 minutes on Monday!") or cautious flags ("It didn't handle X very well."). Importantly, you've proven the agent works in a real scenario, even if it's not perfect yet.

Days 61–75: Feedback Loop and Hardening. Take the lessons from the pilot and make your agent better. In this phase, you'll iterate on the agent's logic, prompts, and UI. Fix any bugs uncovered in pilot (e.g., maybe the agent wasn't parsing a certain input correctly). Adjust the agent's behavior based on user suggestions (perhaps add a little confirmation step if users felt unsure about an automated action). This is also the time to double-check security and guardrails: ensure permissions are set correctly, the agent only accesses what it should, and add any needed fallback paths (what happens if the LLM returns an error or a nonsensical answer?). Re-run any governance review if needed, now that the agent configuration is mostly final. By Day 75, you should have a polished version of the agent (let's call it v1.1) ready for a broader audience.

Days 76–90: Limited Release and Monitoring. In the final stretch, roll out the agent to a wider user group – perhaps an entire department or a second business unit that's interested – but still keep it "limited" in scope (not company-wide just yet). Essentially, this is a broader beta. Announce the agent's availability, provide a brief training or user guide if needed, and let it run in the wild for a few weeks. Closely observe usage and performance during this time. Use the Command Center to watch for any spikes in errors or unusual behaviors now that load is higher. Collect success stories and any final issues. Around Day 90, gather the team to present results: did you hit the success metrics? What value was observed? Also decide what's next: do you iterate further, scale up to more users, or perhaps sunset the pilot if it didn't work out as hoped? Ideally, you'll be in a position to celebrate a win – you delivered a working AI agent in 90 days – and propose the next steps (maybe expanding its user base or tackling a new use case in the next 90 days).

The list below summarizes each phase of the 90-day plan, including the main goal, key inputs, and outputs for each period:

Scope Lock and Design (Days 1–15)

- **Goals or focus:** Finalize agent scope, design the architecture, and secure stakeholder buy-in.
- **Key inputs:** Initial concept, selected agent pattern, stakeholder requirements.
- **Key outputs or deliverables:** Design documentation, initial Agent Builder configuration, project plan, and formal scope sign-off.

Build and Test (Days 16–45)

- **Goals or focus:** Develop the MVP agent and validate functionality in a development environment.
- **Key inputs:** Approved design artifacts, development sandbox, sample data or stubbed responses.
- **Key outputs or deliverables:** Working agent prototype built with Flow and Apex, passing unit tests, and logging enabled.

Internal Pilot (Days 46–60)

- **Goals or focus:** Run the agent with a small user group to gather feedback and performance data.
- **Key inputs:** MVP agent, pilot user group, telemetry and monitoring configuration.
- **Key outputs or deliverables:** Pilot usage logs, qualitative user feedback, and a documented list of issues and improvement opportunities.

Feedback and Hardening (Days 61–75)

- **Goals or focus:** Refine the agent based on pilot feedback and strengthen reliability, safety, and governance.
- **Key inputs:** Pilot feedback, error and performance logs, governance and ethics review inputs.
- **Key outputs or deliverables:** Updated agent version with bug fixes and tuned prompts, enhanced guardrails, and readiness for broader release.

Limited Release (Days 76–90)

- **Goals or focus:** Deploy the agent to a broader audience in a controlled rollout and measure business impact.
- **Key inputs:** Polished agent version 1.1, user training materials, and operational support plan.
- **Key outputs or deliverables:** Agent running in production for a wider group, final metrics and observations, and a go-forward decision on expansion or iteration.

This phased approach ensures that you're not just frantically coding for 90 days and hoping for the best. Instead, you have checkpoints to course-correct and validate that you're on track. Each phase builds confidence: by the end of design you know what to build; by the end of build you know it runs; by the end of pilot you know users find it useful; by the end of hardening you trust it in production; and by the end of limited release you have proven value to show the rest of the organization.

Remember that these timelines are a guideline – adjust them to fit your context. The key is to maintain momentum and not let the project stall. Regular wins (a demo, a pilot result, a metric hit) keep everyone engaged. With a solid 90-day plan in place, you can move on to the fun part: actually building the agent with Salesforce's toolkit, which we'll dive into in the next section.

BUILDING THE AGENT WITH SALESFORCE TOOLS

It's finally build time! By this stage, you have a well-defined plan and a green light from stakeholders. In Salesforce's Agentforce ecosystem, building an agent is a mix of declarative setup and a bit of coding where needed. Think of it like building any Salesforce app – you'll use a combination of tools such as Agent Builder, Flow, and Apex, and possibly add a custom UI or integration for a polished experience. Let's go through the key components of the build toolkit and how they apply to your first agent.

Agent Builder – Laying the Foundation

Salesforce's Agent Builder is the starting point for configuring your AI agent. It's a low-code interface where you define the agent's high-level metadata: its name, description, owning team or person, and importantly the pattern or role it plays. When you create a new agent in Agent Builder, you'll typically:

Specify the Purpose: Write a short description of what the agent does (e.g., "Summarizes employee feedback into weekly insights" or "Closes completed onboarding tasks automatically"). This helps everyone understand the agent's intent at a glance.

Assign an Owner: Just like any asset in Salesforce, an agent should have an owner – the person or team responsible for it. In Agent Builder, you might fill in a field for Owner or Steward of the agent. This ties back to governance; if something goes wrong, we know who is accountable and who will maintain the agent.

Define Inputs and Outputs: Agent Builder lets you list what kinds of inputs the agent expects and what outputs it produces. For instance, does it take a text prompt? Does it output a recommendation record or just a message? In our first agent, this might be simple (e.g., "Input: Slack message text; Output: updated Task record + confirmation message"). Documenting this in the tool ensures clarity.

Tag the Pattern: Since Agentforce is pattern-aware, you may tag the agent as an "Action" or "Presenter" etc. This is important for tracking and for any pattern-specific templates the platform might apply. It also helps down the line when you build an internal Agent Registry (Chapter 17), because you'll categorize agents by pattern.

Set any Guardrails or Settings: Agent Builder might provide toggles or fields for basic guardrails (like "requires human approval" or "data classification"). For now, set these according to your use case (e.g., for an Action agent, you might enable a setting to require certain user permissions to trigger it).

Agent Builder effectively creates the skeleton of your agent. It might provision behind-the-scenes components like a Salesforce metadata entry for the agent, default logging configurations, or connectors for LLM usage. By investing time here, you make downstream steps easier – it's much like creating a custom object and fields correctly before writing Apex.

Flow – Declarative Logic and Orchestration

Salesforce Flow (specifically Flow Builder) is your powerhouse for orchestrating what the agent actually does. Most of your agent's "brain" can often live in a Flow, especially for simpler logic. Using Flow, you can:

Define the sequence of actions: For example, "when triggered, first gather necessary data, then call an Apex action or external API, then decide on outcome, then post a result."

Add decision branches: Flow's decision elements let your agent handle different scenarios without code (e.g., if no feedback is found, branch to an error message; if feedback is found, proceed to summarize).

Incorporate user interactions: If your agent pattern involves user input mid-process (like a Coach that asks a follow-up question), Screen Flows can present a UI to the user. For our first agent, you might not need a screen (especially if it runs in the background or via chat), but know that Flow can handle multi-step dialogs if needed.

Invoke external services or Apex: Flow has elements to make callouts (with the HTTP Callout element or platform-specific actions) and to invoke Apex code (via Invocable Apex). This means you can keep the main structure in Flow and only drop into code for the specialized tasks. For instance, calling a generative AI service might be done via an Apex action that Flow invokes.

Handle errors and timeouts: In an agent context, you might use Flow's fault paths to define what to do if, say, the API call to an AI service fails. You could set a default response or notify an admin – all configurable in Flow without altering code.

One big advantage of building your logic in Flow is maintainability. Non-developers on your team can read the flow and understand the agent's behavior, and future tweaks (like adding a new check or step) can often be done declaratively. Flows also automatically log their executions (especially if integrated with the Command Center), which helps with monitoring.

Invocable Apex – Extending with Code for Brains and Muscles

While Flow is powerful, you'll likely need some Apex to handle tasks that are complex or not provided out-of-the-box. Invocable Apex refers to Apex classes that are annotated so they can be called from Flows or even from outside via API. In the context of your agent, use Apex to:

- Perform complex data transformations or calculations that would be clunky in Flow. For example, merging and formatting text from multiple records before sending it to an LLM might be easier in Apex.
- Implement business rules or validations in code. Perhaps your agent needs to follow a set of company rules (e.g., don't summarize feedback if fewer than 5 responses to avoid anonymity issues). You can code that logic in Apex and have the Flow invoke it, then decide to proceed or not based on the result.
- Call external APIs or services in a more controlled way. If Salesforce doesn't yet have a no-code action for your AI service, you can write an Apex method to make the HTTP request to, say, OpenAI or an Azure function, and return the result to the Flow.
- Provide fallback logic. For instance, if the LLM fails to return a summary, your Apex could detect a null response and maybe substitute a rule-based summary or a polite error message. This ensures the agent always responds gracefully.

When writing Apex for agents, keep it modular. A best practice is to create an Apex action that does one thing (like "SummarizeText" or "ClassifyCase") and test it thoroughly on its own. Then reference that in Flow. Also, respect governor limits and bulk patterns – agents might be invoked in bulk contexts, so avoid assumptions of single-record scope where possible.

User Interface Integration (Lightning Components)

Depending on your agent's design, you might need a user interface component to embed in Salesforce screens or other platforms. Lightning Web Components (LWC) can be used to create custom UI for your agent:

- If your agent is a Presenter or Companion that should appear on a record page (e.g., a component showing "AI Suggestions" or a

summary panel), you'd build an LWC to display the agent's output and maybe provide input controls (like a "Ask Agent" button or a thumbs-up/down feedback).
- LWCs can communicate with Flows and Apex. For example, an LWC could call an Apex method that invokes the agent's logic, or it could trigger a Flow via a dedicated Apex call or the new Flow screens in LWC feature. This way, clicking a button in the UI starts the agent and then the LWC updates to show the result.
- If your agent is accessed via an external UI (like Slack or a mobile app), you might not need an LWC at all – the interface is outside Salesforce. But for anything within Salesforce (Sales Cloud, Service Cloud, Experience Cloud site), LWCs give you flexibility to tailor the UX.

For a first agent, don't over-invest in UI polish. It's perfectly fine to use out-of-the-box options: for example, a quick action that launches a Flow interview, or a Slack command that triggers a flow via Salesforce's Slack app. LWCs are powerful, but you can often get by without them initially. Keep it simple: introduce a custom component only if it significantly improves adoption or usability.

Prompt Design and Generative AI Integration

If your agent uses an LLM or generative AI (common in Presenter, Coach, or Companion patterns), you'll need to design prompts and decide how to integrate the AI:

Prompt Engineering: Craft the prompts your agent will send to the LLM. In our feedback summarizer example, the prompt might be: "Summarize the following employee feedback comments into three key points with a brief intro. Comments: ". You'll want to experiment with the phrasing to get useful output. Keep prompts clear about format and length, and incorporate any needed context (like company tone or specific criteria).

Few-Shot or Templates: Depending on the platform, you might supply examples (few-shot learning) in the prompt. For a first version, it's usually fine not to, unless the model needs guidance. You could include one example of a comment and a desired summary to steer it.

Using Salesforce's AI Services: Agentforce might offer built-in actions for Einstein GPT or other services. If so, you can configure those in Flow or Apex rather than calling third-party APIs directly. This often simplifies authentication and governance (the Einstein Trust Layer can sanitize responses, for instance).

API Integration: If you use an external AI API, handle it via Apex callouts. Be mindful of response time (your Flow might need to wait) and errors. Also, consider cost – perhaps limit the length of text you send or how often the agent calls the API to stay within budget.

Telemetry for AI: It's wise to log what prompts you send and responses you get (maybe not verbatim if they contain sensitive info, but at least metadata like length or an identifier). This will help in debugging if the AI does something unexpected. Salesforce's Command Center or even custom logging objects can be used for this purpose.

Designing the AI interaction is part art, part science. Don't be afraid to iterate on prompts during development and pilot phases. Even minor wording changes can greatly improve relevance or tone of the AI's output.

Example: Building a "Feedback Summarizer" Presenter

To tie it all together, let's walk through how you might build an agent example – a Presenter pattern agent that summarizes employee feedback (perhaps from an internal survey or chatter posts) into a brief report for HR. We'll use Agent Builder, Flow, and an LLM to accomplish this:

Agent Setup in Agent Builder: Create a new agent record, called "Feedback Summarizer". Give it a description like "Analyzes and summarizes weekly employee feedback for HR insights." Assign ownership to the HR analytics team. Tag it as a Presenter pattern. In the inputs field, list "Raw feedback text (list of comments)" and for outputs, "Summary paragraph (text)". This tells everyone that the agent takes a batch of text and returns a shorter text. Save this configuration – behind the scenes, this might create an Agent definition that you can reference in Flow.

Flow Construction: Build an autolaunched Flow (since this agent doesn't need user clicks once triggered; it could be scheduled or kicked off by a button). The Flow might have the following steps:

- A Get Records element to gather the relevant feedback. For instance, fetch all feedback entries from the past week from a custom Feedback__c object (or wherever the comments are stored). Alternatively, the flow could accept those as inputs if triggered via a screen with selected records.

- A Compose step (maybe using a Text Template) to concatenate or format the comments into a single text block. You might insert delimiters or numbers if needed.
- An Action element to call the AI. If using Einstein GPT via a Salesforce provided action, it could be something like "Generate Text (Prompt: [your composed prompt])". If not, you'd call an Apex invocable "SummarizeText" which you write to call an external API. Either way, this step sends the big prompt (with all the comments) and gets back a summary.
- A Create Record or Update Record element to store the summary. Perhaps you create a Summary__c record that has the text, or update a field on a dashboard object. This ensures the summary is saved somewhere for reference.
- Maybe a notification step: e.g., post to a Chatter group or Slack channel "The weekly feedback summary is ready" with the summary text, so the HR team sees it immediately.
- Error handling: add a Fault path on the AI callout. If it fails, maybe have the flow create a Task for the admin or send an alert so it's not silent.

After building the flow, test it with sample data. Use Agent Builder or Flow debug to run it with a subset of comments and see the output.

Apex for AI (if needed): Suppose Salesforce doesn't have a built-in summarization action yet. You write an Apex class FeedbackSummarizerService with an invocable method summarize(List<String> comments) that calls an external API. It might assemble the comments into a JSON and call OpenAI's API. Make sure to handle exceptions and limit the size (maybe only take first 100 comments). Test this class separately with a unit test using a static response to simulate the API.

Review and Iterate: With the flow and components in place, run an end-to-end test. Perhaps input some dummy feedback records ("The new policy is great", "Can we get better coffee?" etc.) and execute the flow. See what summary comes out. If it's too terse or missing important points, tweak the prompt in the Apex or how you format input. Ensure the summary makes sense to an HR person. Check that the Agent Builder entry for "Feedback Summarizer" is complete and accurate (this will serve as documentation).

Through this example, you can see how Salesforce tools come together: Agent Builder gave us a template and place to manage the agent's identity; Flow orchestrated data and actions; Apex extended the capability by interfacing with an AI service; and an LWC (if used) provided a user-friendly touch point. Your first agent likely will have a similar mix.

Keep in mind that building is an iterative process. You might discover mid-way that you need a new field or to tweak a rule – that's okay. Salesforce's agility (metadata-driven development) is on your side. Just remember to keep things as simple as possible. It's your first agent, and done is better than perfect.

Pro Tip: Treat the first agent like an app, not a macro. Give it a proper name, description, and version. Assign a clear owner. Document its intent and design. By formalizing it as a product (even if small), you encourage good habits in maintenance and set expectations that this is a living solution, not a one-off script.

DEPLOYING AND OBSERVING YOUR FIRST AGENT

Deployment day for your agent is a big milestone – but it's not as simple as flipping a switch. A successful go-live requires some preparation to ensure the agent runs safely and you can observe its behavior. In Salesforce, deploying an agent might mean moving your configurations (Flow, Apex, etc.) to production and enabling the agent for real users. Before you do that, run through a quick readiness checklist:

Audit Trail Enabled: Make sure you have logging or audit tracking turned on for the agent's actions. For instance, if the agent updates records or posts messages, those events should be recorded. Salesforce's platform provides logs (Flow logs, Apex logs) and Field History tracking if applicable. Additionally, the Agentforce Command Center automatically logs agent events – verify that your agent is being tracked there. Having an audit trail means if something strange happens, you can trace exactly what the agent did and when.

Inputs Validated: Double-check that your agent handles unexpected inputs gracefully. By the time you're deploying, you likely did this in testing, but it's worth a final pass. If a user provides incomplete info or a field is missing, does the agent handle it (perhaps with a polite error message or by skipping that request)? Also, ensure that any data coming into the agent (like text that might contain special characters or malicious content) is sanitized. For example, if your agent uses a Slack message as input, could someone inject a weird string that breaks the flow? Ideally, incorporate validations in Flow or Apex so the agent doesn't choke on bad data.

Fallback for Users: Plan what happens if the agent cannot fulfill a request. In production, there will be times the agent fails – maybe an API is down or the LLM returns an error. Does the user see a friendly message and know what to do next? Define a fallback path such as: "If agent can't complete action, notify user and create a task for a human to follow up." In an Action agent, this might mean assigning the item to a queue. In a Presenter, maybe showing a "Sorry, I couldn't get that. Try again later." message. The key is to not leave users hanging or confused. Document this behavior and ensure its implemented in your flow (e.g., via fault connectors).

Kill Switch or Limits: Especially for a first deployment, have a way to disable or pause the agent if needed. This could be as simple as a checkbox field "Active" on the agent's record that your Flow checks at start. Or you might limit the agent to certain hours. This isn't in the outline, but as a safety measure: if the agent starts acting odd, you want to quickly turn it off without redeploying code.

Once everything looks good, deploy your agent configuration to the production org (using change sets, unlocked packages, or your CI/CD of choice). It's wise to start with a soft launch: enable the agent for a subset of users initially (maybe the same pilot users, plus a few more) even in production. This is effectively a staged rollout.

Now, how do you observe the agent in action and measure its performance? Salesforce provides the Agentforce Command Center – a monitoring dashboard for agents. In the Command Center (or via your own monitoring if you export logs to Splunk/New Relic, etc.), keep an eye on:

Agent Invocations: How often is the agent being called or triggered? This tells you adoption. If you expected 50 uses a day but see 5, it might indicate low usage or an accessibility issue. Conversely, if it's being spammed unexpectedly, you might need to ensure its handling load.

Error Rates: Watch for any errors the agent is throwing. Command Center can show errors from Flows or Apex. A spike in errors after deployment needs immediate attention – it could be a missing permission in production or an unhandled edge case now surfacing.

Completion and Success: For Action agents, track how many actions were completed vs. failed. For Presenter/Coach types, you might track how often they produce an output and if users engage with it. If the Command Center has a success metric (like "completed without human override"), monitor that. For example, if your agent is supposed to auto-close tasks and you see it attempted 10 but only 6 actually closed, investigate why 4 didn't (were they already closed? Did a validation rule stop it?).

Latency: In the logs, check how long the agent's process takes. If responses are slow (e.g., an average of 8 seconds when you hoped for 2), you might need to optimize or adjust expectations. Sometimes initial runs are slower due to cold starts, so look at steady-state performance.

Beyond system metrics, build a feedback loop with your users. The human perspective will tell you what the charts cannot. Implement simple ways for users to give a thumbs-up or thumbs-down on the agent's output. A few approaches:

- If your agent interacts via Slack, take advantage of reactions. For instance, instruct pilot users to react with 👍 or 👎 on the agent's message if it was helpful or not. You can write a small Slack bot or use Salesforce's Slack integration to catch those reactions and log them (perhaps calling a Flow that updates a Feedback custom object).
- In a Salesforce UI, if you have an LWC or a screen, include quick feedback buttons ("Was this suggestion useful? [Yes/No]"). Tie that to a Salesforce object where you accumulate feedback counts.

Create a Feedback__c object (or use an existing Survey capability) to record any user-submitted comments or ratings about the agent. Make it as frictionless as possible – one-click ratings or a short text field.

Encourage users to report issues in your internal channel or via Chatter. Some teams set up a dedicated Chatter group or Slack channel like "#agent-feedback" where users can post their experiences and the dev team can respond.

If your agent uses prompts and LLMs, consider logging the prompts and responses (perhaps in a secure object) for later analysis. This is optional due to storage and privacy concerns, but it can be invaluable for fine-tuning. For example, you might discover the model often misunderstands a certain phrasing users employ – you can tweak the agent to handle that better.

During the first days or weeks of deployment, review the metrics and feedback daily. This is when you'll catch major issues and also gather success stories. Share those early wins with stakeholders ("In the first week, the agent closed 23 tasks automatically, saving ~5 hours of manual work!"). And any critical issues – address them promptly or use the kill switch if needed while you patch.

Deploying an AI agent isn't a "set and forget" event. It's more like adopting a puppy – you need to watch it, train it, and ensure it adapts well to its new home. By actively observing and guiding your agent in its early life, you'll build trust with users and pave the way for smoother scaling.

Finally, as you approach the end of the 90 days, you should have enough data to evaluate and move into the retrospective phase. We'll cover how to reflect and plan next steps in the following section.

AFTER DAY 90 – REFLECT, REUSE, REPEAT

Congratulations – you've reached (or survived) Day 90! Your first agent is up and running, and you have real data and experience to show for it. This final phase is about reflecting on what happened, capitalizing on the win, and setting the stage for even bigger things. Think of it as a retrospective and a springboard rolled into one.

Start with a structured retrospective with your core team and stakeholders. Gather everyone (virtually or in a room) and discuss:

- What worked? Identify the parts of the project that went well. Maybe your choice of pattern was spot on, or an integration was easier than expected. Highlight these because they're practices to repeat.
- What surprised us? Discuss any unexpected challenges or outcomes. Perhaps users used the agent in a way you didn't anticipate, or a particular feature turned out more valuable (or less useful) than assumed. Surprises often carry key lessons.
- What would we change? Be honest about what could have been better. Maybe the scope could have been narrower, or testing should have included another scenario. This isn't about blame – it's about learning for next time.

Document these retrospective notes on your project wiki page for future reference. They're gold for planning the next agent or iteration.

Next, consider how to apply these learnings:

Can you extend the current agent to increase its value? For example, after 90 days you might find users want the agent to handle a slightly broader task.

You could plan a v2.0 where the agent covers more ground (with new guardrails as needed).

Is it time to introduce a second pattern? Perhaps your first agent was a Presenter; a logical next step might be building a Companion agent that provides a chat interface for the same data, or an Action agent that executes recommendations from the Presenter. Use the credibility from your first success to venture into another pattern with confidence.

Think about multi-agent swarms. This means agents working together. For instance, your Presenter agent could feed insights to a Supervisor agent that routes approvals to managers, or a Companion agent could gather input then invoke an Action agent to do the heavy lifting. Designing a swarm can amplify impact, but it requires careful coordination (and likely is a Chapter 18 topic!). For now, just note if your organization has appetite for more agents and whether they could collaborate.

Don't forget to celebrate and share success – it's crucial for momentum. By now, you likely have metrics or stories that show the agent's value. Spread the word:

- Update that internal wiki page with final results and a short narrative of the project. Make it a mini case study that others in the company can read.
- Host a lunch-and-learn session or a demo day for other teams. Showing a live demo of the agent solving a real problem (perhaps replaying a before-and-after scenario) can inspire other departments to think of use cases.
- Create a short video demo (even an informal screen recording with voiceover). This is handy for executives or teams in other regions who couldn't attend the live demo. It also serves as documentation for onboarding new team members or briefing any new stakeholder.

While the project's fresh in memory, also formalize the agent's existence in your systems. Now is a great time to start (or update) your Agent Registry. If your company doesn't have one, an Agent Registry is essentially a catalog of all AI agents in production – something your team will thank you for as the number grows. Add an entry for your agent with key info: Name, Pattern, Owner, Description, Business Outcome, Status (live/pilot), and links to documentation. Not only does this help govern the agent (who owns it, what it's allowed to do, etc.), it also makes it easier for others to discover and reuse components. For example, six months from now, another team might want a similar agent – if they see yours in the registry, they can reach out to you instead of starting from scratch.

In essence, Day 90 is not an ending but a transition. You move from "project mode" to "operational mode" for your agent. The agent should now have a clear home (an owner who will maintain it, a slot in the weekly metrics review perhaps, and a place in user workflows). Your job shifts to monitoring and continuous improvement for this agent, and championing the next agent initiative.

Take a moment to appreciate how far you've come in 90 days – from zero to a functioning AI teammate. Reflect, reuse what you've built (maybe that Apex class or Flow can serve as a template for the next agent), and then repeat the process with even more ambition. In the next chapter, we'll look at how to scale this single-agent success into a portfolio of agents, ensuring your organization continues to benefit from the Agentforce revolution.

SUMMARY

In this chapter, we walked through the journey of launching your first Agentforce agent from scratch in 90 days. You saw how to choose a manageable first pattern, define a tight MVP scope, rally the right stakeholders, and execute in phased sprints. By using Salesforce's native tools (Agent Builder, Flow, Apex, etc.), you built and deployed a real AI agent safely and observed it in action. We discussed setting up telemetry and feedback loops to continuously learn and improve. Most importantly, you proved that starting from zero is feasible – your small win now stands as a foundation for broader AI adoption.

Your first agent is only the beginning. With one success under your belt, you can confidently reuse your patterns and lessons for future projects. As we move to Chapter 17, we'll shift focus from a single agent to the bigger picture: scaling up to a whole portfolio of agents. You'll learn how to govern multiple agents, ensure consistency across them, and measure their collective impact on your organization. The agent-powered enterprise journey is just getting started – and you're now well-prepared to lead it.

17

MATURING YOUR AGENT PORTFOLIO

Congratulations – you've delivered your first AI agent! Perhaps it's the Presenter agent from the last chapter, a handy "feedback summarizer" that wowed your stakeholders. Now comes the big question: now what? How do you go from one successful agent to an entire ecosystem of them, without chaos? The next phase of your AI journey is not about simply cranking out more agents; it's about cultivating the right agents and doing it intentionally. In this chapter, we'll shift into a progression mindset: moving from a single pilot to a well-governed, scalable portfolio of agents.

This chapter is your guide to operational maturity for AI agents. We'll cover how to transition from a few standalone agents into a coordinated, value-driven portfolio that's governed and observable. Scaling responsibly means putting systems in place: building a registry of all your agents, enforcing naming and documentation standards, reusing components to avoid duplicate work, prioritizing where to invest next, managing each agent's lifecycle, and measuring the business impact of your "digital workforce." In short, growing your portfolio requires more than cloning what worked once – it means establishing standards, reducing redundancy, and treating your agents as reusable products rather than one-off scripts.

Along the way, we'll highlight the Salesforce tools and practices that make this possible. You'll see how to use Salesforce Agent Builder, Invocable Flows and Apex, and custom metadata to classify and manage agents through their lifecycles. We'll look at the Agentforce Command Center for telemetry (monitoring agent performance and usage), and even touch on broader frameworks like the emerging Model Context Protocol (MCP) for connecting your Salesforce agents with external systems. By the end of this chapter, you should have a clear playbook for scaling from that first agent to a thriving ecosystem.

We'll start with understanding what you have – auditing your current agent landscape – and then dive into setting standards and governance. Let's get started with assessing your agent landscape.

AUDITING YOUR AGENT LANDSCAPE

Before you unleash a dozen more agents, it's wise to step back and audit what you have. An audit of your agent landscape gives you a bird's-eye view and prevents unwieldy sprawl. Why start with an audit? Because it helps you:

Prevent sprawl: Catch early if teams are spinning up overlapping agents or too many variants of the same idea.

Spot duplication: Identify if two agents are essentially doing the same thing (perhaps under different names) so you can consolidate efforts.

Identify ownership gaps: Ensure every agent has a clear owner or team responsible for it – no orphaned bots running unmanaged.

The best way to audit is to maintain an Agent Registry – a centralized catalog or custom object that tracks key information about each agent. If you haven't already, build (or adopt) a registry to serve as your single source of truth. Each entry in the registry should capture important attributes such as:

Agent Name: A unique, descriptive name for the agent (we'll discuss naming standards in the next section).

Owner/Team: Who is responsible for the agent's maintenance and success? Every agent should have an owner.

Pattern: The design pattern the agent follows (Presenter, Action, etc.). This provides quick context of its core behavior.

Status: Where the agent is in its lifecycle – for example, Draft, Test/Pilot, Production (Live), or Deprecated. (We'll elaborate on lifecycle stages later.)

Last Used: When the agent was last active or utilized. This could be a timestamp or a simple indication if it's active vs. idle.

Inputs & Outputs: A brief note of what inputs the agent takes and what outputs or actions it produces. This helps others understand its role at a glance.

If you used Agent Builder to create your first agent, some of this information may already exist as metadata. Make it a habit that every new agent goes into the registry from day one. In Salesforce, you might implement the registry as a custom object (e.g. Agent__c) or even leverage the Agent Builder's metadata if it provides a listing of agents. The key is to tag each agent with consistent metadata – pattern, owner, etc. – so that you can query and report on your portfolio easily. For example, Agent Builder could require you to specify a pattern type and business unit when defining a new agent, and you can sync those details into a dashboard.

Beyond just a static catalog, turn your registry into a living dashboard of agent health. Some key metrics to track in your audit include:

Usage frequency: How often is each agent being invoked (daily calls, monthly active users, etc.)? This shows adoption.

Agent-to-agent dependencies: Are some agents calling others? (For example, a Conductor agent orchestrating several Action agents.) Mapping these relationships helps you see clusters and dependencies in your ecosystem.

Manual override or escalation rate: How often does a human need to intervene or approve something the agent does? A high override rate might indicate the agent isn't fully trusted or needs improvement (or that it's doing the right thing by asking humans at appropriate points – context matters).

In practice, you can automate much of this auditing. Salesforce's platform lets you create reports and dashboards off your registry object or metadata. If you tag agents with attributes (like pattern, department, risk level), you can slice and dice the data easily. For instance, you could have a report of all Presenter pattern agents in the Sales department, or find agents that haven't been used in over 30 days (potential retirement candidates). The Agentforce Command Center (more on this later in this chapter) actually provides a unified view of deployed agents, their status, and performance metrics – a great tool to leverage for ongoing audits.

Pro Tip: A good registry doesn't just catalog agents – it sparks smart conversations about them. Use your agent registry to guide portfolio reviews:

Which agents are flourishing and could be scaled up? Which ones overlap and maybe should merge? Which ones show little usage and could be retired or reimagined?

By auditing your landscape first, you set the stage for intentional growth. You've likely already added your Chapter 16 Presenter agent as the first entry in this registry. Now you can see it in context and use it as a benchmark for new additions. With a clear picture of your current agents, let's move on to establishing standards so that every new agent is built and documented consistently.

STANDARDIZING AGENT DEVELOPMENT AND NAMING

As your portfolio grows, consistency is king. Different teams (or even different developers on the same team) might have their own styles, but in an enterprise setting you want agents to feel like a family with a common lineage. This means standardizing how agents are named, built, and documented. Not only does this make your life easier when managing them, it also helps other teams understand and trust agents they didn't personally build.

Naming Conventions: Start with a clear naming scheme for agents. A good convention is to use a prefix that indicates the agent's pattern or role, and a suffix or short description for its specific function or domain. For example:

Pattern Prefix: Use a short code for each pattern type. You might adopt something like ACT- for Action agents, SUP- for Supervisor, CON- for Conductor, PRE- for Presenter, and so on. (If your organization has defined eight core patterns like we introduced earlier, make a little lookup table of prefix codes.)

Descriptive Suffix: Append the agent's primary function or the domain. For instance, an Action agent handling HR onboarding tasks could be named "ACT-HR-Onboard", whereas a Presenter agent summarizing sales call notes might be "PRE-Sales-Notes".

Under this convention, the Presenter agent we built in Chapter 16 might be named "PRE-FeedbackSummary" or similar – immediately conveying its pattern (Presenter) and purpose (summarizing feedback). Consistent naming makes it easier to search your logs and registry; you can tell at a glance what each agent is about.

Development Standards (Flows & Apex): Standardization goes beyond names. It extends into how you structure the agent's logic. Salesforce offers both Flow (low-code) and Apex (pro-code) to implement agent behaviors, and you should leverage both in a standardized way:

Shared Flow Templates: Create reusable Flow templates for common agent patterns. For example, you might have a "Presenter Agent Base Flow" template that includes generic steps like: gather context, call a generative AI (GPT) service, format the output, and handle errors. When building a new Presenter agent, developers can clone this flow template rather than starting from scratch. Similarly, an "Action Agent Template" flow might include steps for validating input, performing an action (like a record update or API call), and logging the result.

Invocable Apex Skeletons: For more complex logic, you might write Apex classes. Define skeleton classes or interfaces for each pattern. For instance, a BaseSupervisorAgent class could enforce methods for evaluation criteria and escalation handling, and automatically log important events. By giving developers a starting point (complete with built-in logging and error handling), you ensure every Supervisor agent has the same robust structure. Even if teams write their own code, if they all extend the same base class or follow the same method patterns, it's easier to maintain and review.

Metadata and Tags: We touched on metadata when building the registry, but it bears repeating as a standard. Whenever you create an agent, fill out its metadata attributes conscientiously. At minimum, tag each agent with:

Pattern (e.g., Action, Presenter, etc.),

Business Domain or department (e.g., HR, Sales, Finance),

Trust Level or risk classification (perhaps a simple High/Medium/Low indicating how sensitive or autonomous it is),

Usage Intent (internal-only, customer-facing, POC vs mission-critical, etc.).

These metadata tags can be implemented via Salesforce's custom metadata types or fields on your Agent object. For example, Agent Builder might allow a "Purpose" field or a "Category" picklist – use those to enforce this info. Consistent metadata makes it possible to enforce governance rules (like "all High Trust agents must go through extra code review" or "show me all Finance domain agents").

Documentation Templates: Don't let documentation be an afterthought. Every agent should have at least a basic README or design doc that follows a standard format. Consider creating a pattern-based README template – a markdown or Confluence template that developers fill in when they create an agent. This template could include sections like:

Overview: A one-liner description of what the agent does.

Pattern: Which pattern it implements (and maybe why that pattern was chosen).

Inputs & Outputs: What it expects, what it produces (almost like an API contract).

Owner: Who to contact about it.

Dependencies: Other systems or agents it relies on, or flows it calls.

Failure Modes: Known edge cases or how it fails (e.g., "if the LLM is unavailable, it falls back to X").

For agents that use GPT or other LLMs, include a section for Prompt Design – documenting the prompt approach, any specific instructions or few-shot examples used. If the agent is part of a multi-agent orchestration, a diagram of dependencies or flow chart can be super helpful (even a simple box-and-arrow diagram showing how data flows through the agent or between agents).

To tie all these standards together, here's a summary in list form of key elements to standardize:

Agent Naming

- **Standard practice:** Prefix agent names with the pattern code and suffix with the function or domain.
- **Tooling or enforcement:** Documented naming conventions and lint checks during code reviews.
- **Example:** ACT-HR-Onboard (Action agent for HR onboarding).

Metadata Tags

- **Standard practice:** Tag each agent with pattern, domain, trust level, and related attributes.
- **Tooling or enforcement:** Agent Builder fields and Custom Metadata types for agent records.
- **Example:** Pattern = Presenter; Domain = Service; Trust = Medium.

Flow Templates

- **Standard practice:** Use standardized base Flow templates per agent pattern.
- **Tooling or enforcement:** Shared Flow library delivered as unmanaged packages or org-level templates.
- **Example:** PresenterTemplateFlow with a predefined LLM invocation structure.

Apex Base Classes

- **Standard practice:** Extend common base classes or interfaces for each agent pattern.
- **Tooling or enforcement:** Shared Apex utility libraries and enforced code review guidelines.
- **Example:** BasePresenterAgent.cls providing common logging and error-handling methods.

Logging and Telemetry

- **Standard practice:** Implement consistent logging for agent start, completion, and error conditions.
- **Tooling or enforcement:** Reusable logging subflows, shared Apex logging classes, and Agentforce Command Center dashboards.
- **Example:** All agents invoke a LogAgentEvent subflow upon completion.

Documentation (README)

- **Standard practice:** Maintain a README for each agent using a standard template.
- **Tooling or enforcement:** Markdown README template and mandatory linkage from the agent registry.
- **Example:** Presenter agent README detailing purpose, inputs, outputs, owner, and sample output.

Prompt Design

- **Standard practice:** Use a consistent prompt style and store prompts in a shared, accessible location.

- **Tooling or enforcement:** Central prompt library implemented via Custom Metadata or a version-controlled repository.
- **Example:** A reusable SummarizationPrompt entry shared across all agents that perform text summarization.

By adhering to standards like the above, your agents will be much easier to manage in the long run. New team members can quickly get up to speed because everything looks familiar. Furthermore, if you ever use open frameworks like LangChain or Microsoft's AutoGen outside of Salesforce, you'll find similar principles apply – those ecosystems benefit from naming conventions and modular design too. The difference with Agentforce is that you have Salesforce's platform to help enforce the standards (through metadata, templates, and tooling) rather than relying on developers to remember everything.

Finally, remember that consistency enables trust. When business users interact with different agents and they all behave predictably (in naming, responses, logs, etc.), it reinforces confidence that the AI system is under control. Now that we have our standards defined, let's talk about one of the biggest benefits of an intentional approach: reusability and modularity.

REUSE, MODULARITY, AND REFACTORING

One agent in isolation can be built any which way. But as soon as you have multiple agents, you'll discover common pieces that shouldn't be reinvented each time. A mature agent portfolio maximizes reuse and modular design – this makes development faster and ensures consistency in behavior. In this section, we'll cover how to avoid duplication by refactoring common logic, and how to set up a culture (and technical framework) of reuse.

Avoiding Duplication: In the early days, two teams might unknowingly build very similar agents or features. For example, imagine you have one agent that summarizes customer feedback (our Presenter from Chapter 16) and another agent that summarizes IT support tickets. Both might be using an LLM to summarize text – do they each need to have their own prompt and flow for summarization? Probably not. Identify such overlaps and centralize shared logic. Salesforce Flow and Apex are great for this:

If you have a piece of logic that could be used by multiple agents, put it in a Subflow or an Invocable Apex method. Then, each agent calls that subflow instead of duplicating the logic. For instance, a "Summarize Text" subflow could take any text input and return a summary via GPT. Your Presenter agents across departments can all invoke this subflow. That way, if you improve the summarization logic (say, add a new prompt or adjust for tone), it benefits all agents using it. Similarly, if multiple agents need to, say, parse an email or fetch a customer record, those can be shared flows or Apex utilities rather than repeated code in each agent's implementation.

Shared Prompt Libraries: For agents leveraging LLMs, prompts and example phrases are essentially code. Duplicating a prompt across many agents leads to inconsistency and extra maintenance work. Instead, consider maintaining a prompt library – perhaps as custom metadata or a dataset – where you store well-crafted prompts for common tasks. Agents can reference these. If the prompt needs tuning, you update it in one place. For example, the prompt for "Provide a one-paragraph summary of text X" can be a named prompt in the library. Your Presenter agent uses it, and so can any future agent that summarizes anything.

Modularize Your Flows: As your portfolio matures, you might have some older, monolithic flows that try to do everything. It's worth refactoring them into modules:

Break out subflows for distinct tasks (data gathering, decision making, output formatting). This aligns with the principle of separating data-gathering from decision-making. For example, one subflow strictly handles "Retrieve all relevant data needed for the agent's decision" (queries, API calls, etc.), and another subflow or step handles "Apply AI or business rules to make a decision or generate output." Decoupling these means you could reuse the data retrieval part for other agents or swap out the decision logic without touching how data is fetched.

If you have legacy agents not built with this modular approach, gradually convert pieces of them into invocable components. Salesforce allows creating invocable methods in Apex and invoking one flow from another. Use these features to create a library of callable components. In effect, you start treating parts of agents like LEGO blocks that can be assembled for new agents.

Create Reference Agents (Templates): Earlier we discussed having Flow templates and base classes for patterns. Take that a step further by designating one or two agents as the "gold standard" for each pattern. For example, the Presenter agent you built in Chapter 16 can now serve as a reference implementation for the Presenter pattern. Ensure that this reference agent is well-documented and peer-reviewed. New teams who need a Presenter-type agent can look at it as a starting point or even clone its project as a template.

This accelerates development and propagates best practices organically – instead of everyone reinventing the wheel, they improve upon an existing, proven design. Over time, try to have at least one exemplary agent per pattern in your registry, with notes in its README like "This is our recommended example of a Supervisor agent handling approval workflows," etc.

AUTOMATE REUSE DETECTION

Humans don't catch all duplication, so put some automation in place.

Use static code analysis tools to scan your Apex (or even prompt text) for similarities. If two classes or flows have a lot of overlap, that's a smell that they could be refactored into a common component. There are code analysis tools that can integrate into your CI pipeline to flag duplicate code blocks.

Leverage metadata reports to spot patterns. For example, if your agent registry has a field for "purpose" or "keywords," run a report to see if multiple agents have similar descriptions. If you find three agents all "summarizing customer input," maybe they are ripe for consolidation or at least sharing a core module. Another trick: use your Salesforce org's dependency API or metadata dictionary to find if the same subflow or Apex is referenced by many agents; if not, perhaps it should be!

Real-world Example: Let's say after Chapter 16, your successful Feedback Summarizer Presenter agent gets attention from other departments. The Support team wants a similar agent to summarize case notes, and Marketing wants one to condense campaign feedback. Instead of building each from scratch, you can reuse the core summarization prompt and flow from your original Presenter agent. You'd simply adjust the inputs (case notes vs. campaign data) and outputs (maybe format the summary slightly differently), but the heavy lifting (LLM prompt, summary generation flow) is a shared component. You might even package the summarization logic as a mini "Summarizer Module" that is maintained centrally. This way, improvements made for one use case immediately benefit all the others.

By enforcing reuse and modular design, you reduce maintenance load (fix one module, update everyone) and improve consistency (all summaries have a similar tone and quality, for example). It's the classic software engineering wisdom applied to AI agents: Don't Repeat Yourself (DRY principle). Plus, your org will thank you when onboarding new developers – it's much easier to grok 10 modules reused by 50 agents than 50 completely unique agents with no common parts.

PRIORITIZING AGENT INVESTMENT

With multiple agents in play, you'll face decisions on where to focus your time and resources. Not all agents are equal in value, and not every cool idea should be built next. A mature approach involves prioritizing which agents (or patterns) to invest in for development, enhancement, or scaling. This is akin to product portfolio management – treating each agent as a product with a ROI to consider.

Score Agents for Value: One useful practice is to come up with a simple scoring system to evaluate each agent's value and potential. Consider factors like:

Adoption: How widely is the agent used? (e.g., number of users or frequency of use). An agent used 100 times a day has more immediate impact than one used 5 times a month.

Impact: How much business value does each successful use of the agent deliver? Does it save time, reduce errors, increase customer satisfaction, generate revenue? Some agents might be used infrequently but when they do run, they save hours of work – that's high impact per use.

Risk Reduction: Does the agent mitigate risks or enforce compliance? For example, an agent that catches potential data privacy violations might prevent major issues – that's a kind of value that isn't direct revenue but extremely important.

Time Savings: Closely related to impact, but you might explicitly estimate how many human hours the agent saves. E.g., "This agent saves 10 minutes per incident, and it handled 300 incidents last month, so ~50 hours saved."

You can create a weighted score out of these to rank agents. Maybe adoption and impact are weighted higher because you care about widely-used, high-value agents first. This scoring helps highlight your "star" agents versus the low performers.

Use Business KPIs: Tie your agent's performance to actual business Key Performance Indicators. This ensures you're not valuing an agent in a vacuum but in context of company goals. For example:

If an agent contributes to SLA compliance (e.g., it auto-triages cases so that response times improve), track the SLA metrics. How much did that improve after the agent was introduced?

If an agent helps sales close deals faster (maybe by automating proposal generation), link it to revenue acceleration or pipeline metrics.

For a compliance-checking agent, measure compliance accuracy or reduction in compliance review time.

By speaking the language of KPIs, you make it easier for executives to see the value of investing in agents. It also helps in prioritization: the agents tied to strategic KPIs likely deserve more love (or faster scaling) than ones with only nice-to-have benefits.

Work with Product Owners: One effective way to manage an agent portfolio is to assign "product owners" or business sponsors to significant agents or agent domains. This person treats the agent as a mini-product – defining its roadmap, advocating for improvements, and measuring its success. For example, your sales department's VP might be the product owner for all sales-related agents, ensuring they align with sales strategy. With owners in place, you can convene a meeting (quarterly, say) to decide which agent gets an upgrade, which new capability to build next, etc., just like feature planning for software.

Encourage evolving agents over quarters, not weeks. In other words, plan out how an agent could grow in the next 3, 6, 12 months. Perhaps your Presenter agent's Q1 goal is to support 2 new languages, Q2 goal is to integrate a sentiment analysis in the summary, etc. This mindset avoids the trap of "fire-and-forget" agents that get launched and never improved. Instead, each important agent has a roadmap and vision for improvement.

Track Pattern Coverage: Another aspect of portfolio maturity is examining which patterns you have deployed and which you haven't. Are there obvious gaps where a certain pattern could add value? For instance, maybe you have lots of Presenter and Action agents but no Sentinel agents (which might monitor and alert on anomalies). That could be an area to explore if your business has monitoring needs. Conversely, check for overuse of certain patterns – sometimes teams default to one pattern for everything (say, using a Presenter agent to do things that really should be an Action or Conductor). If one pattern is overused, it might mean there's an unmet need for more complex coordination (maybe you need a Conductor to orchestrate those many Presenter outputs), or it could indicate a lack of knowledge about other patterns in the org.

A helpful visualization is an Agent Portfolio Quadrant chart, mapping each agent on axes of Value (impact) vs Adoption (usage). This resembles a classic product portfolio matrix:

High Value & High Adoption agents are your All-Stars – these deliver big time and are widely embraced. They deserve protection and continuous investment, and possibly serve as models for further expansion.

High Value but Low Adoption agents are Hidden Gems – they could deliver a lot, but maybe not enough people use them yet. Perhaps they need more user training or broader rollout. Prioritize marketing these agents internally or figuring out why adoption is low (maybe they're hard to access – a UI issue?).

Low Value but High Adoption agents might be Workhorses or possibly Overhyped – people use them a lot, but they aren't giving as much benefit as you hoped. These might need improvements to boost their effectiveness, or you may discover that users use it because it's there, but it's not solving the core pain (opportunity to pivot or enhance).

Low Value & Low Adoption agents are Underperformers – likely candidates for deprecation or major overhaul. They're not providing much and few would miss them if they're gone (but do verify why – it might be salvageable with tweaks).

By plotting agents this way, you can visually communicate where to focus: ideally move everything to high adoption & high value, but reality is you'll have a mix. The goal is to maximize ROI on your agent development efforts by focusing on the agents (or patterns) that promise the biggest return for the business.

In summary, treat your portfolio of agents like a portfolio of products. Use data and business insight to drive decisions on scaling up, improving, or retiring agents. This ensures that as you grow from 1 to 10 to 100 agents, you're not just doing AI for AI's sake – you're constantly aligning with business value.

MANAGING AGENT LIFECYCLE AND DEPRECATION

Agents are not "set and forget." Just like any software product, they go through a lifecycle from idea to maturity, and eventually some will be retired or replaced. Managing this lifecycle deliberately will save you headaches and ensure users are never caught off guard by changes. Let's break down typical lifecycle stages and how to govern them, as well as how to handle deprecation gracefully.

Lifecycle Stages: We suggest defining clear stages for an agent's life. For example:

Draft: The idea or design stage. The agent is not functional yet – perhaps someone is writing a design doc or prototype.

Pilot/Test: The agent is built and being tested, maybe with a limited set of users or in a sandbox environment. It's not broadly released, but it's functional and undergoing refinement.

Production (Live): The agent is fully released to its intended audience and is considered "live" and supported. It should have monitoring and a support plan.

Rework (Revision): This is a cyclic stage – an agent in production might enter a "rework" state if it's pulled back for major updates or improvements. During rework, you might label it differently or even temporarily disable it if needed.

Deprecated: The agent is marked to be sunset. It's no longer recommended for use, perhaps only accessible to certain users or behind a feature flag. Deprecated means a retirement is planned, but it might still be available in read-only or limited capacity.

Retired: The agent is fully shut down or removed from active use.

In Salesforce, you can capture this stage in the agent's metadata (e.g., a field Lifecycle_Status__c with values Draft/Pilot/Production/Deprecated/Retired). This status should also be visible to users if they interact with the agent (for instance, if something is deprecated, perhaps the agent's UI or response can indicate "this agent is being phased out" or similar).

Governance Checkpoints:

Define what needs to happen at each stage.

Draft: At least a basic design or charter should be written. Maybe a sponsor approves the idea. This prevents random half-baked agents from being built without anyone's knowledge.

Pilot: Before moving to pilot, you might require that certain tests are in place or certain guardrails are configured. Maybe the agent needs a security review or a privacy check if it uses sensitive data.

Production: To go live, there should be a deployment checklist: e.g., logging is enabled, telemetry is connected to Command Center, a feedback mechanism is in place, documentation is completed, and the support team knows about it. Essentially, treat it like a mini-go-live for a new app.

Rework: If an agent triggers many errors or user complaints (we'll talk triggers in a second), it might go into rework. In rework, ensure you communicate to stakeholders that "hey, we're doing a V2 of this agent, it might be unstable or temporarily limited." Use feature flags or a "paused" status if needed to hold off usage while reworking (Salesforce Agent Builder might allow marking an agent inactive without deleting it – if not, you can simulate this by removing its triggers or entry points).

Deprecated/Retired: Have a sunset protocol. This typically includes: archiving any data or metadata (so you keep a record of what it was for compliance or historical reasons), updating the registry/status to deprecated, removing the agent from any active orchestrations or UI menus so new users don't start using it, and perhaps leaving a stub that informs anyone who somehow invokes it that it's no longer available. Finally, after a period in deprecated state, fully retire (delete or disable) the agent.

Triggers for Rework or Deprecation

Keep an eye on signals that an agent needs major changes or should be retired.

If an agent has a high error rate (frequent failures in logs) or a high manual override rate (say a Supervisor agent is constantly flagging output for human review, or users frequently click "undo" on the agent's actions), it might indicate the agent's logic isn't keeping up with reality. It may need a redesign or more training data.

Downstream agent failure: In a multi-agent chain, if one agent's outputs consistently cause another agent to stumble, you may need to rework that problematic agent. For example, if a Curator agent is sending bad data to a Presenter agent, maybe the Curator needs improvement.

UX issues via feedback: If you have feedback channels (user surveys, thumbs-down reactions, etc.) and an agent consistently scores low or gets complaints like "it's not helpful" or "it's annoying," that's a sign to either iterate or kill it if it's not salvageable.

On the flip side, an agent might be a candidate for deprecation if the business process changed (perhaps that task is no longer needed or has been absorbed by another agent), or if a new, better agent comes along to replace it.

Dependency Mapping: Before you turn an agent off, make sure you know what other processes or agents depend on it. This is where your registry and documentation saves the day: if Agent A is listed as feeding Agent B, and you want to retire Agent A, you must update Agent B to either handle that or also retire B if it's no longer needed. Use Salesforce tools to trace dependencies: for instance, if Agent A was invoked by a Flow or called via Apex, search your org's metadata (using the Salesforce CLI or Developer Console search) to find references. Also, update any orchestration flows (like a Conductor's steps) to remove or replace the retiring agent. Skipping this step can cause broken processes in production – akin to removing a microservice without telling the others.

When done properly, deprecation doesn't have to be painful. Users should be informed in advance ("this agent will be retired next month, please use the new XYZ agent or manual process Y"). And technically, the removal should be surgical because you prepared for it.

Pro Tip: Keep humans in the loop for agent lifecycle changes. If you're deprecating or updating an agent that people rely on, use a Companion-style agent or notification to inform users proactively. For example, when a user opens the CRM next week, a little chatbot (Companion agent) could pop up: "We've upgraded your Coach agent with new capabilities!" or "The old Contract Analyzer agent is being phased out – meet its successor, the Contract Guru." This ensures that as your ecosystem evolves, your users evolve with it and don't feel blindsided.

In summary, managing lifecycle is about discipline and communication. By formalizing stages and checklists, you avoid wild-west deployments. By monitoring for issues, you catch problems early and either fix or retire agents that aren't delivering. And by gracefully handling deprecations, you maintain user trust even as you clean up the portfolio.

AGENT PORTFOLIO TELEMETRY AND VALUE TRACKING

You can't improve what you don't measure. As your agent portfolio matures, telemetry (monitoring data) and value tracking become your best friends. Salesforce's Agentforce Command Center is built for this purpose – giving you a centralized view of agent performance – but even outside of Command Center, you should set up dashboards to understand how your agents are doing and how much value they're providing.

First, let's talk metrics. Out-of-the-box, you'll want to collect:

Agent Call Frequency: How often each agent is invoked in a given period (daily, weekly, etc.). This shows usage trends and helps spot if an agent suddenly stops being used (which could indicate an incident or that users found a workaround).

Error Rates/Trends: Track how often agents encounter errors or exceptions. Is the error rate going up over time for some agent? That warrants investigation. Command Center can show spikes in errors for each agent, allowing you to quickly pinpoint troublemakers.

Success Confirmation Rate: For agents that have a notion of success/failure or user confirmation (like an Action agent might have a success vs. fallback outcome, or a Presenter agent might have a thumbs-up/thumbs-down from users), measure the percentage of successful or approved outcomes. A low success rate might mean the agent often doesn't complete its job or users are unhappy with the result.

In Agentforce Command Center, you can likely configure KPIs and thresholds for these metrics. For example, an alert if an agent's error rate exceeds 5% in a day, or if an agent hasn't been used at all in 30 days.

Agentforce Command Center provides a unified portfolio dashboard for your AI agents. In this example, you can see at a glance the number of active agents and underperforming agents, as well as key metrics like total sessions and overall consumption. A table lists each agent along with its owner, type (pattern), source, number of sessions, average latency, and a quality score. Dashboards like this help both business and IT teams quickly identify which agents are excelling and which may need attention.

Beyond raw performance metrics, set up value dashboards that translate agent activity into business impact:

Estimated Time Saved: You might create a calculation for each agent (or pattern) estimating how much time it saves per use. Then aggregate that over a month. For instance, "Agent X handled 500 requests this month. If each would've taken a human 5 minutes, that's ~2500 minutes (~42 hours) saved." Present this in a dashboard for leadership to demonstrate tangible benefits.

Human Approval/Intervention Rates: If you have Supervisor agents or any human-in-the-loop processes, track how often humans approve vs reject or override. A high approval rate means the agent is doing well on its own; a low one means humans frequently override (which might reduce the effective value or indicate trust issues).

Impact by Department: Segment usage and outcomes by department or user role. Maybe your agents are heavily used in Sales but not in Marketing – indicating where the value is currently realized and where there's opportunity to expand. Or if some department has unusually higher error rates, perhaps their use cases are more complex – insight for training or improvement.

Feedback Integration: Qualitative feedback is as important as quantitative metrics. Leverage Salesforce's channels for gathering feedback on agents:

Use Slack or chat emoji reactions: If your agent interacts via Slack or Teams, encourage users to react with a 👍 or 👎 emoji to indicate satisfaction. With a bit of integration, you can capture those reactions as feedback signals.

For Presenter agents that show information in the UI, consider adding an inline prompt like "Was this helpful? [Yes/No]" or a 5-star rating on the output. This immediate feedback can be logged.

Create a Feedback__c custom object (or use an existing survey object) to store agent feedback. Every time a user gives a thumbs-down or submits a comment, log it with agent ID, user, timestamp, and context. Over time you can report on this: e.g., see feedback trends, common pain points, etc. You can even integrate this with Command Center, so that for each agent you can drill into qualitative feedback entries.

Trend Alerts: Set up automated alerts for notable trends. For example:

If a Supervisor agent (which intervenes when something might be wrong) suddenly starts firing a lot more interventions than usual, that could mean the underlying agent it's watching has degraded or something in the input data changed. This should trigger an investigation.

A drop-off in interaction with an agent might mean users lost interest or trust. If an agent usage was steadily 100 sessions a week and suddenly it's down to 10, either something broke or users decided it's not useful. Either way, you'd want to know quickly. Command Center or even a simple scheduled report can catch these drops.

Consider integrating with external monitoring or chat ops: Salesforce's telemetry can often be hooked into systems like OpenTelemetry (OTel) or other APM tools. Some organizations pipe agent metrics into Slack channels or pager alerts for the dev team ("Agent X's error rate > 10% today"). The sooner you know about an issue, the faster you can react, which is critical as you scale to many agents.

Dashboards for Different Audiences: It often makes sense to have at least two flavors of dashboards: one for business/executive stakeholders and one for the technical/dev team.

An Executive Dashboard might highlight things like total hours saved this quarter, number of agent-assisted transactions, top 5 agents by value delivered, and overall adoption rates. It should tell the story of how agents are contributing to business outcomes (e.g., "Customer support AI agents handled 30% of Tier-1 issues, saving $X in support costs").

A Developer/Operations Dashboard will be more granular: errors by agent, API usage, performance (latency) stats, maybe a timeline of deployments or changes vs. error spikes (to correlate issues with new releases). This helps the team keep the system healthy and plan improvements.

Salesforce's Agentforce Command Center likely allows you to create custom views or use filters so each role sees what they need. If not, standard Salesforce dashboards or CRM Analytics (Tableau CRM) can be used to mash up the data from the agent registry, feedback objects, and usage logs.

In short, telemetry and value tracking turn your anecdotal agent success into quantifiable data. They illuminate what's working and what's not. As you scale up, this visibility ensures you remain data-driven in evolving your agent portfolio (and it arms you with evidence to justify further investment in AI projects).

GOVERNANCE AND COLLABORATION AT SCALE

When you have one or two agents, governance can be informal (a couple of developers coordinating). But as you scale to dozens of agents spanning multiple teams and business functions, you need formal governance and collaboration structures. This is about putting the right people and processes in place so that your agent ecosystem grows in a controlled, strategic manner – with cross-functional buy-in and oversight.

Portfolio Review Council: It's a good idea to establish a governing body for AI agents – think of it like an extension of an architecture review board specifically for agents. This council would periodically review the portfolio, approve new agent proposals, and enforce standards. Who should be on it? Aim for a mix of technical and business roles, for example:

Pattern Architect: An expert in agent design patterns (possibly you, after reading this book!) who ensures new agents follow known patterns or that any new pattern is well-justified. This person looks at the structural soundness and reusability of agent designs.

Product Owner / Business Sponsor: A representative from the business side (could rotate depending on which department's agents are being discussed) who focuses on business value and alignment with goals. They ensure the agent roadmap ties back to real needs.

AI Ethicist or Risk Officer: Someone focusing on ethical implications, fairness, compliance. They will raise flags if a proposed agent might, for example, introduce bias, violate privacy, or operate without necessary human oversight.

Lead Developer / AI Engineer: A technical lead who knows the nuts and bolts of implementation. They assess feasibility, complexity, and resource needs, and ensure consistency with the engineering practices.

This "AI agent council" should meet regularly (maybe monthly or bi-monthly) or as needed when big decisions arise. They don't necessarily micromanage every little change, but they set guardrails and approve significant changes (like releasing a high-impact agent or deprecating one that has many users).

Agent Intake Process: Just as companies have change management or new product intake processes, do the same for new agents. Rather than someone coding an agent over a weekend and deploying it unchecked, institute an intake workflow:

Idea Submission: A team or individual documents a new agent idea (what problem it solves, which pattern it might use, expected benefit). This could be a simple form or one-page proposal.

Council Review: The portfolio council (or a subset of it) reviews the idea. Is it aligned with strategy? Does it duplicate an existing capability? Is the proposed pattern appropriate? They might ask for adjustments or suggest collaborating with another team if overlap is detected.

Pattern Fit & Design: If approved to explore, ensure the idea is mapped to the right pattern(s). At this stage, an architect might help refine the design – e.g., "This sounds like a Conductor agent use case; make sure to include a Supervisor for the risky step," etc. Essentially, enforce that the design follows the playbook patterns or consciously deviates for a reason.

Prototype/Pilot: The team builds a prototype or pilot. Set a guideline that even at prototype stage, they should use the standard tools (Agent Builder, etc.) and follow naming conventions, so the prototype doesn't become a rogue agent. Once built, perhaps the council or a review team does a quick audit before it goes into any real use.

Go/No-Go Decision: After the prototype shows results, the council (plus relevant stakeholders) give the green light to fully launch, maybe move to production stage, or they might pivot or cancel the effort if the pilot showed it's not worthwhile.

This may sound heavyweight, but it can be scaled appropriately. For trivial agents or ones within a single team's domain, the process can be quick. The point is to avoid ungoverned agents popping up without anyone considering the broader implications.

Change Control: Governance isn't just about new agents; it's also about changes to existing ones. As agents become critical, treat changes with the same rigor as you do for production applications:

Keep an Agent Version in your registry or metadata. Every major update (new feature, new model, significant prompt change) increments a version. This helps in tracking what version of the agent logic is running and correlating any changes with performance shifts.

Require deployment sign-offs for high-impact agents. For example, any change to an agent that deals with customer data might need sign-off from the product owner and maybe the risk officer.

Regression testing: Ideally, you have some automated tests for agents. This is tricky with AI, but you can have deterministic parts tested (e.g., does the flow run through under normal conditions, does it handle a null input gracefully, etc.). If you maintain a library of transcripts or scenarios, you could even test that an agent's responses haven't drifted undesirably after a change (within the stochastic nature of AI). Tools to snapshot and compare AI outputs are evolving. At minimum, when you change something, run the agent through a battery of known test cases (maybe using stored conversations or logs) to ensure nothing major broke.

If you integrate Agentforce with CI/CD, treat agent flows, prompts, and Apex like code – run unit tests, and perhaps use Salesforce DX to validate changes in a testing org before production.

Cross-Functional Working Groups: Encourage ongoing collaboration via specialized groups:

A Shared Prompt Library working group could be responsible for curating and reviewing prompts used by various agents. They can establish guidelines for prompt style (tone, persona, etc.) to keep things consistent. This group might meet to discuss what prompts have been effective and share improvements (this is especially useful as LLMs evolve; a new technique might improve all agents' prompts).

Cross-domain Pattern Reuse Sessions: Set up periodic knowledge-sharing sessions where teams from different business domains show off their agents and how they implemented patterns. For example, the HR team demonstrates their new Supervisor agent for leave approval, the Finance team shows an Action agent for invoice processing. In these sessions, people can identify overlaps or opportunities to reuse something. Often, two departments might realize they can collaborate (e.g., the logic the Finance team uses to parse an invoice could be reused by Procurement's agent that parses purchase orders).

UX Consistency Squads: This is more on the design side – ensure the user experience across agents is unified. If some agents live in Slack, some in Salesforce UI, and some email users, is there a consistent tone or interaction style? A UX group can create guidelines for how agents present themselves (maybe standardizing on first person vs third person voice, how they acknowledge errors, etc.). They might also develop reusable UI components, like a common chat window or feedback widget, that all Presenter or Companion agents use.

All these collaboration efforts help maintain a cohesive ecosystem rather than a collection of siloed bots. It also fosters a community of practice – developers and designers working on AI agents can learn from each other regularly, rather than reinventing the wheel in isolation.

Pro Tip: Don't treat your agents like ad-hoc scripts or one-off utilities. Treat them as software products with clear owners, metrics, and an evolution path. Assigning ownership and following governance processes may feel bureaucratic, but it ensures each agent is cared for throughout its life. In the long run, this yields higher quality, safer, and more impactful AI solutions across your organization.

By instituting governance and encouraging cross-team collaboration, you create a healthy environment for your agent portfolio to grow. Ideas get vetted, best practices spread, and risks are caught early by diverse perspectives. Your AI initiative becomes a coordinated program, not a scatter of disconnected experiments.

SUMMARY

In this chapter, we shifted from zeroing in on a single agent to orchestrating an entire portfolio of AI agents as a strategic asset. You learned how to audit your agent landscape to avoid sprawl and create an agent registry that acts as the system of record for all agents. We established naming conventions and development standards so that every agent is built and documented in a consistent, professional manner. We discussed techniques to enforce reuse and modularity, ensuring that common logic, prompts, and components are shared rather than duplicated – with our Chapter 16 Presenter agent now serving as a template for others to follow.

We also dove into how to prioritize investments across your agents by looking at usage and business value, so you focus your energy where it counts. We outlined the governance of an agent's lifecycle, from inception to deprecation, including how to handle upgrades and retirements in a way that maintains trust and continuity. With Salesforce's Command Center and telemetry tools, you can monitor agent performance in real time, track the value they deliver, and integrate feedback loops for continuous improvement. Finally, we emphasized the importance of governance at scale – from setting up a cross-functional council to manage agent development, to implementing intake processes, change control, and collaborative working groups that promote reuse and consistency across the board.

With these practices, your agent portfolio becomes more than a collection of bots – it becomes a well-managed platform for intelligent work, delivering reliable value and evolving in tandem with your business needs. You're not just deploying AI agents; you're cultivating a sustainable agent-powered ecosystem within your organization.

In Chapter 18, we'll zoom into one particular pattern's evolution. We'll explore how Companion agents can grow from simple helpers into daily work partners, shaping a user's day-to-day experience. We'll see how trust and personalization deepen as Companion agents progress from offering suggestions, to taking actions, to handling delegated tasks autonomously – all within the guardrails and governance we've established. It's a fitting capstone on how an agent portfolio not only grows wider (more agents) but also deeper in capability and relationship with users. Get ready to see what a truly integrated AI Companion can do as it matures alongside its human colleagues.

18

GROWING COMPANION AGENTS INTO DAILY WORK PARTNERS

Every successful AI agent deployment starts small. In Chapter 16, we took an MVP agent from zero to one—delivering a focused win in a controlled scenario. But that was just the beginning. Many agent types (Sentinels, Supervisors, Actions, etc.) deliver value in discrete moments or specialized tasks. Companion agents aim for something more enduring: becoming part of a user's daily rhythm. Rather than handling one-off requests or narrow processes, a mature Companion agent works alongside its user continuously, growing from a helpful assistant into a trusted advisor and eventually an empowered proxy acting on the user's behalf. It's the difference between an occasional helper and an AI colleague you rely on every day.

Imagine logging into Salesforce each morning and being greeted by an agent that already knows your priorities. Early on, it might simply suggest helpful actions—"Here are 3 follow-ups you might want to send" or "Need a quick summary of yesterday's meeting?" Over time, as it learns your preferences, it can execute tasks for you—scheduling a meeting when it sees a gap on your calendar, or updating a record after noticing you took an action elsewhere. Eventually, a truly mature Companion can be delegated certain responsibilities entirely—it operates autonomously within guardrails, handling routine decisions so you can focus on what matters. We can think of this evolution as a maturity curve with three phases:

Phase 1: Suggestion – the agent surfaces helpful nudges or shortcuts for the user.

Phase 2: Execution – the agent carries out tasks on the user's behalf, initially requiring confirmation or based on learned preferences.

Phase 3: Delegation – the agent acts independently within defined guardrails, essentially serving as the user's proxy in certain domains.

This chapter explores how to deliberately build an agent through those phases. The goal isn't just to add more features for the sake of it. It's about earning trust, delivering consistent value, and gradually adapting the agent's behavior to each user's style, needs, and work environment. A Companion that tries to do too much too soon can backfire—users won't hand over the keys to their workday unless the agent proves itself trustworthy and useful at each step. Thus, growing a Companion agent is as much about relationship-building as it is about technology: start with simple help, gain confidence, then step up to heavier automation once you've proven the agent's reliability.

It's important to recognize that while Companion agents often appear simple on the surface (maybe they just greet you, remind you of things, or summarize information), the design challenge behind the scenes is anything but trivial. To truly integrate into a person's daily workflow, a Companion agent needs robust memory, preference tracking, cross-platform awareness, and safety-first execution of actions. For example, remembering a user's preferred communication style (formal vs. casual tone) or knowing which channel to reach them on (Slack vs. email vs. Salesforce UI) at a given moment requires storing and recalling context. The agent must coordinate across surfaces: it might start an interaction in Slack, continue on a Salesforce record page, and finish by sending a mobile notification. And at all times, it must operate with guardrails—never doing anything risky or irreversible without proper checks or approvals. The technical architecture to support this involves a mix of Salesforce-native tools and AI capabilities working in concert.

Fortunately, Salesforce's Agentforce platform is built to handle these exact challenges. We have an entire toolbox at our disposal to craft a personalized, controllable Companion agent. Agent Builder provides a low-code way to define the agent's core parameters and trigger points (for instance, what events or user commands should invoke the Companion). Flows give us a declarative logic canvas to manage the agent's decision trees and interactions step by step, while Invocable Apex lets us extend that logic with custom code for complex or sensitive operations. We can use Lightning Web Components (LWC) to create rich UI elements – perhaps an embedded assistant panel or a floating prompt – ensuring the agent's presence is intuitive on Salesforce pages or in Slack. Custom Metadata and objects allow us to store user preferences, usage statistics, and other configuration data outside of hard-coded logic, so the agent can be tailored and updated without code changes. And of course, GPT-powered services (like Einstein GPT or other LLM integrations) can be woven in where natural language understanding or generation is needed – for example, to interpret a free-form request or to draft a conversational response with the right tone. The combination of these tools allows for highly controlled, user-tailored logic. In other words, we can give our Companion agent a "brain" that's smart enough to be helpful, but also transparent and governable enough that we always know what it's doing and why.

Over the next sections, we'll design and implement a fully matured Companion agent that evolves through suggestion, execution, and delegation. We'll anchor this in real work scenarios to keep things practical – imagine a sales rep's daily assistant, or a project manager's AI aide – and we'll highlight how personalization, memory, escalation paths, and safety measures are built at each stage of the agent's growth. By the end of this chapter, you should have a clear blueprint for turning a modest MVP agent into a daily work partner that users might one day describe as "part of the team."

In the next section, we start with the foundations: the overall architecture of a Companion agent and how to structure it from day one to support growth. We'll lay out the lifecycle (how the agent recognizes context, personalizes its behavior, assists the user, and learns or escalates when needed) and the Salesforce components that make it all possible. This architecture is the backbone that will let our agent mature gracefully from suggestions to autonomy.

THE ARCHITECTURE OF A COMPANION AGENT

Growing a Companion agent begins with a solid architectural foundation. Before diving into features, we need to define how the agent operates in a consistent, extensible way. A mature Companion will cycle through a core lifecycle of steps as it interacts with the user and the environment. One useful model for this lifecycle is: Recognize → Personalize → Assist → Escalate (or Learn). Let's break down these stages:

Recognize: The agent continuously senses context and user state. It "recognizes" who the user is (identity and role), where they are working (which record or screen, which communication channel), and what's happening (events or triggers like a deal closing, an incoming email, or 5pm approaching). Recognizing context might involve listening for platform events, scheduled checks (e.g. a cron-based Flow), or API callbacks. It's the first step where the agent asks, "Is there something I should do for the user right now?" Key inputs at this stage include the User's ID and persona metadata (so the agent knows who you are and maybe your role or department), the current context (like the record in focus, or that you're on mobile vs desktop), and any relevant memory objects (such as your recent interactions or stored preferences). For instance, a Companion agent might detect that the user just finished a sales call (context), recall that the user prefers not to log calls at end of day (preference in memory), and thus decide to step in with a reminder.

Personalize: Once the agent has recognized an opportunity to help, it adapts its behavior to the user's personal style and current needs. Personalization is where the agent fine-tunes what it will do or suggest. Using the inputs mentioned (user metadata, context, and memory), the agent tailors its next action. For example, if our user is an HR manager in the middle of a hiring sprint, the Companion might prioritize assistance related to candidate onboarding tasks. If it knows the user tends to ignore suggestions in the morning but is more receptive after lunch (a pattern gleaned from past interactions), it might schedule its proactive help accordingly. Technically, this involves decision logic that branches based on user-specific settings and history. Salesforce Flow and Invocable Apex are the workhorses here: a Flow can declaratively branch ("if user's role is X and it's after 5pm, do Y") and call Apex for more complex checks ("verify the user hasn't already completed this task"). We might store user preferences like "nudge frequency = low" or "preferred channel = Slack" as Custom Metadata or a Custom Object, which the flow/Apex can query to decide how aggressive or passive to be. By designing this personalization layer, we ensure the Companion's assistance feels relevant rather than one-size-fits-all.

Assist: In this stage, the agent actually provides help – this is the outward action of the Companion agent. Assistance can take a few forms: Suggestions (the agent presents an idea or reminder to the user), Executions (the agent performs an action, such as updating a field or sending a message, either automatically or with one-click confirmation), or Escalations (the agent knows it can't handle something and hands off to another agent or a human). The outputs here are what the user directly experiences. For suggestions, the Companion might generate a friendly prompt: "Don't forget to follow up with Acme Corp about the Q3 proposal." For executions, it might do something on behalf of the user: "I've gone ahead and logged yesterday's call for you." For escalations, it could say: "I'm not sure how to handle this budget exception – bringing in a Supervisor agent for approval." Under the hood, these outcomes are achieved by invoking Salesforce capabilities. Lightning Web Components (LWC) or a Slack message act as the interface to surface a suggestion or confirm an action. If the user approves an action (or if no approval is needed per the design), a Flow or Invocable Apex call will carry out the update or API call safely. In more complex cases, the Companion might even invoke another agent (via Agentforce's agent registry) – for instance, calling a Conductor agent to run a multi-step workflow, then reporting back the result. We'll discuss multi-agent hand-offs later in this chapter.

Escalate or Learn: Finally, after assisting, the agent either escalates the matter if it hit a limit, or learns from the interaction if it succeeded. Escalation means the Companion recognizes it cannot complete the request alone or something went wrong. It might invoke a higher-order agent pattern – e.g., ask a Supervisor agent to double-check a draft or engage a human user for confirmation. In our architecture, we build in safe failure and hand-off paths. Every action the Companion takes can be logged to an audit object (so we have a history), and if an action fails or is outside the Companion's authority, a graceful escalation path (perhaps trigger an email to a human, or call a fallback Flow) is executed. On the other hand, if the outcome was successful, the agent should "learn." This doesn't necessarily imply sophisticated machine learning (though it could involve updating a ML model); at minimum it means updating its memory of the user. For example, if the user manually corrected the agent or chose a different option, the agent notes that preference. If the user ignored three consecutive meeting reminders, maybe the agent learns to reduce its frequency. Technically, this learning can be as simple as updating a custom metadata field like LastFollowUpDismissal__c count, or as advanced as retraining a small recommendation model. The key is that the memory objects get updated: recent interactions, outcomes, feedback are stored for next time. Salesforce provides tools like Platform Events or even just records in a "CompanionInteractionHistory" custom object to record these events. By closing the loop with escalation and learning, our architecture ensures continuous improvement and user safety.

With this core lifecycle in mind, let's map out the key inputs and outputs of a Companion agent's architecture:

Key inputs: (1) User identity & persona – who is the user (ID, role, profile) and what can we infer from that (e.g. a sales rep vs. a support agent might get different styles of assistance). We might use the User object and a Custom Metadata type for "PersonaSettings" that the agent checks. (2) Context – where and when is the agent operating? Is this during a Salesforce record edit? In a Slack channel? What time of day? Context also includes the state of relevant records (e.g. an Opportunity nearing close date). (3) Memory objects – what does the agent already "know" about this user or current scenario from past interactions? This can include preferences (like communication tone, "morning person or evening person", etc.), recent interactions (e.g. tasks the user recently completed or declined), and any long-term goals or patterns (maybe the user always asks for a summary at end of week). In practice, memory can be stored in a combination of Custom Metadata (for admin-defined preferences), Custom Objects (for dynamic data like interaction logs or learned behaviors), and even in LLM vector embeddings or prompt histories if we integrate a GPT model for conversational memory. We will look more into memory storage later in this chapter, but note that up front we plan for a place to put things the Companion will remember.

Key outputs: The architecture should produce three main categories of output, aligned to how the agent assists: (1) Suggestions – e.g. action recommendations, reminder messages, or informational alerts that require user attention. These are usually delivered via UI elements or messaging (an on-screen notification, a chat message, a highlighted tip in a dashboard). (2) Executions – actual task completions like database updates, API calls, file generation. These might happen behind the scenes or with the user's one-click confirmation. (3) Escalations – hand-offs or fallback actions when the Companion can't finish the job. For instance, creating a Case for a human to follow up, or invoking a Supervisor agent to approve something. Architecturally, we ensure that for any suggestion or execution, there's an associated escalation path if needed (even if it's just logging the failure and telling the user "I couldn't do X, please check Y"). By anticipating these outputs, we make our Companion robust and user-friendly – it will always do something appropriate even if it can't do everything.

Now, what Salesforce tools and components support this architecture? We've mentioned several already in passing, but let's list the core ones in one place:

Agent Builder: This is our configuration hub for the agent. In Agentforce, Agent Builder lets you define the agent's metadata – things like its name, description, entry points (triggers), and perhaps its allowed actions or trust level. For a Companion agent, you might configure in Agent Builder that it's a "Companion" pattern, tied to a specific user persona or profile, with certain global settings. For example, Agent Builder could have a field for "Trust Level" which we use later in the Delegation phase (Phase 3) to determine how autonomous the agent can be. It might also let us specify if this agent should be available in Slack, on record pages, or both. Essentially, Agent Builder acts as the front door and blueprint for the agent. By using metadata in this way, we avoid hardcoding behaviors and make it easier to manage the agent lifecycle (e.g. toggling features on/off via config as the agent matures).

Flow and Invocable Apex: Salesforce Flow (particularly screen flows and autolaunched flows) will handle the decision logic and process flow of the agent's actions. For instance, a scheduled flow might run every morning to kick off the Companion's daily routine (recognizing context like "start of day" events). A screen flow might be launched when the agent needs to interact with the user (like presenting options in a modal dialog). Within flows, Invocable Apex actions are crucial for anything that goes beyond what declarative logic can do. Did the agent need to analyze a complex dataset to decide something? An Apex method can do that and return results to the flow. Does the agent need to call an external API (maybe to fetch weather data for a meeting location suggestion)? Apex can handle callouts within the flow's orchestration. We basically use Flow for high-level orchestration and user interaction, and Apex for finer logic, validations, or external integrations – all of which are part of the Companion's brain.

Custom Metadata & Objects: These are the memory bank and configuration settings for the Companion. Custom Metadata is great for defining relatively static preferences or rules that admins can maintain. For example, we could have a Custom Metadata Type called Companion_Preferences__mdt with fields like Tone__c (possible values: Formal, Friendly, Enthusiastic), NudgeFrequency__c (values: Low, Medium, High) or flags like AllowAutoExecution__c. An admin (or the user via some UI) could set these, and the agent's logic will consult them to personalize behavior. Custom Objects, on the other hand, can store dynamic info: e.g. Companion_Memory__c records that log key events ("user dismissed suggestion X on 2025-07-05") or store learned data ("preferred_meeting_time__c = Morning" derived from past acceptance). Having a persistent store for memory means the agent doesn't forget context between sessions – a critical capability if it's truly to be a daily partner. (In contrast, a simple chatbot that forgets everything each day wouldn't earn much trust!)

LWC and Slack (UI surfaces): A Companion agent is only as effective as its interface with the human. If it's annoying or hard to notice, it fails the user. We leverage Lightning Web Components for embedding the agent into Salesforce UIs: for example, a collapsible sidebar component in Lightning App Builder that shows "Your Assistant" where the Companion can post its suggestions or listen for commands. LWCs give us flexibility to create custom layouts, use colorful indicators, or even animations to make the agent's presence clear but not obtrusive. They also allow us to connect to Salesforce data in real-time (using Lightning Data Service) so the Companion's UI can update as records change. Additionally, many users live in Slack or email – a Companion agent should reach them there too. Salesforce offers a Slack integration SDK (Salesforce Platform for Slack) that we can use to send messages or even interactive Slack buttons from our agent. So the architecture might include a Slack bot user that is essentially the Companion's persona in Slack. The agent's core logic (Flow/Apex) would use Platform Events or Slack-specific Apex SDK calls to push notifications to Slack when appropriate (e.g., after recognizing something urgent when the user is away from Salesforce). In summary, designing the UI/UX touchpoints in parallel with the backend logic is part of the architecture – you plan where and how the user will experience the agent from the start.

Before we conclude this section, remember that a good architecture also plans for failure and fallback. One Pro tip to always bear in mind: Companion agents should degrade gracefully. If the agent's fancy personalization data isn't available (say the preference store is empty for a new user), it should still do something sensible by falling back to a default behavior, rather than silently doing nothing or, worse, throwing an error. For instance, if the agent doesn't "remember" the user's preferred task list, it might default to a generic helpful suggestion (like "Let me know if you need anything!") instead of a specific nudge – at least that keeps the interaction open. Graceful degradation builds trust because it avoids situations where the user is left wondering why the agent disappeared or failed. Design your flows with fault paths, use default values in metadata, and add simple checks like "if no recent interactions found, use template X" to ensure the Companion is reliably present even when its ideal data isn't there.

With the foundational architecture in place – a lifecycle that recognizes context, personalizes responses, assists through suggestions/executions, and escalates or learns – and with the key Salesforce tools wired together to support that cycle, we can now start evolving our agent through its maturity curve. Next, we'll dive into Phase One: Suggestion. This is where our Companion starts its journey, offering helpful hints and seeing how the user responds. We'll look at what kinds of suggestions create value, when and how to deliver them using Salesforce tech (like scheduled Flows and GPT for tone), and how to measure success (did the user pick up the suggestion?). This gentle introduction of the agent into daily work sets the stage for deeper trust and heavier lifting down the road.

SUGGESTION – PHASE ONE OF COMPANION EVOLUTION

Every Companion agent should learn to walk before it runs. In practical terms, this means starting in a suggestion capacity. During Phase One of the Companion's evolution, the agent focuses on surfacing timely, relevant suggestions and nudges to assist the user, rather than taking direct action on its own. This approach serves two purposes: it immediately adds value by helping the user notice things or remember tasks, and it allows the user to become comfortable with the agent's presence and judgment without handing over full control. Let's explore how to make the most of this suggestion phase – from what the agent should suggest, to when and how it should do so, using Salesforce's tools to implement this logic.

What to suggest: A good Companion agent feels like it has its user's back. Think of the small things a busy professional might forget or the opportunities they might miss during a hectic workday. Those are prime candidates for suggestions. For example, the agent can remind the user of recently used actions or pending tasks in their workflow. If a sales rep frequently logs customer calls, the Companion might notice when a call is overdue to be logged and suggest: "You had a call with XYZ Corp an hour ago. Log it now to keep the account updated?" Similarly, the agent can flag missed follow-ups – perhaps detecting that an email from a client hasn't gotten a reply in 3 days and gently nudging, "It might be time to follow up with Client A on that proposal." Another rich area is personalized reminders that tie into each user's priorities: for instance, reminding an account manager, "Your quarterly sales report is due tomorrow," or even softer personal cues like "It's been two weeks since you last checked in with your mentor – consider reaching out." Essentially, suggestions fall under anything that helps prevent things from falling through the cracks or helps the user work smarter. To decide what suggestions are relevant, our agent draws on context and memory (from our architecture): upcoming deadlines (from Salesforce records), anomalies (like an Opportunity with no recent activity), or even patterns observed by other agents (maybe a Curator agent summarized some insights and our Companion translates that into a suggestion for the user). It's wise to prioritize suggestions that have clear business value or user value – this isn't Clippy offering generic tips; it should be domain-specific and useful. For example, in a sales context, suggestions about follow-ups and data updates are gold. In a support context, a Companion might suggest knowledge articles to attach to a case or remind the agent to close resolved cases.

How to trigger suggestions: Timing and conditions determine when the Companion speaks up. Poor timing (like spamming suggestions while a user is presenting in a meeting) can annoy users, while well-timed nudges can be incredibly helpful. There are a few common trigger strategies:

Time-based triggers: These are scheduled prompts. Salesforce Flow can run on schedules (e.g., an autolaunched flow every day at 8am for each user) to generate daily or weekly suggestions. For instance, a "morning briefing" suggestion list when the user starts their day, or an end-of-week summary on Friday afternoon. Time-based triggers can also be specific, such as a reminder at 4:30pm to wrap up tasks before the day ends, or on the 1st of each month to prompt some recurring activity. Setting this up in Agentforce is straightforward: using a Scheduled Flow (or even a Cron-triggered Apex if precision is needed) that queries what each Companion agent should do and then dispatches the suggestion. Salesforce's flexibility with scheduling means we could even let the user configure their preferred reminder times (store it in metadata, and the flow reads that to decide when to fire).

Behavior signals: These triggers are reactive – the agent watches for certain user behaviors or events in real-time and responds with a suggestion. Thanks to Salesforce's event-driven capabilities, our Companion can subscribe to things like record updates, platform events, or UI events. For example, if a user changes an Opportunity stage to Closed Won, a Platform Event could be emitted and the Companion (via a Flow or Apex trigger) catches it and suggests: "Congrats on the closed deal! Would you like to send a quick thank-you email to the customer?" Another example: the agent might detect the user has been looking at a case record for 15 minutes (maybe struggling with it) and pop up: "Need help? I can fetch similar past cases or common solutions." These behavior signals can be captured via custom Lightning events in an LWC or via standard platform features (like using a Flow Trigger on Record Change or the "Einstein Next Best Action" framework with conditions). Essentially, the agent is context-aware and event-aware, ready to jump in when something notable occurs.

External or multi-agent signals: Sometimes suggestions are triggered by the output of other AI or data processes. The outline mentions Curator agent summaries as an example trigger. Imagine we have a Curator agent (from earlier chapters) that scans data and produces a summary of, say, important customer sentiment trends this week. The Companion can take that summary and turn it into a personalized suggestion: "Our AI noticed that support tickets about Feature X spiked this week. Maybe reach out to the product team?" In Salesforce, this could be orchestrated via an event or a record – the Curator writes to a "Insight__c" custom object, and our Companion's flow is listening for new Insight records related to the user's domain. When one appears, the flow triggers a suggestion to the user summarizing that insight. This is a glimpse of multi-agent collaboration (which we'll expand on later in this chapter), but it shows that triggers for suggestions can come from various sources – time, user behavior, or other intelligent services – and the Companion is the messenger delivering the right info to the user.

How to surface suggestions: Once the agent decides to make a suggestion, how do we present it to the user so that it's helpful and not intrusive? Salesforce gives us several channels to choose from:

Slack prompt: If the user is often in Slack (perhaps your company uses Slack as the primary communication tool), the Companion can send a direct message or mention the user in a channel with its suggestion. For instance, a message like "🤖 Hey Alex! Don't forget to update the status of the ACME deal in Salesforce." could pop up from the "Salesforce Assistant" bot in Slack. There could even be interactive buttons ("Update now", "Snooze 1 day"). Salesforce's Slack integration (especially with the upcoming MCP for Slack) allows agents to take actions securely in Slack. A Slack prompt is great for immediacy, but we should use it when the suggestion is timely and important, since chat messages can be interruptive.

Screen Flow modal: In the Salesforce web UI, a tried-and-true way to get user attention is a modal dialog or guided prompt via a Screen Flow. The Companion could, upon a trigger, launch a Screen Flow that presents information or asks a question. For example, after a user saves a record, a flow could automatically open saying "I noticed you changed the account owner. Would you like to notify the new owner via Chatter? [Yes/No]". Using a Flow modal ensures the suggestion is front-and-center in Salesforce itself.

However, modals should be used sparingly to avoid frustration. We might configure the agent to only use a modal for high-importance suggestions or when immediate confirmation is useful.

Embedded LWC card: A less intrusive approach is to have a section in the UI where suggestions appear contextually. For example, on a Salesforce Lightning record page, we could embed a custom LWC component (perhaps titled "Assistant") that lights up with suggestions relevant to that record. When there's no suggestion, it could be minimal or hidden; when there is something, it could show a highlighted card like, "🔔 You have 1 suggestion: The last activity on this account was 30 days ago. Consider reaching out." This way, the user sees it when looking at the record, but it doesn't force them to interact immediately. This aligns with a principle from UX: visibility with minimal intrusion. The user can act on or dismiss the suggestion at their leisure. An LWC card could also allow multiple suggestions to queue up (like a small feed of tips), and we can use visual cues (icons, colors) to denote priority.

Often, an effective Companion uses a mix of these surfaces depending on urgency. For quick/time-sensitive suggestions, a Slack DM or toast notification might be best. For informative, less urgent tips, an on-page card or even an email summary could work.

Now, let's consider the tools and implementation details to make suggestion phase real:

Flow Scheduler or Platform Events: As noted, to time suggestions or respond to events, we'll rely on scheduled flows and platform events. A Scheduled Flow can be set up in Salesforce to run at certain times and iterate over users (or relevant records) and create suggestion tasks. For event-driven cases, defining Platform Events (e.g., an event "UserFinishedCall__e" or "HighValueOpportunityIdle__e") and having a Flow subscribed to those events is a powerful pattern. The flow can then create a Notification or a Task, or directly invoke our Companion's suggestion subroutine.

GPT for tone shaping: While the logic of what to suggest is determined by our rules, the phrasing of the suggestion can benefit from a Large Language Model's finesse. We want the agent's tone to be collegial and not too robotic or pushy. We can use an LLM (like OpenAI GPT or Salesforce's Einstein GPT) to generate or refine the message text of suggestions. For example, we could pass a prompt to GPT like: "The user is a sales rep. The agent needs to remind them about logging a call. Tone: friendly and concise." The model might return: "Don't forget to log your call with Acme Corp 📞. I can do it for you if you'd like!" – which we can then display. Using GPT in this way makes the Companion feel more natural and can even incorporate small humor or encouragement appropriately (as long as we keep it professional). Of course, this should be done with guardrails: use approved prompts and templates to avoid any off-brand messages, and have fallback templates in case the API call fails. By leveraging GPT for language, the suggestion doesn't sound like a stiff system alert but like a helpful coworker's ping.

Command Center for tracking: In Phase One, since the agent is only suggesting (not autonomously doing critical things), success will be measured by user engagement. Are users clicking on suggestions? Ignoring them? Dismissing them? This feedback is crucial to decide if the agent is actually helpful or needs adjustment. Salesforce's Agentforce Command Center (introduced in Agentforce 3.0) provides an observability layer where we can monitor agent interactions. We should configure our Companion agent to log each suggestion event to a custom object or telemetry log. For instance, whenever the agent makes a suggestion, we create a record like Companion_Interaction__c with fields: User, Suggestion Type, Time, and whether the user accepted/ignored it. The Command Center can then be set up to display metrics like "suggestions offered per day" and "acceptance rate" or alert us if an agent is spamming too many suggestions (high suggestion count, low acceptance). Monitoring this helps us fine-tune the suggestion algorithm. Maybe we find one type of suggestion is rarely acted on – we can tweak or remove it. Or a certain user never uses the agent – maybe they need onboarding or maybe the agent should adjust its approach for that persona. The Command Center essentially closes the loop at the project management level: ensuring Phase One is delivering value and not nuisance.

As a quick hypothetical example to tie it together: Consider a sales Companion agent named Cora. In suggestion mode, Cora observes that right after a salesperson (Alice) finishes a Google Meet (the system logs a completed event) with a client, there's often a lull where call notes aren't immediately recorded. Using an event trigger (meeting ended event) and context (the related Opportunity), Cora sends Alice a Slack message: "Hope the meeting went well! Do you want to jot down a quick note or next step for Acme Corp while it's fresh? I can open the call log for you." In Slack, Alice sees this and can click "Log Call" which triggers a Salesforce Screen Flow (surfaced via a Slack modal or deep-link to Salesforce) where she can enter a note. If Alice ignores it, Cora's log notes that. If Alice engages, Cora logs that too and maybe even updates her "preference" that Alice responds to Slack prompts. Over time, if Alice consistently ignores these right-after-meeting nudges but does log calls by end of day, Cora might learn to hold off and instead just remind at 5pm ("I've compiled your meetings today, ready to log if you are."). This is how suggestions not only help immediately but also teach the agent about the user.

Pro tip: Early in an agent's life, err on the side of helpful silence over noisy suggestions. One well-timed, contextually spot-on suggestion per day beats ten low-value pop-ups. Quality over quantity will build the user's trust. As a Companion agent designer, use Phase One to tune that quality. If you're unsure whether a suggestion will be welcome, consider logging it internally first (shadow mode) and reviewing with users later, rather than deploying it outright. You can even implement a "suggestion confidence" score and only surface those above a threshold. Remember, the user should feel the agent is looking out for them, not nagging them.

By successfully delivering useful suggestions and responding to the user's feedback, our Companion agent will earn its place in the daily workflow. The user begins to rely on it for gentle reminders and quick tips, and trust builds. Now that the foundation of trust is established, our agent is ready to step up to Phase Two: Execution. In the next section, we'll explore how to let the Companion actually perform actions for the user safely. We'll set criteria for when execution is appropriate, discuss how to implement validations and permissions (so the agent doesn't overstep), and show how using Flow/Apex and Salesforce permissions can enable the agent to take work off the user's plate in a controlled manner.

EXECUTION – SAFELY LETTING THE COMPANION ACT

Suggestions can save time, but eventually an AI assistant should do more than remind – it should help carry the load. In the Execution phase, our Companion agent moves from offering advice to taking action (with the user's blessing). This is a cautious step up in autonomy: the agent can now complete certain tasks directly, like a trusted deputy, rather than just pointing them out. However, with great power comes great responsibility (and risk). We must design this phase so that the agent only acts in safe, appropriate situations and always within boundaries the organization and user are comfortable with. In this section, we'll define when a Companion is ready to execute tasks, how to enforce safeguards (permissions, confirmations, audit logs), and what Salesforce tools to leverage for implementing these agent-driven actions.

When to allow direct execution: Not every suggestion should convert into an automatic action. We need clear criteria for when our Companion has "earned" the right to execute something on behalf of the user without explicit step-by-step instruction. Here are some guidelines:

Low-risk, high-repeatability tasks: The agent should start with tasks that are relatively low stakes and happen often. For example, logging a phone call, scheduling a follow-up task, or updating a single field (like moving a deal stage from "Prospecting" to "Qualifying") are typically low-risk. These are the kind of chores the user would gladly offload. Since they happen frequently, the agent will get lots of practice and feedback, which is good for learning. On the other hand, something like sending an email to a client or deleting a record is higher risk – those might not be in scope for autonomous execution in this phase.

User has accepted this suggestion type before: If our Companion has been suggesting a certain action and the user almost always clicks "Yes, do it", that's a strong signal the agent can start doing it automatically. For instance, if every time after a meeting the user clicks the agent's "Log the call" suggestion, we might begin to skip asking and just do it (with maybe a brief notification "I logged the call from your meeting with Acme Corp."). Essentially, the agent is learning the user's preferences and turning repeated consent into implied permission. We could implement this by tracking acceptance rates per suggestion type and having a threshold: say if the user has accepted a suggestion 5 times in a row, mark that action as "trusted for auto-exec". (We'd likely still offer an undo option or notice, just in case.)

Implicit or embedded confirmation available: Sometimes the nature of the task itself provides a safeguard. For example, if the agent fills out a form or draft but it still requires the user to hit a final "Submit", that's a form of embedded confirmation. Or if company policy says any changes trigger an email to the user, the user will see what happened. In these cases, we can allow execution because even though it's automatic, the user is in the loop. A concrete example: the agent might automatically create a draft opportunity update and save it but not submit if there's an approval process – so the user's manager still approves it like any other update. The agent did the grunt work, but the normal human gate is intact.

In summary, early executions should feel like the agent is helping with the user, not going rogue. Think of it as assisted automation: the Companion holds the tool, the user's hand is still on it lightly.

Use validation layers: To enforce the above and catch any mistakes, we introduce layers of protection:

Salesforce Permission Sets & Roles: If the agent is going to perform actions on behalf of a user, it should fundamentally be limited by what that user (or a dedicated integration user) is allowed to do. Salesforce's permission model is our friend here. For example, if a user doesn't have permission to delete records, the agent obviously shouldn't either. More subtly, if an agent might run as a superuser (some designs use a single "Agent User" with high privileges), then we need to programmatically check the acting user's rights before doing something. A good practice is creating a Permission Set specifically for agent executions – e.g. "CompanionExecBasic" – that includes only the object/field permissions needed for the tasks we intend to automate. Assign this to the agent's running context or ensure the agent only attempts actions covered by those perms. This way even if there's a bug, the platform's security will stop truly out-of-line actions. Additionally, the agent can check user roles; maybe only allow auto-execution for internal users, not for external community users, etc.

Custom metadata triggers & flags: We can make execution decisions dynamic by using metadata. For instance, an admin might toggle a custom metadata setting "AutoExecuteEnabled__c" for certain categories of tasks. If something's not in the whitelist, the agent must revert to suggestion mode. We might also define "safe commands" registry – basically a list of actions the agent is approved to do autonomously. This could be a Custom Metadata Type or Custom Object like Trusted_Agent_Actions__mdt listing actions like "LogCall", "CreateFollowUpTask", "ChangeOpportunityStageToNext". The agent's execution logic will reference this registry: if the intended action is not on the list, it won't execute without user confirmation. This provides a central point to manage and review what an agent can do (and aligns with governance – maybe a committee reviews and adds actions over time as trust grows).

Pre-execution validations in Apex/Flow: Before the agent actually commits an action, build in some sanity checks. For example, if the agent is about to update a record, verify via Apex that the new value meets certain criteria ("I will not set an Opportunity stage backward or to a value that triggers a big workflow, unless explicitly allowed"). Or if the agent is sending an email, perhaps run it by a Supervisor agent or at least ensure the content passes a safety filter (no sensitive data or offensive language – which might come into play if the agent summarizing or generating text). Salesforce Flow has decision elements and Apex can throw exceptions; we use those to halt anything that doesn't look right. Essentially, "trust, but verify" every time the agent is about to act.

Execution patterns: How exactly do we implement the agent doing something in Salesforce? There are a couple of common patterns:

Flow-driven executions with known parameters: If the tasks are straightforward and can be predefined, a Flow can handle them end-to-end. For example, a flow that creates a follow-up task record for a Contact could be set up, and our Companion just calls that subflow whenever needed. If the user normally clicks a button to do something, our agent's logic can mimic that button by invoking the flow behind it. Using Flow ensures that we're using admin-defined logic (which is easier to maintain and see). We likely will use Invocable Flows or subflows triggered from our main Companion flow. We pass in the relevant record IDs or details the flow needs, and it executes the transaction. The advantage is that Flows can have built-in rollback and fault handling (we can configure fault paths to log errors to our audit).

Invocable Apex for structured tasks: For tasks that require complex computation or external calls, Apex comes into play. We might write an Apex method [InvocableMethod] that, say, takes a record ID and a field value, and performs a series of updates or calls an external API, then returns a result. Our Companion would call this Apex via Flow's Apex Action element. By structuring the Apex as invocable actions, we give ourselves modular, reusable building blocks that can be tested independently. For example, an Apex method to "Send Personalized Thank You Email" could accept an Opportunity ID and draft an email content via GPT and send it. Initially, we might use it in suggestion mode (it generates the draft, but user sends). Later, in execution mode, the agent could call it fully to send the email automatically if it's deemed safe. Apex is also where we'd implement any complex multi-step logic for a single action. But note: keep each invocable action fairly granular for clarity and control.

User interface for confirmation (when needed): Sometimes the agent will go ahead and do things invisibly, other times we might give the user a chance to confirm within the flow of work. For example, a Slack shortcut. In Slack, the agent could offer "Yes, do it" button on a suggestion; clicking it effectively transitions the agent from suggestion to execution for that instance. That behind the scenes calls an Apex or Flow to do the task. In the Salesforce UI, using a quick Action or a custom LWC button can serve similarly. This pattern is more "prompted execution" but it's a stepping stone – the logic path is the same as an automatic execution, just with a human trigger. We should build our flows/Apex so that whether the execution was auto or user-clicked, the actual action code is identical. That way, we avoid having two separate implementations and can gradually move tasks from "click to confirm" to "no click needed" by simply automating that click internally.

To illustrate an execution scenario, consider a sample: updating an Opportunity stage from a Companion's Slack prompt. In Phase One, our agent might have suggested "Shall I move this deal to Negotiation stage for you?" after a certain event. Now in Phase Two, if criteria are met (user usually says yes, it's a low risk update), the agent could bypass asking. Once the agent detects the deal should advance (maybe the user marked a related task as done), it directly calls an Apex invocable or Flow to change the Opportunity's Stage field to "Negotiation/Review". We ensure two things around this: (1) That the agent immediately notifies the user of the action: e.g. posting "✅ I updated the deal stage to Negotiation, per our standard process." in Slack or as a toast in Salesforce. This keeps the user in the loop and gives them a chance to object or rollback if needed. (2) That we log this action in our audit object with who/when/what. Ideally, even though the agent did it automatically, any existing Salesforce automation (like field history tracking or platform events on stage change) will capture it as well because either the system user or the user's own context did it. By logging explicitly as well ("Agent X changed Opportunity 123 to Stage=Negotiation at 3:45pm"), we create a human-readable trail too. This addresses the "why did this change happen?" questions later – anyone can see the agent did it, not a mysterious ghost.

And that leads to an important Pro tip: All Companion executions should be logged in an audit object – even if they were user-triggered. This cannot be overstated. In a future state, months down the line, if something weird happened, people will ask "was it the AI or the user who did this?" Having a clear audit log for agent actions ensures accountability and builds trust with stakeholders (including the users and admins). It's easy to implement: make an Agent_Action__c custom object or use the Salesforce Event Monitoring logs if available, and have the agent's flows/Apex do a quick create record or print to logs whenever it performs an action. Include details like the user on behalf of whom it acted (if using a service user, note the real user context), what was done, and any confirmation info. Over time, this audit log can feed into analytics (for example, proving how much time the agent saved by counting how many actions it did).

With Phase Two executed (pun intended) correctly, our Companion agent starts to actually reduce the user's workload. When it only suggested, the user still had to do the work (even if it was just a click). Now the agent is completing tasks – small ones at first – which frees up the user's time and mental energy. Done carefully, the user remains in control and is likely delighted that routine stuff "just happens" without micromanagement. This sets the stage for the boldest step: Phase Three – Delegation, where the agent can take on more autonomy and act proactively even when the user isn't around to green-light every move. Before we get there, though, we must ensure strong guardrails are in place. In the execution phase we implemented technical safeguards; as we move to delegation, we'll also consider policy and preference safeguards to decide if and when an agent should truly run on its own. In the next section, we explore Delegation – how to entrust the agent with autonomy while maintaining oversight. We'll define trust criteria, emergency brakes, and how to expand the agent's reach across multiple systems, all without losing the user's confidence.

DELEGATION – ENTRUSTING AGENTS WITH AUTONOMY

Reaching the Delegation phase is like the moment you hand the car keys to a well-trained teen for the first time: exciting but a bit nerve-wracking. For our Companion agent, delegation means it can initiate and complete certain tasks independently, without waiting for the user's input every time. This might occur when the user is busy, offline, or simply trusts the agent to handle things in the background. To continue our analogy, the agent moves from being a co-pilot to sometimes being the pilot – but only on pre-approved routes and with the ability for the human to take over as needed. In this section, we delineate the criteria that must be met before giving an agent this level of autonomy, the control mechanisms we put in place to manage delegated actions, and how to extend these autonomous capabilities even beyond Salesforce into the broader enterprise ecosystem (safely).

Criteria for delegation: Not every user or scenario will be ready for fully autonomous agent actions. We should establish clear criteria to identify when delegation is appropriate:

Explicit user preference or opt-in: Perhaps the most straightforward criterion is that the user has said, "Yes, I'm okay with the agent doing X without asking me." This could be as simple as a settings toggle, like "Auto-delegate scheduling to my Companion" set to true. If a user proactively opts in for a certain function (e.g., let the agent auto-schedule meetings on my calendar when it sees open slots), that's a green light. We might expose these preferences in a custom UI (maybe a Lightning page "Companion Settings" where checkboxes or picklists allow opting into various automations). A specific example from the outline: a preference flag for "auto-delegate scheduling". If the user flips that on, the agent could, say, find a meeting time with a customer and book it, then just inform the user after the fact, trusting the agent's judgment. Without that flag, the agent would always ask first.

Pattern of trust (confirmed suggestions history): We touched on this in Phase Two but it becomes even more important here. If over time the agent has made, say, 50 suggestions and the user confirmed 45 of them, that's a 90% acceptance – a strong trust indicator. We can quantify this. For each type of task, track how often the user agrees with the agent's recommendation. Once it passes a threshold (both in frequency and recency – e.g., at least 5 occurrences and >80% acceptance in the last month), we could mark that task type as "trusted for delegation". In practical implementation, this could update a custom metadata record for that user (like User_Companion_Trust__mdt with fields per task type). It's a form of individualized learning: the agent doesn't just assume autonomy; it earns it through demonstrated alignment with the user's decisions. In effect, the user has been training the agent what decisions are okay to make solo.

Situational urgency or context where user is unavailable: Sometimes delegation isn't about user preference so much as necessity. Consider a scenario: the user is on a long flight without internet, but something critical comes up that needs action now. If our agent can recognize such a scenario (e.g., time pressure or mobile context where the user can't easily respond), it might step in on the user's behalf to keep things moving, as long as it's confident it's acting in the user's interest. An example might be approving a routine expense report for the user when it's within known limits and the deadline hits, because the user is traveling (the outline gave: a finance Companion approving recurring expense reports within budget for a traveling user). Another scenario: a service agent's Companion notices a high-severity case hasn't been responded to within SLA because the agent is out sick – the Companion could automatically escalate it to another team or provide a placeholder response to the customer. These are cases where doing something autonomously is better than doing nothing. We should use context signals like "user's calendar says OOO" or "the request is time-sensitive (maybe a workflow rule flags it)" to decide this. Of course, these criteria must still operate within bounds of safety and policy.

In summary, delegation is appropriate when either the user has explicitly or implicitly given the agent the nod, or the situation demands quick action and the agent has enough info to act conservatively on the user's behalf.

Control mechanisms: Even when we decide to let the agent off the leash a bit, we keep a long retractable leash attached. Several control features ensure the agent's autonomy doesn't turn into a runaway:

Agent Builder "trust level" field: It would be convenient to have a single setting in Agent Builder that denotes how autonomous a particular Companion agent is allowed to be. We could imagine a field like TrustLevel with values such as "Suggest-Only", "Execute with Confirmations", "Fully Delegated in Domain". An admin could set this per agent (or per user or persona). This provides a top-down control; for instance, maybe your company policy is that new AI agents start at the lowest trust and only after a governance review can an agent be bumped up a level. In our architecture, we would then have the agent's logic check this field before doing any delegated action: if TrustLevel != "Delegation", it won't proceed without user input. The nice thing is this can be dynamic and even automated – e.g., you could have a process that increases the trust level after a certain number of successful interactions, subject to admin override.

Active user presence override: One intuitive rule: if the user is actively using the system right now (e.g., they are typing or clicking around in Salesforce or Slack), the agent should defer to them rather than act autonomously. We don't want the weird scenario of the agent doing something the user was just about to do. We can implement an "if user is active, do not auto-act" check. How to detect activity? In Salesforce, maybe via the streaming API or last page load timestamp; in Slack, whether the user is marked active. If the agent sees the user is currently engaged, it might instead surface a quick "Hey, I noticed X needs doing – shall I handle it?" rather than doing it silently. Conversely, if the user is inactive (away or offline), then the agent might go ahead within its allowed scope. This is a simple but powerful guardrail to ensure the agent doesn't conflict or surprise when the user is present.

Post-action feedback loop: For every autonomous action, the agent should provide a notification or record for the user to review later. Essentially, "log and tell". We already have audit logging, but user-facing feedback is key. That could be as immediate as a notification: "While you were away, I approved 3 low-value invoices per your rules. View details here." And it could include an easy way to undo or question it: perhaps a "Review" button that triggers a Supervisor pattern or simply shows what was done. Another approach is a periodic summary: e.g., daily or weekly "Here's what your Companion did on your behalf." This transparency is vital for user trust; it ensures no mystery actions. And it invites the user to correct the agent if needed ("I didn't want you to do that!"), which is then a learning opportunity to refine criteria or revoke a preference.

Emphasizing feedback: we might even implement a one-click feedback capture after an autonomous action. Imagine the agent posts "I rescheduled your meeting with Bob to tomorrow since you were double-booked. (Good call? 👌 / Undo 🔄)". The user can quickly react with a thumbs-up or click undo, which signals if that was correct. That kind of immediate feedback capture closes the loop nicely.

Now, pushing the envelope, our Companion agent in delegation mode might reach beyond just Salesforce data. Real work involves multiple systems – maybe external calendars, email, ERP systems, etc. Delegating tasks across systems is both an opportunity and a challenge. Salesforce's ecosystem provides some means to do this:

Multi-system delegation with MuleSoft: If our agent needs to perform actions in other enterprise systems (say create an order in an ERP, or pull data from a third-party service), MuleSoft can serve as the bridge. The outline suggests an example of a MuleSoft bridge. We could orchestrate that when an agent needs to do something in another system, it calls a MuleSoft integration (via an HTTP call or MuleSoft's Salesforce Connectors). For instance, your Companion might auto-approve an expense in Concur through a MuleSoft API if criteria match. Using MuleSoft ensures that proper integration protocols and security are maintained – the agent doesn't directly talk to systems it shouldn't; it goes through an approved integration layer. In Agentforce 3.0, the introduction of MCP (Model Context Protocol) also plays a role here, making it easier to plug agents into external contexts. Salesforce described MCP as a "universal plug" for agents to connect to different systems. Concretely, that means our Companion could invoke an external AI or service in a standardized way, or call out to an MCP-compatible endpoint that handles cross-system actions.

External APIs via Apex: Not everything will have a pre-built integration. For custom needs, we can write Apex callouts to external APIs. For example, if our Companion needs to send a message to a third-party messaging platform or update a row in a cloud database, Apex can do an HTTP call. We have to be careful with this – ensure we abide by security (use named credentials, handle secrets properly) and respect rate limits. But Apex callouts effectively let the agent roam outside Salesforce's walls when needed. Perhaps the agent might interface with an external AI service (not unlike how it might use GPT) as part of its delegated task. For instance, auto-creating a presentation slide using an external AI design service when a meeting is scheduled. The sky's the limit, but each API adds complexity and another layer to monitor.

MCP-ready output for external swarms: If we envision a future where multiple agents across platforms collaborate (an "agent swarm"), our Companion might sometimes need to delegate to other agents. For instance, if a request comes in that's beyond its scope, it could formulate a request and send it to an external agent network via MCP. Perhaps something like: a user says "Book my travel for the conference," and the Companion delegates to a travel agent outside Salesforce (through an MCP interface) that coordinates flights and hotels. To do this, our agent would package context in a standardized format (MCP's protocol) including relevant user preferences (from Salesforce data) and send it off. The result might come back asynchronously. While this is an advanced scenario, our design in delegation phase can anticipate it by structuring outputs in a standardized way. For example, the Companion could create a JSON payload of a task (like a mini manifest of what needs doing) and either send it via HTTP or drop it in a queue that an external agent picks up. This goes a bit beyond our core Salesforce focus, but as Agentforce aims for interoperability, it's worth noting that a truly empowered Companion isn't confined to one app – it can represent the user in many contexts.

As an example of delegation at work: recall the finance Companion scenario from the outline. Imagine a finance manager who's traveling. The company has a policy that any expense report under \$1000 that matches past patterns can be auto-approved to not block employees. Our finance manager's Companion agent sees 5 expense reports come in during a week. It knows from preferences that auto-approval is allowed (user opted in and company policy metadata says OK up to \$1000). It also knows the manager is traveling (maybe from calendar or a "Travel Mode" setting the user enabled). So the agent evaluates each report: all under \$1000, all look similar to usual expenses. It then delegates: it goes into the ERP via MuleSoft API or perhaps directly if integrated into Salesforce, marks those reports approved, and triggers the next step (maybe finance system pays them out). The agent then sends a summary Slack message to the manager: "While you were traveling, I auto-approved 5 expense reports (all <\$1000). All within your guidelines. ✅ Let me know if any issues." The manager comes back, sees that, maybe gives a quick thumbs-up reaction. Here, the Companion acted autonomously but within clear guardrails: dollar limit, known pattern, user was unavailable. It saved time and kept things moving. If one of those had been, say, $2000, the agent would have known from criteria "that exceeds my delegation authority" and instead flagged it for the manager or waited.

Another mini example: a sales Companion might notice a big client just sent in a new high-value contract (perhaps via an e-signature integration). The responsible sales rep is on vacation today. The Companion knows that for VIP clients, if a contract comes in, it should immediately create an Opportunity in Salesforce and alert a backup team. It delegates the creation of that record, populates it with info from the contract (maybe using an AI to parse the doc via Apex callout to a PDF service), assigns it to an available colleague, and pings the sales manager that "Contract from ACME received and processed while Alex is out – assigned to Bob for now." This is autonomous, cross-system (involves document system and Salesforce), and showcases how an agent can keep business moving.

To keep things safe and sane:

We tag agents and systems by persona/support in metadata (so the Companion knows which external agents or APIs it's allowed to talk to).

We maintain a registry of trusted call targets (like we did for safe commands but expanded to external endpoints or agent endpoints). For example, only allow calls to known company APIs or partner agent services, deny anything else. This could be configured in Agent Builder or a custom metadata "TrustedEndpoints" list.

Pro tip: When giving agents more autonomy, transparency and throttles are your safety valves. Always inform the user (or relevant people) what the agent is doing, and never let the agent run unchecked in a tight loop. Implement rate limits – e.g., "the agent can only auto-approve at most 10 items per day" or "if more than 3 autonomous actions happen in an hour, require a manual check." These can be simple counters or flows that pause if limits hit. This ensures that if an agent goes a bit wild (say due to a bug or unforeseen scenario), it self-brakes before doing damage. Additionally, consider an "emergency stop" mechanism: maybe a big red button for admins (or even users) – e.g., set TrustLevel to "Suspended" – that immediately puts the agent back to suggestion-only mode. In Salesforce, that could be as easy as a checkbox field "Active" false on the agent's metadata record that all flows check at start.

Having covered suggestion, execution, and delegation phases, we've guided our Companion from a basic helper to a capable proxy. Through careful gating and learning, the agent can handle a surprising amount of daily work autonomously, yet the user remains confident because of the guardrails we put and the continuous feedback loop. At this point, our agent truly behaves like a Daily Work Partner – it anticipates needs, takes initiative, and still knows when to ask for help or step back.

With autonomy comes the need for even more personalization and human touch, which we'll explore next. Delegation doesn't mean one-size-fits-all; in fact, it heightens the need for the agent to deeply understand the user's preferences and company policies. In the following section, we'll focus on Personalization and Growth Over Time – how the Companion adapts and learns as it continues to work with a user, ensuring that its evolution remains aligned with the user's evolving needs and preferences, even as it takes on more autonomy.

PERSONALIZATION AND GROWTH OVER TIME

One of the greatest strengths of a Companion agent (and what sets it apart from a generic chatbot) is its ability to personalize itself to each user over time. Think of it like a workplace buddy that, after months of working together, just gets you – it knows your habits, your preferences, your pet peeves, and tailors its support accordingly. But this kind of personalization doesn't happen magically; we have to design the agent to learn and adapt in a structured, safe way. In this section, we'll discuss what aspects of the agent we personalize for each user, how to store and retrieve that personalized data using Salesforce tools, and how we allow users (and admins) to see or reset the agent's memory to maintain transparency and trust. We'll also cover how the agent's capabilities can "grow" – becoming more sophisticated or broad in scope – and how to manage that growth through configuration and user feedback.

What to personalize: Not every part of an agent needs personalization, but several key dimensions benefit from it:

Preferred channels: Users have different working styles. Some live in email, others in Slack, others in the Salesforce UI all day. A good Companion figures out where to reach a user for maximum impact. For example, if it notices the user always responds to Slack pings but never to Salesforce in-app notifications, it will favor Slack for suggestions. We should store a preference like "Primary Notification Channel = Slack" for that user. Similarly, maybe for urgent issues the user wants a text message – that could be another preference. By personalizing the channel, the agent meets the user where they are, increasing effectiveness.

Tone and verbosity: One user might appreciate a friendly, chatty assistant that throws in a joke occasionally ("Happy Friday! I took care of your timesheet, enjoy the weekend! 🎉"). Another user might prefer a strictly professional, terse style ("Timesheet submitted. Have a good day."). Tone preference can vary by role or personal taste. We can allow a user to set their desired tone (perhaps choices like Formal, Friendly, Humorous, etc.) and how verbose they want the agent to be (concise vs. detailed explanations). For instance, a new employee might want verbose guidance with context ("I've closed the ticket and notified the customer, as per our SLA policy.") whereas a veteran just wants the action confirmation ("Ticket closed and customer notified."). Storing a tone setting and a detail level setting helps the agent's natural language outputs (especially those coming from GPT). In practice, we might pass these as parameters to our prompt templates for GPT: e.g., tone = casual, style = brief and the LLM will adjust phrasing. Even without LLMs, we could have two versions of messages coded and pick based on preference.

Task and content preferences: Over time, the agent can learn which tasks the user likes automated and which they prefer to handle themselves. For example, one manager might love that the agent auto-approves expenses, while another might want to personally review every single one. These preferences can be explicitly set or inferred from behavior. We should personalize which types of suggestions to emphasize. If the user never engages with "update Salesforce data" type suggestions but always engages with "schedule meetings" suggestions, the agent can shift focus. So personalization extends to which features of the agent to highlight or suppress. Technically, we can have flags like EnableCalendarAssist=true/false, EnableDataQualitySuggestions=true/false per user. These could be toggled via a settings UI or automatically toggled off if the agent notices low engagement in an area (with caution – maybe confirm with user if we're turning off a feature).

Timing and frequency: Some people want a daily summary, others find it spammy and prefer weekly. Some don't mind occasional nudges throughout the day, others want the agent to speak only when spoken to unless it's urgent. We personalize how often and when the agent should proactively surface. For instance, store a preferred "Nudge frequency = Low" which the agent interprets as "don't interrupt more than once a day". Or "Quiet Hours" settings (user might set no proactive suggestions after 6pm, for work-life balance). The agent can also deduce: if the user consistently dismisses morning suggestions, maybe they're not a morning person – try afternoon. We could even have an algorithm adjusting suggestion times based on response rates. But simpler is to allow the user to configure times (like do not disturb hours).

Escalation preferences: If something goes wrong, does the user prefer the agent escalate to them first, or directly to someone else? For example, if a delegated action fails, maybe one user wants a Slack alert to themselves, another might want it forwarded to their delegate or team lead. This can be personalized if needed, especially for high-level folks who have assistants.

As you can see, virtually every aspect of the agent's interaction loop can be tuned. But we must balance complexity; we don't want to overwhelm with 50 settings. Often, we pick a handful of impactful ones and implement those first (channel, tone, frequency being common).

How to store and retrieve personalization: Now, where do we put all this data? Salesforce provides multiple options:

Custom Metadata Types: Great for system-wide or profile-level defaults. For example, we might have a CompanionDefaultPreferences__mdt that has a record per Persona or per Org with default values (e.g., salespeople default to Slack channel, support people default to in-app notifications, etc.). Custom metadata is easily deployable and can be referenced in formulas, flows without SOQL. But it's not user-specific unless we make records per user (not ideal because metadata is meant more for config than data and has limits).

Custom Objects (Custom Settings): For user-specific data, a Custom Object like Companion_Preference__c can hold records keyed by User (lookup to User) with fields for each preference. This is straightforward and allows us to query/update easily. Alternatively, a List Custom Setting or Custom Metadata with user scope can be used, but normal custom object might be simplest. We could also split it: e.g., a separate object for "CompanionMemory" versus "CompanionSettings".

- For example, CompanionSettings__c (user, tone, verbosity, primaryChannel, etc).
- And CompanionMemory__c (user, key, value, timestamp) for more dynamic things like last suggestion dismissed timestamp, number of tasks auto-executed, etc., if we want a more generic storage.

Session-based memory vs. long-term memory: Some info might be short-lived (session memory that resets each day or each login). We can leverage the platform cache or even just store in a flow's state if needed. However, most personalization is long-term, so it should persist in the database across sessions.

To retrieve this info, our agent's flows and Apex will query these sources at the start of an interaction. For instance, a flow that prepares a suggestion would do: "Get CompanionSettings where User = currentUser" to fetch their preferences, then branch logic or set variables accordingly (like set a variable tone = result.Tone__c which eventually is used in GPT prompt). We should design queries efficiently (maybe cache some data at login via a Lightning Data Service wire or so, to avoid repeated SOQL every time – but that's an optimization detail).

One crucial aspect is making sure this personalized data is updated as the user or system learns. For explicit settings, the user might update them through a UI (we'll talk about giving user a view of "what your companion knows"). For implicit ones, our flows can update these objects. For instance, if agent notices user always clicks afternoon suggestions, update a field PreferredNudgeTime__c = Afternoon. Or if user clicked "Don't show this again" on a type of tip, set something like ShowDataQualityTips__c = false. Having a robust data model for preferences and memory makes the agent smarter and more tailored with each passing week.

Allowing resets and transparency: No personalization system should be a black box, especially in enterprise. Users (and admins) will rightly ask: "What does this AI think it knows about me?" and "Can I clear it if it's wrong or if I don't want it to remember?" We should build features to:

Reset Companion memory: Perhaps in the user's Companion settings page, have a button "Clear my assistant's memory" which, when clicked, wipes or archives the user-specific data that was accumulated (except maybe essential static preferences). This could delete rows in CompanionMemory__c for that user, reset counters, etc. It's a good practice both for user control and potentially for compliance (similar to a "reset to factory settings" if a user leaves or wants a fresh start).

Session-based memory reset: Additionally, some agents might only remember within a session for privacy. Maybe a flag in Agent Builder configuration "Clear memory each session" if dealing with sensitive contexts. Then after user logs out or after some time, the agent forgets the conversation content (except maybe audit logs). This could be implemented by simply not storing certain data beyond a session ID.

"What your Companion remembers" view: We want to surface the collected preferences and important snippets of memory to the user in a readable form. For example, a panel that says: "Your preferences: Tone=friendly, Channel=Slack, Auto-approve expenses=Yes up to $1000, Last week's key actions: auto-approved 3 expenses, scheduled 2 meetings." It might even list recent learning points: "You often deferred morning reminders, so I've stopped sending those." By being transparent, we demystify the agent and give the user a chance to correct any mislearned behavior ("Actually, I do want morning reminders, I was just busy those days"). Implementing this could be as simple as a Lightning page that queries the preference object and some recent interaction logs and displays them in a readable way (maybe using custom labels to provide friendly descriptions). It might also allow inline editing of some preferences.

Governance of memory scope: On the admin side, define what categories of data the agent is allowed to remember and for how long. For example, maybe by policy, it should not remember exact conversation text beyond 30 days (just aggregate insights), to minimize sensitive info retention. We might enforce that by periodically purging older logs or summarizing them then deleting detail (the Curator pattern could help summarize long chat histories into key points that are stored, then raw logs are wiped). Essentially Memory ≠ infinite history; we curate what is worth keeping. A pro tip from earlier chapters: don't remember everything, only what's meaningful.

By implementing resets and transparency, we address safety and trust: the user remains in ultimate control of their data and can see that the agent isn't hiding a mysterious profile of them.

Let's walk through a quick example of personalization in action: Suppose our user, Alice, initially gets the default Companion settings – it sends suggestions via Salesforce notifications with a formal tone. After a month, Alice finds the agent useful but a bit stiff and easy to miss. She goes to her Companion Settings (maybe a tab in a Lightning app or a command like "Assistant, change your style") and selects a friendly tone and Slack as her preferred channel. Now the agent's Custom Settings for Alice are updated: Tone=Friendly, PrimaryChannel=Slack. Immediately, the agent's behavior shifts – the next suggestion it has, it posts in Slack with a bit more warmth: "Hey Alice, I went ahead and drafted your weekly report. Let me know what you think! 🙂 ". Alice engages more because it's where she chats with team anyway. Later, the agent notices she ignores all suggestions about updating lead data but always accepts calendar scheduling help. It updates an internal flag for Alice: SuggestDataUpdates=false. So it stops bugging her about data quality (maybe her sales ops team will handle that differently) and focuses on calendar and follow-up related help. Alice is happy because the agent "figured out" what she cares about. At any point, Alice can check "What my assistant knows" and see: Preferred Help Areas: Meeting scheduling, Follow-ups (it might list those), Areas on Mute: Data entry suggestions. She can toggle if she decides differently. If something weird happens – say the agent draws a wrong conclusion – she can hit "Reset" and it goes back to defaults and relearns anew (and maybe she also sends feedback to IT to improve the logic).

Pro tip: Treat personalization data with the same care as customer data. It's part of the user's profile and should be protected. Use field-level security and sharing rules appropriately on any custom objects storing potentially sensitive preferences or behavior logs. Also, avoid collecting more than you need – it's better to know 5 things about the user that improve their life than 500 trivia points that never get used. In essence, design the Companion's memory like you'd design a user profile feature: focus on what will drive a better experience, keep it transparent, and make it easy to update.

With a personalized approach, our Companion agent doesn't feel like a generic AI – it comes across as a truly personal aide, tuned to the individual. This increases user affinity for the agent and likely their productivity as well. We've now covered how the agent functions internally and adapts to its user. The next challenge is more human-centric: how do we ensure users embrace this agent as a partner and not as a nuisance or threat? That's a matter of UX design and managing the human-AI relationship. In the next section, we'll dive into UX and Human-AI Relationship Design, discussing how to introduce the agent's presence, keep the user engaged without fatigue, and maintain the right balance of proactivity and humility so that the Companion truly becomes a "daily partner" in the workflow, welcomed by the user rather than tolerated.

UX AND HUMAN-AI RELATIONSHIP DESIGN

Even the smartest Companion agent can fail if it's presented or behaves in a way that doesn't mesh with human workflows and psychology. Designing the user experience (UX) and nurturing a positive relationship between the user and the agent is as important as nailing the technical logic. In this section, we focus on the softer side: how the agent's presence is introduced and contextualized, how to prevent user fatigue or annoyance, and how to ensure the agent remains a helpful colleague rather than a pesky Clippy. We'll cover embedding the agent seamlessly into day-to-day work, giving it a clear purpose (and maybe even personality) that users can relate to, handling cases when the agent isn't sure or needs to defer, and handing off gracefully to humans or other agents when necessary. The tone here is about trust, comfort, and integration into the human workflow.

Give your Companion a purpose (in the user's eyes): From the get-go, the user should understand why this agent exists and what it's meant to do. If an agent just appears and starts doing things, users may be confused or suspicious. So, part of UX is a proper introduction and framing. For instance, when a user first gets the Companion enabled, we could have a welcome message: "Hi, I'm Cora, your Compliance Assistant. I'm here to help you stay on top of compliance tasks and deadlines." This short "job description" sets the stage. It should be descriptive and accurate – if we call it "Your Compliance Assistant", it better handle compliance-related tasks, not scheduling your lunch (unless compliance is about lunch breaks 😁). By describing what it does, we anchor expectations. Many successful AI assistants have a tagline (e.g., "Clara – your scheduling assistant" or "GitHub Copilot – your AI pair programmer"). For our agent, maybe it's "your Sales Companion" or "your Personal CRM Assistant". Along with the description, consider letting the user personalize the agent's identity a bit – like giving it a name or choosing from a few personas (professional vs. playful, etc., within the bounds we set). Some people like to treat their AI like a colleague with a name. Even if it's just cosmetic, allowing "rename or reframe" can increase user affinity. Salesforce might have a default name for the agent, but maybe the user could change it ("Bob's Assistant" or "Eve the Agent"). This isn't just fluff: it gives a sense of ownership and familiarity.

Anticipate and avoid fatigue: One risk of an ever-present Companion is information overload or annoyance. The novelty of a helpful agent can wear off if it interrupts too much or always says the same things. We've touched on controlling frequency in personalization; here are more UX strategies:

Cadence like weekly digests vs. daily pings: Instead of a constant trickle of suggestions, sometimes bundling them is better. For example, the agent could compile a weekly digest email or Slack message: "Here's a recap of what I helped with this week and a few suggestions for next week." This can replace daily pings if the user prefers. Or conversely, maybe micro nudges daily but one big summary weekly. The key is to find a rhythm that doesn't overwhelm. We might allow the user to toggle between live notifications vs. summary mode.

Quiet modes / pause periods: Provide a way for users to say "Not now" or "Do Not Disturb" to the agent. For instance, if someone is in focus mode, they could snooze the Companion for 2 hours. Or set working hours so the agent stays silent outside 9-5. Technically, this can be a quick setting accessible via a click (maybe a bell icon to mute/unmute suggestions). If the agent does try to help during quiet mode (due to an automated trigger), it should either queue it for later or only surface it if it's truly urgent and clearly state why it's breaking silence ("Sorry to interrupt, but a critical case needs attention." – hopefully rare). By respecting quiet times, the agent shows empathy for the user's attention.

Variety and relevance: Part of avoiding fatigue is not repeating oneself or stating the obvious. The agent's content generation (especially if using GPT for phrasing) should add slight variation in greetings or wording so it doesn't feel like spam. More importantly, it should not bring up suggestions that the user consistently ignores or that aren't contextually relevant. If the user always dismisses the "Update contacts" prompt, the agent should stop after a couple of attempts (maybe reintroduce later after a long gap or when context changes, but not every day). Keeping a high relevance bar means the user sees value each time the agent speaks up, which reduces annoyance. Essentially, silence is better than a useless suggestion, from a UX standpoint.

Embed in day-to-day seamlessly

This is about placing the agent's interface in the natural flow of work. We already discussed Slack, record pages, dashboards. Ensure those placements are such that the agent's info is available when needed. E.g., on a record page, maybe the agent's card is near where a user would take actions, so its suggestions appear at the right moment. In Slack, maybe it can join channels relevant to its domain (like a deal room) and provide assistance there rather than a separate DM – if appropriate and if privacy is considered.

Also consider mobile: If users are on Salesforce Mobile or a mobile email, can the Companion reach them? Perhaps via push notifications ("Your assistant has 2 suggestions – tap to view"). Or integrate with a mobile card in Salesforce app that shows the agent feed.

Another day-to-day aspect: perhaps the Companion can integrate with non-Salesforce surfaces like a Chrome extension or Outlook if that's where work happens. That might be beyond our Salesforce scope, but worth noting if a user spends time in Outlook, an Agentforce connector could bring the Companion there ("I see an email from a client, want me to log it in Salesforce?" popping in Outlook UI).

The agent should also have an easy invoke – maybe a fixed icon or chat button in Salesforce that the user can click anytime to ask the agent something. Being there when user initiates is as important as the agent initiating. E.g., a user might click "Companion" and type "summarize this case for me" – crossing into chatbot territory but as a Companion feature. If we have a consistent entry point (like how Copilot is a side panel you can open on demand in Microsoft apps), it becomes part of the routine.

Support graceful fallback: Even the best agent will encounter situations it can't handle or where it gets something wrong. How it behaves in those moments greatly affects user trust. We need to design humility and failsafes into the UX:

Train the agent's responses to admit uncertainty. For example, "I'm not sure how to categorize this request," or "I don't have enough data to answer that." Users prefer an agent that knows its limits. As the outline's pro tip says: agents that admit limits build trust. This might mean the agent sometimes says "Would you like me to try again later after I gather more info?" or simply "I don't know, but I've asked the admin for guidance" (if maybe it triggers a human assist).

Offer alternatives or escalation: If the Companion can't complete something, it should know how to handoff gracefully. For example: "I couldn't find the file you requested. Would you like me to escalate this to IT support (Supervisor agent) or try a different query?" Or "I'm not authorized to approve this request. I've forwarded it to your manager for approval." That handoff could be to a human or to another agent specialized in that task (like a Supervisor or Conductor). Perhaps it triggers a Supervisor agent with the context so that a human can quickly make a decision. The key is the user doesn't just get a "Error, I failed" – they get a next step. Even a simple fallback: "I can't draft this email. Click here to open a template instead." is better than nothing.

Undo and confirm: For delegated actions, always give the user an option to undo if possible. For instance, if the agent sent out a communication or changed a value, perhaps provide a "Undo" link in the notification (which might trigger a compensating action – like if it closed a case, maybe reopen it). Not everything is easily undoable, but even the perception of an undo option reduces anxiety. When things are risky or non-undoable, better to confirm first or involve a human (which we likely did by design).

Beyond failures, to maintain a good relationship, the agent might occasionally solicit feedback or just adapt its behavior as we covered. It should also share credit/success: e.g. if together the user and agent achieved something (like closed a lot of tasks), maybe the agent says "Great job team us – we cleared 10 tasks today!" A bit of positivity can make the relationship feel more like a partnership.

At a higher level, consider accessibility and inclusion in the UX design:

- Ensure the agent's outputs are accessible (if in Salesforce UI, use proper ARIA labels, etc., if voice, speak clearly). If users with disabilities are in play, maybe the agent can have modes like a speech interface.
- The agent's tone should be respectful of different cultures and preferences – e.g., maybe avoid slang unless user's tone preference is explicitly informal.
- We might let users choose how they receive info: some might prefer a visual chart vs. text summary – perhaps the Presenter pattern (in earlier chapters) covers this, but our Companion could coordinate with a Presenter agent to show data in user's preferred style.

Let's do a short scenario to see the UX/relationship in action:

User Bob is introduced to "Assist-o, your Sales Buddy (Companion pattern)" via a pop-up when it's enabled: "Hi Bob! I'm Assist-o, here to help you with follow-ups and data entry so you can focus on selling. I'll pop up suggestions here and in Slack. You're in control – you can adjust my settings anytime." Bob nods and continues. The first week, Assist-o only suggests a couple of things (nothing overwhelming). Bob finds them useful and starts trusting it. Week 2, Bob gets busy and the agent ups its help – scheduling a meeting automatically. It sends Bob a Slack message: "I booked a meeting with ACME Corp for you on Friday at 2pm since you were away. Okay?" Bob's happy because that saved him time; he replies "Thanks" which the agent logs. A month in, Bob decides the agent can even draft emails. He tells it "Go ahead and draft thank-you emails after client calls" by toggling a preference. The agent does so but one draft comes out a bit off. The agent itself flags "I'm not fully confident about the wording, please review." Bob appreciates the honesty, edits the email, and maybe that feedback goes back into improving prompts. Over time, Bob sees the agent as a reliable aide – he even jokes about it with colleagues ("My AI assistant reminded me... good thing, I totally would've forgotten!"). If Bob ever wonders "what has it learned about me?", he checks the transparency page and sees no scary surprises, maybe just "Prefers Slack, rarely needs help with CRM updates, loves scheduling assistance." That aligns with his own view. In short, the agent has fit into Bob's daily work naturally.

Pro tip: Users will personify the agent – leverage that judiciously. Give the agent a bit of character (consistent voice, maybe a light sense of humor if appropriate), but not too much. It should never pretend to be human or over-familiar. Dry humor can be fine ("I promise I'm not procrastinating, but I do need more time to fetch that data 😅") if it fits the company culture, but always secondary to getting the job done. Striking the right tone in the human-AI relationship can turn the agent from a tool into a teammate in the user's mind.

With thoughtful UX design, our Companion agent becomes a welcome part of the user's work life rather than an intrusion. We've now covered designing the agent's brain (architecture, memory) and its personality/presence (UX, relationship). In a modern enterprise, however, an agent rarely lives alone. The final piece of the puzzle is how Companion agents interact within a multi-agent ecosystem – cooperating with other specialized agents and fitting into bigger workflows that span beyond just the user-agent dyad. In the next section, we'll look at Companion Agents in Multi-Agent Ecosystems, exploring delegation patterns between agents, shared contexts, and examples of how our Companion might work hand-in-hand with other agents like Action, Presenter, Supervisor, etc., to deliver even greater value. This will round out our view of the Companion as not only a personal assistant but also a team player in a broader AI workforce.

COMPANION AGENTS IN MULTI-AGENT ECOSYSTEMS

No agent is an island – especially in an enterprise that embraces an agent-first ecosystem. While our Companion agent is focused on serving its individual user, it will inevitably need to interface with other AI agents orchestrating different parts of the business. For instance, a Companion might detect something and hand off to a specialized Action agent to perform a bulk update, or fetch information from a Curator agent's summary. In this section, we explore how Companion agents collaborate with other agent patterns (Action, Presenter, Supervisor, Conductor, Sentinel, etc.), ensuring a seamless network of AI assistance across the organization. We'll outline common delegation patterns between agents, discuss how they share context and data safely, and mention external analogies (like Microsoft's Copilot or multi-agent frameworks such as CrewAI and LangChain) to see how industry patterns align with our approach. The goal is to illustrate that a Companion agent doesn't operate in a vacuum – it can be both a consumer and producer of AI services in a larger ecosystem, all coordinated via Salesforce's Agentforce platform and metadata.

Delegation patterns between agents: Here are a few ways a Companion might coordinate with other agents:

Companion → Action → Presenter: This is a chain where the Companion decides something needs doing, calls on an Action agent to do it, and then a Presenter agent to show the result. For example, the Companion might notice "We need to update 50 records based on this new policy." Rather than doing it one-by-one or bugging the user, it sends a request to an Action agent built for bulk updates. That Action agent executes the changes. Then, to inform the user or broader team, a Presenter agent might come into play to generate a nice summary or dashboard of what changed (or a Chatter post highlighting the outcomes). In practice, this could be implemented by the Companion creating a Platform Event or invoking a Flow that the Action agent subscribes to (with context of which records and what action). Once done, that Action agent could trigger a Presenter (maybe by creating a Summary record or event that the Presenter agent handles). Agentforce's Agent Builder could allow chaining: e.g., a metadata setting like "After Companion X triggers Action Y, invoke Presenter Z with results = true". The user experiences a smooth workflow: they didn't have to manually update records or figure out what happened; the agents coordinated it and presented the outcome.

Companion → Supervisor (draft, validate): If a Companion generates something that requires approval or oversight, it might delegate to a Supervisor agent. Consider an example: the Companion drafts a contract clause for a sales proposal using GPT. Before it's sent to the client, it delegates to a Supervisor agent (trained for policy compliance, perhaps) to validate that the clause meets legal guidelines. The Supervisor agent could either approve it or modify it (or escalate to a human if unsure). Only then does the Companion present it to the user as "ready to send." In terms of integration: the Companion could post the draft to a Supervisor agent's queue or call an invocable method that the Supervisor pattern exposes (like PolicyCheckService.checkText(...)). This is an internal QA step.

Companion → Conductor (multi-step requests): Sometimes a user might ask the Companion something that actually requires orchestrating multiple steps or involving multiple systems – essentially a workflow best handled by a Conductor agent. For instance, the user says, "Assistant, onboard a new employee for me." The Companion alone can't do all that (that might involve IT setup, HR forms, training assignments, etc.). So the Companion delegates to a Conductor agent specialized in onboarding process. The Conductor then kicks off a series of Action agents or flows to create accounts, send welcome emails, etc. The Companion's role becomes to monitor progress and keep the user updated, maybe eventually telling the user "Onboarding complete, all steps done." So, delegation here is handing off a complex goal to another agent orchestrator. Implementation-wise: maybe the Companion creates an "OnboardingRequest__c" record, which a Conductor agent is listening for via a flow trigger, then the Conductor does its thing and updates status which the Companion then reads and informs the user. The interplay might involve the Companion passing the user's context (who's hiring, details) to the Conductor.

These patterns illustrate a principle: the Companion initiates or requests help from other agents when the task is outside its narrow scope or would break the stride of personalized interaction.

Shared context and memory between agents: For such collaborations to work, agents need to share relevant context without breaching privacy or creating inconsistency:

Session memory hand-off: If a user is having a multi-turn interaction that starts with one agent and goes to another, we want to carry over context so the user doesn't have to repeat themselves. For example, a Sentinel agent (monitoring events) might detect a suspicious activity and alert a Companion ("Heads up, this account shows unusual activity"). The Companion when presenting that to the user might then call a Curator agent to summarize the activity. The Curator needs the details from the Sentinel. So either the Sentinel passes its findings (maybe via a record or event) and flags it for that user, and the Curator reads that. Or more systematically, Agentforce might maintain a session context object – something like a ContextId shared across agents in a workflow. Indeed, the outline mentions session memory passed from Sentinel or Curator to Companion. We could implement that with a shared key (like an Incident ID or a Conversation ID). All agents working on that incident attach their outputs to that key in a context store (could be a custom object with child records for each agent's contribution). The Companion then can retrieve the combined context to present to the user.

Preferences passed to Presenter or Coach: Our Companion has gathered user preferences; other agents that serve the user (like a Presenter agent that formats output, or a Coach agent that gives advice) would benefit from knowing those. For instance, if the user's tone preference is friendly and brief, the Presenter agent should present info in that style (maybe fewer details, more informal). The Companion can pass along these preferences when it invokes another agent. If using metadata, one way is that all agents have access to a common Persona profile metadata for the user (maybe loaded by user ID). Or the Companion explicitly calls the Presenter's API with parameters including tone=Friendly, verbosity=Low. The architecture might use Agent Builder metadata to tag agents with what personas or users they support. For instance, the Presenter agent might be tagged as "supports tone adaptation" and the Companion sees that tag and knows it can send tone context. Also, a trusted call registry is likely used to declare which agents can call which (some agents might be forbidden to talk to others for security).

Agent Builder metadata for coordination: Agentforce can act as the directory of agents. In the metadata, we might have entries like:

- Agent Name: "AcmeSalesCompanion", Type: Companion, Persona: Sales Rep, TrustedCalls: [BulkActionAgent, DealReviewerAgent, etc.].
- Agent Name: "BulkActionAgent", Type: Action, AcceptsRequestsFrom: [AcmeSalesCompanion].

This formalizes which agents can delegate to which. It prevents, say, a malicious or buggy agent from calling something it shouldn't. And it helps us design flows because we know the pathways allowed.

The metadata might also include capabilities information that one agent can query about another. For example, the Companion might query "what agents are available for 'send_summary' function?" and find there's a Presenter agent it can use. This dynamic discovery is advanced, but Agentforce could have a registry object or "AgentExchange" for such discovery (the mention of AgentExchange in outline suggests a marketplace or listing of available agents and connectors).

External examples alignment: The outline references a few external analogies that we can mention to frame this multi-agent integration:

Microsoft Copilot's user agents: Microsoft 365 Copilot acts as an assistant across Office apps for a user (similar in concept to a Companion), but it also can call underlying functionalities. We might say: just as Microsoft Copilot is user-centric but uses the whole Office Graph (multiple tools) behind the scenes, our Companion can leverage multiple Salesforce agents under the hood. Microsoft's approach also integrates with external plugins (like in Teams it can schedule meetings, pulling from Outlook, etc.) – it's an ecosystem approach.

CrewAI's embedded user proxies: CrewAI (as an example framework) sometimes uses a "user proxy agent" – an agent that represents a user in a multi-agent collaboration. Our Companion is effectively a user proxy in the Salesforce agent ecosystem: it acts on behalf of the user and coordinates with other agents. CrewAI emphasizes role-based personas in agent clusters, akin to how our Companion has a persona tag and works with other role-defined agents.

LangChain's long-lived memory roles: LangChain/LongChain (as in LangGraph) supports persistent agents that maintain long-term state. Our Companion is a long-lived agent for a user. In LangChain you might have an agent playing a "helper" role with memory across sessions – exactly what our Companion does, storing context and preferences. Additionally, LangChain often orchestrates multiple agents for complex tasks (like one agent for reasoning, one for execution). In our world, we mirror that by splitting Companion vs. Action vs. Presenter, etc., each with a specialized role but working together.

Essentially, industry trends show that having a personalized user agent working in concert with specialist agents/tools is a powerful pattern (e.g., OpenAI's function calling where the assistant decides to call a function – our Companion deciding to call an Action agent is analogous).

To visualize, the outline even suggests a diagram "A Day with Your Companion". Imagine that diagram: morning, a Sentinel agent detects something overnight, passes to Companion which notifies user on mobile; midday, user asks Companion for a summary, Companion gets it from Curator agent; afternoon, user says "execute XYZ", Companion delegates to Conductor agent which involves multiple others, then Companion wraps up and informs the user in Slack in the evening. It's a web of interactions but the user experiences a cohesive help through their Companion.

From a Salesforce implementation perspective, enabling this ecosystem might involve:

Agent Orchestration Flows: flows that route requests between agents, possibly triggered by events or by agents themselves writing to a "handoff" object.

Shared data models: common objects or records that multiple agents can update/read. E.g., an Interaction record with sub-records for each agent's part.

Cross-agent security context: ensure that when one agent passes something to another, it doesn't bypass security. Possibly use something like the Model Context Protocol (MCP) which enforces that context info includes permissions metadata. The article we saw indicates MCP helps maintain security context even when connecting across systems (like Slack's MCP server respects enterprise permissions). In our case, if a Companion passes a user's request to an Action agent, it might include the user's ID or a token that ensures the Action agent only does what that user could do.

Finally, consider that multi-agent doesn't always mean multiple AI systems; it can also mean AI + human. The Companion might coordinate not just with automated agents but trigger a handoff to a human agent (like a support rep or manager). We addressed some of that in delegation and UX (Supervisor pattern). The ecosystem includes humans as ultimate fallback agents, one could say.

We can wrap this section up by highlighting how our design aligns with the broader vision:

We've effectively made the Companion agent the personal layer of a layered AI architecture. Above it might be orchestration (Conductors), beside it specialists (like Supervisor for approvals, Sentinel for monitoring, etc.), and below it, tools and data (Action agents, knowledge bases).

By using Salesforce-native tools (Flow, Apex, metadata) for integration, we ensure governance: for example, our flows can have error handling at each agent handoff, our metadata can quickly turn off a problematic integration if needed (just remove an agent from the trusted list).

The ecosystem approach also future-proofs things: if a new type of agent comes in (say a Planning agent with a new algorithm), the Companion can integrate with it via the same patterns.

To cement the concept, let's narrate "A Day with Your Companion" in multi-agent style (the content that diagram might depict).

Morning: A Sentinel agent in IT detects a server outage at 3 AM and creates an incident. The Companion agent for the IT manager gets the alert when the manager logs in at 8 AM, and using a Presenter agent, it shows a dashboard of overnight incidents with the outage highlighted (so Sentinel → Companion → Presenter chain). The manager acknowledges via the Companion.

Later, the manager asks the Companion, "Summarize yesterday's support tickets for me." The Companion delegates to a Curator agent that specializes in summarizing text. The Curator returns key points, and the Companion relays that summary in Slack (with tone adjusted to manager's preference).

In the afternoon, a sales rep's Companion works with a Conductor agent: The rep says "Assistant, end-of-quarter cleanup: close all deals with no activity 90+ days." The Companion hands this off to a Conductor agent orchestrating a series of checks (maybe consulting a Supervisor agent to ensure none are high-value deals that should stay open) and then an Action agent to close those opportunities. Once done, the Conductor notifies the rep's Companion, which then tells the rep "I closed 12 stale opportunities and notified their owners. (Done via our automation process)." That's Companion → Conductor → (Supervisor + Action) → Companion -> User.

End of day: The executive's Companion compiles a summary of all these happenings by fetching updates from various agents and systems, maybe akin to Microsoft Viva or other cross-domain assistants, and presents a cohesive narrative, showing how multiple agents worked together under the hood.

By now it's clear that our Companion agent, though user-focused, is deeply connected to an ecosystem of AI services. Salesforce's Agentforce provides the glue (metadata, events, flows) to make these connections robust and governable.

Pro tip: Design agents to play well with others. Clearly define each agent's API or invocation interface (inputs/outputs), use common data formats or objects for shared context, and enforce through governance that agents only call permitted agents. This reduces integration headaches and security risks. In essence, treat inter-agent interactions like microservices – with contracts and monitoring. That way, when your Companion delegates a task, you can trust the called agent to do its part and not step on toes, and if something fails, it's easier to locate which agent or handoff had an issue.

By orchestrating multiple agents in concert, we unlock compound value: the sum is greater than the parts. A Companion agent supported by a team of specialized agents can deliver outcomes to the user that neither could achieve alone easily. This multi-agent harmony is the ultimate vision of an AI-augmented enterprise workforce, and our Companion is the friendly face of that complex orchestra for the end user.

SUMMARY

In this chapter, we followed the evolution of a Salesforce Companion agent from a simple assistant into a trusted daily work partner. We saw how it progresses through phases – first offering suggestions to build credibility, then taking on executions of routine tasks under the user's supervision, and finally handling delegated actions autonomously within guardrails. Along the way, we explored the architectural foundations that make this maturity possible: a lifecycle that recognizes context, personalizes responses, assists helpfully, and escalates or learns when needed. We leveraged Salesforce's rich toolkit (Agent Builder metadata, Flows, Invocable Apex, LWCs, and more) to implement a Companion that is both intelligent and governable – every action logged, every decision constrained by permissions and preferences.

Crucially, we emphasized personalization, memory, and UX design as the keys to user adoption. Our Companion agent doesn't treat all users the same; it learns each user's style, preferences, and needs over time, storing those insights in Salesforce's data model and adjusting its behavior accordingly. It remembers context across sessions (while respecting boundaries and offering transparency), so interactions feel continuous and tailored. We implemented safety features like the ability to inspect and reset the agent's memory, ensuring the user stays in control of the relationship. The result is an agent that "gets you" and fits naturally into your workflow – appearing at the right time, in the right channel, with the right tone.

We also tackled the human-AI relationship aspect: giving the agent a clear purpose and identity (so users understand its role), designing it to be polite and non-intrusive (minimizing notification fatigue and gracefully handling uncertainty), and making it a cooperative colleague rather than a clippy antagonist. Through thoughtful UI embedding and interaction design, the Companion becomes a welcome presence across Salesforce, Slack, email, or wherever work happens – always available when needed, but never in the way.

Finally, we zoomed out to see the Companion in the big picture of an agent-first enterprise. Our Companion agent acts as the user's personal proxy in a landscape filled with other AI agents (and humans). We outlined how it delegates to and collaborates with specialized agents – whether calling an Action agent to perform a bulk update, seeking approval from a Supervisor agent, or pulling in a summary from a Curator agent. Thanks to Agentforce's metadata-driven architecture, these multi-agent handoffs are seamless and secure. The Companion carries the user's context and intent into a broader AI network and brings back results, effectively personalizing the power of the whole ecosystem for the individual. In doing so, Companion agents deliver continuity, empathy, and sound judgment, acting as the empathetic front-end to very complex back-end AI processes.

By growing a Companion agent with such care – technically, ethically, and in user experience – we set the stage for an organization where humans and AI agents work side by side in harmony. The Companion pattern shows that AI doesn't have to be a detached system in the background; it can be an engaging, adaptive partner in our daily professional lives, amplifying our capabilities while respecting our autonomy.

Next, Chapter 19 takes us beyond the familiar CRM territory. We will explore how Agentforce and the patterns we've learned (Companion included) can be applied across other enterprise domains like HR, Legal, Finance, Procurement, and more. The journey continues as we discover the opportunities and design considerations for deploying AI agents as daily work partners in every corner of the enterprise, not just in sales or service. Our Companion agents will have many siblings in other departments – and the pattern playbook will guide how to extend our learnings to those new frontiers. Get ready to see AI agents step outside the CRM and into the wider business world, bringing intelligence to every team and process. The skills and insights you've gained in growing a Companion agent will be invaluable as we broaden our scope in the next chapter.

19

AGENTS BEYOND CRM – HR, LEGAL, FINANCE, AND MORE

If Salesforce's Agentforce platform were used only for classic CRM functions, it would be a tremendous missed opportunity. The agent patterns we've explored in this book are inherently cross-functional – nothing about a Sentinel, Supervisor, Companion, or Curator agent limits it to Sales, Service, or Marketing. In fact, all eight core patterns have rich applications beyond the customer domain: a Conductor can orchestrate multi-step workflows in HR or Finance, a Presenter can generate internal reports and briefings, an Action agent can execute routine tasks in IT, and a Coach can guide employees on best practices. The same pattern-driven approach that powers great customer-facing bots can be applied across internal business functions with equal (if not greater) impact.

This chapter broadens our view beyond the traditional Salesforce domains and into the rest of the enterprise. As Agentforce matures, so do the possibilities for deploying AI agents in Human Resources, Legal, Finance, Procurement, IT, Compliance, Facilities, and more – often yielding faster ROI and lower risk than front-office deployments. It's no coincidence that many organizations find their first AI "quick wins" in back-office settings: internal projects show clear value by boosting efficiency without directly touching customers. Internal departments stand to benefit enormously from intelligent automation. These functions are the backbone of day-to-day operations, full of repetitive workflows, policy checks, and data-heavy analysis that agents can handle behind the scenes. By introducing agents "beyond

CRM," organizations can improve employee experience (for example, an HR bot that instantly answers benefits questions), reduce operational risk (a compliance agent that never forgets a required approval), and unlock strategic insight (a finance agent that spots spending anomalies early). Crucially, because these agents work on internal processes, companies can experiment and iterate more freely than with customer-facing bots – mistakes are more contained, and successes directly enhance productivity, compliance, and cost savings.

For instance, imagine a new employee onboarding scenario: an AI Companion in HR greets the new hire on day one, answers their questions, and walks them through orientation. Meanwhile, a Conductor agent behind the scenes coordinates IT and Facilities – creating user accounts, assigning equipment, scheduling training sessions – following the established checklist without human oversight. A Supervisor policy agent ensures all mandatory forms and compliance steps (NDAs, security training) are completed, flagging any missing items for HR to review. By end of day, the new hire's setup is done smoothly and consistently. This kind of cross-team orchestration would be tedious and error-prone manually, but with Agentforce it becomes an automated, audit-friendly workflow that boosts efficiency and employee satisfaction from the start.

In this chapter, we'll explore how each core agent pattern can be applied outside the sales and service arena. Each section focuses on a major enterprise domain – HR, Legal, Finance, Procurement, IT, and others – illustrating practical use cases and the agent patterns that fit them. We'll discuss design considerations unique to each function (for example, how a Legal AI assistant must incorporate human oversight, or how an IT agent handles sensitive security actions), and highlight the Salesforce-native tools that make these agents possible (like Agent Builder, Flow, invocable Apex actions, and Slack integration). Along the way, we'll draw comparisons to the broader AI ecosystem – from Microsoft's workplace Copilots to open frameworks like LangChain or CrewAI – to show how Agentforce's pattern-based approach aligns with industry trends in enterprise AI.

By the end of this chapter, you'll see that Agentforce is not confined to CRM at all – it provides a blueprint for enterprise-wide AI teammates. We'll start in the next section by discussing how to identify prime opportunities for agents across different business functions and how to assess which processes are truly "agent-ready." Let's begin by figuring out where AI agents can make the biggest difference inside your organization.

IDENTIFYING ENTERPRISE AGENT USE CASES

How do you decide where to deploy an AI agent in your enterprise? A good starting point is to evaluate potential tasks against a set of selection criteria derived from the Agentforce patterns. In other words, identify the characteristics of work that agents handle well. Generally, you should look for processes or challenges that meet one or more of the following conditions:

Repetitive, rules-based tasks – Action Pattern: High-volume, routine tasks that follow clear rules are prime candidates for an Action agent. If employees are copy-pasting data between systems or performing the same procedure hundreds of times (for example, entering invoices into a ledger or copying data from emails to a database), an autonomous Action agent can take over those steps and execute them consistently and rapidly without fatigue.

Policy-bound decisions – Supervisor Pattern: Scenarios where decisions are governed by defined policies or approval rules fit the Supervisor agent pattern. Think of expense approvals, compliance checks, or access requests – anywhere a "yes/no" decision must be made by evaluating criteria. A Supervisor agent can enforce business rules impartially, flag or reject out-of-policy items, and escalate to humans only when judgment is truly needed. (For instance, a Supervisor agent might auto-approve routine purchases under a dollar threshold, but route larger or unusual requests to a manager.)

Multi-department coordination – Conductor Pattern: Processes that span multiple teams or systems are ideal for a Conductor agent. These are workflows with several hand-offs or sequential steps (such as employee onboarding, which involves HR, IT, and Facilities, or a customer refund process touching finance and support). A Conductor can orchestrate the entire end-to-end process, ensuring nothing falls through the cracks between departments and everyone gets the right notification at the right time.

Information overload – Curator Pattern: If users or staff are drowning in information – think massive reports, overflowing inboxes, log files, or too many data sources – a Curator agent can help. The Curator pattern excels at filtering, summarizing, and prioritizing information. You might build an agent that digests a 100-page policy document into a one-page brief, monitors various data feeds and surfaces only anomalies, or consolidates customer feedback from multiple channels into key trends for the team.

Behavioral coaching – Coach Pattern: When the goal is to guide or influence user behavior over time (rather than perform a one-off task), consider a

Coach agent. These agents observe behavior and provide tailored feedback or reminders. Use cases include an agent that nudges employees to follow best practices (like a sales coaching bot that notices when opportunities lack next steps and reminds the rep), or a wellness coach that monitors work patterns and suggests breaks/exercises. A Coach agent essentially functions as a personalized mentor or trainer, reinforcing the habits your organization wants to encourage.

Personalized support – Companion Pattern: Any scenario where individuals need on-demand, context-aware assistance is perfect for a Companion agent. This pattern represents a "digital assistant" that users can interact with conversationally or via a convenient UI. From a helper bot that answers employees' HR FAQs one-on-one (instead of filing a ticket), to an in-app guide that adapts to each user's context, Companion agents shine at providing personalized, immediate support. They remember user preferences and can intermediate with other agents/services on the user's behalf.

If a business process or task checks one or more of the boxes above, it's likely a strong candidate for an Agentforce solution. The next step is to scan across your enterprise functions to find where these conditions are most prevalent. Certain departments in particular tend to be rich with opportunities for AI agents. Based on our experience, you should evaluate the following domains first:

Human Resources (HR) & People Operations: HR is full of repetitive processes (benefits enrollment, time-off requests, updating personal info) and multi-step workflows (onboarding, offboarding) that are ideal for automation. It also involves constant Q&A (policies, payroll, benefits) where a Companion agent can provide instant answers. Additionally, HR benefits from agents that do sentiment monitoring or policy enforcement to improve employee engagement and compliance.

Finance & Accounting: Finance has strict policies and data-heavy operations. Expense report auditing, invoice processing, travel approvals, budget tracking – these rule-bound activities are perfect for Supervisor and Action agents to handle. A finance Curator agent could summarize budget variances for managers, while a Sentinel/Supervisor combo flags questionable transactions in real time. By automating routine finance tasks, agents free up the team for analysis and strategic planning.

Legal & Compliance: These functions deal with large volumes of documents and complex rules. An AI agent can scan contracts for risky clauses (using

Curator logic to extract key terms and Supervisor logic to compare against standards), monitor regulatory updates and summarize changes, or ensure processes follow required legal steps (checklists, approvals) – acting as a tireless compliance sentinel. Legal departments can use Presenter agents to draft simple agreements or policy summaries for review, always with a human in the loop for final judgment.

Procurement & Supply Chain: Procurement involves coordinating vendors, purchase orders, inventory levels, and deliveries – often across multiple systems. Agents can streamline vendor onboarding (gathering documents, running compliance checks, setting up records via a Conductor pattern), detect anomalies in supply chain data (Sentinel spotting a delay or an unusual spike in prices), and automatically initiate certain actions. For example, a Companion agent might proactively suggest reordering a product when inventory is low, or even draft an RFP (Request for Proposal) when a contract is due to expire, with a Supervisor agent ensuring policy is followed.

Internal IT & Security: IT operations generate extensive log data and face many repetitive support tasks. Agents can monitor for security threats (a Sentinel agent scanning login patterns and system alerts), automate user provisioning and deprovisioning (an Action agent creating or revoking access based on triggers like new hires or departures), and curate system health summaries (a Curator agent compiling daily IT status reports with a Presenter formatting it for executives). In cybersecurity, AI Sentinels can catch unusual behavior (multiple failed logins, strange network activity) and either alert a human or invoke automated containment via a Supervisor/Action sequence.

Employee Experience & General Operations: Beyond specific departments, consider general employee-facing services – facilities requests, internal help desks, travel coordination, and other services that improve day-to-day employee experience. A Companion agent can serve as a one-stop concierge for employees, handling questions like "How do I reserve a conference room?" or tasks like submitting a facilities ticket for a broken equipment. These cross-cutting use cases improve overall organizational efficiency and morale by providing quick assistance across a range of topics.

Every organization is unique, so you might find agent-ready use cases in other areas as well (from R&D project management to customer feedback analysis) by applying the same pattern lens. The key is to look for the intersections of pain points and pattern-aligned solutions. Once you spot a promising opportunity, also consider its feasibility: does the agent have access to the necessary data, systems, and permissions? Clear data availability and well-defined rules will make it much easier to implement a successful agent. Early projects should ideally target processes that are relatively well-bounded and measurable – you can always expand to more complex scenarios as your team gains experience and trust in the agents.

Pro Tip: The fastest AI wins are often internal. Start where agents can help your employees – not just your customers. Focusing on back-office and operational use cases first lets you demonstrate quick value and refine your agent solutions in a lower-risk environment, paving the way for broader adoption.

HR AND PEOPLE OPERATIONS

Human Resources is a natural starting point for enterprise AI agents. HR teams juggle a mix of repetitive administrative tasks, important but routine employee inquiries, and sensitive compliance requirements – all areas where well-designed agents can make a huge impact. By offloading transactional work to AI and providing employees with self-service tools, HR agents can both improve efficiency for the HR staff and enhance the day-to-day experience of every employee interacting with HR. (Notably, internal-facing agents often face lower risk and regulatory barriers than customer-facing ones, making HR an ideal proving ground for Agentforce.) Below we explore several high-value HR and People Operations use cases for AI agents and how different patterns come into play:

Onboarding Orchestration – Conductor + Action: Bringing a new employee on board involves many coordinated steps across HR, IT, Facilities, and hiring managers. An onboarding agent can act as a Conductor that orchestrates this multi-department checklist. For example, as soon as a candidate is marked "hired," the agent triggers tasks: creating system accounts and email (through an Action sub-task), scheduling required training sessions, shipping a laptop, granting building access, and so on. It ensures all stakeholders (HR coordinators, IT support, the new hire's team) are notified of their responsibilities and tracks completion of each item. The result is a smooth, standardized onboarding process where nothing is forgotten – the new employee shows up on Day 1 with their email, equipment, and accounts ready, and HR didn't have to micromanage dozens of manual emails to make it happen.

Sentiment Monitoring – Sentinel + Curator: HR isn't just about processes – it's also the guardian of organizational health and culture. A Sentinel/Curator agent combo can help HR monitor employee sentiment and engagement in real time. This might involve analyzing pulse surveys, internal chat channels, or anonymized feedback for signs of declining morale, burnout, or issues like harassment. The Sentinel component watches for predefined warning signals (e.g. a spike in negative sentiment in survey comments or certain keywords in feedback), while the Curator aggregates these insights into digestible reports or alerts for HR leadership. For example, the agent could alert HR, "Engagement scores in the Sales team dropped 10% this month, with common themes around remote work challenges," highlighting an issue before it escalates. (Such monitoring must be handled with care – e.g. aggregate data and anonymize identifiers – to protect employee privacy while still surfacing important trends.)

Benefits Coaching – Coach + Presenter: Navigating benefits and wellness options can be confusing for employees, so an AI Coach agent that provides personalized guidance is a welcome addition. Picture a "Benefits Buddy" that employees can consult 24/7. Using the Coach pattern, it can ask the employee a few questions about their needs or life events (e.g. "Having a baby" or "Considering retirement savings options") and then use a Presenter component to show a tailored overview of relevant benefits (health plan options, parental leave policy, 401k contribution suggestions, etc.). During open enrollment, the agent might proactively reach out with tips ("You haven't selected a health plan yet – can I help compare your options based on your family status?") and use company data to make recommendations. The Coach agent can also remind employees of under-utilized benefits ("You have 5 days of PTO left – taking time off can help prevent burnout") or guide managers on supporting their teams' development (like suggesting training programs). By acting as a friendly advisor, the benefits coach agent helps employees make the most of what the company offers.

Time-Off Request Assistance – Companion Pattern: Handling routine HR requests is an ideal job for a Companion agent. A great example is vacation or leave requests. Instead of filling out forms or emailing HR, an employee could simply message an HR chatbot (on Slack or Microsoft Teams) saying, "I'd like to take off the first week of next month." The Companion agent can check the person's vacation balance, cross-reference company holidays and their team's schedule, and interactively ask for any needed details. Finally, it logs the approved time-off in the HR system and notifies the employee's manager for awareness – all in one conversational flow. In fact, companies are already doing this: employees at some organizations can converse with an AI agent in Slack to check their PTO balance, submit leave requests, and receive manager approval through the same channel, with no manual HR intervention. The result is a faster, more convenient process for employees and a lighter load on HR staff who no longer spend time on data entry for leave tracking.

Policy Compliance and Updates – Supervisor + Presenter: HR is responsible for communicating policies and ensuring employee compliance with various requirements (think code of conduct acknowledgments, mandatory training, or new workplace guidelines). A Supervisor agent can take on the enforcement and tracking role, while a Presenter agent handles communication. For instance, when a new HR policy (say, an update to the travel reimbursement policy) is released, a Presenter agent could broadcast a summary of the key changes in an easily digestible format to all employees. The paired Supervisor agent would then monitor acknowledgments – checking off who has read and signed the policy, sending friendly reminders to those who haven't by the deadline, and escalating to HR if certain employees consistently ignore mandatory policies. Similarly, this agent duo could ensure compliance with recurring requirements: it might track completion of annual training modules or paperwork, issue certificates or gentle nudges as needed, and maintain an auditable log. By automating policy communications and compliance tracking, HR can be confident that everyone stays informed and meets obligations without HR teams chasing down each individual manually.

To implement these kinds of HR agents on the Salesforce platform, you can leverage a range of native tools. Experience Cloud (Salesforce's portal framework) allows you to create employee-facing websites or chat interfaces where agents like the onboarding assistant or benefits bot can live, providing a user-friendly front end for interactions. Flow Builder lets you automate HR business processes (like the steps of onboarding or the approval logic for time-off) in a declarative way, which your agents can trigger or call as subroutines. Many HR agents integrate naturally with Slack (thanks to Salesforce's Slack integration and toolkit) – for example, an HR Companion bot can answer questions and push reminders directly in an employee's Slack channel, which drives engagement. And behind the scenes, you might use custom objects in Salesforce to store agent-related data such as sentiment scores over time, onboarding tasks, or policy acknowledgment records. This creates a system of record for the agents' actions and outcomes, enabling HR to analyze trends and demonstrate the agents' impact (e.g.

tracking how much faster onboarding tasks are completed with a Conductor agent in place).

It's worth noting that Salesforce isn't alone in aiming AI at HR – this trend is happening across the industry. Microsoft, for example, has introduced its Viva platform and HR-focused Copilot features to enhance employee experience with AI-driven insights, and Workday's Extend platform enables HR teams to build custom AI apps on top of Workday data. Even open-source multi-agent frameworks like CrewAI have showcased "HR copilot" demos. These validate the opportunity: in fact, Microsoft's internal HR agent pilots have shown significant improvements in both speed and quality of employee support responses. With Agentforce, you can build similar capabilities natively within Salesforce – tightly integrating your HR agents with your core employee data and workflows, and tailoring each agent to your organization's policies and culture.

LEGAL, RISK, AND COMPLIANCE

The Legal, Risk, and Compliance domain is one where AI agents must be applied with particular care – but also one with tremendous opportunity. Legal teams are burdened with reviewing lengthy documents, ensuring regulatory compliance, and managing approvals, all of which involve well-defined rules and lots of text. AI agents can act as force-multipliers for lawyers and compliance officers by handling the heavy lifting of analysis and routing, while leaving final decisions to humans. For example, in 2023 a law firm was sanctioned after an attorney relied on ChatGPT to draft a brief that contained fabricated case citations. This incident underscores that AI outputs in legal matters must be rigorously verified. With that in mind, let's look at some high-impact use cases for agents in legal, risk, and compliance functions:

Contract Clause Analysis – Curator + Supervisor: Contract review is a prime example of a tedious, detail-oriented task perfect for AI augmentation. A Curator agent can scan through lengthy contracts or agreements and extract key clauses, terms, and anomalies. Paired with a Supervisor logic, the agent can then compare these findings against a library of approved standards or checklist criteria set by the legal team. For instance, the agent might flag, "Missing confidentiality clause" or "Indemnification clause deviates from our standard template," highlighting sections that a human lawyer should double-check. The Curator portion reads and summarizes relevant parts of the document (dates, parties, liabilities, unusual language), and the Supervisor portion labels each as acceptable or risky based on predefined rules. This dramatically speeds up contract vetting – an attorney can focus attention only on the flagged points instead of combing through every line. Of course, the lawyer makes the final call on any changes, but the agent's analysis can save hours.

Approval Routing for High-Risk Agreements – Conductor Pattern: Not all contracts are equal – a $5,000 standard purchase may only need a quick legal glance, whereas a $5 million deal with unusual terms needs thorough scrutiny and sign-offs. A Conductor agent can automate the routing of legal documents based on risk thresholds and criteria. When a new contract is submitted, the agent evaluates its characteristics (value, complexity, any unusual terms) and determines the required approval path. Simple, low-risk agreements might be approved with minimal review, while high-risk or non-standard contracts are automatically routed to the appropriate senior counsel, finance, or executive reviewers. The Conductor agent sequences these approvals, notifies each stakeholder of their task, and tracks progress to completion. By handling the coordination, the agent ensures that every contract gets the right level of oversight without legal staff manually chasing approvals. This speeds up cycle times and ensures compliance with internal controls.

Regulation Monitoring – Sentinel + Curator: Compliance teams must stay on top of ever-changing laws, regulations, and industry standards – a daunting task given the volume of information. A Sentinel agent can continuously watch regulatory updates from government websites, legal databases, or news feeds, and a Curator agent can distill those updates into actionable summaries. For instance, a compliance Sentinel might track updates on data privacy laws globally or changes to financial reporting standards. When it detects a new relevant publication (say, a new GDPR guideline or an SEC rule change), it triggers the Curator to summarize the key points and implications. The agent then alerts the legal/compliance team: "New data protection regulation proposed – here's what it covers and how it might affect us." This proactive monitoring ensures the organization isn't caught off-guard by rule changes. The Curator's summary helps experts assess impact quickly or even feed into a Supervisor agent that cross-checks the new rule against company practices (flagging any potential gaps to address). Essentially, the agent becomes an always-on research assistant scanning the horizon of laws and regulations.

Drafting Policy Summaries – Presenter + Coach: Legal and compliance departments often need to communicate complex policies to employees in an understandable way. A Presenter agent can help by generating plain-language summaries or FAQs from dense policy documents, while a Coach agent component can interact with employees to clarify doubts. For example, if a new Code of Conduct is released, a Presenter agent can generate a plain-language "what's changed" memo, while a conversational interface answers employees' questions (e.g., "Does the new policy allow X?") with guidance drawn from the official rules. This uses the Coach pattern by providing interactive guidance and the Presenter pattern by outputting the policy information in a digestible format. By automating first-draft communications and Q&A, legal teams ensure consistent messaging (they would, of course, review any AI-generated policy summary for accuracy before distribution – the agent accelerates the process, but final responsibility stays with the humans).

Escalating Unusual Legal Behaviors – Sentinel → Supervisor: A more advanced scenario is using AI to detect and respond to potential compliance violations or unusual activities that could pose legal risk. A Sentinel agent might monitor certain internal activities or data for red flags – for example, an account experiencing an abnormal number of permission grants, or an employee downloading a large volume of confidential files outside business hours. If it spots something suspicious that falls outside normal parameters, it hands off to a Supervisor agent that applies rules to assess the severity and then routes the issue appropriately (creating a case for the compliance officer or triggering an immediate high-priority alert). For instance, Sentinel detects repeated failed logins on an executive's account → Supervisor flags it as a likely security breach and temporarily locks the account (via an Action agent), while notifying legal and security teams. They don't take action on their own – instead, they ensure human decision-makers are promptly informed with evidence when something looks amiss.

Design Considerations: Legal and compliance agents must be designed with strict human oversight and deterministic logic for critical decisions. Any action involving binding agreements or external parties should require a human in the loop – the agent can draft or recommend, but a lawyer or authorized manager should give final approval. Generative AI (like GPT) can be extremely helpful for analyzing text and suggesting language, but it must be used cautiously in high-stakes domains. Always prefer to have known-good reference data and explicit checks. For example, use a vetted clause library and Apex rules to verify a contract, rather than relying purely on an LLM's "judgment." For example, in 2023 a law firm was sanctioned after an attorney used ChatGPT to write a brief that ended up containing fictitious case citations – a stark reminder that AI output in legal matters needs human validation. Even vendors of legal AI solutions emphasize that their tools complement rather than replace human judgment. A well-implemented legal agent will save time and reduce errors by handling routine analysis, but will always defer to human decision-makers on the final call.

Salesforce Implementation: Building legal and compliance agents in Salesforce will typically combine declarative tools and custom code. Invocable Apex is especially useful here for the more nuanced logic – for instance, an Apex method can score a contract's risk by checking for specific terms or calculate a compliance risk rating, and your Supervisor agent can call that function as part of its decision flow. You can also store key parameters in Custom Metadata (or custom settings): for example, a list of "mandatory clauses" or approval dollar thresholds can live in metadata so that the agent refers to up-to-date policy values without hardcoding them. Salesforce Flow or Agent Builder can orchestrate the stages of an approval or monitoring process (like the contract routing or the insider-trading alert pipeline described above). For user interaction, consider leveraging Experience Cloud to create a secure portal where business users can submit documents for AI review or view compliance reports. Alternatively, a Slack bot interface could let employees ask compliance questions or request a contract check by simply dropping the document into a Slack channel – the agent can then respond in thread after analyzing it. Integrating legal agents with communication channels ensures they fit naturally into existing workflows (e.g., a sales manager uploading a contract draft via a chatbot instead of emailing legal). For traceability, ensure the agent logs its analyses and recommendations (for example, as a custom Legal Review record for each AI-assisted review). Such an audit trail builds trust – letting the legal team see exactly what the agent flagged – and provides evidence of compliance efforts if regulators ever ask.

In summary, legal, risk, and compliance agents can handle a lot of the heavy lifting – reading, cross-checking, alerting – that currently consumes valuable human hours, but they must be deployed in a way that augments, rather than overrides, human expertise. Done right, they function like a diligent junior analyst or paralegal that works 24/7, ensuring nothing is missed and bringing the important things to the attention of the professionals. The legal team can then focus on nuanced analysis and decision-making, confident that the AI is watching the routine details.

FINANCE AND BUDGET MANAGEMENT

Finance and accounting functions run on rules, numbers, and regulations – which makes them fertile ground for AI agents that can ensure policy compliance and surface insights from data. Whether it's monitoring expense reports for misuse or keeping budgets on track, finance-focused agents can help a company protect its money and streamline approvals. At the same time, financial users (like budget owners or accountants) are often skeptical of "black box" decisions. This means our agents need to be not only accurate, but also transparent about their logic (we'll revisit this point shortly). Here are several high-value use cases for agents in Finance and Budget Management:

Expense Review and Flagging – Sentinel + Supervisor: Expense reporting is a classic area where an AI agent can add value by enforcing policy and catching errors or fraud. A Sentinel agent can automatically scan submitted expense reports and receipts, looking for any out-of-policy spend or anomalies (for example, a meal charge above the allowable limit, or two people submitting the same receipt). A Supervisor agent then applies the company's reimbursement rules to determine which expenses can be auto-approved and which need review. In practice, this means routine low-risk expenses might be approved without manager intervention, while questionable items get flagged with an explanation. For instance, if an employee attaches a taxi receipt twice, the agent could flag a duplicate; if a dinner expense exceeds the per diem, the agent might approve only up to the limit and mark the rest as non-reimbursable. AI-powered expense audit tools already achieve this by cross-checking every line item – matching receipts to claims, spotting miscategorized charges, and auto-approving clean reports while highlighting high-risk transactions for audit. The finance team member or approver is then presented with a concise summary of what the agent flagged and why (e.g. "Flight cost is $500 over policy ceiling – needs exception approval"). This speeds up the processing of honest expenses and focuses human attention only where it's truly needed.

Budget Deviation Summaries – Curator + Presenter: Managing budgets involves sifting through piles of financial data to figure out where things are off track. A Curator agent can gather relevant financial data (actuals vs. budget, variances, trends) across departments or projects, and a Presenter agent can turn that into an easy-to-read narrative or visual report. Imagine a monthly "Budget Coach" agent that reviews all departmental budgets at period close and generates a plain-language summary for each budget owner. It might say, "Marketing is 8% over budget this quarter, primarily due to event costs, while Engineering is 5% under budget (saving in travel)." The agent could highlight areas of concern (like spend trending upward every month) or opportunities (funds left unused). By getting automated variance analysis, managers and finance leaders can quickly grasp the state of budgets without poring over spreadsheets. This Curator/Presenter combo essentially automates the first pass of financial analysis – crunching numbers and providing an explanation – so humans can focus on decisions and corrective actions.

Procurement Approvals – Supervisor + Action: Many organizations have approval workflows for purchases or requisitions that follow strict rules (for instance, "if the purchase is under $1,000 and from an approved vendor, it just needs the requester's manager approval; if over that, it needs finance approval," and so on). A Supervisor agent can evaluate each procurement request against these rules, and then an Action agent can automatically execute the appropriate approval steps. For example, say an employee submits a request to buy new software for $300. The agent checks the vendor and amount: it sees the vendor is pre-approved and the amount is under the no-review threshold, so the Action agent automatically marks the request as approved and triggers the purchase order creation. For a larger request – suppose $50,000 – the agent would instead route it to the proper approvers (finance, procurement office, etc.) as defined by policy, possibly using a Conductor pattern to manage the multi-step approval chain. Either way, the agent ensures compliance with spend policies and frees people from having to manually inspect every requisition. This not only accelerates purchasing but also prevents mistakes (the agent will never forget to get a required approval).

Coaching on Compliance Thresholds – Coach Pattern: A Coach agent in finance acts like a financial advisor that keeps the business on the rails with respect to internal policies or targets. This could mean gently coaching managers on spending and compliance. For instance, the agent might monitor each department's travel expenses or training budget and send proactive "coach" messages: "You're nearing the quarterly travel budget limit – consider deferring non-essential trips," or "Only 20% of your training budget has been used this year; consider investing in team development." The Coach agent has context about targets and actuals and provides tailored advice to the responsible person. Another example: a compliance coach for finance might watch key ratios or metrics (say, the percentage of single-source vendor contracts) and nudge the team if a threshold is about to be breached ("Reminder: 10% of our contracts are allowed to be non-competitive – you're at 8% now"). By providing these timely, personalized insights, the AI coach helps managers make informed decisions and avoid accidentally violating policies or blowing budgets. It's like having a financial consultant continuously watching and advising every budget owner.

Travel Companion for Spend Awareness – Companion + Presenter: Business travel is an area where employees have to make spending decisions in real time, and an agent can serve as a helpful travel buddy to keep those decisions within policy. A Companion agent can be available via mobile app or chat to answer questions ("Is this hotel rate within my company's policy?") and provide instant feedback on expenses. Paired with a Presenter, it can also show the traveler a running tally of their trip expenses versus the trip budget or policy limits. For example, an employee could message the agent: "How much of my meal allowance do I have left today?" and the agent would respond with the dollar amount and maybe a friendly tip if needed. Or the agent could proactively ping: "You've spent $80 on meals today, which is near the daily limit – just a heads up." This real-time guidance helps employees stay in compliance and reduces surprises later. After the trip, the same agent might even prepare an expense report draft (compiling all corporate card charges and receipts, using Presenter capabilities to format it) for the traveler to just review and submit. By acting as a personal finance assistant during travel, the Companion agent makes expense compliance almost effortless for employees.

To support these finance agent scenarios, Salesforce provides the building blocks to integrate with financial systems and enforce rules transparently. Accounting Subledger Integration (via MuleSoft or External Services) can connect agents to enterprise finance systems or data warehouses, ensuring they have up-to-date financial data (like actual spend figures or exchange rates) when making decisions. Complex approval workflows can be implemented with Flow Orchestration or standard Salesforce Approval Processes, which our Supervisor agents can trigger or be embedded in. When heavy calculations or custom evaluations are needed – say, computing a variance percentage or detecting duplicates across expense reports – an Invocable Apex method can do the number-crunching and return results to the agent. Finance agents also benefit from integration with collaboration tools: using Slack, an agent can deliver alerts or summaries directly to managers ("Finance Bot: your budget summary for Q2 is ready – click here"), and even let them approve or comment in real time. In Salesforce apps, a Lightning Web Component (LWC) can present the agent's insights in context (for example, an "AI Insights" panel on a budget record showing any anomalies the agent found). Throughout all this, one golden rule for finance agents is explainability. Whenever the agent flags a transaction or makes a recommendation, it should clearly explain why. Providing that rationale (like "Flagged because the amount exceeds the $500 limit for meals") builds user trust in the AI and makes it far more likely that budget owners will embrace the agent's guidance rather than question it.

Pro Tip: Always show your work. In finance, users need to understand why an AI agent made a decision. Having the agent clearly justify each flag or suggestion ("why this was flagged") isn't just nice to have – it's crucial for gaining trust with budget owners and auditors.

PROCUREMENT AND SUPPLY CHAIN

Procurement and supply chain management involves complex workflows that span multiple systems – from sourcing suppliers, to tracking shipments, to managing inventory and payments. AI agents in this domain focus on keeping things running smoothly by automating multi-step processes and flagging risks early. They rely heavily on integrations (since data often lives in ERP or supply chain systems outside of Salesforce) and need to be configured to respect regional or contractual nuances. Here are key use cases where agents can assist:

Vendor Onboarding – Conductor + Supervisor + Action: Bringing a new vendor into your system usually requires collecting documents (tax forms, certifications), performing compliance checks (background, sanction lists), setting up the vendor in internal systems, and obtaining approvals from various departments. A Conductor agent can coordinate this end-to-end onboarding workflow. For example, once a procurement officer initiates a new vendor request, the Conductor agent prompts the vendor to upload necessary documents via a portal (or automatically pulls data from an external source), uses a Supervisor pattern to verify all compliance requirements are met (e.g. checking that a W-9 form is received, running the vendor name through a sanctions API), and then triggers Action tasks to create records in the finance system and notify relevant approvers that the vendor is ready to be used. Throughout the process, the agent can route tasks intelligently – maybe legal needs to sign off if it's a high-value or high-risk vendor, which the Supervisor logic would detect from metadata (like vendor category or region). By automating vendor onboarding, organizations can shave weeks off the time it takes to get a new supplier up and running, and ensure no required step (like a security review or regional compliance check) is overlooked.

Invoice Anomalies – Sentinel Pattern: Invoices from suppliers are another area where agents can maintain oversight. A Sentinel agent can monitor incoming supplier invoices (integrating with the Accounts Payable system) and flag anomalies or potential issues. It might look for duplicates (the same invoice submitted twice), mismatches (an invoice amount that exceeds the purchase order by more than an allowed tolerance), or suspicious patterns (a vendor suddenly invoicing for services outside their usual scope). When something is detected, the agent alerts the finance or procurement team to investigate. This is similar to expense auditing but on the supplier side – for instance, if two different departments submit an invoice from the same vendor with the same invoice number, the agent would notice and flag a possible duplicate payment. By acting as a vigilant bookkeeper, the Sentinel agent helps avoid overpayments and catch errors or fraud that human AP clerks might miss in piles of invoices.

Supply Delay Detection – Sentinel + Curator: Modern supply chains generate event data continuously – shipment updates, production logs, inventory levels. A Sentinel agent can watch these data streams for any signals of trouble, while a Curator agent compiles context to help decision-makers. For example, the Sentinel might be configured to detect if a key raw material shipment is delayed beyond a certain threshold, or if inventory for a top-selling product falls below a safety stock level. Once it spots such an event (say, a delay message from a shipping provider or an inventory dip), the Curator agent gathers relevant information: which orders will be affected by this delay? how long until stockout at current sales rates? It then presents an alert to the supply chain manager: "Alert: Supplier X shipment for Component Y is 1 week late, which may cause stockout of Product Z in 3 days." Armed with this curated insight, the team can act fast – perhaps expediting an alternate shipment or informing customers of a backorder. AI-driven early warning systems like this ensure that potential supply disruptions are caught as early as possible, and the business can respond proactively rather than reactively. Indeed, procurement experts note that AI can continuously monitor supplier signals (financial stability, ownership changes, delivery performance) and proactively flag risks so that procurement teams can intervene before issues escalate.

Auto-Initiated RFP Creation – Companion + Action: Sometimes the need for a new purchase or contract re-negotiation is clear from data – and an AI agent can kick off the process automatically. A Companion agent in procurement could act as an assistant that observes triggers like low inventory, expiring contracts, or frequent spot-buys of a particular item, and then recommends initiating a formal procurement process. For instance, if an ingredient's stock is projected to run out in 2 months and no re-orders are in motion, the agent might alert the sourcing team and even draft a new Request for Proposal (RFP) using a Presenter ability (here we consider the Companion agent leveraging some Presenter skills to prepare documentation). The agent might pre-fill the RFP with known requirements and past vendor performance data, so that a procurement officer only needs to review and publish it. Similarly, for a contract coming up for renewal, the agent could prompt, "The contract with Carrier Co. expires next month. Shall I initiate a renewal process or RFP for other quotes?" By proactively starting these activities, the agent ensures the organization never misses the lead time needed for important procurement actions.

Risk Evaluation of New Partners – Supervisor + Presenter: Before locking in a new supplier or partner, companies often conduct risk assessments – checking the supplier's financial health, compliance records, and operational reliability. A Supervisor agent can automate much of this due diligence. It could pull data from credit rating services, sanction lists, and internal performance databases (via External Services or MuleSoft connectors), then apply risk rules (for example, flag if the supplier has been in business less than 1 year or has a credit score below a threshold). The agent then uses a Presenter component to generate a concise risk report for the procurement team, perhaps with a simple score (e.g. "Risk Rating: Medium – supplier has moderate financial risk and limited capacity history") and a breakdown of factors. This gives procurement officers a head start in understanding potential issues. The agent might even recommend mitigation steps (like "Require upfront payment terms due to lower credit rating"). By standardizing and speeding up partner evaluations, the organization can onboard reliable suppliers faster and avoid ones that might pose hidden risks.

To realize these use cases, integration and configuration are key. Procurement agents often need to connect deeply into ERP and supply chain systems – for example, using MuleSoft or Salesforce External Services to retrieve inventory levels, shipment statuses, or vendor master data from systems like SAP or Oracle. A Conductor agent can then orchestrate across these systems (perhaps creating a case in an ERP when initiating an RFP, or logging a quality incident in a supplier management module). Custom Metadata in Salesforce can be used to maintain regional or category-specific rules – for instance, store different approval workflows or document requirements for EMEA vs. US vendors, which the Supervisor logic will reference when onboarding a vendor or approving a purchase. The agent should also leverage Salesforce's Event Monitoring or platform events coming from integrated systems to stay updated on key events (like a delivery delay event triggering the Sentinel). Designing agents with these integration points ensures they have a full view of the supply chain. Additionally, procurement agents should present themselves as helpers, not gatekeepers, to the users in the business – for example, a Slack integration could allow a user to ask, "Any issues with Supplier ABC lately?" and the agent (leveraging its curated data) can respond with a quick summary of performance and any recent risks. By making the agent accessible via tools employees already use (Slack, Chatter, etc.), you increase adoption and make it easier for teams to collaborate with the AI in procurement decisions.

Overall, agents in procurement and supply chain serve as vigilant coordinators and risk managers. They tirelessly watch process checkpoints, external events, and performance metrics, ensuring that nothing falls through the cracks. When something does require human attention or decision – a flagged invoice, a looming supply risk, a ready-to-go RFP – the agent packages that information and delivers it to the right people with context. The result is a more responsive, efficient supply chain that can adapt quickly to changes, with AI handling the routine drudgery and alerting humans exactly when they're needed.

INTERNAL IT AND SECURITY

IT departments are the troubleshooters and gatekeepers of a company's tech infrastructure. They deal with a flood of routine requests (creating accounts, resetting passwords) and must constantly guard against security threats lurking in system logs. AI agents can act as tireless IT assistants – automating repetitive support tasks and monitoring systems for suspicious events 24/7. The potential impact is huge: incidents can be detected and resolved faster, and IT staff get more time to focus on complex projects instead of firefighting. Below are key IT and security use cases for Agentforce agents:

Auto-Provisioning and Deprovisioning Users – Action Pattern: User lifecycle management (onboarding new hires and offboarding departures) is a natural fit for an Action agent. Whenever HR marks someone as hired or exited, the agent can automatically carry out the IT checklist. For a new employee, it might create accounts in various systems, assign standard access permissions, set up email and collaboration profiles, and even send the welcome email with initial credentials – all by invoking integration scripts or APIs. Conversely, when an employee leaves, the agent can systematically deactivate their accounts, revoke permissions, reclaim licenses, and notify asset management to collect equipment. By automating provisioning and deprovisioning, an Action agent ensures these critical tasks happen immediately and consistently (no waiting days for accounts to be created or – worse – forgetting to disable a former user's access). IT administrators define the rules and connectors (e.g. how to talk to Active Directory, Salesforce, VPN, etc.), and the agent executes them on each trigger event. This improves security and saves IT time on one of their most frequent service desk chores.

Flagging Unusual Access Behavior – Sentinel + Supervisor: Security incident detection is a classic Sentinel agent role. The agent monitors system logs and user activity streams (login attempts, file access patterns, network traffic) for anything that deviates from normal baselines or known safe patterns. The moment it detects a suspicious event – say, an account experiencing a rapid series of failed login attempts, or a user downloading an atypically large amount of data at 2 AM – it raises a flag. At this point a Supervisor agent can evaluate the context and severity according to predefined policies. For example, after 5 failed login attempts, the Supervisor might determine this looks like a probable credential stuffing attack and automatically invoke an Action to lock the account as a precaution. In a less clear scenario, it might simply alert the security team (or create a high-priority incident in the ITSM system) for human investigation. One concrete pattern we can implement is: Sentinel detects repeated failed logins on an admin account → Supervisor agent marks it as a likely breach and triggers Action to lock the account, then notifies security personnel for follow-up. By reacting within seconds to anomalies, the agent can potentially stop security incidents in their tracks or at least limit their impact. Importantly, the rules are under IT's control – you set thresholds and response actions that the Supervisor follows – ensuring the agent's responses align with the organization's risk tolerance.

Daily System Health Summary – Curator + Presenter: IT operators often start their day reviewing system dashboards and log reports to see if anything needs attention. A Curator agent can take over that morning ritual. It can gather overnight logs, system metrics, and monitoring alerts from various tools, filter out the noise, and compile a concise health report. Then a Presenter agent delivers this summary to the IT team (perhaps as an email or Slack message at 8 AM). For example, the agent's report might say: "Server uptime: 99.9%. Backup completed successfully at 3:00 AM. Notable events: Database CPU spiked to 95% at 2:15 AM (resolved), 5 failed login attempts on Server X." This gives IT a quick heads-up on any anomalies or resolved incidents without them digging through multiple systems. The Curator can prioritize what to include (e.g. only errors or metrics beyond certain thresholds) so the team isn't overloaded with trivial details. Essentially, this agent serves as an intelligent operations dashboard that actively pushes insights to IT, enabling a faster start on addressing any issues.

Coaching Admins on Best Practices – Coach Pattern: Even IT staff can benefit from a gentle coach. A Coach agent in IT could observe configuration changes, support responses, or maintenance habits and provide proactive tips. Suppose an administrator frequently creates new users with very broad access privileges; the agent might notice this pattern and advise, "It looks like many of the accounts you created have admin-level rights – consider applying the principle of least privilege for security." Or in an IT support context, if a helpdesk engineer closes tickets without updating the knowledge base, the coach agent can remind them to document solutions for future efficiency. Another example: after a security incident, the agent might monitor that the team implements recommended fixes and periodically remind them of any pending actions (like "It's been 30 days since the last security drill; consider scheduling one"). This sort of AI coach helps enforce IT policies and best practices in a positive, educational manner rather than through after-the-fact audits.

Orchestrating Service Requests – Conductor Pattern: IT service management often involves multi-step workflows cutting across teams. For instance, onboarding a new employee (as touched on above) involves HR, IT, and Facilities; similarly, fulfilling a complex request like setting up a new office location requires coordinating network, hardware, and account configurations. A Conductor agent can take a high-level request and break it into all the requisite subtasks, invoking different systems and notifying responsible teams in sequence. If someone requests a new development environment for a project, the Conductor could automatically create the cloud resources, configure the permissions (via an Action sub-agent), schedule a security scan, and inform the requesting team once it's ready – handling the workflow with minimal human intervention. This pattern ensures standardization and speeds up service delivery. The agent tracks each step's completion; if something fails or needs approval (like additional budget for extra server capacity), it can pause and escalate to an IT manager, then resume once resolved. By serving as the automation glue between IT processes, the Conductor agent reduces the manual coordination effort and error rate that often plague complex IT tasks.

To implement IT and security agents, tight integration with monitoring tools, directories, and ticketing systems is crucial. Salesforce's platform allows for event-driven triggers and API calls that these agents can use. For example, Event Monitoring or platform events can feed login events or system alerts into a Sentinel agent in real time, and the agent can then call out to Apex methods or even external endpoints to handle them. Invocable Apex or Flows can be created for common remediation actions (like disabling a user, restarting a service, or opening a Jira ticket), which the Supervisor or Conductor agents can invoke as needed. Many IT teams rely on Slack for operations collaboration, so integrating agents to post alerts or receive slash-command requests in Slack can make them more accessible (imagine typing "/itbot lock user Alice" in Slack and an Action agent executing that command, with proper verification). Similarly, agents can present information through Lightning components in Salesforce apps or dashboards tailored for IT – for instance, a "Security AI Alerts" component that lists the latest anomaly detections and recommended actions. Because trust is paramount in security, IT agents should be configured to err on the side of caution and log everything they do. Each automated action (like an account lockout by the agent) can write an audit entry or notify the team, so nothing happens quietly. Over time, as the IT team sees the agent making correct calls, confidence will grow and the automation rules can be relaxed to allow the agent more leeway.

In summary, internal IT and security agents work like diligent junior admins and security analysts who never sleep. They execute the repetitive tasks instantly when triggered, watch for threats in the background, and learn the patterns of the environment to know when something's off. By clearly explaining their alerts and involving humans at the right moments, these agents can greatly improve an organization's IT responsiveness and security posture without stepping on the toes of the experts in charge.

DESIGNING FOR CROSS-DOMAIN CONSISTENCY

As organizations deploy agents across different departments, a new challenge emerges: ensuring these agents work in harmony rather than as isolated silos. Consistency in design and governance is key to avoiding a fragmented "wild west" of AI behaviors. In this section, we outline strategies to keep your growing fleet of agents coherent and manageable, even as they span HR, Finance, IT, and beyond:

One Registry to Rule Them All: It's highly recommended to maintain a central registry or inventory of all AI agents in the enterprise. This registry (which could be as simple as a Salesforce custom object or an internal wiki page) should list each agent, its domain or business function, its pattern(s), and the owner/team responsible for it. By tagging each agent with metadata like domain and pattern, you can easily get a bird's-eye view of coverage and quickly identify overlaps or gaps. For example, you might discover you have two "Onboarding" agents in development by different teams – a central registry surfaces that duplication so you can consolidate efforts. The registry also helps with governance: when someone wants to deploy a new agent, they check the registry to ensure similar capability doesn't already exist, and they register their agent so others know about it. This way, agents become enterprise assets that are visible and governed, not hidden scripts sitting under someone's desk.

Shared Presenter and Companion Agents for Continuity: Whenever possible, provide a unified user experience for interacting with agents across domains. One approach is to have a shared Companion agent (or at least a common chatbot interface) that can handle multiple types of queries by delegating to specialized agents behind the scenes. For instance, instead of employees having to remember one bot for IT support and a different bot for HR questions, you might deploy a single "company assistant" in Slack or Teams. This primary Companion agent can identify the user's request context (with some NLP or simple keywords) and route it to the appropriate domain-specific agent logic. The user enjoys a one-stop experience ("Ask the company bot anything") and gets answers that might come from HR, Finance, or IT systems seamlessly. Similarly, certain Presenter functionality can be shared – for example, a standardized way of outputting summaries or reports. If every agent presents its analysis in a different format, users may get confused. Defining some common templates or UI components for agent outputs (like a consistent summary card or alert format) can make interactions feel coherent. Shared components also promote reuse: the HR agent and Finance agent could use the same Presenter sub-module to format an email report, rather than each custom-developing one.

Reuse Metadata for Trust and Control: Consistency isn't just about look-and-feel – it's also about behavior and governance. You should define common metadata that agents across domains reference for critical parameters. For instance, you might establish enterprise-wide trust levels for data or actions: an agent could be marked as "Level 1 – Read-Only" versus "Level 5 – Autonomous Execution," and policies might dictate that Level 5 agents undergo extra approvals before deployment. Role-based access controls should also be consistent – if agents are delivering information to users, ensure they all respect the same role definitions (so that a Sales Manager sees certain data from any agent, but not confidential HR data, etc.). Similarly, you can classify outputs (perhaps tag content an agent produces as public, internal, confidential) in a uniform way and have all agents abide by those classifications when deciding what to show or whom to notify. By reusing metadata configurations, you avoid a situation where, say, the finance agent has a different notion of "sensitive data" than the legal agent. Instead, all agents draw from a centralized definition of sensitivity levels, user roles, escalation paths, and so on. This not only prevents inconsistency, but also makes auditing and adjusting policies easier – change the metadata in one place, and all agents adjust their behavior accordingly.

Cross-Domain Pattern Collaboration: The agent patterns themselves can work together across domains. Encourage a design where agents in different areas communicate or feed into each other when appropriate. For example, a Cross-domain Companion arrangement can allow an employee-facing bot to fulfill requests that span multiple departments in one conversation (as mentioned above). Another scenario: department-specific Coach agents might share their insights upward to a central Supervisor or Presenter agent. Imagine each division has a Coach agent watching for performance or compliance issues internally; those coaches could then report notable findings to a central Supervisor agent that looks for cross-departmental trends or conflicts (ensuring one department's AI-driven decision isn't inadvertently hurting another area). The Supervisor could then produce a consolidated report via a Presenter agent for leadership, combining inputs from HR, Finance, and IT coaches. Likewise, a Curator agent could aggregate signals from multiple domains to give a 360° risk view of a single entity. For example, when evaluating a new project or major client, a Curator could pull compliance risk info from the legal agent, budget health from the finance agent, and resource strain info from the IT agent, merging these perspectives into one composite insight. This kind of pattern synergy ensures that AI agents amplify each other's value rather than operate in isolation.

Ecosystem Integration (MCP and Connectors): Maintaining consistency also means preparing your agents to operate in a multi-platform world. Salesforce Agentforce might be your core, but your enterprise likely uses other AI or automation platforms (Microsoft's Copilots, external RPA bots, etc.). Design agents with interoperability in mind. The emerging Model Context Protocol (MCP) is one way to standardize how agents describe themselves and communicate context – by aligning to MCP standards, your Salesforce agents can more easily hand off tasks or information to agents outside Salesforce if needed in the future. In practical terms, this could mean structuring the data your agents produce (like using standardized JSON payloads or APIs) so any external system can parse it. It also means documenting each agent's capabilities and interfaces clearly (maybe as part of that central registry) – effectively creating an internal API catalog for your AI agents. Meanwhile, leverage MuleSoft and other integration tools as the glue between agent ecosystems: if your HR agent in Salesforce needs to trigger a process in Workday or an Azure function, MuleSoft can bridge that gap in a consistent, managed way. By funneling cross-platform interactions through governed integration layers, you maintain security and oversight even as agents extend beyond Salesforce. The goal is a cohesive "swarm" of agents that can orchestrate together, rather than isolated islands. This topic of cross-platform orchestration is so important that it's the focus of the next chapter.

Agent Ownership and Catalog: Finally, treat your cadre of agents as products or services that need clear ownership and life-cycle management. Just as you wouldn't deploy a bunch of microservices without devops practices, you shouldn't have free-roaming AI agents with no accountability. Establish a simple internal "Agent Services Catalog" – a portal or dashboard that lists all active agents, their purpose, who owns/maintains them, and how to contact those owners or get support. This is similar to the "one registry" principle, but surfaced for general awareness. For example, employees might have access to a page that lists available internal bots and what they do (so they know where to ask their question), and technical teams have a version of the catalog with details like last update, model version, etc. The catalog approach also makes it easier to enforce periodic reviews of agents – you might institute that every agent gets reviewed quarterly to ensure it's still following policy and delivering value. By making ownership explicit, you prevent orphaned agents from drifting out of sync with policy or becoming security liabilities. If someone leaves the company, assign their agents to a new owner. In short: keep a clear map of your AI estate. This will pay off immensely as you scale up, because it allows you to spot redundancies, ensure quality standards, and help users discover the tools available to them.

Pro Tip: Build an internal "AI Council" or governance team that oversees your agent catalog and design standards. Having a regular forum where different business units share their agent use cases and lessons learned can accelerate cross-domain adoption while preventing chaos. Plus, it reinforces a culture that these AI agents are part of a unified strategy, not just ad-hoc experiments. In essence, consistency in principles and oversight will let you enjoy the power of many specialized agents without suffering from inconsistency or conflict among them.

SUMMARY

In this chapter, we expanded our view of Agentforce beyond its CRM origins, demonstrating how the same eight agent patterns can drive transformation in HR, Legal, Finance, Procurement, IT, and other internal functions. We saw practical examples ranging from HR onboarding orchestration and policy compliance monitoring, to AI auditors for expense reports and budgets, to proactive agents in procurement and IT that keep operations running smoothly. Throughout these scenarios, a common theme emerged: by applying a pattern-driven approach, organizations can automate routine work, surface critical insights, and enforce policies consistently across departments – all while keeping humans in control of the strategic decisions.

Crucially, we discussed design strategies to maintain consistency and trust as agents proliferate. A central registry and shared standards ensure that an HR bot and a Finance bot speak the same language (and users aren't confused by a fragmented AI experience). With proper governance, Agentforce becomes more than a set of individual solutions – it forms an integrated ecosystem of digital teammates operating with the same discipline across the enterprise.

Agentforce's applicability beyond CRM means the benefits of AI (efficiency, accuracy, 24/7 vigilance) can be realized in every corner of the business, from onboarding to compliance, budgeting to supply chain. You now have a pattern-driven lens for spotting opportunities in internal processes and for deploying agents safely and effectively in those areas.

Next, in Chapter 20, we will take things a step further and explore how these agents can connect and collaborate across platforms. Modern AI work ecosystems span Salesforce, Slack, Microsoft Copilot, LangChain, MuleSoft, and other orchestration tools. We'll learn how to compose cross-platform "agent swarms" – multi-agent systems that coordinate work across disparate platforms, protocols, and responsibilities. In doing so, we will see how to extend our Salesforce agents to interoperate with external AI assistants via standards like Model Context Protocol (MCP) and how to orchestrate complex workflows that no single agent or platform could handle alone. The journey continues toward an AI fabric that threads through the entire enterprise, bringing all these agents together in concert.

20

COMPOSING THE AGENT SWARM – ORCHESTRATION ACROSS PLATFORMS

Enterprise AI agents don't operate in a vacuum – they live in a sprawling ecosystem of platforms, apps, and services. A single workflow might involve a Salesforce Agentforce agent accessing CRM data, a Slack-based assistant broadcasting updates to a team, a Microsoft 365 Copilot drafting an email, and a LangChain planner orchestrating an external API call. Modern AI work ecosystems span Salesforce, Slack, Microsoft Copilot, LangChain, MuleSoft integrations, and countless other services. For instance, a Salesforce agent might invoke a MuleSoft workflow to retrieve data from an ERP system, while a Slack-based bot kicks off an HR onboarding sequence in tandem. In this context, no agent is an island. Instead, value emerges from how these agents work together, hand in hand across system boundaries.

This chapter tackles the design and governance of agent swarms – coordinated teams of autonomous agents that collaborate across platforms, protocols, and responsibilities to achieve shared goals. We'll explore what it really means to compose a multi-agent system that isn't confined to one application stack. You'll learn how to extend your Salesforce-based agents beyond the Salesforce platform to interoperate with external counterparts, whether that's triggering actions in outside tools or consuming outputs from non-Salesforce AI services. In short, we look at making Salesforce agents both team players and, when needed, effective team leaders in a broader AI ecosystem. And you'll see how to leverage Salesforce's own capabilities –

Agent Builder, invocable Flows and Apex, Flow Orchestration – along with integration tools like MuleSoft to knit these agents together seamlessly.

Crucially, orchestrating agents across platforms poses unique challenges beyond those of a self-contained multi-agent system in Salesforce. Within a single org or application, agents might share databases or event buses. But in a cross-platform swarm, there's no unified event bus or shared memory – each agent often runs on a different stack with its own data schema and interface. As a result, agents must exchange information through explicit contracts, whether via API calls, event messages, or specialized protocols, rather than any implicit integration. We'll introduce the Model Context Protocol (MCP) as an emerging standard to help bridge these gaps – think of MCP as a universal translator that helps diverse agents share state and intentions securely.

By weaving Salesforce agents into broader swarms, you unlock resilience and scale that no single platform could achieve alone. Composability across tech stacks is key: if one component system changes or a new tool emerges, a well-orchestrated swarm can adapt without a total rebuild. It also opens the door to true cross-functional automation – for example, an HR onboarding agent can trigger an IT provisioning agent and update a finance system through specialized agents on each system, instead of forcing one monolithic app to do everything. The patterns and practices in this chapter emphasize loose coupling between agents and platforms so that your solutions remain flexible in the face of change and growth.

Let's begin by defining the core characteristics of a cross-platform agent swarm. In next section, we'll clarify exactly what an "agent swarm" is and how it differs from simpler single-platform orchestrations, setting the foundation for everything that follows.

WHAT IS AN AGENT SWARM?

An agent swarm is a coordinated set of autonomous agents – potentially spread across different platforms – that work together in a distributed fashion to achieve a common goal. In an enterprise context, this might mean a collection of AI agents spanning Salesforce, third-party SaaS tools, and custom apps, all contributing their specialized skills to one overarching process. The swarm behaves like a team: each agent handles its part of the workload, communicating and cooperating to produce an outcome no single agent could deliver alone.

How is this different from running multiple agents inside one system? Think of the distinction between a single application with internal components versus a network of separate services. In a traditional multi-agent setup confined to Salesforce, for example, your agents might all run in the same org – sharing a common database, event bus, or memory store. One agent could invoke another via an Apex method or update the same records. By contrast, in a cross-platform swarm, agents often run on entirely separate tech stacks with no shared runtime or database. A Salesforce agent can't directly call an internal function of a Slack bot or a Microsoft Copilot; instead, they communicate through APIs, events, or message queues. This means hand-offs between agents must be explicit and well-structured. You'll need to account for network latencies, data translation (e.g. converting Salesforce records to a JSON payload an external tool understands), and error handling across system boundaries. Security is another factor – calls across platforms must be authenticated and authorized, whereas internal calls within one platform might implicitly trust the context. In short, composing an agent swarm requires designing clear interfaces and contracts between agents, much like designing integrations between microservices.

To make these swarms work, it helps to define what inputs kick them off and what outputs they produce. The inputs to an agent swarm are typically goals, tasks, or events. A swarm might start because a high-level goal is assigned (e.g. "onboard a new employee"), because a specific task is requested by a user or system (e.g. "generate this month's compliance report"), or because an event triggers it (e.g. a sensor reading or database update that a Sentinel agent detects). These inputs serve as the rallying call that brings the swarm to life. On the other end, the outputs are the coordinated results of the swarm's work: actions completed, decisions made, or artifacts created. That could mean updated records across systems, an approval decision reached and communicated, or a compiled artifact like a report or summary document. In a well-orchestrated swarm, the outputs from one agent often become inputs for another until the final goal is achieved.

Roles within the swarm: Just as effective teams assign members specialized roles, an agent swarm benefits from clearly defined roles for its member agents. While every swarm is unique, we commonly see a few key role types:

Signaler: The agent that initiates the swarm by raising a signal or alert. A signaler spots the trigger condition or receives the initial request. For example, a Sentinel-pattern agent in Salesforce monitoring for anomalies can act as a signaler when it detects an event (like an unusual spending spike or a policy violation) that kicks off the swarm's activity.

Planner: The agent that figures out the game plan once a signal is received. This agent takes the goal or problem and breaks it into discrete tasks, determining which agents (and platforms) should handle each piece. In practice, a planner might be a Salesforce Conductor-pattern agent orchestrating steps via Flow Orchestration, or an external LangChain planner agent that uses an LLM to decide on a sequence of tool calls. The planner sets the stage so that executors know what to do.

Executor: Agents that actually carry out tasks in the swarm. Executors are the doers – they might update a database, call an API, draft content, or perform calculations as needed. Many of the agents you build will fall into this category. For instance, an Action-pattern agent in Salesforce could create a new case or update an opportunity, a MuleSoft integration agent might post a record into an ERP system, or a Copilot agent could compose an email. Executors focus on completing the work assigned to them by the planner.

Validator: The agent that checks or confirms outcomes generated by other agents. Not every swarm includes a validator, but it's common in scenarios requiring oversight or quality control. A validator might review an AI-generated output for accuracy or compliance, or monitor that all tasks were completed successfully. For example, a Supervisor-pattern agent in Salesforce could review a draft contract written by another agent (executor) and ensure it meets policy before it's sent out. Validators provide a safety net and help maintain trust in the swarm's results.

Presenter: The agent responsible for delivering the final output or insight of the swarm to its human stakeholders or to an end system. This agent takes the collective work of the swarm and packages it in an accessible form. A Presenter might generate a summary report, update a dashboard, or send a Slack message with the results. In a customer service scenario, a Presenter-pattern agent could be the one that gathers inputs from several backend agents and presents a resolution to a support agent or customer. Essentially, the presenter ensures the swarm's work doesn't stay hidden – it communicates the outcome where it's needed.

These roles aren't strict categories mandated by a framework, but thinking in terms of roles helps ensure you haven't left any critical function unassigned. In smaller swarms, a single agent might fulfill multiple roles (for example, one agent could both plan and execute simple tasks). However, be cautious about lumping too much responsibility onto one agent. Just as in software architecture we avoid giant, do-everything classes or services, in agent design it's better to have focused agents that collaborate. Clear role definitions prevent confusion and make it easier to swap out or adjust one part of the swarm without unraveling everything.

To illustrate, consider a Salesforce-driven procurement workflow. A Conductor agent on the Salesforce platform might act as the planner, breaking an "Order Materials" goal into steps. It could then invoke a MuleSoft-based integration agent as an executor to fulfill one of those steps – for example, checking inventory in an external SAP system or creating a purchase order. Here the Salesforce Conductor triggers the MuleSoft action and later receives the result, coordinating with an external agent as part of one swarm. None of this requires a human in the loop – the agents negotiate the hand-off via well-defined APIs or events. The Conductor agent doesn't need to know the intricacies of SAP; it just knows to call the MuleSoft agent responsible for that domain, then proceeds once it gets a response. This loose coupling between the Salesforce agent and the MuleSoft service ensures each can do its job independently yet still contribute to the shared goal.

In another example, imagine a pair of Companion agents providing a unified experience to a user across two channels. Say a manager starts an interaction with an HR chatbot in Salesforce (perhaps to initiate an employee onboarding), then later continues the conversation in Slack. Using a standard like the Model Context Protocol, the Salesforce Companion agent can pass the conversation context (the "memory" of what's been discussed and decided so far) to a Slack-based Companion agent. Now the Slack agent instantly knows the manager's intent and the onboarding details already captured, without restarting the process. The two agents effectively exchange memory, so from the manager's perspective it's one continuous assistant. This is a swarm in action: separate agents on different platforms (Salesforce and Slack) working together via shared context to act as one coherent helper. The key is that they agreed on a common context format (MCP provides this) and each sticks to its role – the Slack agent focusing on communication in Slack, the Salesforce agent handling HR data and processes – without stepping on each other's toes.

Pro tip: Define agent roles with the same care as microservice boundaries – loose coupling and clear contracts between agents will make your swarm more robust and easier to maintain.

Having defined what an agent swarm is and how to structure one, we can now look at the patterns that help in actually coordinating all these agents. In the next section, we'll explore design patterns for cross-platform coordination – reusable strategies to trigger, orchestrate, and loop feedback among agents spread out on different systems.

PATTERNS FOR CROSS-PLATFORM COORDINATION

Designing a cross-platform swarm often involves recurring interaction patterns – essentially playbooks for how agents initiate, share work, and return results. By recognizing these swarm design patterns, you can apply proven approaches instead of reinventing the wheel for each integration. Let's look at three common patterns for coordinating agents across systems, and then examine methods to hand off state between platforms.

Trigger + Delegate: In this pattern, one agent detects a need and delegates the heavy lifting to another agent on a different platform. A classic example is a Salesforce Sentinel agent that spots an event or receives a request, and then calls an external planning or processing agent to handle the next step. The Sentinel essentially says "I've detected something important – you, external agent, take it from here." For example, a Salesforce monitoring agent might detect a complex optimization problem (say a large scheduling task or data analysis request). Instead of trying to solve it locally, it uses an API call to invoke a LangChain planner agent running off-platform. The Salesforce agent provides context (the trigger details and relevant data) and then trusts the LangChain agent to figure out a plan or solution. This Trigger + Delegate pattern leverages the strengths of each side: Salesforce handles detection and context (grounded in CRM data and business events), while the delegate agent (perhaps an LLM-based planner or a specialized cloud service) handles intensive reasoning or specialized processing. The trigger agent doesn't micromanage the delegate – it hands off the task and later receives the result. This keeps the initiating agent lightweight and lets external tools do what they're best at.

Orchestrate + Ingest: Here one agent (the orchestrator) proactively calls multiple other agents or services, then ingests (aggregates and processes) their outputs to produce a unified result. This pattern is common when no single agent has all the information or capability needed, so collaboration is required. A Salesforce Conductor agent might exemplify this: it could call out to a knowledge-base agent (say via LangChain) for information, ping a Microsoft 365 Copilot for a draft document or analysis, and perhaps query a third system via MuleSoft – then combine all those inputs. The orchestrator agent acts like a maestro, ensuring each external service plays its part at the right time, and then fusing the outputs into something coherent. For example, consider an internal IT helpdesk scenario: a Conductor agent in Salesforce might query an FAQ bot for known solutions and also ask Copilot to summarize recent related incidents, then merge those into a single response for a support technician. By orchestrating parallel inquiries and ingesting the results, the Salesforce agent delivers a richer outcome than either system could alone. The challenge in this pattern is handling disparate data formats and partial results – the orchestrator must be able to wait for or poll results, check for errors, and assemble the final answer. When done right, Orchestrate + Ingest greatly extends the reach of your Salesforce agents by tapping multiple sources in one go.

Feedback + Loop: This pattern creates a learning or refinement loop between agents. One agent generates an outcome or performs an action, and another agent provides feedback or analysis that leads to an improvement or next step. You can think of it as an agent "review committee." A typical scenario involves a Coach-pattern agent in Salesforce observing what other agents (or users) did and then prompting an external AI (perhaps a Copilot or other LLM service) to reflect or suggest changes. For instance, suppose an AI sales proposal generator (say a Copilot that writes drafts) produces a customer proposal. A Coach agent in Salesforce could take that draft and the customer's response data (e.g. did the customer engage with it? were there questions?) and feed a summary of this back to the Copilot or another analytic agent with a prompt like "Here's what happened, how can we improve the next proposal?" The Copilot might then suggest tweaks to tone or content for future attempts. In another example, a Coach agent might log how often a support chatbot had to escalate to a human, then send those transcripts to a language model with instructions to learn from them or identify patterns. The Feedback + Loop pattern ensures that the swarm isn't a one-and-done execution; it builds continuous improvement into the system. One agent's output (and the outcome it led to) becomes feedback for another agent to analyze, creating a loop that can iteratively make the overall system smarter or more effective over time.

After establishing which pattern (or combination of patterns) fits a given use case, you need to implement the actual handoff of information between these agents and platforms. Cross-platform coordination lives or dies by how well you transfer state – the data, context, and results – through the swarm. Here are a few strategies for state handoff that map to the patterns above:

Direct JSON calls via HTTP (API integration): One straightforward method is to have agents communicate through RESTful APIs or other HTTP endpoints, exchanging information as JSON. For example, a Salesforce Apex action can make an HTTP callout to a webhook exposed by an external agent, packaging the necessary context in a JSON payload. The external agent processes it and returns a JSON response. This direct request-response approach is synchronous and relatively easy to implement with standard tools (HTTP callouts in Salesforce, web service endpoints on the other side). The upside is clarity: you know exactly when you hand off and when you get a reply. However, it does couple the agents rather tightly – the calling agent must know the endpoint and payload schema of the called agent. You should design those schemas as stable contracts. Also consider timeouts and retries – a direct call means the trigger agent is waiting on the delegate. Use this approach when the integration needs to be immediate and you can afford to have one agent pause for another (e.g., delegating a task and needing the result right away).

Event-based messaging (Pub/Sub): Another approach is to decouple the communication using an event or message bus. In this model, an agent publishes an event (containing the context or request), and one or more other agents subscribe to that event and respond asynchronously. Salesforce Platform Events or AWS SNS/SQS topics are examples of this pattern. For instance, a Salesforce agent could publish an event "HighValueTransaction-Detected" with details, and an external fraud-detection agent listening on that channel will pick it up and act. The agents don't call each other directly – they just agree on the event schema. This yields loose coupling: the publishing agent doesn't need to know who exactly will handle the event, just that someone will. It also naturally supports one-to-many scenarios (multiple agents can react to the same event). The trade-off is complexity in tracking and timing – since the response isn't immediate, you may need correlation IDs or a mechanism for the responding agent to post the outcome (perhaps as another event or a callback) that the original system can observe. Event-based handoff is great for long-running processes or cases where many agents might contribute or listen in.

Structured context via MCP (Model Context Protocol): A more recent and powerful strategy is to use a standardized protocol for context exchange like the Model Context Protocol. Instead of ad-hoc JSON structures or custom events, MCP provides a formal way to describe agent capabilities, share memory (state), and include metadata about trust and instructions. Using MCP, a Salesforce agent could package not just raw data but a whole "context object" describing what it wants and what tools it has, and send that to an external agent through an MCP-compliant interface. For example, the Salesforce agent could say (in MCP terms) "Here is a dataset and an intent to get a summary; I have the following functions available for you to call if needed." The external agent (say a data science tool or a Copilot) receives this in a standard format, understands the request and the boundaries, and responds with results plus any updated context. MCP essentially abstracts the handoff so that both sides speak a common language about goals and data. The benefit is interoperability – a variety of vendors and platforms support MCP, which means your Salesforce agents can potentially interoperate with OpenAI, Anthropic, or other AI services with less custom glue code. We'll dive more into MCP in the next section, but it's worth noting here as a state handoff strategy that emphasizes standardization over custom integration.

Error handling and resilience: Expect that cross-platform calls can fail or slow down, and plan accordingly. Agents should anticipate that a partner might be unavailable or could return an error or unexpected result. Design your swarm with checkpoints and fallbacks. If a delegate agent fails to respond in time, should the orchestrator agent retry, call a backup agent, or escalate to a human? If an external service returns a result that doesn't pass validation, can your swarm try an alternative approach? For example, if your Salesforce agent calls a Copilot to draft a message but the content violates a policy, a Salesforce Supervisor agent could catch that and either sanitize the output or ask a different service to try again with stricter guidelines. Plan for network failures too – use timeouts on HTTP calls, subscribe to dead-letter queues for events that couldn't be delivered, and log all cross-system interactions. Implementing retries with exponential backoff or a circuit breaker pattern (to stop calling an external service if it's consistently failing) can save your swarm from grinding to a halt. The bottom line is that in a distributed system, things will go wrong at some point – your coordination patterns should include strategies for detection and recovery of errors so that one failed agent doesn't derail the entire swarm.

These patterns and handoff strategies can be mixed and matched. Real-world swarms often use a combination – for instance, a Trigger + Delegate handoff via an event bus, or an Orchestrate + Ingest sequence that uses MCP for one call and a JSON API for another. The goal is to choose an approach that fits the task: quick synchronous calls for simple delegated steps, events or queues for complex pipelines, and standardized protocols like MCP when you want maximum interoperability and clarity of context.

For instance, in a procurement scenario spanning Salesforce and SAP, a Sentinel agent in Salesforce can detect low inventory and delegate the reorder task to an SAP agent via MuleSoft (a Trigger + Delegate approach). Likewise, in sales enablement (Salesforce and Microsoft 365), a swarm might combine orchestrate and delegate patterns: a Salesforce agent gathers customer data and calls Microsoft Copilot to generate a personalized proposal, then merges the Copilot's output with its own information for the final deliverable.

Having identified how to coordinate agents in principle, we're ready to tackle the challenge of making these hand-offs smoother and more standardized. In the next section, we'll introduce the Model Context Protocol (MCP) – a formal approach to structuring context and actions – which promises to simplify cross-platform agent communication.

LEVERAGING MODEL CONTEXT PROTOCOL (MCP)

Coordinating a swarm of agents across platforms is much easier when everyone speaks a common language. The Model Context Protocol (MCP) has emerged as exactly that – an open interoperability standard that major AI players began adopting in late 2024. (Anthropic, the AI company behind Claude, introduced MCP, and it has since been embraced by others like OpenAI and Microsoft – a sign that the industry is coalescing around a universal agent-to-agent interface.) Think of MCP as the "universal port" for connecting AI agents and tools (akin to a USB-C for data and commands). With MCP, a Salesforce agent and, say, an AWS-hosted agent or a Microsoft agent can exchange information in a structured, agreed-upon format rather than a one-off JSON unique to your integration. This section explores how MCP works and how Salesforce agents can take advantage of it.

Key MCP concepts: MCP provides a formal way for agents to describe themselves, share context, and establish trust in a conversation. Three core elements are:

Agent descriptors: Every agent can publish a descriptor of its capabilities, intents, and constraints. This is essentially a manifest telling others "here's what I can do and how you can interact with me." For example, an agent descriptor might list that an agent can perform actions like "GenerateSummary" or "FetchCustomerData," along with parameters those actions require, and any constraints (like "only operates on data under 10MB" or "requires manager approval for sensitive requests"). Descriptors let a swarm's orchestrator or other agents discover and invoke capabilities dynamically, without hard-coding endpoints – much like a services registry in a microservice architecture.

Memory payloads: This refers to the context data that agents pass around under MCP. Instead of sending unstructured blobs, MCP defines structures for sharing state – things like the current conversation history, the user's preferences or profile, or the results an agent just produced. A memory payload can include past interactions ("Agent A already provided summary X"), current objectives, or environmental context. Because it's standardized, any agent receiving an MCP memory payload knows how to parse and use it. For instance, a memory payload could encapsulate a user's query along with relevant Salesforce records and say "this is the relevant context for the next agent in line to use."

Trust metadata: MCP messages carry metadata that help agents assess origin and validity. This might include the identity of the sending agent or system, a validation token or signature (for example, a digital signature or OAuth token to validate origin) to ensure the message wasn't tampered with, and an expiration or timestamp (e.g. a time-to-live to prevent stale instructions). Trust metadata allows an agent in one platform to decide, for example, "Okay, this request truly came from our Salesforce org's certified agent and hasn't expired – I can proceed." It's essentially the security and governance layer built into the protocol, which is critical when autonomous agents start calling each other across company boundaries.

By using MCP, disparate agents gain a shared vocabulary. A Salesforce agent can package its request or output in an MCP envelope that any compliant service can read, and vice versa. Now, how do we enable our Salesforce-based agents to join this ecosystem?

Making Salesforce agents MCP-aware: Salesforce doesn't natively speak MCP out-of-the-box (at least at the time of writing), but we can configure and extend our agents to participate. Here are a few strategies:

Capability registration via metadata: You can maintain a custom Agent Registry in Salesforce – perhaps as custom metadata or a custom object – where each agent's capabilities and endpoints are listed. For example, you might have a metadata record for a "Contract Analyzer Agent" with entries for what tasks it can do and where it can be reached (URL or API name). This registry can serve both internal use and as a source to generate MCP descriptors. An external orchestrator agent (or an integration middleware) could query this registry to retrieve a Salesforce agent's descriptor and learn how to call it via MCP.

Extensions in Agent Builder for MCP fields: When configuring an agent in Salesforce's Agent Builder, you would ideally have fields to specify things like the agent's trust level (how much authority it has or how much validation it needs), which of its actions are callable via MCP, and what its preferred interaction surface is. For instance, you might mark an agent as "trusted for external calls with token X, exposes actions A/B/C, and is primarily a backend agent with no direct UI." With those settings, an MCP gateway could automatically advertise that agent with the correct descriptor. Similarly, you might configure an agent's "preferred surface" to indicate if it typically outputs to Slack, email, Salesforce UI, etc., so that orchestrators know how to route its results.

MCP adapters and libraries: Enabling MCP might involve deploying an adapter (for example, an MCP server that interfaces with your Salesforce org via API). That adapter could use the above metadata to respond to MCP discovery queries and route incoming MCP requests to the right invocable actions or Apex methods in Salesforce. While this may require some development or third-party tools, the payoff is interoperability – your Salesforce agents become first-class citizens in a multi-platform agent ecosystem.

To make this concrete, let's walk through a simple MCP interaction example. Suppose you have a Salesforce Curator agent that compiles a summary of customer support cases for the week. You also have an external Presenter agent in a separate analytics application that can generate visual reports. Without MCP, the Curator might call a specific API of the Presenter with a custom payload. With MCP, things become more plug-and-play: the Curator agent creates a structured memory payload containing the summary data (say, a list of case metrics and highlights) along with an agent descriptor snippet indicating it's a "SummaryData" artifact intended for presentation. It includes trust metadata – maybe a signed token proving it's from your Salesforce org and a timestamp. The Curator then sends this via an MCP endpoint to the external system. The Presenter agent's MCP listener receives it and immediately understands: Agent descriptor says this is summary data of type X, and the payload contains Y fields of context, and it's verified from a trusted source. Using that information, the Presenter agent can automatically generate a weekly support dashboard, knowing exactly what it was given and that it's safe to use. The entire exchange required no bespoke integration code – just each agent honoring the MCP format.

In short, MCP adds a layer of standardization that can greatly simplify orchestrating complex swarms. It's still early days for the protocol, but it's rapidly gaining traction, and Salesforce teams that adopt it can future-proof their agent interactions. We've discussed how to structure and standardize cross-platform conversations; next, we'll turn to the practical side of actually calling Salesforce agents from other systems. In the next section, we'll explore how to make your Salesforce agents callable participants in a broader swarm.

SALESFORCE AGENTS AS SWARM PARTICIPANTS

Up to now, we've often assumed Salesforce is the center of the universe, orchestrating or initiating actions. But what about when it isn't? In a true multi-platform swarm, sometimes an external agent will need to call into Salesforce – treating a Salesforce-based agent as just another team member that can be invoked on demand. This section covers how to make your Salesforce agents callable from outside platforms, so they can participate in swarms even when Salesforce isn't pulling the strings.

Expose agents via APIs or flows: The most direct way to allow external access is to expose your agent's logic as a callable endpoint. If your agent is implemented as a Salesforce Flow, you can make it an Invocable Flow (with defined input/output variables) and then use Salesforce's REST API to trigger that flow from outside. Similarly, if the agent's brain is in Apex code, you might expose an Apex REST service or a GraphQL endpoint that external systems can hit to activate the agent. In practice, this could mean creating a tiny wrapper around your agent's core logic – for example, an Apex REST class that, when called, executes the agent's process (be it invoking a class or launching a flow) and then returns the result. By doing this, an external orchestrator can simply make an HTTP request to Salesforce to awaken the agent. Be sure to secure these endpoints with OAuth or signed requests, as you would any integration.

Use External Services (or similar) to define tasks: Another approach is to leverage Salesforce's External Services framework in a creative way. Normally, External Services is used to call OUT to external APIs from a flow based on an imported schema. But you can flip the script: define a schema for the "tasks" your Salesforce agent can perform and register it as an External Service (using an OpenAPI spec, for instance). This effectively documents the agent's contract in a standard way. An external system could then call Salesforce through the corresponding auto-generated flow action or endpoint. While this isn't a common use of External Services, it underscores a principle – clearly define the interface of your agent (inputs and outputs) so that any external orchestrator or middleware can invoke it with minimal fuss. Whether via External Services or a custom API, the goal is to present a clean, stable interface for your agent's capabilities.

Allow context injection via metadata or events: When an external platform calls a Salesforce agent, it often brings along some context – say a transaction ID from the external system, user preferences, or intermediate data that the agent will need. You should design a way to inject that context into the agent's execution. One simple method is to accept context data as part of the API request payload (e.g., as JSON fields that map to input variables in a flow or parameters in Apex). Another creative tactic is to use a Platform Event or a custom object as a context carrier: the external system could, for example, create a record in an "Agent_Task__c" object with all details, and then call the Salesforce agent with the ID of that record. The agent would then look up that record to get its full context. This indirection can be useful to avoid overly large payloads or to enable out-of-band updates. The bottom line is to make sure your agent can receive whatever data it needs from the outside world in a structured way, so it can do its job effectively within Salesforce.

Now, as you adapt your agents for external calls, there are a few design strategies to consider in Agent Builder and your overall architecture:

"External-callable" flag: It's helpful to explicitly mark which agents (or which of an agent's capabilities) are meant to be called by external systems. In an ideal world, Agent Builder would let you flip a switch labeled "Expose to external swarms." In current practice, you might implement this by convention – e.g., prefix agent names or actions with something (like "API_") or use a custom metadata flag. The point is to distinguish external-facing agents so you can apply additional governance (like security review, load testing, etc.). External calls can spike unpredictably, so you want to ensure those agents are robust and monitored closely.

Traceability (swarm IDs): When an external orchestrator triggers a Salesforce agent, it's wise to pass along a correlation ID or "swarm ID" that all agents in the chain will use. Salesforce agents should capture and log this ID (for instance, in a log object or even just in debug logs) whenever they start an externally-initiated run. This way, if something goes wrong or you need to audit the multi-agent transaction, you can trace events across system boundaries. You might store the swarm ID in a custom field (perhaps on a

Task or a custom log object) that ties together all actions related to that swarm. Agent Builder could facilitate this by auto-injecting a correlation ID variable into agents configured for external calls.

Choose swarm-friendly patterns: Not every type of agent is equally suited to being invoked from outside. In general, Action agents (which perform a single, well-defined action), Curator agents (which retrieve or summarize data), and Presenter agents (which format or deliver information) make the best candidates for external calls. These patterns have clear inputs and outputs and tend not to maintain long-running state, so an external system can call them like a service. Patterns like Sentinel (event watcher) or Supervisor (oversight) are typically running continuously or on triggers inside Salesforce and aren't naturally request/response – those would usually initiate things, not be invoked. So when designing for external participation, focus on agents that can act as microservices: take a request, do something in Salesforce (e.g., create a record, fetch data, generate content), and return a response. If needed, you can wrap more complex logic in an Action agent so that the external world sees a simple interface.

Example: Suppose your company uses an AI scheduling assistant outside of Salesforce, and it has figured out an optimal meeting time. Now it needs to add the meeting as an event on the Salesforce calendar (and maybe associate it with a customer record). Rather than building a one-off integration, you've prepared a Salesforce Action agent for scheduling. The external planner agent calls a specific Salesforce API endpoint (that you set up, perhaps an invocable flow or Apex REST) and passes the meeting details. The Salesforce Action agent, upon being invoked, creates the Event in Salesforce (and maybe returns the event ID or link). In this way, the Salesforce agent is simply a cooperating member of the swarm orchestrated by the scheduling AI – it fulfills its role (managing Salesforce data) when asked. This handshake could equally apply to other scenarios: an external procurement agent might call a Salesforce agent to update an Opportunity, or a chatbot in another platform might invoke a Salesforce knowledge agent to fetch product info. By making Salesforce agents callable, you ensure that wherever the "brain" of the multi-agent process lives, Salesforce can always be plugged in to do what it does best (data updates, compliance checks, record creation, etc.).

After enabling your Salesforce agents to be triggered by others, the next logical step is to consider the opposite scenario: when should Salesforce itself take the lead in orchestrating a swarm? We'll tackle that in the next section, looking at Salesforce as the swarm orchestrator and how to decide when to put it in charge.

SALESFORCE AGENTS AS SWARM ORCHESTRATORS

We've seen how Salesforce agents can play nicely in swarms led by others – but often, Salesforce will be the one in charge. When does it make sense for a Salesforce agent (or Salesforce as a platform) to orchestrate the entire multi-agent workflow? The short answer: whenever Salesforce is the natural source of truth or control for that process. Let's break down the scenarios and tools for putting Salesforce in the driver's seat of a swarm.

When Salesforce should take the lead: Two big factors are data ownership and process centralization. If the key records or data for the task live in Salesforce (strong data ownership), it's often safest and most efficient for a Salesforce agent to coordinate the flow, ensuring that data stays consistent. For example, consider an order fulfillment swarm – if the customer and order information is in Salesforce, a Salesforce Conductor agent can lead the process, calling out to external inventory or shipping agents as needed but maintaining the authoritative order state in Salesforce throughout. Similarly, if the workflow itself is already centered in Salesforce – say an approval process that involves managers and records in Sales Cloud – it's logical for Salesforce to orchestrate any auxiliary agents (like an external AI that analyzes risk) around that hub. In short, when Salesforce is where the important stuff happens or is stored, having it issue the commands keeps everything aligned with your core system of record.

There's also an element of governance: Salesforce provides robust permissions, auditing, and transactional integrity. If your swarm involves sensitive actions (e.g., approving a finance payment), letting a Salesforce agent control the sequence can enforce checkpoints (maybe leveraging Salesforce's approval processes) and capture a complete audit trail. External agents can still contribute (scoring a risk, providing suggestions), but Salesforce would be the one to say "yes, now execute" based on its internal rules and database state.

Tools for orchestrating multi-agent flows in Salesforce: When you decide that Salesforce is going to be the orchestrator, you have a few powerful tools at your disposal:

Flow Orchestration: This Salesforce feature is designed for coordinating complex, multi-step processes, potentially involving multiple users or long waits. You can use Flow Orchestration not just for human steps but also to weave in automated agent calls. For example, a Flow Orchestration might have a stage where it invokes an Apex action that calls an external AI service (or an invocable action that triggers another agent), then waits for a response or for a human approval, then continues. Orchestration provides a declarative canvas to outline the sequence, branching, and even parallel calls to agents. It's a natural fit when the business process has a clear structure (e.g., first get data from Service Cloud, then ask external AI for analysis, then do X based on outcome, etc.). It also logs the progress, which is great for monitoring swarms.

Conductor pattern + metadata registry: If you need more dynamic control – say your Salesforce orchestrator should be able to call different agents based on context – consider building a metadata-driven Conductor. This is an agent (could be a sophisticated Apex class or set of flows) that doesn't have all its call targets hard-coded. Instead, it references a registry (like the Agent Registry we discussed earlier) to discover which agent to call for a given task. For instance, you might have metadata that maps "If task = TranslateText then call Agent X's API; if task = GetWeather then call Agent Y." Your Conductor agent can read this configuration and route the request accordingly. The benefit is you can add or change external agents without modifying the orchestrator's code – just update the registry. This pattern is powerful for large swarms or where new tools are being introduced frequently. It's essentially implementing a plug-and-play architecture for agent integrations.

MuleSoft for bridging non-AI systems: Oftentimes, an orchestration needs to include systems that aren't themselves AI agents – legacy databases, ERP systems, payment gateways, etc. Salesforce can leverage MuleSoft (or any integration middleware) as a "bridge agent" in the swarm. For example, your Salesforce Orchestrator flow might call a MuleSoft API to execute an SAP transaction or retrieve data from an on-prem system. In the swarm context, MuleSoft acts as an executor agent that interfaces with systems that don't speak MCP or aren't autonomous. By including these calls in your orchestration, Salesforce remains the ringmaster even when steps involve non-AI tasks. The orchestration logic can treat MuleSoft calls similarly to agent calls, and MuleSoft in turn can handle the low-level integration details. The result is a seamless workflow that spans AI and non-AI components under Salesforce's control.

When orchestrating, a few best practices (or "tips") will keep your swarms robust and flexible:

Maintain clear call contracts: Ensure every agent Salesforce might call has a well-defined interface (inputs and outputs) and ideally a version number for that interface. Document these contracts (you might store them in the metadata registry or an internal wiki). This way, if an external agent changes (e.g., a new version of a service with a different API), you can update the contract and adjust the orchestrator logic accordingly. It prevents confusion where Salesforce expects data in one format but the agent sends another. Treat these like API contracts in a microservice architecture.

Plan for fallback agents or paths: As the orchestrator, your Salesforce agent should be ready with plan B and C. If Agent A doesn't respond or returns an unsatisfactory result, can we call Agent B? If the external data service is down, do we queue the request or default to a heuristic? For instance, if your swarm's external AI for sentiment analysis is unreachable, perhaps have a simpler Salesforce rule or secondary service to perform a basic sentiment check so the process doesn't stall. Identify critical points of failure and use Salesforce's automation (like fault paths in Flow, try-catch in Apex, or alternate Flow Orchestration branches) to handle them gracefully.

Annotate agents with patterns/roles: This is more of an organizational tip, but when configuring your orchestrations, it helps to tag or name the participating agents by their pattern or role. Salesforce metadata or even naming conventions can include notes like "(Presenter)" or "-Curator" in an invoked action's description. Why? It gives human operators and developers quick insight into what each external call is meant to do, and it helps ensure you've covered all roles in the process. For example, you might realize "We have lots of Executors being called here, but no Validator – is that okay?" These annotations can also feed into monitoring: you could log that "Called Agent X [Presenter] at 3:00PM, got response..." which helps in debugging and improving the swarm design over time.

Pro tip: Version everything! When you register external agents or define integration points in metadata, include a version identifier. Swarm behaviors can break if an agent's API or response format changes unexpectedly. By tracking versions (and maybe even checking compatibility in your orchestrator logic), you can manage updates deliberately. For example, you might allow calls to Agent v1 and v2 differently, or log a warning if an agent's version doesn't match what was tested. It's akin to having versioned APIs – it will save you from nasty surprises as agents evolve.

In summary, Salesforce should lead a swarm when doing so keeps the process anchored to core data and business rules. With tools like Flow Orchestration and dynamic conductor patterns, plus disciplined management of agent contracts and versions, Salesforce can safely coordinate a diverse cast of agents across the enterprise. Now that we've covered both sides of the coin – being a participant and being the leader – our next focus is on the all-important topics of security, trust, and observability. In the next section, we'll discuss how to maintain strict trust boundaries and get visibility into what your swarms are doing across all these platforms.

SECURITY, TRUST, AND OBSERVABILITY ACROSS PLATFORMS

Having a swarm of agents spread across multiple platforms is powerful – but it also expands the surface for things to go wrong or to be attacked. In this section, we'll cover how to secure your agent interactions and how to monitor and debug a swarm that spans systems. The goal is to ensure that even though the agents operate in different environments, they follow consistent trust rules and provide unified visibility.

Establishing trust boundaries: In a multi-agent ecosystem, every cross-platform call should be treated with the same caution as an external API call. You'll want to implement measures so that an agent in one system can verify that a request or response from another agent is legitimate and authorized. One common practice is signature verification – for instance, if a Copilot agent sends a request to Salesforce, it should include a signed token (JWT or HMAC signature) that Salesforce can check using a shared secret or public key. This proves the call really came from the trusted agent, not an imposter. Similarly, when Salesforce agents call out to other services, sign those requests or use secure credentials so the receiver trusts the source. Alongside identity verification, enforce role-based access controls on cross-platform tasks. Use separate credentials or integration users for each agent where possible, each scoped to just the data and actions it requires. For example, you might give a "SchedulingAgent" integration user permission only to create calendar events and read availability data – if that agent tries to query contacts or perform unauthorized actions, Salesforce's API permissions would block it. Each agent or integration point should be operating under a profile or API role that limits it to its intended scope. By segmenting privileges this way, even if one agent is compromised or goes off-script, it cannot perform other agents' duties or access unrelated data. And of course, all agent-to-agent communications should occur over secure, encrypted channels (HTTPS/TLS) to prevent any eavesdropping or tampering in transit. In short, don't rely on implicit trust just because these are "friendly" agents – use explicit trust mechanisms and least privilege principles at every boundary.

Unified observability and tracing: When something goes wrong in a single Salesforce app, you check debug logs or Event Monitoring. But how do you trace an issue that starts with a Slack bot, goes through MuleSoft, and ends up in a Salesforce action? To achieve end-to-end observability, set up a central logging or monitoring hub where each agent (or the orchestrator) reports key events. This could be as elaborate as aggregating logs into a tool like Splunk or Datadog, or as straightforward as having each agent send event logs to a common database or dashboard. The important part is to include a shared correlation ID (swarm ID) in all those logs (remember that swarm ID we discussed earlier?). That way, you can filter or search the central log by that ID and see the whole story of a particular swarm execution across systems. Implementing distributed tracing is also advisable: if your tools support it, propagate trace headers (like those used in OpenTelemetry or Zipkin) when agents call each other. For instance, an orchestrator agent can generate a trace ID and include it in HTTP headers or payload when invoking external agents; those agents can log the trace ID when they start work and pass it along further if they call others. This gives you a breadcrumb trail to follow in complex scenarios. On a more human-friendly level, many teams set up a dedicated "swarm monitoring" Slack channel where agents post high-level events. You could configure your orchestrator to send a message like ":robot_face: Agent X completed Task Y for Swarm 1234" to a Slack channel that your ops and support teams watch. It's a simple way to get real-time awareness of what the swarm is doing without digging into logs – and to spot when something gets stuck or fails (agents can post an alert message on an error, for example). The Slack channel approach doesn't replace proper logging, but it provides an easy heads-up view across platforms for fast diagnosis or intervention.

Telemetry, feedback, and error handling: Consistency in telemetry is key when multiple systems are involved. Strive to define a common log schema for your agents' important events. For example, decide that every agent log or message should include fields like timestamp, swarmId, agentName, eventType, success/failure, duration and so on. If each platform logs those in its own way, you can use a log aggregator to align them, or at least easily script transformations. This uniformity will make it far easier to analyze swarm performance or identify bottlenecks (perhaps building a dashboard that shows each swarm's timeline and agent success rates) across the ecosystem. Another aspect is designing error escalation pathways. In a single system, an error might just throw an exception that surfaces to a user or triggers a retry. In a swarm, an error might occur deep in another platform where Salesforce or your central team might not notice immediately. Set up mechanisms so that critical failures are bubbled up and handled. For example, if an external agent encounters an error processing a Salesforce request, have it send a specific error response back that your orchestrator in Salesforce can recognize and handle (maybe triggering a compensating transaction or notifying an admin). Or, if a Salesforce agent fails to complete its step (say a flow fault), make sure that failure is signaled to the external orchestrator. You don't want an agent quietly dying without the rest of the swarm knowing. An error routing plan might include automatic retries (with limits) for transient issues, and defined escalation after X attempts – such as logging an incident or notifying a human operator to intervene (for example, by automatically creating a Salesforce Case or sending an email/SMS alert to an on-call team member). Some teams even create a "circuit breaker" logic: if a particular integration keeps failing, the orchestrator stops calling that agent for a while and uses an alternative path, to prevent cascading issues.

In essence, treat your swarm as a distributed system of microservices: apply zero-trust principles at boundaries and invest in robust monitoring and telemetry throughout. That way, you retain control and insight even as your autonomous agents multiply across the enterprise. With these safeguards in place, we can now turn to a concrete illustration of everything coming together. In the next section, we'll walk through an end-to-end example of a cross-platform agent swarm, showing how the patterns, integrations, and guardrails we've discussed play out in a real scenario.

ECOSYSTEM WALKTHROUGH – END-TO-END EXAMPLE

To wrap up, let's walk through a full example of a cross-platform agent swarm in action. This scenario involves an expense management use case touching Finance and HR functions, and we'll highlight how the agents coordinate across Salesforce and external platforms:

Sentinel (Salesforce) – Detects an anomaly: In our company, a Salesforce Sentinel agent monitors employee expense reports in real-time (perhaps using an Einstein Analytics trigger or a scheduled Apex job). It spots an unusual spike in travel expenses for a particular department this month – far outside the normal pattern. Recognizing this as a noteworthy event, the Sentinel agent raises a flag. It creates a swarm instance (assigning a swarm ID) and notifies the next agent in line with relevant details (which expenses, who submitted them, etc.). Since this agent is within Salesforce, it can directly invoke the next step via Apex or Flow.

Curator (Salesforce) – Clusters and analyzes data: The Curator agent wakes up (triggered by the Sentinel or by the abnormal pattern event). Its job is to sift through the expense records and find structure – for example, grouping the expenses by type or employee to see if it's a few big charges or many small ones. The Curator might use an internal Einstein Discovery model or even call an external clustering service, but let's say it does it within Salesforce for now. It produces an analysis: e.g., "All the spike is coming from 5 employees in the Sales team attending the same event, exceeding their meal allowances." This summary of anomalies is now passed on to a Presenter agent. Since both Curator and Presenter are on Salesforce, this hand-off could be in-memory or via a platform event with the summary payload attached.

Presenter (Salesforce) – Generates a human-friendly summary: The Presenter agent receives the analysis and formats it for decision-makers. Perhaps it creates a nicely formatted report or a message: "Expense Spike Alert: 5 sales reps exceeded meal policy by 30% during the Q4 offsite." It could generate a PDF report or a Slack message text. Here's where we cross platforms: the Presenter agent in Salesforce calls out to the collaboration environment where approvals happen. Let's say our company handles approvals in Microsoft Teams via a Copilot-powered assistant. So, the Presenter agent sends the summary (and relevant context like expense IDs, amounts, swarm ID) to the Copilot system – this could be through an HTTP POST to a Copilot API endpoint or using MCP if Copilot supports it. The integration includes the necessary trust token so Copilot knows the data is authentic. Now the baton passes to an external agent.

Supervisor (Microsoft Copilot) – Requests human approval: On the Microsoft side, a Supervisor agent (following the Supervisor pattern) takes over. It's been given the summary of the issue and knows an approval decision is needed (e.g., whether to freeze the expenses or let them through). The Supervisor agent presents an approval prompt to the appropriate manager through Microsoft Teams (for example, it pops up a card saying "Unusual expenses detected: do you approve holding these charges for review?" with Approve/Deny buttons). The manager clicks "Approve Hold".

The Copilot agent then captures that decision (perhaps with some comment) and proceeds to notify the swarm that the hold is authorized. How does it do that? It could call back into Salesforce or directly invoke the next agent responsible for the hold action. Let's say it triggers the next agent via a secure API call, including the context (which expenses to hold, who approved, and the swarm ID for tracking).

Action (MuleSoft) – Executes the expense hold: Now a MuleSoft-based Action agent comes into play. This agent has access to the financial system (which might be an ERP or a payments system) where it can actually put a hold on expense reimbursements or corporate card charges. The Copilot's approval message triggers MuleSoft (perhaps via an HTTP request or an event bus that MuleSoft subscribes to). The Action agent receives the necessary data (employee IDs, amounts, approval auth) and performs the hold operation in the external finance system. For example, it might call an SAP API to freeze those expense reimbursements. MuleSoft then responds back to confirm the action was successful (or not). (If the ERP call failed, that error would bubble up and the orchestrator could alert someone in Salesforce.)

Coach (Salesforce) – Recommends policy changes: With the immediate issue handled (expenses are held pending review), the swarm turns to reflection. A Salesforce Coach agent now looks at the root cause: it analyzes that these employees all exceeded their meal allowance. Perhaps current policy is unclear for offsite events. The Coach agent formulates a recommendation – for instance, "Consider updating the travel policy: meal allowance for offsite events may need to be higher, or enforce pre-approval for exceptions." This suggestion is generated using accumulated knowledge (maybe tapping an internal knowledge base or just simple business rules given the data). The Coach agent then delivers this insight to the HR or Finance team responsible for policies. It might create a Slack message or a Chatter post to the policy owners, or even draft an email to the CFO. The message references the swarm's findings (e.g., "After reviewing the Q4 offsite expense anomaly, I recommend we revisit the meal reimbursement limits for such events to prevent future spikes"). This final step ensures that the organization can learn from the swarm's outcome, not just put out the fire. The swarm's job is now complete.

In this end-to-end narrative, notice how the agents handed off tasks across different platforms while maintaining continuity:

Integration methods and boundaries: Salesforce agents communicated with the Copilot system using a secure web service call (with proper auth and context data), and Copilot triggered MuleSoft via API as well. Each boundary crossing (Salesforce → Copilot, Copilot → MuleSoft, MuleSoft → Salesforce) used a defined interface with the swarm's context attached (for example, an approval ID or expense list). We also see multiple patterns at play: Sentinel and Curator internally, then a Trigger/Delegate style hand-off to Copilot, then Copilot acting as a Supervisor with a human in the loop, then an Action execution via MuleSoft, and finally a Coach feedback loop in Salesforce. All the classic patterns appeared – detection and analysis in Salesforce, delegation to Copilot for approval, external supervision, an integrated action, and a coaching feedback loop – and because the interfaces and context were well-defined, the agents linked up without a hitch.

Error pathways: The swarm design included backup plans. If the manager hadn't responded, the Copilot could have escalated to another person or automatically approved minor expenses after a timeout. If MuleSoft's action failed, that error would flag back to Salesforce so a human or fallback process could handle those charges. (We assumed success in each step here to focus on the flow.)

Agent identities and context sharing: Each agent worked only within its allowed permissions. The external calls carried the swarm ID and only the needed data. For example, the Copilot's request to MuleSoft included the approved expense IDs and a token proving the manager's approval, so MuleSoft knew it was authorized and which records to update. Throughout, the manager and finance team interacted only with their familiar interfaces (Teams and Slack), blissfully unaware of the complex multi-agent choreography happening behind the scenes.

This example ties together many threads we've discussed: multi-agent patterns, cross-platform calls, human-in-the-loop, error handling, and learning. It showcases how a well-orchestrated swarm can respond to an event (spiking expenses), involve the right humans at the right time, leverage the strengths of each platform (Salesforce for data and policy, Copilot for conversational approval, MuleSoft for integration, etc.), and even drive continuous improvement (via the Coach's suggestion). By designing with clear roles, secure integrations, and good observability, such a complex dance of agents becomes not only possible but manageable.

With this concrete journey in mind, you can better envision how to apply these concepts in your own organization. We've now covered everything from patterns and protocols to practical examples. Next, we'll recap the key takeaways from "Composing the Agent Swarm" and prepare to move on to the broader organizational implications in the next chapter.

SUMMARY

This chapter explored how to compose agent swarms that extend beyond Salesforce into the wider AI ecosystem. You learned how to design Salesforce agents that confidently call and respond across platforms, leverage the Model Context Protocol for structured hand-offs, and coordinate work using both Agentforce tools and external services like MuleSoft and LangChain. The key theme is interoperability: in a world of interconnected agents, the ability to seamlessly integrate and orchestrate across systems is a true force multiplier for your enterprise.

Armed with these cross-platform patterns and practices, you're now equipped to tackle multi-agent workflows that span any stack. Next, we shift from technology to strategy: how do you adjust your organization to truly embrace these autonomous agents at scale? In the following chapter, we'll explore what it takes to become an "agent-first" organization – from leadership and culture to budgets and KPIs – so that the human and organizational side keeps pace with the technical innovation.

21

BECOMING AN AGENT-FIRST ORGANIZATION

Becoming an agent-first enterprise isn't about simply adopting a new tool or feature – it's about transforming how work gets done at a fundamental level. In an agent-first organization, AI agents become core participants in business processes and decision-making, not just peripheral assistants. When properly deployed and governed, these agents begin to reshape everything from budget allocations and performance metrics to team structures and cultural norms. For instance, budgets that once went primarily to staffing and manual operations start shifting toward developing AI capabilities and maintaining agent ecosystems. Key performance indicators (KPIs) evolve as well – success is measured not just by human output, but by outcomes achieved through human–AI collaboration and the performance of the agents themselves.

This organizational shift has a broad impact. AI agents affect more than just workflows; they influence decisions, accountability models, and the skills employees need to succeed. Decision-making becomes a shared effort between humans and their digital counterparts, with agents providing data-driven recommendations or taking autonomous actions within guardrails. Accountability also needs rethinking: if an autonomous agent handles part of a process, who is responsible for its outcomes? Leading enterprises assign clear "agent owner" roles to ensure every agent's actions trace back to human oversight. Meanwhile, employees find their skill sets evolving – they spend less time on rote tasks and more time on overseeing agents, tuning their behavior (for example, refining an agent's prompts or business rules), and interpreting agent-provided insights. An agent-first culture encourages continuous learning so that the workforce can effectively guide and collaborate with AI. Skills like prompt design, ethical monitoring, and multi-system orchestration become as important as traditional domain expertise.

Crucially, leadership must align the entire organization – strategy, operations, and incentives – around this agent-driven future. It's not enough for one team or a handful of developers to experiment with AI. Becoming agent-first means executives champion a vision where automation and intelligence are woven into every department's objectives. Operationally, teams incorporate agent management into their daily routines, whether it's monitoring an agent's performance in the field or updating its knowledge base with new business rules. Incentives and KPIs are adjusted to encourage using and improving agents: for example, rewarding a customer service team not just for closing cases, but for how effectively they leverage an AI Agent to resolve issues faster. In an agent-first enterprise, a high-performing team might be one that spends fewer human hours on a process because an agent is handling the heavy lifting – and that efficiency would be celebrated.

Salesforce Agentforce serves as a platform for this kind of organizational transformation. It's not just a collection of AI features bolted onto CRM; Agentforce is a comprehensive ecosystem that acts as a catalyst for change across departments and roles. With tools like Agent Builder and Agentforce Development Tools, teams have a unified environment to design, test, and deploy agents rapidly – using both low-code builders and pro-code Apex or JavaScript as needed. Rich integration points like Invocable Flows and Invocable Apex allow these agents to hook into existing business processes, while Flow Orchestration and event triggers enable multi-step workflows that mix agent and human tasks. Critically, Agentforce bakes in governance and telemetry (via features such as the Command Center and metadata-driven policies), so as you scale up agent usage, you can maintain control and trust. In short, Agentforce provides the connective tissue and guardrails that let a company scale from a few experimental bots to a true digital workforce of enterprise-grade agents.

This chapter takes a strategic look at what it means to become an agent-first organization. We will examine how embracing AI agents changes the way you budget and measure success, how job roles and team structures evolve, and how to manage the cultural change that comes with introducing "digital colleagues" into the enterprise. We'll also highlight why strong governance must be at the heart of an agent-first strategy and how to design your agent ecosystem for long-term scale and continuous innovation. By the end of this chapter, you should understand how to move from tactical agent deployments to a cohesive, enterprise-wide approach where human–AI collaboration is standard operating procedure.

Next, we begin with a foundational question: what does it mean to operate as an agent-first organization?

DEFINING AN AGENT-FIRST ORGANIZATION

What sets an agent-first organization apart is a mindset shift: instead of defaulting to traditional apps or manual steps, the enterprise defaults to AI agents as the primary way work is accomplished. In practice, that means reimagining roles and processes so that autonomous or semi-autonomous agents handle a growing share of tasks, and employees focus on guiding those agents and handling exceptions. To clarify this concept, let's consider some of the key characteristics of an agent-first organization:

Work is increasingly done by agents, not just through apps: In an agent-first enterprise, many tasks that humans used to perform by clicking through software or following scripts are now executed by AI agents. Employees aren't just using applications as tools; rather, they supervise and collaborate with agents that themselves perform the work. For example, instead of a support rep manually checking knowledge articles and composing a response, a Presenter agent might draft the response and a human just approves or tweaks it. Routine data entry, monitoring, and even complex multi-step transactions can be autonomously handled by well-trained agents. The result is that the first line of action on any new workload is often an AI agent, with traditional apps and interfaces becoming the medium through which agents act or the fallback when human input is needed.

Teams focus on overseeing, tuning, and extending agents – not performing routine steps: The human role evolves from doing every step hands-on to managing the agents that do the work. For instance, a finance team in an agent-first company might spend more time defining rules or training data for an expense approval Supervisor agent, rather than manually reviewing every expense report themselves. Team members become "agent supervisors" or "agent trainers" who monitor outcomes, adjust parameters, improve prompts, and handle the edge cases the agents escalate. This doesn't mean people are less important – it means their day-to-day job is less about repetitive tasks and more about ensuring the automation is correct and improving over time. Overseeing a fleet of agents (checking logs, addressing exceptions, updating their knowledge) becomes a core competency. Likewise, building new capabilities might mean extending an agent's skills (for example, adding a new Invocable Action to an existing agent's repertoire) rather than writing a whole new app from scratch.

Metrics reflect outcomes and agent performance, not just human effort: An agent-first organization measures success in terms of results delivered by the human–AI team, rather than input effort alone. Traditional metrics like hours worked or manual throughput make room for metrics like agent-handled transactions, accuracy of agent decisions, or reduction in turn-around time. If a sales agent (AI) drafts proposals, a metric might be the percentage of proposals generated by the agent that lead to deals, or how much faster the process is. You'll see new KPIs such as "percentage of customer inquiries resolved by AI" or "agent suggestion acceptance rate" alongside human productivity metrics. Importantly, outcome-focused metrics (customer satisfaction, resolution time, error rates) take center stage, while it becomes less relevant exactly how many keystrokes a human did – if an agent can achieve the outcome more efficiently, that's success. Agent performance metrics (uptime, response accuracy, model confidence scores) also enter everyday dashboards, treating agents almost like employees whose work quality and reliability can be quantified and improved.

Taken together, these characteristics illustrate a fundamental shift: the organization treats AI agents as an integral part of how work gets done, on par with human employees in many respects. To operationalize this, certain organizational markers start to emerge in agent-first companies:

Formal agent ownership roles are established: Just as one might have application owners or process owners, agent-first enterprises designate Agent Owners or custodians for each important AI agent or agent-led process. This could be a new role or an extension of someone's job, but it's formally recognized. The Agent Owner is accountable for an agent's performance, maintenance, and ethical operation. For example, if you have a contract analysis agent in Legal, there is a named person (perhaps a "Legal AI Product Manager") who is responsible for what that agent does, monitors its outputs, and continually tunes it. By assigning ownership, the organization ensures that agents are not running unchecked – each has human stewardship throughout its lifecycle. This concept was introduced earlier in the playbook (for instance, Chapter 15 on governance) as a critical governance measure, and here it becomes a standard operating practice.

Governance is integrated into standard operating procedures: In an agent-first setting, AI governance isn't a separate or one-time effort; it's woven into the everyday procedures and checkpoints of the business. Whenever a new business process is designed or an existing one changes, the role of AI agents is considered and the governance policies (permissions, risk assessments, compliance checks) are applied. For instance, change management processes include steps like "review by the AI Governance Board" for any new agent deployment. Regular IT audits might include agent behavior audits. There are playbooks for incident response that cover AI missteps (e.g. what to do if an agent makes a critical error). Essentially, governance of AI – covering things like safety, ethics, compliance, version control, and performance monitoring – becomes as routine as financial auditing or cybersecurity practices. Teams might conduct quarterly reviews of all active agents to ensure they still meet standards and business needs. This integration means the enterprise treats agents not as ad hoc experiments, but as persistent elements that must adhere to company policy and industry regulations at all times.

Agent design patterns are reused across the organization: One marker of maturity is that teams speak a common language about agent patterns (like those covered in this book) and reuse them in many domains. It's not just the innovation team or a single department building an agent in isolation – patterns such as Supervisor (human-in-the-loop validator) or Companion (assistive sidekick) are recognized and implemented in both frontline areas (customer service, sales) and back-office functions (HR, finance, IT). For example, a Companion agent might be embedded in an employee helpdesk Slack channel to assist staff internally, while another Companion agent type serves sales reps in the CRM. A Supervisor pattern might govern marketing content approvals as well as legal document checks. By leveraging a set of core patterns enterprisewide, the organization avoids reinventing the wheel for each use case and maintains consistency. This also means best practices learned in one area (say, how to best implement a Coach agent for training support reps) can be quickly transferred to another area (perhaps a Coach agent for employee onboarding in HR), since the pattern is understood by all. Cross-functional architecture reviews might even include a checklist: "Are you using an existing agent pattern for this need?" to encourage reuse and alignment.

Agent lifecycle and usage are tracked centrally (often via Agentforce tools): To support all of the above, agent-first organizations build an internal registry or inventory of all AI agents in use. Salesforce Agent Builder can play a role here by serving as a hub where each agent's metadata is defined – including its pattern, owner, department, risk level, etc. Companies use this registry to track where agents are deployed and how they're performing. For example, they might log each agent's "maturity level," from pilot to fully production, and see which departments are most advanced in agent adoption. This central visibility helps leadership identify gaps (e.g. maybe customer service has many well-governed agents, but finance has few) and opportunities for sharing solutions across teams. By tagging agents with metadata like their primary pattern or business function, you can generate reports such as "show all Action agents in the company and their success rates" or "which agents touch customer data and have a high risk score." In Agentforce, much of this metadata tagging and tracking can be done within the platform, making it easier to manage at scale. A centralized Agent Registry becomes as important as a CMDB (Configuration Management Database) is for IT assets – it's a living catalog that ensures every agent is accounted for, evaluated, and continuously aligned with business strategy.

Pro tip: Treat agents as digital employees. Give each important agent a sort of "job description" (what it's responsible for), set KPIs for its performance (uptime, accuracy, response time, etc.), and even an onboarding process (initial training data, validation before going live). This mindset ensures you're deliberate about how agents operate and integrate into teams, and it reinforces human accountability for every agent's role.

RESTRUCTURING BUDGETS AND KPIS AROUND AGENTS

Adopting an agent-first approach will inevitably lead leadership to rethink budgets and success metrics across the organization. If AI agents are performing significant work and unlocking new efficiency, where and how the company invests resources should change accordingly. Likewise, measuring performance must go beyond human productivity to include the contributions and effectiveness of agents. In this section, we look at how forward-thinking enterprises realign their budgets and KPIs to support a flourishing ecosystem of AI agents.

Reallocating budgets for an AI-driven workforce: One of the first shifts in an agent-first transformation is redirecting investment from manual operations toward agent development and governance. This doesn't necessarily mean cutting people to zero – instead, it means recognizing that scaling up AI capabilities requires its own funding. For example, a customer service org might freeze or slow the growth of hiring for call center reps and channel that budget into an "AI enablement" fund: hiring prompt engineers or Agent Developers, purchasing additional computing resources for AI models, or subscribing to AI services. Departments start proposing budgets that include line items for agent maintenance, training data curation, and continuous improvement, similar to how one would budget for software licenses or system maintenance. Additionally, roles focused on agent governance (like an AI compliance officer or an agent QA lead) might be added, which could come from what used to be purely operations or IT headcount budget. The underlying idea is that money once spent on repetitive manual labor or legacy process overhead can yield a higher return when invested in building robust AI agents that automate those tasks at scale.

To give concrete examples, imagine a finance department that historically budgeted for a team of analysts to manually review transactions for fraud. In an agent-first model, that department might invest in developing a Sentinel agent to monitor transactions in real time. Budget is allocated for the initial development (perhaps using Salesforce Flow plus some Apex for custom logic, and maybe an AI model for anomaly detection), as well as ongoing model retraining and monitoring. The department could justify this by projecting that the Sentinel agent will reduce losses or catch issues faster than the humans could, and free those analysts to focus on investigating the flagged cases rather than sifting everything manually. Similarly, consider the operational cost savings when a single Conductor agent can coordinate a process that used to require a project manager and multiple coordinators – some of the salary savings might be reinvested into improving that agent or building additional agents for other processes.

Investing in tools and infrastructure: Along with shifting headcount or labor budgets into AI capabilities, organizations invest in the infrastructure needed to support agents at scale. This includes things like telemetry and monitoring tools (to track what agents are doing and catch errors), sandbox and testing environments for agents (perhaps using Agentforce Dev Tools to simulate scenarios), and knowledge management efforts to provide agents with quality data. For example, funds might be allocated to develop a library of high-quality prompts and pattern templates that teams can reuse – essentially creating internal IP around agent development. Enterprises may also invest in training programs for employees to upskill in AI (which is an investment in the human capital side of being agent-first). All these investments indicate that the organization treats AI agents as a long-term capability, deserving the same kind of resource planning as any major workforce or IT investment.

New KPIs centered on agent-driven outcomes: Alongside budget changes, an agent-first enterprise updates its performance metrics to capture how well the AI agents are augmenting or replacing traditional work. Some of the novel KPIs that emerge include:

Agent Uptime – a reliability metric tracking the availability and responsiveness of critical agents. Just as we monitor server uptime, if an agent is meant to be "on duty" 24/7 (say a virtual assistant on a customer portal or a monitoring agent watching logs), its uptime percentage and any downtime incidents become important. High agent uptime means business processes supported by that agent are continuously running. For instance, if a Command Center dashboard shows your key sales support agent has 99.9% uptime handling requests, that reliability can be celebrated (and you'd investigate any downtime like a service outage). This KPI reinforces that agents are part of the operational fabric – when they're down, it's like part of your workforce went offline.

Human Touchpoints Reduced – a productivity and efficiency indicator measuring how many manual intervention points have been eliminated thanks to agents. It could be expressed as a percentage decrease in human touches for a given process, or as an absolute number (e.g. "200 hours of human work saved per month"). For example, if previously a customer order required five human checkpoints and now an agent automates three of those, that's a significant reduction in human touchpoints. This KPI focuses on outcomes like speed and effort reduction: fewer touchpoints usually mean faster turnaround and more scalability. Tracking this over time shows how automation is improving. It's also a way to celebrate teams for effectively using agents – if a support team reduced manual escalations by 40% because an agent is handling common cases, that's a win that should reflect in their KPIs.

"Action Agents per Process" (Automation Maturity) – a measure of how deeply agents are embedded into processes. This could literally be counting the number of distinct Action-type agents or automated steps involved in a workflow, or an index that scores processes based on their level of AI automation. The idea is to gauge automation maturity: a higher number means a process is largely automated by specialized agents. For instance, an order fulfillment process might involve a Conductor agent orchestrating steps, a Sentinel agent monitoring for delays, and a Presenter agent generating customer updates – that process would score high on the agent-per-process metric. This KPI might be used by leadership to set targets like "Within one year, 80% of our Tier-1 support processes should have at least one AI agent involved," encouraging teams to continuously look for opportunities to introduce agents. It's a way of quantifying the spread of AI across operations.

Of course, traditional business KPIs (revenue, customer satisfaction, error rates, etc.) remain vital, but these new metrics directly tie into the performance and impact of AI agents. They signal to everyone in the company that agent performance and usage are now first-class components of success.

Using tools to monitor and align these metrics: To manage both budgets and KPIs around agents, organizations lean on dashboards and analytics – often extending existing Salesforce tools:

The Salesforce Command Center (or similar executive dashboard) is configured to display agent activity and health by business unit. For example, an operations leader might have a Command Center view showing number of transactions handled by agents today, the uptime of each critical agent, and any active alerts or exceptions the agents have raised. By monitoring agent activity in real time and historically, leaders can make informed decisions about resource allocation (e.g. if one department's agents are handling dramatically more volume, maybe that department warrants more investment or more oversight).

KPIs are linked with the Agent Registry and metadata. Each agent in Agentforce can carry metadata like its purpose, the business function it serves, its risk level, and performance stats. By aligning KPIs with this metadata, companies can do things like aggregate success rates of agents by function or flag all "High Risk" agents and see if their error rates are within acceptable bounds. For instance, if every agent has a metadata field for "Success_Rate" or "User Override Rate," those can be rolled up to organizational KPIs (like "our agents collectively handle 85% of incoming chats without human intervention, with a 95% success rate as defined by no follow-up needed"). The metadata tagging (covered in governance, Chapter 15) becomes useful for slicing metrics and ensuring the right things are measured. It also helps in transparency: regulators or internal audit can easily retrieve which agents impact a certain compliance metric, because the metadata links them.

ROI dashboards are developed to compare cost and efficiency of agent-handled work versus traditional methods. Finance or strategy teams can build dashboards that show, for example, "cost per transaction" handled by agents vs. cost per transaction if done manually. These often factor in the development and operating cost of the agent (like infrastructure, licensing of AI models, or the salary of the team maintaining it) versus the labor cost and time of human workers. A simple illustration: if an agent processes 1,000 HR helpdesk tickets a month, and the all-in cost of that agent (amortized) is $500 per month, that's $0.50 per ticket – compare that to the $5 or $10 it might cost in human time per ticket. Over time, these ROI metrics help justify further investment in agents and identify where they bring the most value. They also highlight any diminishing returns (perhaps an agent is very complex/expensive but only saves a little bit of time – those would be scrutinized). By making ROI visible, organizations ensure that "becoming agent-first" remains grounded in business value, not just tech for tech's sake.

In summary, restructuring budgets and KPIs around agents means financially committing to AI-driven operations and measuring the impact in tangible ways. Companies on this path treat their AI agents as a new kind of workforce – one that requires upfront investment and ongoing care, but that can yield exponential returns in scale and efficiency. The next step in becoming agent-first is recognizing that with these changes come new roles and team structures to support the hybrid human–AI environment.

EVOLVING ORGANIZATIONAL ROLES AND TEAM STRUCTURES

As AI agents take on a more central role in day-to-day work, organizations will inevitably see the emergence of new roles and a reconfiguration of team structures. People's jobs won't vanish, but what jobs exist and how teams are organized will evolve to support a collaborative environment between humans and agents. In an agent-first enterprise, you begin to find roles explicitly focused on AI agents, and teams that integrate agents as if they were virtual team members. Let's explore some of the emerging roles and how team structures adapt:

Agent Owner: We've touched on this role in the context of governance – an Agent Owner is the person accountable for a specific agent's success and proper function. In practice, this role behaves like a product owner or manager for the AI agent. They define the agent's objectives, ensure its meeting business needs, coordinate improvements, and act as the point of contact if the agent causes an issue or needs a decision. For example, if you have an AI sales assistant agent, the Agent Owner (perhaps someone in Sales Ops or a technically-savvy salesperson) will gather feedback from the sales team, adjust the agent's knowledge or rules, and report metrics about how much that agent is boosting sales productivity. By formally establishing Agent Owners, the company ensures every agent has human stewardship –

no agent is "orphaned" or everyone's responsibility (which often means no one's responsibility).

Prompt Architect: Many AI agents, especially those leveraging large language models (LLMs) or other AI services, rely on well-crafted prompts and dialogues to function effectively. The Prompt Architect role specializes in designing and refining these prompts, conversational flows, and the overall interaction style of agents. Think of this person as part UX designer and part AI psychologist – they figure out how to ask the AI the right questions and provide the right context so that the agent's outputs are accurate and aligned with the brand/requirements. In a customer support scenario, the Prompt Architect might create the template prompts that a Presenter agent uses to answer questions in a friendly yet precise tone. They continuously experiment with improvements as the AI models evolve. This role can overlap with or augment content designers and business analysts, but with a specific focus on optimizing AI behavior. As Agentforce includes tools for managing prompts and conversational contexts (for instance, Agent Builder might have sections for "Agent Instructions" or sample dialogues), the Prompt Architect becomes a key user of those features.

Pattern Librarian: As the organization reuses agent design patterns, having someone (or a team) curating and governing the library of patterns is invaluable. A Pattern Librarian maintains documentation and examples of each agent pattern (Sentinel, Supervisor, Curator, etc.), ensures they are implemented consistently across different projects, and helps teams choose the right pattern for their needs. They also keep track of new patterns or variations emerging from the field. In a way, this is like an enterprise architect but focused on AI agent architectures. For example, if a team in Marketing comes up with a novel "Reviewer" agent pattern that isn't in the standard eight core patterns, the Pattern Librarian would evaluate it, perhaps generalize it, and add it to the playbook for others to use. They might also maintain metadata about which patterns are deployed where (tying in with the Agent Registry). This role ensures that as dozens of agents are built, the underlying approaches remain standardized where it makes sense, which in turn makes maintenance and governance easier.

Agent QA Lead: Quality assurance takes on new dimensions when AI is involved. An Agent QA Lead (or team) is responsible for testing AI agents' behaviors, much like a software QA engineer tests an application – but here it involves testing not only deterministic logic, but also probabilistic AI outputs. This role develops testing frameworks for agents: for example, designing scenarios and sample inputs to feed an agent and verifying it responds correctly, or that a Supervisor agent properly escalates when it should. They also test failure modes (how does the agent handle ambiguity or lack of data?) and bias/ethical considerations (does the agent produce problematic content or decisions under any circumstance?). Using Salesforce's tools, an Agent QA Lead might write Apex tests for invocable actions and flows, and also incorporate mock LLM responses to simulate edge cases. They might leverage the Agentforce Dev Tools to run agents in a sandbox environment with controlled inputs. This role ensures that before an agent goes live – and continuously during its life – there is a rigorous process to catch issues. It's a blend of traditional QA and model evaluation, likely requiring new testing methodologies (like testing an AI's output distributions or using telemetry to spot anomalies in production).

These roles illustrate how job functions can pivot – people move from being general developers, analysts, or support reps into these more specialized positions that revolve around AI agents. Importantly, these roles are highly cross-functional. For instance, an Agent Owner might need to coordinate with IT (for deployments), with business stakeholders (for requirements), and with compliance teams (for approvals). A Prompt Architect may work closely with a copywriter or legal to ensure the agent's tone and content meet standards. The net effect is that silos break down: AI agents often cut across traditional department boundaries (an agent might touch both IT systems and business logic), so the roles around them encourage more interaction between what used to be separate teams.

Beyond individual roles, team structures themselves evolve. Many companies find that organizing around outcomes (with a mix of humans and agents working toward a goal) is more effective than sticking strictly to functional silos in an agent-first world. Some notable shifts include:

From function-based teams to outcome-based pods: Rather than having, say, a marketing team, a sales team, and a service team that rarely intermingle, an agent-first organization might form cross-functional "pods" or squads focused on a particular outcome or process – and those pods include both human members and AI agents as active participants. For example, consider a "Customer Renewal Pod" whose goal is to improve customer renewals. In that pod, you might have a human account manager, a data analyst, and a Companion agent that monitors customer engagement signals, plus maybe a Coach agent that suggests next-best actions. The humans and agents work in tandem: the agent surfaces insights and even takes automated steps (like sending a personalized check-in email via a Flow), while the humans handle relationship nuances and final decisions. By structuring teams around outcomes, the organization ensures that agents are directly embedded where they add value, rather than being an afterthought. It also encourages team members to become fluent in using the agents, because their day-to-day collaboration happens in the context of these pods.

Agents integrated into communication channels (e.g. Slack) as teammates: A very practical change is how teams incorporate AI agents into their daily communications. For many, that means putting agents in chat channels, war rooms, and meetings as informational assistants or even as autonomous participants. Salesforce has robust integration with Slack (via the Salesforce for Slack SDK and various AppExchange apps), enabling agents to post updates or respond to queries in Slack channels. In an agent-first org, it's common to see something like a Slack channel for a project where a Companion Agent is also a member of the channel. Team members might ask the agent questions in natural language ("@DealBot, what's the latest status of Acme Corp renewal?") and get an immediate answer pulled from Salesforce data. Or the agent proactively pings the channel: "I noticed our deployment this morning failed some tests; here are the details..." – behaving as an ever-vigilant team member. By embedding agents in ubiquitous tools like Slack, employees grow accustomed to consulting AI and receiving help in real-time. It blurs the line between an agent and a colleague, reinforcing that the agent is part of the team's workflow. This has cultural benefits too: it normalizes AI assistance and reduces the friction of having to go into a separate interface to interact with the agent.

Adjusting agile rituals and project management to include agents: When your "team" includes AI agents, even the way you plan and review work can change. Progressive organizations include agents in their agile processes. For instance, during daily stand-up meetings, a team might review not only what each human did yesterday and plans to do, but also what the agent accomplished or where it got stuck. Perhaps the agent provides a brief report (via a Slack update or a dashboard) that the team discusses: "Our Lead Qualification Agent triaged 100 inbound inquiries last night – any that it marked as uncertain we should double-check today." In sprint planning, teams assign tasks to improve or update agents as part of the normal backlog (e.g. "Update the pricing rules in the Quoting Agent for the new product line" as a task owned by someone, just like a user story). Some teams even give agents a persona on project boards – for example, in Jira or Trello, creating a card for the agent's "work" or labeling items that the agent will handle. This fosters a sense of partnership: the agent has deliverables and responsibilities just like a human team member. Moreover, retrospectives can include discussing the agent's performance: did it help, were there issues, what can be improved in its behavior for the next cycle? By formally acknowledging agents in team routines, organizations ensure continuous improvement of AI systems and make their integration seamless.

In essence, team structure becomes more fluid and interdisciplinary. A project team might simultaneously involve software developers, operations specialists, a few AI agents, and an AI specialist (like a Prompt Architect) all working together. Hierarchies may flatten somewhat as agents take on some supervisory or coordination duties that middle managers used to do, allowing those managers to focus on more strategic tasks. And because agents can operate around the clock, teams might utilize a "follow-the-sun" model where human work is handed off to agents overnight and vice versa – truly blending automated and human work cycles.

Pro tip: When managing projects or planning work, explicitly include your AI agents as part of the team. For example, add the agent's tasks to your Kanban or sprint board and assign someone to review the agent's outputs. Treating an agent as a team member – with its own backlog of improvements and performance stats – keeps the focus on collaboration. You can even list an agent in an org chart or team roster when communicating to the rest of the company, which reinforces accountability and clarity about what that agent "owns."

MANAGING CHANGE AND ADOPTION

Transforming into an agent-first organization isn't just a technical endeavor – it's a human one. Employees and stakeholders must adapt to new ways of working, and that often comes with concerns, misconceptions, or resistance. Successfully adopting AI agents at scale requires thoughtful change management. In this section, we'll address the common cultural frictions that arise and outline strategies to foster adoption and acceptance of AI agents throughout the enterprise.

Anticipating cultural friction: It's natural for people to be cautious or skeptical when introduced to AI agents working alongside them. Two prevalent concerns often surface:

Job displacement fears: Employees may worry that if AI agents are doing more work, their own jobs could be in jeopardy. For example, a customer support agent might think, "If the new AI chatbot can handle our Tier-1 inquiries, will the company still need me?" This fear can lead to resistance, whether overt or subtle, such as not cooperating with training the AI or underutilizing it to prove it's not effective. Even when leadership frames agents as helping tools, the workforce might suspect a hidden agenda to cut jobs. This concern isn't unfounded historically, so it must be addressed head-on.

Trust and error anxiety: Many employees (and managers) have concerns about AI making mistakes – the fear of errors, "hallucinations" (AI confidently giving false information), or unpredictable behavior. A finance manager might be uneasy about an agent approving transactions, thinking "What if it approves something fraudulent by mistake?" Or a sales rep might hesitate to use an AI-generated proposal, worried it might contain inaccurate data that could embarrass them in front of a client. This anxiety is often amplified by widely publicized instances of AI failures. Essentially, people need to trust that agents are reliable and, importantly, that they won't be blamed for an agent's error if they weren't in control. There's also a general hesitation with any new tech – needing time to understand it and see it proven before fully embracing it.

Acknowledging these concerns internally is important. Change leaders should make it clear that they expect such questions and are prepared to answer them. This sets the stage for the strategies to manage the transition.

Strategies for change management and adoption:

Start with human-in-the-loop designs to build confidence: One effective approach is to use the Supervisor pattern (or similar human-in-the-loop mechanisms) early in the rollout of agents. Instead of immediately giving AI free rein on critical tasks, design agents that assist and make recommendations while humans still have final say. For example, an AI agent might draft responses or flag anomalies, but a human approves the response or decision. In Salesforce, you might implement this with a Supervisor Agent that routes its suggestions through a task or Slack message where a person can click "Approve" or "Adjust." By preserving human oversight in the initial stages, employees see agents as helpers rather than threats. It also provides a safety net – people learn the agent's capabilities and quirks without fearing that one mistake will slip through uncorrected. Over time, as trust in the agent grows (because it proves accurate, or perhaps even more consistent than humans in some cases), those same employees may become comfortable with increasing autonomy for the agent. Essentially, the Supervisor pattern acts as training wheels for the organization's trust: it ensures that for critical operations, nothing fully automated goes unchecked until the stakeholders are ready.

Deploy Coach agents to support and educate users: Another tactic is introducing Coach agents whose job is not to do the user's work, but to help the user do their work better. This addresses adoption on two fronts: it gives users direct value (personal improvement and guidance), and it subtly acclimates them to interacting with AI regularly. For instance, a Coach agent might observe how a new hire uses a software system and provide tips ("You can use shortcut X to do this faster") or gentle corrections ("I noticed you set this field a bit differently than standard; here's why we usually do it the other way"). In the context of Agentforce, you could have a Coach agent integrated into, say, the Sales Cloud UI or Slack, offering sellers real-time advice on best practices. By deploying such agents, you create an environment where AI is seen as a tutor or mentor, not a threat. Employees are likely to be less defensive with an agent that clearly exists to support them (no one thinks a coaching tool is there to replace them). Over time, as users get comfortable taking advice from an AI and see it as part of their growth, they'll naturally be more open to other agent types in the workflow.

Emphasize augmentation, not replacement, in all communications: Leadership and project champions should consistently message that agents are meant to augment human capabilities, not replace the humans. This might sound like buzzwordy reassurance, but it needs to be concrete. For example, highlight use cases where agents handle the drudgery, allowing employees to focus on higher-value tasks. "Our new QA Document Review Agent will take care of checking formatting and basic compliance clauses, so our legal team can spend more time on complex negotiations with clients" – this kind of narrative helps employees envision a positive role for the agent in their daily work. In communications (town halls, emails, training sessions), underscore success stories like: "Since introducing the Scheduling Agent, our support reps now have more time to personally follow up with high-value customers, improving satisfaction scores – the agent didn't remove the human touch, it enhanced it by freeing us from the mundane bits." Also, openly address the job security topic: if the goal is to repurpose people into new roles rather than cut jobs, say so and follow through with actions (like reskilling programs). Consistency here builds credibility. Any sign of dissonance (for instance, saying augmentation but immediately laying off staff after deploying agents) will deeply undermine trust and adoption.

Provide "Agent Impact Briefings" for each function: One practical change management tool is creating short, function-specific briefings or demos that show exactly where and how agents will add value, and what changes for that team. For example, before rolling out an agent in Finance, prepare a brief presentation or document – an "Agent Impact Briefing" – that might include: the current challenges or workload (e.g. too many invoices to approve manually), how the new agent will work (e.g. "Invoice Sentinel will automatically flag out-of-policy expenses and suggest approvals for routine ones"), what the expected benefits are (faster cycle time, fewer errors), and crucially, what the humans in the loop will do before, during, and after the agent's involvement. It should also outline any new skills or training provided. These briefings help demystify the agent for that specific audience. People see a clear mapping: "Here's what stays the same, here's what the agent will do, here's what you'll do differently." It turns abstract AI talk into a concrete change narrative they can prepare for. If possible, include real early results or a pilot demonstration. Seeing an agent in action in a controlled way can turn skeptics into at least curious participants. Each department or function gets their own briefing because the concerns of, say, a Sales team (worry about client relationships and AI tone) are different from an IT team (worry about stability and security). Tailoring the message shows respect for each group's priorities.

Use Companion agents to gather feedback and gauge sentiment: Adoption is not a one-time event – it's ongoing. After agents go live, it's important to keep a pulse on how users are feeling and where issues might be. Interestingly, AI agents themselves can help with this. For instance, you can deploy a Companion agent whose role is to interact with users and solicit feedback about the new AI systems. This might be as simple as a chatbot in your intranet that periodically asks, "Hey, you've been using the new Contract Analyzer agent for a week – how's it going? Any feedback or problems?" and then logs those responses. Or within a Salesforce screen, after an agent assists a user, a pop-up (driven by the agent) asks for a quick rating or comment, similar to how customer service surveys work. These Companion agents can funnel feedback to the implementation team and change managers in real-time. Moreover, by using an agent to do this, it reinforces the notion that the company values the employees' comfort with AI. It also provides psychological safety: some employees might hesitate to openly tell their manager "I don't trust this AI yet," but they might freely tell that to a feedback bot, which can anonymize and aggregate sentiments. In addition, such an agent can track usage patterns (with permission and privacy in mind): e.g. noticing that a particular team isn't using the new agent much and flagging that for follow-up (maybe they need more training or have unresolved concerns). Essentially, the Companion agent acts as an adoption gauge and a facilitator of the continuous improvement loop between users and the AI rollout team.

By implementing these strategies, organizations can significantly smooth the transition to an agent-first way of working. The goal is to create a culture where employees feel part of the process – they are co-evolving with the technology, rather than having it imposed on them. Early wins and positive experiences are crucial: when people see that an agent makes their work easier and that their expertise is still valued (often more than ever), they become advocates for further adoption. This human-centric approach to change is what separates successful agent-first transformations from those that stall due to pushback or poor user engagement.

CENTERING GOVERNANCE IN ENTERPRISE STRATEGY

We've discussed how agents can be woven into the fabric of work, but to do this safely and sustainably, governance can't be an afterthought – it must be a central pillar of your agent-first strategy. By the time an organization is scaling up dozens or hundreds of AI agents, having clear policies, oversight structures, and risk management for those agents is just as important as it is for human employees or core IT systems. In this section, we'll highlight how to integrate strong governance practices (many of which were covered in detail in Chapter 15: Agent Governance and Operational Risk Management) into the enterprise's overall strategy and day-to-day management. This ensures that as you accelerate with AI, you maintain control, compliance, and trust.

Bringing forward the governance fundamentals: As a first step, an agent-first enterprise enforces some fundamental governance requirements for every agent – no exceptions. From the moment an agent is conceived (during its design phase) through its deployment and operation, certain criteria should always be met:

Every agent has an owner, a purpose, and a defined trust/risk score. As mentioned earlier, assigning an Agent Owner is mandatory. This person's name is recorded in the agent's metadata (for example, in Agent Builder's settings or a custom registry object) so everyone knows who is responsible. The agent's purpose (its intended function and scope) is clearly documented – not just in someone's head or a slide deck, but in a living description accessible to stakeholders. This could be part of a standard agent README or record that answers: "What is this agent supposed to do, and what business outcome does it serve?" Finally, a trust score or risk level is attached to each agent. This is effectively a measure of how much autonomy it has and the impact of its decisions. Some organizations use a simple High/Medium/Low risk classification; others might score on multiple dimensions (like data sensitivity, financial impact, etc.). The key is that it's formally assessed, perhaps during a review board process, before an agent goes live. For example, an agent that auto-approves expenses might be labeled Medium risk if it handles small amounts, but High risk if it can approve large payments or affect financial records. That trust score can dictate further governance (e.g. High-risk agents require more frequent audits or more secondary oversight mechanisms). By making these three things prerequisites, you avoid the scenario of "rogue" automations running without clarity on accountability or importance.

Governance squads or committees set and enforce policy across the agent lifecycle. Many companies establishing an agent-first model create a cross-functional AI Governance Committee or dedicate a team (sometimes called an "AI Center of Excellence") to oversee agent deployments. This group's charter is to develop policies for how agents are designed, tested, approved, monitored, and eventually retired. It often includes stakeholders from IT governance, data privacy, security, compliance, and business units. For example, the committee might set a policy like: "Any agent that interacts with customers must undergo a bias and fairness test before deployment" or "LLM-based agents must use only approved foundation models and have prompt logs enabled." These policies become part of the standard operating procedure. The governance squad also decides on things like what the sunset process is for an agent (when and how do you decommission an agent that's no longer needed or that underperforms?). They may create checklists or templates teams must follow (some may leverage Salesforce features, like requiring an approval process in Salesforce that triggers when someone tries to deploy a new agent into production, which routes to the governance team for sign-off). By having a standing body focused on agent governance, the enterprise treats AI agents with the same rigor as financial assets or IT systems – it's a recognition that these agents can have wide-reaching effects and thus need proactive management at the highest level.

Integrate external standards and compliance requirements via metadata and rules: Governance in an enterprise doesn't exist in a vacuum – companies have to comply with external laws and industry regulations (GDPR for data privacy, HIPAA for health info, Sarbanes-Oxley for financial controls, etc.). An agent-first strategy should bake these compliance considerations directly into agent design and deployment. Salesforce's metadata-driven approach can really help here. For example, each agent can have metadata tags for "Compliance Domain" (e.g. GDPR, HIPAA) if it handles relevant data. Suppose an agent processes personal customer data in the EU; it gets tagged with GDPR. Automated checks (perhaps a Flow or Apex trigger in Agent Builder) could then enforce that this agent calls only services or uses only prompts that meet GDPR guidelines (like not asking the LLM to output personal data inappropriately, or ensuring data retention policies are applied to any logs). In practice, you might have a custom metadata type or object listing "Agent Compliance Requirements," and when deploying an agent, a script or checklist ensures all the listed controls are in place. Similarly, if an agent is subject to HIPAA, you might require encryption for any logs it keeps, which could be enforced through platform encryption or shield settings.

By including compliance in the agent's metadata and design, you can even automate enforcement: e.g. a nightly batch Apex job or a real-time rule that scans agents marked "SOX-critical" to confirm they haven't been modified without proper approval. If you integrate with tools like Salesforce Shield or Event Monitoring, you might track all actions taken by a "High Risk" agent and alert if something falls outside of expected parameters. The overarching goal is to treat compliance as an integral part of building and running an agent, not a checkbox after deployment. This approach not only prevents legal issues but also builds trust internally and externally that AI is being handled responsibly. It prepares you for audits where you can show "Here, our Agent X is tagged with GDPR and our system automatically ensures it never stores data longer than 30 days and that removal requests are cascaded."

Building an "Agent Review Board": Many organizations find it valuable to institute an Agent Review Board (which could be part of the governance committee or a separate body) that functions somewhat analogously to a change control board in ITIL frameworks. This board's purpose is to evaluate and prioritize agent initiatives across the enterprise and to approve agents moving from pilot into full production. The board is typically cross-functional: it might include senior leaders from various departments (to ensure alignment with business strategy), representatives from IT/security, and the AI program leaders.

Why have a review board? Because as agent adoption accelerates, you might have dozens of proposals for new agents or major upgrades coming from all corners of the company. The board ensures resources are allocated to the most beneficial and safe projects. They might ask questions like: Does this proposed agent align with our strategic objectives or OKRs? Has the business case been made (e.g. ROI or clear efficiency gains)? Are the necessary governance measures in place (owner assigned, risk assessed, etc.)? If two teams propose similar agents, the board can spot overlap and encourage collaboration or reuse. This prevents fragmentation and "agent sprawl" where redundant agents are being built unbeknownst to each other.

In practical terms, an Agent Review Board could operate through Salesforce as well: imagine using a custom object "AgentProposal__c" where teams submit their agent ideas or requests for go-live, which then go through an approval process (Salesforce's native approvals or even a Slack-integrated approval via Flow). The board meets regularly (maybe monthly) to go over these and give the green light or send back for modifications. Over time, this creates a rhythm where AI developments are consciously steered at the enterprise level, much like major IT projects are reviewed in portfolio management.

Traceability and risk scoring with metadata tagging: We've mentioned metadata a few times – it's worth emphasizing how central it is to enterprise governance of agents. In Salesforce, custom metadata types or custom objects can store tags/attributes for each agent, such as: Business Unit, Owner, Pattern, Risk Level, Compliance Tags, Last Review Date, etc. By tagging agents thoroughly, you gain traceability – you can answer questions like "List all agents that access customer PII" or "Which agents use the Conductor pattern and also integrate with external APIs?" with a simple report or query. This is invaluable for governance because when an issue arises or a new policy comes in, you know where to look.

For example, suppose a new regulation is passed that affects AI decision-making in credit lending. If your agents are well-tagged, you can quickly identify any agent involved in credit decisions and make updates. Without tags, you'd be scrambling through documentation or asking around. Additionally, tags can feed into automated risk scoring. Perhaps you maintain a formula or Apex code that calculates an agent's risk score based on its metadata (number of systems it touches, sensitivity of data, degree of autonomy, etc.). The Command Center can then display a "heat map" of agents by risk vs. performance, or send alerts if a high-risk agent's error count goes above a threshold. These kinds of governance analytics are only possible with good data about the agents themselves, hence the focus on metadata.

Automated policy enforcement: Advanced agent-first organizations incorporate governance checks directly into the pipelines and orchestrations. For instance, using Invocable Apex or flows, you could create a step in every agent's deployment script that calls a "Governance Check" action. This action might automatically verify that the agent has an assigned owner in the system, that it's using only approved APIs, that its prompts don't contain disallowed phrases, etc. If any check fails, the deployment halts and the team is notified. This is analogous to how DevOps pipelines have automated tests and security scans. In Agentforce, you could leverage something like a scratch org or staging environment where an agent is deployed and a suite of Apex tests (covering governance rules) runs before promotion to production. The tests might reference the agent's metadata and simulate some actions to ensure compliance. All this might be overseen by the governance squad but executed via tooling – making governance a continuous, automated process rather than a manual one.

In sum, by centering governance in your strategy, you ensure that scaling up AI does not equate to scaling up chaos or risk. Instead, each new agent is born with a clear lineage of accountability and operates within a framework of rules that align with your enterprise's values and obligations. This gives leadership and stakeholders confidence to accelerate AI adoption – because they know there's a firm hand on the wheel. With governance as the bedrock, we can now look at how to design our agent ecosystem for long-term scale.

DESIGNING FOR LONG-TERM SCALE

Adopting a few agents is one thing; operating an entire ecosystem of agents over the long term is another challenge altogether. An agent-first organization must plan and architect for scale from the outset, so that adding the hundredth or thousandth agent doesn't create unmanageable complexity. Long-term scale isn't just about quantity of agents, but also about sustaining performance, maintainability, and alignment with business goals over years. In this section, we'll discuss key design considerations and practices that enable your AI agent ecosystem to grow in a healthy, controlled, and impactful way.

Prioritize agent patterns that naturally scale across the enterprise: Not all types of agents have equal impact when scaling. Some patterns lend themselves to wide deployment because they provide value in many contexts. Based on the experiences shared in earlier chapters, as well as observing enterprise trends, it's wise to focus on a few patterns as pillars of your long-term strategy:

Companion agents – These are the personalized assistants that help individual employees (or customers) in their daily tasks. Companion agents tend to be broadly useful because almost every role in a company can benefit from a context-aware helper. For example, an internal "Copilot" that helps engineers find documentation or auto-generate code snippets can be replicated for sales (to find collateral, draft emails) or for HR (to answer policy questions). Companion agents scale horizontally across the org, driving productivity in myriad small ways that add up. Designing them well (with user preferences, context awareness, and fail-safes as described in earlier chapters) means you can roll them out to hundreds or thousands of users. By prioritizing Companion agents, you ensure AI is touching the day-to-day work of everyone, not just niche processes.

Conductor agents – These orchestrators coordinate multi-step processes, often across departments or systems. As an organization grows its agent ecosystem, Conductor agents become essential for managing complexity. Think of a Conductor as the "manager" of other agents or processes – for example, coordinating a customer onboarding process that involves a Presenter agent to explain steps, an Action agent to set up accounts, and maybe an external email service. By deploying Conductor agents, you effectively create an automation layer that ties together various siloed tasks into an end-to-end flow. They help avoid fragmentation: rather than humans manually moving data or tasks between different agents or systems, a Conductor handles it. For long-term scale, focusing on Conductor pattern means you're building the integration glue and oversight logic into your AI workforce. These agents will also make it easier to swap components in and out (like replacing one sub-agent with another) without disrupting the whole process, which is key for longevity as technology changes.

Presenter and Coach agents – These patterns focus on human understanding and improvement. Presenter agents surface insights in human-friendly ways, and Coach agents help users learn and adapt. As your organization deploys more "heavy-duty" agents (like action-taking bots), Presenter and Coach agents become indispensable for keeping humans in the loop and the organization learning. From a scaling perspective, Presenter agents ensure that regardless of how complex the underlying agents or data get, there's always a clear interface delivering the right information to people. They prevent the scenario where you have a ton of automation but no one knows what's going on because it's all black-box. A Presenter might summarize a weekly report aggregating what all 50 of your agents did and flag any anomalies – scaling transparency alongside automation. Coach agents, on the other hand, scale the capability of your workforce to effectively work with and improve the AI. They help new employees get up to speed with using agents, and they feedback user struggles or common errors into the system for continuous refinement. By emphasizing Presenter and Coach patterns, you design a future where the more agents you have, the more clarity and skill your human team has (instead of confusion or skill atrophy).

By prioritizing these patterns in your roadmap, you create a core around which other more specialized agents can flourish. It's similar to how in traditional IT you'd focus on core platforms and then allow niche tools around the edges. Here, Companion, Conductor, Presenter, Coach are like core "platform" patterns that will support many use cases and ensure humans remain effective and informed as the agent count grows.

Maintain a centralized Agent Registry and knowledge hub: Earlier we emphasized creating an Agent Registry to track agents. At scale, this registry (or knowledge hub) becomes the source of truth and a coordination mechanism. To design for long-term scale:

Ensure the registry captures usage and performance statistics. It should not just be a static catalog. Ideally, each agent's entry is updated (maybe automatically) with data like how often it's used (transactions per day), its success or error rates, last update time, etc. This turns the registry into a monitoring tool as well. For instance, from the registry you could query "Which agents are underutilized?" and then decide whether to promote them more internally or decommission them. A live registry can integrate with the Salesforce Command Center or other BI tools to visualize the health of your agent ecosystem in one place.

Align the agent roadmap with enterprise OKRs (Objectives and Key Results). This means that for each planning cycle, you use the registry and stakeholder input to plan which new agents to build or which existing ones to enhance, in direct support of the company's strategic goals. If one objective is "Improve customer retention by 10%," you might look at your registry and see opportunities: perhaps invest in a new Coach agent to guide sales reps in outreach, or a Sentinel agent to flag at-risk accounts earlier. By tying agent development plans to OKRs, you prevent random or pet projects from consuming resources and ensure scale is achieved in service of business outcomes. The registry might even have a field linking an agent to a specific OKR or KPI it influences, keeping this alignment explicit.

Use the registry to govern agent lifecycle stages across the org. As in Chapter 15, agents will go through stages (draft, pilot, production, etc.). At scale, you want a clear view: how many agents are in pilot vs fully deployed? Are some lingering in "experimental" phase too long? A centralized dashboard of lifecycle stages (which can be derived from registry metadata) can help manage this. It also signals where more support is needed: if 20 agents are stuck in pilot because of lack of resources to push them to prod, maybe allocate more developers or simplify approval processes.

Leverage Flow Orchestration for multi-agent "service teams": When you have many agents, they often need to work together to deliver value. Salesforce Flow Orchestration is a powerful tool for coordinating multiple steps and actors (including both humans and bots) in a declarative way. Designing for scale means setting up orchestration frameworks so that you're not hard-coding agent-to-agent interactions all over the place, but rather defining them in configurable flows.

For instance, consider a complex employee onboarding process. You might have:

A Conductor agent that triggers on a new hire record.

It then uses Flow Orchestration to invoke a sequence: first, an Action agent creates IT accounts; then a human manager approves some access (human step in the flow); then a Presenter agent sends a welcome email; finally a Coach agent checks in with the new hire after a week to answer FAQs on Slack.

By building this with Flow Orchestration, the entire process is visible as a flow diagram and can be modified without touching code inside each agent. You can swap out an agent (maybe you change the welcome email agent to a new one with a different tone) by editing the flow step to call a different invocable action. You can also handle failures or branching logic in the orchestration centrally. Essentially, orchestration flows act like the meta-controllers for agent collaboration, which is much easier to maintain at scale than a spiderweb of point-to-point triggers.

Additionally, orchestrations can implement service team concepts, where a "team" might consist of several agents each doing their part. You could even create a Flow that serves as a template for multi-agent processes – a standardized way agents hand off tasks. This consistency means as you design new multi-agent solutions, you're not starting from scratch each time; you're following a proven pattern in Flow Orchestration. It also means monitoring is easier: the Flow runtime can track the status of each orchestration, so you can see "Ah, 10 onboarding orchestrations are currently in progress, 2 failed at step X, etc." which is vital for operational oversight.

Plan for resiliency and continuity (agents in business continuity planning): As agents become critical to operations, you must consider how they fit into your business continuity and disaster recovery plans. Long-term scale demands that agents are as resilient as any other critical system.

Some considerations:

Fallback modes: Design each important agent with a fallback if it's unavailable or if the AI service fails. For example, if an AI-powered agent cannot fetch a response from an LLM or hits an error, do you have a rule to automatically route the task to a human or to a simpler rule-based system? Maybe your Customer Chatbot Agent is down – your fallback mode could be to present a web form or immediately escalate to a live chat with a human. These contingencies should be thought out in advance and even automated. In Salesforce flows, you might have fault paths that trigger notifications to a team and switch the process when an agent fails. Metadata can mark whether an agent is in "fallback mode" currently (so that you know it's effectively paused and humans are covering).

Failover logic and redundancy: If an agent is absolutely mission-critical (say an agent that monitors fraud in real-time transactions), consider having a backup agent or method. This could mean running two agents in parallel (perhaps using different models) and if one fails, the other picks up – or even using one as a check on the other's decisions (kind of an active-active redundancy). In Salesforce terms, you might deploy a redundant flow or Apex service that can be toggled on. Or use an external service as a backup via MuleSoft integration – e.g. if your primary AI service is unavailable, route requests to a secondary service via API calls. Testing these failovers is important so you know they actually work under stress.

Inclusion in Disaster Recovery (DR) plans: For enterprise DR planning, ensure that the restoration of AI agents (and their data/state) is part of the plan. If you have nightly backups for Salesforce data, include custom objects that agents rely on or agent definitions themselves if they are stored as metadata. If a data center goes down, how quickly can you redeploy your critical agents in an alternate environment? If using Agentforce on Salesforce, much is handled by Salesforce's own resilience, but if you incorporate external AI components, you need contingencies for those too. For example, if your agent calls out to a third-party AI API, have a strategy if that API is unreachable (like temporarily degrade the agent's functionality or throttle its operations).

Escalation workflows for exceptions: At scale, even with high accuracy, agents will encounter novel situations or make errors. Design an escalation workflow such that when an agent is unsure or an error is detected, the issue is immediately escalated to the right human or another oversight agent (like a Supervisor pattern) and logged for later analysis. Many companies implement an "AI operations center" concept – similar to IT operations center – where significant agent incidents are tracked. For instance, if an agent produces an output that triggers a manual override or a customer complaint, a case might be automatically created in Salesforce for an AI operations team to review. This ensures nothing falls through the cracks just because a machine was doing it. Over time, analyzing these escalations will highlight where to improve agents or where certain tasks might always need a human touch.

By including agents in your business continuity and resilience planning, you acknowledge that they are becoming as critical as human staff or IT systems. This mindset avoids nasty surprises – like a key process grinding to a halt because an agent crashed – and it demonstrates to all stakeholders (including regulators or customers) that you run a tight, reliable ship even with heavy AI usage.

All these design-for-scale measures help create an environment where adding more agents adds more value, not more risk or confusion. They help your organization avoid plateauing after a handful of agents due to complexity. Instead, with strong patterns, central oversight, orchestration, and resilience, you can keep expanding the agent workforce in a controlled, strategic manner.

BECOMING AN ENTERPRISE-WIDE INNOVATION PLATFORM

Once the foundational pieces are in place – agents are working across the enterprise, governance is tight, and you've designed for scale – the organization can shift focus to a powerful question: how do we leverage this agent-first model to drive continuous innovation? The ultimate stage of becoming agent-first is not just doing what you used to do more efficiently; it's unlocking new possibilities and fostering a culture of experimentation and improvement that spans the entire enterprise. In this section, we discuss how agents can turn your organization into an innovation platform, where ideas can be rapidly prototyped, tested, and scaled, and how connecting your internal agent ecosystem to the broader tech landscape keeps you at the cutting edge.

Using agents as innovation enablers: With Agentforce tools readily available, individual teams and even individual employees can start turning their creative ideas into working solutions faster than ever. Think of each agent as a mini-app or micro-service that can be spun up to test a concept. For example, an employee in the Operations department might think, "Wouldn't it be great if we had an agent that could automatically remind project managers of pending tasks every Friday?" In a traditional IT setup, that idea might die due to lack of resources or get delayed in a long dev queue. But in an agent-first company, that employee could open Agent Builder, define a quick Flow or two, maybe write a bit of Invocable Apex if needed, and have a basic "Task Nudge" agent running in a sandbox in days. The barrier to entry for innovation is lowered significantly.

To capitalize on this, many organizations encourage internal hackathons or innovation days focused on AI agents. These are events where employees from various departments come together (physically or virtually) to build new agent-based solutions in a short time frame (say 24-48 hours or a week). Salesforce's low-code environment shines here: mixed teams of developers and non-developers can use Flow Builder, Apex Actions, and pre-built connectors (like MuleSoft APIs) to prototype agents that solve real problems they face. One team might prototype an agent that integrates with a legacy ERP system via MuleSoft to automatically update inventory levels (something that was manual before). Another might use an LLM and Apex to create a sentiment-analysis agent that scans internal surveys and flags issues. The point is, the enterprise becomes a sandbox of ideas where agents are the building blocks. And because of the standardized patterns and governance in place, these hackathon projects can potentially be turned into production solutions more easily – they're not completely disconnected skunkworks, they're using the sanctioned tools and frameworks (perhaps even pattern libraries provided by the Pattern Librarian role).

Leadership can fuel this by providing resources and recognition. For example, set quarterly or biannual hackathons with themes ("Next-Gen Customer Experience Agents" or "AI for Internal Efficiency") and then celebrate the winners, fund their projects to become real. Some companies establish an internal "Agent Innovation Fund" that provides budget to teams that want to develop a promising prototype into a fully supported agent. The message is that innovation isn't top-down; anyone with a smart idea and the initiative can create a new agent that benefits the company.

Creating agent enablement centers and communities: To sustain momentum, organizations invest in structures to support ongoing learning and sharing about agents. This often takes the form of an internal Center of Excellence (CoE) or "Agent Enablement Center." What does this involve?

Internal training programs: The CoE might develop training specifically for different roles – e.g. a workshop for business analysts on how to use Agent Builder to create basic agents, or an advanced course for developers on how to implement complex multi-agent orchestrations with Flow Orchestration and custom Apex. These programs could be akin to internal Trailhead modules or lunch-and-learn sessions. The idea is to raise the baseline skill level so more people can participate in agent innovation. There might also be training on AI ethics and responsible design, ensuring your innovators are considering those aspects from day one.

Pattern playbooks and best practices: Building on this very playbook, the CoE could maintain internal documentation that translates these patterns and lessons into the company's specific context. For example, they might have a "Catalog of Agent Patterns with Internal Examples" – essentially a knowledge base where anyone can look up "Supervisor Pattern" and see how your organization has implemented it in a few cases, including code snippets or flow designs that they can mimic. There could be best practice guides like "How to properly tag your agent with metadata in our org" or "Checklist for deploying an agent to production." These resources accelerate innovation because teams don't have to reinvent the wheel or guess at the right approach; they have proven guidelines to follow.

Agent reuse catalogs: Over time, you'll accumulate a lot of agent components that could be reused. The CoE or an enablement team might run an internal catalog or marketplace for these. For instance, if someone built a great Invocable Flow that takes a customer issue and suggests a Knowledge Article (a mini AI service), they can list that in the catalog so others can incorporate it rather than build their own. Or a set of Apex classes that connect to a popular internal API – put that in the catalog for easy reuse. Even full agent templates ("Onboarding Agent Template") can be shared so teams can clone and tweak rather than starting from scratch. By promoting reuse, you not only speed up development, but also move toward consistent, tested components which improves quality at scale. Salesforce's AgentExchange concept externally mirrors this idea – internally, you can have your own mini-AppExchange for agent parts.

Communities of practice: Encourage formation of interest groups or regular meetups where those working with agents share knowledge. Maybe all "Prompt Architects" across the company have a monthly call to discuss new techniques for better LLM prompts. Or an internal chatter/Slack channel (#agentforce) where people ask questions ("Has anyone integrated an Agent with System X? Any tips?") and others chime in. This social aspect of innovation ensures that as more people join the agent-first journey, they're supported by peers and can learn collectively.

Connecting to the broader ecosystem: No matter how much innovation happens internally, it's wise to stay connected with the fast-moving external AI ecosystem. An agent-first organization should be somewhat porous to new ideas and technologies. Here are a few ways to do that:

Align with emerging standards like Model Context Protocol (MCP): As AI agents become popular across industries, standards are being proposed to allow agents on different platforms to interoperate or at least share a common "language." The Model Context Protocol (MCP) is one such concept – it's about standardizing how agents describe their context, capabilities, and state so they can work together or be managed uniformly. By aligning your internal metadata and agent descriptions to MCP (even if loosely at first), you future-proof your ecosystem. For example, if MCP specifies a JSON schema for an agent's capability declaration, you might structure your agent registry in a similar way. Why? Down the line, if you want your Salesforce agents to interact with, say, an external agent running in a supplier's system or a partner's platform, having that common protocol can make integration much easier. It could enable scenarios like an Agentforce Conductor agent triggering an action in a Microsoft Power Platform agent because both understand a shared MCP-based handshake. Also, if regulators or auditors start expecting AI systems to expose certain standard info (like an agent's purpose, data usage, etc.), being MCP-aligned means you can generate those reports readily.

Leverage MuleSoft and other integration tools to extend agents beyond Salesforce: Salesforce Agentforce is powerful within the Salesforce world, but enterprises have many systems. Using MuleSoft (Salesforce's integration platform) or similar tools, you can give your agents access to data and actions in external systems (ERP, databases, third-party services) without having to build custom connectors from scratch each time. For example, if you have an inventory management system outside Salesforce, MuleSoft can expose a reusable API or flow that your Action agents or flows can call to check stock or place an order. Syncing with MuleSoft means your agents remain part of a unified enterprise architecture – they won't become siloed AI that only know about CRM data. In an innovation context, this means teams can dream up agent uses that involve multiple systems relatively easily. One team might integrate an agent with a legacy mainframe via a MuleSoft connector, another might pull data from a Data Warehouse – all using the standard integration pipelines rather than reinventing integration logic. Essentially, the agent platform extends to wherever your data and processes live.

Incorporate complementary AI technologies (Slack, Copilot, LangChain, etc.): Being agent-first doesn't mean Salesforce-only. It means using the best tools for the job in harmony. If your company uses Slack heavily, you might integrate Slack's own AI features or toolkits alongside Agentforce – for instance, using Slack's SDK to create an interactive agent interface, or connecting a Salesforce agent to trigger a Slack Workflow. If you use Microsoft 365 heavily, perhaps Microsoft's Copilot is generating content or summaries from documents – you could loop that into your processes. For example, a Salesforce agent might detect a need for a document and call out to Microsoft Graph or Copilot to retrieve or summarize something, then feed it back into Salesforce context. LangChain and similar frameworks can be leveraged for advanced reasoning or when you want to quickly prototype something outside the Salesforce platform that later integrates back in. Some teams might experiment with LangChain to orchestrate a complex multi-tool reasoning process, and if it proves valuable, the outcome can be connected via an API to Salesforce (or even ported into a Salesforce-based flow if feasible). The point is to remain technology-agnostic enough that you can bring in external innovation. You might even allow some agents to run outside of Salesforce (on a cloud function or another platform) but register them in your Agent Registry and control them via Salesforce events – effectively mixing your internal Agentforce agents with external ones into one big "agent mesh."

Metadata alignment for interoperability: We mentioned MCP, but even simpler, ensure that your agent metadata can map to what other systems might expect. For example, if every agent in your registry has a clear description of inputs/outputs, you can expose that via APIs to a central enterprise catalog or AI governance tool. Some companies are starting to adopt enterprise AI management software that inventories models and agents across the organization; if your data is well-structured, plugging into those higher-level management tools becomes easier. This might also help if you acquire another company or merge – having standard descriptors means you can merge agent inventories and figure out overlaps or integration points more quickly.

Innovation metrics and incentives: To truly become an enterprise-wide innovation platform, leadership can set targets that encourage experimentation and cross-functional collaboration with agents. For example, an organization might set a quarterly target like: "Each department should propose at least one new AI agent idea that drives improvement in their KPIs." Or KPIs like number of processes improved by AI, or percentage of employees who have built or configured an agent (to encourage democratization). The Pro tip below captures a key idea: measure success not by how fancy the tech is, but by cross-functional outcomes – e.g. a hackathon solution that involved Marketing and IT and actually improved lead conversion by X%. By rewarding teams for those outcomes, you incentivize not just building agents, but building agents that matter.

Pro tip: Establish quarterly goals for agent-driven innovation that tie to business results. For instance, challenge teams to deliver an AI improvement that cuts a process time by 50% or improves customer NPS, and celebrate those wins. By focusing on cross-functional outcomes (like customer satisfaction, speed to market, cost savings) rather than just technical metrics (number of models used, etc.), you ensure that innovation efforts stay aligned with what really moves the needle for the enterprise.

In summary, at this stage the organization isn't merely using agents – it's continuously reinventing itself with agents. Every employee feels empowered to contribute ideas, the structure is in place to develop and deploy those ideas safely, and the enterprise is plugged into a larger network of technology advancements. Your company becomes a kind of innovation platform where human creativity and AI capability intersect fluidly, driving competitive advantage and adaptability. That's the hallmark of a true agent-first organization: not just efficiency, but agility and ingenuity at scale.

SUMMARY

In this chapter, we explored what it takes to evolve from implementing a few tactical AI solutions to truly becoming an agent-first organization. This transformation is as much about people and process as it is about technology. We began by defining an agent-first enterprise as one where AI agents are embedded in the core of work – handling an increasing share of tasks, while humans focus on higher-level oversight and collaboration with these digital teammates. Key characteristics include shifting work to agents, redefining team roles to manage and improve those agents, and measuring success in terms of outcomes and agent performance rather than just human effort.

We then examined the practical shifts needed in budgets and KPIs. Embracing AI at scale means reallocating resources: investing in AI development, training, and governance instead of simply adding headcount for manual work. New performance metrics come into play – from "Agent Uptime" indicating reliability, to "Human Touchpoints Reduced" reflecting efficiency gains – ensuring the organization quantitatively tracks the impact of agents. These changes send a clear signal that the enterprise values and monitors the contributions of its AI workforce alongside its human workforce.

As agents become pervasive, entirely new roles emerge (like Agent Owner, Prompt Architect, Pattern Librarian, Agent QA Lead) and team structures adapt. We discussed how teams can reorganize into hybrid pods where agents and humans work together towards outcomes, and how even daily routines (stand-ups, Slack channels, etc.) start to include AI agents as active participants. Successfully integrating agents requires thoughtful change management: addressing employees' fears of job displacement and their concerns about trust. Strategies such as deploying human-in-the-loop Supervisor agents, using Coach agents to assist and train users, and maintaining open communication that emphasizes augmentation over replacement are crucial. By actively managing this cultural shift – through education, feedback loops (often aided by Companion agents gathering input), and celebrating wins – companies can bring their people along on the journey and foster widespread adoption of AI tools.

A major theme of the chapter was that governance must be front and center. We reinforced that every agent should have a named owner, a clear purpose, and risk assessments (a "trust score") established from the start. Enterprises need to integrate governance into their strategy via policies, review boards, and metadata-driven controls to keep the rapidly expanding agent ecosystem safe, compliant, and aligned with corporate principles. This includes tying into external standards and ensuring things like privacy, security, and ethical guidelines are baked into every agent's design (with the help of tools like metadata tags, approval workflows, and Salesforce's Command Center for oversight). Governance, far from stifling innovation, provides the confidence and structure that allow innovation to scale without igniting chaos.

Designing for long-term scale was another critical piece. We highlighted how focusing on scalable patterns (Companion, Conductor, Presenter, Coach) and maintaining a robust Agent Registry set the stage for managing many agents effectively. The organization treats its agent ecosystem as an evolving system – orchestrating multiple agents through Flow Orchestration, planning for resilience with fallback modes and failovers, and including agents in business continuity plans so that the enterprise can depend on them just as it would any mission-critical system or team. By doing this homework upfront, the enterprise avoids hitting a wall when the number of agents grows; instead, it has the frameworks to accommodate growth gracefully.

Finally, we looked at the endgame of agent-first transformation: turning the enterprise into an innovation platform. With Salesforce Agentforce tools and a culture that supports experimentation, companies can accelerate solution development and problem-solving. AI agents become building blocks that employees across departments can combine and recombine to prototype new ideas quickly, whether through hackathons, internal incubators, or just empowered individuals automating their day-to-day challenges. We discussed establishing centers of excellence, internal training, and knowledge-sharing mechanisms to continuously elevate the organization's AI proficiency. And we stressed staying connected to the wider AI world – aligning with standards like MCP for interoperability, integrating with other platforms via MuleSoft and APIs, and leveraging complementary technologies (from Slack integrations to external AI services) to ensure the enterprise remains at the cutting edge and not siloed.

In sum, becoming an agent-first organization means moving beyond isolated AI projects to a holistic reimagining of work with AI at the heart. Budgets, roles, and culture all shift to support a partnership between humans and a growing "digital workforce" of agents. Thanks to Salesforce Agentforce and thoughtful strategy, what starts as a handful of AI use cases can mature into an enterprise-wide capability – one that is scalable, governed, and continuously driving innovation. With this foundation in place, your organization is poised to lead with confidence in a world increasingly defined by intelligent automation. As we transition to the Epilogue of this playbook, we'll zoom out to reflect on the broader leadership mindset required in the age of AI agents, ensuring that you not only deploy agents, but also inspire and guide your teams through the transformative changes ahead.

EPILOGUE: BEYOND THE PATTERNS – BECOMING A LEADER IN THE AGE OF AGENTS

The journey through this playbook has taken you from the nuts-and-bolts of agent patterns and technical implementation to the high-level realms of system design, governance models, and full organizational transformation. Along the way, you haven't just learned how to build AI agents – you've learned how those agents fit into a bigger picture of enterprise strategy and culture. In reflecting on this journey, it's clear that something profound has changed. You, the reader, are no longer simply a developer writing Apex or a solutions architect configuring Salesforce flows. You are now stepping into a new role: an orchestrator of intelligent systems, a steward of automation, and a designer of human–AI partnerships. This epilogue is about embracing that new kind of leadership.

In earlier chapters, we treated AI agents as powerful tools – but tools nonetheless. Now, in this conclusion, we reframe that perspective. Agents are no longer passive assistants confined to executing tasks. They actively shape decisions, workflows, and customer experiences through the insights they surface and actions they take. As a leader in the age of agents, your responsibility shifts from simply deploying technology to cultivating an ecosystem of AI teammates within your organization. It's a transition from tool-use to team-building: from asking "How do I use this agent to get a job done?" to "How do I empower this agent (and those who work with it) to continuously improve our work?"

This shift requires a broadening of mindset. Technical proficiency with Salesforce Agent Builder, Invocable Apex, and Flow is still important – but equally important is your ability to align these agent capabilities with your company's mission, values, and goals. Leadership now means understanding how to scale AI in alignment with your culture and desired outcomes. It means setting clear roles and guardrails for agents, integrating them across departments, and nurturing the human team's trust and acceptance of their non-human colleagues. In short, leading in an agent-first world means designing organizations where human talent and AI agents learn and execute side by side toward shared objectives.

The opportunity in front of you is enormous. Intelligent agents promise to eliminate drudgery, surface real-time insights, and adapt processes on the fly – but these benefits are only fully realized under thoughtful guidance. The challenge for modern leaders, then, is not simply keeping up with what AI can do; it's figuring out how to guide, govern, and grow AI agents within a living enterprise. Just as a great manager mentors human employees, a great agent-era leader will mentor AI agents – shaping their "careers" through training, feedback, and well-defined responsibilities.

The pages ahead explore what this means in practice. We'll reflect on how information asymmetry in organizations is ending (and what that means for leadership authority). We'll discuss the mindset shift of treating agents as teammates with training plans. We'll weigh the trade-offs between giving agents autonomy and maintaining control. We'll look at how leaders need to operate across silos and technology stacks, uniting systems through standards and collaboration. We'll paint a picture of effective leadership attributes in this new era – from curiosity and experimentation to ethical stewardship. Finally, we'll outline practical next steps for you to continue growing as an AI-first leader, and we'll end with a call to action: the baton is now in your hands to shape an agent-powered future.

THE END OF INFORMATION ASYMMETRY

One of the greatest shifts in the agent-first enterprise is the end of information asymmetry. Traditionally, leadership authority was reinforced by exclusive access to information – managers had reports that line employees did not, experts held knowledge that newcomers couldn't easily obtain. Decisions often tilted toward whoever held the most data (or simply whoever spoke with the loudest voice) rather than toward whoever had the best idea. This "knowledge is power" dynamic meant that critical insights trickled slowly from the top, and front-line teams operated with only a partial understanding of the business.

Today, AI agents and modern data platforms are rapidly democratizing information. The same real-time dashboards and analytics once reserved for executives can now be put in the hands of every employee – and even customers or partners. Intelligent agents break down silos by pulling data from across Salesforce, Slack, ERP systems, customer feedback channels, and more, merging it into a unified view of the truth. There's no need to wait for a monthly report from Finance when a well-tuned agent can pull live data on demand. A sales rep's assistant agent can compile pipeline trends across regions in seconds, just as the VP of Sales's dashboard can. Frontline employees, managers, and even external stakeholders are increasingly on equal footing when it comes to data access. For example:

- Then: A regional manager might have been the only one with full visibility into sales figures, using that private insight to set targets and make decisions.
- Now: Every salesperson's AI Companion can access up-to-the-minute sales data across regions, and even customers see personalized data (like order status or usage metrics) through AI-driven portals. The manager's role shifts from gatekeeping information to coaching the team on how to interpret shared information and act on it.

Forward-looking organizations intentionally link formerly isolated data sources so that all teams operate on a shared dataset. When DevOps, Marketing, and Customer Support can all query the same AI-powered knowledge base, no department stays in the dark. As one industry report notes, integrating data across teams (customer feedback, engineering progress, roadmaps) ensures decisions are made with a full 360° view rather than fragmented insights. The result? Advantage shifts to those who can interpret and act on information the fastest – not those who simply hold it.

Even externally, information asymmetry is vanishing. Customers now use their own AI tools to research products, compare options, and read reviews – often knowing as much about a product's pros and cons as the sales team does. Likewise, the same market datasets and AI analytics available to you are available to your competitors. If there's a sudden shift in customer behavior or a new trend emerging, chances are everyone's agents will notice it sooner or later. The playing field of raw information is leveling not just within organizations, but across entire industries. What will separate winners and losers is how quickly each can move from observation to action. Imagine two firms receive identical real-time alerts from their analytics agents about a spike in demand for a certain product feature. Company A has empowered its team (human and AI) to immediately interpret and respond – by that afternoon, their Salesforce Command Center has spun up a targeted campaign addressing the new demand. Company B, however, waits for a traditional meeting the next week to discuss the data. By then, they've missed the window. Both had the same information; Company A's insight velocity turned that information into value first—securing a clear competitive edge.

Even science fiction anticipated this power shift. In Robert A. Heinlein's The Moon Is a Harsh Mistress, a self-aware AI nicknamed Mike shares its strategic knowledge with an oppressed colony, helping ordinary people outmaneuver a ruling Authority that once had total information control. In that story, liberated data (and a friendly AI agent) tipped the balance of power. Likewise, in today's enterprise, when information flows freely and AI helps everyone interpret it, old hierarchies based on information hoarding give way to new models based on agility and wisdom.

In this new landscape, knowledge alone isn't a differentiator – insight is. When every competitor and every team member has access to the same facts, competitive advantage comes from how quickly and wisely you can leverage those facts. We are moving from information asymmetry (only a privileged few have the data) to insight asymmetry (everyone has data, but few can extract its full value). Real-time, insight-driven decision-making is becoming the norm. The most effective leaders and teams cultivate the ability to sift signal from noise, to contextualize raw data into strategy, and to turn observations into proactive decisions. In short, it's not about what you know (since in principle everyone can know the same things) – it's about how adeptly you can use that knowledge for impact.

The speed at which you and your agents can generate actionable insight from shared data – not just how fast you gather data – will define future enterprise performance. Modern AI copilots excel at analyzing live data streams to highlight trends or anomalies in seconds, leveling the informational playing field. Organizations that emphasize this rapid cycle from data to decision are already outpacing those that cling to old hierarchical reporting structures. Simply put, when data flows freely, the winners will be those with the fastest insight response time, not merely those with the biggest data warehouse. Some enterprises even track time-to-insight as a key metric – how quickly a new data point (a customer complaint pattern, a supply chain delay) is detected by agents, disseminated to teams, and translated into action. In the agent era, compressing this loop is a critical source of value.

For you as a leader, the end of information asymmetry demands a transparent, empowering style. Instead of hoarding knowledge, you'll succeed by enabling your teams (human and AI alike) to access data and learn from it continuously. It also means cultivating data literacy and critical thinking across your workforce – a flood of information is only an asset if people and agents know how to swim in it. Encourage your teams to ask the right questions of their AI tools, and make insight-sharing a regular habit. You might institute open dashboards, cross-functional "insight huddles," or AI-driven daily briefings that keep everyone informed. Your job is no longer to dispense information, but to foster a collaborative environment where insights emerge from everywhere. In many ways, it's a paradigm shift: you move from being the person with all the answers to the person who ensures that everyone has the ability to find answers. Measure success not by the information you personally control, but by the insights and innovations your collective organization can produce from a shared base of knowledge.

In short, you cease being a hoarder of knowledge and become a catalyst for insight throughout your organization. This sets the stage for our next topic. If information is now widely accessible to all, what does that mean for the way we design and deploy our AI agents? The answer begins with reimagining those agents not as mere tools, but as collaborative teammates in the enterprise.

AGENTS AS TEAMMATES, NOT JUST TOOLS

A fundamental mindset shift for an AI-first leader is to start treating AI agents as teammates, not just tools. Up to now, you may have viewed bots and algorithms as convenient assistants – perhaps powerful, but essentially static utilities that you configure and deploy. The agent-first approach goes further. It asks you to envision agents as digital employees or co-workers: entities with defined roles, responsibilities, and even growth paths within your organization. In other words, your AI isn't just something you use; it's something (or someone) you work with. As one Salesforce engineering leader put it, "We've been experimenting with what it means to treat AI agents not as tools, but as true team members – that collaborate, learn, and add value." This means designing your agents with the same intentionality as you would hire and develop a human teammate.

Practically, treating an agent as a teammate starts from day one of its "employment." Just as you would onboard a new hire, you need to onboard your AI agents with clear scope, guidelines, and support. Define what the agent's job is: what tasks it should handle, what decisions it can make on its own, where it should defer to humans, and how it should communicate. In Salesforce's internal practice, they introduce their Agentforce AI to teams with explicit parameters: "Here's what it can do. Here's what it can't. And here's how we'll supervise it." Framing an agent's role explicitly helps human colleagues understand and trust it, and it gives the agent a well-bounded sandbox to operate in. You're essentially writing a job description for the AI – and using tools like Salesforce Agent Builder to translate that into technical constraints (permitted actions, data access, conversational tone, etc.), and wiring up Invocable Apex methods or Flow actions that the agent can safely invoke as its way of executing tasks.

Next comes ongoing management and improvement. An AI agent, like any team member, requires feedback and oversight to reach its full potential. A leader should establish mechanisms to audit an agent's performance and provide iterative coaching. Think of this as the "one-on-one meetings" you'd have with a direct report, except here you might be reviewing analytics and logs. Did the agent meet its KPIs (e.g. resolution rate, accuracy, response time)? Is it drifting off-script or producing errors? What do users (employees or customers) say about interacting with it? These questions ensure you're not deploying and forgetting an agent, but actively managing it. In fact, Salesforce teams encourage employees to give feedback and suggestions to their AI counterparts – treating that feedback as fuel for the agent's improvement. One manager described it to her team this way: "You're not just managing AI – you're mentoring it." That captures the essence of this new leadership task.

To systematize this, forward-thinking organizations are adding new agent management practices to their playbooks. Consider adopting some of these strategies:

Assign "Agent Owners": Just as a product has a product owner, give each major AI agent an owner on the team – a human accountable for that agent's success and compliance. This Agent Owner monitors the agent's output, handles its "training" (updating prompts or model versions), and serves as the point of contact if the agent misbehaves or needs an upgrade.

Establish Feedback Loops: Require regular reviews of agent performance. This can include monitoring telemetry (usage stats, error rates), collecting user feedback after agent interactions, and feeding those insights back into development. For example, if an agent in Salesforce Service Cloud is handling customer chats, you might log cases where it had to hand off to a human or where customer sentiment dropped, and then analyze those for improvements. Some companies even share agent performance metrics transparently on team dashboards – treating an agent's stats like a colleague's progress report.

Promotion and Retirement Plans: Include AI agents in your governance workflows for role changes. If an agent consistently excels at its tasks, you might broaden its scope or deploy it to new teams (a kind of "promotion"). Conversely, if an agent becomes obsolete (say, a pricing bot made redundant by a new ERP feature) or falls short of expectations despite coaching, have a process to retire or replace it. This ensures you don't accumulate deadweight bots that no one trusts or uses. In an agent-first organization, every agent should either be growing in value or gracefully sunset.

Embracing AI as teammates also brings a cultural shift. Leaders should set the tone that interacting with AI agents is a normal and valued part of everyday work. In team meetings, that might mean acknowledging the contributions of an AI ("Our scheduling agent coordinated all these interviews for us – let's recognize that efficiency"). It also means encouraging human employees to treat agent outputs with neither unwarranted skepticism nor blind faith, but with the same constructive scrutiny and collaboration they'd give to a human colleague's work. The psychological shift here cannot be understated: your team is no longer only flesh and blood. It now includes code and algorithms working alongside people. Great leaders help their staff see the opportunity in that – freeing humans from drudge work, extending their capabilities – rather than seeing the AI as a threat or gimmick.

Importantly, treating an agent as a teammate doesn't imply pretending it's human or granting it human-level authority. Rather, it's about respecting the agent's role and ensuring it fits smoothly into the team's workflows. Just as you'd ensure two human teammates have clearly defined responsibilities and handoff points, you do the same for human-agent collaboration. For example, if your sales forecasting agent provides a weekly prediction, make it clear that the agent "owns" the data crunching and initial forecast, while the human sales director "owns" final judgment calls incorporating context the agent might miss (like an upcoming marketing campaign or one-off event). By delineating roles, the agent becomes a reliable partner in its domain, and humans understand where their expertise continues to be essential.

The payoff to this approach is a team – humans plus AIs – that can achieve more together than either could alone. Your human employees are liberated from rote tasks and supported with real-time insights. Your AI agents continuously learn from human feedback and handle scale and complexity that people cannot. The synergy creates a new kind of high-performing organization. But it only works if you, as a leader, cultivate it. That means investing time and thought into your AI agents' "professional development" just as you do for people. It means celebrating wins where human-agent collaboration produced something great. And it means being prepared to adjust roles and rules as you learn what these digital colleagues excel at and where they need guidance.

This agent-as-teammate philosophy sets the foundation for balancing autonomy and control, which we'll explore next. Once you start treating agents like part of the team, you face nuanced decisions about how much authority to give them. The next section dives into those trade-offs of autonomy, trust, and oversight in enterprise AI.

YOUR DECISIONS SHAPE THE SYSTEM

Adopting AI agents into your enterprise isn't just a technical installation – it's a series of leadership decisions. Now that you have a sense of agents' capabilities and are treating them as part of the team, you must decide where and how to deploy them, and under what rules. These design choices will shape your AI-powered system's effectiveness and integrity. In essence, every pattern you implement and every permission you grant is a reflection of your leadership philosophy.

One key decision point is which agent pattern to apply to a given problem. Do you use a light-touch Companion agent that offers suggestions to a human operator, or do you use an autonomous Conductor agent that coordinates tasks across multiple systems with minimal human input? This isn't just an engineering question – it's a values question. For instance, choosing a "Human-in-the-loop" pattern (like a sales Companion that recommends next steps but lets a human finalize actions) reflects a priority on human judgment and accountability. On the other hand, deploying a fully autonomous Conductor to, say, handle end-to-end software deployments or financial reconciliations indicates a comfort with automation taking the driver's seat to maximize efficiency. Neither is categorically right or wrong; as a leader you weigh the context. High-risk domains (healthcare decisions, legal approvals) might warrant a Supervisor or Companion pattern by design, whereas high-volume, low-risk workflows (log file analysis, routine data entry) could be orchestrated by autonomous agents without slowing things down. The crux is that every agent architecture decision carries a philosophical stance – how much you're willing to delegate to machines versus where you insist on human oversight. As a pro tip from earlier chapters put it, every pattern is also a philosophy.

Another set of decisions involves the guardrails and governance you establish around your agents. An agent given free rein can be incredibly powerful – and potentially problematic. So ask: what constraints will you impose? This can range from hard technical limits (e.g. an agent cannot delete records, or it can only email drafts to a supervisor for approval) to process checkpoints (e.g. requiring human sign-off for an AI-generated customer communication). These guardrails are your way of dialing the autonomy knob to the appropriate level. You might implement simple permissioning via Salesforce's permission sets or OAuth scopes for agents that call APIs. For critical decisions, you could enforce a "two sets of eyes" rule – for example, any expense approval the AI makes over $1,000 might automatically require a human manager's click before its final. You might schedule regular reviews of an agent's decisions, especially early in its deployment, to ensure it's not drifting into unwanted behavior. Some organizations create an AI oversight board or include AI-specific scenarios in their change management and risk audits. The point is that leadership must actively design the rules of engagement for each agent: what it's allowed to do, when it must yield to a human, and how it logs and explains its actions.

This leads to the broader theme of autonomy vs. control. Granting an agent more autonomy can unlock speed, scale, and cost savings – the agent might complete tasks in seconds that would take humans hours, and do so 24/7. However, with autonomy comes risk. An unsupervised agent might execute a flawed trade, deploy buggy code, or simply make decisions that don't align with human values or intent. One member of Salesforce's AI ethics board put it bluntly: "Autonomy creates significant risks: unchecked actions, unintended data sharing, and difficulty attributing accountability." In other words, if you let the AI loose, you had better be confident in its alignment with your goals and ethics. Science fiction has long warned of AIs operating beyond human intent – for example, William Gibson's Neuromancer envisioned rogue AIs requiring special police to keep them in check. In the real world, the "rogue AI" scenario might simply look like an agent that corners itself into a bad decision because it lacked context a human would have provided. As the leader orchestrating this system, you carry a dual responsibility: enable productivity gains without undermining trust and safety.

Don't be lulled by the term "AI copilot" into thinking the agent will always steer correctly. Even advanced agents can and will make mistakes or odd choices. Treat autonomous outputs with healthy caution. For example, if your AI Copilot for code suggests changes, you still run tests and code reviews; if your AI sales advisor drafts an email, you (or another agent with a review role) give it a quick sanity check. Never assume an AI's first answer is the right answer – build in checks, at least until an agent has earned a high level of trust through consistent performance.

Before granting any AI agent expansive autonomy in a production environment, stress-test it in a sandbox. Simulate edge cases and even adversarial conditions to probe how the agent reacts. Does a customer service agent remain polite and accurate when a customer is irate, or does it go off-script? Will a finance agent catch an obviously fraudulent transaction or blindly approve it? Engage your QA team to "red team" the AI – intentionally try to break or confuse it – and see where its failure points lie. This hands-on testing helps you refine guardrails and provides confidence that when you do let the agent operate freely, you won't be caught off guard by predictable errors.

Ultimately, determining the right level of autonomy is an iterative learning process. Early on, you might err on the side of caution: deploy agents in advisory roles or with narrow scope until they prove their reliability. As confidence builds, you can relax some constraints – perhaps moving a forecasting agent from recommendation-only to auto-executing certain inventory orders within set boundaries. Throughout, maintain transparency with stakeholders about how decisions are being made. Employees should know if a decision came from an AI agent or a person; customers, too, should be informed (in appropriate terms) when an AI is driving an outcome that affects them. This transparency reinforces trust: people are more likely to trust autonomous systems if they understand when and how those systems are in play.

As you craft these rules, remember that how you choose to use AI is sending a signal to your organization. If you automate without oversight and something goes wrong, that's on leadership. If you under-utilize AI due to fear, missing out on benefits, that's also on leadership. Finding the balance is a new part of the job description. And it's not static – you'll continually adjust as agents become more capable and as your team becomes more comfortable.

The next dimension to explore is how this leadership extends beyond one team or system. It's one thing to manage AI within a single department, but what about leading across multiple business silos and technology stacks? In the next section, we'll look at scaling your agent strategy horizontally across the organization.

LEADING ACROSS SILOS, STACKS, AND SYSTEMS

Up to this point, we've largely considered leading AI agents within a team or a process. The next challenge is scaling that leadership horizontally – across the many silos of a large organization and the diverse technology stacks in your ecosystem. In an enterprise, it's common for Sales, Finance, HR, and Operations to each develop their own AI assistants or automations in isolation. But true agent-first transformation happens when these agents can interoperate and when leaders champion cross-functional collaboration rather than isolated innovation.

To lead across silos, start by thinking horizontally. Look for workflows that span departments – for example, an employee onboarding process touches HR (creating a profile), IT (provisioning accounts), Finance (payroll setup), and perhaps Facilities (access badges). Rather than each department's agent handling its piece in a vacuum, envision a swarm of agents coordinating that workflow end-to-end. That might mean the HR agent kicks off the process, then signals the IT agent to create accounts, which then notifies the Facilities bot, and so on. As an AI leader, you must orchestrate agent systems across org boundaries much like you break down silos among human teams. Encourage your department heads and product owners to share their agent strategies early and often. Form cross-functional working groups to design inter-agent touchpoints. This prevents a scenario where, say, Marketing's AI and Legal's AI make conflicting decisions because they were never "introduced" to each other. Open governance is key: by bringing diverse stakeholders into a common AI steering committee or "center of excellence," you set unified policies (security, ethics, escalation paths) that apply to agents enterprise-wide.

Technically, leading across stacks means ensuring your Salesforce agents can talk to your other tools and vice versa. In modern enterprises, you might have AI components in Salesforce Cloud, another in Slack or Teams (think

Microsoft 365 Copilot), another in a cloud data warehouse, etc. Leading in this context requires embracing interoperability standards and integration platforms. One emerging standard, the Model Context Protocol (MCP), provides a common fabric for connecting AI systems regardless of where they run. MCP acts like a universal adapter – or as Cloudflare's engineers put it, "a USB-C port for AI applications". Using MCP, an agent running in Salesforce could securely query a vector database or call an external AI service, with all parties understanding the request/response format and context. Even if you don't implement MCP specifically, the principle stands: invest in making your agents modular and able to exchange information through well-defined APIs or event messages. If your CRM agent can trigger a workflow in your ERP system via MuleSoft, or your Service Cloud agent can hand off a complex query to an AWS Lambda function, you unlock compounded value. For instance, an AI-driven procurement workflow might start in Salesforce (an employee request) and seamlessly pass through an SAP agent (to generate a purchase order) before notifying a supplier via a custom integration – all orchestrated without manual handoffs. The goal is an ecosystem of agents that can each specialize yet still collaborate across platforms.

When connecting agents across systems, favor loose coupling. In one project, our Salesforce Conductor agent didn't call the finance system's internals directly; instead, it dropped a structured task message into a MuleSoft integration layer. The finance side's agent picked it up, executed the transaction, and returned a result message. This design meant each agent/system could evolve independently as long as they honored the message contract. By using event buses, API gateways, or middleware like MuleSoft, you avoid brittle entanglement and make cross-cloud workflows more resilient.

Leading across silos also means stretching your organizational culture. You want your AI initiatives to be collaborative, not competitive. Often, different departments may choose different tooling (one team likes a Python-based AI stack, another prefers Salesforce's low-code approach). Rather than force everyone onto one platform, a good leader facilitates communication between platforms. This could mean something as simple as scheduling demos where teams show off their agents to each other, or sharing a common "agent registry" where anyone in the company can see what automations exist (reducing duplicate efforts). It also means championing data sharing agreements across silos – your agents in Marketing can only be as smart as the data they can legally and ethically learn from in Sales or Support, for example. Break down those data barriers where possible, with proper consent and security, so agents have the richest context to work with.

We've seen this story before in traditional IT: isolated systems lead to duplicate work and inconsistent results, prompting past movements toward enterprise integration. The same caution applies now – don't let "islands of AI" proliferate without bridges between them. We can draw a parallel here to science fiction's visions of distributed intelligence. In Ann Leckie's Ancillary Justice, the starship's AI inhabited dozens of bodies at once, operating in different locations but unified in purpose. Enterprise AI isn't so far-fetched – you might have a dozen semi-autonomous agents across various software environments, and your leadership role is to ensure they function as a cohesive whole rather than disjointed fragments. Just as the starship AI shared one memory across many "ancillaries," your agents should share context and goals across departments. Achieving this might involve creating a centralized knowledge hub or adopting Model Context Protocol to pass state between agents seamlessly. It certainly involves fostering a mindset in your human leaders that we're all working with parts of the same AI-enabled organism.

Cross-platform agent strategy also has a human dimension: you must encourage cross-domain skill development. Your Salesforce developers might need to learn about Azure AI services, and your data science team might need to integrate with SAP's AI APIs. As a leader, model this interdisciplinary approach – show that you value solutions that span multiple systems, and reward teams that reach across the aisle to leverage each other's tech.

Finally, be prepared to handle the governance at scale. More agents across more systems means more potential points of failure or misuse. Make sure your security and compliance teams are involved in the design of inter-agent communications. For example, ensure that an agent passing information to another doesn't violate data policies (no personal data leaking from HR to a marketing bot, for instance). Logging and observability become crucial – when an outcome is produced by a chain of three different agents, you need a trace to explain what happened. But with the right groundwork – standards like MCP, integration middleware, and a collaborative culture – these challenges are surmountable. In return, you gain an organization whose AI capabilities are far greater than the sum of its parts.

At this stage, we've looked at managing agents individually and as an interconnected network. Now, let's examine the qualities that leaders themselves must embody to drive such an AI-first organization. The next section turns the focus onto you – what traits and disciplines make for truly effective leadership in the era of intelligent agents.

WHAT GREAT AGENT LEADERSHIP LOOKS LIKE

By now it's clear that leading in the age of agents demands more than the traditional playbook. So what traits do the most successful agent-era leaders exhibit? Through this book (and observing pioneers in the field), a set of key characteristics emerges:

Curious and Experimental, but Disciplined: Great AI leaders are avid experimenters. They stay curious about new technologies, run pilot projects, and encourage a culture of trying new agent ideas. But they pair that curiosity with rigor. They don't launch half-baked bots into critical workflows without testing; they set hypotheses, measure results, and iterate methodically. This blend of open-minded exploration and engineering discipline ensures steady innovation without chaos.

Clear-Eyed About Risks, but Bold in Intent: Agent-era leaders neither ignore AI's pitfalls nor are paralyzed by them. They develop a keen sense of where things can go wrong – data biases, security holes, regulatory concerns – and they put mitigations in place. Yet, they remain bold about what their organization can achieve with AI. They communicate a vision of intelligent automation that excites stakeholders, even as they frankly acknowledge the safeguards needed. This balanced outlook earns trust: the team knows the leader isn't drinking the "AI Kool-Aid" blindly, but also isn't hiding under a rock.

Collaborative Across Functions (Not Isolated in IT): In the past, some organizations treated AI projects as the sole domain of IT or data science teams. Modern leaders break this silo. They personally work across departments – bringing HR, legal, operations, and others into the AI conversation. They might rotate AI champions through different departments or hold cross-functional design sessions for new agents. The result is that AI isn't a side project in a server room; it's a company-wide endeavor with shared ownership. These leaders also seek external collaboration, learning from industry peers and open-source communities to stay on the cutting edge.

Design-Driven and Ethically Grounded: The best agent leaders think like product designers and guardians of ethics. They care about the quality of the agent's design – its reliability, its user experience, its maintainability –

not just quick wins. They put in the work to refine prompts, streamline workflows, and reduce technical debt in automation. And critically, they imbue an ethical perspective throughout, perhaps instituting AI ethics checklists or bias audits as standard procedure for new deployments. They set guidelines on data privacy, fairness, and transparency for AI behaviors, and they ensure their teams follow them. They know that every automation has human impact, so they strive to make that impact positive and aligned with the organization's values.

These qualities manifest in tangible behaviors. You'll see an agent-savvy leader spending an afternoon personally testing a new bot, just to understand its quirks (curiosity in action), and then insisting on a staging environment for it (discipline). You'll hear them in meetings openly discuss "What could go wrong if we let the pricing AI auto-adjust discounts?" (clear-eyed about risk) and in the next breath, "If we manage those risks, think of how much more agile our sales could be" (bold intent). They will proactively reach out beyond their turf: a CIO might invite Marketing and Compliance heads to co-create an AI use policy – demonstrating that AI leadership is a team sport. And when their developers present an impressive new agent, these leaders will ask not only "How does it work?" but also "Is it doing the right thing for customers and employees?"

Great agent-era leadership also involves leading by example with AI tools. The leaders themselves often leverage AI agents to enhance their work, signaling to the organization that it's okay (even encouraged) to work alongside smart machines. For instance, a product director might use a personal Companion agent to gather daily customer feedback highlights, which she then shares with her team – showing how AI can keep everyone more informed. A sales manager might deploy a Coach agent to junior reps, providing real-time tips or flagging missed follow-ups, thereby championing continuous learning with AI assistance. And a VP of Operations might rely on a Supervisor agent to monitor key metrics across all other agents (like an AI audit assistant), exemplifying that even oversight can be intelligently automated. In short, effective leaders leverage Companion agents to enhance communication with stakeholders, Coach agents to elevate team capabilities, and Supervisor agents to maintain oversight of the AI ecosystem – all as part of their leadership toolkit. By visibly using these tools, leaders send a powerful message: that AI isn't just an abstract project for "others" to do, but a practical part of everyone's job – including theirs.

One striking commonality in effective leaders is their design discipline in implementing AI. They don't treat agents as disposable scripts; they treat them as products or team members that evolve. That means setting up proper version control, documentation, and maintenance cycles for automations. It means tracking metrics for agents (uptime, error rates, value delivered) just as they would for human staff performance. It also means knowing when to pull the plug – if an AI tool isn't delivering or poses unexpected issues, these leaders aren't afraid to pause, reassess, and if needed, retire it. Their ego isn't tied up in "my AI must succeed"; it's focused on outcomes and doing what's best for the organization in the long run.

Perhaps the most important trait, though, is a sense of stewardship. Top leaders in the agent era see themselves as stewards of both human and artificial team members. They foster an environment of learning and adaptation for people (reskilling, upskilling in tandem with AI rollout), and they shepherd their AI agents through training and iteration. They act as mediators when there's friction – maybe employees are unsure about a new agent, or an agent is overrunning a process – stepping in to set guidelines or recalibrate expectations. They take accountability: when AI causes an error, they address it openly rather than scapegoating the technology. This sense of responsibility and care builds a culture where innovation with AI can flourish because trust is high.

In summary, great agent leadership looks much like great traditional leadership – but augmented with new skills and sensitivities. It's curious and courageous, yet methodical and conscientious. It's collaborative and communicative across technical and business divides. It's principled and people-centric, even as it eagerly embraces automation. Leaders with these qualities are not just directing tools; as we've said, they're nurturing ecosystems – guiding a dynamic interplay of humans and AIs toward meaningful goals.

With these personal qualities in mind, the final pieces of our journey are about action – how do you, the reader, continue to grow and drive change in an AI-first world? The last two sections will outline practical next steps and issue a call to arms for shaping the future of work with agents.

HOW TO KEEP GROWING

The journey of becoming an agent-first leader doesn't end with finishing this book – in fact, it's just beginning. The AI field evolves rapidly, and maintaining momentum requires continuous learning and proactive leadership. Here are some practical next steps and habits to help you keep growing and extend your influence in an AI-driven workplace:

Host an Internal "Agent Showcase" Day: Set up a regular forum (quarterly or biannual) where teams demo their latest AI agents, automations, and experiments to the whole organization. Think of it like a science fair or hackathon expo. This encourages teams to innovate (they'll want something cool to show) and spreads awareness across silos. At one company, an "Automation Fair" uncovered that multiple departments had built similar approval bots; they were able to consolidate the best ideas into one enterprise-wide solution on the spot. An agent showcase day also surfaces duplicate efforts and opportunities for collaboration. As a leader, you can kick it off with a keynote highlighting successes and learnings (including failures). Celebrate the contributors publicly. This builds excitement and normalizes the presence of AI in every corner of the company.

Start a Prompt Library or "Agent Guild": One very actionable step is to create a shared repository of effective prompts, patterns, and agent templates that anyone in your org can reuse. This could be as simple as a Confluence page or Slack channel where people share "recipes" for using AI (for example, a tried-and-true prompt for summarizing customer support tickets, or a reusable Flow for an approval bot). Some organizations formalize this into an AI Guild (a concept akin to a Center of Excellence) – a cross-functional working group of enthusiasts and experts who meet to swap tips, run trainings, and define best practices. By institutionalizing knowledge sharing (say, turning common prompts into pre-built "blocks" that anyone's Flow or code can call), you help everyone level-up faster and avoid each team reinventing the wheel.

Contribute to Standards and Communities: The future of enterprise AI is being shaped now – and you can be part of that shaping. Get involved in the wider community of AI practitioners. This might mean contributing use cases or feedback to groups developing interoperability standards like MCP, or writing a case study for an industry blog about your agent implementation. It could mean joining an online forum/Discord with other prompt engineers to swap techniques, or contributing to an open-source project on GitHub that aligns with your needs or joining a standards working group such as the one around Model Context Protocol. By engaging externally, you not only stay ahead of the curve on emerging technologies, you also put your company on the map as an AI thought leader. Moreover, you'll build relationships with peers, which is invaluable when troubleshooting or brainstorming new ideas.

Bridge with Peers, Vendors, and Academia: Don't grow in isolation. Connect with other leaders who are on the AI journey. This can be through informal meetups, LinkedIn groups, or formal conferences. It's amazing how a casual conversation with a peer at another company can spark an idea or save you from a pitfall they already experienced. Engage with your technology vendors (for instance, join customer advisory boards or beta programs to get an early look at new AI features) – often, they have insider knowledge and training that can accelerate your projects. Also consider liaising with academic institutions or taking advantage of online courses or even collaborating with universities on research projects to keep your skills sharp. The landscape will keep shifting – new model architectures, new regulations, new ethical dilemmas will emerge – so continuous education is your ally. Subscribe to AI research newsletters, follow relevant thought leaders, and keep an experimental mindset to adapt to whatever comes next.

Embrace Lifelong Learning (for Yourself and Your Team): Adopting an AI-first mindset is not a one-and-done journey; it's a perpetual evolution. Commit to your own development – for example, pair up with a technical mentor to learn new skills, or dedicate a few hours each week to studying AI trends. Maybe you'll decide to get hands-on and learn a bit of Python to better prototype agents, or maybe you'll dive into AI ethics literature to deepen your governance approach. Encourage your team members to do the same – provide them with time and resources to attend workshops or obtain certifications (e.g. a Salesforce AI Specialist credential or a Coursera Machine Learning certificate). Create a culture where staying current is part of the job. This not only prevents skills atrophy, it also helps you attract and retain talent – people want to work in places that invest in their growth, especially in cutting-edge fields.

Throughout these steps, maintain a growth mindset. There will be setbacks (perhaps your first chatbot deployment flops with users or an algorithm produces bias you didn't anticipate), but treat those as learning opportunities. For instance, if an agent fails to perform as expected in a pilot, dissect why – was the training data insufficient? Did the workflow need tweaking? Use that insight to make version 2.0 better. Model that mindset for your colleagues: show them that every sprint with AI, even if it doesn't meet the goal, yields insights that inform the next iteration. By cultivating resilience and adaptability, you prepare your organization to handle the twists and turns of the AI revolution.

By taking these steps, you ensure that both you and your organization remain on the cutting edge. In effect, you're cultivating a living, breathing AI-first culture – one that evolves with the technology, constantly learns, and stays resilient amid change.

Finally, remember that your influence comes not just from technical know-how or hierarchical position, but from your ability to inspire and guide others through change. Share your vision consistently and tie it to your organization's mission. People need to understand why becoming agent-first matters – whether it's to serve customers faster, free up time for creativity, or remain competitive. By linking AI initiatives to purpose, you rally broader support. Pair every new agent deployment with a narrative about how it benefits the team or customers. Mentor up-and-coming leaders in your org who show interest in AI. In doing so, you create a network of champions who push the agent-first agenda alongside you. This collective leadership is what truly embeds AI-first thinking into an organization's DNA.

As we approach the conclusion of this playbook, take stock of how far you've come and how far you can go. The next section will conclude our journey with a call to action – an invitation for you to shape the future as an agent-first leader armed with knowledge, tools, and the right mindset.

YOUR TURN TO SHAPE THE FUTURE

You've studied the patterns. You've seen the architecture. You've explored governance and transformation. Now it's your time to build, lead, and influence the next era of AI-powered enterprise. The final step in this journey is simple yet profound: to take action and become a catalyst for change.

As a leader equipped with the Agentforce playbook, you are uniquely positioned to drive innovation. Start with something tangible: pick that one high-impact opportunity in your department where an AI agent could make a difference and champion it. Don't wait for perfect certainty – in this fast-moving field, action creates clarity. Launch a well-scoped pilot project, perhaps with a single, well-defined agent. It could be as modest as an AI helper that saves your team an hour a day, or as ambitious as a multi-agent workflow that reimagines a customer experience. What matters is that you begin.

When you deploy that first agent (or the next one), do so with intention. Shape it according to the principles you've learned: give it a clear role, put the right guardrails around it, and set up feedback loops so it improves. Involve your team in its design and rollout – make it a collective mission. This not only yields a better agent, it also creates buy-in. People support what they help create.

Parallel to building, continue leading by influence. Share success stories widely – nothing inspires adoption like real examples of agents making work better. If your pilot agent reduced response times by 50% or uncovered a new sales opportunity, broadcast that story in internal newsletters, at town halls, and up the chain of command. Conversely, be transparent about lessons learned when things don't go as expected. Your credibility as an AI leader comes from being realistic as well as optimistic.

Also, empower others to step up. Encourage your lieutenants to initiate agent projects of their own, using the patterns and best practices you now champion. Support them with resources and air cover, but let them take ownership and grow as leaders in their own right. The more agent-savvy leaders your organization has, the stronger your agent-first future will be. Over time, aim to make yourself less of a single point of drive and more of a hub in a wheel of many motivated, AI-fluent leaders across the business.

As you push forward, remember to consider the broader impact. Being an agent-first leader isn't just about efficiency or profit – it's about shaping a future of work that is more dynamic, creative, and humane. By offloading drudgery to machines, you're freeing human potential for higher-order problem solving and connection. By weaving AI into decision-making, you're moving toward a reality of real-time, insight-rich strategy. By thoughtfully governing AI, you're helping ensure this transformation is responsible and trusted.

This is a pivotal moment. Technology is accelerating, and organizations everywhere are grappling with how to adapt. You have the knowledge and vision to not only adapt, but to set the pace. Embrace the role. Be the orchestrator, the experimenter, the bridge-builder, the ethicist. Cultivate curiosity in your teams, and lead with both head and heart as you integrate AI into the fabric of your enterprise.

The playbook in your hands is a starting point. The real playmaking happens next – on the field of your company, in the projects you spearhead, the standards you influence, and the people you inspire. Think of the next week, month, and year as your proving ground. What will you automate? What new insights will you uncover? Whom will you mentor into an AI champion? Each action, however small, is a step toward the agent-first organization you've envisioned throughout this book.

To borrow a phrase: Don't wait for perfect certainty. You won't have all the answers, and that's okay. Start with one well-shaped agent, one empowered team, one trusted insight – and grow from there. Adapt as you learn. Keep your principles in view. You'll find that momentum builds, and what once seemed futuristic becomes second nature in your leadership practice.

The future isn't just happening to us – we are shaping it with every line of code, every policy decision, every empowered employee. Now it's your turn to shape the future. Go forth and lead with confidence, creativity, and compassion in the age of agents.

SUMMARY

This epilogue has reframed the playbook's technical and organizational lessons into a personal leadership journey. You are no longer just a participant in the age of agents – you've grown into a designer of its systems, a mentor to its agents, and a steward of its impact. Leadership in this new era isn't about directing tools; it's about nurturing ecosystems of intelligence, trust, and transformation. Armed with patterns, principles, and the right mindset, you stand ready to orchestrate the next chapter of innovation. The future is yours to shape – go forth and lead with an agent-first vision.

ABOUT THE AUTHORS

Cynthia Qiao is an accomplished Salesforce Certified Technical Architect (CTA) and a recognized leader in agentic AI, enterprise architecture, and large-scale digital transformation. With nearly two decades of experience guiding complex programs across multiple industries, she has helped organizations modernize operations, improve decision-making, and design technology strategies that support long-term business goals.

As one of the earliest women to earn the CTA credential, Cynthia brings both technical depth and a strong sense of leadership to her work. She is known for her ability to simplify complexity—turning multi-cloud architectures, data strategy challenges, and emerging AI capabilities into clear, actionable guidance that executive stakeholders and delivery teams can trust.

Her background spans AI-driven process design, data and CRM integration, business transformation, and program architecture. She has led end-to-end initiatives for global enterprises, coached teams through complex system landscapes, and developed innovative approaches for aligning AI and CRM capabilities with real business outcomes.

In *Designing Salesforce Agents: The Pattern-Based Guide to Agentforce*, Cynthia brings her practical experience to the forefront—helping readers understand how to design AI agents that are scalable, predictable, and ready for enterprise use. Her focus is on providing clear patterns and guidance that teams can apply immediately, regardless of where they are in their AI journey.

Cynthia regularly shares insights on AI, architecture, and technology strategy, and enjoys connecting with readers who are exploring the next wave of intelligent systems and agent-driven business processes. Readers who want to explore the ideas in this book can follow Cynthia on LinkedIn.

Andy Forbes is a Salesforce architect and practitioner with deep experience helping organizations modernize their operations and prepare for the emerging era of AI-driven work. He has worked across multiple Salesforce "clouds" as well as the emerging AI ecosystem, giving him a practical understanding of how real-world enterprises adopt new technologies and the challenges they face along the way.

Andy's interest in AI is rooted in delivery reality: how teams actually work, where processes tend to break down, how data behaves in the wild, and what it takes to design solutions that stand up to complexity. That perspective shapes *Designing Salesforce Agents: The Pattern-Based Guide to Agentforce*, which focuses on giving architects, developers, and business analysts a clear, repeatable structure for building agents that are effective, reliable, and ready for production use.

Andy currently spends much of his time helping organizations think through AI-first delivery models, intent-driven process design, and the practical steps required to integrate agents into existing systems and teams. He enjoys translating emerging capabilities into approaches that teams can use right now, without hand-waving or hype. He shares his work and research sporadically on LinkedIn. Readers who want to explore these ideas further - or who are beginning their own AI journey - are welcome to connect with him there.

Made in the USA
Monee, IL
05 November 2026

67914371R00439